ANNUAL REVIEW OF ANTHROPOLOGY

ANNUAL REVIEW OF ANTHROPOLOGY

VOLUME 21, 1992

BERNARD J. SIEGEL, *Editor*
Stanford University

ALAN R. BEALS, *Associate Editor*
University of California, Riverside

STEPHEN A. TYLER, *Associate Editor*
Rice University

ANNUAL REVIEWS INC.   4139 EL CAMINO WAY   P.O. BOX 10139   PALO ALTO, CALIFORNIA   94303-0897

ANNUAL REVIEWS INC.
Palo Alto, California, USA

International Standard Serial Number: 0084–6570
International Standard Book Number: 8243–1921–4
Library of Congress Catalog Card Number: 72–821360

Annual Review and publication titles are registered trademarks of Annual Reviews Inc.

The paper used in this publication meets the minimum requirements of American National Standards for Information Sciences—Permanence of Paper for Printed Library Materials, ANZI Z39.48-1984

Annual Reviews Inc. and the Editors of its publications assume no responsibility for the statements expressed by the contributors to this *Review*.

Typesetting by Ruth McCue-Saavedra and the Annual Reviews Inc. Editorial Staff

PRINTED AND BOUND IN THE UNITED STATES OF AMERICA

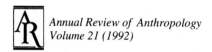

Annual Review of Anthropology
Volume 21 (1992)

CONTENTS

SOME RELATED ARTICLES IN OTHER *ANNUAL REVIEWS*

From the *Annual Review of Sociology,* Volume 18 (1992)

From the *Annual Review of Psychology,* Volume 43 (1992)

From the *Annual Review of Public Health,* Volume 13, (1992)

From the *Annual Review of Ecology and Systematics,* Volume 23 (1992)

From the *Annual Review of Earth and Planetary Sciences,* Volume 20 (1992)

W.W. Howells

Annu. Rev. Anthropol. 1992. 21:1–17

YESTERDAY, TODAY AND TOMORROW

W. W. Howells

Peabody Museum, Harvard University, Cambridge, Massachusetts 02138

KEYWORDS: physical anthropology, history

Although attuned to dinosaurs and cave men as a boy, I never heard of anthropology. Certainly not as a college freshman tentatively pointed for English literature. That pointing was stopped dead by the list of summer readings I was handed. Concealed from consciousness at first was an older friend's mention of enjoying a course in anthropology, and now a light went on in the attic. I went to see Professor Tozzer, the anthropology chairman, who made it plain that the department did not need every Tom, Dick, or Harry, and admitted me as a concentrator only after determining that my freshman grades were above a certain not very high minimum.

Like some others, I was captured for good by the essential appeal and viewpoint, both intellectual and aesthetic, of anthropology as a whole. Naturally, this viewpoint was reflected in our teachers. None of the three limited himself to one subdiscipline. Roland B. Dixon's courses were mostly labeled "Races and Cultures of" Oceania, North America, etc, which included archaeological outlines of these areas; he also taught the prehistory of China, India, and Mesopotamia, as well as a seminar in linguistics. Alfred Tozzer taught social anthropology and religion, although his own field was Middle American archaeology. Earnest Hooton supplemented physical anthropology with a very good course on Africa, the only gap in Dixon's perimeter, and also a course on European prehistory good enough to capture a Movius. We were supposed to cover all the fields, and even in my graduate years I took Tozzer's seminars on Mexico and the Mayas, to my great gratification then and later.

From Tozzer and Dixon I learned, or was at least exposed to, the beauties of organization. Tozzer was serious and methodical in lectures. He wrote nicely arranged outlines on the board, but in a hand that did not distinguish well

0084-6570/92/1015-0001$02.00

1

between i's or o's or n's or u's, so that when he wrote a word like "communion" it was apt to look as much like a healthy cardiogram as like actual handwriting. His seminars were different: Held in his office, they were also appealing presentations of the solid information of the day, but laced with anecdotes about Middle American archaeologists reputable or disreputable, delivered with a delighted half chuckle. It is easy and pleasant to remember his face in action and the sound of his voice—the things that live on in the memory of one more generation after you die, before they are gone forever.

Dixon had to be experienced to be known. He was reserved and, I think, shy; but on the other hand he was kindly, amiable, and helpful in course contact. His erudition was enormous: He knew a number of European and American Indian languages, without linguistic training; and he had wide first-hand ethnographic knowledge. He was a walking HRAF: Each subregion in one of his area courses got exactly the same treatment; he needed no outline on the board, because by the second week any new student knew what was coming next. First, remarks on physical anthropology. Then a capsule archaeology. Then material culture: food-getting, house form, clothing, artefacts of every kind, weaponry offensive and defensive, and so on, followed by similarly structured social organization and religion. Dixon had only to take a breath, and the student wrote the next heading down in his notes. But this approach was not dry; it was interesting, and the student left the lecture with sore tendons in his hand but satisfied that he had gotten his money's worth.

Dixon was extraordinarily meticulous and immensely systematic. His systematic nature also expressed itself in the organization and cataloging of the Peabody Museum library (now the Tozzer Library of the Harvard University Libraries, and always unequaled in anthropology). It was he who planned the exhibits in those halls that were devoted to ethnography: beautiful epitomes of all culture areas, without concessions to artistic canons of display. He must have collected a great many of the materials himself. Now thoroughly out of date and dismantled, they were nevertheless gems of visual information.

Hooton, of course, was a phenomenon. He was genuine, forceful, and reflective. Entirely without self-consciousness, he never gave a thought to presenting a persona. He was not one to look over his shoulder to see if any were following him. Nor would I call him merely charismatic. I do not think his students had a "Cher Maître" attitude toward him. All this may seem strange, considering his public image. Based upon my first memories of him, I doubt he was originally aware of his gift for the vivid and the comic; but gradually he became a formidable public speaker. Owing to his richness of expression, and to the fact that he knew his own mind, Hooton was much in demand at Harvard alumni clubs and elsewhere. He felt strongly that in tastes, ideals, and breeding habits the American public was going downhill—has he been proved wrong? wait and see—and he said so constantly enough to create a misanthropist image. Despite his deep pessimism (e.g. 19), he illustrated many of his general writings with humorous cartoons. He was not a first-class draftsman like Adolph Schultz, but he was good at making his point, and his blackboard drawings were excellent.

Hooton never expressed his dark views in the classroom. He was a completely practical teacher, who could in fact dictate a lot of numbing statistics in his courses. In the midst of such a delivery, naturally, he might suddenly give way to a humorous or colorful diversion. His witticisms were not set pieces, asterisked in his notes, but spontaneous and appropriate excursions.

He was patient, listening seriously to his students and never brushing anything off. He was not a glad-hander. He laughed easily, and liked to, but he didn't go around smiling all the time. Behind a practical exterior he was warm and hospitable. He and Mrs. Hooton had tea for all comers every day, and everyone was welcome. At the first department meeting after he died, someone asked who would now offer daily afternoon tea? The answer, alas, was that nobody would. We had lost an institution along with the man.

He was always mindful of his graduate students, past and present. It was probably only later that they realized how much thought he gave them, and how many opportunities, large and small, he put in their way. In my youth I was asked by a publishing house to write a popular book on human evolution. There were not many such books then. The publishers had asked Hooton to do it but he, being too busy, recommended me for the job. To show me what they had in mind, they gave me another of their books—of the "Story of Chemistry" brand of glop, as I remember. I thought I could do better, fell to work, and sent them half a dozen chapters. They said sorry, not really what they wanted, there's a war on, etc. I tried another publisher; no luck. I thought my work was not really so bad, and asked Hooton if he would look at it. In a way I was actually competing with him, at his behest. He read it over and on his own hook advised the publishers to reconsider it. Properly awed, they told me they had heard from Hooton how much my book had been improved, and requested another look. Along with the same old chapters I now sent additional ones, and after some further dithering they brought the book out as *Mankind So Far* (23). By any modern standard this work is old-fashioned, of course, as such books get; but it was successful then and did me a lot of good. However, it was Hooton who started me on it and helped it through by taking a little trouble. That was by no means the only time he gave me substantial help or put me onto interesting things. Nor did I butter him up; far from it. I was too naive for that.

He was simply large souled. He was incapable of taking offense—or at least he never did so in my presence. He couldn't give offense either, even when (being no Mr. Chips) he spoke sharply. In that remote day it was permissible to turn in hand-written papers. He forcefully told me several times that my handwriting was dreadful, which it was; the criticism never seemed harsh to me. Later, when I was the new Secretary of the AAPA, I was with him one day in his study at home discussing the next meeting. He suggested having a session on new methods of body-typing. I was not conscious of the fact that he had recently become interested in Sheldon's approach. In my callow way I suggested that such a session would only open the door to a lot of constitutional stuff. Mrs. Hooton had just come into the room; she laughed heartily and went out again. I don't know why Hooton didn't kick me. He simply gave a kind of dismissing grunt and passed it off. Only later did I realize what I had said.

Around this time Hooton showed his unflappability at a meeting of the AAPA. Ashley Montagu had considerable gifts in anatomy and anthropological history, as well as one for treading on his seniors' toes. His listed paper was on the pyramidalis muscle in the primates, but he announced a change of title and launched into an attack on some recent writing of Hooton's. Hooton, seated right in front of him, listened with utter amiability, thanked Montagu and offered to give a paper on the pyramidalis muscle.

It is commonly said that a whole generation of physical anthropologists was "trained by Hooton." This does not sound right: If there had been more coaching, his students would have tended more to follow parallel tracks. Instead, they set off in many directions. As he said himself, he was pleased that none of them were yes-men. Of course, anthropometry was the available technique, whether for measuring growth (Garn), for evaluating the effect of environment (Shapiro) or, in the bulk of cases, for comparing and describing populations to various ends. He even influenced some cultural anthropologists to bring back highly useful data—e.g. Lloyd Warner, Douglas Oliver, Clyde Kluckhohn. In his *Up From the Ape* (15), he included instructions in measuring; but I do not remember any drill in such work, of the kind implied by "training." The only process that could be called training involved practice in bone identification, along with a little desultory work in bone measuring, and some rudimentary statistics.

Rather, he educated us. He profoundly respected education in the basic sense, from his own experience. Beyond that, the effective element was the way he treated us, in conversation and suggestion, and in putting in our way opportunities for thesis work and later projects and jobs. And behind it all lay his attitude: his verve and his honest interest in his own work and that of others. Some of his students could speak well, and some could write well, but he excelled them all at both. Although we did not actually see him at it, I think he was also more industrious than any of his students, possibly excepting Carl Coon. He helped and influenced archaeologists as well as physical anthropologists. He showed his gift for synthesis in his books, above all *Up From the Ape* (15). With that book and *Man's Poor Relations* (22), he introduced primates to the public at large, showing an engaging affection for his subjects. Such writing was a major gift to both the profession and the public.

Naturally, it was course work that drew undergraduates and graduates under the Hooton spell. The mainstays were his human evolution and bone courses, the latter having some coverage of the living. His other offerings involved his own interests, race mixture and anthropology of the criminal.

These may seem bizarre choices now, but given the embryonic state of human genetics at the time, I suppose the study of racial hybridization seemed a useful approach.

I can think of only one student who took up "race mixture": Harry Shapiro worked with the descendants of the *HMS Bounty* mutineers. Nobody followed Hooton into the anthropology of criminals, although he employed some students in his work. In a major lifelong investment of time and energy, Hooton pursued connections between soma and psyche, body and behavior. He lectured at length on Cesare Lombroso, who claimed to distinguish physical marks of criminal man, and on Charles Goring who, in *The English Convict* (11), employed biometry instead of ear lobes, and satisfied himself by statistical analysis that few if any measurable aspects distinguished malefactors from benefactors. Hooton felt strongly that this was a wrong conclusion, and once said in a radio talk: "See what a rent the envious Goring made [in Lombroso's mantle]."

Yet it was Goring's system of statistics that Hooton taught us then, and which he used for the rest of his life. It had been suggested to Goring by Karl Pearson, consisting essentially of the *t*-test for the signficance of a difference between two samples. (Hooton got the correlation coefficient from Kendall and Yule, and taught us that also.) Is has to be said that Hooton had no mathematical background and, more important, little natural feeling for the relation between statistics and data. He taught us how to compute the standard deviation but said nothing about either the normal curve of error which it expresses or the whole matter of sampling. All this, I think, cost him dearly in effort. He mounted a massive project on US prison populations in a number of states and believed he had detected correlations between physical differences and types of crime (20). Both his selection of samples and his ideas of control were denounced by statisticians right and left. He never thought simply to compare convicts with their unincarcerated siblings or to use similar controls. Such a technique might not have been easy, but even limited samples would have yielded better answers than he got from his massive but rather ill-chosen bodies of data.

Statisticians were not alone in belaboring him. He was constantly under attack by those whose dogma absolutely denies all connections between biology and behavior. Such connections were indeed among Hooton's avowed interests, but he was never, as I think many believed, a racist. One need only peruse his many public pronouncements, as in *Apes, Men and Morons* (18), or *Why Men Behave Like Apes* (21), to see that this was not the case. On the other hand, he berated social scientists for ignoring the variable nature of the human animal.

He eventually felt frustration with the methods prevalent in his early career. He became discontented with types and measurement, out of his own philosophy. He thought there should be a holistic science of body, function, and behavior, and that physical anthropology should, as the Chinese say, serve the people. (This has not been a general attitude among us, then or since.) He made his view known repeatedly, especially in public lectures. "In its beginning physical anthropology was pure science, in the sense of being completely useless," he said. He did arouse the interest of various local researchers in child development and dental medicine, but what to offer in more positive terms remained a problem. He wrote: "A few medical scientists turned to physical anthropology.... They asked us for a comprehensive scheme of body build and we gave them the cephalic index—which is the scientific equivalent of asking for bread and getting a stone. Medical science looked at the data of physical anthropology and saw a mass of unrelated measurements, coefficients and probable errors. It turned away in disgust, leaving the anthropologist to rattle his calipers in the Valley of the Dry Bones."

So it was that, in about 1940, he looked to Sheldon's methods of body typing, which had a double appeal: scales in place of measurements or types, and a promise of body/behavior connections. But Hooton soon discarded Sheldon's formalized scales of temperament, simplified and objectified his scales of body typing, and, in his late work, addressed himself to possible physical variations in military personnel by function and performance.

For practical ends, of course, things have now changed at many points. One need only think of growth studies, or the introduction of more sophisticated insights coming from anthropology into medicine.

Hooton's earliest principal field of endeavor was craniometry. The work itself did not last beyond the 1930s, but the interest persisted in his osteology course and in his view of race and populations, and, I think, best reveals his train of thought. As his other interests show, he was a self-made anthropologist. His mentors at Oxford and elsewhere were anatomists, but he did not follow that line. And, strange to say, he took no note of Karl Pearson's school, of which more below. So there was not much to guide him outside of the French and German formalized methods of measurement. He got some instruction in the Broca school from Hrdlička. He practiced these techniques industriously in major works, but I think in the end he found them rather sterile.

Unlike the continentals, he was not interested in straight racial classification. (He did suggest some rather tortuous racial genealogies, but not as a result of his own research.) Both he and the Europeans can certainly be called typologists, but there is a distinction: The Europeans were more interested in distinguishing among whole populations as types or as representing preconceived "races." Hooton was more concerned with the dynamics, with looking at the variation within populations, although in such work typology was indeed prominent.

His first major work, on Canary Island skulls (13), was an attempt to find significant subdivisions within that population. Let him tell it (17): The Canary Island study taught him "that the analysis of a racially mixed population whose antecedents are individually unknown, can best be approached by the division of skull series into morphological impressional types, on the basis of general resemblance. Such types may then be validated by statistical tests." This was actually written after his well-known Pecos Pueblo study (14), which was carried out exactly along those lines.[1] The Pecos cranial types were assigned designations partly with suggestive connotations: "Pseudo-Negroid," "Long-faced European," "Plains Indian." Given the process of selection, it is not surprising that the statistics appeared to support the distinction among types. But he also found that his "Pseudo-Australoids" and "Plains Indians" failed to approach their proposed affiliates. This work founded his perception of American Indian racial origins, and of racial history generally. However, his interpretation (e.g. 16) was by no means as simple or specific as the above labels might suggest.

With our latter-day wisdom it is easy to see the a priori flaws—i.e. using statistics to validate what were nonrandom samples to begin with, and departing from the assumption that skeletal populations, whether Canary Island or Pecos, were racially mixed, not normal breeding populations. Hence the types. But it was Dixon, in an unlucky foray into physical anthropology (5), whose racial types were based strictly on divisions of three cranial indexes—e.g. long skull + broad nose + long face would be one of eight such possible combinations, each of the eight in search of a primeval parent race. In a mammoth analysis Dixon subjected cranial series the world over to such subdividing, and created a scenario of migrations of the eight primeval races that was not persuasive. Chastened by the reviews that met the publication, he retreated into his excellent work on cultural evolution and diffusion, and he ever after spoke of his *Racial History of Man* as The Crime. It is interesting that Dixon's Crime was too mechanical for Hooton. They worked independently, even though they shared certain assumptions and were similarly vague about the ultimate origins of the supposed racial components involved.

However the results may look today, the Pecos study was impressive as a thoughtfully designed and fully executed major project of craniology, and it was correspondingly influential. Like others of the day, I used means of measurements and indexes for description and comparison, trying to relate populations in this way. I gave Hooton's approach a try with two cranial series, one Irish and one Melanesian, but was unable to discern anything persuasive as to types; also, I was dubious about dissecting populations in this way, having some idea of normal variation. I take no credit for this; it was a limitation that seemed to enforce itself. In comparing populations, running the

---

[1] I am here addressing only the matter of types. The Pecos study was also a detailed tabulation of the characters and variations of the series of the whole; it included statistical testing of the type series against known sets of African, Asian, etc skulls, and also statistical comparisons of stratigraphic subgroups. The impressive combination of inventiveness and much detailed work is the reason for the general effect of the Pecos project.

eye up and down columns of means was minimally rewarding but seemed to me the only recourse. For statistical support there was Pearson's Coefficient of Racial Likeness, which entailed a lot of labor, and Mahalanobis's D^2 distance, which entailed a great deal more, although on the face of it a better statistic. I became disappointed and disenchanted with available methods. So, of course, did Hooton, who had been the most inventive in his own endeavors, both with crania (Pecos) and with the living (Irish; the data having been collected on a large scale by Wesley Dupertuis).

The second major figure of the time was, of course, Alex Hrdlička. Tenacious of purpose, he made great contributions: founding the *AJPA* and supporting it partly out of his own pocket; bringing the American Association of Physical Anthropologists into being; building up the cranial collections of the Smithsonian and indefatigably traveling to collect data on crania elsewhere; and cleaning up many dubious claims of ancient American human remains.

He was certainly a diligent measurer of skulls. At one dinner of the AAPA Raymond Pearl toasted Hrdlička with a rather wooden jest about how many skulls Hrdlička could measure in a day, beginning with six before breakfast. Hrdlička, as I remember, was not amused. As to methodology, he was indeed keeper of the flame. He was true to the methods he had learned in Paris, and he explicitly saw firm standardization of measurements as a gift to the future. In the 1930s he endeavored to reinforce standardization by means of special small studies, published in the *AJPA*, on particular points of craniometric methodology. I was obliged to do one by the sheer force of his personality, brought to bear on this very junior colleague. I remember riding back from a New Haven meeting on the train, observing Hrdlička trying to persuade Adolph Schultz to do a similar thing, with Schultz uncomfortably but successfully managing to evade the job. I think Hrdlička also approached Hooton, also unsuccessfully.

Hrdlička compiled and published large numbers of measurements and their means but did not use them effectively to demonstrate anything. Statistics flowed easily from Boas; Hooton used them lavishly but did not understand them well; Hrdlička detested them and warned the young away from them. As Alice Brues says (1), Hrdlička suffered from "math anxiety," a temperamental disposition not unknown in later anthropologists.

Biological anthropology in America might have a different face today if Franz Boas had been teaching in a university with more students interested in that field and in evolution, and if Boas had not eventually been so occupied with the Kwakiutl. At Columbia he had only one PhD in physical anthropology, Marcus Goldstein, who tells me he thinks Herskovits may also have started in physical. Boas actually did more in our field than might generally be remembered today: influence of the environment (changing cephalic index in immigrants), growth studies (spotting different rates in individuals, etc; see

32), and biometrical genetics (unexpected stature values in hybrids; importance of variation among family lines within a population).

His German education was strong, beginning with classics. Boas was fascinated by physics and mathematics, which obviously came easily to his intellect. He thus saw the biological and the mathematical aspects of problems and data at the same time. He admired Karl Pearson and his work; he did not go as far as Pearson in actually formulating statistics, although he adumbrated analysis of variance before Fisher introduced it. Though he used and warmly advocated measurements, specifically for purposes of classification of existing humanity, his classification was broad and loose, unlike those of his contemporaries. In 1899 he wrote (2): "The function of measurement is ... solely that of giving greater accuracy to the vague verbal description ... . Measurements must be selected in accordance with the problem that we are trying to investigate." Put that with what Fawcett (see below) wrote a couple of years later, and anthropology would seem to have been poised for a more rapid advance along such lines than actually ensued.

I wish I knew more about Boas. As with Hooton, I am inclined to think his influence was not that of simple charisma (in spite of his being "Papa Franz" at Columbia), but rather came from personal force, ideas, and industry. He never downplayed the biological aspect vis-à-vis the cultural, although many of his students tended to do so. That is to say, I think some members of the "Boas school" developed attitudes that were not those of Boas himself. At the same time his mathematical viewpoint defended him against ideas of "types" and fueled his devastating review of Dixon's *Racial History of Man* (5).

In the early part of the century, craniometry seemed to be the only game in town as far as bones were concerned. Of the major players, Boas sat osteology out, allowing Bruno Oetteking to give courses at Columbia that were pure and dense methodology. Boas seems only to have taught a grueling course in statistics.

With respect to developments then and later it is a pity that there was not more transatlantic communication, specifically between Americans and the Biometric Laboratory under Karl Pearson. Pearson proceeded from statistical principles to the measuring of crania as test material, instead of the other way around. He got his good friend Flinders Petrie to harvest large series of skulls in Egypt, where Petrie was the leading archaeologist of the time. In due course Pearson and such coworkers as G. M. Morant and Miriam Tildesley became more interested in the anthropological problems, and used various sets of crania for comparison. Pearson devised the Coefficient of Racial Likeness as the first multivariate measure of distance among samples or populations.

At the turn of the century Cicely Fawcett, under Pearson's guidance, published on the Naqada crania (8). This paper introduced the measurement designations and definitions used henceforth in the Biometric Laboratory, borrowed with modifications from the Frankfurt Agreement of 1884. [In Hooton's very first cranial reports, on the Madisonville (12) and Turner (36) mound burials, he noted that the methods in use in the Peabody Museum and in the National Museum conformed instead to the Monaco Agreement, implicitly acknowledging Hrdlička's influence.]

Fawcett had this to say: "We do not contest the value of anatomical appreciation in the hands of the master, but we do contest the cloaking of such appreciation by an apparent array of craniometric data, which are statistically inadequate," going on to assert that most data published by anatomists were hopelessly inadequate and further, as Pearson had made clear, that large numbers of specimens would be needed. This statement seems to answer beforehand some objections made later, especially those about the relative virtues of anatomical versus statistical assessments.

But the main point is this: The Biometric Lab people knew why they were measuring, whereas many craniometrists—and I would have to include Hrdlička—did not. There remained the problem of computation: The CRL was a makeshift. R. A. Fisher, in his well-known paper (9) of 1936, pointed out that the CRL was a measure of significance of difference, not a measure of likeness or of distance. He also complained that things were in a primitive state if specialists were not being taught even simple statistics, and said "the fact is, whether it be necessary or accidental, that the majority of anthropologists, as of biologists, feel so unfamiliar with statistical reasoning as to accept, in some cases, alleged statistical conclusions with something akin to credulous awe, or in others to reject them with indignation as introducing unnecessary confusion into otherwise plain issues." By this time Fisher had already formulated analysis of variance and the discriminant function, and he knew what he was talking about.[2]

Mahalanobis (25) in the 1920s tried to point out to Pearson another defect in the CRL: that it did not take account of the correlation among measurements, as Fisher also noted later (9). He did not prevail, but then himself introduced D^2, the accepted best measure of distance today. Lionel Penrose in 1954 (28) published his size and shape distances, also subject to the effects of correlation; but because of greater ease of computation several people argued that they were close enough in results to D^2 to be preferable. Computers have naturally made that appeal pointless.

Thus for the first half of the century there was a certain stagnation at the center of this kind of work, owing to lack of both computers and communication. Again, Boas practically invented analysis of variance himself but only in the form of a mathematical expression to point out the importance of variation within populations, not only the differences between them. To Hrdlička all this

---

[2]

I met Professor Fisher late in 1961 in Adelaide, where he had retired. In the course of conversation he said he thought Africans were most distant among modern populations, essentially today's Out-of-Africa position. To my lasting regret I did not press him as to why he thought so; he died a month later.

was obscenity. Hooton always employed a small staff in compiling and computing, by hand and using punched cards, testing the significance of differences among types, criminals, or army jobs. Even Pearson, who could project multivariate statistics mentally, was cowed by the actual work—hence the CRL. In *Anthropology Today,* published in 1953, John Rowe (29) dealt with technical aids, and for biological anthropology discussed only punchcard methods of data compilation, which Hooton had been using for years. At that time, electronic computers were great vacuum tube dragons, slow and unreliable, though nonetheless effective.

So much for the first half of the century. A very few years, centered on 1950, brought change from many directions. In the 1940s Boas, Hrdlička, and Weidenreich died, with Hooton surviving only until 1954. The same decade saw major books by Dobzhansky (6), Simpson (30), and Mayr (26), followed by the synthesis in evolutionary theory datable to 1947 (24), as well as the recognition of *Australopithecus* as a hominid. In anthropology Boyd (3, 4) and Washburn (33, 34) were particularly effective in exorcising some of the past.

Boyd had a good grasp of the genetic aspects of evolution and was a hard-working blood-group man. The ABO data were well known, but other systems like the Rh were only just coming over the horizon. A mild and pleasant man personally, Boyd nevertheless minced no words in plowing under simpler ideas of multiple races, with their supposedly clear edges and long persistence, as well as any and all ideas of types. His 1950 book was a well-informed and balanced presentation and criticism. His subtitle was "An Introduction to Modern Physical Anthropology"; and perhaps because he came into the field from immunology, and so was not one of the boys, some physical anthropologists were nettled. He was a major force in civilizing the unreconstructed (myself included), even if his effect was not instantaneous.

Washburn has been an acute and articulate critic (33, 34), and had particular effect through helping organize the 1952 Wenner-Gren Conference, and especially the Cold Spring Harbor Symposium of 1950. With clarity of style he pointed out the logical difficulties underlying past conceptions of race, types, and classifications, and emphasized the role of problem- and hypothesis-testing. Later on he was ahead of the curve in fostering studies in primate behavior and molecular biology.

The 1953 publication of *Anthropology Today* is now far in the past. As a sign of how far, we might remember that carbon-14 dating was then brand new.[3] What has been happening to physical anthropology since that distant time? The field is of course far too broad for facile indexing. Nor, unfortunately, is it governed by well-developed theory of its own, as Washburn

---

3

Its entrance would have been further delayed if Paul Fejos had not instantly seen the importance of Libby's discovery and called a group of anthropologists together to consider it (7).

apparently hoped it could be—unless such theory is limned in such prevailing controversies as that over the origins of modern *Homo sapiens:* replacement versus regional continuity. Naturally, present work follows the past along the same obvious avenues to the human animal: his primate relatives; his remains, fossil or recent; his living biology.

Weidenreich precipitated the "origin of *sapiens*" argument as early as 1939 (35); however, nobody in 1950 foresaw the avalanche of fossil hominid material coming after 1960, something that is now fodder for a large number of professionals. That development has been important in fusing several main interests in human population history. Not long ago, paleoanthropologists and molecular workers disagreed in dating hominid emergence, and the latter won general acceptance of their solution. In today's work the molecular people, the paleontologists, and the cranial-morphology and distance people are all avidly looking into each other's materials, and symposia show that this has become a natural grouping of workers, informed also by archaeologists and paleoclimatologists.

The other main avenue has been broadened and extended: human biology and variation. This is really Hooton's main interest, freed from its earlier limitations. Blood and serum polymorphisms are perhaps less vigorously pursued than when they were the one new alternative to anthropometry, and before the appearance of DNA analysis.

In population studies especially, Hooton's frustrated hopes are being fulfilled: interaction of anthropology and medicine (in the broad sense). In particular, the Harvard Solomon Islands Project (10), with sizeable teams, has gathered a wealth of biological, anthropological, and medical data, on eight Melanesian communities comprising a spectrum of degrees of contact effects, over a 15-year period of particularly rapid acculturation. (On Bougainville, the team arrived at a reportedly pristine village to be greeted by a boy with a transistor radio clasped to his ear; on Ontong Java, visits spanned the changeover from wood-hulled to fiberglass canoes.) The Project yielded immediate significant findings on the health effects of changing diet, as well as providing a future data base, established at a critical point in time—notably, before the powerful impact of copper mining on Bougainville.

Another well-focused recent example is an assemblage of papers (31), on epidemiological topics from an anthropological perspective, recognizing especially the co-evolution of culture and pathogens, as well as population and individual genetics. Writers specifically recognize that 40 or 50 years ago neither anthropology nor medicine was in a technical or conceptual position to produce such integrated work. Today the vista is one of unlimited progress in the same direction. Again, Hooton felt deeply that this direction was needed, but he could not even envision the shape of things to come.

In general, it seems to me that the 1980s have seen the lifting of physical anthropology to a new plane. The number of workers is greater, of course, but in addition students now serve real apprenticeships in one line or another (see my remarks above about being "trained by Hooton"). Primate behavior has, so to speak, developed stereoscopic vision, now comparing multiple populations of a given species and of many separate species. Molecular workers are doing things I understand only in outline. Analysts of fossils carry interpretations of the functional anatomy of single bones to impressive lengths, often using forbiddingly mathematical methods. Similar studies of cranial form and function also use special measurements and demanding statistical analysis.

As an example of such sophistication let me cite recent studies by Oxnard (27), actually an old primate hand. A longtime form-and-function man, using morphometrics, Oxnard has lately devised continuous numerical scales for behavior, diet, and other aspects of life style, over many primate species, so as to apply factor analysis and canonical variates to the whole. Such analysis elicits fuller detailed information about kinds of adaptation than could be found when simpler categories of locomotion were used; at the same time, almost paradoxically, the analysis appears to sustain the existing taxonomy of species even though species related in this way may arrange themselves differently along adaptive axes. Work like that of Oxnard brings together various approaches—anatomical, behavioral, quantitative—at a new level. Needless to say, such studies could not have been accomplished in the pre-computer period, which constrained even so energetic a man as Schultz to tabulations of osteometric data; he was limited to demonstrating the range of variation in ape species, valuable though that was.

Certain other interests in current physical anthropology, though active, are more parochial: forensics, for example, or paleopathology. These have their special journals, and there is a *Journal of Quantitative Anthropology* to serve the whole field. When Hrdlička retired as editor of the *AJPA* he stipulated that a new series of volumes should be started, to distinguish them from his own legacy. If he could see recent numbers of the journal, containing formidably mathematical work and using ad hoc measurements not covered in the Frankfurt or Monaco Agreements, I feel sure he would be satisfied he had done the right thing.

Foretelling future activity was chancy in 1950 and is chancy now—a warning against pontification. Washburn at that time believed experiment would become important, but it is really not in the nature of physical anthropology to be experimental; non-invasive work like Tuttle's on muscle performance is representative of what can be done. Beyond a safe bet that things will proceed by further intensification of what is being done at the moment, it is highly probable that DNA analysis, nuclear and mitochondrial, still has a great deal of mileage in it, and might do more to elucidate the history of human populations than blood polymorphisms did.

It is easier to point to historical problems that should find answers. Preoccupation with modern human origins should continue for a while, advancing only by fits and starts (for example, with new datings of the Middle Paleolithic Near Eastern fossil remains). The answers are bound to come eventually, but probably through much painstaking study of existing materials—there are good recent examples—and through piece-by-piece fossil finds, not through a dramatic solution. Mitochondrial Eve has been a stimulus but needs more scrutiny and samples. Long ago Weidenreich, who had plenty of imagination, constantly insisted that fossils, and only fossils, could settle such questions.

Similarly, continuing finds of late Miocene hominoid fossils should close in on an actual ape/australopithecine ancestor, whose emergence may reveal some unprophesied aspects. Here, matters of climate and general environment must invade a problem that was once all anatomy and teeth. These are things that must captivate anthropologists, as dinosaurs do the public. Biomedically important studies like those of human growth, or even reconstructions of language origins, are sure to have a hard time competing with the products of the Rift Valley silts.

Speculation is ultimately idle. More important are questions of education for physical anthropologists. In my own day, the PhD called for a reading knowledge of French and German—now merely pleasant luxuries—and for conversance with Hooton's bone identification. Today, a streamlined course in human and primate anatomy would seem essential. For those who can stomach it, at least a reading knowledge of statistics is needed. This surely means some basic mathematics of the high school level. Unfortunately, streamlined statistics appropriate for anthropologists are hard to come by. I once remarked to M. J. R. Healy, who is good at such things, that the statistics department at Harvard required a year or more of calculus for admission to a course in so relatively simple a method as multivariate analysis, and he was indignant. My own mathematical background does not equip me to understand some of what is being published today, and a higher level of learning is really demanded by computer availability and the opportunities for modern investigation. Like Healy I can see no reason not to teach the appropriate statistics without demanding previous servitude in advanced math.

Further enormous changes over the past 40 years are obvious. At the founding meeting of the AAPA, for example, only a few of the eighty-odd present were physical anthropologists in their own right. And the Association was hardly yet national; it was some years before it met as far west as Pittsburgh—after all, in those train-bound days, baseball's western horizon was St. Louis.

And what about anthropology as a whole? Around the house I happen to have the Harvard course lists for 1891, 1931, and 1991. In the first of these, the complete course offerings of the college occupy 41 pages, devoting the first 20 to ancient and modern languages. On the last page, one paragraph announces a three-year course in Archaeology and Ethnology, for graduate students; no prerequisites—other than knowledge of French, Spanish, elementary chemistry, geology, botany, zoology, drawing, and surveying. By 1931 anthropology had forged ahead, having two and a half pages of course listings all to itself, and three officers of instruction (this was a major department). By 1991 both these numbers had increased tenfold. (These may be ho-hum figures to anthropologists of this moment, but they awe one whose career has spanned the interval.) I do not feel that all this signifies that today's graduating senior is ten times as educated as I am, or, for that matter, as Hooton or Thomas Jefferson were. Still, her or his training and professional focus will certainly be informed and scientific at a much higher level.

As all of anthropology grows, the ties between the biological and cultural domains have become looser—a depressing fact. At least in this country, anthropologists of two generations ago explicitly favored a more unified discipline. Nowadays it is too much to expect individuals to have authority in several fields, but I think we are only the losers when contacts diminish and subjects like sociobiology or population attributes are addressed from *ex parte* positions.

Those earlier physical anthropologists were the frontiersmen, free spirits. Can one imagine a new Hooton, Hrdlička, or Boas? Technology was simple and laboratories hardly deserved the name. Work was individual, and jointly authored papers were almost unknown. Hooton and Dixon, both at Harvard, did not consult over cranial types. Schultz and Straus, both at Johns Hopkins, both working on primates, published jointly only once, as far as I know. Now, collaborative papers are more the rule, although we have not yet reached the point of a paper published this year in *Nature,* on an Einsteinian problem, by 35 coauthors. Charles Darwin, are you listening?

As for myself, I am well content with what I got. Teachers like Boas, Hooton, and Dixon were making their own anthropology, on the grand scale, and we had the luxury of a general view of the field. As an undergraduate I was surprised and delighted to hear so much from Dixon about China, India, Mesopotamia, Majapahit Indonesia, the Incas, and others, and I agree that we should all know a great deal more about such cultural springs. And we should all know a great deal more about Western civilization. The current drive to dilute study of the latter, by which the nation lives, with a sort of cultural bazaar, does not seem to me to be the anthropological perspective at all. We learn about humanity from other cultures but we do not live by them.

In obedience to anthropology's mission, professionalism has led to some particularized and recondite interests, certain of them downright peculiar, and I wonder if some of this baggage will still seem rewarding to today's graduate student 20 or 30 years from now. I had a couple of such courses, in and out of anthropology, but I still benefit and take pleasure from most of my work. I cannot imagine a professional life that would have been more congenial, or one that would have given me more admired and amusing friends.

It is pleasant to be retired. The news from anthropological front lines arrives in ever greater quantities. The discipline of teaching obliges you to try to present important matters in well-rounded, balanced fashion, even as you make your own views known. A nice ideal, but now I can lean back, read without having to revise lecture notes, and tell myself (in private) just what I think of things. It's sort of like spending capital, and why not?

Literature Cited

1. Brues, A. M. 1990. 60 years of physical anthropology, including false starts and dead ends. Paper presented at 1990 Meet. Am. Anthropol. Assoc.
2. Boas, F. 1940. *Race, Language and Culture,* p. 647. New York: Macmillan
3. Boyd, W. C. 1950. *Genetics and the Races of Man. An Introduction to Modern Physical Anthropology,* p. 453. Boston: Little, Brown & Co
4. Boyd, W. C. 1953. The contributions of genetics to anthropology. In *Anthropology Today. An Encylopedic Inventory,* ed. A. L. Kroeber, pp. 488–506. Chicago: Univ. Chicago Press
5. Dixon, R. B. 1923. *The Racial History of Man,* p. 583. New York: Charles Scribner's Sons
6. Dobzhansky, T. 1941. *Genetics and the Origin of Species,* p. 364. New York: Columbia Univ. Press
7. Dodds, J. W. 1973. *The Several Lives of Paul Fejos. A Hungarian-American Odyssey,* p. 113. New York: The Wenner-Gren Found.
8. Fawcett, C. D. 1902. A second study of the variation and correlation of the human skull, with special reference to the Naqada crania. *Biometrika* 1:408–67
9. Fisher, R. A. 1936. "The Coefficient of Racial Likeness" and the future of craniometry. *J. Roy. Anthropol. Inst.* 66:57–63
10. Friedlaender, J. S., ed. 1987. *The Solomon Islands Project. A Long-Term Study of Health, Human Biology, and Culture Change.* Res. Monogr. Hum. Pop. Biol. Oxford: Clarendon
11. Goring, C. 1913. *The English Convict. A Statistical Study,* p. 440. London: H. M. Stationery Office
12. Hooton, E. A. 1920. Indian village site and cemetery near Madisonville, Ohio. *Peabody Mus. Pap.* 8(1):137
13. Hooton, E. A. 1925. *The Ancient Inhabitants of the Canary Islands Harvard African Studies,* Vol. 7. Cambridge, MA: Peabody Mus. Harvard Univ. xxv + 401 pp.
14. Hooton, E. A. 1930. *The Indians of Pecos Pueblo. A Study of Their Skeletal Remains.* Papers of the Southwestern Expedition, Phillips Andover Academy, Vol. 4. New Haven: Yale Univ. Press. xxvii + 391 pp.
15. Hooton, E. A. 1931. *Up From the Ape,* p. 626. New York: Macmillan
16. Hooton, E. A. 1933. Racial types in America and their relation to Old World types. In *The American Aborigines. Their Origin and Antiquity,* ed. D. Jenness, pp. 133–63. Toronto: Univ. Toronto Press
17. Hooton, E. A. 1935. Development and correlation of research in physical anthropology at Harvard Univ. Proc. Am. Philos. Soc. Philadelphia
18. Hooton, E. A. 1937. *Apes, Men, and Morons,* p. 307. New York: G. P. Putnam's Sons
19. Hooton, E. A. 1939. *Twilight of Man,* p. 308. New York: G. P. Putnam's Sons
20. Hooton, E. A. 1939. *The American Criminal. An Anthropological Study.* Cambridge, MA: Harvard Univ. Press. 309 + app.
21. Hooton, E. A. 1940. *Why Men Behave Like Apes and Vice Versa,* p. 234. Princeton: Princeton Univ. Press
22. Hooton, E. A. 1942. *Man's Poor Relations,* p. 412. New York: Doubleday, Doran
23. Howells, W. 1944. *Mankind So Far,* p. 319. New York: Doubleday, Doran
24. Jepsen, G. L., Mayr, E., Simpson., G. G. 1949. *Genetics, Paleontology, and Evolution,* ed. G. L. Jepsen, E. Mayr, George Gaylord Simpson, p. 474. Princeton: Princeton Univ. Press
25. Mahalanobis, P. C. 1949. Appendix 1. Historical note on the D^2-statistic. Sankhya. *Indian J. Stat.* 9(2,3):237–40
26. Mayr, E. 1942. *Systematics and the Origin of Species.* New York: Columbia Univ. Press. xiv + 334 pp.
27. Oxnard, C. E., Crompton, R. H., Lieberman, S. S. 1990. *Animal Lifestyles and Anatomies: The Case of the Prosimian Primates,* p. 174. Seattle: Univ. Washington Press
28. Penrose, L. S. 1954. Distance, size and shape. *Ann. Eugen.* 18:337–43
29. Rowe, J. H. 1953. Technical aids in anthropology: a historical survey. See Ref. 4, pp. 895–940
30. Simpson, G. G. 1944. *Tempo and Mode in Evolution,* p. 237. New York: Columbia Univ. Press
31. Swedlund, A.C., Armelagos, G. J., eds. 1990. *Disease in Populations in Transition. Anthropological and Epidemiological Perspectives.* New York: Bergin and Garvey
32. Tanner, J. M. 1959. Boas' contribution to knowledge of human growth and form. In *The Anthropology of Franz Boas,* ed. W. Goldschmidt, pp. 76–111. Mem. Am. Anthropol. Assoc., Vol. 89.
33. Washburn, S. L. 1951. The new physical anthropology. *Trans. NY Acad. Sci.* 13/2:261–63
34. Washburn, S. L. 1953. The strategy of

physical anthropology. See Ref. 4, pp. 714–27

35. Weidenreich, F. 1939. The classification of fossil hominids and their relation to each other, with special reference to *Sinanthropus pekinensis. Bull. Geol. Soc. China* 20(1):64–75

36. Willoughby, C. C. 1922. The Turner group of earthworks, Hamilton County, Ohio, with notes on the skeletal remains by Earnest A. Hooton. *Peabody Mus. Pap.* 8(3):132

Annu. Rev. Anthropol. 1992. 21:19–42

THE CARIBBEAN REGION: An Open Frontier in Anthropological Theory

Michel-Rolph Trouillot

Department of Anthropology, The Johns Hopkins University, Baltimore, Maryland 21218

KEYWORDS: culture theory, complex societies, history, native voice, units of analysis

The encounter between anthropological theory and any region of the globe says as much about anthropology as it does about that region. Caribbean anthropology is a case in point. This region where boundaries are notoriously fuzzy has long been the open frontier of cultural anthropology: neither center nor periphery, but a sort of no man's land where pioneers get lost, where some stop overnight on their way to greater opportunities, and where yet others manage to create their own "new" world amidst First-World indifference. Accordingly, the object of this essay is dual: I write here about the Caribbean as viewed by anthropologists, but also about anthropology as viewed from the Caribbean. The review dwells on the coincidence between some zones of weakness in anthropological theory and areas of concern for Caribbeanists. I claim neither exhaustiveness nor statistical representativeness in dealing with the literature, and my boundaries are both arbitrary and fuzzy. I emphasize a present that encompasses most of the last 20 years, but my framework—not to mention the absence of any Caribbean focus in previous issues of this series— justifies forays into more distant pasts. I concentrate on works available in English, which happens to be the predominant language of Caribbean ethnology; but this emphasis here is no less arbitrary. More importantly, since I am addressing outsiders and insiders alike, I flatten some rough edges and over-

19

0084-6570/92/1015-0019$02.00

look inevitably some segments of the corpus, notably the anthropology of healing and that of religion, and urban studies as such (but see 59, 87, 156, 181). Issues in Creole linguistics, the ethnography and politics of language in the Caribbean, have generated many solid studies and deserve separate treatment. So does the literature on migration. The reader can consult other review essays on specific topics or earlier periods, bibliographies, as well as bibliographies of bibliographies (19, 27, 45, 112, 136, 165).

The essay is organized around three major themes: "heterogeneity," "historicity," and what I refer to as "articulation" (matters relating to levels, boundaries—the nature and limits of the unit of observation or analysis) and their ramifications. I do not see these themes as natural groupings of a self-contained Caribbean corpus but as markers highlighting the encounter between Caribbean studies and anthropology, scattered posts on the open frontier.

AN UNDISCIPLINED REGION

Christopher Columbus's landing in the Caribbean in 1492 provided a nascent Europe with the material and symbolic space necessary to establish its image of the Savage Other (188, 191). Not surprisingly, it is in the Caribbean islands and in the surrounding mainland that a certain kind of comparative ethnography was born in the 16th century, with the writings of Spanish scholars (134). But the Caribbean was also where Europe first achieved the systematic destruction of the Other, with the genocide of the Caribs and Arawaks of the Antilles. By the time the Enlightenment returned to the myth of the noble savage, recycling with a vengeance the debates in philosophical anthropology that had marked the Renaissance, most of the Antilles were inhabited by African peoples who had crossed the Atlantic in chains, and their Afro-Creole descendants, also enslaved. Many of these slaves worked on plantations run by profit-conscious Europeans on quite "modern" lines (119).

Slavery ended in the Caribbean at about the same time that the social sciences diverged from law and history in Europe and the United States; but by then the Caribbean had become an oddity in Western scholarship. The swift genocide of the aboriginal populations, the early integration of the region into the international circuit of capital, the forced migrations of enslaved African and indentured Asian laborers, and the abolition of slavery by emancipation or revolution all meant that the Caribbean would not conform within the emerging divisions of Western academia. With a predominantly nonwhite population, it was not "Western" enough to fit the concerns of sociologists. Yet it was not "native" enough to fit fully into the Savage slot where anthropologists found their preferred subjects. When E. B. Tylor published the first general anthropology textbook in the English language in 1881, Barbados had been "British" for two and a half centuries, Cuba had been "Spanish" for almost four, and Haiti had been an independent state for three generations—after a long French century during which it accounted for more than half of its metropolis's foreign trade. These were hardly places to look for primitives. Their very existence questioned the West/non-West dichotomy and the category of the native, upon both of which anthropology was premised.

The entire corpus of Caribbean cultural anthropology from the early decades of this century up to the present can be read against the background of this basic incongruity between the traditional object of the discipline and the inescapable history of the region. In that light, many riddles of the encounter fall into place, including North American anthropology's relative avoidance of the Caribbean (112). Up to the fourth decade of this century, native scholars from Haiti, Cuba, or Puerto Rico were more willing than foreigners to apply the tools of anthropological analysis to the study of their own folk. Later on, as Caribbean anthropology developed its specific interests, some of the weakest zones of anthropological theory came to overlap with concerns that Caribbeanists could not fully escape. Even the increased interest in Afro-American anthropology in the early 1970s (83, 198) failed to accord full legitimacy to the Caribbean within the guild. Today, as anthropology continues to nurture a legacy of tropes and concepts honed through the observation of societies once deemed "simple" (if not "primitive"), outsiders continue to confront the fact that Caribbean societies have long been awkwardly, yet definitely, "complex" (if not "modern").

No Gates on the Frontier

Three related features of this complexity sustain the lines of tension between anthropological discourse and Caribbean ethnology. First, Caribbean societies are inescapably heterogeneous. If savages elsewhere once looked the same to most anthropologists, the Caribbean has long been an area where some people live next to others who are remarkably distinct. The region—and indeed particular territories within it—has long been multiracial, multilingual, stratified and, some would say, multicultural (49, 50, 122, 150, 158, 161, 193). Second, this heterogeneity is known to be, at least in part, the result of history. Caribbean societies are inescapably historical, in the sense that some of their distant past is not only known, but known to be different from their present, and yet relevant to both the observers' and the natives' understanding of that present (6, 28, 102, 139). There is no general agreement on the extent of this relevance, but some of the earliest attacks on "the fallacy of the ethnographic present" (157:76–77) were launched from the Caribbean.

To be sure, the Caribbean is not the only area where heterogeneity and historicity have haunted the practitioners of a discipline that once made sociohistorical depth the exclusive attribute of Western societies. Elsewhere, however, anthropologists often blocked the full investigation of that complexity by posting "gatekeeping concepts": hierarchy in India, honor-and-shame in the Mediterranean, etc (10), a maneuver that, in my view, reflected as well the West's ranking of certain Others. Anthropological gatekeeping notwithstanding, "Sinology" was—and is—more likely to be taken as a separate field, and any reunion of "Orientalists" as an academic meeting, than similar bodies or institutions of knowledge—and power—dealing with many other parts of the world. Would anyone open Pandora's box by suggesting that such implicit rankings are based on "objective" grounds?

Still, gatekeeping as a specific anthropological strategy was relatively successful in many complex societies outside of the Caribbean because anthropologists dealing with these regions could pay lip service to history while using that same history as a buffer against historical investigation (cf 3). With history kept at a comfortable distance, anthropologists could resurrect the "native" while forsaking the primitive. Gatekeeping concepts are so-called "native" traits mythified by theory in ways that bound the object of study. They act as theoretical simplifiers to restore the ethnographic present and protect the timelessness of culture.

Gatekeeping has never been successful in the Caribbean. Here, heterogeneity and historicity opened up new vistas, deflecting energies from theoretical simplification. Each in its own way pointed to a third feature of the sociocultural landscape, the fact that Caribbean societies are inherently colonial. It is not only that all Caribbean territories have been conquered by one or another Western power. It is not only that they are the oldest colonies of the West and that their very colonization was part of the material and symbolic process that gave rise to the West as we know it. Rather, their social and cultural characteristics—and, some would say, individual idiosyncrasies of their inhabitants (59)—cannot be accounted for, or even described, without reference to colonialism.

This inescapable feature precludes the resurrection of the native, even when colonialism is not evoked explicitly. Here, there is no way to satisfy anthropology's obsession for "pure" cultures (109, 148, 167). Even populations such as the Island Caribs of Dominica and St. Vincent or the mainland Garifuna are known to be products of complex mixtures (65, 67, 69, 180). Whereas anthropology prefers "pre-contact" situations—or creates "no-contact" situations— the Caribbean is nothing but contact.

Understandably, disciplinary fences are quite flexible. Anthropologists engage historians, economists, and policy makers (35, 70, 71, 99, 126, 185), and many publish as much in historical or regional journals as in publications regimented by the guild. Gatekeeping themes never muster a partisan following large enough within the discipline to allow for fermentation. Anthropological master tropes have rather short tenures on the frontier, as competing topics sneak through the open lands and establish new lines of exchange. Theory alone cannot enclose the object of study, not because Caribbean reality is messier than any other but because anthropological theory has yet to deal with the mess created by colonialism with handles as convenient as honor-and-shame, the caste system, or filial piety. Yet, in part also because of colonialism, empirical boundaries are no clearer in this region of prefabricated enclaves and open frontiers where the very "unit of empirical existence" (171:2), let alone that of analysis, is a matter of open controversy.

HETEROGENEITY

If complexity is what first strikes the anthropologist when looking at Caribbean societies, and if heterogeneity is at least one marker of this complexity, what, then, holds these societies together? Michael G. Smith's answer to this question has remained consistent over the years. "[T]he monopoly of power by one cultural section is the essential precondition for the maintenance of the total society in its current form," writes Smith (160:183), quoting himself 24 years later. For Smith, Caribbean societies are "plural": They exhibit antagonistic strata with different cultures. They stand as essentially political shells, filled with juxtaposed—and incompatible—value-systems, different sets of institutions being held together solely by the vertical power of the state (158, 161).

The debate over Smith's use of the "plural society" concept has been long—much too long, some would say (14, 18, 49, 50, 145, 146, 159, 160, 162). Caribbeanists of various persuasions fail to see the insurmountable wall that Smith erects between his corporate groups. Moreover, the distinction between plural and nonplural societies never seemed convincing to the rest of the guild, and few scholars (51, 130) embraced Smith's framework. Yet, his inflexibility notwithstanding, Smith does raise eloquently the issue of the relation between heterogeneity and power, an issue that remains to be taken more seriously by anthropologists, in the Caribbean and elsewhere. For Smith is right in suggesting that in the Caribbean case, at least, one cannot presume "culture," if by this we mean a principle of homogeneity, determined by fiat, that would somehow find its parallel in an equally bounded entity referred to as "society."

Cite, Praise, or Paraphrase?

M. G. Smith makes much of the respective birthplaces, nationalities, and races of his various opponents. Smith himself is Jamaican-born and faces continuous insinuations that his application of the plural society is local middle-class ideology passing for social theory (145, 146, 159, 161, 162). Unfortunately, the serious issue of the status of native discourse remains only in the subtext of this debate. For although many Caribbean-born scholars have rightly questioned some of the assumptions behind the plural society framework, we need to ask why approaches that emphasize ethnic or cultural segmentation constitute a cross-generational stream in Caribbean studies and letters (130, 135, 142). These approaches are singularly effective when translated into the realm of state politics by a self-trained ethnologist such as Haiti's François Duvalier, by self-anointed "natives" such as Forbes Burnham in Guyana or Balaguer in the Dominican Republic, or by dissidents and potential coup leaders in Suriname and Trinidad. In an obvious reference to the local persuasiveness of his views, Smith himself notes that those "who participate in those processes and who are most directly affected by them" implicitly know which side is right (161:35). This "proof of the pudding" argument is not convincing to those of us who believe that social science is possible and that Goebbels does not necessarily provide the best analysis of Nazism. Yet the fact that Smith's viewpoint indeed reflects Jamaican elite ideology does not change by an iota the fact—equally "obvious"—that the presumption of order and homogeneity that has been a hallmark of Western social science is itself a reflection of dominant Euroamerican consciousness, a by-product of the ideological invention of the nation-state.

The issue is not trivial. Even a superficial inquiry reveals that the pronouncements of Caribbean peoples of various origins have long made their way into anthropological accounts with unequal value added. Recently, Richard Price has systematically undertaken to record the Saramaka Maroons' voices and narratives from and about the past and present them to an academic audience (137, 138). Price excels at inventing intellectual quotation marks, new ways of marking on the published page both the boundaries and the dialogs between voices; but he keeps prudently away from epistemological issues. Advancing along the path Price broke with *First-Time, Alabi's World* masterfully mixes four voices on the page. Price gives us tips on how to "hear" three of these voices (Moravian missionaries, Dutch planters, and native Saramakas) but none on how to read his own prose and "passages from other scholars." Yet it may be worth asking which philosophy of knowledge we should use to evaluate native historical or sociological discourse or, for that matter, that of any participant (140). How do we handle the overlaps and incompatibilities of participants' judgments with Euroamerican scholarship (54, 195)? How does anthropology handle the similarities between, say, Puerto Rican discourses on virility and nationalism and Peter Wilson's construct on reputation and respectability (about which more below), or the affinities between the social criticism of Haitian scholars in the 1930s and Herskovits's notion of "socialized ambivalence"? To identify scholars independently of nativeness reopens the epistemological issues we might have wanted to postpone. Yet even if we set aside the issue of knowledge *qua* truth, who is the outsider who assigns differential semiotic relevance to alternative native voices (139)? And who is to bestow nativeness, anyway (54, 129, 195)? In the Caribbean, there is no "native" viewpoint in the sense that Geertz assumes nativeness (61), no privileged shoulder upon which to lean. This is a region where Pentecostalism is as "indigenous" as Rastafarianism, where some "Bush Negroes" were Christians long before Texans became "American," where some "East Indians" find peace in "African" rituals of Shango (16, 76, 138).

Anthropology has yet to reach a consensus on both the epistemological status and semiotic relevance of native discourse anywhere. Is native discourse a citation, an indirect quote, or a paraphrase? Whose voice is it, once it enters the discursive field dominated by the logic of academe? Is its value referential, indexical, phatic, or poetic? The problem is compounded in the Caribbean by colonial domination whose duration and intellectual reach defy most under-standings of nativeness. At least some resident intellectuals have long been interlocutors in European debates about the region (64, 90, 142, 146). No discursive field is fully "ours," or "theirs." Diane Austin's suggestion that Caribbean anthropology is marked by an analytical antinomy between, on the one hand, conflict-resistance and, on the other, integration-domination is tell-ing (13), for similar dualities obtain in Caribbean intellectual discourse (90). But such dualities stand correct only if we do not try to push every single author toward one or the other pole.

At any rate, the real debate is not over whether heterogeneity exists but about where to locate it and—quite literally—what to do with it. The answer to that question turns on one's idea of what Caribbean societies are about and, equally important, on one's theory of culture and society. This is also what I mean by saying that the inescapable fact of Caribbean heterogeneity poses fundamental questions for anthropological theory that most anthropologists have chosen to ignore. Raymond T. Smith, one of M.G. Smith's earliest intellectual opponents, said as much long ago, though in more muted terms and in a different context.

Gender, Social Organization, and the Wider World

In a 1963 review of family and kinship studies in the Caribbean, then the dominant field of Caribbean ethnology, R. T. Smith states: "The major prob-lem is what it has always been; to relate patterns of familial and mating behaviour to other factors in the contemporary social systems and to the cultural traditions of the people concerned. Here progress is less impressive because we are still unclear about the nature of these societies" (165:472).

Smith's concern should not be read only as the reflection of a functional-ist's search for structuring principles. The assumption that fieldwork will somehow reveal the nature of the entity under study, however persuasive it may look in cases of apparent homogeneity, breaks down completely on the frontier. Smith's statement shows how the inescapable manifestations of com-plexity turn the anthropologist's eye toward a larger horizon. It suggests why the glut of kinship studies did not lead in turn to enduring gatekeeping con-cepts in Caribbean anthropology: the heterogeneity of the ensemble precluded the domestic unit, the matrifocal family, or the allocation of gender roles to generate theoretical simplifiers, in spite of a flow of publications recycling a restricted number of themes.

I cannot do justice to this abundant corpus (more than 200 titles between 1970 and 1990), which has sparked, in turn, a number of anthologies, bibliog-raphies, and reassessments (e.g. 92, 136, 143, 147, 177). The streams are multiple, though they tend to crisscross around the role—or the plight—of women as mothers, as child-bearers and rearers, and as mates. In their own way, Caribbean kinship studies have always been gender studies, and they have always insisted that gender is a two-way street. This had to do, ironically, with an early concern for policy on the part of officials who saw Afro-Caribbean families as "deviant" simply because they did not fit the nuclear folk-model of Western consciousness (147, 148, 168, 170). Just as in the United States, these bureaucrats' views were echoed by social scientists who wanted to explain—or explain away—such "abnormalities" as "missing fathers."

Two early studies continue to influence the tone of the research: Edith Clarke's *My Mother Who Fathered Me* and R.T. Smith's *The Negro Family In British Guiana* (42, 163). Smith's legacy may well be, to his despair, the often misused notion of matrifocality. Smith insists that he coined the word not to mean female-headed or even consanguineal families, as others would believe, but to underline the role of women as mothers (166, 167). Clarke's legacy goes more in the direction of a social pathology. More recently, Peter Wilson's construct of "reputation and respectability," which neatly ties gender roles to the wider society, came close to becoming the master trope of Caribbean anthropology, precisely because it did not treat the domestic as a closed domain. Criticizing the fact that "social organization" was a code word for limited studies of the purely "domestic," Wilson postulates a pan-Caribbean opposition between an internal value system ("reputation"), emphasizing equality, virility, and lower-class norms, and an external one emphasizing ranking, womanhood, and elitist respectability (201, 202). The scheme is more ingenious than most of the dualities that plague Caribbean studies; hence its continuous impact on the literature (e.g. 1, 148). But it is too neat for comfort; hence the reluctance of most Caribbeanists to use it as an overall simplifier. Wilson's polarity requires strong qualifications when the observer tackles the historical and social particulars of specific territories and especially the relations among gender, the dual value system, and colonialism (132).

New paradigms have yet to emerge in spite of an abundance of refreshing positions on gender and the family. I can note only a few: the call to incorporate an emic approach to kinship into ethnographies of "social organization" (95, 136, 141); the call for yet more careful distinctions between household and family (147), or for a reconceptualization of the consanguineal household (66); the call for a more systematic study of the wide realm of female responsibility (56) or for the delineation of gender-specific estates, spheres, or domains against the background of economic roles (26). The last two strategies do not always point to a simplistic division that would consign women to the home and leave the world to men. Neither among the relatively isolated Maroons of Suriname nor in Barbados, arguably one of the most Westernized islands, do the cultural ideals and the practice of gender roles duplicate fully dominant Western patterns (48, 141, 179). Further, the case for female-centered domains, material or symbolic, is usually made on more sophisticated grounds than a base/superstructure model where gender would duplicate the division of labor (16, 178, 202). Furthermore, the division of labor itself does not always operate as most Westerners would expect. Specialization in independent economic activities, notably marketing, often helps open for rural *women* certain gender-specific vistas upon the wider world (106, 121, 128). Men may occupy street corners and engage in lewd behavior in nonfamilial settings (37, 91, 98), but the woman's world is by no means "private," as North Americans would understand this word (20, 21, 88). The evidence does not prove that gender equality is a widespread Caribbean phenomenon, but it does indicate indigenous forms and designs of female autonomy. In that context, female independence does not necessarily mean the breaking of traditional ties; it may signify the reinforcement of certain "networking" practices (21). Nor does modernization always mean the demise of a putative "feudal" patriarchy. On the contrary, recent Western inroads often create or renew forms of gender inequality. Off-shore industries, Christian churches, professionalization, monetization, or remittances from migrants may reduce traditional female autonomy or increase gender-specific risks (35, 68, 73, 89, 106, 149, 179, 187). The complexity of gender roles recorded by Caribbean ethnographers implicitly begs feminist theory to de-Westernize its premises further.

Caribbean analyses of kinship and gender keep encroaching upon the wider world. Sally Price's rich ethnography of Saramaka shows how the production and flow of art reflect and reinforce cultural understandings about gender (141). In an equally acclaimed study of mating patterns in 19th-century Cuba, Martinez-Alier centers on the relationship between sexual values and social inequality. She argues convincingly that the battles between sexes, races, and classes intertwine and that, in the final analysis, it is "the hierarchical nature of the social order" (100:128) that generates sexual codes as well as gender roles and relations. One cannot adequately abridge Martinez-Alier's superb exposition of these arguments. I note here that, in the end, they echo R. T. Smith's earlier intimation to look at "the nature" of these societies. How revealing, then, it is of the relationship between the Caribbean frontier and the discipline that a leading feminist theorist found it necessary to state five years ago that "analyses of marriage must be based on analyses of entire social systems" (43:197).

If Martinez-Alier's work remains the concrete standard for studies tying marriage and the family to the entire social system, Raymond Smith remains the most consistent advocate for studies that meet this standard. For him, the strongest critique levied against any analysis of Caribbean kinship, including his earlier work on Guyana, is that which undermines the linkages that the researcher establishes between family and society (167). Smith repeatedly emphasizes that kinship relations are not mere derivatives of a larger social structure and especially not epiphenomena or consequences of the economic order (166–168, 170, 171). Rather he sees domestic organization tied to the wider world by way of multiple subsystems (households, sex roles, etc), each of which can be explored more systematically as potential linkages to the totality.

Smith's views of that totality and of the ways to deal with it reflect changes in emphasis and a capacity to incorporate multiple influences. One detects a distinct shift from structure and stratification (163, 164) to culture, and at times, a less clear-cut move from culture to culture-history. The second mode pervades Smith's recent essay on race, class, and gender in the Americas, one of his most powerful to date (172). In the first and more familiar mode, Smith distinguishes culture as an analytically distinct system of symbols and meanings, but he replaces David Schneider's "conglomerate" cultural level with a plane of "ideas in action," the "norms which mediate" (rather than govern) behavior. Smith then tends to locate on an intermediary level the two messy fields that I call here heterogeneity and historicity.

Heterogeneity and Hegemony

The intermediate level has served as the emergency exit of social science since at least Talcott Parsons. If Smith, to his credit, tries not to treat it as residual, it took younger scholars to make the very heterogeneity that this level embodies the stuff of anthropological inquiry. Lee Drummond draws on fieldwork in Guyana to question the homogeneity of culture and on Creole linguistics to propose a "creole metaphor" that posits a set of intersystems with no uniform rules, no invariant properties, and no invariant relationships between categories (55). The proposal is refreshing in light of the dominance of Western folk-models of cultural homogeneity in anthropological theory but, as Brackette Williams notes, Drummond's continuum is unidimensional and overlooks hierarchy. For Williams, who also did fieldwork in Guyana, the construction of mixed hierarchies is a chief concern, and multidimensional complexity a theoretical litmus test. Multidimensionality is what makes the hitherto intermediate level—where putative purities evaporate, where neither thought nor action constitutes an unruffled web, let alone an harmonious system—both pivotal and amenable to study. Williams's research strategy on ethnicity (partly colored through Gramscian lenses) emphasizes the process of homogenization of national cultures (199, 200).

Williams seems unaware of Andrès Serbin's work on ethnicity and politics in Guyana, published in Venezuela in 1981. This unawareness would confirm that various anthropologists now tackling the relationship between heterogeneity and power in the Caribbean consider Gramsci a stimulating interlocutor, since Serbin's treatment of Guyana is explicitly Gramscian. Yet if both Serbin and Williams agree on the limits of hegemony (in the Gramscian sense) in Guyana, Serbin insists on the state-wide mechanisms that foster both dominant and counter "ethnic ideologies," while Williams documents the cultural struggle in a back-and-forth movement from the "community" to the national scene.

Race, class, and power—and Gramsci—are also present in the work of Austin-Broos. Austin's theoretical reformulations include a distinction between culture (values and their embodiments) and ideology (the interpretation of that culture in a contested field); a rejection of the old oppositions between ideology and knowledge, between the symbolic and the structural-practical (11–13, 16). Austin's ethnographic comparison of two Jamaican neighborhoods exposes a situation where conflict is constrained by a dominant (and, in her view, hegemonic) ideology of education (15).

The conflation of color, class, and power and the fiction of the nation-state return in my book on the Haiti of the Duvaliers, which rests on a reevaluation of Benedict Anderson's notion of the nation as "imagined community" and on yet one more reading of Gramsci that emphasizes the role of the state (189). The nation is not a political fiction but a fiction in politics, culture-history projected against the background of state power. In both Haiti and Dominica, the state is part of the stakes and yet, at times, is an actor competing for the very stakes that it helps to define (192). The requisite gap between state and nation creates a field where both homogeneity and heterogeneity are simultaneously created and destroyed.

The contention that sameness and heterogeneity intermesh necessarily in so-called "complex" societies was not always a given of anthropological practice. Nor is it an explicit premise of most anthropological strategies today. It is thus further illustration of the ambiguous relationship between the Caribbean frontier and the discipline that an early quest to untangle the roots of heterogeneity remained for long on the outer orbit of anthropological discourse. Individual assessments of *The People of Puerto Rico* vary (144, 204); but when Steward and his associates launched that seminal project, it was an extraordinary attempt to look beyond the singular community study and treat an entire society as a complex structural whole. Further, in spite of its intellectual contradictions, the collective book did set out a proposition central to the themes that structure this review: Communities need to be studied in reference to a "larger context" that includes networks of local institutions but also the development of colonies and empires (176:32, 505–6). In short, heterogeneity cannot be grasped without serious reference to history.

HISTORICITY

The Puerto Rico project did not introduce historicity in debates about Caribbean cultures, even though two of its participants, Sidney W. Mintz and Eric Wolf, have become well-known proponents of a historically oriented anthropology (112, 120, 203). Dutch scholar Rudy Van Lier, a pioneer of 20th-century Caribbean studies, also leaned toward history in his dealings with Caribbean heterogeneity, as would his compatriot H. Hoetink, later in the century (79, 80, 194). In the 1920s and 1930s, many Caribbean-born writers, such as Price-Mars in Haiti and Pedreira in Puerto Rico, saw the study of culture as inevitably tied to history (135, 142). In 1940, anteceding some of Mintz's work, Cuban writer Fernando Ortiz (133) saw in the history of export crops the framework within which to look at sociocultural patterns in Cuba.

In the United States, by the mid-1930s, Melville Jean Herskovits had also concluded that Caribbean heterogeneity made the use of historical data "almost mandatory" (78:329). Herskovits saw the Afro-Americas and especially Caribbean territories as ideal laboratories for anthropologists suspicious of the theoretical assumptions underpinning analyses of "simple" societies. Within the framework of acculturation studies, anthropologists could map out the differential evolution of European and African traits in the Americas and, ultimately, discover the nature of culture, understood as a continuous process of retention and renewal.

This research program paralleled a political agenda marked by the US experience. Herskovits was anxious to demonstrate that cultural legacies were innate entitlements of all humans; they were neither the exclusive property of whites, as believed by the general public, nor an awkward accoutrement of some American Indians, as demonstrated by anthropologists (78:297–330). Herskovits saw culture-history as one of the most powerful antidotes to North American racism. It is fair to say, however, that in spite of this political goal and in spite of an explicit attention to the workings of culture under strain, the model itself cannot deal with the differential access to power that conditioned the encounter between Europeans and Africans in the Americas—only with its consequences. Thus, the investigation of slave culture can take on a life of its own; the description of past or present cultural traits (or their ascription to African, European, or Creole roots) can become an end in itself.

The extent to which Caribbeanists still engage in such exercises and manage to avoid the Herskovitsian pitfalls depends very much on their view of the region, but also on their perspective on both racism and the nature and role of culture theory (e.g. 124). Holland & Crane (81) rely more on industrialization than on the past in studying current developments in Trinidadian Shango. For Roger Abrahams and John Szwed, the vision of Americans of African descent as misadapted individuals, stripped of their cultural heritage, is very much alive and should be challenged on Herskovitsian grounds (2:1–48). Abrahams & Szwed's compilation of travel accounts and residents' journals from the British Caribbean shows enslaved Africans and their descendants busily building a distinctive Afro-American culture patterned after African models. The extracts cover various aspects of slave life, with an emphasis on religion, patterns of performance, and expressive continuities (2). One or another of these emphases returns in a number of works published in the 1980s (47, 53, 156, 181)—but see Glazier (63) for an exception to Herskovits's influence, and Dirks (52) for a more narrowly materialistic treatment of a slave ritual.

The rigidity of Herskovits's model became an open secret after developments in the historiography of slavery in the 1960s and early 1970s, but few anthropologists before Sidney Mintz and Richard Price (122) dared to revise the scheme. Rejecting the backward search for the retention of alleged African forms, Mintz & Price argue that the African influence on Afro-American cultures is best defined in terms of underlying values and "grammatical" orientations, and that the culture-history of the Afro-Americas should rest upon historical knowledge of the concrete conditions under which the slaves operated and interacted with Europeans. Although they do not address frontally the role of power in the making of Afro-American cultures, Caribbeanists from various disciplines addressing the issue of African and European continuities in the New World must now take into account their influential reevaluation of the Herskovits model (40). Mintz & Price's methodological framework for the study of culture contact also has important implications for the guild, now that anthropologists admit, more readily than in Herskovits's time (77), that we are living in a global village. Richard Price's subsequent work, often in collaboration with Sally Price, greatly advances our knowledge of the Afro-Caribbean past (137–140).

The explicit reevaluation of Herskovits and the reevaluation of Steward implicit in the addenda to—and contradictions of—the Puerto Rico book are the intersecting lines with which Sidney Mintz scissors his space on the Caribbean frontier. For Mintz, heterogeneity cannot be grasped without history (as knowledge) because heterogeneity is the product of history (as process). Historical knowledge is not just a succession of facts—though its empirical grounds must be sound; nor can it pass as explanation—though it illuminates patterns and trends (107, 112). Rather, history provides the only context within which to make sense of human beings as subjects (121). Thus, the historical study of the material and symbolic rise of sugar in the modern world provides the context within which to observe the connection between culture and power (120). What is true for a world commodity is also true for a localized religion: "*Vaudou* cannot be interpreted apart from its significance for the Haitian people, and for Haitian history" (105:11).

Mintz's view of historicity thus encompasses the natives' conscious sense of the past emphasized by Price, the "conditioning fact of historicity" emphasized by Alexander Lesser (119:59), and the sweeping movements so well captured by Eric Wolf (203). Mintz's historicism reminds us of C. L. R. James and E. P. Thompson (but note that the former influenced the latter), insofar as it takes the great tides of history (107, 114, 116, 120) as seriously as it does the petty details of individual lives (111). But individuals manifest themselves only in cultural guise and within the constraints of historically defined social roles. Indeed, social positioning can steer the employment of the same cultural materials in opposite directions (117, 118). Mintz repeatedly uses Afro-American slavery, as the most repressive and influential institution of recent Western history, to underscore the necessary dialectics between institutions and individuals, system and contingency, adaptation and resistance, and structure and creativity (115, 121): "The house slave who poisoned her master's family by putting ground glass in the family food had first to become the family cook" (107:321).

From that viewpoint, history is never just about the past; that is, the historical process never stops. History is, altogether, part of anthropology, part of what anthropology studies, and part of why anthropology matters; it is material, tool, and context of anthropological discourse. "Culture must be viewed historically if it is to be understood at all" (117:508). Culture itself is cleansed of ahistorical assumptions of homogeneity. Mintz agrees with Wolf that "culture" and "society" are neither "perfectly coherent in themselves nor necessarily congruent with each other" (117:509). A favorite axis along which to follow the play between the social and the cultural is the plantation-peasantry complex. Mintz sees Caribbean peasantries and the cultural patterns they recreated, developed, or renewed over time as one of the most vibrant signs of resistance on the part of Caribbean peoples (especially Afro-Caribbeans) against a system imposed from the outside and dominated by the capitalist plantation (108, 115, 116, 121).

Unfortunately, many of the metatheoretical insights that Mintz draws from the Caribbean and that serve him so well in the study of the plantation-peasantry complex are hidden in over 100 publications, most of which stand outside disciplinary lines. He rarely packages theory for immediate consumption (but see 108, 110, 120, 121). Understandably, some students of the Caribbean freely adopt any combination of the themes that he refines or generates: the proto-peasantry, slave marketing and its impact on social organization, etc. Others follow similar directions but on parallel lines. Still, the peasant-plantation complex is a major theme in the anthropology of the region, in part because of Mintz's work. Historians, sociologists, geographers, and anthropologists continue to raise cognate questions about the transition from slavery to free labor in the Caribbean, about the relation between the cultural and the social before and after slavery, and about the relation between agrarian systems and cultural traditions (29–32, 38, 46, 99, 101, 182, 185). Accommodation and resistance are the organizing themes of Karen Fog Olwig's monographic study of St. John, a work that spans three centuries and combines effectively oral history, archival research, and ethnographic fieldwork (131). Marilyn Silverman (155) retraces the factional politics in a rice-producing village of East Indians in Guyana over a 70-year period. My own book on Dominica spans more than two centuries, combining historical and ethnographic research to situate a Caribbean peasantry in a changing world. I explicitly use the case as a contribution to peasant studies and social theory (187). In richly different ways, Jean Besson, Hymie Rubenstein, and Drexel Woodson look at customary forms of land tenure and the perception of land in Jamaica, St. Vincent, and Haiti. Woodson's work is well grounded in history and explores the dialectic of similarity and dissimilarity as it relates to person, place, and forms of tenure (205). Besson emphasizes "family land" as an institution of resistance in Martha Brae, Jamaica; but Carnegie, in turn, sees customary tenures as probable African retentions (29–32, 40). Rubenstein's contributions to the field are numerous. His monograph on a St. Vincent village uses primarily ethnographic data to address both the Caribbean and general literature on issues of livelihood, kinship, and household structure and social life outside the family. But, as Robert Manners long insisted, even community studies in the Caribbean must take cognizance of the past and use archival materials (97).

BOUNDARIES AND ARTICULATIONS

Historicity, once introduced, is the nightmare of the ethnographer, the constant reminder that the groupings one tends to take for natural are human creations, changing results of past and ongoing processes. Caribbean ethnography long faced the issue of the boundaries of observation and analysis (42, 176), but this concern increased lately with the greater awareness of history. I disagree with Rubenstein's statement that Caribbean ethnography has been marked by too much theory running after too little descriptive data (148:3–4). Caribbean ethnographers are no worse than others. Rather, the complexity of the frontier makes the application of many models inherited from the guild simplistic—a realization often deterred in other regions of the world by gatekeeping and the adoption of unproblematized units. To Radcliffe-Brown's search for a "convenient locality of suitable size," Baber replies (18:95) that "social boundaries can never be a matter of convenience" and that their setting is crucial in analyses of multicultural situations. Elsewhere, Baber warns us that Turner's notion of social drama may be misleading without proper attention to the context within which this drama is played out (17).

But in the Caribbean, context is not uniform and the individual actor, this basic unit of methodological individualism, not an obvious entity of which the boundaries are known—even though individualism may be quite evident (51, 121, 202, 205). Ever since Comitas's influential article (44), Caribbean anthropology has tried to deal with "occupational multiplicity," the simultaneous or sequential engagement in a number of economic activities. Of course, there are obvious reasons why the urban and rural poor, women heads of households, migrants, and other people eking out a living under social and economic strain would want to be skeptical and bank on multiple adaptive strategies (21, 39, 41). Yet I suspect that what strikes most ethnographers is something more than risk management. First, the systematicity with which people maintain multiplicity is prevalent enough for observers to phrase it not in terms of movement between roles or types but in terms of types or roles that include movement (44, 60). Second, Caribbean peoples seem to have fewer problems than most in recognizing the fuzziness and overlap of categories, and multiplicity is not confined to the economic realm or to the poor. What appears to some as divided political, economic, or social loyalties has a long history on the frontier (33, 135, 139, 142). Middle-class individuals engage in behavior similar to the economic strategies of the poor—but further research is required because few anthropologists have enhanced our knowledge of the Caribbean middle classes (5, 96). Still, what seems to be at stake here is a way to live what the post-Enlightenment West calls—and anthropology uncritically accepts as—individual oneness. Herskovits's comments on Haitian "socialized ambivalence" seem to rest on an assumption of universal univalence, and a good deal of symbolic anthropology is premised on individual oneness.

The presumption of a microcosm, to paraphrase Manners (97), is no easier to maintain when studying a "community" on the frontier. The village tradition of the anthropological monograph becomes problematic in the Caribbean, where the line between rural and urban folk is not clear-cut (103). Anthropologists have noted the scarcity of book-length community studies in the region (40, 148). This deficiency is not just a reflection of the politics of the guild; it is also a healthy sign that Caribbean ethnographers often realize that the story they were after does not end with their village. How does one package ethnography with such an awareness? Williams ties her descriptions of Cockalorum to the national space in Guyana. Rubenstein admits that his village is open to the world (148:83–84) but stops short of drawing from this confession any fundamental shift in the scope of description. Still, Rubenstein goes much further than the expected chapter on history and the nation. He takes 78 pages to get to his village and, once there, he returns to history for a proper introduction of his core unit of observation. Woodson also rejects the perfunctory historical introduction: In his dissertation, historical chapters spanning the Haitian space come after the ethnographic introduction of his community and before his institutional analysis (205). My own study of Dominica also takes on the joint issues of historicity and boundaries. I use three units of description and analysis, The Nation, The World, and The Village—three different vantage points from which to look at Dominican peasants. History generates the first unit; political economy helps make sense of the second. The reader enters the village-level ethnography only two thirds of the way through the book (187).

The simultaneous use of multiple units of analysis by a single author or a team is one of the many strategies that reveals the search by many Caribbeanists for a way to tie their immediate units of observation to the wider world (42, 120, 176, 183, 186, 187). The overwhelming evidence for the intrusion of outside forces makes Caribbean anthropologists attentive to—if not always uncritical of—world system theory, dependency theory, or cognate approaches that allow them to read their data beyond the traditional boundaries of the colonial or national state (17, 35, 36, 58, 68, 72, 73, 101, 127, 154, 167, 168, 171, 183). But once the world is acknowledged, one must deal with "local response," of which the Caribbean is a powerful illustration precisely because it is so colonial (114). Potential methodologies include analyses moving down, through concentric circles, from the level of the world system to as small a unit as the plantation by way of increasingly smaller units, such as the region or the territory (183).

Fortunately, at the level of the region, the conceptualization of units and boundaries is well advanced. Mintz's overview of the Caribbean stands as one of the most sophisticated conceptualizations of a sociocultural area in the anthropological literature. Neither a laundry list of necessary particulars nor a covert reference to an immanent essence, it is doubly open. First, it ties the Caribbean to the rest of the world, notably to the continental Americas, and to Europe and Africa, by way of the Atlantic. Second, it does not superimpose homogeneity upon its internal units but views Caribbean territories along a multidimensional continuum informed by history. Colonial domination, African substrata, ecological limits, forms of labor extraction, cultural and ideological ambiance, and now US domination intermix in this scheme, which I read as an exemplar of "family resemblance" à la Wittgenstein (104, 107, 109, 123).

The concern for a regional multilevel methodology is explicit in the Women in the Caribbean Project, a multidisciplinary study covering a number of Caribbean territories that is the focus of two special issues of *Social and Economic Studies* and that has already spurred one book (151). Unfortunately, in line with most of the works published or sponsored by the University of the West Indies (but see 7), the project concentrates on territories where English is the official language, a weak commonality if we take seriously the idea of family resemblance. What makes Guadeloupe look like St. Lucia is not what makes Dominica look like Antigua; what makes Barbados look like Cuba is not what makes Cuba look like the Dominican Republic; and even Haitian exceptionalism is, to a large extent, a myth (190). There are good grounds for arguing that a comparison of women in Jamaica and Haiti would be at least as interesting as one between women in Jamaica and Trinidad; good grounds to suggest that we may understand better the degree to which Barbados is British if we also look at Martinique; good reasons to suppose that studies of local consciousness in Curaçao may throw a better light on Puerto Rican nationalism. More important, everything we know about each of these territories confirms one thing: It is as a complex package that the Caribbean presents such stimulating challenge to Western social science and to anthropology in particular.

CONCLUSION

The domination of English on Caribbean studies reflects and reinforces boundaries and rankings inherited from the colonial past, as well as current US domination. It is also a scholarly handicap that amplifies intellectual parochialism within disciplinary, linguistic, or colonial spheres. It restricts the range of comparison and the number of territories studied (Jamaica, Barbados, Guyana, Trinidad), and promotes superficial similarities. Few students of Caribbean culture (especially Caribbean-born or African-American scholars) dare to cross linguistic or colonial borders, with only a few exceptions in recent years (e.g. 17, 18, 205). Few dare to bring explicitly to the discipline the political or metatheoretical lessons learned on the frontier (74, 190, 191). Fewer dare to be comparative across linguistic boundaries (101, 121, 123, 139). Yet as language gives fieldworkers the impression of being on familiar territory, chances increase for them to be off guard and also to ignore works done in other languages.

Yet Dutch scholars continue to produce a small but steady stream of works on the Caribbean, only a few of which are available in English (e.g. 79, 80, 82). In the 1970s, PhD theses on the Caribbean outnumbered those dealing with every other non-Western area in departments of anthropology and sociology in the Netherlands (19). Works in Dutch and in other languages are covered in the yearly update on Caribbean Studies of the *Boletin de Estudios Latinoamericanos y del Caribe*. A few titles by historians in Spanish (e.g. 125) and a number of works in French, on the French Antilles, Guyane, and Haiti, should be also of interest to English-speaking anthropologists (4, 8, 9, 22–25, 28, 62, 75, 85, 86, 93). To be sure, while the Dutch tend to match North Americans in empiricism, works in Spanish and French are rarely based on the kind of ethnographic fieldwork required by most US universities. On the other hand, the latter works often partake of an ancient and fundamental debate about the the nature of Caribbean societies and their relation to the West. A number of writers (mostly linguists and literary critics writing in French, many of whom are Caribbean-born) are asking questions about Creolité, or what it means for Caribbean people to be part of societies and cultures born out of contact (e.g. 28, 64, 85). The multidisciplinary periodical *Etudes Créoles* extends beyond the technical issues of Creole linguistics and ties the Caribbean to societies and cultures of Africa and the Indian Ocean. In short, the concerns that I have highlighted here as scattered posts on the frontier are not the exclusive domain of Caribbean anthropologists nor are they exclusively expressed in English. A number of academics and intellectuals, writing in at least four languages, have dealt in different ways with what I here call heterogeneity, historicity, and articulation. That some think this endeavor possible without anthropology reveals their intellectual preference and prejudices. Yet it also suggests some of the limits to anthropological theory, at least as seen from the frontier.

ACKNOWLEDGMENTS

I thank Flor Ruz, Sara M. Springer, and especially Paul Kim for their research assistance. I am grateful to Suzan Lowes, Sidney W. Mintz, and Drexel G. Woodson for their comments on an early version of the manuscript. I alone remain fully responsible for the substance of the argument and the final text.

Literature Cited

1. Abrahams, R. D. 1983. *The Man-of-Words in the West Indies: Performance and the Emergence of Creole Culture*. Baltimore and London: Johns Hopkins Univ. Press
2. Abrahams, R. D., Swzed, J., assisted by

Baker, L. and Stockhouse, A. 1983. *After Africa: Extracts from British Travel Accounts and Journals*. New Haven: Yale Univ. Press
3. Abu-Lughod, L. 1989. Zones of theory in

the anthropology of the Arab world. *Annu. Rev. Anthropol.* 18:267–306

4. Affergan, F. 1983. *Anthropologie à la Martinique.* Paris: Anthropos

5. Alexander, J. 1977. The culture of race in middle-class Kingston, Jamaica. *Am. Ethnol.* 4(3):413–36

6. Alexander, J. 1984. Love, race, slavery and sexuality in Jamaican images of the family. In *Kinship, Ideology and Practice in Latin America,* ed. R. T. Smith, pp. 147–80. Chapel Hill: Univ. North Carolina Press

7. Allman, J. 1985. Conjugal unions in rural and urban Haiti. *Soc. Econ. Stud.* 34(1):27–57

8. André, J. 1987. *L'inceste focal dans la famille noire antillaise.* Paris: Presses Universitaires de France

9. Ans, A. M. d'. 1987. *Haiti: Paysage et société.* Paris: Karthala

10. Appadurai, A. 1986. Theory in anthropology: center and periphery. *Comp. Stud. Soc. Hist.* 28:356–61

11. Austin, D. J. 1979. History and symbols in ideology: a Jamaican example. *Man* 14:447–514

12. Austin, D. J. 1981. Born again ... and again and again: communities and social change among Jamaican Pentecostalists. *J. Anthropol. Res.* 37:226–46

13. Austin, D. J. 1983. Culture and ideology in the English-speaking Caribbean: a view from Jamaica. *Am. Ethnol.* 10(2):223–40

14. Austin, D. J. 1984. Reply to M. G. Smith. *Am. Ethnol.* 11(1):185

15. Austin, D. J. 1984. *Urban Life in Kingston, Jamaica: The Culture and Class Ideology of Two Neighborhoods.* New York: Gordon and Breach

16. Austin-Broos, D. J. 1987. Pentecostals and Rastafarians: cultural, political, and gender relations of two religious movements. *Soc. Econ. Stud.* 36(4):1–39

17. Baber, W. L. 1985. Political economy and social change: the Bissette Affair and local-level politics in Morne-Vert. *Am. Ethnol.* 12(3):489–504

18. Baber, W. L. 1987. The pluralism controversy: wider theoretical implications. *Caribbean Q.* 33(1/2):81–94

19. Banck, G. A. 1988. Anthropological research on the Caribbean and Latin America. *Bol. Estud. Latinoam. Caribe* 44:29–38

20. Barrow, C. 1986. Male images of women in Barbados. *Soc. Econ. Stud.* 35(3):51–64

21. Barrow, C. 1986. Finding the support: a study of strategies for survival. *Soc. Econ. Stud.* 35(2):131–76

22. Bastien, R. 1985 [1951]. *Le Paysan haïtien et sa famille.* Paris: ACCT-Karthala

23. Bebel-Gisler, D. 1985. *Léonora: L'Histoire enfouie de la Guadeloupe.* Paris: Editions Seghers

24. Bebel-Gisler, D. 1989. *Le Défi Culturel Guadeloupeen.* Paris: Editions Caribbéennes

25. Benoist, J. 1972. *L'Archipel inachevé: Culture et société aux Antilles francaises.*

Montreal: Les Presses de l'Université de Montréal

26. Berleant-Schiller, R. 1977. Production and division of labor in a West Indian peasant commune. *Am. Ethnol.* 4(2):253–72

27. Berleant-Schiller, R. 1981. Plantation society and the Caribbean present (1): history, anthropology. *Plantation Soc.* 1(3):387–409

28. Bernabé, J., Chamoiseau, P., Confiant, R. 1989. *Eloge de la créolité.* Paris: Gallimard

29. Besson, J. 1979. Symbolic aspects of land in the Caribbean: the tenure and transmission of land rights among Caribbean peasantries. In *Peasants, Plantations and Rural Communities in the Caribbean,* ed. M. Cross, A. Marles, pp. 86–116. Guilford, UK; Leiden, Netherlands: Univ. Gurney and Roy. Inst. Linguist. Anthropol.

30. Besson, J. 1982. Family land and Caribbean society: toward an ethnography of Caribbean peasantries. In *Perspectives on Caribbean Identity,* ed. E. M. Thomas-Hope, pp. 57–83. Liverpool: Cent. Latin Am. Stud., Univ. Liverpool

31. Besson, J. 1984. Land tenure in the free villages of Trelawny, Jamaica: a case study in the Caribbean peasant response to emancipation. *Slavery Abolition* 5(1):3–23

32. Besson, J., Monsen, J., eds. 1987. *Land and Development in the Caribbean.* London: Macmillan

33. Bilby, K. M. 1989. Divided loyalties: local politics and the play of states among the Aluku. *New West Indian Guide* 63(3/4):143–74

34. Bolland, O. N. 1986. Labour control and resistance in Belize in the century after 1838. *Slavery & Abolition* 7(2):175–87

35. Bolles, A. L. 1983. Kitchens hit by priorities: working class women confront the IMF. In *Women, Men, and the International Division of Labor,* ed. J. Nash, M. P. Fernandez-Kelly, pp. 138–60. Albany: State Univ. NY Press

36. Bolles, A. L. 1986. Economic crisis and female-headed households in Jamaica. In *Women and Change in Latin America,* ed. J. Nash, H. Safa, pp. 65–83. South Hadley: Bergin and Garvey

37. Brana-Shute, G. 1989. *On the Corner: Male Social Life in a Paramaibo Creole Neighborhood.* Prospect Heights, IL: Waveland

38. Brierley, J. S., Rubenstein, H., eds. 1988. *Small Farming and Peasant Resources in the Caribbean.* Winnipeg: Dept. Geogr., Univ. Manitoba

39. Carnegie, C. V. 1982. Strategic flexibility in the West Indies: a social psychology of Caribbean migration. *Caribbean Rev.* 2(1):10–13, 54

40. Carnegie, C. V., ed. 1987. Afro-Caribbean villages in historical perspective. *African-Caribbean Inst. Jamaica Res. Rev.* 2. Spec. Issue

41. Chibnik, M. 1980. Working out or working in: the choice between wage labor and cash

cropping in rural Belize. *Am. Ethnol.* 7(1):86–105

42. Clarke, E. 1957. *My Mother Who Fathered Me: A Study of Three Selected Communities in Jamaica.* London: George Allen and Unwin

43. Collier, J. F. 1987. Rank and marriage: or why high-ranking brides cost more. In *Gender and Kinship: Essays Toward a Unified Analysis,* ed. J. F. Collier, S. J. Yanagisako, p. 197–220. Stanford: Stanford Univ. Press

44. Comitas, L. 1964. Occupational multiplicity in rural Jamaica. In *Proceedings of the American Ethnological Society,* ed. E. Garfield, E. Friedl, pp. 41–50. Seattle: Univ. Washington Press

45. Comitas, L. 1977. *The Complete Caribbeana.* Millwood: KTO Press

46. Cross, M., Marles, A., eds. 1979. *Peasants, Plantations and Rural Communities in the Caribbean.* Guilford/Leiden: Univ. Surrey and Roy. Inst. Linguist. Anthropol.

47. Dance, D. C. 1985. *Folklore from Contemporary Jamaica.* Knoxville: Univ. Tennessee Press

48. Dann, G. 1987. *The Barbadian Male: Sexual Attitudes and Practice.* Kingston: Macmillan Caribbean

49. Deosaran, R. 1987. The social psychology of cultural pluralism: updating the old. *Caribbean Q.* 33(1/2):1–19

50. Deosaran, R. 1987. Some issues in multiculturalism: the case of Trinidad & Tobago in the Post-Colonial Era. *Caribbean Q.* 33(1/2):61–80

51. Despres, L., ed. 1975. *Ethnicity and Resource Competition.* The Hague: Mouton

52. Dirks, R. 1987. *The Black Saturnalia: Conflict and Its Ritual Expression on British West Indian Slave Plantations.* Gainesville: Univ. of Florida Presses

53. Dobbin, J. D. 1986. *The Jombee Dance of Montserrat: A Study of Ritual Trance in the West Indies.* Columbus: Ohio State Univ. Press

54. Dominguez, V. 1986. Intended and unintended messages: the scholarly defense of one's "people". *New West Indian Guide* 60(3/4):208–22

55. Drummond, L. 1980. The cultural continuum: a theory of intersystems. *Man.* 15:352–74

56. Durant-Gonzales, V. 1982. The realm of female familial responsibility. In *Women and Family.* Cave Hill: ISER

57. Farmer, P. 1988. Bad blood, spoiled milk: bodily fluids as moral barometers in rural Haiti. *Am. Ethnol.* 15(1):62–83

58. Farmer, P. 1988. Blood, sweat and baseballs: Haiti in the West Atlantic system. *Dialect. Anthropol.* 13:83–99

59. Fisher, L. E. 1985. *Colonial Madness: Mental Health in the Barbadian Social Order.* New Brunswick: Rutgers Univ. Press

60. Frucht, R. 1967. A Caribbean social type:

neither peasant nor proletarian. *Soc. Econ. Stud.* 16(3):295–300

61. Geertz, C. 1976. "From the native's point of view": on the nature of anthropological understanding. In *Meaning in Anthropology,* ed. K. H. Basso, Henry A. Selby, pp. 221–37. Albuquerque: Univ. New Mexico Press

62. Giraud, M. 1979. *Race et Classes à la Martinique.* Paris: Anthropos

63. Glazier, S. D. 1983. *Marchin' the Pilgrims Home: Leadership and Decision-Making in an Afro-Caribbean Faith.* Westport: Greenwood

64. Glissant, E. 1989. *Caribbean Discourse: Selected Essays,* transl. J. M. Dash. Charlottesville: Univ. Virginia Press

65. Gonzalez, N. L. 1983. New evidence on the origin of the Black Carib with thoughts on the meaning of tradition. *New West Indian Guide* 57(3/4):143–72

66. Gonzalez, N. L. 1984. Rethinking the consanguineal household and matrifocality. *Ethnology* 23:1–12

67. Gonzalez, N. L. 1988. *Sojourners of the Caribbean: Ethnogenesis and Ethnohistory of the Garifuna.* Urbana: Univ. Illinois Press

68. Griffith, D. C. 1985. Women, remittances, and reproduction. *Am. Ethnol.* 12(4):676–90

69. Gullick, C. J. M. R. 1985. *Myths of a Minority: The Changing Traditions of the Vincentian Caribs.* Assen: Van Gorcum, Stud. Dev. Countries

70. Handler, J. S. 1982. Slave revolts and conspiracies in Seventeenth-Century Barbados. *New West Indian Guide* 56(1/2): 5–42

71. Handler, J. S. 1984. Freedmen and slaves in the Barbados militia. *J. Caribbean Hist.* 19(1):1–25

72. Harrison, F. V. 1987. Gangs, grassroots politics, and the crisis of development capitalism in Jamaica. In *Perspectives in U. S. Marxist Anthropology,* ed. D. Hakken, H. Lessinger, pp. 186–210. Boulder: Westview

73. Harrison, F. V. 1988. Women in Jamaica's urban informal economy: insights from a Kingston slum. *New West Indian Guide* 62(3/4):103–28

74. Harrison, F. V. 1991. Ethnography as politics. In *Decolonizing Anthropology,* ed. F. V. Harrisson, pp. 88–109. Washington, DC: AAA

75. Helly, D. 1979. *Idéologie et Ethnicité: Les Chinois Macao de Cuba.* Montreal: Les Presses de l'Université de Montréal

76. Henry, F. 1983. Religion and ideology in Trinidad: the resurgence of the Shango religion. *Caribbean Q.* 29(3/4):63–69

77. Herskovits, M. J. 1937. The significance of the study of acculturation for anthropology. *Am. Anthropol.* 39:635–43

78. Herskovits, M. J. 1971 [1937]. *Life in a Haitian Valley.* Garden City: Anchor Books

79. Hoetink, H. 1971. *Caribbean Race Relations: A Study of Two Variants,* transl. E. M. London Hooykaas. Oxford/New York: Oxford Univ. Press
80. Hoetink, H. 1982. *The Dominican People, 1850–1900: Notes for a Historical Sociology,* transl. S. K. Ault. Baltimore: Johns Hopkins Univ. Press
81. Holland, D. C., Crane, J. G. 1987. Adapting to an industrializing nation: the Shango cult in Trinidad. *Soc. Econ. Stud.* 36(4):41–66
82. Hoogbergen, W. S. M. 1990 [1984]. *The Boni Maroon Wars in Suriname.* Leiden/New York: Brill
83. Horowitz, M., ed. 1971. *Peoples and Cultures of the Caribbean: An Anthropological Reader.* Garden City: The Natural History Press
84. Horowitz, M. 1983. *Morne Paysan.* New York: Irvington
85. Jolivet, M. J. 1986. *La Question créole: Essai de sociologie sur la Guyane.* Paris: Orstrom
86. Labelle, M. 1978. *Idéologie de couleur et classes sociales en Haïti.* Montréal: Univ. Montréal
87. Laguerre, M. S. 1982. *Urban Life in the Caribbean.* Cambridge: Schenkman
88. Lazarus-Black, M. 1991. Why women take men to Magistrate's Court: Caribbean kinship ideology and law. *Ethnology* 30(2):119–33
89. Leo-Rhynie, E., Hamilton, M. 1983. Professional Jamaican women—equal or not? *Caribbean Q.* 29(3/4):70–85
90. Lewis, G. K. 1983. *Main Currents in Caribbean Thought: The Historical Evolution of Caribbean Society in Its Ideological Aspects, 1492–1900.* Baltimore and London: Johns Hopkins Univ. Press
91. Lieber, M. 1981. *Street Scenes: Afro-American Culture in Urban Trinidad.* Cambridge, MA: Schenkman Publishing Co.
92. Lorona, L. V. 1983–1987. *Bibliography of Latin American and Caribbean Bibliographies.* Madison: U.W. SALALM
93. Louillot, G., Crusol-Baillard, G. 1987. *Femmes Martiniquaises: mythes et réalités.* Fort-de-France: Editions Caribéennes
94. Lowenthal, D. 1972. *West Indian Societies.* London: Oxford Univ. Press
95. Lowenthal, I. P. 1987. *Marriage is 20, children are 21: the cultural construction of conjugality and the family in rural Haiti.* PhD thesis, Johns Hopkins Univ.
96. Lowes, S. 1987. Time and motion in the formation of the middle class in Antigua, 1834–1940. Paper presented at the Annu. Meet. AAA, Chicago
97. Manners, R. 1957. Methods of community analysis in the Caribbean. In *Caribbean Studies: A Symposium,* ed. V. Rubin, pp. 80–92. Seattle: Univ. Washington Press
98. Manning, F. E. 1973. *Black Clubs in Bermuda: Ethnography of a Play World.* Ithaca: Cornell Univ. Press
99. Marshall, W. K. 1990. *The Post-Slavery Labour Problem Revisited.* (Elsa Goveia Memorial Lecture). Kingston: Univ. West Indies
100. Martinez-Alier, V. 1974. *Marriage, Class and Colour in Nineteenth-Century Cuba.* London: Cambridge Univ. Press
101. McGlynn, F., Drescher, S., eds. 1992. *The Meaning of Freedom: Economics, Politics and Culture after Slavery.* Pittsburgh: Univ. Pittsburgh Press
102. McWatt, M. 1982. The preoccupation with the past in West Indian literature. *Caribbean Q.* 28(1/2):12–19
103. Mintz, S. W. 1953. The folk-urban continuum and the rural proletarian community. *Am. J. Sociol.* 59:136–43
104. Mintz, S. W. 1971. The Caribbean as a socio-cultural area. See Ref. 83
105. Mintz, S. W. 1971. Introduction. In *Voodoo in Haiti,* ed. A. Metraux, pp. 1–15. New York: Schoken Books
106. Mintz, S. W. 1971. Men, women and trade. *Comp. Stud. Soc. Hist.* 13:247–69
107. Mintz, S. W. 1971. Toward an Afro-American history. *Cah. Hist. Mond.* 13:317–32
108. Mintz, S. W. 1973. A note on the definition of peasantries. *J. Peasant Stud.* 1:91–106
109. Mintz, S. W. 1974. The Caribbean region. In *Slavery, Colonialism, and Racism,* ed. S. W. Mintz, pp. 45–71. New York: Norton
110. Mintz, S. W. 1974. The rural proletariat and the problem of rural proletarian consciousness. *J. Peasant Stud.* 1:291–325
111. Mintz, S. W. 1974 [1960]. *Worker in the Cane.* New York: Norton
112. Mintz, S. W. 1975. History and anthropology: a brief reprise. In *Race and Slavery in the Western Hemisphere: Quantitative Studies,* ed. S. L. Engerman, E. D. Genovese, pp. 477–94. New Jersey: Princeton Univ. Press
113. Mintz, S. W. 1977. North American anthropological contributions to Caribbean studies. *Bol. Estud. Latinoam.* 22:68–82
114. Mintz, S. W. 1977. The so-called world system: local initiative and local response. *Dialect. Anthropol.* 2(4):253–70
115. Mintz, S. W. 1978. Was the plantation slave a proletarian? *Review* 2(1):81–98
116. Mintz, S. W. 1979. Slavery and the rise of peasantries. *Hist. Reflect.* 6(1):135–242
117. Mintz, S. W. 1982. Culture: an anthropological view. *Yale Rev.* 71:499–512
118. Mintz, S. W. 1984. American anthropology and the Marxist tradition. In *On Marxian Perspectives in Anthropology,* ed. J. Macquet, N. Daniels, pp. 11–34. Malibu: UCLA
119. Mintz, S. W., ed. 1985. *History, Evolution and the Concept of Culture: Selected Papers by Alexander Lesser.* New York: Cambridge Univ. Press
120. Mintz, S. W. 1985. *Sweetness and Power: The Place of Sugar in Modern History.* New York: Viking

121. Mintz, S. W. 1990 [1974]. *Caribbean Transformations*. New York: Columbia Univ. Press
122. Mintz, S. W., Price, R. 1992 [1976]. *The Birth of African-American Culture: An Anthropological Perspective*. Boston: Beacon
123. Mintz, S. W., Price, S., eds. 1992. *Caribbean Contours*. Baltimore: Johns Hopkins Univ. Press
124. Moreno Fraginals, M. R., ed. 1984. *Africa in Latin America,*. transl. L. Blum. New York/London: Holmes & Meier
125. Moreno Fraginals, M. R. et al. 1987. Apuntes para una historia economico-social de la cultural Cubana: cultural Indocubana. *Temas.* 12:53–84
126. Moya Pons, F. 1986. *El Batey: Estudio Socioeconomico de los Bateyes del Consejo Estatal del Azucar*. Santo Domingo, Republica Dominicana: Fondo Para el Avance de las Ciencias Sociales, Inc.
127. Murphy, M. 1991. *Dominican Sugar Plantations: Production and Foreign Labor Integration*. New York: Praeger
128. Murray, G., Alvarez, M. 1975. Haitian beans circuits: cropping and trading maneuvers among a cash-oriented peasantry. In *Working Papers in Haitian Society and Culture*, ed. S. W. Mintz, pp. 85–126. New Haven: Antilles Res. Prog., Yale Univ.
129. Nettleford, R. 1972 [1970]. *Mirror, Mirror: Identity, Race and Protest in Jamaica*. Kingston, Jamaica: W. Collins & Sangster/William Morrow
130. Nettleford, R. 1979. *Caribbean Cultural Identity: The Case of Jamaica*. Los Angeles: UCLA Latin Am. Cent. Publ.
131. Olwig, K. F. 1985. *Cultural Adaptation and Resistance on St. John: Three Centuries of Afro-Caribbean Life*. Gainesville: Univ. Florida Press
132. Olwig, K. F. 1990. The struggle for respectability: Methodism and Afro-Caribbean culture on 19th-century Nevis. *New West Indian Guide* 64(3/4):93–114
133. Ortiz, F. 1970. *Cuban Counterpoint: Tobacco and Sugar*. New York: Vintage
134. Pagden, A. 1982. *The Fall of Natural Man: The American Indian and the Origins of Comparative Ethnography*. Cambridge: Cambridge Univ. Press
135. Pedreira, A. 1968 [1934]. *Insularismo*. Rio Piedras: Edil
136. Price, R. 1971. Studies of Caribbean family organization: problems and prospects. *Dedaldo Rev. Mus. Arbe Archeol. Univ. Sao Paulo* 4(14):23–58
137. Price, R. 1983. *First Time: The Historical Vision of an Afro-American People*. Baltimore and London: Johns Hopkins Univ. Press
138. Price, R. 1990. *Alabi's World*. Baltimore: Johns Hopkins Univ. Press
139. Price, R. 1990. *Ethnographic History, Caribbean Pasts*. College Park: Univ. Maryland, Work. Pap. No. 9
140. Price, R., Price, S., eds. 1988. *Narrative of a Five Year Expedition against the Revolted Negroes of Suriname in Guiana on the Wild Coast of South America from the year 1772 to the year 1777 by John Gabriel Stedman*. Baltimore: Johns Hopkins Univ.
141. Price, S. 1984. *Co-Wives and Calabashes*. Ann Arbor: Univ. Michigan Press
142. Price-Mars, J. 1983 [1928]. *So Spoke the Uncle*. Washington, DC: Three Continents Press
143. Rawlins, J. M. 1987. *The Family in the Caribbean, 1973–1986: An Annotated Bibliography*. Cave Hill, Barbados: ISER
144. *Revista/Review Interamericana.* 1978. 8(1). Spring
145. Robotham, D. 1980. Pluralism as an ideology. *Soc. Econ. Stud.* 29:69–89
146. Robotham, D. 1985. The why of the cockatoo? *Soc. Econ. Stud.* 34(2):111–51
147. Rubenstein, H. 1983. Caribbean family and household organization: some conceptual clarifications. *J. Comp. Fam. Stud.* 14(3):283–98
148. Rubenstein, H. 1987. *Coping with Poverty: Adaptive Strategies in a Caribbean Village*. Boulder: Westview
149. Safa, H. I. 1986. Economic autonomy and sexual equality in Caribbean society. *Soc. Econ. Stud.* 35(3):1–21
150. Safa, H. I. 1987. Popular culture, national identity, and race in the Caribbean. *New West Indian Guide* 61(3/4):115–26
151. Senior, O. 1991. *Working Miracles: Women's Lives in the English-Speaking Caribbean*. Cave Hill/Bloomington: ISER/Indiana
152. Serbin, A. 1981. *Nacionalismo, etnicidad y politica en la Republica Cooperativa de Guyana*. Caracas: Editorial Bruguera Venezolana
153. Serbin, A. 1985. Procesos etnoculturales y percepciones mutuas en el desarollo de las relaciones entre el Caribe de Habla Ingles y America Latina. *Bol. Estud. Latinoam. Caribe* 38:83–98
154. Silverman, M. 1979. Dependency, mediation, and class formation in rural Guyana. *Am. Ethnol.* 6(3):466–90
155. Silverman, M. 1980. *Rich People and Rice: Factional Politics in Rural Guyana*. Leiden: Brill
156. Simpson, G. E. 1980. *Religious Cults of the Caribbean: Trinidad, Jamaica and Haiti*. Rio Piedras: Inst. Caribbean Stud., Univ. Puerto Rico, Caribbean Monogr. Ser. No. 15
157. Smith, M. G. 1962. History and social anthropology. *J. Roy. Anthropol. Inst. Great Britain and Ireland* 92:73–85
158. Smith, M. G. 1965. *The Plural Society in the British West Indies*. Berkeley: Univ. Calif. Press
159. Smith, M. G. 1983. Robotham's ideology and pluralism. *Soc. Econ. Stud.* 32:103–39
160. Smith, M. G. 1984. Comment on Austin's "Culture and ideology in the English-

speaking Caribbean". *Am. Ethnol.* 11(1):183–85

161. Smith, M. G. 1984. *Culture, Race and Class in the Commonwealth Caribbean.* Mona, Jamaica: Dept. Extramur. Stud., Univ. West Indies

162. Smith, M. G. 1987. Pluralism: comments on an ideological analysis. *Soc. Econ. Stud.* 36(4):157–91

163. Smith, R. T. 1956. *The Negro Family in British Guiana.* London: Routledge and Kegan Paul

164. Smith, R. T. 1970. Social stratification in the Caribbean. In *Essays in Comparative Stratification,* ed. L. Plotinov, A. Tuden, pp. 43–76. Pittsburgh: Univ. Pittsburgh Press

165. Smith, R. T. 1971. Culture and social structure in the Caribbean. See Ref. 83, pp. 448–75

166. Smith, R. T. 1973. The matrifocal family. In *The Character of Kinship,* ed. J. Goody. London: Cambridge Univ. Press

167. Smith, R. T. 1978. The family in the modern world system: some observations from the Caribbean. *J. Fam. Hist.* 3:337–60

168. Smith, R. T. 1982. Family, social change and social policy in the West Indies. *New West Indian Guide* 56(3/4):111–42

169. Smith, R. T. 1982. Race and class in the post-emancipation Caribbean. In *Racism and Colonialism,* ed. E. Ross, pp. 93–119. The Hague: Martinus Nijhoff

170. Smith, R. T. 1987. Hierarchy and the dual marriage system in West Indian society. In *Gender and Kinship: Essays Toward a Unified Analysis,* ed. J. Collier, S. Yanagisako, pp. 163–96. Stanford: Stanford Univ. Press

171. Smith, R. T. 1988. *Kinship and Class in the West Indies.* Cambridge/New York: Cambridge Univ. Press

172. Smith, R. T. 1992. Race, class and gender in the transition to freedom. See Ref. 101

173. *Social and Economic Studies.* 1986. 35(2) Spec. Issue: Women in the Caribbean, Pt. 1

174. *Social and Economic Studies.* 1986. 35(3) Spec. Issue: Women in the Caribbean, Pt. 2

175. Stephen, H. J. M. 1985. *Winti: Afro-Surinaamse religiee en magische rituelen in S. en Ned.* Amsterdam: Karnak

176. Steward, J., et al. 1956. *The People of Puerto Rico.* Urbana: Univ. Illinois Press

177. Stuart, B. A. C. 1985. *Women in the Caribbean: A Bibliography.* Leiden: RILA, Dept. Caribbean Stud.

178. Stubbs, J. 1988. Gender construct of labour in prerevolutionary Cuban tobacco. *Soc. Econ. Stud.* 37(1/2):241–70

179. Sutton, C., Makiesky-Barrow, S. 1981. Social inequality and sexual status in Barbados. In *The Black Woman Cross-Culturally,* ed. F. Steady. Cambridge: Schenkman

180. Taylor Steady, D. 1946. Kinship and social structure of the island Carib. *Southwest. J. Anthropol.* 2:180–212

181. Thoden van Velzen, H. U. E., van Wetering, W. 1988. *The Great Father and the Danger: Religious Cults, Material Forces, and Collective Fantasies in the World of the Surinamese Maroons.* Dordrecht/Providence, MA: Foris Publications

182. Thomas-Hope, E. M., ed. 1982. *Perspectives on Caribbean Identity.* Liverpool: Cent. Latin Am. Stud., Univ. Liverpool

183. Trouillot, M.-R. 1982. Motion in the system: coffee, color, and slavery in 18th-century Saint-Domingue. *Review* 5(3):331–88

184. Trouillot, M.-R. 1983. The production of spatial configurations: a Caribbean case. *New West Indian Guide* 57(3/4):215–29

185. Trouillot, M.-R. 1984. Labour and emancipation in Dominica: contribution to a debate. *Caribbean Q.* 30(3/4):73–84

186. Trouillot, M.-R. 1987. Discourses of rule and the acknowledgement of the peasantry in Dominica, W. I., 1838–1928. *Am. Ethnol.* 16(4):704–18

187. Trouillot, M.-R. 1988. *Peasants and Capital: Dominica in the World Economy.* Baltimore: Johns Hopkins Univ. Press

188. Trouillot, M.-R. 1990. Good day, Columbus: silences, power and public history (1492–1992). *Publ. Cult.* 3(1):1–24

189. Trouillot, M.-R. 1990. *Haiti: State Against Nation: The Origins and Legacy of Duvalierism.* New York: Monthly Review Press

190. Trouillot, M.-R. 1990. The odd and ordinary: Haiti, the Caribbean and the world. *Cimarron* 2(3):3–12

191. Trouillot, M.-R. 1991. Anthropology and the savage slot: the poetics and politics of otherness. In *Recapturing Anthropology,* ed. R. G. Fox, pp. 17–44. Santa Fe: Sch. Am. Res. Press

192. Trouillot, M.-R. 1992. The inconvenience of freedom: free people of color and the aftermath of slavery in Dominica and Saint-Domingue/Haiti. See Ref. 101

193. Van Lier, R. A. J. 1950. *Development and Nature of Society in the West Indies.* Amsterdam: K. Vereen. Ind. Inst., Med. XCII, Afdeling Cult. Phys. Anthropol. 37

194. Van Lier, R. A. J. 1971 [1949]. *Frontier Society.* The Hague: Marinus Nijhoff

195. Vega, B., ed. 1981. *Ensayos Sobre Cultura Dominicana.* Santo Domingo: Meseo del Hombre Dominicano

196. Warner, K. Q. 1982. *Kaiso! The Trinidad Calypso.* Washington, DC: Three Continents Press

197. Watts, D. 1987. *The West Indies. Patterns of Development, Culture and Environmental Change since 1492.* New York: Cambridge Univ. Press

198. Whitten, N. E., Szwed, J. F., ed. 1970. *Afro-American Anthropology.* New York: Free Press

199. Williams, B. F. 1989. A class act: anthropology and the race to nation across ethnic terrain. *Annu. Rev. Anthropol.* 18:401–44

200. Williams, B. F. 1991. *Stains on My Name, War in My Veins. Guyana and the Politics of Cultural Struggle.* Durham: Duke Univ. Press

201. Wilson, P. J. 1969. Reputation and respectability: a suggestion for Caribbean ethnology. *Man* 4:70–84

202. Wilson, P. J. 1973. *Crab Antics: The Social Anthropology of English-Speaking Negro Societies of the Caribbean.* New Haven/London: Yale Univ. Press

203. Wolf, E. 1982. *Europe and the People without History.* Berkeley: Univ. California Press

204. Wolf, E. 1990. Facing power—old insights, new questions. *Am. Anthropol.* 92(3):586–96

205. Woodson, D. G. 1990. *Tout Mounn se Mounn, Men tout Mounn pa Menm: sociocultural aspects of land tenure and marketing in a Northern Haitian locality.* PhD thesis, Univ. Chicago

206. Yamagushi, M., Naito, M., eds. 1987. *Social and Festive Space in the Caribbean.* Tokyo: Inst. Stud. Lang. Cult. Asia and Africa

Annu. Rev. Anthropol. 1992. 21:43–66

MOBILITY/SEDENTISM: CONCEPTS, ARCHAEOLOGICAL MEASURES, AND EFFECTS

Robert L. Kelly

Department of Anthropology, University of Louisville, Louisville, Kentucky 40292;
Bitnet: RLKELL01@ULKYVM

KEYWORDS: stone tool technology, enculturation, inequality, site structure, foraging

INTRODUCTION

There is hardly a more romantic image in anthropology than that of a small band of hunter-gatherers setting off into the bush, their few belongings on their backs. Mobility, in fact, has long been considered a defining characteristic of hunter-gatherers. At the *Man the Hunter* conference, for example, Lee & DeVore (101:11) assumed that all hunter-gatherers "move around a lot." This is not entirely accurate, for many hunter-gatherers move infrequently—some less than many "sedentary" horticultural societies. Early concepts of mobility blinded us to the fact that mobility is universal, variable, and multi-dimensional.

Partly because of these concepts, and partly because we do not understand the relationships between movement and material culture, archaeologists have had difficulty identifying different forms and levels of mobility. This is especially true in defining and then detecting sedentism.

It is important that we learn to recognize the various forms of mobility archaeologically, because the ways people move exert strong influences on their culture and society. In his classic study, Mauss (105), for example, related the Inuit's seasonal mobility to their moral and religious life. Sahlins (136) saw mobility as conditioning cultural attitudes towards material goods. Currently, archaeologists focus attention on the sedentarization process because reduced mobility precipitates dramatic changes in food storage, trade, territoriality, social and gender inequality, male/female work patterns, subsis-

0084-6570/92/1015-0043$02.00

tence, and demography (44, 69, 71, 73, 89, 93, 124, 126, 152) as well as cultural notions of material wealth, privacy, individuality, cooperation, and competition (170).

Here I consider concepts of mobility/sedentism, archaeological measures of mobility, and the effects of reduced mobility, focusing on foraging and, secondarily, on horticultural societies. (Space prohibits discussion of nomadic pastoralists; for reviews see 36, 40, 98.)

CONCEPTS INVOLVED IN THE STUDY OF MOBILITY

While some archaeologists refer to a settlement continuum from mobile to sedentary, many in practice think of mobility in typological terms. One early scheme divided hunter-gatherers into four categories (11): *free-wandering groups,* with no territorial boundaries; *restricted-wandering groups,* constrained by territorial limitations; *center-based wandering groups,* who seasonally return to a central village; and *semi-permanent sedentary groups,* who occupy a village year-round but move it every few years. Murdock (111) modfied these terms and categorized societies as fully nomadic, semi-nomadic, semi-sedentary, and fully sedentary. Many archaeologists still use a variant of this typology, or, more simply, distinguish only between mobile and sedentary societies (2).

These categories have analytic utility (e.g. 17, 21), but they collapse the several different dimensions of mobility and encourage us to think of it in terms of a single scale of group movement. However, mobility is a property of individuals (25, 47), who may move in many different ways: alone or in groups, frequently or infrequently, over long or short distances. Some sorts of individuals may move more than others (e.g. men vs women, parents vs nonparents, young vs old, good vs poor foragers), and movement also occurs on daily, seasonal, and annual scales.

Binford (17) began to unpack the concept of mobility by differentiating between *residential mobility,* movements of the entire band or local group from one camp to another, and *logistical mobility,* foraging movements of individuals or small task groups out from and back to the residential camp. Binford used these descriptions to categorize two ideal hunter-gatherer settlement systems. *Collectors* move residentially to key locations (e.g. water sources) and use long logistical forays to bring resources to camp. *Foragers* "map onto" a region's resource locations. In general, foragers do not store food; they make frequent residential moves and short logistical forays. Collectors store food; they make infrequent residential moves but long logistical forays. However, the main difference between foragers and collectors is not the frequency or length of movement, but the relationship between the placement of consumers and the tasks of individual foragers—that is, the organizational relations between movements of individuals as individuals and movements as a group. The Anbarra of northern Australia, for example, move residentially only a few times each year (107) while the Aeta of the northern Philippines move residentially much more frequently (90). Both, however, are foragers since they move consumers to resources; the difference in the frequency of movement is related to the food density of their respective environments.

Binford did not intend that the concepts of foragers and collectors become types. Instead, he used them as conceptual tools that helped him to think about the organization of camp movement relative to foraging activities and thus to understand the role mobility plays in creating archaeological sites. Many have misunderstood this aspect of Binford's original paper. The archaeological literature is replete with examples of "foragers" and "collectors," along with efforts to critique the behavioral descriptions of the two concepts while ignoring the more important organizational differences they encompass (e.g. 6, 164).

Binford (18, 20) later added another dimension, what we might call *territorial* or *long-term mobility,* encompassing cyclical movements of a group among a set of territories. For example, the Nunamiut's specific annual range changes as caribou populations rose and fell, and as resources such as firewood became depleted at particular locations (3, 20). While the Nunamiut change the location and size of their territory every decade or so, they eventually return to a previously used tract of land. Thus, they circulate through a series of territories. Long-term mobility is often seen as a conservation measure (51), but it is more likely a response to subsistence stress (65). In either case, the land required by a foraging (or horticultural) population over the long term is much larger than the area used during a single year. Constraints on the long-term territory rather than on the annual territory may be important in conditioning evolutionary change (133).

Finally, to residential, logistical, and long-term mobility we can add permanent migration from a former territory. Such migration can be intentional or unintentional, and it can result from movement of groups or from gradual abandonment by individuals or families. It is probably caused by population growth, but there may be other reasons as well. This aspect of mobility is poorly studied because modern foragers and horticulturalists are encapsulated and circumscribed by agricultural and industrial societies. However, because most of the world was initially populated by foraging peoples, migration must have been an important dimension of mobility in the past (for discussion of free-wandering, see 11).

As should be apparent, most definitions of mobility are behavioral. Mobility has, of course, a cultural component, in that cultural conceptions of the environment affect the way a locality is treated, as Steward pointed out many years ago (85, 148). Hunter-gatherers who leave a place physically and conceptually, for example, may treat it differently from those who leave a locale physically but who still think of it as a place on the landscape, perhaps because of facilities located there (20) or because of a cultural attachment to it. Some researchers differentiate between hunter-gatherers and pastoralists, arguing that the former develop concepts of "relatedness" to land while the latter do not (40)—concepts that generate differences in mobility in addition to those associated with feeding livestock. Some prehistoric foragers may have had little attachment to land under some conditions and so could more easily migrate from one area to another. [The populations who colonized North America, for example, may fall into this category (94).] Thus, current behavioral descriptions may need to expand and include cultural and cognitive factors affecting mobility, such as cultural concepts of and knowledge of the environment.

Bettinger & Baumhoff (15, 14:100–3) offer an alternative to Binford's forager-collector scheme. Their model proposes a continuum from *travelers*, who have high mobility (presumably residential and logistical) and take only high-return-rate food resources, especially large game, to *processors*, who are less mobile and use intensively a diversity of resources, especially plant foods. The difference in subsistence generates differences in demography as well, with high rates of female infanticide lowering the growth rate among travelers. According to these authors, such a model specifies precise relationships between population and resources, and settlement and subsistence. Both the forager/collector and traveler/processor models, however, collapse several dimensions of adaptation (primarily mobility, subsistence, and demography). Nevertheless, the detail of these models cannot help but encourage us to think less typologically and more theoretically about the issue of mobility.

Foraging and Mobility

Although many variables affect mobility, subsistence—and therefore foraging strategy—is certainly a primary one (17, 90). Since the introduction of optimal foraging theory to anthropology there have been numerous ethnographic studies of hunter-gatherer and horticultural foraging strategies (e.g. 66, 142, 143, 171). These studies focus on foraging time, location and group size, and diet breadth but are rarely related to residential movement because they are often conducted with foragers settled by government policy, or with trekking horticulturalists who move residentially only every few years. Thus, arguments relating daily foraging to group movement are largely theoretical.

As they consume food around their camp, foragers reach a point of diminishing returns, where "they may stay on only by absorbing an increase in real costs or a decline in real returns: rise in costs if the people choose to search farther and farther afield, decline in returns if they are satisfied to live on the shorter supplies or inferior foods in easier reach. The solution, of course, is to go elsewhere" (136:33). Many ethnographic cases demonstrate that foragers move not when all food has been consumed within reach of camp but when daily returns decline to an unacceptable level (72). Although the Tanzanian Hadza, for example, can forage for roots up to 8 km from camp, they generally do not go beyond 5 km, preferring instead to move camp (160). It is likely that foragers move when the returns of logistical forays from the current camp drop below those to be expected from another camp, after allowing for the cost of moving (92).

We should point out that foragers do not always move as a group; forager social units, in fact, can have an extremely fluid composition. Relieving social tension is a reason often given for this fluidity, and subsistence can often be a source of this tension. Large families, for example, will reach the point of diminishing returns more quickly than small families, and may move on a different schedule. The degree to which everyone's subsistence is tied to the same resource (e.g. fish runs, communal hunting) will also condition the degree to which families move together. Since many plant foods provide lower returns than large game, the point of diminishing returns will be reached at shorter distances for plant gathering than for hunting large game. Since large game is usually procured by men (with a few ethnographic exceptions), women's foraging should by and large determine when camp is moved. This is important in considering the effect of reduced residential mobility on women's and men's activities (see below).

At the heart of the relationship between daily foraging and group movement is perceived "costs" of camp movement and foraging. While it is unclear what period (e.g. per hour, day, or week) should be used in assessing the cost and benefits of moving and foraging, we still might predict that as the cost of camp movement increases relative to the benefit of foraging in a new location, foragers will remain longer in the current camp (92). Several variables enter into the decision to move. One important variable is the return rate of the exploited foods. As resource return rates decline, foragers reach the point of diminishing returns at shorter and shorter distances and must move more frequently. Likewise, if a resource appearing elsewhere provides higher return rates than current foraging provides, the forager may also elect to move. (This, rather than "affluence," probably explains why foragers pass up some resources; see 70.) Another variable is the "cost" of moving, determined not only by the distance to the next camp but also by what must be moved (e.g. housing material), the terrain to be covered (e.g. mountains versus prairie), and availability of transport technology (such as dogsleds or horses) to move housing, food, and/or people. If food has been stored, then the cost of moving it must be balanced against the next camp's anticipated resources. Models predicting how far resources can be transported (87, 128) show that a resource's return rate does not necessarily predict how far that resource can be carried.

Perceived costs of moving must include evaluations of the risk involved in transferring to a new location. "Risk" involves several components, such as the likelihood of an event's occurring and the magnitude of that event. If foragers perceive the next camp's resources to be more risky, they may elect to remain where they are and accept lower mean foraging rates. Some desert hunter-gatherers, called *tethered nomads* by Taylor (151), remain at a water source at the expense of decreasing foraging return rates (moving only when water runs out) because they are uncertain of the status of other water holes. Some Australian Aborigines, for example, will consume only 800 kcal/day and forage up to 15 km from camp rather than move to an insecure water source (33).

Finally, the number of people who forage for each family, and their specific tasks, can affect mobility. The usual assumption is that adults forage, with women gathering plant food and men hunting. However, in some societies children forage and can provide much of their daily food needs (24); in others, women sometimes hunt (50). Understanding variability in age and sex division of labor is a prerequisite to understanding mobility.

Non-Energetic Variables

Foraging is an important variable, but by no means does it alone determine mobility. People also respond to religious, kinship, trade, artistic, and personal obligations. This does not negate the importance of foraging efficiency. In fact, if nonforaging activities are as important as we presume they are, then they require that one forage or garden as efficiently as possible (142). Nonetheless, not all residential movements are directly controlled by subsistence. People move to gain access to firewood or raw materials for tools, or because insects have become intolerable. Movements can be socially or politically motivated, as people seek spouses, allies, or shamans, or move in response to sorcery, death, and political forces (64, 159). Kent (96, 97), for example, found that Basarwa and Bakgalagadi gave political or social motives for 57% of their movements. However, some movements made for social/political reasons can ultimately be related to foraging concerns. For example, during a period of drought-induced food stress, /Xai/Xai Basarwa stated that they were going elsewhere to trade, but the decision followed two weeks of bickering over food (165).

Finally, residential mobility itself may be culturally valued. Formerly mobile hunter-gatherers often express a desire to move around in order to visit friends, to see what is happening elsewhere, or to relieve boredom (92). The Kaska, for example, did not like "sitting in one place all the time like white men" (81:92). On the other hand, the coastal Tlingit used dance to parody interior groups who, in their opinion, wandered about in a pathetic search for food (106:96). Cultural ideals valuing movement might encourage mobility even where sedentism is possible, although they are unlikely to account for large-scale evolutionary trends. They may, however, help perpetuate cultural and niche differences between populations of horticulturalists/agriculturalists and hunter-gatherers or pastoralists, since mobility can be a strategy to maintain cultural autonomy.

SEDENTISM

One of the most important topics in archaeology today is the question of the origins of sedentism, especially sedentism among hunter-gatherers. For many years, sedentism was thought to be incompatible with a foraging lifeway except in a few favored locations, North America's Northwest Coast being the classic example. However, it is now clear from archaeological and ethnohistoric data that significant reductions in residential mobility occurred without benefit of agriculture (or with agriculture playing only a minor role) in a number of areas, including the Gulf Coast of Florida (163), the Levant (8–10, 30), the American Midwest (29, 28, but see 115), and perhaps coastal/highland Peru (1, 130). Recognition of these prehistoric cases has caused many archaeologists to reexamine the concept of sedentism.

What Does "Sedentism" Mean?

The term sedentism is used in many different ways and encompasses a range of settlement forms (25). What one author labels sedentary another may label semi-sedentary; some authors focus on settlement permanence, others on settlement size (47, 126). Even where sedentism is defined, ambiguity may remain. Higgs & Vita-Finzi (77:29), for example, defined sedentary economies as those "practiced by human groups which stay in one place all the year round," but these authors also recognized *sedentary-cum-mobile* societies having "a mobile element associated with sedentary occupation." Most authors see sedentism as a process "whereby human groups reduce their mobility to the point where they remain residentially stationary year-round" (80:374), and sedentary settlement systems as "those in which at least part of the population remains at the same location throughout the entire year" (G. Rice, in 30:183). For the sake of convenience, I use these definitions here.

Sedentism is usually considered a relative rather than an absolute condition (e.g. 130:270). "Sedentary" settlement, therefore, usually means a condition less mobile than some previous one. Thus, Brown & Vierra (29:189) refer to the settlement systems of the Middle Archaic Period of the American Midwest as ones of "increasing degrees of sedentary settlement." Bar-Yosef & Belfer-Cohen (9:490, 10:186) refer to the Natufian Phase in the Levant as the period of the "emergence" of sedentism, a period of increasing "degrees" of sedentism, a trend to be "deepened" during the succeeding Early Neolithic Phase (see also 27). Archaeologists envision the "emergence" of sedentism as a process akin to a settlement system's batteries running down: People move less and less until they are not moving at all. The transition is thus quantitative, not qualitative. It is not clear, however, whether the slow "emergence" of sedentism is always real, or is in some cases a product of a poor sample of the archaeological record. Depending on chronological controls and sites' temporal distribution, a slow transition could appear to be quick, or vice versa.

This view of gradual quantitative change also comes from archaeologists' tendency to think of mobility in terms of a single scale, a single continuum of residential mobility, rather than as a multi-dimensional phenomenon. But in thinking about sedentism as a point on a continuum of residential mobility, or as a system-state opposed to "mobile," archaeologists conflate the many different dimensions of mobility—individual mobility, group residential movements, territorial shifts, and migration—each of which can vary independently of the others (90). There is no single continuum of mobility (47), and continuing to rely on one diverts attention from the relationship between camp movement and foraging. The question of what causes sedentism actually subsumes many different questions: What controls whether people move as a camp, as families, or as individuals? What controls how far an individual can travel in a logistical foray? What controls how frequently or how far a group moves over the course of a year (90)? What controls how frequently a group shifts its annual range?

Is Sedentism a Threshold Phenomenon?

Not only do archaeologists tend to see sedentism as emerging slowly along a continuum of residential mobility, but many also see it as an important social and behavioral threshold, a "point of no return" (9:490), after which sedentary peoples cannot return to a mobile life-style. In most cases this concept is probably correct, but Ames (2) provides a potential counter-example. In evaluating radiocarbon dates from sites in the plateau region of the northwestern United States, he argues that pithouse construction, indicative of seasonal sedentism, is episodic rather than continuous. While periods without house construction could result from many factors, they may indicate intermittent sedentism. The nature of archaeological data makes it difficult to assess the accuracy of a model in which sedentism develops continuously over time. Imagine a settlement system oscillating between states of greater and lesser residential mobility. In all likelihood, sites produced when people are less residentially mobile will be more visible archaeologically; those produced by an intervening period of high residential mobility will be less visible, and if undated may even be interpreted as special-purpose camps of the sedentary system (see 158). The assumption that sedentism "emerges" slowly and is a "point of no return" might erroneously appear to be confirmed.

Even when sedentary settlement systems develop, they do not necessarily involve all of a region's people. As some people reduce their residential mobility, others may continue to be residentially mobile, perhaps developing a mutualistic relationship with the sedentary villages. We must recognize that statements such as "sedentism slowly emerged" do not capture the totality of the prehistoric social landscape. Hunter-gatherers today are encapsulated by and interact with nonforaging peoples (see review in 112), and the interstices between horticultural societies are frequently filled with nomadic foragers or pastoralists (145, 146). It is highly likely that mobile foraging or pastoral peoples filled the interstices between horticultural or agricultural settlements in the past as they do today, influencing the nature of those sedentary societies and in turn being influenced by them (109). A growing number of archaeological studies of forager-farmer interaction, e.g. for the Neolithic in central Europe (e.g. 62, 63) and Ireland (61), and for the late prehistoric period of the southwestern United States (145, 146), testifies to the importance of these interactions.

Recent studies of horticultural societies suggest new insights into the relationships among gardening, foraging, and village movement, especially for Amazonia (56, 58, 66, 88, 123, 159). The variables that affect foraging are also relevant to horticulture, for both can be evaluated in terms of time, returns, cost, and risk. Both Vickers (159) and Heffley (75), for example, use Horn's Model to describe Siona-Secoya and Athapaskan residential movements, respectively; the only difference is that where Heffley discusses seasonal changes, Vickers refers to multi-year changes.

Archaeological studies of horticulturalists' mobility strategies are changing received views of prehistory. Archaeologists in the American Southwest, for example, are reevaluating the concept of sedentism, and many think the agriculturalists there, those occupying pueblo villages as well as those who lived in pithouses, were more mobile than previously assumed (55, 122, 123, 166, 167; papers in 108). Preucel (123), for example, argues that the larger the population the greater the distance some farmers must walk, and the greater the probability that daily or periodic logistical moves will develop into seasonal residential movements. (This was the situation of many Puebloan settlements at the time of contact.) Seasonal rather than year-round sedentism might account for the archaeological record of the Basketmaker and Puebloan periods. Seasonal settlement may also account for variability in Natufian sites in the Levant (30).

In sum, sedentism need not be a threshold phenomenon. Not everyone is equally involved in changes in mobility, and the inception of village life entails changes in (but not a cessation of) movement. Additionally, reductions in residential mobility produce changes in mobility on different levels and scales under different conditions, resulting in considerable variability among cases currently classed together as "sedentary" (25).

The Causes of Sedentism

THE "PULL" AND "PUSH" HYPOTHESES Price & Brown (125) label the two basic hypotheses explaining hunter-gatherer sedentism as the pull and push hypotheses. In the pull hypothesis, the presence of abundant resources is both a necessary and a sufficient condition for sedentism to appear. To an earlier generation of theorists, it seemed a straightforward assumption that humans would take advantage of the opportunity to reduce mobility: "in general sedentary life has more survival value than wandering life to the human race, and... , other things being equal, whenever there is an opportunity to make the transition, it will be made" (11:134). Sedentism, it was argued, is a more efficient form of resource procurement, because it saves the effort of moving—in particular, the effort of moving children, the elderly, and the infirm (126, 147). Part of the reason for assuming sedentism to be efficient is that Western society sees movement as burdensome and undesirable; but many other societies do not (41).

Many archaeologists continue to rely upon the "pull" hypothesis. "Resource abundance" allegedly accounts for sedentism among the Ainu and Owens Valley Paiute (161); paleoindians of California (110); the aboriginal inhabitants of coastal eastern North America (120), coastal areas of the arctic (172, 117) and northern Europe (134); and Archaic hunters of the Andean puna (130), central Mexico (113), the midwestern United States (29), and the Great Basin (76, 103). Marine and wetland resources are the usual candidates for resource abundance. (We leave aside the issue of whether sedentism is actually demonstrated in each of these studies.)

The pull explanation of sedentism seems reasonable, but it is fraught with empirical difficulties. Archaeologists long assumed that agriculture, for example, would always result in sedentism because people could then produce abundant food resources. However, we now know that agricultural practices often precede sedentism, sometimes by many centuries, in the American Southwest (166, 167), Mesoamerica (53), and the American Midwest (29). Furthermore, although few agricultural societies change residences throughout the year (126), some are nonetheless residentially mobile, even ones like the Raramuri, for whom agricultural products constitute nearly 100% of diet (42, 59, 68). It was long assumed that the transition from pithouses to aboveground pueblos, a transition that almost surely indicates a reduction in annual residential mobility, was associated with an increased use of maize. However, in at least some parts of the southwest, the settlement transition does not appear to be associated with an increased use of maize (e.g. 55, 162; papers in 108). The relationship between agriculture and mobility is now open to question (68).

Sedentism may not reduce mobility, nor may it be as efficient, as was once thought. Binford (17) suggested that when residential mobility is constrained, logistical mobility must increase. Eder (47:851) found this to be true among the Batak, where mobility was shifted from local groups as whole units to lower levels of social organization. As the Nata River Basarwa became less residentially mobile, men made increasingly longer foraging trips, and women gathered a wider range of bush foods, including lower-quality foods, working longer hours to process them (44, 79). In both cases, reduced residential mobility does not seem to have reduced overall energy use; instead, it reorganized it (and may even have increased it). We should point out that the Basarwa, the Batak, and other foraging societies undergoing sedentization today are instances of secondary or contact sedentism—a change in settlement behavior imposed upon nomadic peoples by outside governments for purposes of census and control. While it is difficult to separate the effects of reduced mobility from those of a hostile political environment, we nonetheless cannot assume that a sedentary existence is more efficient than a residentially mobile one.

It is true, of course, that if hunter-gatherers are to become sedentary (and remain hunter-gatherers) then food must be available in a single location year-round, either continuously or as a stored resource. Binford (19) argued that hunter-gatherers would forgo such opportunities to become sedentary because residential mobility allows them to collect information continually about their natural and social environment, and thus to prepare for local resource failure. However, others point out that environments fluctuate on different scales and that ethnographic cases come from environments that fluctuate widely from year to year (57). In areas where resource fluctuation is infrequent or less severe there may be little need to remain mobile to gather information.

Even where the conditions for sedentism appear to exist (e.g. resource abundance and/or large-scale storage), there is not always archaeological evidence of sedentism (28, 144). One simple simulation study suggests that if foragers wish to maintain maximum foraging return rates they should move residentially even if it is energetically possible to remain in one location (92). Resource abundance may be a necessary but is probably not a sufficient condition for sedentism.

As an alternative to the "pull" hypothesis, the "push" hypothesis proposes that hunter-gatherers are forced into sedentism by subsistence stress. In this scenario, as efficiently gathered resources become scarce, foragers intensify their subsistence efforts, taking a greater range of foods and spending more time in harvesting and processing them. Researchers invoke several factors to explain intensification, including population increase, climatic change, and territorial constriction (37, 126). In essence, these all involve resource stress—a shortage of food supply relative to population size. Rafferty (126) developed a model in which three different settlement patterns—nonsedentary, nucleated sedentary, and dispersed sedentary—result from different environmental conditions and different cultural responses to resource stress, including emigration, population limitation, and technological/organizational change. To this useful model one might add greater attention to the concept of stress. Does stress result from one lean season or does it require a series of lean seasons? Is stress a periodic or a chronic state of subnormal caloric intake?

Understanding sedentism involves understanding the relationship between residential and logistical mobility, between movement of the camp and foraging. Assuming that foragers (or horticulturalists) wish to maximize the return rate from foraging (or gardening), the decision to move is based not solely on whether they can stay where they are but also on the difference between the expected returns of the current and the next potential camp, after allowing for the cost of moving. Local resource abundance must be weighed in terms of the regional foraging potential. Many variables can affect this basic equation, including the cost of moving, the regional population density (displacing others increases the "cost" of moving), and the degree of risk attached to the resources of different areas. Much creative research remains to be done in this area.

NON-MATERIALIST APPROACHES   The push and pull hypotheses are both firmly grounded in a materialist paradigm. In both, sedentism occurs initially (for whatever reason), and as a result foragers intensify production. (Many studies of sedentization indicate that intensification is coeval with or soon follows the appearance of sedentary villages.) However, some argue that sedentism results from the perceived need for intensification. In this scenario, what we might call the social competition hypothesis, effort expended in mobility is channeled to producing resources for competitive feasts, long-distance trade, or other prestige-seeking activities (12, 73). Lourandos (102), for example, argues that a shift towards semi-sedentism was driven by the development of increasingly complex social networks and alliance systems. (Note that many archaeologists would argue the reverse.) Lourandos suggests that environment and demography play a role in establishing the initial need for social competition, but others find the reasons less clear why some hunter-gatherers intensify (and become sedentary) and others do not (e.g. 12). Determining whether or not sedentism precedes intensification and social competition is critical to testing the social competition hypothesis. To date, discussion relies upon generalized archaeological sequences where it is not easy to say which comes first.

STUDYING MOBILITY FROM ARCHAEOLOGICAL REMAINS

To this point I have mentioned a number of archaeological studies purporting to demonstrate changes in mobility. I cannot evaluate all these studies here, but I can note that it is difficult to study mobility archaeologically. Both the resource base and mobility itself are difficult to document.

Measuring Resource Abundance

Evaluating hypotheses of sedentism requires that archaeologists document actual availablility of food in a particular locality. Many archaeologists simply assume food abundance from subjective evaluations of a region's potential. Continuous, year-long occupation of villages and continual seasonal availability of food within a feasible foraging distance have been documented only for a few cases (e.g. 127, 134). Food abundance must be measured objectively and must take harvesting and processing rates into consideration—for these are crucial factors in selecting resources to use (142). Measures of sheer abundance are not adequate. The biomass per hectare of forest is greater for mice than for deer, for example, yet prehistoric hunters hunted deer, not mice, because deer provide much higher return rates than do mice.

Even where the resource base is well documented it is normally limited to those resources for which there is archaeological evidence of use. But in order to test hypotheses about mobility and sedentism the nature of both used and unused resources (or regions) must be documented, because "abundance" is relative. To know what one resource offers means knowing what it offers relative to others.

Stone Tool Technology

For many years, archaeologists have measured the size of prehistoric foraging territories and thus the degree of mobility through the distribution of stone tools relative to the geologic sources of their raw material (e.g. 82, 138). Paleoindian Clovis and Folsom projectile points, for example, are often found 100–300 km from their sources. Some archaeologists argue that this indicates high residential mobility (see papers in 48 and 149) or a combination of residential, logistical, and territorial mobility (94). Such information provides a rough indicator only of range, rather than mobility, since the raw material could have been acquired through residential or logistical movements, or trade.

Archaeologists have tried recently to reconstruct mobility by examining the organization of stone tool technologies (e.g. 4–7, 16, 23, 86, 91, 114, 118, 154, 155). Organization here refers to "the selection and integration of strategies for making, using, transporting, and discarding tools and the materials needed for their manufacture and maintenance" (114:57). Many factors affect tool production, use, and discard; but currently the relationship between technology and mobility takes precedence in research (156).

Archaeologists debate the relationship between mobility and technology. Bifacial tools or cores are generally associated with frequent and/or lengthy residential or logistical movements (26, 91, 94), while expedient flake tools and bipolar reduction are associated with infrequent residential moves (118). However, the distribution of lithic raw material could alter these associations significantly (5). Other researchers focus on the statistical relationship between tool assemblage size and diversity. Shott (141) suggests that collectors produce assemblages with no correlation while foragers produce assemblages with a strong positive correlation; additionally, he suggests that there should be an inverse relationship between technological diversity and residential mobility (140). However, correlations between assemblage size and diversity could be related to many factors (104, 153). Torrence (157), for example, argues that technological diversity relates directly to the degree of risk involved in prey capture rather than mobility per se.

Reconstructing mobility strategies from prehistoric technology is hampered by several difficulties. First, there are no simple relationships between mobility and tool manufacture. Many other variables intervene—e.g. tool function, raw material type, and distribution, hafting, and risk. Second, the reconstruction of different tool manufacturing methods from debitage is fraught with interpretive difficulties. Third, stone tools are not routinely used to a significant extent by any living foragers, making it difficult to test ideas relating stone tools to mobility. Analyses of ethnographic data often make the unverified assumption that as the total technology goes (including its organic parts) so goes the (usually absent) stone tool component. At present, then, many interpretations of stone tool assemblages as indicators of mobility are subjective, intuitive, and sometimes contradictory.

Site Structure

Another avenue of research into mobility lies in the analysis of site structure, the spatial distribution of debris within a site (54, 97a). Studying changes in modern Basarwa residential sites, Hitchcock (80) found that as residential mobility decreased, the abundance and diversity of debris left in a site increased, as did site size and the number of storage features (although group size did not increase). Site size and artifact density are frequently used as indicators of reduced residential mobility (10, 126), although they can be attributed to several other factors as well, such as frequency of reoccupation (31). The distribution of remains may be a better indicator of residential mobility since it appears to be directly related to the length of time a location is occupied. Specifically, instead of simply throwing or sweeping trash off to the side (as mobile foragers do; see 116), sedentary Basarwa used secondary trash dumps located farther from houses than those in camps of residentially mobile groups. They also used specific areas for specific activities; thus, as residential mobility decreased, internal site differentiation increased (80). While many factors (e.g. social organization and cultural conventions) affect the use of space, the site structures among nonresidentially mobile horticulturalists and recently settled foragers and pastoralists appear to be more internally differentiated than those of residentially mobile peoples (e.g. 42, 43, 59, 97, 100).

Much of this space differentiation seems to be directed toward the privatization of space (40, 100, 170) and may be related to a change in methods of conflict resolution. One way conflict is generated among foragers is through one individual's refusal to meet demands to share. (Contrary to many claims, foragers do not always share freely and gladly.) Mobile foragers use movement to resolve social conflict; but if this option is not available, people may "privatize" space (170) by placing houses further apart or by building enclosed houses and fenced households to hide food and goods and discourage demands to share (80). Criteria for recognizing mobility strategies archaeologically must develop hand-in-hand with a theoretical understanding of how social relations change as residential mobility decreases.

Houses

Reduced residential mobility can be demonstrated through indicators other than site structure. The presence of human commensals—house mice, for example—may indicate a continuous supply of fresh trash and hence year-round occupation (9). Perhaps the most commonly used archaeological indicator of a reduction in residential mobility is the presence of houses. Cross-cultural studies demonstrate that investing labor in houses is related to low (or no) residential mobility (e.g. 55). But even substantial housing may not indicate a cessation of residential movements. Cedar plank houses built by Northwest Coast peoples, for example, were partially dismantled in the spring and moved to fishing locations.

Unfortunately, the presence of any kind of dwellings, even of those requiring little energy investment, is often taken as evidence of year-round sedentism. Unless we understand the factors involved in house construction (21), differential preservation of indications of houses can lead to erroneous reconstructions of mobility. For example, as a group of people become territorially constrained, they may visit the same places repeatedly each season. Binford refers to such arrangements as *embedded mobility* (19, 60). Under these circumstances, people may construct facilities, including houses, at some locations. This may be why houses appear in rockshelters when settlement systems appear to be becoming sedentary (1, 9). But these houses could indicate redundant use of locations through residential or logistical mobility due to territorial circumscription or a reduction in long-term mobility options. Evidence of house scavenging (168) likewise could indicate continuous or seasonal use, or be a product of reoccupation on even longer time scales.

Individual Differences in Mobility

Finally, it is important that we understand the differences in individual mobility patterns within a society. For example, in some foraging societies good hunters remain out longer (and thus travel more) than poorer hunters, while in other societies the reverse is true (78). Ethnographic accounts suggest that men generally travel further than women in daily foraging trips, even remaining out for one or several nights (this appears to be true even when women hunt); thus, there can be gender differences in degrees of logistical mobility. Such variability is extremely difficult to detect archaeologically, although one avenue lies in detecting different kinds or degrees of mechanical stress on human osteological remains. Larsen et al (99) show that the femurs of males sustained greater mechanical stress than the femurs of females for a prehistoric adult hunting and gathering population in the Great Basin. This difference in stress suggests that males were more mobile than females.

THE EFFECTS OF MOBILITY

The difficult task of recognizing different patterns of mobility from archaeological data is important to an understanding of how changes in mobility relate to other aspects of human society. Research suggests that changes in logistical, residential, and long-term mobility strongly affect sociopolitical organization, trade, territoriality, demography, and enculturative processes. Particularly important are the effects of reduced residential mobility.

Sociopolitical Organization

While foragers are often characterized as "egalitarian," a concept undergoing increasing scrutiny (52), many are clearly nonegalitarian, with political hierarchies, wealth competition, and extreme social and gender inequality (125). Keeley (89) demonstrates that groups occupying one camp for more than five months of the year live at substantially higher population densities, rely more heavily on stored food, and have greater wealth distinctions than foragers who are more residentially mobile. It is likely, therefore, that a reduction in residential mobility encourages or is part of a process resulting in inequality.

Some see sedentism as lifting the constraints residential movements impose upon a foraging society. Following the argument that sedentism is a product of resource abundance and increases efficiency, many assume that sedentary hunter-gatherers simply have more time and resources to devote to what Gould (57) calls "aggrandizing" behavior. Here, inequality appears to be the inevitable response of human nature to the accumulation of surplus made possible by sedentism.

But sedentism probably does not lift previous constraints as much as it replaces them (93). Specifically, sedentism probably occurs under, or soon results in, conditions where residential and/or long-term mobility are no longer viable solutions to local resource failure. Sedentary hunter-gatherers must use other mechanisms to reduce the risk inevitably associated with reliance on a single resource or location (38, 73). These may include efforts to increase household production and storage by restricting sharing networks, by using slaves, and by permitting men to control the labor of women (wives or sisters) and affinals, thus fostering gender and social inequality (39, 74, 93, 137).

Additionally, more time and effort may be put into alliance formation, entailing for example competitive feasting (73) and the manipulation of marriages to ensure access to another group's resources. Accordingly, trade may change as societies become sedentary; trade may in addition become more critical as a symbolic indicator of social alliances (35). Territoriality may also increase as competition for resources escalates with population growth (34, 37). Such competition might also increase perceived cultural or ethnic differentiation between groups. Given that sedentism requires methods other than mobility to reduce risk, the temporal and spatial parameters of resource variability probably condition the specific forms of social, trade, and territorial relations (93, 129, 135).

Demography

The association of certain behaviors with sedentism implies that they are generated not only under conditions of low residential mobility but also under conditions of population pressure (89). In some cases population growth may eventually force sedentism. However, as mobile populations today become sedentary, their populations grow, often dramatically (e.g. 22, 79, 131, 132). Medical care plays a role in this growth, but changes in women's foraging behavior may also increase fertility and the rate of population increase.

The nature of the relationship between mobility and fecundity is not clear (13, 169, 49). As pointed out above, a reduction in residential mobility generally increases resource processing. Adults in sedentary Basarwa camps are busier at home than adults of mobile camps (45). For women, this transition could increase fecundity in two ways. First, by increasing the amount of work women do, increased resource processing may decrease the frequency and intensity of breastfeeding, a primary factor in increasing fecundity (32). Second, a reduction in female traveling, through a trade-off of foraging for resource processing, may also decrease aerobic activity and, through a still poorly understood physiological process, increase fecundity (13). These trends could be affected by changes in diet as well, by increasing caloric intake and/or by using storage which, by leveling out seasonal fluctuations in food intake, could maintain long-term energy balance and increase fecundity (49, 84). Children may also become incorporated into the work force of adults (45), decreasing the perceived cost of children, and encouraging fertility (46).

Reduced residential mobility may also decrease child mortality, which may be more critical to population growth than an increase in fertility (67). While it has long been assumed that sedentism increases the rate of contagious disease, Pennington & Harpending (119) point out that mobility encourages "traveler's diarrhea," producing a chronic state of poor health in the children of mobile populations that eventually takes its toll. Reducing mobility could increase child survival and hence population growth.

Enculturation and Cultural Change

The changing adult work patterns associated with the changing resource harvesting and processing requirements of sedentism may also affect childrearing (83) and alter enculturation. As the Basarwa became sedentary, for example, men spent more time away from home and women spent more time at home processing resources and doing other work (45, 79). These factors may conspire to reduce the time men and women spend with children, encouraging young children to work more, especially in the care of infants, and thus cause a shift from parental to peer-group enculturation (46, 45). Although the process is by no means clear (and many factors are involved), peer-group enculturation appears to encourage processes of gender role enculturation (46) and the formation of modal personalities different from those of parental enculturation. Such a shift in enculturation patterns could alter culture in sedentary communities.

CONCLUSION

There are no Gardens of Eden on earth, no single locales that can provide for all human needs. Mobility—residential, logistical, long-term, and migration—was the first means humans used to overcome this problem. Changes in the way humans choose to be mobile dramatically affect other aspects of human life, from demography to enculturation. Theoretically, then, mobility must be critical to understanding human evolutionary change. From this perspective, it is encouraging to see theoretical and archaeological scrutiny of early hominid foraging and mobility patterns (137a). Potts, for example, has asked whether the concentrations of fauna and stone tools at places such as Olduvai Gorge are evidence of home bases or are intentional caches of stone to be used by foraging hominids, perhaps in scavenging carcasses (121). The foraging and mobility patterns of early hominids were in all likelihood quite different from those of any known foragers or nonhuman primates. Documenting variability in these patterns is important to an understanding of how selective processes shaped human evolution [see Potts's (121) comparison of the archaeology of Olduvai and Koobi Fora].

By deconstructing the concepts of mobility and sedentism, we see the need to construct more useful approaches than a simple polarization of mobile vs sedentary societies. Indeed, it is no longer useful to speak of a continuum between mobile and sedentary systems, since mobility is not merely variable but multi-dimensional. No society is sedentary, not even our own industrial one—people simply move in different ways. The dimensions of movement need to be disentangled and studied independently so that we can understand how factors altering one component affect other areas of behavior and culture. We will also need more detailed theoretical arguments linking group movement and daily activities with economic structures, labor requirements, childcare, marriage, and trade. Numerous technical and theoretical difficulties surround the archaeological study of mobility, and archaeological, ethnographic, and ethnohistoric data must be used creatively in developing methodological tools for the study of prehistoric mobility. Such middle-range research promises a large reward, for the analytical study of mobility and foraging will provide a clearer understanding of important evolutionary processes.

ACKNOWLEDGMENTS

I thank Lin Poyer for her patient consideration of previous drafts, and W. H. Wills and T. Rocek for their thoughts on sedentism.

Literature Cited

1. Aldenderfer, M. S. 1989. The Archaic Period in the south-central Andes. *J. World Prehist.* 3:117–58
2. Ames, K. M. 1991. Sedentism: a temporal shift or a transitional change in hunter-gatherer mobility patterns? See Ref. 63, pp. 108–34
3. Amsden, C. 1977. *A quantitative analysis*

of *Nunamiut Eskimo settlement dynamics.*
PhD thesis. Univ. New Mexico, Albuquerque
4. Andrefsky, W. 1991. Inferring trends in prehistoric settlement behavior from lithic production technology in the southern Plains. *North Am. Archaeol.* 12:129–44
5. Bamforth, D. B. 1986. Technological efficiency and tool curation. *Am. Antiq.* 51:38–50
6. Bamforth, D. B. 1990. Settlement, raw material, and lithic procurement in the central Mojave Desert. *J. Anthropol. Res.* 9:70–104
7. Bamforth, D. B. 1991. Technological organization and hunter-gatherer land use. *Am. Antiq.* 56:216–35
8. Bar-Yosef, O. 1987. Late Pleistocene adaptations in the Levant. In *The Pleistocene Old World: Regional Perspectives,* ed. O. Soffer, pp. 219–36. New York: Plenum
9. Bar-Yosef, O., Belfer-Cohen, A. 1989. The origins of sedentism and farming communities in the Levant. *J. World Prehist.* 3:447–98
10. Bar-Yosef, O., Belfer-Cohen, A. 1991. From sedentary hunter-gatherers to territorial farmers in the Levant. See Ref. 63, pp. 181–202
11. Beardsley, R. K., Holder, P., Krieger, A., Meggers, M., Rinaldo, J., Kutsche, P. 1956. Functional and evolutionary implications of community patterning. *Sem. Archaeol., 1955. Soc. Am. Archaeol. Mem.* 11:129–57
12. Bender, B. 1985. Prehistoric developments in the American midcontinent and in Brittany, Northwest France. See Ref. 124, pp. 21–57
13. Bentley, G. 1985. Hunter-gatherer energetics and fertility: a reassessment of the !Kung San. *Human Ecol.* 13:79–109
14. Bettinger, R. L. 1991. *Hunter-Gatherers: Archaeological and Evolutionary Theory.* New York: Plenum
15. Bettinger, R. L., Baumhoff, M. 1982. The Numic spread: Great Basin cultures in competition. *Am. Antiq.* 47:485–503
16. Binford, L. R. 1979. Organization and formation processes: looking at curated technologies. *J. Anthropol. Res.* 35:255–73
17. Binford, L. R. 1980. Willow smoke and dogs' tails: hunter-gatherer settlement systems and archaeological site formation. *Am. Antiq.* 45:4–20
18. Binford, L. R. 1982. The archaeology of place. *J. Anthropol. Archaeol.* 1:5–31
19. Binford, L. R. 1983. *In Pursuit of the Past.* London: Thames and Hudson
20. Binford, L. R. 1983. Long-term land use patterns: some implications for archaeology. In *Working at Archaeology,* by L. R. Binford, pp. 379–86. New York: Academic
21. Binford, L. R. 1990. Mobility, housing, and environment: a comparative study. *J. Anthropol. Res.* 46:119–52

22. Binford, L. R., Chasko, W. J. 1976. Nunamiut demographic history: a provocative case. In *Demographic Anthropology,* ed. E. Zubrow, pp. 63–143. Albuquerque: Univ. New Mexico Press
23. Bleed, P. 1986. The optimal design of hunting weapons: maintainability or reliability. *Am. Antiq.* 51:737–47
24. Blurton-Jones, N. G., Hawkes, K., O'Connell, J. F. 1989. Modelling and measuring costs of children in two foraging societies. In *Comparative Socioecology: The Behavioural Ecology of Humans and Other Mammals,* ed. V. Standen, R. A. Foley, pp. 367–90. Oxford: Blackwell Scientific
25. Bocek, B. 1991. Prehistoric settlement pattern and social organization on the San Francisco peninsula, California. See Ref. 63, pp. 58–86
26. Boldurian, A. T. 1991. Folsom mobility and organization of lithic technology: a view from Blackwater Draw, New Mexico. *Plains Anthropol.* 36:281–95
27. Bonnier, E., Rozenberg, C. 1988. From shrine to hamlet: about the Neolithic process in the central Andes highlands. *L'Anthropologie* 92:982–96
28. Brown, J. A. 1985. Long-term trends to sedentism and the emergence of complexity in the American Midwest. See Ref. 124, pp. 201–23
29. Brown, J. A., Vierra, R. K. 1983. What happened in the Middle Archaic? Introduction to an ecological approach to Koster Site archaeology. In *Archaic Hunters and Gatherers in the American Midwest,* ed. J. L. Phillips, J. A. Brown, pp. 165–96. New York: Academic
30. Byrd, B. F. 1989. The Natufian: settlement variability and economic adaptations in the Levant at the end of the Pleistocene. *J. World Prehist.* 3:159–98
31. Camilli, E. 1989. The occupational history of sites and the interpretation of prehistoric technological systems: an example from Cedar Mesa, Utah. See Ref. 155, pp. 17–26
32. Campbell, K. L., Wood, J. W. 1988. Fertility in traditional societies. In *Natural and Human Fertility: Social and Biological Determinants,* ed. P. Diggory, M. Potts, S. Teper, pp. 39–69. London: MacMillan Press
33. Cane, S. 1987. Australian Aboriginal subsistence in the Western Desert. *Hum. Ecol.* 15:391–434
34. Cashdan, E. 1983. Territorality among human foragers: ecological models and an application to four bushman groups. *Curr. Anthropol.* 24:47–66
35. Cashdan, E. 1987. Trade and its origins on the Botletli River, Botswana. *J. Anthropol. Res.* 43:121–38
36. Casimir, M. J., Rao, A., eds. 1992. *Mobility and Territoriality: Social and Spatial Boundaries among Foragers, Fishers, Pastoralists and Peripatetics.* New York: Berg

37. Cohen, M. N. 1977. *The Food Crisis in Prehistory*. New Haven: Yale Univ. Press
38. Cohen, M. N. 1981. Pacific Coast foragers: affluent or overcrowded? In *Affluent Foragers. Senri Ethnol. Stud.*, ed. S. Koyama, D. H. Thomas, 9:275–95. Osaka: Natl. Mus. Ethnol.
39. Collier, J. F. 1988. *Marriage and Inequality in Three Classless Societies*. Stanford: Stanford Univ. Press
40. Cribb, R. 1991. *Nomads in Archaeology*. Cambridge: Cambridge Univ. Press
41. DeVine, J. 1985. The versatility of human locomotion. *Am. Anthropol.* 87:550–70
42. Dodd, W. 1989. *Determinants of site structure among Guarijio horticulturalists*. PhD thesis, Univ. Utah, Salt Lake City
43. Doershuk, J. F. 1989. *Hunter-gatherer site structure and sedentism: the Koster site Middle Archaic*. PhD thesis, Northwestern Univ., Evanston
44. Draper, P. 1975. !Kung women: contrasts in sexual egalitarianism in foraging and sedentary contexts. In *Toward an Anthropology of Women*, ed. R. Reiter, pp. 77–109. New York: Monthly Review Press
45. Draper, P., Cashdan, E. 1988. Technological change and child behavior among the !Kung. *Ethnology* 27:339–65
46. Draper, P., Harpending, H. 1987. Parent investment and the child's environment In *Parenting Across the Lifespan: Biosocial Dimensions*, ed. J. B. Lancaster, A. S. Rossi, J. Altmann, L. R. Sherod, pp. 207–35. New York: Aldine de Gruyter
47. Eder, J. 1984. The impact of subsistence change on mobility and settlement pattern in a tropical forest foraging economy: some implications for archaeology. *Am. Anthropol.* 86:837–53
48. Ellis, C. J., Lothrop, J. C., eds. 1989. *Eastern Paleoindian Lithic Resource Use*. Boulder, CO: Westview Press
49. Ellison, P. 1990. Human ovarian function and reproductive ecology: new hypotheses. *Am. Anthropol.* 92:933–52
50. Estioko-Griffin, A., Griffin, P. B. 1981. Woman the hunter: the Agta. In *Woman the Gatherer*, ed. F. Dahlberg, pp. 121–51. New Haven: Yale Univ. Press
51. Feit, H. A. 1973. The ethno-ecology of the Waswanipi Cree; or how hunters can handle their resources. In *Cultural Ecology*, ed. B. Cox, pp. 115–25. Toronto: McClellend & Stewart, Ltd.
52. Flanagan, J. G. 1989. Hierarchy in simple "egalitarian" societies. *Annu. Rev. Anthropol.* 18:245–66
53. Flannery, K. V. 1972. The origins of the village as a settlement type in Mesoamerica and the Near East: a comparative study. In *Man, Settlement, and Urbanism*, ed. P. J. Ucko, R. Tringham, G. W. Dimbleby, pp. 23–53. London: Duckworth
54. Gamble, C. S., Boismier, W. A., eds. 1991. *Ethnoarchaeological Approaches to Mobile Campsites: Hunter-Gatherer and Pastoralist Case Studies*. Ann Arbor, MI: Int. Monogr. Prehist.
55. Gilman, P. A. 1987. Architecture as artifact: pit structures and pueblos in the American Southwest. *Am. Antiq.* 52:538–64
56. Good, K. 1989. *Yanomami hunting patterns: trekking and garden relocation as an adaptation to game availability in Amazonia, Venezuela*. PhD Thesis, Univ. Florida, Gainesville
57. Gould, R. 1982. To have and have not: the ecology of sharing among hunter-gatherers. In *Resource Managers: North American and Australian Hunter-Gatherers*, ed. E. Hunn, N. Williams, pp. 69–92. Boulder, CO: Westview Press
58. Gragson, T. L. 1992. Comparative ecological structure of tropical rainforests and savannas and its functional role in the subsistence ecology of South American foragers. In *Research in Economic Anthropology*, ed B. Isaac. Vol. 14: In press
59. Graham, M. 1989. *Raramuri residential site structure: an ethnoarchaeological approach to settlement organization*. PhD thesis, Univ. New Mexico, Albuquerque
60. Graham, M., Roberts, A. 1986. Residentially-constricted mobility: a preliminary investigation of variability in settlement organization. *Haliksa'i* 5:105–16
61. Green, S. W. 1991. Foragers and farmers on the prehistoric Irish frontier. See Ref. 63, pp. 216–44
62. Gregg, S. A. 1988. *Foragers and Farmers: Population Interaction and Agricultural Expansion in Prehistoric Europe*. Chicago: Univ. Chicago Press
63. Gregg, S. A., ed. 1991. *Between Bands and States. Cent. Archaeol. Invest. Occas. Pap. No. 9*. Carbondale: S. Ill. Univ. Press
64. Griffin, P. B. 1989. Hunting, farming, and sedentism in a rain forest foraging society. See Ref. 95, pp. 60–70
65. Hames, R. 1987. Game conservation or efficient hunting? In *The Question of the Commons*, ed. B. J. McCoy, J. M. Acheson, pp. 92–107. Tucson: Univ. Arizona Press
66. Hames, R. B., Vickers, W. T., eds. 1983. *Adaptive Responses of Native Amazonians*. New York: Academic
67. Handwerker, W. 1983. The first demographic transition: an analysis of subsistence choices and reproductive consequences. *Am. Anthropol.* 85:5–27
68. Hard, R. J., Merrill, W. L. 1992. Mobile agriculturalists and the emergence of sedentism: perspectives from Northern Mexico. *Am. Anthropol.* 94: In press
69. Harris, D. R. 1978. Settling down: an evolutionary model for the transformation of mobile bands into sedentary communities. In *The Evolution of Social Systems*, ed. J. Friedrich, M. S. Rowlands, pp. 401–17. London: Duckworth

70. Hawkes, K., O'Connell, J. F. 1981. Affluent hunters? Some comments in light of the Alyawara case. *Am. Anthropol.* 83:622–26
71. Hayden, B. 1981. Research and development in the Stone Age: technological transitions among hunter-gatherers. *Curr. Anthropol.* 22:519–28
72. Hayden, B. 1981. Subsistence and ecological adaptations of modern hunter-gatherers. In *Omnivorous Primates: Hunting and Gathering in Human Evolution,* ed. G. Teleki, R. Harding, pp. 344–422. New York: Columbia Univ. Press
73. Hayden, B. 1990. Nimrods, piscators, pluckers, and planters: the emergence of food production. *J. Anthropol. Archaeol.* 9:31–69
74. Hayden, B., Deal, M., Cannon, A., Casey, J. 1986. Ecological determinants of women's status among hunter/gatherers. *Hum. Evol.* 1:449–74
75. Heffley, S. 1981. Northern Athabaskan settlement patterns and resource distributions: an application of Horn's Model. In *Hunter-Gatherer Foraging Strategies,* ed. B. Winterhalder, E. A. Smith, pp. 126–47. Chicago: Univ. Chicago Press
76. Heizer, R. F., Napton, L. 1970. Archaeology and the prehistoric lacustrine subsistence regime as seen from Lovelock Cave, Nevada. *Contrib. Univ. Calif. Archaeol. Res. Facil.* 10
77. Higgs, E. S., Vita-Finzi, C. 1972. Prehistoric economies: a territorial approach. In *Papers in Economic Prehistory,* ed. E. S. Higgs, pp. 27–36. Cambridge: Cambridge Univ. Press
78. Hill, K., Hillard, K., Hawkes, K., Hurtado, M. 1987. Foraging decisions among Aché hunter-gatherers: new data and implications for optimal foraging models. *Ethol. Sociobiol.* 8:1–36
79. Hitchcock, R. K. 1982. Patterns of sedentism among the Basarwa of eastern Botswana. In *Politics and History in Band Society,* ed. E. Leacock, R. B. Lee, pp. 223–67. New York: Cambridge Univ. Press
80. Hitchcock, R. K. 1987. Sedentism and site structure: organzational change in Kalahari Basarwa residential locations. In *Method and Theory for Activity Area Research,* ed. S. Kent, pp. 374–423. New York: Columbia Univ. Press
81. Honigmann, J. J. 1949. Culture and ethos of Kaska society. *Yale Univ. Publ. Anthropol.* 40
82. Hughes, R. E., ed. 1984. Obsidian studies in the Great Basin. *Contrib. Univ. Calif. Archaeol. Res. Facil.* 45
83. Hurtado, A. M., Hawkes, K., Hill, K., Kaplan, H. 1985. Female subsistence strategies among Aché hunter-gatherers of eastern Paraguay. *Hum. Ecol.* 13:1–47
84. Hurtado, A. M., Hill, K. R. 1990. Seasonality in a foraging society: variation in diet, work effort, fertility and sexual division of labor among the Hiwi of Venezuela. *J. Anthropol. Res.* 46:293–346
85. Ingold, E. 1987. *The Appropriation of Nature: Essays on Human Ecology and Social Relations.* Manchester: Manchester Univ. Press
86. Johnson, J. K., Morrow, C. A., eds. 1987. *The Organization of Core Technology.* Boulder: Westview Press
87. Jones, K. T., Madsen, D. B. 1989. Calculating the cost of resource transportation: a Great Basin example. *Curr. Anthropol.* 30:529–34
88. Keegan, W. F. 1986. The optimal foraging analysis of horticultural production. *Am. Anthropol.* 88:92–107
89. Keeley, L. H. 1988. Hunter-gatherer economic complexity and "population pressure": a cross-cultural analysis. *J. Anthropol. Archaeol.* 7:373–411
90. Kelly, R. L. 1983. Hunter-gatherer mobility strategies. *J. Anthropol. Res.* 39:277–306
91. Kelly, R. L. 1988. The three sides of a biface. *Am. Antiq.* 53:231–44
92. Kelly, R. L. 1990. Marshes and mobility in the western Great Basin. In *Wetlands Adaptations in the Great Basin. Museum of Peoples and Cultures Occasional Papers,* ed. J. C. Janetski, D. B. Madsen, 1:259–76. Provo: Brigham Young Univ.
93. Kelly, R. L. 1991. Sedentism, sociopolitical inequality, and resource fluctuations. See Ref. 63, pp. 135–58
94. Kelly, R. L., Todd, L. C. 1988. Coming into the country: early paleoindian mobility and hunting. *Am. Antiq.* 53:231–44
95. Kent, S., ed. 1989. *Farmers as Hunters.* Cambridge: Cambridge. Univ Press
96. Kent, S. 1989. Cross-cultural perceptions of farmers as hunters and the value of meat. See Ref. 95, pp. 1–17
97. Kent, S., Vierich, H. 1989. The myth of ecological determinism—anticipated mobility and site spatial organization. See Ref. 95, pp. 96–130
97a. Kent, S. 1991. The relationship between mobility strategies and site structure. In *The Interpretation of Archaeological Spatial Patterning,* ed. E. M. Kroll, T. D. Price, pp. 33–59. New York: Plenum
98. Khazanov, A. M. 1984. *Nomads and the Outside World.* Transl. J. Crookenden. Cambridge: Cambridge Univ. Press (from Russian)
99. Larsen, C. S., Ruff, C. B., Kelly, R. L. 1991. Skeletal structural adaptations in prehistoric Western Great Basin hunter-gatherers. Presented at Annu. Meet. Am. Assoc. Phys. Anthropol., 60th, Wisconsin
100. Layne, L. 1987. Village-Bedouin: patterns of change from mobility to sedentism in Jordan. In *Method and Theory for Activity Area Research,* ed. S. Kent, pp. 345–73. New York: Columbia Univ. Press
101. Lee, R. B., DeVore, I., eds. 1968. *Man the Hunter.* Chicago: Aldine
102. Lourandos, H. 1985. Intensification and

64   KELLY

Australian prehistory. See Ref. 124, pp. 385–423

103. Madsen, D. B. 1982. Get it where the gettin's good: a variable model of Great Basin subsistence and settlement based on data from the eastern Great Basin. In *Man and Environment in the Great Basin*. Soc. for Am. Archaeol. Sel. Pap. No. 2, ed. D. B. Madsen, J. F. O'Connell, pp. 207–26. Washington, DC: Soc. Am. Anthropol.

104. Magne, M. P. R. 1989. Lithic reduction stages and assemblage formation processes. In *Experiments in Lithic Technology. BAR International Series 528*, ed. D. S. Amick, R. P. Mauldin, pp. 15–32. Oxford: Brit. Archaeol. Rep.

105. Mauss, M. 1906. Essai sur les variations saisonnières des sociétés Eskimos: étude de morphologie sociale. *L'Année Sociol.* 9:39–132

106. McClellan, C. 1975. My old people say: an ethnographic survey of southern Yukon Territory. *Natl. Mus. Man Publ. Ethnol.* 6

107. Meehan, B. 1982. *Shell Bed to Shell Midden.* Canberra: Austral. Inst. Aborig. Stud.

108. Minnis, P. E., Redman, C. E., eds. 1990. *Perspectives on Southwestern Prehistory.* Boulder: Westview Press

109. Misra, P. K. 1986. Mobility-sedentary opposition: a case study of the nomadic Gadulia Lohar. *Nomadic Peoples* 21–22:179–87

110. Moratto, M. 1984. *California Archaeology.* New York: Academic

111. Murdock, G. P. 1967. The ethnographic atlas: a summary. *Ethnology* 6(2)

112. Myers, F. R. 1988. Critical trends in the study of hunter-gatherers. *Annu. Rev. Anthropol.* 17:261–82

113. Neiderberger, C. 1979. Early sedentary economy in the Basin of Mexico. *Science* 203:131–42

114. Nelson, M. C. 1991. The study of technological change. In *Archaeological Method and Theory*, ed. M. B. Schiffer, 3:57–100. Tucson: Univ. Arizona Press

115. O'Brien, M. J. 1987. Sedentism, population growth, and resource selection in the Woodland Midwest: a review of coevolutionary developments. *Curr. Anthropol.* 28:177–97

116. O'Connell, J. F. 1987. Alyawara site structure and its archaeological implications. *Am. Antiq.* 52:74–108

117. Pálsson, G. 1988. Hunters and gatherers of the sea. In *Hunters and Gatherers, Vol. 1: History, Evolution and Social Change*, ed. T. Ingold, D. Riches, J. Woodburn, pp. 189–204. London: BERG

118. Parry, W., Kelly, R. L. 1987. Expedient core technology and sedentism. See Ref. 86, pp. 285–304

119. Pennington, R., Harpending, H. 1988. Fitness and fertility among Kalahari !Kung. *Am. J. Phys. Anthropol.* 77:303–19

120. Perlman, S. M. 1980. An optimum diet model, coastal variability and hunter-gatherer behavior. *Advances In Archaeological Method and Theory*, ed. M. B. Schiffer, 3:257–310. New York: Academic

121. Potts, R. 1988. *Early Hominid Activities at Olduvai.* Hawthorne, NY: Aldine de Gruyter

122. Powell, S. 1983. *Mobility and Adaptation: The Anasazi of Black Mesa.* Carbondale: S. Ill. Univ. Press

123. Preucel, R. 1990. *Seasonal Circulation and Dual Residence in the Pueblo Southwest: A Prehistoric Example from the Pajarito Plateau, New Mexico.* Hamden, CT: Garland

124. Price, T. D., Brown, J. A., eds. 1985. *Prehistoric Hunter-Gatherers: The Emergence of Cultural Complexity.* New York: Academic

125. Price, T. D., Brown, J. A. 1985. Aspects of hunter-gatherer complexity. See Ref. 124, pp. 3–20

126. Rafferty, J. 1985. The archaeological record on sedentariness: recognition, development, and implications. In *Advances in Archaeological Method and Theory*, ed. M. B. Schiffer, 8:113–56. New York: Academic

127. Renouf, M. A. P. 1988. Sedentary coastal hunter-fishers: an example from the Younger Stone Age of northern Norway. In *Archaeology of Prehistoric Coastlines*, ed. G. Bailey, J. Parkington, pp. 102–15. Cambridge: Cambridge Univ. Press

128. Rhode, D. E. 1990. Transportation costs of Great Basin resources: an assessment of the Jones-Madsen model. *Curr. Anthropol.* 31:413–19

129. Richardson, A. 1982. The control of productive resources on the Northwest Coast of North America. In *Resource Managers: North American and Australian Hunter-Gatherers*, ed. E. Hunn, N. Williams, pp. 93–112. Boulder, CO: Westview Press

130. Rick, J. 1980. *Prehistoric Hunters of the High Andes.* New York: Academic

131. Roth, E. A. 1981. Sedentism and changing fertility patterns in a northern Athapascan isolate. *J. Hum. Evol.* 10:413–25

132. Roth, E. A., Ray, A. K. 1985. Demographic patterns of sedentary and nomadic Juang of Orissa. *Hum. Biol.* 57:319–26

133. Rowley, S. 1985. Population movements in the Canadian Arctic. *Etudes Inuit Stud.* 9(1):3–22

134. Rowley-Conwy, P. 1983. Sedentary hunters: the Ertebølle example. In *Hunter-Gatherer Economy in Prehistory*, ed. G. Bailey, pp. 111–26. Cambridge: Cambridge Univ. Press

135. Rowley-Conwy, P., Zvelebil, M. 1989. Saving it for later: storage by prehistoric hunter-gatherers in Europe. In *Bad Year Economics*, ed. P. Halstead, J. O'Shea, pp. 40–56. Cambridge: Cambridge Univ. Press

136. Sahlins, M. D. 1972. *Stone Age Economics.* Chicago: Aldine
137. Schalk, R. 1981. Land use and organizational complexity among foragers of northwestern North America. In *Affluent Foragers. Senri Ethnological Studies,* ed. S. Koyama, D. H. Thomas, 9:53–76. Osaka: Natl. Mus. Ethnol.
137a. Sept, J. 1992. Archaeological evidence and ecological perspectives for reconstructing early hominid behavior. In *Archaeological Method and Theory,* ed. M. B. Schiffer, 4:41–56. Tucson: Univ. Arizona Press
138. Shackley, M. S. 1990. *Early hunter-gatherer procurement ranges in the Southwest: evidence from obsidian geochemistry and lithic technology.* PhD thesis, Ariz. State Univ., Tempe
139. Deleted in proof
140. Shott, M. J. 1986. Technological organization and settlement mobility: an ethnographic examination. *J. Anthropol. Res.* 42:15–51
141. Shott, M. J. 1990. Stone tools and economics: Great Lakes paleoindian examples. In *Early Paleoindian Economies of Eastern North America. Research in Economic Anthropology,* ed. K. B. Tankersley, B. L. Isaac, Suppl. 5, pp. 3–44. Greenwich, CT: JAI Press
142. Smith, E. 1983. Anthropological applications of optimal foraging theory: a critical review. *Curr. Anthropol.* 24:625–51
143. Smith, E. A. 1991. *Inujjuamiut Foraging Strategies.* Hawthorne, NY: Aldine de Gruyter
144. Soffer, O. 1989. Storage, sedentism, and the Eurasian Palaeolithic record. *Antiquity* 63:719–32
145. Spielmann, K. A. 1986. Interdependence among egalitarian societies. *J. Anthropol. Archaeol.* 5:279–312
146. Spielmann, K. A., ed. 1991. *Farmers, Hunters, and Colonists: Interaction Between the Southwest and the Southern Plains.* Tucson: Univ. Arizona Press
147. Stark, B. L. 1981. The rise of sedentary life. In *Supplement to the Handbook of Middle American Indians,* Vol. 1: *Archaeology,* ed. J. Sabloff, pp. 345–72. Austin: Univ. Texas Press
148. Steward, J. H. 1936. The economic and social basis of primitive bands. In *Essays in Anthropology Presented to Alfred Louis Kroeber,* ed. R. Lowie, pp. 331–50. Berkeley: Univ. Calif. Press
149. Tankersley, K. B., Isaac, B. L., eds. 1990. *Early paleoindian economies of eastern North America. Res. Econ. Anthropol.* Suppl. 5
150. Deleted in proof
151. Taylor, W. W. 1964. Tethered nomadism and water territoriality: an hypothesis. *XXXV Congr. Int. de Am.,* 2:197–203. Mexico City: Inst. Nac. Antropol. Hist.
152. Testart, A. 1988. Some major problems in the social anthropology of hunter-gatherers. *Curr. Anthropol.* 29:1–31
153. Thomas, D. H. 1989. Diversity in hunter-gatherer cultural geography. In *Quantifying Diversity in Archaeology,* ed. R. D. Leonard, G. T. Jones, pp. 85–91. Cambridge: Cambridge Univ. Press
154. Torrence, R. 1983. Time budgeting and hunter-gatherer technology. In *Hunter-Gatherer Economy in Prehistory,* ed. G. Bailey, pp. 11–22. Cambridge: Cambridge Univ. Press
155. Torrence, R., ed. 1989. *Time, Energy and Stone Tools.* Cambridge: Cambridge Univ. Press
156. Torrence, R. 1989. Tools as optimal solutions. See See Ref. 155, pp. 1–6
157. Torrence, R. 1989. Re-tooling: towards a behavioral theory of stone tools. See Ref. 155, pp. 57–66
158. Upham, S. 1984. Adaptive diversity and Southwestern abandonment. *J. Anthropol. Res.* 40:235–56
159. Vickers, W. T. 1989. Patterns of foraging and gardening in a semi-sedentary Amazonian community. See Ref. 95, pp. 46–59
160. Vincent, A. 1984. Plant foods in savanna environments: a preliminary report of tubers eaten by the Hadza of northern Tanzania. *World Archaeol.* 17:131–47
161. Watanabe, H. 1968. Subsistence and ecology of northern food gatherers with special reference to the Ainu. See Ref. 101, pp. 69–77
162. Whalen, M. E. 1981. Cultural-ecological aspects of the pithouse-to-pueblo transition in a portion of the Southwest. *Am. Antiq.* 46:75–92
163. Widmer, R. J. 1988. *The Evolution of the Calusa: A Nonagricultural Chiefdom on the Southwest Florida Coast.* Tuscaloosa: Univ. Alabama Press
164. Wiessner, P. 1981. Measuring the impact of social ties on nutritional status among the !Kung San. *Soc. Sci. Inform.* 20:641–78
165. Wiessner, P. 1982. Risk, reciprocity and social influences on !Kung San economics. In *Politics and History in Band Societies,* ed. E. Leacock, R. B. Lee, pp. 61–84. Cambridge: Cambridge Univ. Press
166. Wills, W. H. 1988. Early agriculture and sedentism in the American Southwest: evidence and interpretations. *J. World Prehist.* 2:445–88
167. Wills, W. H. 1988. *Early Prehistoric Agriculture in the American Southwest.* Santa Fe: Sch. Am. Res. Press
168. Wills, W. H. 1991. Organizational strategies and the emergence of prehistoric villages in the American Southwest. See Ref. 63, pp. 161–80
169. Wilmsen, E. N. 1986. Biological determinants of fecundity and fecundability: an application of Bongaarts' model to forager fertility. In *Culture and Reproduction: An Anthropological Critique of Demographic*

Transition Theory, ed. W. P. Handwerker, pp. 59–82. Boulder, CO: Westview Press

170. Wilson, P. J. 1988. *The Domestication of the Human Species.* New Haven: Yale Univ. Press

171. Winterhalder, B., Smith, E. A., eds. 1981. *Hunter-Gatherer Foraging Strategies: Ethnographic and Archaeological Analyses.* Chicago: Univ. Chicago Press

172. Yesner, D. R. 1980. Maritime hunter-gatherers: ecology and prehistory. *Curr. Anthropol.* 21:727–50

Annu. Rev. Anthropol. 1992. 21:67–91

PREHISTORIC ARTHRITIS IN THE AMERICAS

Patricia S. Bridges

Department of Anthropology, Queens College and CUNY Graduate Center, Flushing, New York 11367

KEYWORDS: Degenerative Joint Disease, rheumatoid arthritis, ankylosing spondylitis

Trauma, infection and deficiency diseases have a gratifying precision as causes of pathological change. Conditions described as "degenerative" are much less understood but are none the less important because among them is osteoarthritis which has the distinction of being one of the commonest, most widespread and most antique of all diseases (119:59).

INTRODUCTION

Arthritic conditions are among the most commonplace diseases affecting humans, not only today, but in the past as well. Although arthritis means literally "inflammation of the joints," the term is used to encompass an array of conditions affecting the joints, many of which do not involve inflammation. Perhaps the most familiar of these conditions is osteoarthritis (OA) or degenerative joint disease (DJD), caused by what is sometimes described as "wear and tear" on the joints (82). Because of the role that activities play in the etiology of OA, it is often used as an indicator of activity levels in prehistoric societies, or of the prevalence of specific activities (e.g. spear-throwing).

Here I focus on osteoarthritis in prehistoric Amerindians and on what may be inferred from its prevalence about differences in the level and type of activities in these groups. With respect to several other forms of arthritis

67

0084-6570/92/1015-0067$02.00

suggested to be present in prehistory—rheumatoid arthritis and ankylosing spondylitis—I discuss only the evidence for their appearance and prevalence in pre-Columbian America.

Among the factors implicated in the etiology of osteoarthritis, age and physical activities (or trauma) are the most common. In OA, destruction of articular cartilage of synovial (or freely movable) joints leads to characteristic bony changes, including peripheral osteophytes or bony "lipping," porosity of the joint surface, and eburnation—the development of dense smooth areas where cartilage has been destroyed, exposing underlying bone (48, 74, 105, 106). Degeneration of the vertebral disks results primarily in bony lipping around the margins of the vertebral bodies called osteophytosis (OP). The apophyseal facets at the back of the spine are synovial joints and exhibit the typical features of OA described above.

Rheumatoid arthritis (RA) is characterized by inflammation of appendicular joints, especially the hands and feet. The disease usually manifests itself symmetrically on both sides of the body. Its victims typically go through periods of remission and recurrence. The etiology of RA is unknown, although a number of factors (including allergies, diet, hormonal influences, genetic predisposition, infections, stress, and autoimmune reactions) have been implicated. Females are more prone to RA than males. RA results in resorption and osteoporosis around the articular ends of the bones. It is therefore primarily a lytic or bone-destroying process rather than a proliferative arthritis like DJD (26, 85, 106). Leisen et al (60) and Rothschild et al (95) discuss the identification of RA in skeletal material.

Juvenile rheumatoid arthritis (JRA) differs from RA in adults in a number of ways. Its onset is frequently associated with fever, and it may affect only a few of the larger joints, such as the knee. Rheumatoid factor is usually absent, and the patient may completely recover. However, growth disruption (especially of the mandible) and widespread joint destruction occur in a minority of cases (12, 17, 26).

Ankylosing spondylitis (AS), also called Marie-Strümpell disease after two of its early describers, is characterized by inflammation and eventual bony fusion or ankylosis of various joints. It preferentially attacks males. Generally it begins in the sacroiliac joints and moves upward in the vertebral column. It affects primarily the small apophyseal joints at the back of the vertebral column rather than the vertebral discs themselves, although the annulus fibrosus (consisting of ligaments running down the sides of the vertebral bodies) also becomes ossified, fusing together the vertebrae. This leads to a unique form of ankylosis sometimes called "bamboo spine." In advanced cases, appendicular joints may also be affected, especially the hip and shoulder. Although the etiology of AS is uncertain, it is related in part to heredity, since the majority of its sufferers share the HLA-B27 antigen (62, 85, 100, 106). AS is one of a series of related diseases—the seronegative spondyloarthropathies (SNS), so called because rheumatoid factor is absent in the bloodstream and because they primarily affect the vertebral column. Other forms of SNS have rarely been diagnosed in prehistory largely because paleopathologists were unaware of the distinctions between them and AS (6, 88).

OSTEOARTHRITIS

Historical Survey of Osteoarthritis in the Americas

Arthritis has been noted in prehistoric Amerindian skeletal remains for well over a century. In early reports, it was frequently referred to as the most common ailment of prehistoric peoples; perhaps because of its ubiquity, it was often ignored, except for a description of exceptional cases (see, for example, 29, 31, 38, 40, 56, 61, 72, 104, 118, 120).

As part of a study on the paleopathology of prehistoric Peruvians, Hrdlička (39) listed the prevalence of arthritis on individual long bones and vertebral regions. He suggested that arthritis first appeared in the lumbar vertebrae and distal femur. His published figures, when converted to percentages, show that osteophytosis was present between the fifth lumbar vertebra and the sacrum in 14.6% of the bones studied, and in 8.3% of the second cervical vertebrae examined. Other vertebrae, as a group, showed bony reactions in 11.2% of cases. The greatest frequency of appendicular lesions actually occurred at the elbow (5.3%, as seen in the proximal ulna), followed by the glenoid fossa of the scapula (4.8%), the acetabulum (3.6%), and knee (3.0%) (39).

In the 1940s, T. Dale Stewart began a more comprehensive analysis of arthritis in human populations (107–110, 112). In addition to his well-known work on the relationship between arthritis and aging (109), Stewart compared vertebral and sacroiliac osteophytosis in Eskimos, Pueblo Indians, and American whites (107, 110-112). He found differences in frequency of osteophytosis and osteoarthritis of the articular facets, as well as variability in which regions of the spine were most involved. Variation in osteophytosis in a number of Amerindian groups was further described by Chapman (20–23). These studies suggested that there were populational differences not only in level of arthritis, but also in its patterning. The reasons for this variability were not clear.

J. Lawrence Angel, another pioneer in the study of arthritis, endeavored to link types of arthritis with specific activities. He coined the term "atlatl elbow" to refer to DJD of the radiohumeral joint in several skeletons from California (3). Angel believed that this form of arthritis was caused by use of the spearthrower, although he noted its presence in females as well as males and suggested that for them it was precipitated by seed-grinding.

Early work on arthritis in the Americas, then, started with a descriptive period, during which OA was noted but not considered remarkable. It continued with Stewart's studies, growing into a branch of research that recognized populational differences and that, with Angel's work, tried to relate these differences to specific prehistoric activities. Later researchers have built on these goals through more sophisticated techniques and analyses, and have begun to test more rigorously how these differences might relate to aspects of subsistence economy.

Ortner (73), for example, carried out a thorough examination of DJD at the humeral component of the elbow in Eskimos and Peruvians. He considered in detail the structure of the elbow, relating this to the degenerative changes occurring at different regions of this joint. "Atlatl elbow" and bilateral asymmetry were significantly more prevalent in Eskimos than in the Peruvian skeletons. This paper is important not only for its careful look at the structure of the elbow but also because it statistically compared samples from different regions (73).

During the last two decades, a number of studies on osteoarthritis have been completed (including a series of as-yet-unpublished doctoral dissertations). A few notable examples include Jurmain's work assessing populational differences in DJD (42–45), and Merbs's study (64) on patterns of arthritis in the Sadlermiut, which he related to their activities. In addition, scholars have compared arthritis levels in Native American populations with different economic strategies (discussed below). A good deal of information is now available on arthritis in a variety of Amerindian groups.

Major problems remain, however, in the interpretation of these findings, given the differences in methodologies and means of analysis used in the studies (89, 116; also see 86 for suggestions regarding classification and description of lesions). Since the coding of arthritis scores relies on visual inspection, it is necessarily subjective. But perhaps the most critical problem is that many studies fail to control adequately for age differences between samples, even though the development of arthritis is closely linked to increasing age. In addition, there are differences among studies in how arthritis is scored, in the recording of scores for data presentation or analysis, in which parts of joints are examined and how they may be lumped together to form composite scores, in whether average or maximum scores are assigned to composite joints, and in the presentation of statistical findings.

Although the impact of differing techniques is hard to assess, it may be illustrated by a discussion of several reports that have examined various types of arthritis at Indian Knoll, often in comparison with other groups. For example, three studies looking at vertebral osteophytosis found average prevalences of 39%, 60%, and 72% (19, 50, 104). The large differences among these figures are due in part to different methods of data presentation—i.e. whether or not "arthritis" included all individuals with minor to severe arthritis, or only those with at least moderate arthritis.

I wish to emphasize that none of the above-mentioned studies presented "wrong" information. Different research protocols and techniques of data analysis simply affected the findings presented. As a result, it is often not possible to compare directly levels of osteoarthritis in different groups. At least some inter-observer error may be eliminated by comparing the patterning of arthritis—i.e. which joints are most commonly affected within groups. Appendicular arthritis shows a strong pattern among Amerindians that differs, often strikingly, from that among contemporary Americans.

Patterning of Osteoarthritis

The four major appendicular joints (shoulder, elbow, hip, and knee) are compared below for 25 skeletal samples from the Americas (2, 11, 15, 24, 33, 39, 42, 45, 46, 50, 57, 64, 66, 77, 80, 90, 113, 117). These joints were chosen for comparison because they are the most widely reported. Data from both sexes, the left and right sides, and individual joint surfaces, when given, have been averaged to create a composite score for each joint.

Of the 25 skeletal groups, 17 have the greatest prevalence of DJD at the knee. The level of elbow arthritis falls in first or second place in 15 groups (and ties for second in two other instances). In contrast, modern American Whites and Blacks show the lowest levels of arthritis at the elbow, with the most DJD at the hip in Whites and the shoulder in Blacks (42). Another autopsy sample from Germany showed the most arthritis at the knee and the least at the elbow (74). It is unlikely that these results reflect genetic differences alone. In a prehistoric skeletal collection from Iran and Iraq (83), the knee shows the most DJD and the hip the least—a pattern more like that seen in many Native American skeletal samples. A skeletal sample from medieval Nubia, on the other hand, shows the greatest amount of OA at the knee but the least at the elbow (53).

The subsistence economies of groups with high levels of both knee and elbow arthritis are varied, including a series of hunter-gatherers (33, 46, 50, 57, 80, 90, 117, 118), agriculturalists (50, 57, 80), and fishers (117). Eskimos tend to show fairly high levels of shoulder arthritis and so do not fit this pattern (42, 64). However, a number of other groups also have the most (or second most) arthritis at the shoulder, including hunter-gatherers (11, 15, 77, 118) and a wide variety of agriculturalists (2, 15, 39, 42, 45, 66, 113). Therefore, the patterning of arthritis does not correlate with subsistence economy, although the relative lack of hip arthritis in prehistoric samples may be significant.

Although I have concentrated on the four major appendicular joints, some evidence suggests wide variation in the prevalence of OA at the hands and feet. OA of the hands and feet is less widely reported owing to the large numbers of small joint surfaces present there. Degenerative changes are more subtle and difficult to observe. Studies that do present data on these lesions are usually not comparable because they look at different combinations of joint surfaces. Jurmain (46) found the highest levels of appendicular OA at the hands (including the wrist) and feet (including the ankle) in a sample from prehistoric California. Hand or wrist arthritis was similarly high in another hunter-gatherer group from California, as well as in a Great Lakes Archaic sample (77, 117). Other groups with relatively widespread arthritis of the hands include California fishers, the Sadlermiut, and hunter-gatherers from the

Georgia Coast and Indian Knoll (50, 57, 64, 117). However, a variety of groups show lower levels of arthritis at the hands, including Alabama and Mobridge hunter-gatherers (15, 50) and agriculturalists from Alabama, Kentucky, Ontario, Arizona, and Peru (15, 24, 39, 50, 113). Contemporary Eskimos also have low levels of hand and wrist arthritis (9). Generally, the groups with high levels of wrist or hand arthritis tend not to be agriculturalists, although not all hunter-gatherers have increased amounts of DJD at these joints. Ankle or foot arthritis is usually less common than that of the hands (but see 46, 50, 113).

Patterning of Osteophytosis

A clear-cut patterning of vertebral osteophytosis (OP) appears in Native American samples (several Eskimo groups, Aleuts, California hunter-gatherers, and two Alabama series) that is broadly comparable with that of other populations (16, 34, 46, 64, 110, 112, 122). Within the cervical region of the spine, the articulation between C5 and C6 invariably has the greatest prevalence of arthritis. Within the thoracic segment, the peak is less certain and varies between the middle and lower thoracic vertebrae (T7 through about T11). The lumbar vertebrae usually show their greatest lipping between L2 and L4, although L5 is occasionally strongly involved. The region between C7 to about T3 is always the least affected by osteophytosis (16, 34, 46, 64, 110, 112).

Studies on American White and Black vertebral columns show again that C5/C6, the area in the mid-lower thoracics, and L3/L4 are the most involved articulations within their segments of the spine. T1/T2 shows the least OP of any vertebral articulation (70, 110). The patterning seen in American Indian spines, then, is broadly similar to that in other populations in being related to areas of maximum curvature of the spine (53, 70).

However, there is some variation in which segment shows the highest level of arthritis. Osteophytosis in prehistoric Amerindians is usually greatest in the lumbar region. Fourteen of 17 populations (2, 16, 34, 46, 57, 64, 79, 90, 107, 112, 113, 117, 118, 122) have more arthritis in the lumbar spine than elsewhere, but the Sadlermiut have greater frequencies in the cervicals, California hunter-gatherers at the thoracic vertebrae, and Aleuts high levels at both the cervicals and thoracics (64, 117, 122). Twelve of the remaining groups show their second highest level of arthritis at the cervical vertebrae. Although two Eskimo series show sharp peaks in the mid-thoracics (34, 64), most Native Americans other than the Aleuts and California hunter-gatherers mentioned above show much lower levels of arthritis in this region.

The White and Black specimens studied by Nathan (70), which came in part from the Hamann-Todd Collection, show high maximum levels of arthritis in the mid-lumbars and lower thoracics, with lower involvement in the cervicals. In contrast, the Whites from the Terry Collection show maximum lipping in the cervical portion of the spine, with the lumbar vertebrae second

(110). Osteophytosis in Nubian skeletons resembles those of most Native American groups, with maximum lipping in the lumbars, followed by the cervicals and then the thoracics (53). The locus of maximum OP, then, varies somewhat among populations of both Amerindians and other groups. Most samples show the greatest lipping in the lumbars, followed by the cervical vertebrae. The general similarity among most groups may be due to the forces imposed by bipedalism (53). The differences may be a result of variation in types of normal posture, methods of carrying burdens, or activities. It is interesting to note that except for Stewart's sample (110, 112), Arctic groups have high levels of both cervical and thoracic OP (34, 64, 121), which could be related to differences in activities, burden carrying, or normal posture between them and other Native American populations.

Bilateral Asymmetry

Since most humans are right-handed, it might be expected that DJD should show strong bilateral asymmetry, especially in the upper limb. It has also been suggested that in groups that used spears or harpoons, males should show more asymmetry of the arms than females because of the stresses associated with throwing (64, 79). These suggestions are not completely supported by available data (14, 79). Below are included results from Native American skeletal groups for which we have arthritis data for both sides of the major appendicular joints (15, 24, 42, 46, 64, 77, 80).

For males, four of nine Native American groups show the most bilateral asymmetry at the knee, two each at the elbow and shoulder, and one at the hip. For females, five show the most asymmetry at the knee, an additional three at the elbow, and one at the hip. In a combined sex sample, the knee also has the greatest asymmetry, with the elbow next (24). The knee, then, tends to show more widespread asymmetry than the other major appendicular joints, with elbow asymmetry second in prevalence.

Data on hand and foot arthritis are not as frequently given, but the wrist (and in one case, the ankle) occasionally shows higher levels of asymmetry than the major appendicular joints (15, 46, 64). For the wrist, stronger right-side involvement is invariable.

Generally, the joints of the upper limb (shoulder and elbow) have more arthritis on the right side than on the left. The only exception to this trend in males is an agricultural group from Alabama, where there is more arthritis in the left arm for both joints (15). Females show a more mixed pattern. Three of seven groups examined here have more arthritis on the right side for both the shoulder and elbow, two show more on the left, and the remaining two groups have right dominance for one joint and left for the other. Males, then, do seem to show more widespread right-side dominance in the upper limb.

Degree of asymmetrical arthritis at the major appendicular joints varies between the sexes. Males are more likely to show greater asymmetry at the shoulder and knee, nearly always right-sided. Females are more likely to show greater asymmetry at the hip and elbow, and in about half of these cases the left side has the most arthritis. While this confirms that right dominance is more frequent in male arthritis, it is surprising to see that asymmetry itself is often higher in females—particularly at the elbow, where the influence of activities is thought to be much greater than at the hip (43, 47).

Unfortunately, side differences are generally not tested statistically, so these findings must be considered tentative. In one of the few explicit tests of bilateral asymmetry (using a skeletal sample from Nubia), Kilgore found no significant differences between the sides in prevalence of arthritis (53). In a series from the Lower Illinois Valley, there were no significant differences between the sexes in bilateral asymmetry (79). In addition, the greater amount of asymmetry in the knee than in the shoulder in most Native American groups makes it clear that factors other than handedness may be important in the development of DJD.

Bilateral asymmetry is also present in the vertebrae, both in the distribution of osteophytes on the centra and in arthritis of the apophyseal joints, but it has rarely been examined in detail. The Sadlermiut show more osteophytosis on the right side, primarily in the thoracic region (64). This generally fits the pattern seen in other populations and may be related to the position of the aorta, which lies on the left side of the column at that level (53, 70).

Osteoarthritis of the articular facets shows somewhat more asymmetry. The cervical vertebrae tend to show more involvement of these joints on the left side in the Sadlermiut and two Alabama series, as well as in a medieval Nubian group and modern Americans (53, 64, 109; P. S. Bridges, in preparation). In the Sadlermiut the thoracic facets have more OA on the right side, particularly around T2 through T6 (64). However, for remains from an Iroquois ossuary, only the combined lumbar region was asymmetric, with more arthritis on the left side (24).

Sex Differences

Sex differences with respect to arthritis are often easier to evaluate than inter-populational ones because each researcher typically compares both sexes using the same methodology. However, such differences are not always statistically tested. I compare first those studies that do present statistical analyses of sexual dimorphism.

A surprisingly wide variation in the sexual dimorphism of arthritis is evident in prehistoric samples. Males often show higher levels of OA, but sex differences are not always significant. In a pre-agricultural group from Georgia, Larsen found males to have significantly higher levels of OA at the shoulder and OP in the lumbar region. Agriculturalists from the same area have more widespread sexual dimorphism, again with more prevalence of arthritis in males, at the elbow, at the knee, and in the cervical, thoracic, and lumbar segments of the spinal column (57).

In hunter-gatherers and agriculturalists from Alabama, sexual dimorphism is less common. None of the major appendicular joints (shoulder, elbow, wrist, hip, knee, or ankle), nor the combined vertebral segments (cervical, thoracic, lumbar) show significant sexual dimorphism in the hunter-gatherers (15; P. S. Bridges, in preparation). Slightly greater sexual dimorphism in the vertebral column is evident in the agricultural group, but in contrast to Larsen's observations, thoracic OP is significantly greater in agricultural females than in males, while OA of the apophyseal facets is higher in males at the cervical level.

Pickering (79) found no significant sex differences in combined arthritis scores for the arms and legs in several prehistoric Illinois groups in either age at onset or severity. An earlier study on a single Lower Illinois Valley site (Ledders) had suggested that while females showed earlier onset of DJD in the arms, males eventually had greater prevalence and severity (78). There are also no significant differences between the sexes at Dickson Mounds (Illinois) when comparing combined arthritis scores for both appendicular and vertebral joints. However, males, especially in the Mississippian agricultural series from this site, have more OP than females (32, 55).

Males generally have higher levels of appendicular arthritis than females at both Indian Knoll and the Averbuch sites. The hunter-gatherers from Indian Knoll show significant sex differences at the shoulder, hip, and knee. Males have significantly greater arthritis at the shoulder and hip alone for the Averbuch Mississippian agriculturalists (80). For combined arthritis scores, males at Indian Knoll have higher rates overall than females, but the differences between the sexes are not significant (19).

A number of other studies present data on sex differences, many of which show great variability in patterning of arthritis between the sexes. At Indian Knoll, Mobridge, and Grasshopper Pueblo, males tend to have more arthritic lesions than females. This is particularly true for the Grasshopper Pueblo sample, with Mobridge and then Indian Knoll showing lesser overall differences between the sexes. However, females from all three sites have higher frequencies of temporomandibular arthritis (50).

Among the Sadlermiut, males, except in the temporomandibular joint, also have much higher levels of arthritis than females. The greatest differences occur in the lower limb, at the foot, ankle, and hip, followed by the shoulder and wrist. For the vertebral column, results are more varied; females have greater OP in the mid-thoracics but males show significantly more at the lumbar region (64). Among Koniag Eskimos, on the other hand, for the entire combined vertebral column, males have both more osteophytosis and more osteoarthritis of the articular facets (34).

Jurmain's (42) analysis of appendicular arthritis also reveals high levels of sexual dimorphism in Eskimos, with males showing more OA than females, mostly at the shoulder, but also at the elbow, knee, and hip. Other groups in this study, which included Pecos Pueblo Indians and American Blacks and

Whites, show fewer sexual differences; the prevalence of arthritis is some-times greater in females than males.

In skeletons from a California site, males show greater involvement at the elbow (especially on the right side) while females have more arthritis at the left knee. Other joints show smaller differences between the sexes (46). A com-parison of two other California groups finds no significant differences between the sexes of either sample in combined arthritis scores, although the patterning of lesions varies. The hunter-gatherer series shows the most differences be-tween the sexes, with males having higher levels of arthritis at the hand, shoulder, and elbow. Females have more arthritis at the knee and the vertebral column as a whole. For the later group, which engaged in intensive fishing, males and females have more nearly equal levels of arthritis (117).

Males also show generally more arthritis than females in a Great Lakes Archaic group, especially at the knee and ankle, followed by the wrist and hand. Females have somewhat (but not significantly) greater levels of OA at the temporomandibular joint (77).

Two Arikara samples show differences in the level of sexual dimorphism, possibly related to the adoption of horseback riding in the later group. The earlier sample has generally greater levels of arthritis in females, especially in the vertebral column and knee. In the later population, males show a higher level of arthritis than females in the lower limbs and sacroiliac joints (11).

Females from the Chiggerville site in Kentucky have more widespread arthritis than males for both appendicular and vertebral joints, but especially at the sacroiliac and thoracic levels. The only joint where males outrank females is at the shoulder (113). In skeletal samples from Peru and Chile, commoner females have more OP of the cervical and lumbar segments than do males of the same social rank (1).

Comparative data, from outside prehistoric America, also show mixed re-sults. In a Nubian skeletal sample there are no significant differences between the sexes at the appendicular joints (where females nonetheless have higher levels of OA, especially at the knee) or in OP of the vertebral bodies. Females do show significantly higher levels of OA of the apophyseal joints in the lumbar region (53). On the other hand, in a study of American Black and White vertebral columns, Nathan (70) found significantly higher levels of OP in both male groups between T9 and T11, where arthritis is most prevalent. Appendicular arthritis in contemporary Whites and Blacks, however, does not show consistent levels of sexual dimorphism. Males have more arthritis at the elbow, whereas females may have more at other joints, especially the knee (42). Females also tend to have more arthritis of the hands, especially the distal interphalangeal joints of the fingers, in living populations (51, 81). Unfortu-nately, these joints have not been examined in detail in most prehistoric collections, so it is not clear whether this pattern was present in the past.

This survey clearly shows differences in the level of sexual dimorphism among Native American groups, as well as between them and modern skeletal samples. For cases in which statistical information is presented, either males show higher levels of DJD or there is no significant difference between the sexes. Other groups on occasion show higher frequencies of arthritis in females. Significant sexual dimorphism is observed more frequently in the agricultural than in the hunter-gatherer groups surveyed (15, 32, 50, 55, 57). In the various Eskimo groups men also tend to exhibit more arthritis than women. Given the strenuous life-style of the pre-contact Eskimo, which emphasized hunting, it is not surprising that sexual differences are well marked. The high levels of arthritis in males of many agricultural societies may suggest a fundamental shift in the division of labor when agriculture was adopted. Male activities leading to joint degeneration may have increased or those of females declined. Another possibility is that traumatic arthritis subsequent to injuries suffered in warfare is more widespread in the agricultural groups. The lower or variable amounts of sexual dimorphism found in other prehistoric groups suggest that for them, sex roles were more similar, or that in some cases females had more strenuous duties than males. Of course, factors besides activities—including age differences between the sexes—could be important.

Females tend to show more DJD than males in the temporomandibular joint (50, 64, 77). In Eskimos, this observation has been related to hide-processing techniques, although it could also be associated with differences in diet. Not all world populations show sexual dimorphism in arthritis of this joint (e.g. 37).

Populational Differences

As noted above, comparisons among groups are often impossible owing to the varied methodologies used by researchers. Of course, when one worker compares several groups, this problem is precluded. Here I consider studies of populational differences in prevalence of arthritis.

Stewart (107, 110, 112) compared differences in vertebral osteophytosis and osteoarthritis among Eskimos, Pueblo Indians, and modern American Whites. These groups differ in both levels and patterning of pathology. Both Native American groups show the highest OP in the lumbar region, while Whites have more at the cervicals. In Stewart's sample Eskimos evidence little OP above the lumbars and Pueblo Indians show somewhat more. Eskimos, however, have greater OA of the apophyseal facets than the other groups.

Jurmain (42–44) examined appendicular arthritis in Pueblo Indians, Eskimos, and modern American Whites and Blacks. He found a number of significant differences in prevalence that contrast with Stewart's findings on vertebral OP. Eskimos show a significantly higher frequency of arthritis than modern Americans or Pecos Pueblo Indians at many joints. This is particularly true for the males, and for the right side. The Pueblo sample has less arthritis in many cases than the sample of modern Americans. Eskimos tend to have more arthritis of the arms (especially at the elbow) than the other groups. This high level of arthritis at the elbow in Eskimos has also been demonstrated in Ortner's (73) comparison of Eskimos and Peruvians.

California hunter-gatherers show levels of arthritis much lower than those of the Eskimos and generally closer to those of Pueblo Indians. The California series shows more elbow and knee arthritis than the Pueblo Indians. The California Indians have very high levels of hand and foot arthritis approaching those of the Eskimos (46).

Varying activity patterns in different subsistence economies may explain some of these observed differences. This suggestion has been examined by comparing Native American groups that practiced different subsistence economies. Such studies emphasize the transition to, or intensification of, maize agriculture; but at least one has also examined the change to a maritime economy (117). The results of these studies are mixed. Cohen & Armelagos (25) note that in many cases from around the world, arthritis declines with the introduction of agriculture, implying a reduction in workload. In at least some cases from the New World, however, the level of arthritis increases with agriculture.

Larsen (57, 58) found a number of decreases in the prevalence of arthritis in Coastal Georgia with the introduction of agriculture. Agricultural females have significantly lower levels of arthritis than hunter-gatherers at the lumbar and cervical vertebrae, and at the knee, elbow, ankle, and hip. Male agriculturalists have significantly less arthritis at the lumbar vertebrae, the shoulder, and wrist. Combined with other information on the biomechanical attributes of the arms and legs, this work suggests a major decrease in activity levels with the introduction of agriculture (57, 58, 97, 98).

Similarly, in a comparison of three Native American skeletal samples (Indian Knoll Archaic, Mobridge Arikara, and Grasshopper Pueblo), Kelley found the highest overall level of appendicular arthritis at Mobridge, with Indian Knoll second. The agricultural Pueblo Indians show the lowest levels. Spinal arthritis is most prevalent at Indian Knoll, while the Pueblo group again has the lowest frequency of spinal lesions (50).

These studies suggest that the agricultural way of life involves less joint stress than does hunting/gathering or simple horticulture. Jurmain (42–44), Ortner (73), and Stewart (107, 109, 110) also found lower levels of arthritis in the agricultural groups they surveyed than in Eskimos.

However, other work demonstrates that in some cases the level of arthritis increases with the introduction of agriculture in prehistoric America. In a comparison of three cultural groups from Dickson Mounds, Lallo (55) found an increase in overall frequencies of arthritis over time, with the greatest change occurring with the intensification of maize agriculture in the Mississippian period. Vertebral arthritis also increases significantly in the later groups, more so in males than in females (32, 55).

Results from the Lower Illinois Valley are similar, though not identical, to those from Dickson Mounds. Spinal osteophytosis is greater in the later groups who relied on maize agriculture than in earlier horticultural populations. In this case females rather than males show significant increases in the cervical, upper thoracic, and lumbar vertebrae. Agricultural females also have higher levels of DJD in the left arm. These findings are attributed to greater female involvement in agriculture-related chores, such as food processing (79).

In addition, Mississippian agriculturalists from Averbuch, Tennessee have significantly higher frequencies of arthritis than hunter-gatherers from Indian Knoll at the knee, hip, elbow, and shoulder (80). In short, several groups from the Eastern Woodlands clearly demonstrate increases in DJD with the advent of maize agriculture; but other studies in the same region show little significant change over this period.

For example, a comparison of Indian Knoll with the Hardin Village Mississippian sample found no significant differences between the groups with respect to vertebral arthritis. However, age at onset is lower in the later group, possibly suggesting an infectious origin (19). Another Archaic group from northern Alabama resembles a later Mississippian series from the same area in terms of appendicular DJD, when the effects of age differences between the samples are taken into consideration (15). However, there is a significant decline in OP of the cervical vertebrae of older adult males from the agricultural group in this region (27). These findings contrast with a biomechanical study that suggested workload had increased in the agricultural sample (13, 15).

The complexity of the response to agricultural adoption and intensification is well illustrated by a series of works on remains from the Mississippi River Valley and regions to its west. In the Lower Mississippi Valley, the direction of change differs between northerly and southerly regions. In the north, DJD declines with the intensification of agriculture in the Late Mississippian period. To the south, OP and OA decreases with the introduction of agriculture, while OP alone later rises sharply in the Late Mississippian (35, 91).

A pattern of decreased arthritis at the transition to maize agriculture, followed by an increase during its intensification, is also characteristic of parts of the Caddoan region to the west (18, 91). However, south and east of the Upper Red River, less arthritis is observed in the late Caddoan groups than in earlier ones (18). In short, no single consistent response to the introduction or intensification of agriculture can be inferred.

Many factors likely account for the observed differences in how the introduction of agriculture affected the prevalence of arthritis. These include activity differences among both agricultural and hunter-gatherer groups. For example, Eskimos must certainly have had a more strenuous life-style than the Archaic Indians of the Eastern Woodlands. Similarly, Pueblo dwellers and Southeastern Indians clearly had different agricultural systems, presumably involving different activity patterns. Arthritis levels at the Pueblo sites examined so far are consistently lower than those among Eskimos and many other hunter-gatherer groups from North America.

As agricultural practices were introduced and intensified, regions may have differed both in new tasks adopted and in former activities retained. The intensification of agriculture may have meant an overall increase in activity; on the other hand, as crop-growing and -processing technology became more sophisticated, physical activity may have decreased.

Of course, changes not directly related to subsistence may also influence the development of joint lesions. Such factors include increased warfare (with subsequent traumatic arthritis), decreased mobility (presumably with less wear and tear on the skeletal system), and increased social complexity (perhaps involving conscription of crops by local authorities and a consequent need to produce more). An increase in the prevalence of infectious diseases due to population growth could result in higher levels of infectious arthritis and a subsequent degeneration of the joints that can be mistaken for OA. Finally, any change in life expectancy would lead to different age profiles and arthritis prevalence between groups. In short, regional differences in how the introduction of agriculture affected arthritis prevalence suggest that local factors are just as important as the type of subsistence system in determining levels of DJD.

One study has examined the consequences of a shift from hunting/gathering to a maritime economy in coastal California (117). Arthritis is higher in the group relying on intensive fishing, especially in males. Historically, males fished more than females. The level of activities likely increased with the adoption of a fishing economy, and the division of labor probably changed as well. Males may have assumed more of the new chores associated with this subsistence system.

Arthritis and Specific Activities

Because osteoarthritis can be a response to localized trauma or overuse of a joint, the activities carried out within populations have often been inferred from its occurrence. J. L. Angel endeavored to draw such a link in a variety of human groups, using muscle markings and arthritic lipping as indicators of occupation (e.g. weaver, laundress, skilled craftsman) or specific activities (horseback riding, heavy labor, or digging) (4, 5, 49). In his report on the Tranquillity skeletons from California, Angel noted the extremely high prevalence of arthritis at the elbow. He suggested that in males the lesions might be related to spear-throwing (hence "atlatl elbow") and in females to seed-grinding (3).

A landmark study tying arthritis to specific activities was Merbs's 1983 work on the Sadlermiut. Merbs first reconstructed the usual behaviors of both sexes, using historical, archaeological, and comparative data from other Inuit groups, and then interpreted patterns of arthritis in light of this reconstruction. He suggested that the patterning of arthritis in this group was caused mainly by such activities as (for women) preparation of hides to make clothing and (for men) harpoon throwing and kayak paddling. According to Merbs, high levels of vertebral osteophytosis were related to sledding injuries and (in women) to carrying heavy loads (64).

Several studies have examined changes in the elbow that might be related to spear-throwing. Ortner, for example, showed that "atlatl elbow" was more prevalent in Eskimos than in Peruvians, supporting the idea that atlatl use was its primary cause (73). However, other workers have not found a similar relationship between use of the atlatl and arthritis at the elbow and elsewhere. Pickering (79) compared two groups of Illinois Indians, one of which used the atlatl, the other relying on the bow. He found no difference between the groups for males in arm arthritis. In addition he found greater bilateral asymmetry in females than in males for arm arthritis, the opposite of what would be expected if males were the primary hunters.

Similarly, Bridges (14) compared a series of joint lesions suggested to result from either throwing or archery in two groups from northwestern Alabama. Neither "atlatl elbow" nor any other lesion of the arm associated with throwing was more prevalent among males in the group that used the atlatl. In fact, arthritis in females more closely fit the pattern predicted for weapon use. Either use of the atlatl in Eastern Woodlands groups was rare or other activities were more important in the etiology of elbow arthritis (14, 79).

An alternative explanation for arthritis at the elbow has followed on Angel's suggestion that processing of seeds might cause these lesions. In a paper on pathology in a California female skeleton dated at 3000–4000 BP, Merbs suggested that DJD, especially at the right elbow, could be termed "metate elbow" (63). Similarly, arthritis at the elbow at a Pueblo Indian site (Nuvakwewtaqa) dated 1000–1400 AD has been attributed to use of the mano and metate, in this case to grind corn (67). Lesions are found on both sides but are more common at the left humerus than the right. Because both males and females exhibit elbow arthritis, however, activities besides grinding maize must have contributed to deterioration of the joint surfaces.

Moreover, in the southeastern United States, where corn was processed by pounding it in large wooden mortars, we have no evidence of more arthritis in agricultural than in earlier hunter-gatherer females, even though studies have suggested that greater arm strength in the later group was related to pounding corn (13, 15). Processing corn in a wooden mortar may place stresses on the elbow different from those occasioned by grinding it with a metate, accounting for the lower frequency of elbow arthritis in Southeastern Indian agricultural groups. However, the prevalence of elbow arthritis across many groups with widely varying subsistence regimens suggests strongly that high levels of DJD at this joint cannot be tied to any specific activity.

In a paper comparing prehistoric and historic Arikara groups, Bradtmiller looked for changes in arthritis associated with the introduction of the horse (11). Increased arthritis of the pelvic and lumbar joints has been associated with horseback riding in groups from other parts of the world (5, 28). Contrary to expectations, in the Arikara there is more arthritis in the earlier group; but differences in the age structure of the samples may explain this result. The patterning of arthritis occurrence varies between the groups in a way that may indeed have been due to horseback riding: Although in the earlier group the females had more arthritis than the males, in the later period males exhibited higher levels of DJD in the vertebral column, sacroiliac joint, hip, knee, and ankle (11).

In short, many types of arthritis—especially at the elbow—have been linked with specific activities. In certain cases where the behavior of earlier peoples is fairly well understood (such as the hunting methods of the Inuit), it may be possible to suggest that these activities contributed to the development of later arthritis. However, in most cases it is not possible to associate specific types of arthritis with particular behaviors, precisely because so many kinds of activities or injuries can result in joint trauma. Increased arthritis may be a sign of a change in the level or type of physical activity, but it is not generally possible to specify which activity or combination of activities caused joint deterioration (47).

Status Differences

Few studies have examined the relationship between social status and arthritis. If higher-status individuals were engaging in different sorts of activities or in fewer strenuous chores overall, one would expect them to show less joint degeneration. In a study of Middle Woodland burials from the Lower Illinois Valley, higher-status individuals (those buried in log tombs) have significantly less arthritis of the elbow than those buried elsewhere (114). Both sexes show significant differences: males differ in both the radiohumeral part of the joint (involving rotational movement) and the ulnohumeral component (flexion-extension), while females differ for the rotational component only.

In a study on remains from northern Chile dating to about 1000 AD, burials identified as shamans have less arthritis of the cervical and lumbar vertebrae than either commoner males or females. Commoner females have the greatest amount of arthritis at these joints, which may be related to the use of tumplines to carry burdens (1).

In short, the limited evidence available suggests that in some populations arthritis patterns varied by social status. Such variation may correlate with activity level. Additional work with larger samples is needed to clarify these issues.

Relationship with Age

The relationship of osteoarthritis to age is well known in human populations (53, 70, 84, 105, 109). The association between age and OA has also been confirmed for skeletal samples from North America (42, 50, 80). Jurmain's (42) comparison of Eskimos and Pueblo Indians with American Whites and Blacks documents differences in the development of DJD among the four samples: Eskimos show the earliest age of onset, while the Pueblo Indians are less affected at all ages than even the two contemporary American groups. Not all the joints examined show the same degree of deterioration with age. The elbow is the least correlated with age effects, suggesting that activities are an important determinant of arthritis developing there. Arthritis of the hip and to a lesser degree the shoulder shows a greater correlation with age (42, 47).

Other studies on prehistoric Amerindians also demonstrate an increase in female arthritis in late middle age (42, 50). Contemporary research also finds that the percentage of women with arthritis exceeds that of males after age 55 (84), which suggests a hormonal influence on the development of arthritis. The consistent association between arthritis and age indicates that the age profiles of groups must always be considered when examining differences in OA.

ANKYLOSING SPONDYLITIS

An early case from Ohio of what was probably ankylosing spondylitis (AS) was described in the 1880s (56). Additional reports of what may be AS come from Alaska (74), a Huron ossuary (36, 52), the Great Plains (7, 33), a late prehistoric site in Arizona (65), the Maya (99), and the Archaic through Mississippian periods in Illinois (68, 71), Ohio, and the southwestern United States (106).

The antiquity of AS in the Americas is therefore thought to be well established, as it is for the Old World. Indeed, it has been suggested to be present in a variety of other animals, going back as far as the Mesozoic (10, 123). We are not certain that all of these cases represent AS rather than another seronegative spondylarthropathy such as Reiter's syndrome or Diffuse Idiopathic Skeletal Hyperostosis (DISH). Until recently there has been little attempt to differentiate these diseases in skeletal material (88). An exception is Arriaza's recent study (6) of prehistoric Chilean remains, which found seronegative spondyloarthropathies and a DISH-like condition, although in low frequencies. Arriaza was able to differentiate among several forms of vertebral arthritis, even though in many cases the skeletons did not exhibit the classic forms of the lesions associated with these diseases today. In general, it is clear that some sort of vertebral arthropathy, often leading to ankylosis, has long been occurring in the Americas.

Today, ankylosing spondylitis occurs with great frequency in some Native American groups (30, 102). Since the disease has a genetic component (62, 100), its prehistoric presence is certainly plausible. Some Indian groups also show high frequencies of Reiter's syndrome (69), a seronegative spondylarthropathy that differs from AS in the nature and distribution of skeletal lesions (86).

RHEUMATOID ARTHRITIS

The first clear-cut description of a disease similar to rheumatoid arthritis (RA) in the living appeared in 1676. As a result, Short has suggested that the disease is of recent origin (101). A few examples of a polyarticular resorptive condition similar to modern RA have been found in the Old World and dated prior to 1492, but they are rare (87, 115). A candidate for a predecessor syndrome has been suggested, but it differs from RA in a number of features (54). On the other hand, some recent work suggests that RA may have appeared prehistorically in the New World first and spread to Europe after 1492.

Rothschild et al have found evidence for a polyarticular resorptive arthritis that resembles RA in its predilection for peripheral joints, as well as in the appearance of its lesions, both visually and radiographically (92; also see 95). It first appears during the Archaic period (1000–4000 BC) in a region encompassing northern Alabama and western Kentucky. It is also found in later Mississippian cultures of the same area, as well as at a Woodland site (Libben) in Ohio (93, 96, 121). Rothschild and coworkers argue that RA is confined to the Tennessee River Valley area until the Woodland period and only later expands to other parts of North America, and eventually the world (94). The early restricted distribution might suggest some sort of local influence in its transmission (rather than, for example, simple person-person contact), but its later rapid spread throughout the rest of the world makes this scenario less likely. The presence of a polyarticular arthritis similar to RA in a prehistoric Kodiak Island skeleton also suggests that it may have been more widespread than is currently substantiated (75). Unfortunately, given the dearth of information about the etiology of RA in general, any suggestions about manner of its origin and later dispersal must remain speculative.

Rheumatoid arthritis afflicts Native Americans to various degrees today (8, 9, 59). Differences in prevalence may be due in part to genetic influences, since RA has been associated with HLA type DR4 (26, 102).

The RA-like disease seen in pre-Columbian America may not have been true RA, but may instead have been caused or triggered by an infective agent. A variety of bacterial, viral, and even parasitic diseases have been known to cause rheumatoid symptoms. Hudson et al (41) suggested that one of these, the *Erysipelothrix* bacterium, caused many cases of arthritis in the southeastern United States. The mode of transmission to humans would have involved the handling of contaminated meat, and the authors tied the widespread distribution of symptoms to known cultural practices of historic tribes in the region.

Hudson and coworkers did not attempt a differential diagnosis based on skeletal pathology, and many of the cases they cite as evidence are certainly the result of other kinds of arthritis, including osteoarthritis. Their suggestion is nonetheless plausible for some instances of reactive arthritis. *Erysipelothrix* is common in a number of mammalian species, including swine and deer, and can cause a disease like rheumatoid arthritis in infected individuals (103). It can be transmitted to humans through handling of contaminated animal parts. In fact, many infective arthritides mimic rheumatoid arthritis, and it is possible that at least some of the reported cases from around the world are the result of infection, rather than RA.

JUVENILE RHEUMATOID ARTHRITIS

Until recently, juvenile rheumatoid arthritis (JRA) had not been identified in prehistoric skeletal populations. In a thorough description and differential diagnosis of a juvenile from Southern Peru (900–1050 AD), Buikstra et al (17) argue that this individual had a disease closely resembling JRA. The skeleton is characterized by widespread degenerative changes of the joints; reduced growth in the long bones, face, and mandible; and disuse atrophy of much of the skeleton. The disease was obviously of long standing and closely resembles systemic or polyarticular JRA in modern populations (17).

DISCUSSION

Osteoarthritis

A good deal of new information is now available on the prevalence of OA, but the new data do not simplify the situation. Can anything be said about arthritis in general in the Americas? Certain broad, if perhaps simplistic, statements can indeed be made.

First, the patterning of arthritis among the major appendicular joints in prehistoric populations often differs widely from that in modern groups, with elevated levels of lesions especially at the elbow. In both the elbow and (to a lesser extent) the knee, variations in arthritis prevalence are thought to reflect differences in physical activity levels; development of arthritis at the shoulder and hip is more closely related to age and less affected by activities (47). The greater prevalence of prehistoric elbow and knee arthritis suggests high physical activity levels in a variety of prehistoric populations.

Prehistoric males frequently show more arthritis than females. This pattern reverses that seen in some modern groups, where females may have significantly more arthritis than men, either at such joints as the distal finger joints (51, 81) or in the older age categories (76, 84). Studies examining changes in arthritis with age in American Indians demonstrate a marked increase of the disease in older females, which may parallel the situation seen in contemporary populations. In fact, larger sample sizes for the different age groups may reveal the pattern of sexual dimorphism to be similar in prehistoric and modern populations.

On the other hand, substantiation of a tendency towards more arthritis in males might suggest more rigidly defined sex roles in some prehistoric societies than in modern ones, with males subject to a greater risk of joint injury.

Such reasoning makes sense for groups like the Eskimo, but it is not obvious why arthritis is more prevalent among settled agriculturalist males than among male hunter-gatherers (especially in societies where females are thought to do much of the agricultural work). One explanatory factor may be the increase in warfare and associated traumatic injuries seen across parts of the Eastern Woodlands in later prehistory.

The effects on the body's joints of the economic shift to agriculture vary both between and within regions. Even when a general trend is seen—e.g. when arthritis increases with the introduction of agriculture—variability is observed in which sex and which part of the body is affected most. Type of subsistence economy and level or patterning of arthritis cannot be coupled directly.

Nor can arthritis be linked conclusively to any specific economic activity. Correlation of arthritis with particular activities in the past was often simplistic; it ignored the wide range of individuals' activities as well as the traumatic injuries they may have suffered.

Future Research

Future work should standardize the coding of arthritis on joint surfaces and present data in a form readily interpreted, using appropriate statistical techniques.

The presentation of percentages of individuals with moderate–severe arthritis is easier to interpret than average arthritis scores (especially since scoring varies among researchers). Most useful for comparative purposes are data on individual joint complexes (such as the "knee" or "elbow"); for more specific purposes it may be necessary to present information on separate components of each joint. The maximum arthritis score on any joint surface should be assigned to the joint complex as a whole, rather than averaging scores for different parts of the joint.

Controlling for age is essential. Perhaps the best technique is to give data for different age categories. While categorizing by life decade often leads to unacceptably small sample sizes, testing for mean age differences between samples is not specific enough. For example, the mean age in a sample where everyone is 35 might be identical to that in one where the ages ranged from 15 to 65.

Only a handful of reports present statistical analyses of sexual dimorphism or bilateral asymmetry. Work has been completed on such special topics as the change in arthritis prevalence with the introduction of agriculture, or the association of some type of arthritis with a particular activity, while certain more basic topics have been given short shrift. Also, while a good deal of work has been done in the Eastern Woodlands, with various Arctic groups, and with coastal California samples, data on arthritic diseases in the rest of the Americas are scarce.

Finally, anthropologists tend to use arthritis levels or patterns as direct indicators of normal activities; but although mechanical loading is thought to be a major contributor to the development of arthritis, it is not the only cause of joint degeneration (47). High-intensity, infrequent forces may injure the joint while lower-level habitual activities may not (25). The duration of activities may be as important as their level. In short, while arthritis is undoubtedly related in part to forces placed on the joint, it is not a straightforward indicator of the level or type of normal activities.

Much less is known about other arthritic conditions in prehistory. Although AS has been widely reported in the literature, in few of the specimens mentioned has AS been differentiated from other forms of arthritis. Until differential diagnosis has been carried out in a number of populations, the prevalence of AS must remain uncertain. Rheumatoid arthritis has been more methodically examined in recent years, but its origins and spread must be more thoroughly scrutinized in populations outside the Eastern Woodlands.

CONCLUSIONS

The complexity of the etiology of osteoarthritis seems daunting. Basic prevalence patterns characterize different Native American groups, but these are not related to activity level in any simple way. Understanding the meaning of these differences will require more careful, statistically oriented research.

As Kellgren (51:5243) put it over 30 years ago,

> The history of osteoarthrosis is long, for degenerative joint changes can be seen in fossil skeletons of prehistoric animals and in the joints of ancient Egyptian mummies. Despite this long history our knowledge of the disease is incomplete, perhaps because it is one of those dull commonplace disorders that are hard to study with enthusiasm, but new knowledge of osteoarthrosis must be gained if the later years of our lengthening lives are not to be plagued by increasing pain and disability.

ACKNOWLEDGMENTS

I thank all those who offered advice, reprints, or other help, including B. Bradtmiller, T. Bromage, R. Jurmain, C. Merbs, J. Rose, K. Rosenberg, S. Stinson, D. Ubelaker, and especially M. Powell. R. Jurmain and K. Rosenberg made a number of valuable comments on the manuscript. I gratefully acknowledge the assistance of L. Carroll and the Interlibrary Loan Service at Rosenthal Library, Queens College. My own work on arthritis was supported by the PSC-CUNY Research Award Program, and was carried out largely at the University of Alabama Laboratory for Human Osteology. I thank K. Turner of that institution for many useful discussions on this topic.

Literature Cited

1. Allison, M. J. 1984. Paleopathology in Peruvian and Chilean populations. In *Paleopathology at the Origins of Agriculture*, ed. M. N. Cohen, G. J. Armelagos, pp. 515–29. Orlando: Academic
2. Anderson, J. E. 1963. The people of Fairty. An osteological analysis of an Iroquois ossuary. *Natl. Mus. Can. Contrib. Anthropol. Bull.* 193(1):28–129
3. Angel, J. L. 1966. Early skeletons from Tranquillity, California. *Smithson. Contrib. Anthropol.* 2:1–19
4. Angel, J. L. 1971. *The People of Lerna*. Washington: Smithson. Inst. Press
5. Angel, J. L., Kelley, J. O., Parrington, M., Pinter, S. 1987. Life stresses of the free black community as represented by the First African Baptist Church, Philadelphia, 1823–1841. *Am. J. Phys. Anthropol.* 74:213–29
6. Arriaza Torres, B. 1991. *The search for seronegative spondyloarthropathies and diffuse idiopathic skeletal hyperostosis in ancient South America*. PhD thesis. Ariz. State Univ., Tempe
7. Bass, W. M., Gregg, J. B., Provost, P. E. 1974. Ankylosing spondylitis (Marie Strumpel Disease [sic]) in historic and prehistoric Northern Plains Indians. *Plains Anthropol.* 19(66):303–5
8. Bennett, P. H., Burch, T. A. 1968. The genetics of rheumatoid arthritis. In *Population Studies of the Rheumatic Diseases*, ed. P. H. Bennett, P. H. N. Wood, pp. 136–47. Amsterdam: Excerpta Medica
9. Blumberg, B. S., Bloch, K. J., Black, R. L., Dotter, C. 1961. A study of the prevalence of arthritis in Alaskan Eskimos. *Arth. Rheum.* 4:325–41
10. Bourke, J. B. 1967. A review of the paleopathology of the arthritic diseases. In *Diseases in Antiquity*, ed. D. Brothwell, A. T. Sandison, pp. 352–70. Springfield, IL: C. C. Thomas
11. Bradtmiller, B. 1983. The effect of horseback riding on Arikara arthritis patterns. Presented at Annu. Meet. Am. Anthropol. Assoc., 82nd, Chicago
12. Brewer, E. J., Giannini, E. H. 1983. Juvenile rheumatoid arthritis. *Clin. Rheum. Dis.* 9:629–40
13. Bridges, P. S. 1989. Changes in activities with the shift to agriculture in the Southeastern United States. *Curr. Anthropol.* 30:385–94
14. Bridges, P. S. 1990. Osteological correlates of weapon use. In *A Life in Science: Papers in Honor of J. Lawrence Angel*, ed. J. E. Buikstra, pp. 87–98. Cent. Am. Archeol. Sci. Pap. 6
15. Bridges, P. S. 1991. Degenerative joint disease in hunter-gatherers and agriculturalists from the Southeastern United States. *Am. J. Phys. Anthropol.* 85:379–91
16. Bridges, P. S. 1992. Vertebral arthritis in a northwestern Alabama skeletal sample. *Am. J. Phys. Anthropol. Suppl.* 14:54 (Abstr.)
17. Buikstra, J. E., Poznanski, A., Cerna, M. L., Goldstein, P., Hoshower, L. M. 1990. A case of juvenile rheumatoid arthritis from Pre-Columbian Peru. In *A Life in Science: Papers in Honor of J. Lawrence Angel*, ed. J. E. Buikstra, pp. 99–137. Cent. Am. Archeol. Sci. Pap. 6
18. Burnett, B. A. 1990. The bioarcheological synthesis of the eastern portion of the Gulf Coastal Plain. *Ark. Archeol. Surv. Res. Ser.* 38:385–418
19. Cassidy, C. M. 1984. Skeletal evidence for prehistoric subsistence adaptation in the Central Ohio River Valley. In *Paleopathology at the Origins of Agriculture*, ed. M. N. Cohen, G. J. Armelagos, pp. 307–45. Orlando: Academic
20. Chapman, F. H. 1962. Incidence of arthritis in a prehistoric Middle Mississippian Indian population. *Proc. Indiana Acad. Sci.* 72:59–62
21. Chapman, F. H. 1964. Comparison of osteoarthritis in three aboriginal populations. *Proc. Indiana Acad. Sci.* 74:84–86
22. Chapman, F. H. 1972. Vertebral osteophytosis in prehistoric populations of Central and Southern Mexico. *Am. J. Phys. Anthropol.* 36:31–38
23. Chapman, F. H. 1973. Osteophytosis in prehistoric Brazilian populations. *Man* 8:93–99
24. Clabeaux, M. S. 1976. Health and disease in the population of an Iroquois ossuary. *Yrb. Phys. Anthropol.* 20:359–70
25. Cohen, M. N., Armelagos, G. J. 1984. Paleopathology at the origins of agriculture: editors' summation. In *Paleopathology at the Origins of Agriculture*, ed. M. N. Cohen, G. J. Armelagos, pp. 585–601. Orlando: Academic
26. Condemi, J. J. 1987. The autoimmune diseases. *J. Am. Med. Assoc.* 258:2920–29
27. Dobbs, W. H. 1988. Vertebral osteophytosis among Archaic and Mississippian populations of the Tennessee River Valley in North Alabama. *Am. J. Phys. Anthropol.* 75:204 (Abstr.)
28. Edynak, G. J. 1976. Life-styles from skeletal material: a medieval Yugoslav example. In *The Measures of Man*, ed. G. Giles, J. S. Friedlander, pp. 408–32. Cambridge: Peabody Mus. Press
29. Funkhouser, W. D. 1939. A study of the physical anthropology and pathology of the osteological material from the Wheeler Basin. In *An Archaeological Survey of*

Wheeler Basin on the Tennessee River in Northern Alabama, ed. W. S. Webb, pp. 109–25. Bur. Am. Ethnol. Bull. 122

30. Gofton, J. P., Lawrence, J. S., Bennett, P. H., Burch, T. A. 1968. Sacroiliitis in eight populations. In *Population Studies of the Rheumatic Diseases*, ed. P. II. Bennett, P. H. N. Wood, pp. 293–98. Amsterdam: Excerpta Medica

31. Goldstein, M. S. 1957. Skeletal pathology of early Indians in Texas. *Am. J. Phys. Anthropol.* 15:299–311

32. Goodman, A. H., Lallo, J., Armelagos, G. J., Rose, J. C. 1984. Health changes at Dickson Mounds, Illinois (A. D. 950–1300). In *Paleopathology at the Origins of Agriculture*, ed. M. N. Cohen, G. J. Armelagos, pp. 271–305. Orlando: Academic

33. Gregg, J. B., Gregg, P. S. 1987. *Dry Bones. Dakota Territory Reflected.* Sioux Falls: Sioux Printing

34. Gunness-Hey, M. 1980. The Koniag Eskimo presacral vertebral column: variations, anomalies and pathologies. *Ossa* 7:99–118

35. Harmon, A. M., Rose, J. C. 1989. Bioarchaeology of the Louisiana and Arkansas study area. *Ark. Archeol. Surv. Res. Ser.* 37:323–54

36. Harris, R. I. 1949. Osteological evidence of disease amongst the Huron Indians. *Univ. Toronto Med. J.* 27:71–75

37. Hodges, D. C. 1991. Temporomandibular joint osteoarthritis in a British skeletal population. *Am. J. Phys. Anthropol.* 85:367–77

38. Hooton, E. A. 1930. *The Indians of Pecos Pueblo. A Study of Their Skeletal Remains.* New Haven: Yale Univ. Press

39. Hrdlička, A. 1914. Special notes on some of the pathological conditions shown by the skeletal material of the ancient Peruvians. *Smithson. Misc. Coll.* 61:57–69

40. Hrdlička, A. 1916. Physical anthropology of the Lenape or Delawares, and of the Eastern Indians in general. Bur. Am. Ethnol. Bull. 62

41. Hudson, C., Butler, R., Sikes, D. 1975. Arthritis in the prehistoric Southeastern United States: biological and cultural variables. *Am. J. Phys. Anthropol.* 43:57–62

42. Jurmain, R. D. 1977. Stress and the etiology of osteoarthritis. *Am. J. Phys. Anthropol.* 46:353–66

43. Jurmain, R. D. 1977. Paleoepidemiology of degenerative knee disease. *Med. Anthropol.* 1:1–23

44. Jurmain, R. D. 1978. Paleoepidemiology of degenerative joint disease. *Med. Coll. Va. Q.* 14:45–56

45. Jurmain, R. D. 1980. The pattern of involvement of appendicular degenerative joint disease. *Am. J. Phys. Anthropol.* 53:143–50

46. Jurmain, R. D. 1990. Paleoepidemiology of a Central California prehistoric population from Ca-Ala-329. II. Degenerative disease. *Am. J. Phys. Anthropol.* 83:83–94

47. Jurmain, R. D. 1991. Degenerative changes in peripheral joints as indicators of mechanical stress: opportunities and limitations. *Int. J. Osteoarchaeol.* 1:247–52

48. Keefer, C. S., Myers, W. K. 1934. The incidence and pathogenesis of degenerative arthritis. *J. Am. Med. Assoc.* 102:811–13

49. Kelley, J. O., Angel, J. L. 1987. Life stresses of slavery. *Am. J. Phys. Anthropol.* 74:199–211

50. Kelley, M. A. 1980. *Disease and environment: a comparative analysis of three early American Indian skeletal collections.* PhD thesis. Case Western Reserve Univ., Cleveland

51. Kellgren, J. H. 1961. Osteoarthrosis in patients and populations. *Br. Med. J.* 2(1 July):5243–48

52. Kidd, K. E. 1954. A note on the palaeopathology of Ontario. *Am. J. Phys. Anthropol.* 12:610–15

53. Kilgore, L. 1984. *Degenerative joint disease in a Medieval Nubian population.* PhD thesis. Univ. Colo., Denver

54. Klepinger, L. L. 1979. Paleopathologic evidence for the evolution of rheumatoid arthritis. *Am. J. Phys. Anthropol.* 50:119–22

55. Lallo, J. W. 1973. *The skeletal biology of three prehistoric American Indian societies from Dickson Mounds.* PhD thesis. Univ. Mass., Amherst

56. Langdon, F. W. 1881. The Madisonville pre-historic cemetery: anthropological notes. *J. Cincinnati Soc. Nat. Hist.* 4:237–57

57. Larsen, C. S. 1982. The anthropology of St. Catherines Island. 3. Prehistoric human biological adaptation. *Am. Mus. Nat. Hist. Anthropol. Pap.* 57:159–270

58. Larsen, C. S. 1984. Health and disease in prehistoric Georgia: the transition to agriculture. In *Paleopathology at the Origins of Agriculture*, ed. M. N. Cohen, G. J. Armelagos, pp. 367–92. Orlando: Academic

59. Lawrence, J. S., Behrend, T., Bennett, P. H., Bremner, J. M., Burch, T. A., et al. 1966. Geographical studies on rheumatoid arthritis. *Ann. Rheum. Dis.* 25:425–31

60. Leisen, J. C. C., Duncan, H., Riddle, J. M. 1991. Rheumatoid erosive arthropathy as seen in macerated (dry) bone specimens. In *Human Paleopathology. Current Syntheses and Future Options*, ed. D. J. Ortner, A. C. Aufderheide, pp. 211–15. Washington: Smithson. Inst. Press

61. MacCurdy, G. G. 1923. Human skeletal remains from the highlands of Peru. *Am. J. Phys. Anthropol.* 6 (Old Ser.):218–330

62. McDaniel, D. O., Acton, R. T., Barger, B. O., Koopman, W. J., Reveille, J. D. 1987. Association of a 9.2-kilobase Pvu II Class I major histocompatibility complex restriction fragment length polymorphism with ankylosing spondylitis. *Arth. Rheum.* 30:894–900

63. Merbs, C. F. 1980. The pathology of a La Jollan skeleton from Punta Minitas, Baja California. *Pac. Coast Archaeol. Soc. Q.* 16:37–43

64. Merbs, C. F. 1983. Patterns of activity-induced pathology in a Canadian Inuit population. *Archaeol. Surv. Can. Pap.* 119:1–199

65. Merbs, C. F., Vestergaard, E. M. 1985. The paleopathology of Sundown, a prehistoric site near Prescott, Arizona. In *Health and Disease in the Prehistoric Southwest,* ed. C. F. Merbs, R. J. Miller. Tucson: Ariz. State Univ. Anthropol. Res. Pap. 34, pp. 85–103

66. Miles, J. S. 1966. Diseases encountered at Mesa Verde, Colorado. II. Evidences of disease. In *Human Palaeopathology,* ed. S. Jarcho, pp. 91–97. New Haven: Yale Univ. Press

67. Miller, R. J. 1985. Lateral epicondylitis in a prehistoric central Arizona Indian population from Nuvakwewtaqa. In *Health and Disease in the Prehistoric Southwest,* ed. C. F. Merbs, R. J. Miller. Tucson: Ariz. State Univ. Anthropol. Res. Pap. 34, pp. 391–400

68. Morse, D. 1978. Ancient disease in the Midwest. *Illinois State Mus. Rep. Invest.* 15:1–181

69. Morse, H. G., Rate, R. G., Bonnell, M. D., Kuberski, T. 1980. High frequency of HLA-B27 and Reiter's Syndrome in Navajo Indians. *J. Rheumatol.* 7:900–2

70. Nathan, H. 1962. Osteophytes of the vertebral column. An anatomical study of their development according to age, race, sex with considerations as to their etiology and significance. *J. Bone Joint Surg.* 44-A:243–68

71. Neumann, H. W. 1967. The paleopathology of the Archaic Modoc Rock Shelter inhabitants. *Illinois State Mus. Rep. Invest.* 11:1–68

72. Newman, M. T., Snow, C. E. 1942. Preliminary report on the skeletal material from Pickwick Basin, Alabama. In *An Archaeological Survey of Pickwick Basin in the Adjacent Portions of the States of Alabama, Mississippi and Tennessee,* ed. W. S. Webb, D. L. DeJarnette, pp. 393–507. Bur. Am. Ethnol. Bull. 129

73. Ortner, D. J. 1968. Description and classification of degenerative bone changes in the distal joint surfaces of the humerus. *Am. J. Phys. Anthropol.* 28:139–56

74. Ortner, D. J., Putschar, W. G. J. 1981. Identification of pathological conditions in human skeletal remains. *Smithson. Contrib. Anthropol.* 28:1–488

75. Ortner, D. J., Utermohle, C. J. 1981. Polyarticular inflammatory arthritis in a pre-Columbian skeleton from Kodiak Island, Alaska, U. S. A. *Am. J. Phys. Anthropol.* 56:23–31

76. Peyron, J. G. 1986. Osteoarthritis. The epidemiologic viewpoint. *Clin. Orthop.* 213:13–19

77. Pfeiffer, S. 1977. The skeletal biology of Archaic populations of the Great Lakes region. *Archaeol. Surv. Can. Pap.* 64:1–384

78. Pickering, R. B. 1979. Hunter-gatherer/agriculturalist arthritic patterns: a preliminary investigation. *Henry Ford Hosp. Med. J.* 27:50–53

79. Pickering, R. B. 1984. *Patterns of degenerative joint disease in Middle Woodland, Late Woodland, and Mississippian skeletal series from the Lower Illinois Valley.* PhD thesis. Northwestern Univ., Evanston

80. Pierce, L. K. C. 1987. *A comparison of the pattern of involvement of degenerative joint disease between an agricultural and non-agricultural skeletal series.* PhD thesis. Univ. Tenn., Knoxville

81. Radin, E. L., Parker, H. G., Paul, I. L. 1971. Pattern of degenerative arthritis: preferential involvement of distal finger-joints. *Lancet* 1:377–79

82. Radin, E. L., Paul, I. L., Rose, R. M. 1972. Role of mechanical factors in pathogenesis of primary osteoarthritis. *Lancet* 1:519–22

83. Rathbun, T. A. 1984. Skeletal pathology from the Paleolithic through the Metal Ages in Iran and Iraq. In *Paleopathology at the Origins of Agriculture,* ed. M. N. Cohen, G. J. Armelagos, pp. 137–67. Orlando: Academic

84. Roberts, J., Burch, T. A. 1966. Prevalence of osteoarthritis in adults by age, sex, race, and geographic area. United States—1960–1962. *Natl. Cent. Health Stat. Ser.* 11(15):1–27

85. Rodnan, G. P., ed. 1973. Primer on the rheumatic diseases. *J. Am. Med. Assoc.* 224:663–805

86. Rogers, J., Waldron, T., Dieppe, P., Watt, I. 1987. Arthropathies in palaeopathology: the basis of classification according to most probable cause. *J. Arch. Sci.* 14:179–93

87. Rogers, J., Watt, I., Dieppe, P. 1981. Arthritis in Saxon and medieval skeletons. *Br. Med. J.* 283:1668–70

88. Rogers, J., Watt, I., Dieppe, P. 1985. Palaeopathology of spinal osteophytosis, vertebral ankylosis, ankylosing spondylitis, and vertebral hyperostosis. *Ann. Rheum. Dis.* 44:113–20

89. Rogers, S. L. 1966. The need for a better means of recording pathological bone proliferation in joint areas. *Am. J. Phys. Anthropol.* 25:171–76

90. Roney, J. G. Jr. 1959. Palaeopathology of a California archaeological site. *Bull. Hist. Med.* 33:97–109

91. Rose, J. C., Burnett, B. A., Nassaney, M. S., Blaeuer, M. W. 1984. Paleopathology and the origins of maize agriculture in the Lower Mississippi Valley and Caddoan Culture areas. In *Paleopathology at the Origins of Agriculture,* ed. M. N. Cohen,

G. J. Armelagos, pp. 393–424. Orlando: Academic
92. Rothschild, B. M., Turner, K. R., DeLuca, M. A. 1988. Symmetrical erosive peripheral polyarthritis in the Late Archaic Period of Alabama. *Science* 241:1498–501
93. Rothschild, B. M., Woods, R. J. 1990. Symmetrical erosive disease in Archaic Indians: the origin of rheumatoid arthritis in the New World? *Sem. Arth. Rheum.* 19:278–84
94. Rothschild, B., Woods, R. 1991. Eastern migration of rheumatoid arthritis from the Archaic to the Historic. *Am. J. Phys. Anthropol. Suppl.* 12:154 (Abstr.)
95. Rothschild, B. M., Woods, R. J., Ortel, W. 1990. Rheumatoid arthritis "in the buff:" erosive arthritis in defleshed bones. *Am. J. Phys. Anthropol.* 82:441–49
96. Rothschild, B. M., Woods, R. J., Turner, K. R. 1989. Regional persistence of symmetrical erosive polyarthritis from the Archaic to the Mississippian. A tale of two "cities." *Am. J. Phys. Anthropol.* 78:293 (Abstr.)
97. Ruff, C. B. 1987. Postcranial adaptation to subsistence changes on the Georgia coast. *Am. J. Phys. Anthropol.* 72:248 (Abstr.)
98. Ruff, C. B., Larsen, C. S., Hayes, W. C. 1984. Structural changes in the femur with the transition to agriculture on the Georgia Coast. *Am. J. Phys. Anthropol.* 64:125–36
99. Saul, F. P. 1972. The human skeletal remains of Altar de Sacrificios. An osteobiographic analysis. *Pap. Peabody Mus. Archaeol. Ethnol. Harv. Univ.* 63(2):1–123
100. Schlosstein, L., Terasaki, P. I., Bluestone, R., Pearson, C. M. 1973. High association of an HL-A antigen, W27, with ankylosing spondylitis. *New Eng. J. Med.* 288:704–6
101. Short, C. L. 1974. The antiquity of rheumatoid arthritis. *Arth. Rheum.* 17:193–205
102. Sievers, M. L., Fisher, J. R. 1981. Diseases of the North American Indians. In *Biocultural Aspects of Disease,* ed. H. R. Rothschild, pp. 191–252. New York: Academic
103. Sikes, D., Neher, G. M., Doyle, L. P. 1956. The pathology of chronic arthritis following natural and experimental *Erysipelothrix* infection of swine. *Am. J. Pathol.* 32:1241–51
104. Snow, C. E. 1948. Indian Knoll skeletons. *Univ. Kentucky Rep. Anthropol.* 4:371–545
105. Sokoloff, L. 1969. *The Biology of Degenerative Joint Disease.* Chicago: Univ. Chicago
106. Steinbock, R. T. 1976. *Paleopathological Diagnosis and Interpretation.* Springfield, IL: C. C. Thomas
107. Stewart, T. D. 1947. Racial patterns in vertebral osteoarthritis. *Am. J. Phys. Anthro-*

pol. 5:230–31 (Abstr.)
108. Stewart, T. D. 1957. Rate of development of vertebral hypertrophic arthritis and its utility in age estimation. *Am. J. Phys. Anthropol.* 15:433 (Abstr.)
109. Stewart, T. D. 1958. The rate of development of vertebral osteoarthritis in American whites and its significance in skeletal age identification. *Leech* 28:144–51
110. Stewart, T. D. 1966. Some problems in human palaeopathology. In *Human Palaeopathology,* ed. S. Jarcho, pp. 43–55. New Haven: Yale Univ. Press
111. Stewart, T. D. 1976. Sacro-iliac osteophytosis. *Am. J. Phys. Anthropol.* 44:210 (Abstr.)
112. Stewart, T. D. 1979. Patterning of skeletal pathologies and epidemiology. In *The First Americans: Origins, Affinities, and Adaptations,* ed. W. S. Laughlin, A. B. Harper, pp. 257–74. New York: Gustav Fischer
113. Sullivan, N. C. 1977. *The physical anthropology of Chiggerville: demography and pathology.* MA thesis. Western Michigan Univ., Kalamazoo
114. Tainter, J. A. 1980. Behavior and status in a Middle Woodland mortuary population from the Illinois Valley. *Am. Antiq.* 45:308–13
115. Thould, A. K., Thould, B. T. 1983. Arthritis in Roman Britain. *Br. Med. J.* 287:1909–11
116. Waldron, R., Rogers, J. 1991. Inter-observer variation in coding osteoarthritis in human skeletal remains. *Int. J. Osteoarchaeol.* 1:49–56
117. Walker, P. L., Hollimon, S. E. 1989. Changes in osteoarthritis associated with the development of a maritime economy among Southern California Indians. *Int. J. Anthropol.* 4:171–83
118. Webb, W. S., Snow, C. E. 1974. *The Adena People.* Knoxville: Univ. Tenn. Press
119. Wells, C. 1964. *Bones, Bodies and Disease.* London: Thames and Hudson
120. Whitney, W. F. 1886. Notes on the anomalies, injuries and diseases of the bones of the native races of North America. *Peabody Mus. Rep.* III:433–48
121. Woods, R. J., Rothschild, B. M. 1988. Population analysis of symmetrical erosive arthritis in Ohio Woodland Indians (1200 years ago). *J. Rheumatol.* 15:1258–63
122. Yesner, D. R. 1981. Degenerative and traumatic pathologies of the Aleut vertebral column. *Arch. Calif. Chiropractic Assoc.* 5:45–57
123. Zorab, P. A. 1961. The historical and prehistorical background of ankylosing spondylitis. *Proc. Roy. Soc. Med.* 54:415–20

Annu. Rev. Anthropol. 1992. 21:93–123

THE CULTURAL ANTHROPOLOGY OF TIME: A CRITICAL ESSAY

Nancy D. Munn

Department of Anthropology, University of Chicago, Chicago, Illinois 60637

KEYWORDS: temporal theory, space, symbolic anthropology

Writing a review of the cultural anthropology of time is something like reading Borges's (19a) infinite "Book of Sand": as one opens this book, pages keep growing from it—it has no beginning or end. Borges's book could be taken as the space of time: A page once seen is never seen again, and the book's harried possessors keep trying to escape its "monstrous" self-production by surreptitiously selling or losing it.

The diffuse, endlessly multiplying studies of sociocultural time reflect time's pervasiveness as an inescapable dimension of all aspects of social experience and practice. This apparently "infinite complexity" (1:200) seems to be both a cause and a product of insufficient theoretical attention to the nature of time as a unitary, focal problem (cf 1:200, 119a:152). When time is a focus, it may be subject to oversimplified, single-stranded descriptions or typifications, rather than to a theoretical examination of basic sociocultural processes through which temporality is constructed (cf 39a, 51:42, 178a:182). Anthropological reviews or summaries of the field (51, 71, 127a, 164) are both sparse and, with the exception of Gell's (62) major new study,[1] relatively superficial despite the importance of the topic.

Thus the problem of time has often been handmaiden to other anthropological frames and issues (political structures, descent, ritual, work, narrative, history, cosmology, etc, as well as, at another level, general theories of anthropological discourse) with which it is inextricably bound up. In short, the topic of time frequently fragments into all the other dimensions and topics anthropologists deal with in the social world.

---

[1]
Gell considers selected anthropological work and draws on the philosophies of Mctaggart and Husserl to develop his own theoretical approach to the anthropology of time. Because the work is unpublished at this writing, I do not examine its argument here.

0084-6570/92/1015-0093$02.00

Time's inescapability emerges in another way. Like all other discourses, those about time themselves take temporal form. We cannot analyze or talk about time without using media already encoded with temporal meanings nor, in the course of doing so, can we avoid creating something that takes the form of time—as I am doing here. We and our productions are in some sense always "in" time (the socioculturally/historically informed time of our activity and our wider world)[2] and yet we make, through our acts, the time we are in. These inescapable convolutions are critical features that, as I argue below, anthropologists should incorporate into their models of sociocultural time.

A further complication appears in the fact that, as in the infinite book of sand, time and space are integral to each other. Although Western theory frequently treats space as time's antithetical "Other," time's Other turns out somewhat embarrassingly to be its Other Self. In a lived world, spatial and temporal dimensions cannot be disentangled, and the two commingle in various ways (for different perspectives on these connections see 6a, 28b:106–7, 73, 82, 134, 142:279–83, 143:8–11, 153a, 173a:42, 175a, 178b, 183, 191:284–85, 196). Anthropologists have only sometimes understood these connections, which were early emphasized by Granet (73) in his important account of Chinese formulations of time and space. Discussing time apart from space is necessary in a study of this length; but I also use the separation to show, where possible, some of the basic articulations.

Finally, I delimit this review[3] by a selective framing of the topic in terms of ways anthropological writings have dealt with time in relation to action, actors, and space. I offer critiques of some of these dealings and sketch a few ideas of my own.

BACKGROUND: BETWEEN COLLECTIVE CONCEPT AND RHYTHMIC ACTIVITY

The anthropology of time emerged in an era when there was a complex polemic in Western society and thought regarding notions of temporal diversity ("local times") and heterogeneity, as opposed to temporal singularity and homogeneity; conceptions of time as "atomistic" units ("instants," "clock minutes," etc) as opposed to conceptions of time as motion or "flux" (99:11, 15, 19, 139; cf 84:260ff, 149:55ff). Durkheim and his colleagues (42, 43, 91, 127) founded time in the image of social diversity (cf 155:117),[4] qualitative hetero-

---

[2] The expression "in time" has drawbacks because it tends to reify time (28a:312). I use the phrase simply to express the inextricable temporality of human being, experience, and practice.

[3] I have excluded certain specialized subjects such as narrative time (6a, 163, 179); time allocation studies (133a); and studies of diachrony and synchrony, time and structure and related problems in anthropological meta-language (6c, 51, 53a). Much that deserves closer attention I mention only in passing; for instance, life time and age-grading (10, 83, 106, 114, 168a) and the many relevant ritual-symbolic or cosmological studies (114a, 150, 185, 193a).

[4] The notion of the multiple forms of social time is a leitmotif of the literature (e.g. 40a, 75, 78:106–112, 78b, 157, 158, 178a), but what kind of diversity is meant varies. The notion has also been linked to questions of cross-cultural temporal relativity (e.g. 6b:331f, 18, 62).

geneity, and a conceptual segmentation that nonetheless remained connected to activity or motion. In their paradigm, social time consists of "collective representations" or "categories" that derive from and reflect the groupings and varied "rhythms" of social life. These categorical divisions (days, seasons, etc) form a meaningful, qualitatively varied rather than an abstract, homogeneous temporality.

The influential notion of qualitative time (e.g. 5, 118:119f, 170, 171) actually derives from Bergson's (15, 16) characterization of inner *durée* as a qualitatively differentiated but unsegmented, temporal movement. Although Durkheim & Mauss (43:86) briefly use the notion, Hubert (91) explicitly appropriates it for social time in the heart of his partial rapprochement with Bergson and his opposition to the latter's subjective derivation of human temporality. For Hubert, the calendric periodization of time, established in religio-magic practices, segments time but does so qualitatively: Periods are defined by specific social activities or "facts" (*choses*) whose particularities and varying intensities give "active qualities" to these categories of duration. Calendars do not so much measure time as give it rhythmic form. In his view, the homogeneous notion of time may be due to the separation of temporality from the "things" of social life (91:129; cf 96:202). Thus Hubert turns Bergson on his head, grounding qualitative temporal rhythms in objective, social life and giving them a morphology of segmenting categories that Bergson regarded as quantified, static "spatialization."

Similarly, Durkheim (42:441) divides the "personal time" of subjective consciousness—the undifferentiated flow of "duration which I feel passing within me"—from social time's morphology of cognizable units that imposes itself on "all minds." Indeed, Durkheim's notion of personal time accords well with Bergson's *durée* or James's "stream of consciousness," to which Durkheim (41:12) refers [cf Pocock's (158:307) Durkheimian distinction between collective, social time and the "mere duration" of personal time]. For Durkheim, of course (in contrast to Bergson), social time has primacy in human temporality.

In fact, if carried to its logical conclusion, Durkheim's argument would require personal time itself to be infused with collective time representations and activity rhythms. Halbwachs (76–78) later takes up this implication. Resituating the problem of time within a subject-centered process of "remembering," he asks how the past is formed in consciousness through the "mnemonic agencies" (144a) of social relationships, as well as of objects and landscapes invested with social meanings. Recent anthropological (and historical) concern with memory, and with "the past in the present" (see below), has aroused new interest in Halbwachs's work (30, 40, 186a), ignored in Anglo-American anthropology despite Bastide's (8a) classic study.

Other ambiguities appear in the Durkheimian paradigm. On the one hand, Durkheim's notion of temporal category is ambiguous, because it blends substantive, variable cultural categories with Kant's transcendental mental forms (121:447–48; see 62 for a detailed critique). On the other hand, although time consists of collective representations or "categories," not of "becoming" or "motion," this Durkheimian notion of time as collective concepts looks ever behind itself at social "rhythms"—i.e. time as process constituted in the unfolding of activities. The locus of time thus retains a subterranean ambiguity, although overtly located in concepts or representations.

Time Reckoning: Malinowski and Evans-Pritchard

In Malinowskian functionalism time concepts emerge as "time-reckoning" (147), suggesting emphasis on time as the measure of motion (to use Aristotelian terms). Malinowski views time-reckoning as a means of "coordinating activities," dating events, and gauging the length of time spans (124:203). Time puts on mundane, empiricist clothing, instead of the "qualitative," myth-ritual dress (e.g. 73) of Durkheimian representations.

In this approach—which Rigby (164: 429, 432ff) calls "both abstract and empiricist"—temporal representations are frequently indigenous vocabulary concepts, such as terms for the seasons, the day and its parts, etc (11, 12, 19, 48, 49).[5] Action is also carried along in the time-reckoning frame due in part to concern with the kinds of repetitive processes used to reckon time. Thus, in contrast to Nilsson's (147) designation of a natural source for time-reckoning, Malinowski (124:210–11) argues that gardening activities rather than natural sequences are the ordinary media of Trobriand time-reckoning, although gardening experts make use of an "independent [natural] scheme of time-reckoning" (namely, the lunar cycle). However, the emphasis on agricultural activities also integrally links the notion of "action" with "nature."

Evans-Pritchard's (48, 49) well-known notion of "oecological time" crystallizes the unresolvable ambiguities of the Functionalist and Durkheimian versions of the locus of time. Oecological time is identified essentially with time-reckoning concepts that convey "social activities" or a "relation between activities" (49:96, 100, 102). To the extent that he adopts this representational model, Evans-Pritchard takes time's passage to be "perceived" (49:103) through a lens of cultural concepts referring to activities (i.e. via the time-reckoning "system"), rather than experienced through immersion in the activities. But time also consists for him of the "rhythms" of basic activity cycles linked to natural cycles (such as the daily cattle movements and the seasonal passages between villages and camps) as well as each season's distinctive "tempos" [cf here the influence of Mauss (127; see 55b:13f)]. In this sense time is understood as motion or process, not static units or concepts functioning to reckon time.

5

    In a "Piagetian" study of "primitive thought," Hallpike (80:340–65) makes problematic use of such verbal categories of time-reckoning as evidence for the level of abstract time capacities culturally available in a given society. Hallpike's reductive notion of time requires more critical attention than I can give it here. For a general criticism see Schweder (167a).

When he turns to long-term, "structural time" Evans-Pritchard's gaze shifts away from activities (which provide a sense of concrete movement) to entirely conceptual frames referring to abstract "relations between groups of persons"; in his view, these concepts provide only an "illusion" of temporal "movement" (49:105, 107). Thus the study of transgenerational relations of age grades and lineage/descent constructs as forms of long-term time, or time-reckoning, enters the anthropological literature (e.g. 6b, 10, 18, 32, 33, 47, 59, 83, 114, 164, 186) in the now well-known form of an abstract space of "structural distance." Lineage time, for instance, is "not a continuum, but a … relationship between two points," with a "constant number of steps" (49:105–8) between ancestors and living groups or persons. Because it is noncumulative, engaging a limited set of nonprogressive positions rather than an incremental movement, the genealogical grid creates only an immobilized "illusion" of time (49:107). The space of Evans-Pritchard's structural time is thus not concrete and qualitative but geometrical (cf 58:67) and quantitative—rather like a social-structural version of Bergson's spatialized time. I argue below that this static vision derives from excising the concrete and meaningful lived space of activity from this kind of time, thus creating an anthropological "synoptic illusion" (21:97f).

The theoretical turn that treats structural time as an abstract space also detaches oecological time from concrete oecological space. "Oecological space," like Evans-Pritchard's "structural space," is defined in terms of distance. The latter consists of abstract social distance between groups (e.g. tribes); the former of concrete socio-geographical distances between communities, specified "in terms of density, and distribution," and described as if from the perspective of an airplane "fly[ing] over Nuerland," rather than (as in oecological time) from the perspective of people's activities within it (49:109f). Activity space is thus deleted.

Yet when describing "oecological time," Evans-Pritchard obviously draws on spatiotemporal periodicity (e.g. the phased movements between camp and village). This co-constitution of time and space in activity is ignored, however, in his analytic frame. I infer that Evans-Pritchard equates activity (and natural cycles) with time, and opposes time to space.

We can see from this pattern of oppositions and identifications that intrinsic to the vision of structural time as illusory is the tendency to set it loose from the concrete constructions of activity space-time and treat it as an abstract geometry of social distance. This "loosening" includes the separation of Nuer historical accounts of ancestral spatiotemporal activities (164:448ff) from the model of structural time, but I use another kind of example to reinforce my point. Burton's (28:114) critique of Evans-Pritchard's detachment of kinship and descent models from (concrete) space cites a song image of the Nilotic Atuot: "the ashes of the dung fire in my [cattle] camps are so very deep," meaning that "the singer is a descendent of an ancient ancestor whose people occupied the same space for uncountable years" (cf 50:3). The image of the deepening ash suggests the experience of temporal increment from the originating past (an "ancient ancestor"). Such images do not simply represent time in spatial metaphors. They are built on the spatiotemporal constitution of the world (the increasing ash in the hearth; the sense of a continuous or recurrent spatial occupation) emerging in and from daily activities, which conveys the connection of people with their ancestors. I return to other images of temporal increment below.

THE NOTION OF "STATIC" TIME

The idea of a noncumulative structural illusion of time is obviously not the only anthropological stereotype of "static" cultural formulations of time. An exemplar of another sort is Whorf's (192:139) argument that in European languages the "subjective 'becoming later' which is the essence of time" is "covered under" homogeneously quantifying and spatializing time concepts. If Whorf then takes the contrasting Hopi language to contain no "time"-referring forms (as commentators have often stressed; see 124a), it is apparently, because of his Bergsonian dichotomy of *durée* (non-spatialized, "psychological time") and spatialized "time" (192:57f., 216). Since, in his view, Hopi expresses *durée* only, he calls it (paradoxically) "timeless (192:216). (For linguistic evidence that Hopi does in fact "spatialize" time, see 124a.)

The use of the Bergsonian dichotomy to signify cross-cultural difference is part of a larger discourse of dichotomous temporal stereotypes that posit the notion of "static" time. This discourse necessarily entails an independent locus of (nonstatic) temporality, which explicitly or implicitly defines the writer's view of quintessential features of time. In this kind of "objectivism" (see 105:xii, 160f; cf also 164a), certain cultural time concepts do not accurately "mirror" these features but, according to the dichotomous model, deform them.[6]

This model appears in Geertz's (57) pioneering attempt (cf 98, 106) to articulate Balinese views of person and time. In a "configurationalist" version of Evans-Pritchard's structuralist illusory time, he argues that Balinese culture as a whole detemporalizes experience. Thus Balinese kinship terms, teknonymy, and calendric categorizations provide at the most an "illusion" of temporality [as Geertz (57:375) says explicitly of the kinship terms].

As a foil against which to define this Balinese pattern of time, Geertz employs a broad interpretation of certain temporal features implicated in Schutz's (167:15–19, 218–22) notion of consociative interaction and his paradigm of "consociates," "contemporaries," "successors," and "predecessors" (who frame different "time perspectives" of Ego's social field). Schutz's com-

---

6
    The notion of "static" time also has a more self-conscious, critical function as part of a meta-language concerned with the adequacy of anthropological discourse. An example is Bourdieu's (21:97) well-known notion of the "synoptic illusion" (see below).

munication-based model grounds social time in consociative processes in which people actively create intersubjectivity and a sense of coordinated life times in the "vivid present" (167:220) of daily interaction. Geertz argues that Balinese culture mutes this experience by reformulating interaction in terms of "an unperishing present" of anonymous "stereotyped contemporaries" (57:379, 389). The temporal experiences generated in consociation are thus detemporalized. This includes the concrete experience of "biological aging" and its implicate, "a sense of temporal flow," emerging in the consociative process of "growing older together"; as well as the capacity of successors and predecessors to perceive "one another in terms of origins and outcomes and ... experience the ... linear [measurable] progress of standard, transpersonal time" (57:391, 406; after 167:221–22).

Geertz adopts this Schutzian phenomenological model of intersubjective process as an acultural frame of reference: By characterizing time in these acultural terms, he defines, in effect what he means by cultural detemporalization.[7] But it is also as if the Schutzian model inserts within Geertz's discussion a social space where interacting subjects reside, actively constructing "true" temporal experience. Conversely, Balinese cultural time is shown not as an interactive process but largely as a set of forms or elements of a worldview [an *opus operatum* (21:18)] whose supposedly atemporal implications mute this intersubjective time. To transpose a point of Fabian's (51:56): the temporality of praxis is removed from the realms of Balinese culture and given its place in an acultural world.

Geertz's view that Balinese teknonymy emphasizes "social regenesis" might not seem to imply detemporalization, but for Geertz (57:377–79; cf pp. 389–91) this emphasis obscures the "processes of biological aging" as well as historical progression from an ancestral past, focussing instead on descendants and a person's "procreative status." On the face of it, this suggests an emphasis on dynamic growth, looking forward to the child (in this sense, to the future). It is detemporalizing only by reference to an "essentializing," selective presupposition about what constitutes temporality, which Geertz specifies largely via his Schutzian world of interpersonal time.

Teknonymy is also abstracted from a wider Balinese scene. Geertz's own data point to past as well as future references engaged, as one might expect, in Balinese residential and descent group genesis. The Balinese notion of "origin" (60:52–53; cf 57:395) is applied to a household from which new houseyards have hived off. Members of the houseyard—"one emergence"—maintain links with the past; temples of newer locales refer to their earlier "sources." Because any given Balinese or social group is situated within this developmental process, the fact of this "situatedness" could be incorporated into an account of Balinese temporality as a process in which the "present" of

7
    Geertz has been read as attempting to refute Schutz's universalism (4:151). I offer an additional reading based on his rhetorical use of Schutz's model.

the subject (individual or group) is the reference point from which one looks backward to origins or "pasts" and forward to what might emerge from the present (making the subject into an originating source for a future growth). Such a perspective takes the position of a subject into the anthropologist's model of cultural time (and cultural time into the model of the subject), thus suggesting another way of incorporating a phenomenological framework into a cultural account. The model does not yet animate cultural forms with agentive action (or interaction); I return to this notion below.

Temporal illusions re-emerge as Marxian "mystifications" in Bloch's (18) much-discussed Malinowski lecture (3a, 24, 27, 51:44f, 62, 90, 182, 186c:11). Opposing both Durkheim's view of the social source of time "cognition" and Geertz's that Balinese culture wholly detemporalizes time, Bloch divides Balinese time into socio-ritually derived, ideological "mystifications" involving "static," "cyclic," "nondurational" time forms; and universal, unmystified knowledge of "durational," "linear" time (18:284). The latter derives from practical (agricultural) activities constrained only "by the requirements of human action on nature" (18:278). Bloch's binary framework is thus reminiscent of Evans-Pritchard's contrast between structural (static) and oecological (nature/daily-life-activity) time (see above). But it transforms this contrast into a theory—influenced by Marxism—of temporal cognition, illusion, and reality. Practical activity provides an extra-societal vantage point enabling cross-cultural communication: The mind escapes from social illusions of time into true temporal knowledge based on an "empirically" derived cognition that has somehow bypassed any sociocultural constitution of reality (cf 186:189)—not to mention what the Balinese themselves may count as empirical reality.

Howe (90) has opposed Bloch's Maginot Line dividing Balinese time, pointing to a coherent cultural time concept operative in agriculture and rite, which entails both repetition ("circularity") and fixed sequence ("linearity"). Both cohere in Balinese "notions of duration." In Howe's view, people universally "perceive" time's passage—the "succession of events" Howe calls "duration" (90:222, 231)—only via such differentiated cultural concepts (including images) or modes of "time-reckoning." Howe is, one presumes, opposing an illusionary model of time; but even so, time defined as the "succession of events" (90:231) still stands outside cultural time understood as representations or concepts that merely reflect this succession (i.e. time as ongoing duration) in cross-culturally varied formulations. We are back to the impasse of these different objectivist frameworks in which cultural time consists of fixed concepts of time that may or may not, in the author's view, adequately represent the temporal process excluded from them. In short, cultural time is not itself viewed as temporal. These frameworks are not merely simplified; at the minimum, they cannot take account of the problem that people are "in" cultural time, not just conceiving or perceiving it.

Time Typifications and Images of Repetition and Growth

The illusional model of time often draws on dichotomous abstractions like cyclic-circular vs linear, and spatial vs temporal. Used for a wide spectrum of purposes (not necessarily involving the idea of "static" time) to characterize or "synopsize" patterns of time (45, 52, 82a, 74, 113, 198:113ff), such dichotomies have a long history in Western time theory (see e.g. 135, 190:128, 131ff, 167c). The geometric labels refer to the temporal "aspects" (cf 113:125) of repetition and succession actually cohering within concrete temporal processes, which are thus analytically detached and opposed as binary typifications contrasting intra- or inter-cultural "types" of time. Similarly, as noted above, stereotypically opposed space and time are aspects of each other within the lived world.

The circular-linear opposition has also been questioned on the basis that so-called "circular" (repetitive) time does not logically exclude "linear" sequencing because each repetition of a given "event" necessarily occurs later than previous ones (7:126–29; 62:sec. 4; 90:231f; 146:57). The analogy between time and a circle closing back on itself misleads here (146:57).

These points return us to the notion of noncumulative time. Not only does it seem to persist as a general stereotype (5:332; 47:198–203), but the view that the time implications of lineage structures are typically noncumulative warranted a critique as late as 1990 (186). In his examination of this and related issues concerning the historical representation of time as process, Valeri (186:158) argues, for instance, that such forms as the "status lineage" entail a cumulative time "since birth order in a previous generation overrules birth order in a later one."

Varied ethnographic accounts since the 1970s give substantial evidence of the widespread view of long-term time as an incremental process, often conveyed in organic images of "continuous and progressive" growth (153:164; 55, 153), or in ancestral, creative place-to-place travel involving increasing extension from an origin place (70:178; 88, 93, 154, 164).

South American studies of time and space (see especially 152), combining developmental ideas of descent groups with Lévi-Straussian semiotic frames, emphasize this point. C. and S. Hugh-Jones (92-94), for instance, show that the Northwest Amazonian Barasana view their patrilineal descent groups as incrementally traveling or growing away from their ancestral origins: "as generations pile up like leaves [on the forest floor], living people are taken further and further away from the ancestors" (94:215; see also 93:167). This increasing separation is undesirable: Repetitive male initiation "squashes the pile" (94:209), reversing through human action the growth of generations from the originating past.

This leaf imagery shows how repetition, successiveness, and developmental components may be bound in dense spatiotemporal images that iconically convey time's form within their own form. Thus generational succession appears as incremental repetition uniting the qualitative dimension of "leafiness" with quantity or measure grasped as a process of leaf piling (recall the growing ash pile in the Atuot example). Far from "repetitive" and "nonrepetitive events" involving "logically" distinct "aspects of time" only artificially connected, as Leach (113:125) would have it, repetition here is inextricable from the nonrepetitive growth it produces. Nor do these homogeneous units (the leaves) define a static segmentation: When reiterated, the leaf "reflected in itself" changes from a "delimited meaning" unit into "an indefinite semantic ambience" (138:41) of leafy potential for increase, and implication of past increase.

Barasana must "squash" this transgenerational increase back to the beginning, operating dialectically on self-reproductive increment. Putting time "into reverse" (113:128) is thus time-creative or renewing (61:344; 113:135), but as C. Hugh-Jones (93) has effectively argued for the similar space-time patterns in a range of Barasana practices, it is the dialectical relations that define the form of this time (her "space-time") as they produce it. One is thus reluctant to "flatten" these complex processual forms into Leach's (113:135) static Durkheimian view that reversals *"create time* by creating intervals" (Leach's emphasis)—thus, that intervals in themselves define time's basic form.

TIME RECKONING: ANOTHER LOOK

A significant part of the anthropology of time has been concerned with how time is "counted" (measured) or "told," and with calendric categories, schedules, and the periodization of activities. Often using the portmanteau labels of "time-reckoning," the "calendar," or other notions such as "temporal orientations" (79), the relevant literature covers a wide range of perspectives; accounts may also be encapsulated in studies with broader intent (7, 10a, 11, 18, 27, 28d, 34, 35, 37, 56, 79, 83, 95a, 111, 112, 123a, 124, 125, 148b, 158, 160a, 172, 175, 176, 178a, 182, 185, 198, 199).[8] An interconnecting historical literature examines the history of clocks (e.g. 28c, 107, 139).

Strictly construed, "time-reckoning" refers to the use of selected cultural categories, or contingent events ["time indications" (147)] to "tell time"—to ask "when" something happened, will or should happen—and to "measure" duration—to ask "how long" something takes, or to "time" it. The relevant categories may segment natural processes (including diurnal, solar, and lunar cycles) or human activities into successive intervals. But the presence of category series involving, for example, task sequences or lunations does not in itself imply their generalized use in time-telling or measurement (79:230; 49:100). Like contingent events, they become a time-reckoning in the strict sense only if used to define "reference points" (79:216) or "axes of orienta-

---

8

One approach meriting more study examines exchange cycles as ways of segmenting and measuring life-cycle time (31, 106).

tion" (26:7) for these specific purposes. In this sense, time-reckoning is a particular kind of "comportment towards time" (85:259).

Time-telling is operationalized by formulating a conjunction or synchronization (cf 19:316; 26:8; 17:618; 174:59f) between the reference point and the event to be located—for instance, in planning to meet at sunrise, or in recalling an event's occurrence in World War II.[9] Time-telling also implicitly measures duration. For instance, it implies a temporal distance between the deictic "here-now" (82:5; 167:133) of the time-teller and the conceptualized conjunction. However, the aim of measurement may be explicit in notions of duration (as, "a long visit") or through counting homogeneous intervals such as hours, moons, or "sleeps" (79:222). In addition to questions of "how long" or "how many," the related question of "how fast" (62:sec. 12; 141:41; 142:284ff; 153:160; 168:507) is especially significant because, as we shall see, it forms a direct bridge to body time.

Two related concerns have been paramount in the time-reckoning literature: 1. the procedures and kinds of knowledge involved in determining "what time it is" at any given moment—for example, how people determine what lunar month they are in, or how lunar and solar cycles are articulated through intercalating months, etc (34, 111, 112, 124, 182); and 2. the connection between task or activity sequences (especially agricultural tasks) and natural phenomena in seasonal time-reckoning concepts and procedures (49, 79, 83, 124). Since Malinowski, the importance of sequences of tasks as "reference points" used in time-reckoning has been regularly noted. However, the emphasis on activities and activity sequences as time-reckoning media merely highlights the failures of the models of time discussed above to consider time-reckoning as itself a temporal activity. The notions of action available in this tradition—as a referent of time concepts or medium of time-reckoning, or as a "rhythmic" round of activities—do not carry the idea of action as an intrinsically temporal "project" (166:91ff; 167:68–96) of purposeful human agency.

This latter view of time-reckoning can be explained by way of an example involving the concern of Nebilyer Valley (Highland New Guinea) peoples (130:238) with "energetic planning." Preparing events, people use remarks like " the sun/time is finishing (i.e. time is passing, we must get on with things)." The implication is that workers need to hurry because relative to the sun (the term for "time" in Nebilyer usage), they are behind. Such remarks are even "made early in the day ... [so they are not merely] references to the actual time of day, but are part of the construction of events"—an attempt to "move events along and discover what they hold in store" (130:238).

9

  The reference point may entail a "temporal zero-point" or "deictic center" as in deictics such as "They will come later" (115:73ff; 123:683). Anthropological time-reckoning studies (in contrast to linguistics) give little attention to these forms.

Thus the time being told relates to the time of one's purposes: to the sense that one is not (in our own expression) "on time." This concern requires relating the actor's speed to some defined standard of timing. In this instance, time is measured through correlating bodily activity with the sun's motion, thus conjoining body time and an external motion used as a reference point to reckon people's time relative to a desired accomplishment (cf 168:507f). Moreover, "being slow" is not a neutral state. As an index of temporal distance from the accomplishment of certain purposes it carries "negative value" (143). A tensional relationship to the sun time, involving a striving to overcome this distance, is being created.

Through such procedures a nonbodily spatiotemporal motion (operating as a timing device) is symbolically referred to a bodily motion, and vice versa. In the 19th-20th century urban West, for instance, the developing control of the finegrained "demanding" structure of clock time involves an increasingly pervasive emphasis upon this mutually referring process. Not only is close determination of the speed of activity (as in work time) involved, but also the increasing use of the clock in telling time for other purposes (cf 99:110ff; 148a:199f; 146a, 149, 177). Both body time and clock time are being mutually refashioned in this process, as each takes on meanings from the other (see e.g. 149:175–79; Marx cited in 120:89).[10]

Of course, measuring the speed of activity represents only one kind of time-reckoning. But like this example, time-reckoning in general is constituted not merely in the conceptual reference point or codified system of timing, but also in the actor's "attending to" (160:34) such a reference point as part of a project that engages the past and future in the present—the space-time or "here-now" of the project. Actors are not only "in" this time (space-time), but they are constructing it and their own time (143:11ff) in the particular kinds of relations they form between themselves (and their purposes) and the temporal reference points (which are also spatial forms). The latter are not simply "natural" phenomena or clocks but may also involve other media such as visual charts of prescribed production sequences (e.g. 25a). This whole symbolic process may be called, following Fabian (51:74), "temporalization" (technically, "spatiotemporalization"). Time-reckoning is only one mode of temporalization. We may think of temporalization as going on in multiple forms, "all the time," whether it entails relatively "tacit knowing" (159, 160) or varying degrees of attention to time dimensions during the course of a project.

From this perspective, we can consider Wagner's (186b:81–95) view of time-reckoning. For Wagner, "literal time" "reduces" life time to a "common

---

   Such interchanges between time media and body time are not confined to time-reckoning: consider, for instance, the complex interchanges being formed between the body of the Quiche diviner-"daykeeper" and the crystals and "breath" of the calendar ("days/sun") during the divinatory questioning (176).

denominator" of intervals but does not express the "presence of time" ("epoch")—time's "nowness"—in our experience. Wagner's aim is to compensate for the failure of anthropologies of time to confront the latter temporal aspect. This is certainly a valid concern, but in dichotomizing literal and epochal time Wagner reproduces the problem he is attempting to overcome. I have argued instead that the experience of the "presence of time" is intrinsic to time-reckoning (subsumed under Wagner's "literal time"). All we need do is put time-reckoning back into time (and vice versa), where it belongs.

Ricoeur (162:169) poses another critique of the reduction of time to intervals and measurement, one that draws on Heidegger (see also 65:133). For Ricoeur, time measurement derives from the more fundamental imperative of "reckoning *with* time," or "taking [it] ... into account" (85:258), that derives from our being in the time of everyday activities. Time-telling or measurement presupposes, for instance, that "there is a [right and wrong] *time to do* this" (162:169, emphasis in the original). Without some sort of presupposition like this, time-telling or measuring would hardly take place.

One can see particular cultural forms of this premise in concepts like the Benedictine concern with the "appointed time" (198), and in calendars emphasizing "what kind of time it is" (57:393; cf 172, 175) in which the qualities defined in the conjunctions of different day sequences establish "auspicious" and "inauspicious" days for particular activities (cf also 98:744 and 172 for related concepts).[11] Cultural notions like these convey certain aspects of the underlying relevance of time-telling emerging in the purposes or practices of a particular lived world.

ACTOR, ACTION, AND TEMPORAL STRATEGY

I turn now to a consideration of action- or practice-based models of time (20–23, 40c, 64–68, 82, 141–144; cf also 51, 97:pt. 4). These models often frame relations among time, action, and the subject in terms influenced by phenomenological philosophies and Marxist notions of praxis, although elements of a Geertzian/Parsonian influence also appear (40a). Rather than being perched uncomfortably outside the world in temporal limbo "timelessly" (cf 51:41; 166a:191) perceiving or conceptualizing time, the subject in these models is situated within time and space, and may sometimes be envisioned as constructing the time and space he/she is in. Efforts have also been made to get subjects back into their bodies and (in certain symbolic studies) cultural formulations of the spatiotemporal back into bodily being (21, 28e, 38, 53, 61, 143, 180).

Varying attention has been given to formulating the complex relations among actor/subject, action, time, and space in a unitary framework. My own

---

11
   Contrary to Geertz (57), such calendars do not exclude a concern with time measurement (90, 176:3; see also 108:64ff).

studies directly address this problem but construe these relations in somewhat different ways. They all view action as a symbolic (meaningful, and meaning-forming) process in which people ongoingly produce both themselves as spatiotemporal beings and the space-time of their wider world (140–144; for a related emphasis from a linguistic perspective see 82).

Giddens's (64–67) effort to make time and space flow through his theory of structuration seems to falter on these points. In his work "no real account is provided as to how human agency is chronically implicated in the very structuring of time and space" (184:160; cf 143:10–11). Such an account would at the least have to view the spatiotemporal as comprising meaning relations being generated by actors in and through their already meaningful practices. But Giddens's actors and their spatiotemporal world receive only impoverished handouts of cultural meaning. His rather positivist agents act "in" time and space, make or follow "time-space paths" (67:133), or overcome the "restraints" of time-space through increasing technological "storage capacity" (65:91ff), etc. So, for instance, Giddens's notion of spatiotemporal "distantiation" or "presence and absence in human social relations" (65:38) lacks a vision of practices as "symbolic (meaning-forming) processes whereby distanced events or relations become meaning horizons of an actor's present" (144:1).

Bourdieu also incorporates time and space into his theory of practice (21, 23). In his early studies (20, 22), combining Marxian, Weberian, and phenomenological influences, he frames time through an agent-oriented lens. Thus he argues that pre-capitalist economies (exemplified by "traditional" Algeria) encourage "foresight" of the immediate future that is "implicit in the directly perceived present" (22:2, 8; cf 20). In capitalist economies, however, "forecasting" depicts "the [indefinite] future as a field of possibles to be explored … by calculation …" (22:8). Modes of future orientation rather than geometric models of circular vs linear time thus become characterizations of a society's time orientations [cf related temporal stereotypes of "past or future-oriented" (148:326) societies or social classes; of societies as annihilators or incorporators of historical change (116:233f; 55c:176ff)]. Clearly, such typifications do not confront the complexities of future constructions in multiple experiential contexts.

We may readily question Bourdieu's mode of differentiating future orientations in capitalist and noncapitalist societies, even in the specifically economic contexts to which it refers. For instance, societies practicing long-distance exchange do indeed regard the future as a "field of possibles to be explored … with calculation" in making long-range plans to obtain desired objects or returns, in the preparation of exchange networks for major transactions, and so forth.

More interesting is Bourdieu's phenomenologically influenced view of the actor looking forward through different modes of formulating the future beyond the present moment but experientially anchored within a present that engages both past and future horizons in one "context of meaning" (20:60). This forward-looking agent turns up in Bourdieu's recent work (21, 23) in the form of the game or exchange strategist (see below).

In these later studies, the temporality of action is integral to Bourdieu's theory of practice. Descriptions of practices should take account of the irreversible, ongoing time of activities, as well as of the agent's strategic manipulation of this time, rather than accounting for practices in terms of fixed "rules" external to practical time (21:9; 23:98). Such "totalizing" notions as "rules" and "reciprocity" (in exchange), or "linear" calendars used to describe temporally disparate activity cycles, take the time out of practices (21:97ff; 23:81–82, 105).[12]

When he examines calendric rhythms and periodization (21, 23), Bourdieu's agent-oriented lens tends to disappear (especially in Ref. 21) in the more conventional focus on the multiple rhythms of different production activities. But Bourdieu does not follow these "incommensurable islands of duration" into the microlevel of daily life where situated actors, operating in the light of expectations and past references available within their fields of meaning (see 20:60), strategically develop the sequences and tempos of work. Instead, he pursues the symbolic homologies that relate the different task cycles in a general "logic of practice."

The concept of "rhythm" in the sense of concrete movement does, however, connect Bourdieu's concept of time with space and the bodily actor (23:75–77). In a well-known passage, he points out that bodily activities or movements "make" and are "made by" the space of their enactment (21:90). Thus the body is continuously invested with the cultural meanings of space as space is invested with bodily meanings (21:90; 23:75–77). Furthermore, through the body's immersion in activity rhythms (including verbal action) it becomes imbued with "a whole relationship to time" (23:76). Spatiotemporality is thus constituted as part of the actor's habitus, held in bodily memory.

Only when Bourdieu switches to interactional models of "games" or "exchanges" does he again view activity as purposeful strategy that engages the future. For instance, in the immediacy of action the ballplayer "adjusts ... to what he foresees ... [and so] passes the ball not to ... where his team-mate is but to the spot he will reach ... [thus launching himself] into the impending future" (23:81, 82).

In these contexts one encounters Bourdieu's actor strategically manipulating time (e.g. the interval in exchange) but not (at least in Bourdieu's explicit formulation) space. In *Outline of a Theory of Practice* (21), Bourdieu markedly privileges time over space in contexts of strategizing, and space over time

---

12

Weiner (187) also opposes the use of the notion "reciprocity" in describing exchange, but for reasons relating to another aspect of time. For her, the label implies that a given exchange is a completed temporal sequence, whereas in fact it may be a "moment" in a long-term regenerative exchange cycle.

in contexts of bodily motion. We have seen that special attention is later (23:76) paid to the temporality of bodily motion. However, space as a strategic medium of the competitive actor remains in the background. Significantly, strategic action is brought to the foreground in the chapter titled "The Work of Time" (23:98–111, my emphasis).

In accord with this dichotomy is Bourdieu's frequent introduction of strategic uses of time to illustrate the descriptive inadequacies of what he calls "detemporalizing science" (23:82f; 98ff; 20:4–9). Practice theory must take into account the "properties [practice] ... owes to the fact that it is constructed in time, that time gives it its form" (23:98). It seems that time is privileged over space in these contexts because it is invoked as the rhetorical opposite of object-oriented "science," which is typified as "detemporalizing." But in fact, space as well as time "gives [practice] its form," as shown in Bourdieu's example of the ballplayer passing the ball to a position where he expects the receiver to be. Obviously, the properties this practice owes to construction "in time" are also spatial (and vice versa). As the philosopher Ströker (173a:42) puts it, "temporal components are traceable in the spatial structure and spatial ... in the temporal."[13] Although Bourdieu's theory would seem to enjoin this sort of perspective, an implicit opposition of space and time appears to be at work in his thought (cf Evans-Pritchard, above), subtly undercutting the unified spatiotemporal framework his theory of practice requires.

Well-known among Bourdieu's ideas about time is his notion of the strategic play of transactors on the "interval" between giving and receiving (21:4ff, 15, 171ff; 23:98ff). From this perspective, exchange acts can be seen as a mode of temporalization (in the sense used above) in which the tempo and irreversibility of activity time are politically efficacious, symbolic media that actors manipulate. Bourdieu argues that the giver manipulates time ("irreversibility") by concealing "reversibility" (reciprocity with its implication of "interestedness;" cf 126). The delay between giving and returning enables the gift-act to be experienced as if it were "without any past or future" (21:171). Bourdieu's strategist thus obscures temporality by masking the pasts and futures embedded in the present.

The assimilation of "delay" to a Marxian notion of mystification does not accord well with the evidence from classic cases such as kula. For instance, the transactor of an opening kula gift may denigrate a recipient's kula abilities in order to make him "remember" his obligation to return a shell later. The giver deliberately evokes awareness of the future in the present (143:64). (For another critique using the kula case, see Ref. 62:sec. 27.) Nevertheless, this case also reinforces the importance of examining political strategies of timing in exchange.

---

[13] Some languages succinctly reflect this mingling of time and space by using one general category term for both (see 28g:199; 97a:92; 161:21; 167b:36). Pervasive, more general time-space connections in languages are well-known (cf 178b).

Developing this concern of Bourdieu's in connection with Cretan animal theft and retaliation, Herzfeld (87) stresses that Cretans both manipulate tempo to increment raids "gradually" and also introduce "timeless" oaths in an effort to suspend increasing distrust (87:306). An oath recasts "the suspect's word" in terms of the deities' immortal time (87:317). The oath-taking can be viewed as a transformative temporalization both of and in the time of the argument. Attention is then focused on an eternal continuum from past to future and an associated image of society's past condition of harmony between shepherds.

The strategic manipulation of tempo is also discussed in a study of waiters in Florida restaurants for fine dining (52b). Regulating timing to accommodate their clients' desires to "escape the harried industrial rhythm of food production and consumption," waiters must coordinate these time expectancies with the timing of the restaurant's "production techniques"; thus they avoid "misshaping duration, making its temporal quality overly present through excessive extension or excessive interaction [with clients]" (52b:20, 30). Part of the wider problem of managing time in work contexts (see e.g. 25a:103f; cf; also the Nebilyer Valley case discussed above), such strategic temporalizations illuminate ways in which time is not merely "lived," but "constructed" in the living.

TIME AND CHANGING TIME AS COSMO-POLITICAL POWER

Control over time is not just a strategy of interaction; it is also a medium of hierarchic power and governance (3, 27, 28f, 54, 73, 104:223ff; 108, 149, 177, 197). Here I consider some aspects of this problem partly in the context of changing time, a subject requiring more attention in anthropology (3, 27, 28f, 29:234, 44, 79:223ff; 157, 158, 168).

Authority over the annual calendar (the chronological definition, timing, and sequence of daily and seasonal activities), or of other chronological instruments like clock time, not only controls aspects of the everyday lives of persons but also connects this level of control to a more comprehensive universe that entails critical values and potencies in which governance is grounded. Controlling these temporal media variously implies control over this more comprehensive order and its definition, as well as over the capacity to mediate this wider order into the fundamental social being and bodies of persons. Hence, the importance of calendric and related time shifts connected with sociopolitical changes is more than political in the narrow pragmatic sense. It has to do with the construction of cultural governance through reaching into the body time of persons and coordinating it with values embedded in the "world time" of a wider constructed universe of power.

As an example, consider the pre-colonial "keeper of the calendar" on Simbu (Solomon Islands) (27). A member of the island's founding descent group, he controlled the coconut shell model (and associated knowledge) used to define the lunar cycles. These cycles reflected the symbolism and underlying "pendulum model of time" (27:255, after 113:133) organizing the informal temporal reference points known to all islanders, and in daily use. This group also controlled shell rings that drew on mana from the gods, giving power over the motility of winds, rains, and earthquakes. Through manipulating these rings and the coconuts, it regulated "the very motion of time" (27:259). Extending Burman's point, one can consider the "motion of time" they controlled as the motion of the people's daily activities in addition to that of the cosmic process.

Missionization affected this structure by introducing the abstract, numerical Gregorian calendar (with which the alternating winds were articulated) and subsidiary cycles like the seven-day week with its "pivotal" Sunday and twice-daily church services (27:262–63). The resulting transformed calendar is located especially in the control of the exogenous "Church and its agents" rather than the island's "root" clan (27:264). Indeed, the people view the missionaries' arrival as the founding act of these "new ways" (27:263). This common post-colonial notion of "new ways" shifts the relations of historic past to present. The present derives its meaning as a departure from earlier ways, but the latter are then dialectically implicated in the very idea of the new (cf 30:7f). Overall there is a different world time—regulated by a changed source of potency and political agents—in which the governance of daily and seasonal activity is grounded. Such transformations are familiar in the context of European colonization (see e.g. 29:xi, 234–36).

We need not go so far afield to demonstrate the cosmo-political significance of changing calendars. The French Republican calendric reform (197, 198) aimed at creating a radical "discontinuity between the [historico-political] past and present" (198:83) not merely by substituting one ordering chronology for another but also by using chronological features that conveyed the new cosmo-political vision of the state. For instance, its substitution of the rationalized decimal system for the septimal model of the Gregorian calendar was part of a systematic deletion of "the existing system of units of time [and] ... dating frameworks" (198:83). The decimal system defined a "new" world that opposed the Judaic-Christian tradition, grounding calendric time in another vision of the socio-cosmic foundation of political power.[14]

The changing regulation of work time in the West with its so-called "commodification" of time (66:130; 173:98; cf 156a:31–39) also illustrates control over timing as a mode of governance grounding the person and daily activity in a wider world order. A recent history of 19th century American time (149) argues that the development of standard time with its increased emphasis on clocks and watches substituted industrial and scientific authorities linked with "efficiency and convenience" for "religious guidelines for dividing up the day" that were grounded in the "natural law" of "God." Emerging amid conflicts

---

[14] On the structuring principles of codified calendars see (14:71f; 156, 163a:106–9).

about time at local and national levels, the over-all effect of standard time was thus a "reconstruction of ... the authority Americans used to govern themselves" in daily life (149:ix).

Behind standard time lay the "natural law" of astronomy, mediated through the observatories and the techno-industrial control of the railroads. When the Lowell Mills' 1851 timetable pointed out that the "divisions of the work day were based in standard time as defined by 'the meridian of Lowell'" (indicated by a local "regulator clock"), the mills thus "allied themselves with astronomy and science to invest their factory bells with an unimpeachable authority" (149:52). Later, bells could be triggered by synchronized clocks instead of being rung by personnel. As a result, "human authority merges with the clock's" (149:156).[15]

Clock time is thus concretized in experience reaching (partly through the sonorous bells and increasing visibility of the clock) into the body to fuse with body time[16] and space and back out into the visible object world of clocks and bells which cohere with the wider cosmic order of industry, science, and technology. We can see from this that an analytical perspective that views clock time as a "lifeless time," "a chronological series of points on a string" (97:7), is misleading. Considered in the context of daily activity, clock time is quite alive, embodied in purposeful activity and experience. Coordinately, people are ongoingly articulated through this temporalization into a wider politico-cosmic order, a world time of particular values and powers. This articulation may include conflicts over clock time, as well as daily operations carried on in its terms. Endowed with potency and affect, the clock may be "hated, endured ... [and] manipulated" (148a:199), or taken as a "moral timepiece" (177:87), etc. It is precisely in considering the spanning or ongoing movement between micro- and macro-levels and the complexity of such processes, with their embedded conflicts and attitudes, that we can say [to adjust a point of Merleau Ponty's (131:415) to the present argument]: "it is of the essence of [sociocultural-political] time to be in process of self production, and not to be; never, that is, to be completely constituted."

Examining the body's disciplining through the "temporal elaboration of the act," Foucault (54:151ff; cf 68) pursues this dynamic into the micro-level of body time. Commenting on an 18th-century French military ordinance on marching steps, he argues that an "anatomo-chronological" schema or "programme" for constructing an "obligatory rhythm" is set out which systemati-

---

[15] I do not address historical-cultural issues about the degree of current control of Western work time by the clock. For critiques of Thompson's (177) well known "linear progression from task-based time to clock time," see Refs. 169 and 189 (cf 173:111). On variably-based timing and other relevant time constructs in a North American high-technology work place, see Refs. 25a, 178c. On the continuing importance of "natural god-driven time" in American responses to daylight-saving time, see Ref. 136.

[16] This is one way in which number can enter bodily experience as time (cf 146a). For a study examining how this occurs through counting on the body see Ref. 133:43–44, 133–39.

cally segments the body into spatiotemporal units (54:152). These units reto-
talize bodily motion into a preplanned "rhythm" imposed by a "disciplinary"
militancy. "Time penetrates the body and with it all the meticulous controls of
power" (54:152; cf Bourdieu's view of bodily rhythm cited above).

Thus we return to the notions of temporal units or categorizing schema, and
"rhythm"—now viewed as media of diffuse political control, exerted as power
in the embodying process. This vision of body time may be brought together
with Bourdieu's bodily "geometer," embodying spatial boundaries and seg-
mentations within itself as it moves through space.

It would seem that the body is not only the fundamental means of tacit
temporalization (or spatiotemporalization) but also part of the vital means of
constant movement back and forth between the self and world time. The body
"lends itself to the practice of reconstructing the world" (28e:564)—here,
world time (or world space-time)—just as the latter lends itself to reconstructing body time (cf 28e).

TEMPORALIZATIONS OF PAST TIME; NOTES ON THE FUTURE

A cursory reading of the literature on historico-mythic time might initially
suggest a problem quite different from those just discussed. As Rigby
(164:437) has noted, anthropologists tend to treat historical (historico-mythic)
time as "a separate dimension of time, ... an analytically distinct conceptual
element among other such elements." In this context, converging perspectives
from Western historiography and anthropological studies of myth have led to a
focus on cultural concepts of successive "ages," including the originating
"mythic" phase with its distinctive, temporally ambiguous relation to a society's "present" (46, 128, 129, 132, 137, 154, 181). Since these studies examine
categories and modes of temporal distance constructing the past-present horizons of a society—the framework for relative temporal "locations" of events
(cf 55a)—they overlap with those examining genealogical, or age-grading
categories as sequential positions along this distance axis (see above).

One concern of these studies has been the mode of causal-temporal continuity and discontinuity between different "eras" (44, 46, 128; cf 63). Some issues
are similar to those discussed above in connection with "static time." For
instance, rather than modeling change in a causal-temporal continuum, "episodic" temporal phasing is said to form the past in terms of discontinuous
modes of existence, or to emerge through "transformative" acts. These concepts run into difficulties when they imply a radical difference from Western
thought. Similar episodic notions are available in past Western traditions of
history (193:52–53) as well as in contemporary Western ideas (155:120).

But the other side of temporal distance is the question of how such distances, or how various historico-mythic "pasts," are brought into the "here-

now" of the ongoing social world—i.e. how "presence" implicates "pastness." This concern enters variably into all the above studies, and numerous additional anthropological and related works concentrate on it, sometimes under the rubric of "historical (or collective) memory" (2, 3a, 6, 9, 25, 30, 36, 39, 47, 76–78, 81, 87a, 103, 110, 119, 155, 186, 186a, 186c, 191). I use this question to return finally to reconsidering anthropological compartmentalization of historical time.

Concern with the way the past enters the present foregrounds the implications of the meaningful forms and concrete media of practices for apprehension of the past. For instance, certain "views of time" are contained in the ways Ijesha (Nigerian) histories are embodied in the narrator's person (155:118, 123). Ijesha regard *itan* historical narratives as an active force "transformed from an immaterial transcendant state into a material creation through the [performer's] body" (109:272, cited in 155:118). A lineage title owner's use of the first person pronoun to tell an *itan* referring to his predecessors has an import similar to reincarnation [*atunbi,* containing *tun* ("to do something again")] (155:118, 123). It is part of the means by which a narrated ancestral event is given "presence" [cf similar identifications in positional succession elsewhere (e.g. 32, 33)].

In Apache narrations (8), ancestral place names orient listeners' minds to "look 'forward' into space," thus positioning them to "look 'backward' into time." Names identify "viewing points" "in front of" places; "as persons imagine themselves standing in front of a named site, they may imagine [themselves] ... standing in their 'ancestors tracks'" (8:112.) By taking the ancestor's position, a viewer transforms an ancestral "there-then" (what was for the ancestor, of course, a "here-now" of travel) into his/her own "here-now." Incorporated into the latter-day viewer's biography, ancestral events then become a particular form of "lived history" in Halbwachs's (78:43) sense. Coordinately, "A [specific] past [becomes] charged with the time of the now" (13:261), which also implies that it is charged with the expectancies or "possible futures" entailed in the "now." The time of the viewer, and that of the relevant landscape spaces with their ancestral meanings, "are being [mutually] refashioned in this process" (cf above).

The Apache case exemplifies the well-known concretizing of mythic-historical pasts in named places and their topographies through ancestral activities, especially travel (1a, 69, 77, 88, 110, 145, 154; cf also 52a:86ff; 165, 166b:178ff, on more immediate biographical pasts embedded in places). For instance, in desert Australian societies, ancestral travels make bodily "marks" that form the landscape (69, 140, 145). Concurrently, the landscape is created with an interior ("inside/underneath") dimension, as ancestors go "inside" where they remain hidden yet available to externalization in contemporary ritual performances (69, 140). This spatiotemporal complexity has posed problems to Australianists regarding the appropriate way to conceptualize Aboriginal formulations of the (ancestral) past-present relation (see 69:91ff; 174a). However, the interpretive issues raised go beyond the present discussion.

Here I wish merely to note that an immobile, enduring topography of ancestral "camps" and "paths" is created out of transient, sequential activities. This transformation accords with Parmentier's (154:136) notion of traveling as a "paradigmatic cultural act" establishing "spatiotemporal linkages" (the passage visibly marking the land with a path) that can transcend the given moment. Indeed, desert Australian notions of ancestral transformation can themselves be broadly understood as symbolic condensations of the sense of ongoing experience of connection between people and country generated in the traditional mobile existence.

From a different perspective, we can see that the expectancies and immediate past-references entailed in ordinary activities (for instance, food gathering) involve people in temporalizations which go on in a landscape invested with remembered ancestral events. These past events may be momentarily "out of focus," but they may also be brought into "focal awareness" (159:55ff), as in narrative commentaries often evoked by topographic features. Another kind of temporalization is then formed in which present activities become "charged" with the ancestral past, and the ancestral past with the present.

Of course, the multifeatured spaces people live in are "saturated" with varied temporal meanings (82:390; cf 87a, 122), including different kinds of pasts [some of which may be contested (see Refs. 87a, 110)]. A particular spatiotemporal formulation of past-present relations occurs when relative geospatial distance from a given reference point such as one's homeland is roughly correlated with the relative temporal distances of different eras from the present (e.g. 51, 72:29ff, 232ff; 86:33-49; 132). Similarly, a generic "pastness" relative to "present-futurity" may be introduced into the time coding of regions. Consider, for instance, the Portuguese variant (157) of a modern Western "nationalizing" mode of inflecting rural and non-industrialized regions with pastness while urban spaces are inflected with the progressive or future-oriented present (cf 194).[17]

I return now to Rigby's remark regarding the compartmentalization of historical time. My critique diverges from Rigby's Marxian concerns, without excluding his point that (Maasai) history is constructed in the consciousness of a movement embodying "the relations of past and present in the creation of a future" (164:451). I emphasize a similar view but also aim to release the past-present-future relation from its restrictive lodging in "myth" and "history."

---

[17]
Studies of the investment of moveable objects (rather than landscapes) with meanings about the past include accounts of heirlooms (188), memorials (103, 195), and archives and historical manuscripts (110, 116:241–42; 163a:116ff). Such media may be regularly reproduced rather than relatively enduring (103).

To begin with, examples like the Ijesha and Apache cases are clearly modes of temporalization that focus on ancestral/historical pasts. But the past-present-future relation, as I have argued, is intrinsic to all temporalizations irrespective of focus, inasmuch as people operate in a present that is always infused, and which they are further infusing, with pasts and futures or—in Husserl's (95) subject-oriented language—with relevant "retensions" and "protensions" (cf 144:5, 13).

Ways of attending to the past also create modes of apprehending certain futures (17, 52, 155; cf also 101) or of reconstructing a particular sense of the past in the present that informs the treatment of "the future in the present" (cf 144). Thus the Dinka man once "imprisoned in Khartoum called one of his children Khartoum [both] in memory of the place" and to exorcise the continuous agential power 'Khartoum' (the disturbing past) might have over him in the present and future (117:149).

Prophecy, including attention to the millenarian "figure of the End" (100:6), may focus on the future, but futures are projected out of construals made of or in relation to the present; and these construals in turn, as I have pointed out, cannot be detached from the ways pasts are felt to be in or excluded from the present. So, for instance, the Iraqw prophet (178:177f) speaks of the future as "the matter which I see"; the future is thus contained "*in potentia* at the [prophetic] moment." Since Iraqw historical narrative proceeds in such a way that the fulfillment of this potential "is the inescapable denoument of the episode," previously prophesied events enter into the listener's present as inevitable outcomes (178:177f). The past's realized prophecies thus argue that the future the prophet is seeing in a given present will indeed be realized. Obviously, it is not just Western scientists who "have the future in their bones" (C. P. Snow, cited in 89:169). On the one hand, the past-present-future relation is integral to temporalization in general; on the other, any part of the relation also tacitly implicates the other parts.

The difficulty is that the usual anthropological context for viewing this relation has been long-term historical-mythic time where, for anthropologists at least [unlike historians (e.g. 99, 100)], the problem of the future has typically been displaced by the past-present relation. Exceptions occur to this contextualization (20, 22, 78a, 123a) and to the anthropological neglect of the future within it (46, 155, 164); increasing attention is also being paid to futurity in non-Western societies (17, 52, 128, 130, 142–144). Yet even in accounts of prophecy and millenarianism, futurity is poorly tended as a specifically temporal problem (for exceptions see 17, 46, with brief comments in 71:40–41; 178:177ff; 182:592).[18] Thus anthropologists have viewed the future

---

18 The traditional anthropological focus on non-Western societies stereotyped as "past-oriented" has no doubt been a factor in this displacement. [Contrast sociological emphasis on the study of "future orientation" (see 14a, 148, 148a)]. Biersack's (17:232) recent point that "the future is at the heart of the [Papua New Guinea] Paiela cultural vision" exemplifies the increasing dissolution of this stereotyping.

in "shreds and patches," in contrast to the close attention given to "the past in the present" (a title evoking a whole field of study). In short, the future tends to be a displaced temporal topic, absent from its homeland in the past-present-future relation, whereas this relation itself has been kept in history rather than accorded its wider place in time.

CONCLUSION

The problem of time in anthropology, as in other disciplines, is subject to the Augustinian lament: how difficult to find a meta-language to conceptualize something so ordinary and apparently transparent in everyday life. Of course, this kind of difficulty is a problem of anthropology more generally; but if so, time with its pervasiveness, inescapability, and chameleonic character is the epitome of that problem. In this review, I have pointed out what seem to me to be some of the more embedded conceptual difficulties in the anthropology of time by looking at different senses in which our theoretical understandings of temporality hinge on the way we conceptualize its connections to space, action, and actor.

With these difficulties in mind, I have tentatively sketched a notion of "temporalization" that views time as a symbolic process continually being produced in everyday practices. People are "in" a sociocultural time of multiple dimensions (sequencing, timing, past-present-future relations, etc) that they are forming in their "projects." In any given instance, particular temporal dimensions may be foci of attention or only tacitly known. Either way, these dimensions are lived or apprehended concretely via the various meaningful connectivities among persons, objects, and space continually being made in and through the everyday world. This review has merely pointed to some kinds of temporalizations and anthropological visions of them by turning time briefly through a few of its traditional topics (e.g. time-reckoning, calendric patterns, cultural constructions of the past, time as a medium of strategy or control, etc). Obviously, many critical issues remain untouched in this limited exercise.

I conclude by returning to the book of sand with which I began. In that haunting parable, Borges's narrator, trying to lose the book, finally succeeds only by leaving it in a library of innumerable dusty books. Thus he lodges infinity in the place of its infinite reproduction—in the encompassing architecture of its own imaginings. Of course, by this act he merely shows us how it cannot be escaped. I have tried to show a little of that here.

ACKNOWLEDGMENTS

I am grateful to Jean Comaroff for a helpful reading of this paper in its final hours.

Literature Cited

1. Adam, B. 1988. Social versus natural time, a traditional distinction re-examined. In *The Rhythms of Society*, ed. M. Young, T. Schuller. London: Routledge
1a. Allen, N. 1981. The Thulung myth of the Bhume and some Indo-Tibetan comparisons. In *Asian Highland Societies in Anthropological Perspective*, ed. C. von Furer-Haimendorf, pp. 168–81. New Delhi: Sterling
2. Alonso, A. 1988. The effects of truth: representations of the past and the imagining of community. *J. Hist. Soc.* 1(1):33
3. Anderson, B. 1983. *Imagined Communities*. London: Verso
3a. Appadurai, A. 1981. The past as a scarce resource. *Man* 16:201–19
4. Austin-Broos, D. 1987. Clifford Geertz: culture, sociology and historicism. In *Creating Culture: Profiles in the Study of Culture*, ed. D. Austin-Broos, pp. 141–59. London: Allen & Unwin
5. Aveni, A. 1989. *Empires of Time: Calendars, Clocks and Cultures*. New York: Basic Books
6. Babb, L. 1984. Amnesia and remembrance in a Hindu theory of history. *Asian Folklore* 41:49–66
6a. Bakhtin, M. 1981. Forms of time and of the chronotope in the novel. In *The Dialogic Imagination*, pp. 84–258. Austin: Univ. Texas Press
6b. Barden, G. 1973. Reflections of time. *Hum. Context* 5(2):331–44
6c. Barnes, J. 1971. Time flies like an arrow. *Man* 6(4):537–52
7. Barnes, R. 1974. *Kedang: a Study of the Collective Thought of an Eastern Indonesian People*. Oxford: Clarendon
8. Basso, K. 1988. Speaking with names: language and landscape among the Western Apache. *Cult. Anthropol.* 3(2):99–130
8a. Bastide, R. 1960. Problems of the collective memory. In *The African Religions of Brazil*, pp. 240–59. Baltimore: John Hopkins Press
9. Battaglia, D. 1990. *On the Bones of the Serpent: Person, Memory and Mortality in Sabarl Island Society*. Chicago: Univ. Chicago Press
10. Baxter, P., Almagor, U., eds. 1978. *Age, Generation, and Time*, pp. 197–210. New York: St. Martin's Press
10a. Becker, J. 1979. Time and tune in Java. In *The Imagination of Reality: Essays in Southeast Asian Coherence Systems*, ed. A. Becker, A. Yengoyam. Norwood: Ablex
11. Beidelman, T. 1963. Kaguru time reckoning: an aspect of the cosmology of an East African people. *Southwest. J. Anthropol.* 19:9–20
12. Beidelman, T. 1986. Persons and time. In *Moral Imagination in Kaguru Modes of Thought*, pp. 84–104. Bloomington: Indiana Univ. Press
13. Benjamin, W. 1969. Theses on the philosophy of history. In *Illuminations*, pp. 253–64. New York: Schocken
14. Benveniste, E. 1974. *Le langage et l'experience. Problémes de linguistique generale*, 2:67–78. Paris: Gallimard
14a. Bergman, W. 1992. The problem of time in sociology: an overview of the literature on the state of theory and research on the "Sociology of Time," 1900–82. *Time & Society* 1(1):81–134
15. Bergson, H. 1927. (1889). *Essai sur les données immediates de la conscience*. Paris: P. U. F.
16. Bergson, H. 1946. (1896). *Matière et Mémoire*. Paris: P. U. F.
17. Biersack, A. 1991. Prisoners of time: a millenarian praxis in a Melanesian valley. In *Clio in Oceania: Toward a Historical Anthropology*, ed. A. Biersack, pp. 231–96. Washington, DC: Smithsonian Inst. Press
18. Bloch, M. 1977. The past and the present in the present. *Man* 12:278–92
19. Bohannon, P. 1967. (1953). Concepts of time among the Tiv. In *Myth and Cosmos*, ed. J. Middleton, pp. 315–30. New York: Natural History Press
19a. Borges, J. 1977. "The Book of Sand." In *The Book of Sand*. Transl. N. di Giovanni. New York: Dutton
20. Bourdieu, P. 1964. The attitude of the Algerian peasant towards time. In *Mediterranean Countrymen*, ed. J. Pitt-Rivers, pp. 55–72. The Hague: Mouton
21. Bourdieu, P. 1977. *Outline of a Theory of Practice*. Cambridge: Cambridge Univ. Press
22. Bourdieu, P. 1979. (1963). The disenchantment of the world. In *Algeria 1960*, pp. 1–94. Cambridge: Cambridge Univ. Press
23. Bourdieu, P. 1990 [1980]. *The Logic of Practice*. Stanford: Stanford Univ. Press
24. Bourdillon, M. 1978. Knowing the world or hiding it: a response to Maurice Bloch. *Man* 13:591–99
25. Bourguet, M., Lucette, V., Wachtel, N., eds. 1986. Between memory and history. *History and Anthropology*:2(Part 2)
25a. Bucciarelli, L. 1988. Engineering design process. See Ref. 40c, pp. 92–122
26. Bull, W. 1971 [1963]. *Time, Tense and the Verb*. Berkeley: Univ. Calif. Press
27. Burman, R. 1981. Time and socioeconomic change on Simbo, Solomon Islands. *Man* 16(2):251–68
28. Burton, J. 1983. Same time, same space: observations on the morality of kinship in pastoral, Nilotic societies. *Ethnology* 22(2):109–19
28a. Burton, R. 1975–1976. The human aware-

ness of time: an analysis. *Philos. Pheno-
menol. Res.* 36(3):303–18
28b. Cassirer, E. 1955. *The Philosophy of Symbolic Forms,* Vol. 2. New Haven: Yale
Univ. Press
28c. Cipolla, C. 1978 [1967]. *Clocks and Culture: 1300–1700.* New York: W. W. Norton
28d. Colson, F. 1926. *The Week: An Essay on
the Origin and Development of the Seven
Day Cycle.* Cambridge: Cambridge Univ.
Press
28e. Comaroff, J. 1985. Bodily reform as historical practice: the semantics of resistance
in modern South Africa. *J. Int. Psychol.*
20(4/5):541–67
28f. Comaroff, J. 1991. Missionaries and Western clocks: an essay on religion and history
in South Africa. *J. Relig.* 71(1):1–17
28g. Comaroff, J., Comaroff, J. L. 1987. The
madman and the migrant: work and labour
in the historical consciousness of a South
African people. *Am. Ethnol.* 14:191–209
29. Comaroff, J., Comaroff, J. L. 1991. *Of
Revelation and Revolution: Christianity,
Colonialism and Consciousness in South
Africa,* Vol. 1. Chicago: Univ. Chicago
Press
30. Connerton, P. 1989. *How Societies Remember.* Cambridge: University Press
31. Coppet, D. de. 1970. 1, 4, 8; 9, 7. la mon-
naie: présence des morts et mesure du
temps. *L'homme* 10(1):17–38
32. Cunnison, I. 1956. Perpetual kinship: a political institution of the Luapula people.
Rhodes Livingston Inst. J. 20:28–48
33. Cunnison, I. 1957. History and genealogies
in a conquest state. *Am. Anthropol.* 59:20–
31
34. Damon, F. 1982. Calendars and calendrical
rites on the northern side of the kula ring.
Oceania 52(3):221–39
35. Damon, F. 1990. Time and values. In *From
Muyuw to the Trobriands: Transformations
along the Northern Side of the Kula Ring,*
pp. 16–53. Tucson: Univ. Arizona Press
36. Davis, N., Starn, R., eds. 1989. *Representations* 26 (Spec. Issue: *Memory and
Counter-Memory*)
37. Davis, R. 1976. The northern Thai calendar
and its uses. *Anthropos* 71:3–32
38. Devisch, R. 1985. Symbol and psychoso-
matic symptom in bodily space-time: the
case of the Yaka of Zaire. *J. Int. Psychol.*
20(4/5):589–616
39. Dillon, M., Abercrombie, T. 1988. The destroying Christ: an Aymara myth of conquest. See Ref. 87b, pp. 50–77
39a. Doob, L. 1978. Time: cultural and social
anthropological aspects. In *Timing Space
and Spacing Time,* ed. T. Carlstein, D. Par-
kas, N. Thrift, 2:57–65. London: Arnold
40. Douglas, M. 1980. Introduction. See Ref.
78, pp. 1–21
40a. Dubinskas, F. 1988. Cultural constructions: the many faces of time. See Ref. 40c,
pp. 3–38
40b. Deleted in proof
40c. Dubinskas, F., ed. 1988. *Making Time:
Ethnographies of High-Technology Organizations.* Philadelphia: Temple Univ.
Press
41. Durkheim, E. 1953 [1898]. Individual and
collective representations. In *Sociology
and Philosophy.* London: Cohen & West
42. Durkheim, E. 1915 [1912]. *The Elementary
Forms of the Religious Life.* London: Allen
& Unwin
43. Durkheim, E., Mauss, M. 1963 [1903].
Primitive Classification. London: Cohen &
West
44. Eickelman, D. 1977. Time in a complex
society: a Moroccan example. *Ethnology*
16(1):39–55
45. Eliade, M. 1954 [1949]. *Cosmos and History: The Myth of the Eternal Return.* New
York: Harper & Row
46. Errington, F. 1974. Indigenous ideas of order, time and transition in a New
Guinea cargo movement. *Am. Ethnol.*
1(2):255–68
47. Errington, S. 1989. Forgetting genealogies.
In *Meaning and Power in a Southeast
Asian Realm,* pp. 203–31. Princeton:
Princeton Univ. Press
48. Evans-Pritchard, E. 1939. Nuer time reckoning. *Africa* 12:189–216
49. Evans-Pritchard, E. 1940. *The Nuer.* Oxford: Clarendon
50. Evans-Pritchard, E. 1951. *Kinship and
Marriage among the Nuer.* Oxford: Clarendon Press
51. Fabian, J. 1983. *Of Time and the Other:
How Anthropology Makes its Object.* New
York: Columbia Univ. Press
52. Farriss, N. 1987. Remembering the future,
anticipating the past: history, time and cosmology among the Maya of Yucatan.
Comp. Stud. Soc. Hist. 29(3):566–93
52a. Feld, S. 1982. *Sound and Sentiment: Birds,
Weeping, Poetics and Song in Kaluli Expression.* Philadelphia: Penn. Univ. Press
52b. Felz, G., McDonogh, G. 1989. Waiting:
Temporality, manipulation and service in
fine dining. Paper presented at Am. Ethnol.
Soc. Meet., Spring 1989, Santa Fe.
53. Fernandez, J. 1982. *Bwiti: An Ethnography
of the Religious Imagination in Africa.*
Princeton: Princeton Univ. Press
53a. Fortes, M. 1949. Time and social structure:
an Ashanti case study. In *Social Structure:
Studies Presented to A. R. Radcliffe-
Brown,* ed. M. Fortes, pp. 54–84. New
York: Russell & Russell
54. Foucault, M. 1979. Docile bodies. In *Discipline and Punish.* New York: Vintage
Books
55. Fox, J. 1971. Sister's child as plant: metaphors in an idiom of consanguinity. In *Rethinking Kinship and Marriage,* ed. R.
Needham, London: Tavistock
55a. Fox, J. 1979. Standing in time and place:
the structure of Rotinese historical narratives. In *Perceptions of the Past in South-*

east Asia, ed. A. Reid, D. Marr. Singapore: Heinemann

55b. Fox, J. 1979. Translator's forward. In *Seasonal Variations of the Eskimo*, M. Mauss, H. Beuchat, pp. 1–17. London: Routledge & Kegan Paul

55c. Friedman, J. 1985. Our time, their time, world time: the transformation of temporal modes. *Ethnos* 50(3–4):169–82

56. Gaborieau, M. 1982. Les Fêtes, le temps et l'espace: structure du calendrier Hindou dans sa version Indo-Nepalese. *L'Homme* 22(3):11–29

57. Geertz, C. 1973 [1966]. Person, time and conduct in Bali. In *The Interpretation of Cultures*, pp. 360–411. New York: Basic Books

58. Geertz, C. 1988. *Works and Lives: The Anthropologist as Author.* Stanford: Stanford Univ. Press

59. Geertz, H., Geertz, C. 1964. Teknonymy in Bali: parenthood, age grading and genealogical amnesia. *J. Roy. Anthropol. Inst.* 94:94–108

60. Geertz, H., Geertz, C. 1975. *Kinship in Bali.* Chicago: Univ. Chicago Press

61. Gell, A. 1975. *The Metamorphosis of the Cassowaries.* London: Athlone Press

62. Gell, A. 1992. *The Anthropology of Time.* London: Berg. In press

63. Gellner, E. 1971. Our current sense of history. *Arch. Eur. Sociol.* 12:159–79

64. Giddens, A. 1979. *Central Problems in Social Theory: Action, Structure and Contradiction in Social Analysis.* Berkeley: Calif. Univ. Press

65. Giddens, A. 1981. *A Contemporary Critique of Historical Materialsm.* Berkeley: Univ. Calif. Press

66. Giddens, A. 1981. Time, labour and the city. See Ref. 65, pp. 129–56

67. Giddens, A. 1984. *The Constitution of Society: Outline of the Theory of Structuration.* Berkeley: Calif. Univ. Press

68. Giddens, A. 1984. Foucault on timing and spacing. See Ref. 67, pp. 145–61

69. Glowczewski, B. 1988. *Du rêve á la loi chez les Aborigenes: Mythes, rites et organisation sociale en Australie.* Paris: Presses Universitaires de France

70. Goldman, I. 1977. Time, space and descent: the Cubeo example. See Ref. 152, pp. 175–84

71. Goody, J. 1968. Time: social organization. In *The International Encyclopedia of the Social Sciences,* ed. D. Sills. New York: Macmillan

72. Gossen, G. 1974. *Chamulas in the World of the Sun: Time and Space in a Maya Oral Tradition.* Cambridge: Harvard Univ. Press

73. Granet, M. 1968 (1934). Le temps et l'espace. In *La pensee Chinoise.* Paris: Albin Michel

74. Gurevich, A. 1976. Time as a problem of cultural history. In *Cultures and Time,* L. Gardet, A. Gurevich, A. Kagame, C. Laree,

A. Naher, et al, pp. 229–43. Paris: UNESCO Press

75. Gurvitch, G. 1964. *The Spectrum of Social Time.* Dordrecht: Reidel

76. Halbwachs, M. 1925. *Les cadres sociaux de la mémoire.* Paris: F. Alcan

77. Halbwachs, M. 1971 [1941]. *La topographie légendaire des Evangiles en Terre Sainte: Etude de mémoire collective.* Paris: Presses Universitaires de France

78. Halbwachs, M. 1980 [1950]. *The Collective Memory.* New York: Harper & Row

78a. Hall, E. 1959. *The Silent Language.* New York: Doubleday

78b. Hall, E. 1983. *The Dance of Life: The Other Dimension of Time.* New York: Doubleday

79. Hallowell, A. 1955 [1937]. Temporal orientations in western civilization and in a preliterate society. In *Culture and Experience,* pp. 216–35. Philadelphia: Penn. Univ. Press

80. Hallpike, C. 1979. *The Foundations of Primitive Thought.* New York: Oxford Univ. Press

81. Handelman, D., Shamgar-Handelman, L. 1990. Shaping time: the choice of the national emblem of Israel. In *Culture Through Time,* ed. E. Ohnuki-Tierney, pp. 193–226. Stanford: Stanford Univ. Press

82. Hanks, W. 1990. *Referential Practice: Language and Lived Space Among the Maya.* Chicago: Univ. Chicago Press

82a. Harkin, M. 1988. History, narrative and temporality: examples from the Northwest Coast. *Ethnohistory* 35(2):99–130

83. Harrison, S. 1982. Yams and the symbolic representation of time in a Sepik River village. *Oceania* 53(2):141–62

84. Harvey, D. 1989. *The Condition of Postmodernity.* Oxford: Basil Blackwell

85. Heidegger, M. 1982. *The Basic Problems of Phenomenology.* Bloomington: Indiana Univ. Press

86. Helms, M. 1988. *Ulysses Sail: An Ethnographic Odyssey of Power, Knowledge and Geographical Distance.* Princeton: Princeton

87. Herzfeld, M. 1990. Pride and perjury: time and the oath in the mountain villages of Crete. *Man* 25(2):305–22

87a. Herzfeld, M. 1991. *A Place in History: Social and Monumental Time in a Cretan Town.* Princeton: Princeton Univ. Press

87b. Hill, J., ed. 1988. *Rethinking History and Myth: Indigenous South American Perspectives on the Past.* Urbana: Univ. Illinois Press

88. Hill, J., Wright, R. 1988. Time, narrative and ritual: historical interpretations from an Amazonian society. See Ref. 87b, pp. 78–105

89. Horton, R. 1970 [1967]. African traditional thought and Western science. In *Rationality,* ed. B. Wilson, pp. 131–71. Oxford: Blackwell

90. Howe, L. 1981. The social determination of

knowledge: Maurice Bloch and Balinese time. *Man* 16:220–34

91. Hubert, H. 1905. Etude sommaire de la representation du temps dans la religion. *Annu. Ecole Pratique des Hautes Etudes* (section des sciences religieuses), pp. 1–39. (Reprinted 1909 in *Mélanges d'histoire des religions,* H. Hubert, M. Mauss. Paris: Librairies Félix Alcan et Guillamin Réunies)

92. Hugh-Jones, C. 1977. Skin and soul: the round and the straight. Social time and social space in Pira-Parana society. See Ref. 152, pp. 185–204

93. Hugh-Jones, C. 1979. *From the Milk River: Spatial and Temporal Processes in Northwest Amazonia.* Cambridge: Cambridge Univ. Press

94. Hugh-Jones, S. 1977. Like the leaves on the forest floor: space and time in Barasana ritual. See Ref. 152, pp. 205–17

95. Husserl, E. 1964. *The Phenomenology of Internal Time Consciousness.* Bloomington: Indiana Univ. Press

95a. Ingham, J. 1971. Time and space in Ancient Mexico: the symbolic dimensions of clanship. *Man* 6(4):615–29

96. Isambert, F. 1979. Henri Hubert et la sociologie du temps. *Rev. Française Sociol.* 20(1):183–204

97. Jaques, E. 1982. *The Form of Time.* New York: Crane Russak

97a. Kagame, A. 1976. The empirical apperception of time and the conception of history in Bantu thought. See Ref. 74, pp. 89–117

98. Kemper, S. 1980. Time, person and gender in Sinhalese astrology. *Am. Ethnol.* 7(4):744–58

99. Kern, S. 1983. *The Culture of Time and Space: 1880–1918.* Cambridge, MA: Harvard Univ. Press

100. Kosellek, R. 1985. *Futures Past: on the Semantics of Historical Time.* Cambridge, MA: MIT Press

101. Kosellek, R. 1985. Modernity and the planes of historicity. See Ref. 100, pp. 3–20

102. Deleted in proof

103. Kuchler, S. 1988. Malangan: objects, sacrifice and the production of memory. *Am. Ethnol.* 14(4):625–37

104. Kuper, H. 1947. *An African Aristocracy: Rank among the Swazi.* Oxford: Oxford Univ. Press

105. Lakoff, G. 1987. *Women, Fire and Dangerous Things: What Categories Reveal about the Mind.* Chicago: Univ. Chicago Press

106. Lambek, M. 1990. Exchange, time and person in Mayotte. *Am. Anthropol.* 92(3):647–71

107. Landes, D. 1983. *Revolution in Time: Clocks and the Making of the Modern World.* Cambridge, MA: Harvard Univ. Press

108. Lansing, S. 1991. *Priests and Programmers: Technologies of Power in the Engineered Landscape of Bali.* Princeton: Princeton Univ. Press

109. La Pin, D. 1977. *Story, medium and masque,* Vol. 1. PhD thesis. Univ. Wis., Madison

110. Lass, A. 1988. Romantic documents and political monuments: the meaning-fulfilment of history in Czech nationalism. *Am. Ethnol.* 15:456–71

111. Leach, E. 1950. Primitive calendars. *Oceania* 20(4):245–62

112. Leach, E. 1957. Primitive time-reckoning. In *A History of Technology,* ed. C. Singer, E. Holmyard, A. Hall, pp. 11–27. London: Oxford Univ. Press

113. Leach, E. 1961. Two essays concerning the symbolic representation of time. In *Rethinking Anthropology,* pp. 124–236. London: Athlone

114. Legesse, A. 1973. *Gada: Three Approaches to the Study of an African Society.* New York: Free Press

114a. Leon-Portilla, M. 1973. *Time and Reality in the Thought of the Maya.* Boston: Beacon

115. Levinson, S. 1983. *Pragmatics.* Cambridge: Cambridge Univ. Press

116. Lévi-Strauss, C. 1966. *The Savage Mind.* Chicago: Univ. Chicago Press

117. Lienhardt, G. 1961. *Divinity and Experience.* Oxford: Oxford Univ. Press

118. Lloyd, G. 1976. Views on time in Greek thought. See Ref. 74, pp. 117–48

119. Lowenthal, D. 1985. How we know the past. In *The Past Is a Foreign Country.* Cambridge: Cambridge Univ. Press

119a. Luckmann, T. 1991. The constitution of human life in time. In *Chronotypes: The Construction of Time,* ed. J. Bender, D. Wellbery, pp. 151–66. Stanford: Stanford Univ. Press

120. Lukacs, G. 1971. Reification and the consciousness of the proletariat. In *History and Class Consciousness.* Cambridge, MA: MIT Press

121. Lukes, S. 1972. *Emile Durkheim: His Life and Work.* New York: Harper & Row

122. Lynch, K. 1972. *What Time Is This Place?* Cambridge, MA: MIT Press

123. Lyons, J. 1977. *Semantics,* Vol. 2. Cambridge: Cambridge Univ. Press

123a. Mahieu, W. de. 1973. Le temps dans la culture Komo. *Africa* 43:2–17

124. Malinowski, B. 1927. Lunar and seasonal calendar in the Trobriands. *J. R. Anthropol. Inst.* 57:203–15

124a. Malotki, E. 1983. *Hopi Time: A Linguistic Analysis of the Temporal Concepts in the Hopi Language.* Amsterdam: Mouton

125. Maltz, D. 1968. Primitive time reckoning as a symbolic system. *Cornell J. Soc. Relat.* 3:85–111

126. Mauss, M. 1990 [1950]. *The Gift: the Form and Reason for Exchange in Archaic Societies.* New York: Norton

127. Mauss, M., Beuchat, H. 1968 [1904-1905]. Essai sur les variations saisonnières des

sociétés Eskimos. In *Sociologie et anthropologie*, M. Mauss, pp. 389–475. Paris: Presses Universitaires de France
127a. Maxwell, R. 1971. On social time. In *The Future of Time: Man's Temporal Environment*, ed. H. Yaker, H. Osmond, F. Cheek, pp. 36-72. Garden City: Doubleday
128. McDowell, N. 1985. Past and future: the nature of episodic time in Bun. In *History and Ethnohistory in Papua New Guinea*, ed. D. Gewertz, E. Schieffelin. *Oceania Monogr.* 28:26–39
129. McKinley, R. 1979. Zaman dan Masa, eras and periods: religious evolution and the permanence of epistemological ages in Malay culture. In *The Imagination of Reality*, ed. A. Becker, A. Yengoyan, pp. 303–24. Norwood: Ablex
130. Merlan, F., Rumsey, A. 1991. *Ku Waru: Language and Segmentary Politics in the Nebilyer Valley, Papua New Guinea*. Cambridge: Cambridge Univ. Press
131. Merleau-Ponty, M. 1962. *Phenomenology of Perception*. London: Routledge & Kegan Paul
132. Middleton, J. 1967 [1954]. Some social aspects of Lugbara myth. In *Myth and Cosmos*, ed. J. Middleton, pp. 47–62. New York: Natural History Press
133. Mimica, J. 1988. *Intimations of Infinity*. Oxford: Berg
133a. Minge-Klevana, W. 1980. Does labor time decrease with industrialization? A survey of time-allocation studies with CA comment. *Curr. Anthropol.* 21(3):279–98
134. Mitchell, W. 1974. Spatial form in literature: toward a general theory. In *The Language of Images*, ed. W. Mitchell, pp. 271–99. Chicago: Univ. Chicago Press
135. Mitchell, W. 1986. Space and time: Lessing's Laocoon and the politics of genre. In *Iconology: Image, Text, Ideology*, pp. 95–115. Chicago: Univ. Chicago Press
136. Mohavede, S. 1985. Cultural preconceptions of time: can we use operational time to meddle in God's time? *Comp. Stud. Soc. Hist.* 27:385–400
137. Morphy, H., Morphy, F. 1984. The 'myths' of Ngalakan history: ideology and images of the past in northern Australia. *Man* 19(3):459–78
138. Mukarovsky, J. 1977. *On Poetic Language. The Word and Verbal Art*, pp. 1–64. New Haven: Yale Univ. Press
139. Mumford, L. 1964 [1934]. *Technics and Civilization*. New York: Harcourt
140. Munn, N. 1970. The transformation of subjects into objects in Walbiri and Pitjantjatjara myth. In *Australian Aboriginal Anthropology*, ed. R. Berndt, pp. 141–63. Nedlands: Univ. West. Australia Press
141. Munn, N. 1977. The spatiotemporal transformations of Gawa canoes. *J. Soc. Océanistes* 33(54–55):39–53
142. Munn, N. 1983. Gawan kula: spatiotemporal control and the symbolism of influence.

In *The Kula: New Perspectives on Massim Exchange*, ed. J. Leach, E. Leach, pp. 277–308. Cambridge: Cambridge Univ. Press
143. Munn, N. 1986. *The Fame of Gawa: A Symbolic Study of Value Transformation in a Massim (Papua New Guinea) Society*. Cambridge: Cambridge Univ. Press
144. Munn, N. 1990. Constructing regional worlds in experience: kula exchange, witchcraft and Gawan local events. *Man* 25(1):1–17
144a. Munn, N. 1991. An essay on the cultural construction of memory in the Kaluli Gisaru. Paper presented at Soc. Cult. Anthropol. Meet., Boston
145. Myers, F. 1986. *Pintupi Country, Pintupi Self: Sentiment, Place and Politics among Western Desert Aborigines*. Washington, DC: Smithsonian Inst.
146. Newton-Smith, W. 1980. *The Structure of Time*. London: Routledge & Kegan Paul
146a. Nguyen, D. 1992. The spatialization of metric time: the conquest of land and labour in Europe and the United States. *Time & Society* 1(1):29–50
147. Nilsson, M. 1920. *Primitive Time-Reckoning*. Lund: C. W. K. Gleerup
148. Novotny, H. 1975. Time structuring and time measurement: on the interrelation between timekeepers and social time. In *The Study of Time II*, ed. J. Fraser, N. Lawrence, pp. 325–42. New York: Springer-Verlag
148a. Novotny, H. 1989. Mind, technologies and collective time consciousness: from the future to the extended present. In *Time and Mind: the Study of Time VI*, ed. J. Fraser, pp. 197–216. Madison, CT: Int. Univ. Press
148b. Ohnuki-Tierney, E. 1973. Sakhalin Ainu time reckoning. *Man* 8(2):285–99
149. O'Malley, M. 1990. *Keeping Watch: A History of American Time*. New York: Penguin Books
150. Ortiz, A. 1969. *The Tewa World: Space, Time, Being and Becoming in a Pueblo Society*. Chicago: Chicago Univ. Press
151. Deleted in proof
152. Overing Kaplan, J., org. 1977. *Social Time and Social Space in Lowland South American Societies*. Paris: Soc. Am., Mus. de l'Homme
153. Panoff, M. 1969. The notion of time among the Maenge people of New Britain. *Ethnology* 8:153–66
153a. Parkes, D., Thrift, N. 1978. Putting time in its place. In *Timing Space and Spacing Time*, ed. T. Carlstein, D. Parkes, N. Thrift, Vol. 2, pp. 119–29. London: Arnold
154. Parmentier, R. 1987. *The Sacred Remains: Myth, History and Polity in Belau*. Chicago: Univ. Chicago Press
155. Peel, J. 1984. Making history: the past in the Ijesha present. *Man* 19(1):111–32
156. Pepper, S. 1935. The order of time. In *The Problem of Time*. Univ. Calif. Publ. Philos. 18:3–20. Berkeley: Univ. Calif. Press

156a. Pillet, G., Leimgruber, R., Bourrit, A. 1981. Les donneurs de temps. (Titre 2). In *Les donneurs de temps,* P. Sansot, G. Pillet, P. Amphoux, R. Leimgruber, A. Bourrit, et al, pp. 23–150. Albeuve: Editions Castella

157. Pina Cabral, J. de. 1987. Paved roads and enchanted Mooresses: the perception of the past among the peasant populations of the Alto Minho. *Man* 22(4):715–35

158. Pocock, D. 1967 [1964]. The anthropology of time reckoning. In *Myth and Cosmos,* ed. J. Middleton, pp. 303–14. New York: Natural History Press

159. Polanyi, M. 1964. *Personal Knowledge: Towards a Post-Critical Philosophy.* New York: Harper & Row

160. Polanyi, M., Prosch, H. 1975. *Meaning.* Chicago: Univ. Chicago Press

160a. Poole, D. 1984. *Ritual-economic calendars in Paruru: the structure of representation in Andean ethnography.* PhD thesis. Univ. Ill., Urbana-Champaign

161. Reeve, M. 1988. Cauchu Uras: lowland Quichua histories of the Amazon rubber boom. See Ref. 87b, pp. 19–34

162. Ricoeur, P. 1981. Narrative time. In *On Narrative,* ed. W. Mitchell, pp. 165–86. Chicago: Univ. Chicago Press

163. Ricoeur, P. 1984–1985. *Time and Narrative,* Vols. 1, 2. Chicago: Univ. Chicago Press

163a. Ricoeur, P. 1988. *Time and Narrative,* Vol. 3. Chicago: Univ. Chicago Press

164. Rigby, P. 1983. Time and historical consciousness: the case of Ilparakuyo Maasai. *Comp. Stud. Soc. Hist.* 25(3):428–56

164a. Rorty, R. 1979. *Philosophy and the Mirror of Nature.* Princeton: Princeton Univ. Press

165. Rosaldo, R. 1980. *Ilongot Headhunting: 1883–1974.* Stanford: Stanford Univ. Press

166. Sartre, J. P. 1968 [1963]. *Search for a Method.* New York: Random House

166a. Sartre, J. P. 1966. *Being and Nothingness.* New York: Pocket Books

166b. Schieffelin, E. 1976. *The Sorrow of the Lonely and the Burning of the Dancers.* New York: St. Martins

167. Schutz, A. 1962. *The Problem of Social Reality.* The Hague: Martinus Nijhoff

167a. Schweder, R. 1982. Review of Hallpike, *The Foundations of Primitive Thought.* Am. Anthropol. 84(2):354–66

167b. Skar, S. 1981. Andean women and the concept of space/time. In *Women and Space: Ground Rules and Social Maps,* ed. S. Ardener, pp. 35–49. New York: St. Martin's Press

167c. Smith, J. 1991. A slip in time saves nine: prestigious origins again. In *Chronotypes: the Construction of Time,* ed. J. Bender, D. Welbery, pp. 67–76. Stanford: Stanford Univ. Press

168. Smith, M. 1982. Bloody time and bloody scarcity: capitalism, authority and the transformation of temporal experience in a Papua New Guinea Village. *Am. Ethnol.* 9(3):503–18

168a. Smith, R. 1961. Cultural differences in the life cycle and the concept of time. In *Aging and Leisure,* ed. R. Kleemeier, pp. 84–112. Oxford: Oxford Univ. Press

169. Smith, T. 1986. Peasant time and factory time in Japan. *Past and Present* 111:165–97

170. Sorokin, P. 1943. *Sociocultural Space, Time, Causality.* Durham: Duke Univ. Press

171. Sorokin, P., Merton, R. 1937. Social time: a methodological and functional analysis. *Am. J. Soc.* 47(5):615–29

172. Stanley, J. 1977. Special time, special power: the fluidity of power in a popular Hindu festival. *J. Asian Stud.* 37(1):27–43

173. Starkey, K. 1988. Time and work organization: an empirical and theoretical analysis. In *The Rhythms of Society,* ed. M. Young, T. Schuller, pp. 95–117. London: Routledge & Kegan Paul

173a. Ströker, E. 1987 [1965]. *Investigations in Philosophy of Space.* Athens, OH: Ohio Univ. Press

174. Strong, W. 1935. Time in operational analysis. In *The Problem of Time.* Univ. Calif. Publ. Philos. 18:51–80. Berkeley: Univ. Calif. Press

174a. Swain, T. 1988. The ghost of space. In *Aboriginal Australians and Christian Missions: Ethnographic and Historical Studies,* ed. T. Swain, D. Rose, pp. 452–69. Bedford Park: Austr. Assoc. for Study of Religions

175. Tannenbaum, N. 1988. Shan calendrical systems: the everyday use of esoteric knowledge. *Mankind* 18(1):14–25

175a. Taylor, R. 1955. Spatial and temporal analogies. *J. Philos.* 52(22):599–612

176. Tedlock, B. 1982. *Time and the Highland Maya.* Albuquerque: Univ. New Mexico Press

177. Thompson, E. 1967. Time, work and discipline in industrial capitalism. *Past and Present* 38:56–97

178. Thornton, R. 1980. *Space, Time and Culture among the Iraqw of Tanzania.* New York: Academic

178a. Thornton, R. 1989. Time scales and social thought. In *Time and Mind: Disciplinary Issues. The Study of Time VI,* ed. J. T. Fraser, pp. 181–96. Madison, CT: Int. Univ. Press

178b. Traugott, E. 1978. On the expression of spatio-temporal relations in language. In *Universals of Human Language,* ed. J. Greenberg, C. Ferguson, E. Moravcsik, 3:370–99. Cambridge, MA: MIT Press

178c. Traweek, S. 1988. Discovering machines: nature in the age of its mechanical reproduction. See Ref. 40c, pp. 39–91

179. Turner, T. 1969. Oedipus: time and structure in narrative form. In *Forms of Symbolic Action,* ed. R. Spencer, pp. 26–68. Seattle: Univ. Washington Press

180. Turner, T. 1980. The social skin. In *Not Work Alone,* ed. J. Cherfas, R. Lewin, pp. 112–40. Beverly Hills: Sage

181. Turner, T. 1988. Ethno-ethnohistory: myth and history in native South American representations of contact with Western society. See Ref. 87a, pp. 195–213

182. Turton, D., Ruggles, C. 1978. Agreeing to disagree: the measurement of duration in a southwestern Ethiopian community. *Curr. Anthropol.* 19(3):585–600

183. Urry, J. 1985. Social relations: space and time. In *Social Relations and Spatial Structures,* ed. D. Gregory, J. Urry, pp. 20–48. New York: St. Martin's Press

184. Urry, J. 1991. Time and space in Giddens' social theory. In *Giddens' Theory of Structuration,* ed. G. Bryant, D. Jary, pp. 160–75 London: Routledge

185. Urton, G. 1981. *At the Crossroads of the Earth and the Sky.* Austin: Univ. Texas Press

186. Valeri, V. 1990. Constitutive history: genealogy and narrative in the legitimation of Hawaiian kingship. In *Culture Through Time: Anthropological Approaches,* ed. E. Ohnuki-Tierney, pp. 154–92. Stanford: Stanford Univ. Press

186a. Wachtel, N. 1986. Memory and history: introduction. See Ref. 25, pp. 207–24

186b. Wagner, R. 1986. *Symbols that Stand for Themselves.* Chicago: Chicago Univ. Press

186c. Warrell, L. 1990. Historicizing the cosmogony: naming the Asala Perahara in Buddhist Sri Lanka. *Aust. J. Anthropol.* 1(1):3–17

187. Weiner, A. 1980. Reproduction: a replacement for reciprocity. *Am. Ethnol.* 7:71–85

188. Weiner, A. 1985. Inalienable wealth. *Am. Ethnol.* 12(2):210-27

189. Whipp, R. 1987. 'A time to every purpose': an essay on time and work. In *The Historical Meanings of Work,* ed. P. Joyce, pp. 210–36. Cambridge: Cambridge Univ. Press

190. Whitrow, G. 1988. *Time in History.* Oxford: Oxford Univ. Press

191. Whitten, N. 1988. Historical and mythic evocations of chthonic power in South America. See Ref. 87b, pp. 282–306

192. Whorf, B. 1956. *Language, Thought and Reality,* ed. J. B. Carroll. New York: MIT/Wiley

193. Wilcox, D. 1987. *The Measure of Times Past: Pre-Newtonian Chronologies and the Rhetoric of Relative Time.* Chicago: Univ. Chicago Press

193a. Williams, D. 1975. The brides of Christ. In *Perceiving Women,* ed. S. Ardener, pp. 105–25a. New York: Wiley

194. Williams, R. 1973. *The Country and the City.* London: Chatto & Windus

195. Young, J. 1989. The biography of a memorial icon: Nathan Rapoport's Warsaw Ghetto monument. See Ref. 36, pp. 69–106

196. Zentner, H. 1966. The social time-space relationship: a theoretical formulation. *Sociol. Inq.* 36(1):61–79

197. Zerubavel, E. 1977. The French Republican calendar: a case study in the sociology of time. *Am. Sociol. Rev.* 42:868–77

198. Zerubavel, E. 1981. *Hidden Rhythms: Schedules and Calendars in Social Life.* Chicago: Univ. Chicago Press

199. Zerubavel, E. 1985. *The Seven Day Circle: The History and Meaning of the Week.* New York: The Free Press

Annu. Rev. Anthropol. 1992. 21:125-41

ORIGINS AND SPREAD OF PASTORALISM IN AFRICA

Andrew B. Smith

Department of Archaeology, University of Cape Town, Rondebosch 7700, South Africa

KEYWORDS: archaeology, African pastoralists, transition to food-production

The antiquity of African pastoralism is no longer in dispute. We now have information about more than the broad outlines of the origins and spread of herding societies in the continent. Several regional studies, when combined, allow a coherent picture of the wider scope of pastoral adaptation.

We start with a basic ecological model of adaptation to the grassland environments of Africa, against which we then can understand the socio-political relationships between the different groups that can be identified in the archaeological record. None of this means that we have worked out the whole picture. As will be seen in the ensuing narrative, fundamental theoretical disagreements remain—for example, about what constitutes a "domesticated" animal, or with respect to the problems of understanding the transition from hunting to food production; and these indicate the need for more data. Pastoral archaeology in Africa is currently a growth area, and it is to be hoped that this article will encourage entry both into the arguments and into research efforts to fill gaps in our knowledge.

To understand early pastoralism in Africa we must look at its precursors and estimate the degree to which culture and environment influenced early food production

THE ENVIRONMENTAL BACKGROUND

Evidence is widespread in the Sahara of fluctuating environmental conditions throughout the Holocene (57, 83). Such fluctuation is most apparent in (*a*) diatomite exposures found over a wide area in Mali (75) and Niger (25), indicating standing water in the form of lakes over considerable periods as

125

0084-6570/92/1015-0125$02.00

well as high beach levels around Lake Chad (91), and (*b*) data from sediment cores in Sebkha Mellala (Algeria) and the Manga Plateau (Niger) (27). In the Aïr Mountains, Niger, a relict sub-Mediterranean flora, such as olive and cypress trees, is still to be found; in the Ténéré (Niger) we find evidence from charred wood of a savanna vegetation 400 km north of its present distribution 7000 years ago (65). Archaeological data back up the evidence of a considerably ameliorated environment in the past: Rock engravings and paintings, as well as cultural debris, are found in areas with less than 20 mm annual rainfall today. This rock art shows giraffe, hartebeest, ostrich, etc, all of which, though dry area adapted, need vegetation to survive, even if water is not available. Cattle paintings indicate that water had to exist, at least seasonally. The Tassili n'Ajjer (southeastern Algeria) (53) or Jebel Uweinat (where Egypt, Sudan and Libya meet) (72), where many of these paintings are to be found, are presently stark desert environments.

SAHARAN EARLY HOLOCENE LACUSTRINE/RIVERINE ADAPTATION

During the wet phase between 10,000 and 8000 BP, which affected all of north and east Africa (66, 105, 108), we can find the cultural and economic remains of people who lived around lakes and rivers and exploited aquatic resources. This would appear to have been a period of experimentation, as the equipment used differed markedly from what had preceded it. Bone tools, particularly harpoons, in association with a microlithic industry, have been found across a wide area stretching from the Nile Valley, at the confluence of the White and Blue Niles (1, 15) and the Atbara and Nile Rivers (36), to the central Sahara in Niger (16, 96), Mali (26), and Chad (18), and even around Lake Turkana in northern Kenya (7, 74). Not all the sites were located around lakes or along rivers, as the area just to the east of the Nile was occupied at such sites as Shaqadud (59) by similar people at this time. But perhaps more significant is the appearance of associated ceramics, first found around Khartoum (4), whose antiquity has only recently been recognized (e.g. 6, 37, 84, 85).

This early cultural expression has also been found in the western desert of southern Egypt (106, 107). Large bovid bones, identified as cattle, have been found with this material (30). The rest of the faunal material is dominated by hares and gazelles, and, as the argument goes, the environment that can only support small mammals will be inadequate for large bovids without human intervention. Therefore the cattle are considered to have been domesticated. In addition, pits have been identified dug into the center of the playas. These are interpreted as water holes used for watering the stock.

Domestication of cattle here by 9500 BP would be earlier than anything found in the the Near East, so research designs are being created to determine the Sahara's influence on Europe, via the Maghreb, Sicily, Sardinia, and Corsica (James Lewthwaite, personal communication).

A part of the mind-set of those claiming very early domestication in North Africa sees ceramics as an indicator of food production. As Camps (12:217) has said: "L'abondance des poteries dans le Néolithique saharo-soudanais du Sahara méridional sera donc considérée par nous comme une preuve indirecte d'un développement de l'agriculture."

Not everyone is convinced, however, that this early ceramic tradition indicates a food producing society. A number of questions remain to be resolved. These revolve around the interpretation of the environment at the time the sites were occupied. Proponents of the interpretation discussed here are explicit about the grassland conditions that would have existed around the playas during the phases in which they held water. Williams writes that "The monotony of the large samples of fauna collected at both Bir Kiseiba and Nabta reflects the restricted environmental characteristics of the North African Sahel. Vegetation must have been limited, and almost all of it concentrated around the seasonal playas" (108:408); but Williams also concedes that the environment could have looked like Kordofan and Darfur with "stands of grasses and herbs on the uplands, and by galleries of bushes and trees ... along drainages and around basins" (p. 408). Why, then, could the environment support only hares and gazelles? Where are the medium-sized bovids: oryx, hartebeest, or even the extremely arid-adapted addax? These animals can get the water they need from the vegetation they eat (89). Where in Africa does an environment occur in which only hares and gazelles are found? Because no such environment is to be found, the faunal sequences at Nabta and Bir Kiseiba do not accurately reflect the environment. A clue to the fact that the faunal sequence may be incomplete can be seen in Gauthier's (29) re-identification of some of the "cattle" bones as medium-sized bovids (30:59).

Fayum, site 2, shows a similar pattern of exploitation (11). The animals found in the earliest of the Fayum industries, called Qarunian and dated between 7th and 6th millennium BC (50), include hares, canids, gazelles and cattle, none of which the analyst can identify as domesticates (11:130).

Because standing water was available in the playas of southern Egypt and around the Fayum (some 30 km from the Nile) at time of occupation, and because grass was present as well, cattle would likely have survived without human intervention; the circumstantial environmental evidence for domestication is thus questionable.

As the hunters appear to have been selective about what they took out of the environment, and thus were probably in control of their food resources, we might ask why they would have assumed the additional responsibility of keeping stock. What pressures on the society brought about involvement in food production? Would the minor environmental fluctuations outlined by Wendorf & Schild (107: Figure 2.33) have been sufficient stressors, or would the long-term aridity that affected all of North Africa after 8000 BP have been required (91, 108)? The question is not an arbitrary one, because it is only after 7700 BP that ovicaprids begin to show up in a North African context, including both at Nabta Playa and Fayum. Only one wild ovine is found in Africa—the Barbary sheep (*Ammotragus lervia*)—an animal eliminated as a source of genetic material for African domesticates (58); thus animals found in Africa likely originated in the Levant.

Potential connections between Africa and the Near East can be found in sites along the Mediterranean coast south of Tel Aviv (24, 109). These sites have produced stone knives with an invasive retouch "characteristic of arrow-heads and knives at Fayum" (109:131). Other artefacts that have analogs in Africa are the flaked axes with polished tips (24: Figure 4:14; 109: Figure 15:3) and a human figurine of a type unknown elsewhere in Israel but found in Egypt (62). One such site, Nizzanim, produced a radiocarbon date of 6740 ±90 BP (Hv-8509); an unpublished date of 7th millennium BP in association with cattle and small stock has also come from Qatif, a similar site in the Gaza area (I. Gilead, personal communication).

Another argument in favor of a later date for the introduction of domestic cattle lies in the size of the animals. Gauthier (31:180) has argued that the size differences between, on the one hand, the larger cattle of the Mediterranean sites, Fayum, and the Nile Valley, and, on the other, the smaller Saharan variety were due to poor grazing in the Sahara. The larger cattle are in no way distinguishable from the Pleistocene cattle found in the Nile Valley (13) or from Europe (21; see 101 for discussion). The Saharan cattle are all later than those from the so-called "Early Neolithic" at Nabta Playa and Bir Kiseiba, and would fall within the date of the later sites (with ovicaprids) from those two areas.

Gauthier would like to believe that because they are due to ecological conditions, size differences in the earliest phases of the domestication process would be insignificant. However, experience of farmers with wild game, such as eland, have shown that it takes very few generations for an appreciable difference in size to manifest itself in animals constrained by humans, unless wild genetic material is introduced continuously. When the gene pool is re-stricted, succeeding generations of animals become rapidly smaller.

THE GRASSLAND ECOLOGICAL NICHE IN THE SAHARA: c. 7500–4500 BP

Clearly identifiable domestic stock in the form of ovicaprids first appeared in the African continent after 7700 BP (107). Their bones have been found at the Haua Fteah in Cyrenaica c. 6800 BP (41, 48) and the Fayum c. 6400 BP (11, 40, 50). All this coincided with the opening up of a grassland niche in the Sahara which was increasingly occupied by pastoral people—e.g Tin-Torha (Libya) from 7400–5300 BP, Uan Muhuggiag (Acacus Mountains, Libya) c. 6000 BP, Adrar Bous (Ténéré Desert, Niger) c. 5800 BP, Meniet (Hoggar Mountains, Algeria) c. 5400 BP, Erg d'Admer (Algeria) c. 5400 BP, and Arlit (Niger) c. 5200 BP (Figure 1).

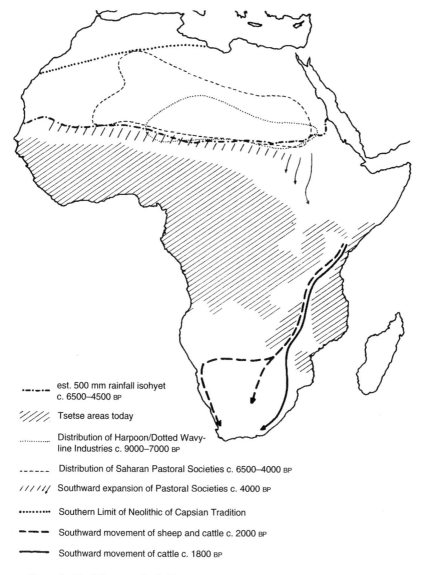

est. 500 mm rainfall isohyet
c. 6500–4500 BP

Tsetse areas today

Distribution of Harpoon/Dotted Wavy-
line Industries c. 9000–7000 BP

Distribution of Saharan Pastoral Societies c. 6500–4000 BP

Southward expansion of Pastoral Societies c. 4000 BP

Southern Limit of Neolithic of Capsian Tradition

Southward movement of sheep and cattle c. 2000 BP

Southward movement of cattle c. 1800 BP

Figure 1   The Sahara grassland niche.

The gradual movement southwestwards that can be discerned in the radiocarbon dates supports the idea of a Near Eastern connection. Our real problem
in understanding this relationship lies in the crucial area of the Nile Delta,
where continuous silting has buried Neolithic sites beyond recovery by modern archaeological methods. The closest source of information is Merimde
beni-Salame on the eastern edge of the Delta where settled villagers kept

cattle, ovicaprids, and pigs. The dates of occupation and cultural material are similar to those of Fayum (39). One piece of information that may have relevance for a considerably wider area of North Africa is the burial pattern of Merimde. Cemetaries, as found in the Badarian of Upper Egypt, do not occur in this period. Also significantly different is the fact that the Merimde graves lack the profusion of grave goods associated with the Badarian skeletons. The Merimde grave goods are limited to a few personal possessions, such as a bead, an amulet, or a reed mat (42:174). As we shall see below, this pattern is repeated among prehistoric pastoralists in the southern Sahara and Sahel.

During this period rock paintings depicting domestic stock and their keepers appear in the Sahara (the "bovidien period"; 55, 56). Art from the Tassil n'Ajjer has been dated by means of small fragments of the painted panels that exfoliated and were buried by subsequent occupational debris. At one such site, Uan Muhuggiag, a stone fragment with two oxen on it had fallen in. The deposits overlying the painted stone were dated to 4730 BP (indicating the paintings were older). At another site, Uan Telocat, the dating was obtained from deposits that had built up sufficiently in the cave to conceal painted figures on the wall. The cultural material from the deposit was similar to that of Uan Muhuggiag, but the date of 6754 BP adds strength to the idea of pastoral occupation of the area around 7000 BP (61).

The paintings offer more than just pictures of domestic stock. Cultural information is also encoded that indicates two separate groups: a dark-skinned group whose activities resemble those of modern Fulani; and a light-skinned, long-haired group with Ancient Libyan affinities (52; see also 101 and 102 for discussion).

Excavation of graves at Adrar Bous (92) showed the skeletons to be tightly flexed, and grave goods were limited to a single bead around the neck and the remains of a skin garment worn by the corpse.

The cultural material of these pastoral people in the Central Sahara can be separated on the basis of projectile points and other stone tools. This has allowed a spatial distribution of cultural groupings (96) perhaps analogous to the various Tuareg sub-groups found in Niger, Mali, and Algeria today. The southern limits of these sites is clearly a line across the 18° N parallel (Figure 1). Annual rainfall in the southern Sahara during this period has been estimated at less than 500 mm, which, because the tsetse fly requires at least 500 mm of annual rainfall for breeding (64), would support the hypothesis that southward movement of domestic stock was restricted by tsetse infestation (95, 98).

Owing to the perennial waters of the river itself, which offered conditions conducive to agriculture, in the Nile Valley at this time food production was much more varied than in the Sahara to the west. Communities could rely on grain production and were able to make use of the more marginal environment away from the river as a pasture zone (35). Esh Shaheinab was the first of the so-called Khartoum "Neolithic" sites to be described (5). It produced a particular flaked stone adze with polished tip and edges, found in the central Sahara at places like Adrar Bous, suggesting some cultural connection at this time.

More recent work at other Khartoum "Neolithic" sites such as Kadero (51) and surrounding areas has allowed modeling of seasonal activities and exploitation of the resource base of people along the river and away from it (35). The development and integration of herding societies into more complex social organisations along the Nile are comprehensively treated by Sadr (86). His thesis is that as far as northeast Africa is concerned, all nomadic groups developed on the edges of state level societies. He bases this hypothesis on his work in the Atbai area of Sudan where he is confident that the mixed economy, like that described above for the Kadero area, developed into agro-pastoralism before specialization took place either towards fully fledged agriculture or pastoralism.

THE SPREAD OF AFRICAN PASTORALISM

Around 4500 BP a major climatic shift caused increasing aridity in the Central Sahara, resulting in conditions similar to today's (63, 65, 91). At this time the weather systems appear to have been influenced by the Intertropical Convergence Zone, which moved southwards. As the rain belt retreated, so did the tsetse, thus allowing occupation of areas hitherto closed to pastoralists (71, 95).

The first pastoral occupation of the present Sahel occurred around 4000 BP. At this time seasonal fishing camps were occupied by herders at Karkarichinkat in the Tilemsi Valley, Mali, north of Gao. The cultural equipment, while stylistically different from what has been found earlier in the southern Sahara, nonetheless shows affinities with the pastoral societies of the north. This can be seen in the large numbers of projectile points, flaked stone axes, and globular pots. It is also apparent in the flexed burials with a single bead around the neck (28, 92–94).

Evidence for a similar southward occupation of the Sahel by people with domestic stock comes from Kobadi, near Namapala to the west of the Central Niger Delta, Mali (71), and Chin Tafidet, west of Tegidda n Tesemt, Niger (67). The brief descriptions indicate that the sites overlap with the end of the occupation at Karkarichinkat (c. 3300 BP), but the two groups had different funerary practices. Cemetaries with large numbers of individuals were found in both places, but while the Kobadi skeletons had no grave goods, the Chin Tafidet burials had pots in association.

On the eastern side of the continent the movement of stock-keepers had a pattern similar to that seen in the West African Sahel. Occupation of the area lying between the Upper White Nile (49) and Kenya (8) did not occur until c. 4000 BP. In the Lakes Province of Sudan, high lake levels during the mid-Holocene would have flooded the toich, and prevented occupation of much of the area by pastoral people prior to 4000 BP (78, 82). Even today, tsetse are concentrated on the ironstone substrate, so during the wet season cattle are kept on the toich away from the homesteads, some 13–20 km distant (82:144). Further south in Sudan, the sites that have been excavated and dated to this period in Eastern Equatoria Province all appear to have been occupied by Later Stone Age hunters of the Lokabulo ceramic tradition, with domestic stock coming in much later (19, 81).

The same explanation for the spread of pastoralism can be invoked for what happened further west, in this case a southwesterly retreat of the 500 mm rainfall isohyet, taking with it tsetse infestation. A tsetse-free corridor to the east along the foothills of the Ethiopian highlands (Figure 1) would have allowed pastoral expansion into East Africa and possibly even into the highlands of Ethiopia (10, 14).

EARLY PASTORALISM IN EAST AFRICA

The earliest dates for pastoralism in East Africa come from Lake Turkana in northern Kenya. At the site of GaJi4, Barthelme (7–9) excavated the bones of both cattle and ovicaprids in association with ceramics, and at another site, at Ileret, he found similar material, with the addition of fish bones and stone bowls. Both these sites were dated to c. 4000 BC. This industry, called the Lowland Savanna Pastoral Neolithic (3), is earlier by about 1000 years than a similar cultural expression found further south in the Central Rift Valley and named the Highland Savanna Pastoral Neolithic (see 76 for later sites in the Turkana area).

These names, however, have proved to be too general, since the sequence is complex and varies from area to area in Kenya. In the Central Rift Valley Later Stone Age, hunters (Eburran Phase 5) interfaced with Olmalenge herders, while up on the Mau escarpment resided Elmenteitan herders. On the border with Tanzania, in the Loita-Mara area, the Elmenteitan is dated between c. 2400 and 1400 BP (80).

Attempts have been made to reconstruct linguistic history of pastoral societies in East Africa (see 77 for discussion). The people living on both sides of the Nile in the southern Sudan are assumed to have been agro-pastoral Central Sudanic speakers prior to 4000 years ago. Around 4000 BP Southern Cushites moved out from Ethiopia into Equatoria Province and southwards to northern Kenya, and later into the Central Highlands (2, 22). A later movement of Southern Nilotes, suggested as represented by the Elmenteitan industry, penetrated from the Sudan, displacing many of the Cushitic speakers. All this assumes a period of contact between Central Sudanic and Cushitic speakers sufficient to allow the transfer of stock. Since the archaeology of pastoralism in Ethiopia is at best weak, and an inferred date of c. 4000 BP for the entry of stock from the Upper Nile is given by Clark (14:75), it would appear that there was not much time for new economies based on herding to have developed in Ethiopia before the opening up of tsetse-free zones. More work needs to be done in southwestern Ethiopia to show that cultural contact with the southern Sudan, as well as northern Kenya, did indeed occur.

At Prolonged Drift in the Central Rift Valley, 81% of the animals by Minimum Number of Individuals (MNI) were wild (32, 33), while at Ngamuriak and other sites in the Loita-Mara area only 0.5% of the animals were wild (80). This raises questions about the economy of prehistoric herders in Kenya. Among the Gabbra Boran of northern Kenya today, no wild meat is taken back to a camp for fear of disease among the domestic stock (Hussein Isack, personal communication), so virtually no wild animal bones would be found at settlements of herders. In contrast, Wak hunters, who live on the periphery of herding society, take their game catches back to camp, and occasionally they are given a cow or small stock in payment for services rendered. Thus their camps would have a mixture of wild and domestic animal bones, with more of the former. Robertshaw (80), in his interpretation of the Prolonged Drift samples, would see them as "poor pastoralists" trying to re-establish their herds after loss. Such an interpretation is at odds with his later assertion that the relations of production of hunting ought to be considered separately from herding. In theoretical terms, a herder need not fall back on hunting for survival, but can gain access to breeding stock by calling in debts or obligations from bond friends.

Ngamuriak also produced ceramic vessels with lugs and spouts—attributes that seem to have been common among East African pastoralists (see 54).

We have no evidence that the early pastoral people in East Africa used grain. This does not mean that the herders did not practice some cultivation, but their sites are on the savanna grasslands of Kenya, rather than the richer, more fertile soils of the eastern Highlands (79). Pastoral societies existed in East Africa for about 1500 years before iron-using agriculturalists penetrated from the west and settled in the highlands. This incursion appears to have occurred at the time when East African weather patterns changed to a dual rainfall system that allowed the development of a more specialized pastoral subsistence based on higher milk yields and improved herd fecundity (60). The results were clusters of semi-permanent house structures and kraals, as found among the Maasai today. At Ngumuriak a single horizon extending over some 8000 square meters was identified (80). This site showed a culling pattern of small stock consistent with the practices of modern pastoral people who are relatively unstressed. Of the small stock faunal remains, 45% were of mature animals (Table 1). Marshall (60:878) suggests this is a strategy of herders "who are able to feed surplus animals until they reach an age when growth has slowed and maximum culling gain can be obtained." She also noted differences in fragmentation patterns between cattle and small stock. Cattle bones were more broken up, indicating "intensive use of within bone nutrients" (60:879) from animals whose condition was good enough for such nutrient extraction to be attractive.

Since grain could now be traded (or stolen) from the agriculturalists, herding could become a full-time occupation. The relations between the different economic groups have yet to be determined archaeologically. We can surmise, however, that the pastoralists would have put constant pressure on agricultural societies, at one level, while interacting and trading with them at another. It is probable that domestic stock were transferred into agricultural economies, with the farmers storing their wealth in the form of cattle (see 34).

STOCK MOVEMENT INTO SOUTHERN AFRICA

When Iron Age agriculturalists modified the landscape by means of their superior technology, they may have opened up a greater pastoral environment by removing woody vegetation. Thus pastoralists may have pressured farmers not only for the product of their fields but also for the fields themselves. We know little about why agriculture spread southward in Africa. We know only that about 2000 years ago iron-using people arrived in Southern Africa (43). The coastal group, or Matola tradition, coming through Mozambique to Natal, may not have had domestic stock, but the people coming down through Zambia (Huffman's Lydenburg or Bambata tradition) certainly had (44). At the site of Salumano in Zambia, dated to c. 2400 BP (69), both cattle and ovicaprids were identified (70). Another reference point for early domestic stock is the site of Bambata in Zimbabwe, where sheep remains were dated to c. 2100 BP. At the latter site the sheep bones were associated with pottery (one vessel of which had a spout) and stone tools, indicating a probable interface with hunting groups.

Contact between the agro-pastoralists and the aboriginal hunting people of Southern Africa, the San, had important ramifications for the continued spread of pastoralism into the rest of Southern Africa. The transfer of stock and ceramics from agro-pastoralists to hunters presumably resulted in the development of Khoikhoi society, which was to colonize the western and southern coasts of Namibia and South Africa (100).

Where the transfer took place is as yet unknown. Current archaeological knowledge suggests it was somewhere in southeastern Angola or southwestern Zambia. Two models of the spread of Khoi pastoralism have been proposed. The first, by Stow (104) and Cooke (17), hypothesized that stock-keepers came across northern Namibia and down the Atlantic coast to the Cape. The second, by Elphick (23), suggested, on the basis of a similarity between the Khoe spoken by Bushmen of northern Botswana and the language spoken by the Khoi at the Cape, that pastoralism spread down through the Kalahari in Botswana to the Orange River, then either downriver to the Atlantic from whence it spread both north and south, or southwards to the coast of South Africa, following one of the major valleys (e.g. of the Seekoe River), whence it spread east and west.

Archaeological research in the Seekoe River Valley, to the south of the Orange River (38, 87), indicates that pastoral occupation of the area did not take place until the 14th century AD. The Namibian connection, however, is more hopeful. Dates of 2100 BP for ceramics have come from Falls Rock in the Brandberg (46), and ceramics and possibly sheep were recovered from levels dating to c. 2000 BP at Geduld (45; L. Jacobsen, personal communication). Further south in Namaqualand, L. Webley (personal communication) dates sheep and ceramics to 1900 BP at Spoegrivier; at Kasteelberg on the Cape west coast the earliest dates for sheep are at least c. 1400 BP but may be as old as 1800 BP (99, 103).

Thus a gradual Atlantic Coast connection seems at first glance to be the best scenario, but it has to be admitted that the archaeological evidence for the earliest herders at the Cape must be more firmly fixed. Uncertainty is due partially to the small samples of sheep bones so far recovered from the period 1900 to 1600 BP at such sites as Die Kelders and Hawston, and partially to the uncertain dating controls within the stratigraphy. If indeed sheep were introduced at this time, the density of population was apparently low and a significant presence did not make itself felt in the Cape landscape until after 1600 BP. So far no cattle bones have been identified unequivocally from this early period. The earliest cattle probably appear just before 1300 BP, when they were to be found at Kasteelberg. Again the density of large stock is low in the beginning (10 sheep to one cow) but increases by around 1000 BP to 4.7 sheep to one cow (99), a ratio closer to that which existed by trade between the Khoikhoi at the Cape and the first European colonists in the 17th century (20:353).

The original source of the large stock has yet to be identified. A connection is possible with the Eastern Cape, where the summer and winter rainfall areas overlap; this was the western extent of Iron Age adaptation. In this area hunters performed important tasks for agro-pastoralists (e.g. rain-making), so cattle from this source could have come west along the south coast.

The mortality profiles of small stock from Kasteelberg (47) (Table 1) may be compared with those from Ngamuriak in East Africa. The older site (KBA), dated to at least c. 1400 BP, shows a bimodal distribution of young and mature animals. This contrasts with the upper part of KBB, dated between 1000 and 800 BP, where there are more juveniles than mature animals. As can be seen in Table 1, this pattern is exaggerated at the South Coast site of Die Kelders (47).

HUNTERS AND HERDERS IN THE CAPE LANDSCAPE

The identities of various aboriginal economies in the southwestern Cape are currently controversial. The argument has anthropological, historical, and archaeological components. First, how permeable was the social boundary between hunters and herders, and second, how easy is it for groups to change relations of production, in this case for hunters to become pastoralists? Using

Table 1   Mortality rates of small stock (MNI's)

	0-14 mos.	14-28 mos.	>28 mos.	Total
Ngamuriak	24 (35%)	14 (20%)	31 (45%)	69
Kasteelberg "A"	20 (43%)	6 (13%)	20 (43%)	46
Kasteelberg "B"	40 (63%)	13 (21%)	10 (16%)	63
Die Kelders	25 (83%)	3 (10%)	2 (7%)	30

historical records, Elphick (23) surmised that the difference between the two economic groups was one of degree rather than kind. When a person had stock he was a herder; when he lost the animals through theft, disease, or drought he could fall back on hunting for a livelihood.

Would sites with these different economic emphases have a similar cultural identity? Schrire & Deacon (90) found the indigenous cultural material from a small 17th-century Dutch redoubt to be no different from what has been found on many prehistoric sites in the Cape. Since the Khoikhoi interacted with the Dutch when the site was occupied by colonists, these must be Khoi artefacts. Here, the authors suggested, was proof that hunters and herders had similar archaeological signatures.

The counter-argument is based on evidence from various sites dating to the last 3000 years in the region of the Dutch redoubt. The largest site in the area is Kasteelberg, some 4 km from the coast (99). Analysis of the faunal remains has shown it to have been a sealing camp of ceramic-using herders (47), although a pre-ceramic/pre-herder occupation dated to 2150 BP has also been identified. Of importance to the issue now before us is the frequency of small bovids (*Raphicerus* spp.)—79% in the preherder deposit, compared with 3.8–8.6% (depending on depth) in the herder deposit. Seals make up only 6% of faunal remains in the pre-herder levels but 36–70% of those in the herder levels. Formally retouched stone tools constitute 2% of the total tools in the pre-herder levels compared with only 0.2% in the herder deposit. (In addition, because in these later levels the tools are made from material not generally selected for other uses, they are likely intrusive from the earlier period.)

At Witklip, a small rock shelter coeval with Kasteelberg, some 10 km to the south and 9 km from the coast, small bovids constitute 53% of the fauna in the pre-2000 BP levels, and 55–63% in the upper levels; seals make up 4.5% of the fauna below, and 0–0.4% above (103). It might be argued that distance from the coast would correlate with the presence of seals at a site, but at Heuningklip, a herder site 13 km from the sea, faunal percentages are similar to Kasteelberg's. The low frequency of sheep at Witklip (<8% of faunal remains in the post-2000 BP levels) suggests that not herders but hunters of small antelope occupied this site, who had access to small stock from theft or payment for services. The formally retouched stone artefacts constitute 5% of the total.

The Witklip and pre-herder Kasteelberg pattern of stone tool frequencies is repeated at small limited-occupation sites in the hills directly above the Dutch redoubt examined by Schrire & Deacon (90). These tools, similar in form and predominantly in the same raw material as those from the redoubt, suggest that we are dealing with hunters who are distinct from herders. Thus the artefacts in the redoubt were made not by Khoi herders but by coastal foragers, or "soaqua," who existed even up to the colonial period on the fringes of herding society (68).

If indeed two distinct economic and cultural groups occupied the area, how did they maintain their cultural separateness? Since the hunters presumably derived from the aboriginal population at the Cape they and the colonizing herders would have spoken different languages. More important would have been the difficulties of changing the relations of production from those of an egalitarian foraging society, where people would come for their share, to those of a society based on private or corporate ownership, where the individual "shares his food with others because he has the right to dispose of it, not because they have an equally legitimate claim to it" (88:321). Smith (100) thinks that herders would not have wished to have additional competition for grazing, and so would have denied hunters access to the means of production, especially when cattle became symbols of wealth and prestige.

There is good evidence, however, that such social and cultural distinctions broke down by the beginning of the 18th century under pressure from the expanding Dutch colony at the Cape. The Khoi gradually lost their stock through nonproductive exchange (for metals, tobacco, liquor, etc), theft by the Dutch, interference in raiding between Khoi groups by the colonists, and loss of some of their best pasture lands (see 97 for discussion). The final blows appear to have been a devastating smallpox epidemic in 1713 and a series of drought and stock-disease episodes up to 1720 (23). At this time the surviving Khoi had the choice of becoming stock-keepers for the Dutch or moving away from the Cape into the hinterland where they relied upon hunting for survival, and joined forces with local hunting/foraging populations.

CONCLUSIONS

Studies of pre-colonial pastoralist societies that began in the 1970s in West Africa (91–93) continued in Northeast Africa (84, 106) and in East Africa (60, 78). They are now coming to fruition in Southern Africa (46, 47, 99, 103). Many questions remain to be answered about the intervening, archaeologically poorly understood areas. Ethiopia, Tanzania, and Angola remain terra incognita in this reasearch.

Anthropologists (73, 74) and historians (23) have tried to project their data back in time to determine how the early colonial period changed traditional social and economic patterns. The development and spread of African pastoralism do not end with the colonial period but continue today, with San hunters shifting to herding (100).

Literature Cited

1. Adamson, D., Clark, J. D., Williams, M. A. J. 1974. Barbed bone points from Central Sudan and the age of the "Early Khartoum" tradition. *Nature* 249:120–23
2. Ambrose, S. H. 1982. Archaeology and linguistic reconstructions of history in East Africa. In *The Archaeological and Linguistic Reconstruction of African History*, ed. C. Ehret, M. Posnansky, pp. 104–57. Berkeley: Univ. Calif. Press. 299 pp.
3. Ambrose, S. H. 1984. The introduction of pastoral adaptations to the highlands of East Africa. See Ref. 15a, pp. 212–39
4. Arkell, A. J. 1949. *Early Khartoum*. Oxford: Oxford Univ. Press
5. Arkell, A. J. 1953. *Shaheinab*. Oxford: Oxford Univ. Press
6. Barich, B. E. 1987. Adaptation in archaeology: an example from the Libyan Sahara. See Ref. 16a, pp. 189–210
7. Barthelme, J. 1977. Holocene sites northeast of Lake Turkana: a preliminary report. *Azania* 12:33–41
8. Barthelme, J. 1984. Early evidence for animal domestication in eastern Africa. See Ref. 15a, pp. 200–5
9. Barthelme, J. 1985. *Fisher-Hunters and Neolithic Pastoralists in East Turkana, Kenya*. Oxford: BAR Int. Ser. 254
10. Brandt, S. A. 1984. New perspectives on the origins of food production in Ethiopia. See Ref. 15a, pp. 173–90
11. Brewer, D. J. 1989. A model for resource exploitation in the prehistoric Fayum. See Ref. 51a, pp. 127–37
12. Camps, G. 1974. *Les Civilisations préhistoriques de l'Afrique du Nord et du Sahara*. Paris: Doin. 366 pp.
13. Churcher, C. S. 1972. Late Pleistocene vertebrates from archaeological sites in the plain of Kom Ombo, Upper Egypt. *Life Sci. Contrib.* 28:1–172
14. Clark, J. D. 1976. The domestication process in sub-Saharan Africa with special reference to Ethiopia. In *Origine de l'Elevage et de la Domestication*, ed. E. Higgs, pp. 56–115. Nice: IXth Congr. IUSPP
15. Clark, J. D. 1989. Shabona: an Early Khartoum settlement on the White Nile. See Ref. 51a, pp. 387–410
15a. Clark, J. D., Brandt, S. A., eds. 1984. *From Hunters to Farmers: the Causes and Consequences of Food Production in Africa*, pp. 212–39. Berkeley: Univ. Calif. Press. 433 pp.
16. Clark, J. D., Williams, M. A. J., Smith, A. B. 1973. The geomorphology and archaeology of Adrar Bous, central Sahara: a preliminary report. *Quaternaria* 17:245–97
16a. Close, A. E., ed. 1987. *Prehistory of Arid North Africa*. Dallas: Southern Methodist Univ. Press. 357 pp.
17. Cooke, C. K. 1965. Evidence of human migrations from the rock art of Southern Rhodesia. *Africa* 5:3:263–85
18. Courtin, J. 1966. Le Néolithique du Borkou, Nord-Tchad. *L'Anthropologie* 70(3–4):269–82
19. David, N., Harvey, P., Goudie, C. J. 1981. Excavations in the southern Sudan 1979. *Azania* 14:7–54
20. Deacon, J. 1984. *The Later Stone Age of Southernmost Africa*. Oxford: BAR Int. Ser. 213. 441 pp.
21. Degerbol, M., Fredskild, B. 1970. The URUS (*Bos primigenius Bojanus*) and Neolithic domesticated cattle (*B. taurus domesticus* L.) in Denmark. *Det. K. Danske Videns. Sels. Biol. Skrifter* 17:1
22. Ehret, C. 1982 Population movement and culture contact in the southern Sudan, c. 3000 BC to AD 1000: a preliminary linguistic overview. See Ref. 56a, pp. 19–48
23. Elphick, R. 1977. *Kraal and Castle*. New Haven: Yale Univ. Press. 266 pp.
24. Epstein, C. 1984. A pottery Neolithic site near Tel Qatif. *Isr. Explor. J.* 34(4):209–19
25. Faure, H., Manguin, E., Nydal, R. 1963. Formations lacustres du Quaternaire supérieur du Niger oriental. *Bull. Bur. Rech. Geol. Minieres* 3:41–63
26. Gallay, A. 1966. Quelques gisements néolithiques du Sahara malien. *J. Soc. Afr.* 36:2:167–208
27. Gasse, F., Tehet, R., Durand, A., Gibert, E., Fontes, J.-C. 1990. The arid-humid transition in the Sahra and the Sahel during the last deglaciation. *Nature* 346:141–46
28. Gaussen, M., Gaussen, J. 1962. Apercu sur les divers facies neolithiques du Tilemsi et nouveaux objets en quartz poli. *Bull. Soc. Prehist. Fr.* 59:98–108
29. Gauthier, A. 1980. Contributions to the archaezoology of Egypt. See Ref. 106, pp. 317–44
30. Gauthier, A. 1984. Archaeozoology of the Bir Kiseiba region, eastern Sahara. See Ref. 107, pp. 49–72
31. Gauthier, A. 1987. Prehistoric men and cattle in North Africa: a dearth of data and a surfeit of models. See Ref. 16a, pp. 163–87
32. Gifford, D. P., Isaac, G. L., Nelson, C. M. 1980. Evidence for predation and pastoralism at Prolonged Drift: a Pastoral Neolithic site in Kenya. *Azania* 15:57–108

33. Gifford-Gonzalez, D. P. 1984. Implications of a faunal assemblage from a Pastoral Neolithic site in Kenya: findings and a perspective on research. See Ref. 15a, pp. 240–51
34. Haaland, G. 1972. Nomadism as an economic career among the sedentaries of the Sudan savannah belt. In *Essays in Sudan Ethnography*, ed. I. Cunnison, W. James, pp. 149–72. London: Hurst. 256 pp.
35. Haaland, R. 1987. *Socio-Economic Differentiation in the Neolithic Sudan.* Oxford: BAR Int. Ser. 350. 249 pp.
36. Haaland, R., Magid, A. A. 1991. Atbara research project: the field seasons of 1985, 1987, 1989, and 1990. *Nyame Akuma* 35:36–43
37. Hakem, A. M. A., Khabir, A. R. M. 1989. Sarourab 2: a new contribution to the Early Khartoum tradition from Bauda site. See Ref. 51a, pp. 381–86
38. Hart, T. J. G. 1989. *Haaskraal and Volstruisfontein: later Stone Age events at two rockshelters in the Zeekoe Valley, Great Karoo, South Africa.* MA thesis. Univ. Cape Town. 254 pp.
39. Hassan, F. A. 1985. Radiocarbon chronology of Neolithic and Predynastic sites in Upper Egypt and the Delta. *Afr. Archaeol. Rev.* 3:95–116
40. Hassan, F. A. 1986. Holocene lakes and prehistoric settlements of the western Faiyum, Egypt. *J. Archaeol. Sci.* 13:483–501
41. Higgs, E. S. 1967. Early domesticated animals in Libya. In *Background to Evolution in Africa*, ed. W. W. Bishop, J. D. Clark, pp. 165–73. Chicago: Univ. Chicago Press. 935 pp.
42. Hoffman, M. A. 1980. *Egypt Before the Pharaohs.* London: Routledge & Kegan Paul. 391 pp.
43. Huffman, T. N. 1982. Archaeology and ethnohistory of the African Iron Age. *Annu. Rev. Anthropol.* 11:133–50
44. Huffman, T. N. 1990. Broederstroom and the origins of cattle-keeping in Southern Africa. *Afr. Stud.* 49(2):1–12
45. Jacobson, L. 1987. More on ostrich eggshell bead size variability: the Geduld early herder assemblage. *S. Afr. Archaeol. Bull.* 42:174–75
46. Kinahan, J. 1989. *Pastoral nomads of the Central Namib desert.* PhD thesis. Univ. Witwatersrand. 206 pp.
47. Klein, R. G., Cruz-Uribe, K. 1989. Faunal evidence for prehistoric herder-forager activities at Kasteelberg, western Cape Province, South Africa. *S. Afr. Archaeol. Bull.* 44:82–97
48. Klein, R. G., Scott, K. 1986. Re-analysis of faunal assemblages from the Haua Fteah and other late Quaternary sites in Cyrenaican Libya. *J. Archaeol. Sci.* 13:515–42
49. Kleppe, E. J. 1984. Village Life in the Upper White Nile Region Over a Period of 3500 years. Presented at Dymaczewo

Conf. Nile Basin and the Sahara, 2nd, Poznan, Poland
50. Kozlowski, J. K., Ginter, B. 1989. The Fayum Neolithic in the light of new discoveries. See Ref. 51a, pp. 157–79
51. Krzyzaniak, L. 1984. The Neolithic habitation at Kadero (Central Sudan). In *Origin and Early Development of Food-Producing Cultures in North-Eastern Africa*, ed. L. Krzyzaniak, M. Kobusiewicz, pp. 309–15. Poznan: Muzeum Archeologiczne. 503 pp.
51a. Krzyzaniak, L., Kobusiewicz, M., eds. 1989. *Late Prehistory of the Nile Basin and the Sahara*, pp. 387–410. Poznan: Muzeum Archeologiczne. 547 pp.
52. Kuper, R. 1978. *Sahara: 10,000 Jahre zwischen Weide und Wuste.* Köln: Museen der Stadt. 470 pp.
53. Lajoux, J-D. 1963. *The Rock Paintings of Tassili.* London: Thames & Hudson. 204 pp.
54. Leakey, M. D. 1945. Report on the excavations at Hyrax Hill, Nakuru, Kenya Colony, 1937–38. *Trans. R. Soc. S. Afr.* 30:271–409
55. Lhote, H. 1958. *A la Découverte des Fresques du Tassili.* Paris: Arthaud. 237 pp.
56. Lhote, H. 1976. *Vers d'Autres Tassilis.* Paris: Arthaud. 257 pp.
56a. Mack, J., Robertshaw, P., eds. 1982. *Culture History in the Southern Sudan.* Nairobi: Br. Inst. East Africa. 179 pp.
57. Maley, J. 1977. Palaeoclimates of central Sahara during the early Holocene. *Nature* 269:573–77
58. Manwell, C., Baker, C. M. A. 1975. *Ammotragus lervia:* progenitor of the domesticated sheep or specialized offshoot of caprine evolution. *Experimentia* 31:1370–71
59. Marks, A. E., Mohammed-Ali, A., Peters, J., Robertson, R. 1985. Prehistory of the central Nile Valley as seen from its eastern hinterlands: excavations at Shaqadud, Sudan. *J. Field Archaeol.* 12:261–78
60. Marshall, F. 1990. Origins of specialized pastoral production in East Africa. *Am. Anthropol.* 92:4:873–94
61. Mori, F. 1965. *Tadrart Acacus.* Torino: Einaudi
62. Mozel, I. 1979. Three stone objects from Nizzanim. *Tel Aviv* 6:133–35
63. Munson, P. J. 1974. Late Holocene climatic chronology of the southwestern Sahara. Presented at Bienn. Meet. Am. Quat. Assoc., 3rd, Madison
64. Nash, T. A. M. 1969. *Africa's Bane.* London: Collins. 214 pp.
65. Neumann, K. 1989. Vegetationsgeschichte der Ostsahara in Holozan Holzkohlen aus prahistorischen Fundstellen. In *Forschungen zur Umweltgeschichte der Ostsahara*, ed. R. Kuper, pp. 13–81. Koln: Heinrich Barth Inst. 341 pp.
66. Nicholson, S. E., Flohn, H. 1980. African environmental and climatic changes and the general atmospheric circulation in the

late Pleistocene and Holocene. *Climatic Change* 2:313–48
67. Paris, F. 1984. La region d'In Gall-Tegidda n Tesemt (Niger), programme Archeologique d'Urgence (1977–81). III. Les sepultures du Néolithique final a l'Islam. *Etud. Niger.* 50:1–233
68. Parkington, J. 1984. Soaqua and Bushmen: hunters and robbers. In *Past and Present in Hunter Gatherer Studies,* ed. C. Schrire, pp. 151–74. New York: Academic. 299 pp.
69. Phillipson, D. W. 1989. The earliest South African pastoralists and the Early Iron Age. *Nsi* 6:127–34
70. Plug, I., Voigt, E. A. 1985. Archaeozoological studies of Iron Age communities in southern Africa. *Adv. World Archaeol.* 4:189–237
71. Raimbault, M., Dutour, O. 1990. Decouverte de populations mechtoides dans le Neolithique du Sahel malien (gisement lacustre de Kobadi); implications paleoclimatiques et paleoanthropologiques. *C. R. Acad. Sci. III* 310:631–38
72. Rhotert, H. 1952. *Libysche Felsbilder.* Darmstadt: Wittich. 146 pp.
73. Rigby, P. 1985. *Persistent Pastoralists: Nomadic Societies in Transition.* London: Zed Books. 198 pp.
74. Rigby, P. 1987. Class formation among East African pastoralists: Maasai of Tanzania and Kenya. In *Power Relations and State Formation,* ed. T. C. Patterson, C. W. Gailey, pp. 57–80. Washington, DC: Am. Anthol. Assoc. 169 pp.
75. Riser, J., Hillaire-Marcel, C., Rognon, P. 1983. Les phases lacustres holocenes. In *Sahara ou Sahel?: Quaternaire recent du Bassin de Taoudenni (Mali),* ed. N. Petit-Maire, J. Riser, pp. 65–86. Luminy: Lab. Geol. Quat., CNRS. 473 pp.
76. Robbins, L. H. 1984. Late prehistoric aquatic and pastoral adaptations west of Lake Turkana, Kenya. See Ref. 15a, pp. 206–11
77. Robertshaw, P. T. 1982. Eastern Equatoria in the context of later eastern African prehistory. See Ref. 56a, pp. 89–100
78. Robertshaw, P. T. 1987. Prehistory in the Upper Nile basin. *J. Afr. Hist.* 28:177–89
79. Robertshaw, P. T. 1989. The development of pastoralism in East Africa. In *The Walking Larder Patterns of Domestication, Pastoralism and Predation,* ed. J. Clutton-Brock, pp. 207–14. London: Unwin Hyman. 384 pp.
80. Robertshaw, P. T. 1990. *Early Pastoralists of Southwestern Kenya.* Nairobi: Br. Inst. East Africa. 318 pp.
81. Robertshaw, P. T., Mawson, A. 1981. Excavations in eastern Equatoria, southern Sudan 1980. *Azania* 14:55–95
82. Robertshaw, P. T., Siiriainen, A. 1985. Excavations in Lakes Province, Southern Sudan. *Azania* 20:89–151
83. Rognon, P. 1976. Essai d'interpretation des variations climatiques au Sahara depuis

40,000 ans. *Rev. Geogr. Phys. Geol. Dyn.* 18(2–3):251–82
84. Roset, J.-P. 1983. Nouvelles donnees sur le probleme de la Neolithisation du Sahara meridional: Air et Tenere, au Niger. *Cah. ORSTOM Ser. Geol.* 13(2):119–42
85. Roset, J.-P. 1987. Paleoclimatic and cultural conditions of Neolithic development in the early Holocene of northern Niger (Air and Tenere). See Ref. 16a, pp. 211–34
86. Sadr, K. 1991. *The Development of Nomadism in Ancient Northeast Africa.* Philadelphia: Univ. Penn. Press. 180 pp.
87. Sampson, C. G. 1988. *Stylistic Boundaries among Mobile Hunter-Foragers.* Washington, DC: Smithsonian Inst. Press. 186 pp.
88. Schapera, I. 1930. *The Khoisan Peoples of South Africa.* London: Routledge & Kegan Paul. 450 pp.
89. Schmidt-Nielsen, K. 1964. *Desert Animals.* Oxford: Oxford Univ. Press. 277 pp.
90. Schrire, C., Deacon, J. 1989. The indigenous artefacts from Oudepost 1, a colonial outpost of the VOC at Saldanha Bay, Cape. *S. Afr. Archaeol. Bull.* 44:105–13
91. Servant, M., Servant-Vildary, S. 1980. L'environnement Quaternaire du bassin du Tchad. In *The Sahara and the Nile,* ed. M. A. J. Williams, H. Faure, pp. 133–62. Rotterdam: Balkema. 607 pp.
92. Smith, A. B. 1974. *Adrar Bous and Karkarichinkat: examples of post-palaeolithic human adaptation in the Saharan and Sahel zones of West Africa.* PhD thesis. Univ. Calif., Berkeley. 382 pp.
93. Smith, A. B. 1974. Preliminary report of excavations at Karkarichinkat Nord and Sud. *W. Afr. J. Archaeol.* 4:33–55
94. Smith, A. B. 1975. A note on the flora and fauna from the post-palaeolithic sites of Karkarichinkat Nord and Sud. *W. Afr. J. Archaeol.* 5:201–4
95. Smith, A. B. 1979. Biogeographical considerations of colonisation of the lower Tilemsi Valley in the 2nd millenium B. C. *J. Arid Environ.* 2:355–61
96. Smith, A. B. 1980. The Neolithic tradition in the Sahara. In *The Sahara and the Nile,* ed. M. A. J. Williams, H. Faure, pp. 451–65. Rotterdam: Balkema. 607 pp.
97. Smith, A. B. 1983. The disruption of Khoi society in the 17th century. *Africa Seminar: Collected Papers,* 3:257–71. Univ. Cape Town, Centre Afr. Stud.
98. Smith, A. B. 1984. Origins of the Neolithic in the Sahara. See Ref. 15a, pp. 84–92
99. Smith, A. B. 1987. Seasonal exploitation of resources on the Vredenburg Peninsula after 2000 B. P. In *Papers in the Prehistory of the Western Cape, South Africa,* ed. J. Parkington, M. Hall, pp. 393–402. Oxford: BAR Int. Ser. 332. 529 pp.
100. Smith, A. B. 1990. On becoming herders: Khoikhoi and San ethnicity in southern Africa. *Afr. Stud.* 49:2:51–73

101. Smith, A. B. 1992. *Pastoralism in Africa: Origins and Development Ecology.* London: Hurst. In press

102. Smith, A. B. 1992. New approaches to Saharan rock art of the 'bovidian' period. In *L'Arte e l'Ambiente del Sahara Preistorico: Dati e Interpretazioni*, ed. G. Calegari. Mem. Soc. Ital. Sci. Naturali Museo Civico Storia Naturale Milano. In press

103. Smith, A. B., Sadr, K., Gribble, J., Yates, R. 1991. Excavations in the southwestern Cape, South Africa, and the archaeological identity of prehistoric hunter gatherers within the last 2000 years. *S. Afr. Archaeol. Bull.* 46:71–91

104. Stow, G. W. 1905. *The Native Races of South Africa.* London: Swan Sonnenschein. 618 pp.

105. Street, F. A., Grove, A. T. 1976. Environmental and climatic implications of late Quaternary lake-level fluctuations in Africa. *Nature* 261:385–90

106. Wendorf, F., Schild, R., eds. 1980. *Prehistory of the Eastern Sahara.* New York: Academic. 414 pp.

107. Wendorf, F., Schild, R., eds. 1984. *Cattlekeepers of the Eastern Sahara: the Neolithic of Bir Kiseiba.* Dallas: South. Methodist Univ. 452 pp.

108. Williams, M. A. J. 1984. Late Quaternary prehistoric environments in the Sahara. See Ref. 15a, pp. 74–83

109. Yeivin, E., Olami, Y. 1979. Nizzanim, a Neolithic site in Nahal Evtah: excavations of 1968–1970. *Tel Aviv* 6:99–133

Annu. Rev. Anthropol. 1992. 21:143–70
Copyright © 1992 by Annual Reviews Inc. All rights reserved

NUTRITIONAL ADAPTATION

Sara Stinson

Department of Anthropology, Queens College, City University of New York, Flushing, New York 11367

KEYWORDS: diet, enzyme polymorphisms, thrifty genotype, undernutrition, body size

INTRODUCTION

Human diet and food use have always been subjects important to anthropologists. Over the past several decades interest in these topics has grown into an area of research, nutritional anthropology, that crosscuts cultural, archaeological, and biological anthropology. One focus of nutritional anthropology, particularly among biological anthropologists, has been on how nutrition affects human adaptation (see 87 for an earlier review). Nutrition plays a major role in human adaptation because it acts both as an independent stressor (e.g. food scarcity) that may necessitate adjustment and as an important modifier of other stressors (e.g. disease severity) (88). Because nutrition is important to human functioning, behaviors and biological traits that lessen the impact of nutritional stress or improve the capacity of nutrition to buffer the effects of other stressors should be advantageous. Such behaviors and biological traits can be considered nutritional adaptations when their benefits in terms of function, survival, or reproduction are greater than their costs. As will be apparent below, the assessment of both costs and benefits and the demonstration that characteristics are in fact relatively advantageous (157) remain major challenges. Many attributes of living humans have been characterized as nutritional adaptations. These include species-wide characteristics thought to have evolved early in our evolutionary history, traits found only in some populations that may be adaptations to specific past conditions, and responses that can be interpreted as adjustments to present environmental constraints. Here I concentrate on the last two categories of nutritional adaptation. The review is not exhaustive but rather focuses on frequently used examples of nutritional adaptation and on topics that have been the subject of recent research and debate.

143

DIET AND FOOD PREPARATION TECHNIQUES

The Diet of Our Species

Is our species adapted to any particular diet? Eaton and coworkers (50, 51) have argued that we are biologically adapted to the diet of our Pleistocene ancestors and that a return to this diet would reduce the frequency of many chronic diseases associated with the high fat, salt, and sugar diets typical of industrialized countries. Their dietary reconstruction, based primarily on analogy with modern hunter-gatherers, indicates that our ancestral diet was healthier than the current US diet, providing adequate calcium and vitamin C, less fat and sodium, but more fiber. However, Garn & Leonard (69) have criticized several aspects of this reconstruction. They argue that early hominid diets were frequently deficient in nutrients and that food preparation techniques may have resulted in food unsafe to eat.

In addressing the question of whether our species is adapted to a particular diet we confront several problems. First is the difficulty in determining the diets of our ancestors. Dietary reconstructions have usually been based on some combination of information on nonhuman primate diets, archaeological evidence of food use, dental indicators of the types of foods consumed, and analogy with modern hunter-gatherers (1, 50, 69, 81, 89, 168, 239). As pointed out by many of the reconstructors, all of these methods have their problems. Techniques based on bone chemistry promise to provide information on individual diets (127, 203). While these techniques have been applied to fossils (137), current limitations prevent their being generally suitable for analysis of fossilized remains. Even if we could accurately reconstruct the diets of our ancestors, the question would remain: Which diet are we adapted to—that of early *Homo sapiens, H. erectus, H. habilis,* the Australopithecines, or some earlier primate (69, 89)? This problem is intensified by debates about which species are, in fact, our ancestors. Data beyond those of dietary reconstruction alone will be needed to determine whether our species is adapted to a particular diet and, if so, what that diet is.

In another line of inquiry, researchers look for evidence of physiological or morphological adaptation to a particular diet. Several investigators have compared the relative proportions of the compartments of the human digestive system to those of other mammals in an attempt to infer the type of diet our digestive system is adapted to handle (150, 168, 239). Human gut proportions generally imply a diet high in nutrient-dense foods, but whether these foods are necessarily of animal origin is controversial. As all these authors note, gut proportions in other mammals can be modified by dietary change. It is therefore not certain to what extent the human results reflect only the usual diets of the individuals examined. Further research on humans consuming different diets will be necessary to ascertain whether studies of digestive tract proportions will be of use in the determination of a basic human dietary adaptation.

NUTRITIONAL ADAPTATION 145

Advantages of Particular Foods

At a more specific level than studies of species-wide diet are investigations examining the benefits of individual dietary components. Katz & Schall (118, 120, 121) have examined the potential beneficial effects of the consumption of fava beans in malarial areas. Fava beans are a common cultivar in the Mediter- ranean where glucose-6-phosphate dehydrogenase (G6PD) deficiency, an X- linked enzyme deficiency whose major harmful effect is a potentially severe hemolytic anemia following fava bean consumption, is also common. But what appears to be a case of dietary maladaptation—a food is consumed that is harmful to a sizable portion of the population—may, in fact, be the opposite. Fava bean consumption by individuals who are not G6PD deficient may increase their resistance to falciparum malaria. In addition, processing tech- niques and cultural beliefs about fava beans lessen the risk to potentially sensitive individuals. To date, in vivo evidence of the antimalarial action of fava beans is still lacking, although much in vitro evidence supports the hypothesis of beneficial effects (165).

Pica, the ingestion of substances not commonly considered to be food, and more specifically, geophagia, the consumption of soil, are other examples of seemingly harmful dietary behaviors that may have nutritional benefits. It has been proposed that geophagia can provide needed minerals (101), but this remains only one of several hypotheses about the behavior (40).

Another food that may interact with falciparum malaria and with the associ- ated genetic trait, sickle cell anemia, is manioc (cassava) (106, 118). The proposed effects of manioc consumption on malaria and the *hemoglobin S* allele result from the abundant cyanide contained in some varieties of the root. Although much of the cyanide is removed prior to ingestion, blood levels of cyanide metabolites in individuals consuming manioc diets may still be sub- stantial (45). Some investigations indicate that cyanate, a metabolite of cya- nide, prevents sickling of red blood cells in sickle cell anemia, but toxic effects have also been reported at the levels necessary for therapeutic effect (128). Were a diet high in manioc to prevent sickling, selection against homozygotes for *hemoglobin S* would be reduced (107, 109). The effect of cyanide ingestion on selection at the *hemoglobin S* locus is complicated by the fact that cyanate has also been shown to inhibit the growth of malaria parasites in vitro (174). If this effect were seen in manioc eaters, then malarial selection against "normal" homozygotes would be reduced (107). A further complication is the observa- tion that cyanate decreases the activity of G6PD (108) and may have anti- malarial action in this manner as well (118). Jackson (106) has recently examined the pattern of *hemoglobin S* allele frequencies in Liberia in terms of the different possible effects of cyanide intake on selection at the locus in the 400 years since cassava was introduced into Africa from South America. She suggests that in areas of low cassava intake the predominant effect is an increase in the fitness of SS homozygotes, leading to an increase in the frequency of the *hemoglobin S* allele. In areas of high cassava intake, inhibition of the growth of malaria parasites is the main effect, resulting in less selection for *hemoglobin S* and a reduction in S allele frequencies.

Interest in the adaptive value of particular diets also has focused attention on populations such as the Inuit (Eskimo) and African herders, who traditionally consume a diet high in fat and cholesterol but who evidence much less heart disease than do the populations of industrialized countries (11, 104, 105, 147, 212). The Inuit do not exhibit cholesterol-lowering physiological adaptation (105), and researchers have argued that their diet is a major factor in their low levels of heart disease. A series of studies of Greenland Inuit by Bang and Dyerberg (10, 11, 12, 49) suggest that the consumption of marine mammals and fish, rich in omega-3 polyunsaturated fatty acids, is the dietary factor responsible. Subsequent epidemiological and clinical investigations of the effects of fish oils on non-Inuit populations have generally supported the protective effects of fish oils on cholesterol levels and ischemic heart disease (9, 28, 98, 126, 134), although there have been exceptions (202, 263).

The causes of low blood cholesterol levels and low rates of heart disease in African herders are less clear than in the Inuit. In terms of dietary factors, Mann and coworkers (146, 148) have argued that yogurt lowers blood cholesterol levels and that the high intake of fermented milk by Kenyan Maasai is responsible for their low cholesterol levels. This hypothesis is in doubt given the contradictory results of studies of the effect of yogurt consumption (97, 146, 155, 162, 196). Other explanations for low blood cholesterol levels in African herders include a physiological adaptation that reduces cholesterol synthesis (20, 104), high levels of physical activity (147), and alternating periods of high and low fat intake (73, 211, 212). Given recent evidence of substantial seasonality in diet among African pastoralists (139), the last explanation seems most reasonable at present.

Food Processing

In addition to their work on the benefits of certain foods in the diet, Katz and coworkers (118, 119) have examined the potential advantages of food processing techniques. Based on this work, Katz (118) has suggested a "lock and key" hypothesis in which knowledge of food processing techniques is the key that unlocks the full nutritional potential of cultivated plants. He further argues that effective food processing techniques are most likely to develop where a crop is first domesticated and heavily consumed, but that knowledge of these techniques is less likely to spread than the crop itself, leading to less efficient use of the crop outside its core area. Illustrations of this concept include Asian soybean processing techniques that remove potentially harmful compounds (118) and the better-known case of alkali processing of maize by many Amerindian groups (119). Based on studies indicating that the nutritional value of maize is improved by the traditional method of lime boiling used to prepare maize for tortillas (25, 160), Katz and coworkers (119) tested and confirmed the hypothesis that indigenous New World groups that relied heavily on corn also would use alkali processing techniques. Although the cultivation of maize has spread to groups other than Amerindians, alkali processing techniques have not. Pellagra, a niacin deficiency disease, illustrates the "lock and key" hypothesis. Pellagra is extremely rare in groups using alkali cooking of maize. It is, however, associated with corn diets in areas to which the crop, but not its processing technique, has spread (118, 119). Absence of alkali cooking techniques has certainly contributed to many outbreaks of pellagra, but it is not always the most immediate cause. It has been argued that the pellagra outbreak in the US south early in this century occurred at a time when the consumption of maize was probably declining; the outbreak may have been related to the introduction of degermed corn meal at about this time (29). It should also be noted that economic inequality plays an immediate role in the occurrence of pellagra by determining which groups will be forced to subsist on a diet composed primarily of corn (195).

POPULATION DIFFERENCES IN NUTRIENT UTILIZATION

Lactose and Sucrose

The best-known example of variation in nutrient utilization involves differences between populations in the ability of individuals to digest lactose, the sugar in milk (159, 217, 218). The distribution, genetics, origin, and implications of this variation have been reviewed many times (61, 63, 96, 111, 180, 198, 205, 219). In only a few of the world's populations, mainly northern Europeans but also some herding groups in Africa and the Middle East, do most individuals retain high intestinal activity of the enzyme lactase into adulthood. Without this enzyme, lactose cannot be broken down into glucose and galactose, and cannot be absorbed in the small intestine. Adults in most populations have low levels of lactase activity and may suffer from intestinal symptoms of intolerance including bloating, flatulence, and diarrhea upon the ingestion of milk products high in lactose.

Individuals who do not retain the ability to digest lactose have customarily been called lactase deficient, lactose malabsorbers, or lactose intolerant; those who retain the ability have been termed lactose sufficient, lactose absorbers, or lactose tolerant. Several authors have questioned this terminology (61, 112). They note that the inability to digest lactose is frequently not associated with symptoms of intolerance. Further, the terms *malabsorber* and *lactase deficient* mislead by implying that a condition is abnormal that is present in most people. Finally, the term *malabsorber* is inaccurate because the primary problem concerns the digestion of lactose. Flatz (61) suggests new terms for the two phenotypes: *high lactose digestion capacity/persistence of lactase activity* and *low lactose digestion capacity/restriction of lactase activity.* Although somewhat unwieldy, these terms more accurately describe the phenotypes.

Most evidence suggests that adult lactase persistence is inherited as an autosomal dominant trait (61). Although certain findings are not entirely consistent with this mode of inheritance (61, 96, 112), apparent exceptions may result from the inaccuracy of standard lactose tolerance tests in which blood glucose levels are measured following lactose ingestion (61). Suggestions that lactase is an inducible enzyme and that the ability to digest lactose is maintained into adulthood simply by the continued consumption of lactose-rich dairy products after the age of weaning (22) have not been supported by experiment (61, 96).

Since it first received systematic attention, population variation in lactose digestion capacity has been explained primarily in terms of what Simoons (218) called the culture-historical hypothesis. According to this hypothesis, low lactose digestion capacity in adulthood is the normal condition in humans (as in other mammals), and high frequencies of adult persistence of lactase activity resulted from selection only after humans domesticated animals and only in populations relying heavily on lactose-rich dairy products (159, 217, 218). Such selection occurred because individuals with high lactose digestion capacity would have been at a nutritional advantage as a result of their ability to consume large quantities of milk products without experiencing the symptoms of lactose intolerance. Although this hypothesis has received wide support, alternative explanations for persistence of lactase activity have been proposed. In a slight modification of the culture-historical hypothesis, Cook (38) has suggested that high lactose digestion capacity originally evolved among desert nomads in the Arabian peninsula and was selected for mainly because those with the trait would have been better able to absorb the water and electrolytes in milk, an advantage in a hot, dry environment.

Flatz & Rotthauwe (61, 62, 63) have argued that the culture-historical hypothesis is insufficient to explain the high frequency of persistence of lactase activity in northern European populations. Because many individuals with low lactose digestion capacity can consume moderate amounts of high-lactose milk products without experiencing symptoms of intolerance, they suggest that selection due to general nutritional advantage best explains the high lactose digestion capacity in pastoral nomads who consume large amounts of fresh milk. Flatz & Rotthauwe assert that northern European populations probably did not consume such large quantities of milk and that the late introduction of domesticated animals into northern Europe (in particular into Scandinavia, where the highest frequencies of persistent lactase activity are found) is too recent to allow selection due to general nutritional advantage. Their explanation for the high frequency of lactase persistence in northern Europe follows from Loomis's (141) hypothesis about skin color variation in human populations. Loomis suggested that light skin color would be selected for in areas of low ultraviolet light intensity because individuals with light skin would be able to produce more vitamin D and would therefore be less likely to develop rickets. Flatz & Rotthauwe argue that hydrolysis of lactose by lactase has the same effect as vitamin D, increasing intestinal absorption of calcium; persistence of lactase activity would therefore also have been selected for in northern Europe. While there is some experimental support for the calcium absorption hypothesis (35), more recent studies (84, 244) suggest that the hydrolysis of lactose by lactase does not increase calcium absorption; the hypothesis that high lactase activity would have been adaptive because it increases calcium absorption seems in doubt.

In the strongest departure from the culture-historical hypothesis, Nei & Saitou (178) suggest that variation in lactose digestion capacity is unrelated to milk consumption. According to these investigators the polymorphism was established as a result of natural selection or genetic drift long before animal domestication. They argue that the gene for persistence of lactase must have evolved at least 40,000 years ago because the gene is present in Asians, Europeans, and Africans, who, according to their calculations, diverged between 40,000 and 100,000 years ago. As further support for the early evolution of high lactose digestion capacity, they point out that some nonhuman primates have high frequencies of the trait (257). The early-polymorphism hypothesis, however, has been criticized because it ignores the possibility that the gene for lactase persistence arose by mutation before 40,000 years ago but did not become frequent until it was selected for in parallel in many populations after animal domestication (61).

At present the culture-historical explanation of the distribution of high lactose digestion capacity seems the best supported, but questions raised by proponents of other hypotheses remain to be answered. What dietary proportion of lactose-rich dairy products confers a nutritional advantage to high lactose digestion capacity? Were such quantities consumed in prehistoric northern Europe? Also puzzling is the fact that many human groups with no history of milking are polymorphic in terms of lactose digestion capacity. Although this is usually explained in terms of gene flow, the observation that some nonhuman primates have high frequencies of lactase persistence raises the possibility of earlier evolution of appreciable frequencies of the trait.

Humans also vary in their ability to digest sugars other than lactose. Some Inuit groups have a high prevalence of inability to digest the sugar sucrose as a result of lower activity of the intestinal enzyme sucrase (15, 52, 161). It is questionable whether this can be considered a dietary adaptation because no one suggests that it is advantageous; it probably results from genetic drift made possible by the fact that the low sugar content of the traditional Inuit diet would not have selected for the persistence of sucrase activity.

Ethanol

There is considerable evidence of population variation in ethanol metabolism. Comparisons of the rate of clearance of ethanol from the blood have generally found faster rates in Amerindians than in Europeans (17, 56, 57, 193). Less consistent results are found in comparisons of ethanol metabolism per unit body weight. Metabolism seems to be faster in Chinese and Japanese than in Europeans (91, 193), but comparisons of Amerindians and Europeans have yielded contradictory results (17, 56, 57, 59, 193). A major complication in interpreting population comparisons of rate of disappearance of blood ethanol or rate of ethanol metabolism per unit body weight is that neither of these measures controls fully for differences in body composition, although the latter, as usually calculated, does so at least partially (58, 115, 192, 201). Given this problem, attention has focused on variation in blood levels of acetaldehyde, the product of the first step in the metabolism of ethanol. Several studies report higher acetaldehyde levels following alcohol ingestion in north Asians than in Europeans (53, 54, 209, 271). These high acetaldehyde levels have been explained as resulting either from an atypical form of alcohol dehydrogenase (ADH), the enzyme responsible for the conversion of ethanol to acetaldehyde (232), or from the lack of the more active form of aldehyde dehydrogenase (ALDH), the enzyme that metabolizes acetaldehyde to acetate (76, 77, 79). [The more active form of ALDH, which is found in the mitochondria, was previously referred to as ALDHI, but is now called ALDH2 (223); some authors still use the older terminology.] Goedde and coworkers (4, 5, 79) argue that the atypical ADH is not responsible for high acetaldehyde levels because, although the atypical form of ADH has higher activity in vitro, alcohol metabolism has not been found to be faster in individuals with atypical ADH. They support the lack of ALDH2 as the cause of high acetaldehyde levels because acetaldehyde levels have been found to be higher in Japanese deficient in ALDH2 (77, 92, 133, 171). While their arguments are convincing, atypical ADH cannot be totally excluded as a cause of high acetaldehyde levels because even though individuals with atypical ADH do not metabolize ethanol more rapidly over the long term, they may metabolize it more rapidly in the period immediately after alcohol consumption and therefore have higher early levels of acetaldehyde (3).

Atypical ADH has been found in most north Asians but in fewer than 25% of Europeans tested (4). ALDH2 deficiency is common (approximately 30% are deficient) in north Asians, but absent in Europeans and north Africans (78). Few Amerindian groups have been tested to date, but three South American groups have frequencies of ALDH2 deficiency similar to those of north Asians, while groups in North America have much lower levels of ALDH2 deficiency (78, 270). Goedde and coworkers (77, 79) suggest that high levels of acetaldehyde as a result of ALDH2 deficiency are responsible for the facial flushing frequently observed in north Asians following alcohol ingestion. This idea is supported by findings that facial flushing is much more common in deficient than in nondeficient Japanese subjects (92, 170, 171, 214), but it is puzzling that North Amerindians, who also exhibit facial flushing in response to alcohol (264), do not have high frequencies of ALDH2 deficiency. It has also been suggested that those who experience facial flushing and associated symptoms of alcohol sensitivity will be less likely to become alcohol abusers and that the high frequency of these characteristics in north Asians may explain their low rate of alcoholism (77). High rates of alcoholism among Amerindians contradict this hypothesis. Social factors rather than variation in alcohol metabolism seem the best explanation for differences in alcoholism rates among populations (156, 201).

Variation in ethanol metabolism, whatever its present effect, is usually considered to have arisen as the result of genetic drift rather than natural selection (178). Several authors, however, have recently suggested potential mechanisms for selection for high ADH activity or ALDH2 deficiency. These include selection based on the possible roles of ADH and ALDH in neurotransmitter and hormone metabolism (64), and selection favoring individuals deficient in ALDH2 because their higher acetaldehyde levels inhibit the growth of intestinal parasites (80).

BENEFICIAL TRAITS MADE HARMFUL BY CHANGED ENVIRONMENTS

Diabetes

In 1962, Neel (176:353) suggested that diabetes mellitus was the result of "a 'thrifty' genotype rendered detrimental by 'progress'." He hypothesized that the quick release of insulin in response to hyperglycemia would have been advantageous to our hunter-gatherer ancestors as a means to store calories during times of plenty; this quick insulin response became disadvantageous, leading to overproduction of insulin and diabetes mellitus, in environments with (over)abundant food supplies. Neel (177) has updated his hypothesis to take into account new understandings of diabetes, in particular the distinction between juvenile-onset or insulin-dependent diabetes and maturity-onset or non-insulin-dependent diabetes (NIDDM), and has outlined several possible metabolic pathways whereby a "thrifty genotype" could result in NIDDM.

The thrifty-genotype hypothesis has been used frequently to explain the high prevalence of NIDDM among North Amerindians (16, 129, 131, 184, 215, 256, 258). Several kinds of evidence have been used to support the idea that Amerindians have a genetic predisposition to NIDDM and that this predisposition originally evolved as a thrifty trait that became harmful with Westernization. Diabetes was rare in North Amerindians before 1940, but today most tribes have diabetes prevalence rates greater than those of US whites; and diabetes has become a major health problem in most North Amerindian groups (172, 215, 216, 259). The highest prevalence of diabetes is found in the Pima, with 50% of individuals over age 35 having diabetes; a number of other groups have adult diabetes prevalence rates over 20% (216, 256). Although it has been argued that high levels of obesity, a major risk factor for NIDDM, can explain the high rates of diabetes in North Amerindians (260), even lean Pima have a much greater incidence of diabetes than US whites (130). Diabetes is also common in Mexican-Americans (233), and again this high prevalence cannot be explained on the basis of obesity alone (234). Findings that diabetes prevalence in Mexican-Americans is positively associated with amount of Amerindian admixture further support an Amerindian genetic predisposition to NIDDM (30, 31, 68). It is interesting, however, that studies to date find such associations using group admixture levels but not on the basis of individual admixture estimates (30, 90).

Knowler and coworkers (129, 131) have argued that the thrifty-genotype hypothesis could well explain diabetes in the Pima, who traditionally practiced irrigated desert agriculture in an area with unpredictable rainfall. Among the Pima, the ability of insulin to cause cellular uptake of glucose is impaired even in nondiabetics, but the action of insulin to inhibit the breakdown of fat is retained in severe diabetics. Knowler et al hypothesize that this retention would lead to increased fat storage when food is abundant. Such storage would have been advantageous under the Pima's previous conditions, but it results in obesity, insulin resistance, and diabetes under today's greater food availability. At a wider level, Weiss et al (256) have proposed that the thrifty-genotype hypothesis could account for the evolution among all Amerindians of a predisposition to obesity, diabetes, cholesterol, gallstones, and gallbladder cancer, a constellation of conditions they refer to as the New World Syndrome. They suggest that the circumstances under which the New World was originally populated—small groups of individuals living under severe arctic conditions—would have been ideal for the spread of thrifty genes through the original founding population by a combination of selection and genetic drift. Inuit, who have lower rates of diabetes than Amerindians (216, 240, 256), are not at present included among those susceptible to the New World Syndrome, but Weiss and coworkers do not rule out the possibility that Inuit may begin to experience the New World Syndrome in the future as their diet becomes more Westernized.

A slightly different scenario employing the thrifty-genotype hypothesis was presented recently by Wendorf (258). He suggests that selection for thrifty genes took place at the point when the ancestors of Amerindians had migrated south of the northern ice-free corridor and were abruptly confronted with unfamiliar non-arctic hunting conditions. These conditions precipitated food shortages and selection favoring those able to store calories efficiently as fat. Based on the suggestion that there occurred three migrations to the New World (83), and on the possibility of lower rates of NIDDM in speakers of Athapascan languages, Wendorf further proposes that the ancestors of speakers of Athapascan languages would not have been subject to selection for thrifty genes because by the time of their migration environmental conditions had changed. This is an interesting suggestion, but it is not clear that differences in diabetes rates between Athapascan and non-Athapascan speakers need an evolutionary explanation. Canadian speakers of Athapascan languages do have low rates of diabetes (240, 266), but this is not the case for many US Athapascan speakers (16, 216, 259), suggesting that environmental factors play an important role.

Although the thrifty-genotype hypothesis is used widely to explain the high prevalence of diabetes in Amerindians, it is not universally accepted (194, 240, 241). Based on her studies of the Canadian Dogrib, Szathmary (240, 241) argues that the postulated quick release of insulin in response to hyperglycemia would not have been likely to occur during the early stages of migration to the Americas because the high-protein, low-carbohydrate diet then current would have prevented hyperglycemia. As an alternative to the thrifty-genotype hypothesis she suggests that adaptation to a high-protein diet could have resulted in inappropriate response to carbohydrate, leading to hyperglycemia, oversecretion of insulin, and NIDDM when individuals with such an adaptation began to consume a high-carbohydrate diet. While this hypothesis might explain abnormalities of glucose tolerance among northern American groups, who have (or had until very recently) a high-protein diet, it does not seem to apply as well to agricultural groups such as the Pima who have a long history of high carbohydrate intake but have developed NIDDM only recently. However, the Pima case is potentially reconcilable with Szathmary's hypothesis given the fact that traditional Pima carbohydrate sources are more slowly digested and raise glucose and insulin levels less than do Western cereal products (24). Thus the traditional diet may have placed less stress on a system adapted to high protein intake.

It is not only in Amerindians that NIDDM prevalence is high. Westernized Polynesian and Australian Aborigine populations also show high rates of diabetes (273), and on the island of Nauru in Micronesia over 30% of individuals over age 15 have diabetes (274). Given that the settlement history of these areas involved colonization by small numbers of people under severe circumstances, the thrifty-genotype hypothesis also has been used as an explanation for diabetes in these populations (272, 273). Recently, the prevalence of NIDDM in second-generation Japanese-American men in the Seattle area was found to be twice that of US males of European ancestry and four times that in Japan (67). The thrifty-genotype hypothesis does not seem to fit this case well, and the finding of high rates of diabetes in Japanese-Americans raises the possibility that a genetic predisposition to NIDDM is an Asian (or north Asian) characteristic rather than one specific to colonized regions.

Hypertension

The idea that a thrifty genotype might become harmful with environmental change has also been used to explain the high prevalence of hypertension among US blacks. Gleibermann (75) suggested that an increased ability to retain sodium evolved in parts of Africa as an adaptation to a combination of high sweat rate, made necessary by the tropical climate, and low salt availability. This salt conservation adaptation became disadvantageous in environments with abundant salt, resulting in an increased predisposition to develop high blood pressure. Subsequent investigation of the history of salt supplies in West Africa found that salt was, in fact, rare in most of the region and suggested that blood pressures in West African cities today, where salt is readily available, are inversely related to past salt availability (262). While these studies support selection for salt conservation taking place in Africa, Wilson & Grim (262a) have recently suggested that selection took place as a result of conditions imposed by slavery, especially the high frequency of salt-depleting diseases such as diarrhea that would have occurred on slaving ships. While their hypothesis is interesting and deserves further study, it rests on there being more hypertension in US blacks than in Africans living in comparable circumstances, a situation that has not been shown to exist (5a).

The idea of a sodium conservation adaptation in US blacks is supported by the finding that blacks with normal blood pressure have lower renal sodium excretion following saline infusion than do whites (142). There is also evidence that hypertension in US blacks has a different basis than that in whites. Blacks with high blood pressure are much more likely than hypertensive whites to have low levels of the hormone renin, they generally respond better to diuretics, and they may have higher plasma volumes (7, 39, 135, 200, 251, 265). As these authors note, differences in sodium handling provide one possible explanation for these differences between black and white hypertensives.

The salt conservation hypothesis implies that blacks have a genetic predisposition to develop hypertension, but environmental factors could also contribute to blood pressure differences between US blacks and whites. Among dietary factors, high sodium intake and low intakes of potassium and calcium have been suggested to increase blood pressure (114, 117, 125, 143, 158, 255). The sodium intake of US blacks has not generally been found to be higher than that of whites, but potassium intakes have been found to be lower (65, 74, 86, 265). The higher ratio of sodium to potassium intake among blacks, however, could not explain all of the difference in blood pressure between US whites and blacks in the first National Health and Nutrition Examination Survey (NHANES) (65). Similarly, although calcium intakes of blacks in the first and second NHANES were lower than those of whites, this difference could not account fully for blood pressure differences between the two groups (210). While differences in blood pressure between US whites and blacks cannot be explained easily on the basis of dietary differences, the possibility that they result from increased stress among blacks as a result of poverty and racial discrimination is difficult to reject (7, 74).

If the higher prevalence of hypertension in US blacks is the result of selection for salt conservation that occurred either in Africa or early in slavery, one might expect blood pressure to be higher in individuals with a greater percentage of genes of African origin. The most frequent test of this hypothesis involves studies that have used skin color as an indicator of admixture. While some of these investigations have found that darker skin color in US blacks is associated with higher blood pressure (23, 93, 94), others have found that skin color is not a strong predictor of blood pressure (122, 123, 126a). The studies that have found a relationship between skin color and blood pressure have been criticized because socioeconomic status, which has been found to be correlated with both skin color and blood pressure, was not always controlled; furthermore, in some of the studies (93, 94), skin color was rated with a subjective scale (246). Problems in the interpretation of studies relating skin color and blood pressure are not resolved by studies of the relationship between blood pressure and estimates of admixture based on blood polymorphisms. Blood pressure has been found to be positively associated with African admixture among blacks in Rochester, New York (144) and on the Caribbean Island of La Désirade (41), but not among Caribbean Black Caribs or Baltimore blacks (102, 103, 167a). These results are no more consistent than those relating skin color and hypertension.

Even if darker skin or amount of African admixture were found to be associated with higher blood pressure, it is open to question whether this would fully support a genetic basis for hypertension in US blacks. Skin color is not a socially neutral characteristic. Studies reporting a positive correlation between skin color and blood pressure in US blacks may measure not genetic effects on blood pressure but the increased social stress associated with dark skin color (246). Since degree of African admixture as estimated from blood polymorphisms might reasonably be expected to correlate with skin color, these studies can be criticized on the same grounds.

ADAPTATIONS TO PROTEIN ENERGY UNDERNUTRITION

Metabolic Adaptation

As noted by Waterlow (253) in his review of metabolic adaptations to undernutrition, the ability of humans to adjust to a range of protein intakes is well documented. As levels of protein intake are reduced, amino acids are reutilized more efficiently; protein breakdown and synthesis are reduced such that intake balances obligatory nitrogen losses (55, 206, 268, 269). While increased efficiency of amino acid utilization appears to be without harmful consequences, it has been argued that reduced protein turnover may have a negative impact because it reduces the organism's ability to respond to trauma and infection (206, 253, 267).

Most studies providing information on responses to low protein diets involve the restriction of protein intake for relatively short periods in previously well-nourished adults. We have few data on whether additional adaptations occur in individuals experiencing chronically low protein intakes throughout their life spans. Although the most recent FAO/WHO/UNU (55) statement on energy and protein requirements concluded that there were no differences between groups in average protein requirement, Waterlow (253) argues that several studies suggest lower requirements in individuals with habitually low protein intakes. Interesting in this regard is Oomen's (179) suggestion that nitrogen-fixing bacteria might be present in the large intestines of people in the Mount Hagen region of New Guinea. Nitrogen-fixing bacteria were subsequently found in human intestines (18), but doubts have been raised about whether such bacteria actually supply nitrogen to their hosts (100, 268).

There is also debate about the extent of metabolic adaptation to low calorie intakes. Evidence of metabolic adaptation comes from the classic Minnesota starvation studies of Keys and coworkers (124), which showed a reduction in basal metabolic rate (BMR) of about 36% after a six-month period of energy restriction. Although most of the decline in BMR resulted from a reduction in metabolically active tissue because of weight loss, a substantial portion of the decline was the result of a decrease in BMR/kg active tissue (110).

Does this same sort of metabolic adjustment occur in chronic undernutrition? A number of studies report measured caloric intakes well below accepted standards in moderately undernourished but active adults (46). These low caloric intakes might be considered to suggest some sort of adaptation to long-term, low energy intakes, but this conclusion does not seem justified (46, 110): Individuals supposedly subsisting on very low caloric intakes frequently lose weight when they are placed in metabolic wards and fed the same number of calories as ingested in their previously measured diet (8, 46). In terms of BMR, there is evidence that residents of tropical areas have a lower BMR per unit body weight than do individuals of European ancestry (96a, 204), but the extent to which this is due to climatic, dietary, or other factors is unclear. Studies directly comparing metabolic rates of individuals differing in nutritional status have yielded contradictory results. Gambian men have been found to have lower BMR in relation to fat free mass than European men (169), and one comparison of undernourished and well-nourished workers in India found that the resting metabolic rate was significantly lower in the undernourished group both in absolute terms and expressed relative to body weight or lean body mass (213). On the other hand, no evidence of lower BMR relative to weight or lean body mass in undernourished individuals was found in comparisons of rural Indian agriculturalists differing in socioeconomic status (163) or of undernourished and well-nourished Colombian children (229). The results of these studies are difficult to assess owing to inadequate determinations of body composition. In only some of the studies (169, 229) was the equation used to estimate lean body mass validated on the subject population. Even when lean body mass is accurately determined, differences or lack of differences between well- and poorly nourished individuals in BMR per unit lean body mass cannot necessarily be taken as evidence for or against metabolic adaptation, because the lean tissue of undernourished individuals may not contain the same proportion of metabolically active tissue as that of well-nourished individuals (60, 223a, 261).

A further question of interest in terms of metabolic response to low energy intakes is whether additional energy-saving adaptations occur during pregnancy and lactation. This possibility is suggested by studies reporting that women's energy intakes during pregnancy and lactation do not appear to cover their energy costs (2, 26, 48, 186, 190, 191, 245, 248). Several explanations have been suggested for these findings. The best evidence for metabolic adaptations during pregnancy comes from studies of Gambian women subsisting on marginal food intakes in whom BMR during pregnancy is lower, on average, than in the nonpregnant state because of a substantial decrease in BMR during early pregnancy (136). That the reduction in BMR occurs in response to low food intakes is shown by the fact that BMR is much higher in pregnant Gambian women given food supplements (136). Although metabolic adaptation to low food intake during pregnancy does appear to occur in undernourished Gambian women, it must be noted that birth weight increases after maternal supplementation (187), indicating that the metabolic responses are not completely successful in buffering the fetus from the adverse effects of food shortages. Reductions in BMR have also been observed in well-nourished pregnant and lactating women, although not universally (188, 189).

Another possible explanation for the apparently low food intake of pregnant and lactating women is that changes in the release of digestive hormones during pregnancy and lactation increase digestive capacity (247), a finding that may explain the observation, almost 40 years ago, of improvement in digestive tract functioning during pregnancy in a woman who had undergone extensive small intestine resectioning (173). While there is some evidence to support the existence of metabolic adaptations during pregnancy and lactation, given methodological problems in accurately measuring energy expenditure (47) and food intake (140, 221), it is also possible that the difference between energy intakes and costs may have been overestimated in many studies. If this is the case, there is less need to invoke metabolic adaptation to explain these results.

Body Size

One of the most frequently discussed and debated aspects of responses to undernutrition is whether small body size (low height for age but adequate weight for height, also referred to as stunting) is an adaptation to malnutrition. It has been suggested that small body size is advantageous under conditions of nutritional stress because small individuals require fewer nutrients for growth and maintenance (235, 236, 242), and it has been proposed that fast-growing children would be more likely than their slower-growing peers to become severely malnourished when food supplies are limited (70).

Small body size does reduce the caloric costs of performing certain tasks. For example, Spurr & Reina (228) compared the energy cost of carrying a load while walking on a treadmill in undernourished and well-nourished individuals and found that undernourished boys expended less energy because their smaller body size meant that they were moving less total weight (body weight + load).

Related to studies of task efficiency are investigations comparing the efficiency of work (in a technical sense) in individuals differing in body size. Spurr et al (227) compared undernourished and adequately nourished Colombian boys in terms of their work efficiency in treadmill walking and found that the smaller, undernourished boys did not perform work more efficiently (and by some measures were actually less efficient). While this result may seem to contradict the idea that small body size is advantageous, it must be kept in mind that the result pertains to work as technically defined—weight moved over distance—and not to *work* used informally to mean a task performed. In this study, the work performed was the movement of body weight on the treadmill; because the smaller boys weighed less, they had to move over a greater distance than did the larger boys in order to perform the same amount of work. In contrast to the results of the Colombian study are the results of two recent studies, one comparing Gurkha and British soldiers matched for body weight (237), and the other comparing Gambian and European men matched as closely as possible for body mass index and percentage body fat (169). These studies found Gurkha and Gambian men performed work more efficiently than did European men. Although neither non-European group was considered malnourished, both groups were significantly shorter than their European controls. However, it should be noted that small body size is not necessarily the cause of the greater work efficiency. In the case of the Gambian men, greater economy of movement during walking may account for their greater efficiency (169); in the case of the Gurkha soldiers, greater muscular development in the legs may explain their greater efficiency during step tests (237). The results of these studies indicate that although small body size enables individuals to perform certain tasks at a lower energy cost, it does not necessarily result in greater work efficiency.

Proposed advantages of small body size are also examined in investigations of the relationship between body size and children's performance in strength and motor tasks. If small body size is advantageous in terms of task efficiency, one might expect superior performance relative to body size in undernourished children. Some studies do find this to be the case (181). For example, undernourished boys in Kinshasha, Zaire, generally performed worse than well-nourished boys from the same city in terms of grip strength, throwing, running and jumping (72). After controlling for body weight, however, the performance of the undernourished boys was equal to or better than that of the well-nourished boys. Similarly, for their body weight, Efe pygmy children performed better in most tasks than did larger Lese children (71). Results of a comparison of moderately undernourished children from Pere, New Guinea, and Oaxaca, Mexico, with well-nourished Philadelphia children present a somewhat different picture (145). After controlling for body size, the New Guinea children performed better than the Philadelphia children in most tasks, but the Mexican children's performance was worse than that of Philadelphia children in running and jumping. This study, then, suggests variation between tasks and populations and does not fully support the idea that smaller-bodied individuals show superior performance relative to body size.

A number of studies have examined another aspect of the possible advantage of small body size under conditions of nutritional stress by investigating whether small body size is associated with greater reproductive success in undernourished populations. Studies have variously found that shorter women have a higher percentage of offspring surviving (66), that shorter women have a lower percentage of offspring surviving (153), and that there is no relationship between maternal stature and offspring survival rate (44, 138). Looking at the actual number of surviving children, a better measure of reproductive success, the relationship between maternal stature and number of surviving offspring in undernourished populations has been found to be negative (44), positive (153), curvilinear (27), and nonsignificant (138). These results point once again to population variability.

A further complication in examining the effect of body size on reproductive success is that studies of maternal body size and child survival relate only to the differential fertility component of reproductive success and do not take into account size-associated differential mortality before reaching adulthood. Investigations of the relationship between height and childhood mortality in undernourished populations consistently report that children who die are shorter than survivors (6, 19, 99, 222). This finding illustrates the difficulty of applying data on mortality and fertility differences to the larger evolutionary question of body size selection. It would be difficult to argue that children who die are genetically small; it is much more likely that their smallness (and deaths) result from their poor health and nutritional status. It is also difficult to determine to what extent associations between fertility and adult body size are the result of genetic differences in body size rather than environmental factors that affect both height and reproductive performance (27).

The recent "small but healthy" hypothesis proposed by Seckler (207, 208) has raised considerable debate about the adaptive value of small body size (14, 151, 166, 167, 183, 206). Seckler argues that individuals who would be considered to suffer from mild to moderate malnutrition because of their stunted growth (short stature but adequate weight for height) represent successful adaptation to undernutrition because they have adjusted their growth rates and nutrient needs to limited food supplies without suffering functional impairment. They are small but healthy (207, 208). Margen (149) has expressed a similar view.

The proposal that body size reduction is a no-cost response to undernutrition, with no harmful consequences to the individual or the population, has been criticized on several grounds. Marginally undernourished children and adults have reduced maximal work capacity compared to well-nourished individuals, and this reduction is related to their smaller lean body mass (224,

225). The effect of body size on maximal work capacity is shown by a study comparing undernourished and well-nourished Colombian boys (231). Boys with low weight (and height) for age but normal weight for height, who were considered to have been undernourished in the past but to be normally nourished at the time of study, had lower maximal work capacity than well-nourished boys. Furthermore, the work capacity of the stunted boys was virtually identical to that of boys with low weight for height who were judged to be undernourished at the time of study.

Since work for long periods only can be maintained at about 35–40% of maximal work capacity, undernourished individuals, with their lower work capacity, would be expected to be less productive in prolonged energy-demanding activities (224). Studies of workers in the high-energy output task of harvesting sugar cane indicate that maximal work capacity is positively related to worker productivity (42, 43, 226). As Martorell & Arroyave (152) point out, studies of workers in energy-demanding activities do not provide universal support for the idea that stunting reduces productivity, because not all of them have found that reduced height adversely affects productivity. In this regard it would be interesting to know whether workers employed in jobs such as sugar cane harvesting represent the full range of work capacity and body size among undernourished (stunted) populations. It seems likely that they do not, because some degree of self-selection is probably involved in determining who becomes employed in such energy-demanding activities. If sugar cane workers are not representative of the population, this might partially explain the failure to find that productivity is always related to body size. One of the few studies to examine productivity in a less intense activity found that the number of detonator fuses produced per day by factory workers in India (who were judged to have variable nutritional histories) was significantly correlated with both weight and height (199).

Moderate undernutrition has harmful consequences other than reduced maximal work capacity. Physical activity is reduced in undernourished individuals (82, 124, 197) and increases when supplemental food is given (34, 230, 243, 249). While the reduction in physical activity could be viewed as an energy-saving adaptation, decreased activity in young children may damage their behavioral development by reducing their interaction with people and surroundings (13, 32, 33). Viteri & Torun (250) have suggested that reduction in physical activity may directly cause growth retardation in undernourished children. In addition, impairments in immune function have been associated with moderate undernutrition (154). Although reductions in immune function and activity levels are not the direct result of small body size, they are the result of the undernutrition and poor health that lead to small body size. In these terms, it is not being small per se that is harmful; rather, the process that results in small body size is harmful (14, 151).

Is small body size an adaptation to undernutrition? This depends in part on how one defines adaptation. Scrimshaw & Young (206:21–22) make the distinction between adaptation, the achievement of "a long-term, steady state ... while function is maintained within an 'acceptable' or 'preferred' range," and accommodation, "responses ... that, while they favor survival of the individual, result simultaneously in significant losses in some important functions." Scrimshaw & Young consider small body size to be an accommodation to undernutrition, not an adaptation, because of the harmful consequences discussed above. This distinction between adaptation and accommodation usefully underscores the harmful aspects of small body size and counters a potential implication of the "small but healthy" argument—that there is no urgent need to direct nutritional resources to the vast majority of undernourished individuals because they are well adapted to their environment. With respect to the customary use of the term adaptation in anthropology, however, Scrimshaw & Young's definition seems narrow. Although there is no consensus definition of the term, anthropologists generally do not require *adaptations* to be free of harmful consequences. As pointed out by Pelto & Pelto (182), our most frequently used example of a genetic adaptation, the increased frequency of *hemoglobin S* in geographic regions where falciparum malaria is prevalent, is hardly a no-cost adaptation: The polymorphism is preserved at the expense of having some individuals die from sickle cell anemia. Adaptations are traits that are relatively advantageous (157). In this sense we do not yet know whether small body size is an adaptation to undernutrition because we cannot measure its costs and benefits accurately.

CONCLUSIONS

There is still much work to be done on the subject of nutritional adaptation. Even the most frequent textbook example of nutritional adaptation, high lactose digestion capacity, is not yet fully understood. Perhaps this is because we have tended to accept explanations too readily for the adaptive value of particular attributes. Such acceptance forecloses research on topics about which major questions remain to be answered. Much of the research reviewed here is that of non-anthropologists. Anthropologists have long been consumers of research in other fields, and the topic of nutritional adaptation necessarily includes several disciplines; but if anthropologists seek to answer questions about population variation and evolution they cannot necessarily rely on research from disciplines in which these issues may not be major concerns.

ACKNOWLEDGMENTS

I am grateful to Ian Carmichael and Gillian Harper for their bibliographic assistance. This paper is dedicated to Ian's memory.

Literature Cited

1. Abrams, H. L. 1979. The relevance of paleolithic diet in determining contemporary nutritional needs. *J. Appl. Nutr.* 31:43–59
2. Adair, L. S. 1984. Marginal intake and maternal adaptation: the case of rural Taiwan. See Ref. 185, pp. 33–55
3. Aebi, H. E., von Wartburg, J.-P., Wyss, S. R. 1981. The role of enzyme polymorphisms and enzyme variants in the evolutionary process. In *Food, Nutrition and Evolution*, ed. D. N. Walcher, N. Kretchmer, pp. 143–53. New York: Masson
4. Agarwal, D. P., Goedde, H. W. 1986. Ethanol oxidation: ethnic variations in metabolism and response. See Ref. 116, pp. 99–112
5. Agarwal, D. P., Harada, S., Goedde, H. W. 1981. Racial differences in biological sensitivity to ethanol: the role of alcohol dehydrogenase and aldehyde dehydrogenase isozymes. *Alcohol. Clin. Exp. Res.* 5:12–16
5a. Akinkugbe, O. O. 1985. World epidemiology of hypertension in blacks. In *Hypertension in Blacks*, ed. W. D. Hall, E. Saunders, N. B. Schulman, pp. 3–16. Chicago: Year Book Medical Publisher
6. Alam, N., Wojtyniak, B., Rahaman, M. M. 1989. Anthropometric indicators and risk of death. *Am. J. Clin. Nutr.* 49:884–88
7. Anderson, N. B., Myers, H. F., Pickering, T., Jackson, J. S. 1989. Hypertension in blacks: psychosocial and biological perspectives. *J. Hypertension* 7:161–72
8. Ashworth, A. 1968. An investigation of very low calorie intake reported in Jamaica. *Br. J. Nutr.* 22:341–55
9. Ballard-Barbash, R., Callaway, C. W. 1987. Marine fish oils: role in prevention of coronary artery disease. *Mayo Clin. Proc.* 62:113–18
10. Bang, H. O., Dyerberg, J. 1980. Lipid metabolism and ischemic heart disease in Greenland Eskimos. *Adv. Nutr. Res.* 3:1–22
11. Bang, H. O., Dyerberg, J., Nielsen, A. B. 1971. Plasma lipid and lipoprotein pattern in Greenlandic west-coast Eskimos. *Lancet* 1:1143–46
12. Bang, H. O., Dyerberg, J., Sinclair, H. M. 1980. The composition of Eskimo food in north western Greenland. *Am. J. Clin. Nutr.* 33:2657–61
13. Barrett, D. E., Frank, D. A. 1987. *The Effects of Undernutrition on Children's Behavior.* New York: Gordon & Breach
14. Beaton, G. H. 1989. Small but healthy? Are we asking the right question? *Hum. Organ.* 48:30–39
15. Bell, R. R., Draper, H. H., Bergan, J. G. 1973. Sucrose, lactose, and glucose tolerance in northern Alaskan Eskimos. *Am. J. Clin. Nutr.* 26:1185–90
16. Bennett, P. H., Rushforth, N. B., Miller, M., LeCompte, P. M. 1976. Epidemiologic study of diabetes in the Pima Indians. *Recent Prog. Horm. Res.* 32:333–76

17. Bennion, L. J., Li, T. K. 1976. Alcohol metabolism in American Indians and whites. *N. Engl. J. Med.* 294:9–13
18. Bergersen, F. J., Hipsley, E. H. 1970. The presence of N_2-fixing bacteria in the intestines of man and animals. *J. Gen. Microbiol.* 60:61–65
19. Billewicz, W. Z., McGregor, I. A. 1982. A birth-to-maturity longitudinal study of heights and weights in two West African (Gambian) villages, 1951–1975. *Ann. Hum. Biol.* 9:309–20
20. Biss, K., Ho, K. J., Mikkelson, B., Lewis, L., Taylor, C. B. 1971. Some unique biologic characteristics of the Masai of East Africa. *N. Engl. J. Med.* 284:694–99
21. Blaxter, K., Waterlow, J. C., eds. 1985. *Nutritional Adaptation in Man.* London: John Libbey
22. Bolin, T. D., Davis, A. E. 1970. Primary adult lactase deficiency: genetic or acquired? *Am. J. Digest. Dis.* 15:679–92
23. Boyle, E. 1970. Biological patterns in hypertension by race, sex, body weight, and skin color. *J. Am. Med. Assoc.* 213:1637–43
24. Brand, J. C., Snow, B. J., Nabhan, G. P., Truswell, A. S. 1990. Plasma glucose and insulin responses to traditional Pima Indian meals. *Am. J. Clin. Nutr.* 51:416–20
25. Bressani, R., Scrimshaw, N. S. 1958. Effect of lime treatment on in vitro availability of essential amino acids and solubility of protein fractions in corn. *Agric. Food Chem.* 6:774–78
26. Brewer, M., Bates, M. R., Vannoy, L. P. 1989. Postpartum changes in maternal weight and body fat depots in lactating vs nonlactating women. *Am. J. Clin. Nutr.* 49:259–65
27. Brush, G., Boyce, A. J., Harrison, G. A. 1983. Associations between anthropometric variables and reproductive performance in a Papua New Guinea highland population. *Ann. Hum. Biol.* 10:223–34
28. Burr, M. L., Fehily, A. M., Gilbert, J. F., Rogers, S., Holliday, R. M., et al. 1989. Effects of changes in fat, fish, and fibre intakes on death and myocardial reinfarction: Diet and Reinfarction Trial (DART). *Lancet* 2:757–61
29. Carpenter, K. J. 1981. Effects of different methods of processing maize on its pellagragenic activity. *Fed. Proc.* 40:1531–35
30. Chakraborty, R., Ferrell, R. E., Stern, M. P., Haffner, S. M., Hazuda, H. P., et al. 1986. Relationship of prevalence of non-insulin-dependent diabetes mellitus to Amerindian admixture in Mexican Americans of San Antonio, Texas. *Genet. Epidemiol.* 3:435-54
31. Chakraborty, R., Weiss, K. M. 1986. Frequencies of complex diseases in hybrid populations. *Am. J. Phys. Anthropol.* 70:489–503

32. Chavez, A., Martinez, C. 1979. Consequences of insufficient nutrition on child character and behavior. In *Malnutrition, Environment, and Behavior,* ed. D. A. Levitzky, pp. 238–55. Ithaca, NY: Cornell Univ. Press

33. Chavez, A., Martinez, C. 1984. Behavioral measurements of activity in children and their relation to food intake in a poor community. See Ref. 185, pp. 303–21

34. Chavez, A., Martinez, C., Bourges, H. 1972. Nutrition and development of infants from poor rural areas. 2. Nutritional level and physical activity. *Nutr. Rep. Int.* 5:139–44

35. Cochet, B., Jung, A., Griessen, M., Bartholdi, P., Schaller, P., et al. 1983. Effects of lactose on intestinal calcium absorption in normal and lactase-deficient subjects. *Gastroenterology* 84:935–40

36. Deleted in proof

37. Collins, K. J., Roberts, D. F., eds. 1988. *Capacity for Work in the Tropics.* Cambridge: Cambridge Univ. Press

38. Cook, G. C. 1978. Did persistence of intestinal lactase into adult life originate on the Arabian peninsula? *Man* 13:418–27

39. Cruickshank, J. D., Beavers, D. G. 1982. Epidemiology of hypertension: blood pressure in blacks and whites. *Clin. Sci.* 62:1–6

40. Danford, D. E. 1982. Pica and nutrition. *Annu. Rev. Nutr.* 2:303–22

41. Darlu, P., Sagnier, P. P., Bois, E. 1990. Geneological and genetical African admixture estimations, blood pressure and hypertension in a Caribbean community. *Ann. Hum. Biol.* 17:387–97

42. Davies, C. T. M. 1973. Relationship of maximum aerobic power output to productivity and absenteeism of East African sugar cane workers. *Br. J. Ind. Med.* 30:146–54

43. Davies, C. T. M., Brotherhood, J. R., Collins, K. J., Dore, C., Imms, F., et al. 1976. Energy expenditure and physiological performance of Sudanese cane cutters. *Brit. J. Ind. Med.* 33:181-86

44. Devi, M. R., Kumari, J. R., Srikumari, C. R. 1985. Fertility and mortality differences in relation to maternal body size. *Ann. Hum. Biol.* 12:479–84

45. Dufour, D. L. 1988. Dietary cyanide intake and serum thiocyanate levels in Tukanoan Indians in Northwest Amazonia. *Am. J. Phys. Anthropol.* 75:205 (Abstr.)

46. Durnin, J. V. G. A. 1979. Energy balance in man with particular reference to low intakes. *Bibl. Nutr. Dieta* 27:1–10

47. Durnin, J. V. G. A. 1987. Energy requirements of pregnancy: an integration of the longitudinal data from the five-country study. *Lancet* 2:1131–33

48. Durnin, J. V. G. A., McKillop, F. M., Grant, S., Fitzgerald, G. 1987. Energy requirements of pregnancy in Scotland. *Lancet* 2:897-900

49. Dyerberg, J., Bang, H. O., Hjorne, N. 1975. Fatty acid composition of the plasma lipids in Greenland Eskimos. *Am. J. Clin. Nutr.* 28:958–66

50. Eaton, S. B., Konner, M. 1985. Paleolithic nutrition: a consideration of its nature and current implications. *N. Engl. J. Med.* 312:283–89

51. Eaton, S. B., Shostak, M., Konner, M. 1988. *The Paleolithic Prescription.* New York: Harper and Row

52. Ellested-Sayed, J. J., Haworth, J. C., Hildes, J. A. 1978. Disaccharide malabsorption and dietary patterns in two Canadian Eskimo communities. *Am. J. Clin. Nutr.* 31:1473–78

53. Ewing, J. A., Rouse, B. A., Aderhold, R. M. 1979. Studies of the mechanism of Oriental hypersensitivity to alcohol. *Curr. Alcohol.* 5:45–52

54. Ewing, J. A., Rouse, B. A., Pellizzari, E. D. 1974. Alcohol sensitivity and ethnic background. *Am. J. Psychiatry* 131:206–10

55. FAO/WHO/UNU Expert Consultation. 1985. *Energy and Protein Requirements. World Health Organization Technical Report Series* 724. Geneva: World Health Organization

56. Farris, J. J., Jones, B. M. 1978. Ethanol metabolism and memory impairment in American Indian and white women social drinkers. *J. Stud. Alcohol* 39:1975–79

57. Farris, J. J., Jones, B. M. 1978. Ethanol metabolism in male American Indians and whites. *Alcohol. Clin. Exp. Res.* 2:77–81

58. Feldstein, A. 1978. The metabolism of alcohol: on the validity of the Widmark equations, in obesity, and in racial and ethnic groups. *J. Stud. Alcohol* 39:926–32

59. Fenna, D., Mix, L., Schaefer, O., Gilbert, J. A. L. 1971. Ethanol metabolism in various racial groups. *Can. Med. Assoc. J.* 105:472-75

60. Ferro-Luzzi, A. 1986. Range of variation in energy expenditure and scope for regulation. In *Proceedings of the XIII International Congress of Nutrition,* ed. T. G. Taylor, N. K. Jenkins, pp. 393-99. London: John Libbey and Co.

61. Flatz, G. 1987. Genetics of lactose digestion in humans. *Adv. Hum. Genet.* 16:1–77

62. Flatz, G., Rotthauwe, H. W. 1973. Lactose nutrition and natural selection. *Lancet* 2:76–77

63. Flatz, G., Rotthauwe, H. W. 1977. The human lactose polymorphism: physiology and genetics of lactose absorption and malabsorption. *Prog. Med. Genet.* 2:205–49

64. Fong, W. P., Ho, Y. W., Lee, C. Y., Keung, W. M. 1989. Liver alcohol and aldehyde dehydrogenase isozymes in a Chinese population in Hong Kong. *Hum. Hered.* 39:185–91

65. Frisancho, A. R., Leonard, W. R., Bollettino, L. A. 1984. Blood pressure in blacks and whites and its relationship to dietary sodium and potassium intake. *J. Chronic Dis.* 37:515–19

66. Frisancho, A. R., Sanchez, J., Pallardel, D., Yanez, L. 1973. Adaptive significance of small body size under poor socio-economic conditions in southern Peru. *Am. J. Phys. Anthropol.* 39:255–61

67. Fujimoto, W. Y., Leonetti, D. L., Kinyoun, J. L., Newell-Morris, L., Shuman, W. P., et al. 1987. Prevalence of diabetes mellitus and impaired glucose tolerance among second-generation Japanese-American men. *Diabetes* 36:721–29

68. Gardner, L. I., Stern, M. P., Haffner, S. M., Gaskill, S. P., Hazuda, H. P., et al. 1984. Prevalence of diabetes in Mexican Americans. Relationship to percent of gene pool derived from native American sources. *Diabetes* 33:86–92

69. Garn, S. M., Leonard, W. R. 1989. What did our ancestors eat? *Nutr. Rev.* 47:337–45

70. Garrow, J. S., Pike, M. C. 1967. The long-term prognosis of severe infantile malnutrition. *Lancet* 1:1–4

71. Ghesquiere, J., D'Hulst, C. 1988. Growth, stature and fitness of children in tropical areas. See Ref. 37, pp. 165–79

72. Ghesquiere, J., Eeckels, R. 1984. Health, physical development and fitness of primary school children in Kinshasa. In *Children and Sport,* ed. J. Ilmarinen, I. Valimaki, pp. 18–30. Berlin: Springer-Verlag

73. Gibney, M. J., Burstyn, P. G. 1980. Milk, serum-cholesterol, and the Maasai. *Atherosclerosis* 35:339–43

74. Gillum, R. F. 1979. Pathophysiology of hypertension in blacks and whites. A review of the basis of racial blood pressure differences. *Hypertension* 1:468–75

75. Gleibermann, L. 1973. Blood pressure and dietary salt in human populations. *Ecol. Food Nutr.* 2:143–56

76. Goedde, H. W., Agarwal, D. P. 1986. Aldehyde oxidation: ethnic variations in metabolism and response. See Ref. 116, pp. 113–38

77. Goedde, H. W., Agarwal, D. P. 1987. Polymorphism of aldehyde dehydrogenase and alcohol sensitivity. *Enzyme* 37:29–44

78. Goedde, H. W., Agarwal, D. P., Harada, S., Rothhammer, F., Whittaker, J. O., et al. 1986. Aldehyde dehydrogenase polymorphism in North American, South American and Mexican Indian populations. *Am. J. Hum. Genet.* 38:395–99

79. Goedde, H. W., Harada, S., Agarwal, D. P. 1979. Racial differences in alcohol sensitivity: a new hypothesis. *Hum. Genet.* 51:331–34

80. Goldman, D., Enoch, M. A. 1990. Genetic epidemiology of ethanol metabolic enzymes: a role for selection. *World Rev. Nutr. Diet.* 63:143–60

81. Gordon, K. D. 1987. Evolutionary perspectives on human diet. See Ref. 113, pp. 3–39

82. Gorsky, R. D., Calloway, D. H. 1983. Activity pattern changes with decreases in food energy intake. *Hum. Biol.* 55:577–86

83. Greenberg, J. H., Turner, C. G., Zegura, S. L. 1986. The settlement of the Americas: a comparison of linguistic, dental, and genetic evidence. *Curr. Anthropol.* 27:477–97

84. Griessen, M., Cochet, B., Infante, F., Jung, A., Bartholdi, P., et al. 1989. Calcium absorption from milk in lactase-deficient subjects. *Am. J. Clin. Nutr.* 49:377–84

85. Deleted in proof

86. Grim, C. E., Luft, F. C., Miller, J. Z., Meneely, G. R., Battarbee, H. D., et al. 1980. Racial differences in blood pressure in Evans County, Georgia: relationship to sodium and potassium intake and plasma renin activity. *J. Chronic Dis.* 33:87–94

87. Haas, J. D., Harrison, G. G. 1977. Nutritional anthropology and biological adaptation. *Annu. Rev. Anthropol.* 6:69–101

88. Haas, J. D., Pelletier, D. L. 1989. Nutrition and human population biology. In *Human Population Biology,* ed. M. A. Little, J. D. Haas, pp. 152–67. New York: Oxford Univ. Press

89. Hamilton, W. J. 1987. Omnivorous primate diets and human overconsumption of meat. See Ref. 95, pp. 117–32

90. Hanis, C. L., Chakraborty, R., Ferrell, R. E., Schull, W. J. 1986. Individual admixture estimates: disease associations and individual risk of diabetes and gallbladder disease among Mexican-Americans in Starr County, Texas. *Am. J. Phys. Anthropol.* 70:433–41

91. Hanna, J. M. 1978. Metabolic responses of Chinese, Japanese and Europeans to alcohol. *Alcohol. Clin. Exp. Res.* 2:89–92

92. Harada, S., Agarwal, D. P., Goedde, H. W. 1981. Aldehyde dehydrogenase deficiency as cause of facial flushing reaction to alcohol in Japanese. *Lancet* 2:982

93. Harburg, E., Erfurt, J. C., Hauenstein, L. S., Chape, C., Schull, W. J., et al. 1973. Socioecological stress, suppressed hostility, skin color and black-white male blood pressure: Detroit. *Psychosom. Med.* 35:276–96

94. Harburg, E., Gleibermann, L., Roeper, P., Schork, M. A., Schull, W. J. 1978. Skin color, ethnicity and blood pressure I: Detroit blacks. *Am. J. Public Health* 68:1177–83

95. Harris, M., Ross, E. B., eds. 1987. *Food and Evolution. Toward a Theory of Human Food Habits.* Philadelphia: Temple Univ. Press

96. Harrison, G. G. 1975. Primary adult lactase deficiency: a problem in anthropological genetics. *Am. Anthropol.* 77:812–35

96a. Henry, C. K. J., Rees, D. G. 1991. New predictive equations for the estimation of basal metabolic rate in tropical peoples. *Eur. J. Clin. Nutr.* 45:177–85

97. Hepner, G., Fried, R., St. Jeor, S., Fusetti, L., Morin, R. 1979. Hypocholesterolemic effect of yogurt and milk. *Am. J. Clin. Nutr.* 32:19–24

98. Herold, P. M., Kinsella, J. E. 1986. Fish oil consumption and decreased risk of cardio-

vascular disease: a comparison of findings from animal and human feeding trials. *Am. J. Clin. Nutr.* 43:566–98

99. Heywood, P. F. 1983. Growth and nutrition in Papua New Guinea. *J. Hum. Evol.* 12:133–43

100. Huang, P.-C., Lee N.-Y., Chen S.-H. 1979. Evidence suggestive of no intestinal nitrogen fixation for improving protein nutrition status in sweet potato eaters. *Am. J. Clin. Nutr.* 32:1741–50

101. Hunter, J. M. 1973. Geophagy in Africa and in the United States: a culture-nutrition hypothesis. *Geogr. Rev.* 63:170–95

102. Hutchinson, J. 1986. Relationship between African admixture and blood pressure variation in the Caribbean. *Hum. Hered.* 36:12–18

103. Hutchinson, J., Crawford, M. H. 1981. Genetic determinants of blood pressure level among Black Caribs of St. Vincent. *Hum. Biol.* 53:453–66

104. Ho, K. J., Biss, K., Mikkelson, B., Lewis, L. A., Taylor, C. B. 1971. The Masai of East Africa: some unique biological characteristics. *Arch. Pathol.* 91:387–410

105. Ho, K. J., Mikkelson, B., Lewis, L. A., Feldman, S. A., Taylor, C. B. 1972. Alaskan artic Eskimo: responses to a customary high fat diet. *Am. J. Clin. Nutr.* 25:737–45

106. Jackson, F. L. C. 1990. Two evolutionary models for the interactions of dietary organic cyanogens, hemoglobins, and falciparum malaria. *Am. J. Hum. Biol.* 2:521–32

107. Jackson, L. 1986. Sociocultural and ethnohistorical influences on genetic diversity in Liberia. *Am. Anthropol.* 88:825–42

108. Jackson, L. C., Chandler, J. P., Jackson, R. T. 1986. Inhibition and adaptation of red cell glucose-6-phosphate dehydrogenase (G6PD) in vivo to chronic sublethal dietary cyanide in an animal model. *Hum. Biol.* 58:67–77

109. Jackson, L. C., Oseguera, M., Medrano, S., Kim, Y. L. 1988. Carbamylation of hemoglobin in vivo with chronic sublethal dietary cyanide: implications for hemoglobin S. *Biochem. Med. Metab. Biol.* 39:64–68

110. James, W. P. T., Shetty, P. S. 1982. Metabolic adaptation and energy requirements in developing countries. *Hum. Nutr. Clin. Nutr.* 36C:331–36

111. Johnson, J. D., Kretchmer, N., Simoons, F. J. 1974. Lactose malabsorption: its biology and history. *Adv. Pediatr.* 21:197–237

112. Johnson, R. C., Cole, R. E., Ahern, F. M. 1981. Genetic interpretation of racial/ethnic differences in lactose absorption and tolerance: a review. *Hum. Biol.* 53:1–13

113. Johnston, F. E., ed. 1987. *Nutritional Anthropology.* New York: Alan R. Liss

114. Joint National Committee. 1988. The 1988 report of the Joint National Committee on Detection, Evaluation and Treatment of High Blood Pressure. *Arch. Intern. Med.* 148:1023–38

115. Kalant, H., Reed, T. E. 1978. Limitations of the Widmark calculation: a reply to Feldstein's critique. *J. Stud. Alcohol* 39:933–36

116. Kalow, W., Goedde, H. W., Agarwal, D. P., eds. 1986. *Ethnic Differences in Reactions to Drugs and Xenobiotics.* New York: Alan R. Liss

117. Karanja N., McCarron, D. A. 1986. Calcium and hypertension. *Annu. Rev. Nutr.* 6:475–94

118. Katz, S. H. 1987. Food and biocultural evolution: a model for the investigation of modern nutritional problems. See Ref. 113, pp. 41–63

119. Katz, S. H., Hediger, M. L., Valleroy, L. A. 1974. Traditional maize processing techniques in the New World. *Science* 184:765–73

120. Katz, S. H., Schall, J. 1979. Fava bean consumption and biocultural evolution. *Med. Anthropol.* 3:459–76

121. Katz, S. H., Schall, J. I. 1986. Favism and malaria: a model of nutrition and biocultural evolution. In *Plants in Indigenous Medicine and Diet,* ed. N. L. Etkin, pp. 211–28. Bedford Hills, NY: Redgrave

122. Keil, J. E., Sandifer, S. H., Loadholt, C. B., Boyle, E. 1981. Skin color and education effects on blood pressure. *Am. J. Public Health* 71:532–34

123. Keil, J. E., Tyroler, H. A., Sandifer, S. H., Boyle, E. 1977. Hypertension: effects of social class on racial admixture. The results of a cohort study in the black population of Charleston, South Carolina. *Am. J. Public Health* 67:634–39

124. Keys, A., Brozek, J., Henschel, A., Mickelsen, O., Taylor, H. L. 1950. *The Biology of Human Starvation.* Minneapolis: Univ. Minnesota Press

125. Khaw, K. T., Barrett-Conner, E. 1988. The association between blood pressure, age, and dietary sodium and potassium: a population study. *Circulation* 77:53–61

126. Kinsella, J. E., Lokesh, B., Stone, R. A. 1990. Dietary n-3 polyunsaturated fatty acids and amelioration of cardiovascular disease: possible mechanisms. *Am. J. Clin. Nutr.* 52:1–28

126a. Klag, M. J., Whelton, P. K., Coresh, J., Grim, C. E., Kuller, L. H. 1991. The association of skin color with blood pressure in US blacks with low socioeconomic status. *J. Am. Med. Assoc.* 265:599–602

127. Klepinger, L. L. 1984. Nutritional assessment from bone. *Annu. Rev. Anthropol.* 13:75–96

128. Klotz, I. M., Haney, D. N., King, L. C. 1981. Rational approaches to chemotherapy: antisickling agents. *Science* 213:724–31

129. Knowler, W. C., Pettitt, D. J., Bennett, P. H., Williams, R. C. 1983. Diabetes mellitus in the Pima Indians: genetic and evolutionary considerations. *Am. J. Phys. Anthropol.* 62:107–14

130. Knowler, W. C., Pettitt, D. J., Savage, P. J., Bennett, P. H. 1981. Diabetes incidence in Pima Indians: contributions of obesity and

parental diabetes. *Am. J. Epidemiol.* 113:144–56

131. Knowler, W. C., Savage, P. J., Nagulesparan, M., Howar, B. V., Pettitt, D. J., et al. 1982. Obesity, insulin resistance and diabetes mellitus in the Pima Indians. See Ref. 132, pp. 243–50

132. Kobberling, J., Tattersall, R., eds. 1982. *The Genetics of Diabetes Mellitus.* London: Academic

133. Kogame, M., Mizoi, Y. 1985. The polymorphism of alcohol and aldehyde dehydrogenase in the Japanese and its significance in ethanol metabolism. *Jpn. J. Alcohol Stud. Drug Dependency* 20:122–42

134. Kromhout, D., Bosschieter, E. B., Coulander, C. L. 1985. The inverse relation between fish consumption and 20-year mortality from coronary heart disease. *N. Engl. J. Med.* 312:1206–9

135. Langford, H. G. 1981. Is blood pressure different in black people? *Postgrad. Med. J.* 57:749–54

136. Lawrence, M., Lawrence, F., Coward, W. A., Cole, T. J., Whitehead, R. G. 1987. Energy requirements of pregnancy in The Gambia. *Lancet* 2:1072–76

137. Lee-Thorpe, J. A., van der Merwe, N. J., Brain, C. K. 1989. Isotopic evidence for dietary differences between two extinct baboon species from Swartkrans. *J. Hum. Evol.* 18:183–90

138. Little, B. B., Malina, R. M., Buschang, P. H., Little, L. R. 1989. Natural selection is not related to reduced body size in a rural subsistence agricultural community in southern Mexico. *Hum. Biol.* 61:287–96

139. Little, M. A. 1989. Human biology of African pastoralists. *Yearb. Phys. Anthropol.* 32:215–47

140. Livingstone, M. B. E., Prentice, A. M., Strain, J. J., Coward, W. A., Black, A. E., et al. 1990. Accuracy of weighed dietary records in studies of diet and health. *Brit. J. Nutr.* 300:708–12

141. Loomis, W. F. 1967. Skin-pigment regulation of Vitamin-D biosynthesis in man. *Science* 157:501–6

142. Luft, F. C., Grim, C. E., Higgins, J. T., Weinberger, M. H. 1977. Differences in response to sodium administration in normotensive white and black subjects. *J. Lab. Clin. Med.* 90:555–62

143. MacGregor, G. A. 1983. Dietary sodium and potassium intake and blood pressure. *Lancet* 1:750–53

144. MacLean, C. J., Adams, M. S., Leyshon, W. C., Workman, P. L., Reed, T. E., et al. 1974. Genetic studies on hybrid populations. III. Blood pressure in an American black community. *Am. J. Hum. Genet.* 26:614–26

145. Malina, R. M., Little, B. B., Shoup, R. F., Buschang, P. H. 1987. Adaptive significance of small body size: strength and motor performance of school children in Mexico and Papua New Guinea. *Am. J. Phys. Anthropol.* 73:489–99

146. Mann, G. V. 1977. A factor in yogurt which lowers cholesteremia in man. *Atherosclerosis* 26:335–40

147. Mann, G. V., Shaffer, R. D., Anderson, R. S., Sandstead, H. H. 1964. Cardiovascular disease in the Masai. *J. Atheroscler. Res.* 4:289–312

148. Mann, G. V., Spoerry, A. 1974. Studies of surfactant and cholesteremia in the Maasai. *Am. J. Clin. Nutr.* 27:464–69

149. Margen, S. 1984. Energy-protein malnutrition: the web of causes and consequences. In *Malnutrition and Behavior: Critical Assessment of Key Issues,* ed. J. Brozek, pp. 20–31. Lausanne: Nestle Found.

150. Martin, R. D., Chivers, D. J., MacLarnon, A. M., Hladik, C. M. 1985. Gastrointestinal allometry in primates and other mammals. In *Size and Scaling in Primate Biology,* ed. W. J. Jungers, pp. 61–89. New York: Plenum

151. Martorell, R. 1989. Body size, adaptation and function. *Hum. Organ.* 48:15–20

152. Martorell, R., Arroyave, G. 1988. Malnutrition, work output and energy needs. See Ref. 37, pp. 57–75

153. Martorell, R., Delgado, H. L., Valverde, V., Klein, R. E. 1981. Maternal stature, fertility and infant mortality. *Hum. Biol.* 53:303–12

154. Martorell, R., Ho, T. J. 1984. Malnutrition, morbidity, and mortality. In *Child Survival: Strategies for Research,* ed. W. H. Mosley, L. C. Chen. *Popul. Dev. Rev.* 10:49–68 (Suppl.)

155. Massey, L. K. 1984. Effect of changing milk and yogurt consumption on human nutrient intake and serum lipoproteins. *J. Dairy Sci.* 67:255–62

156. May, P. A. 1982. Substance abuse and American Indians: prevalence and susceptibility. *Int. J. Addict.* 17:1185–209

157. Mazess, R. B. 1975. Biological adaptation: aptitudes and acclimatization. See Ref. 254, pp. 9–18

158. McCarron, D. A., Morris, C. D., Henry, H. J., Stanton, J. L. 1984. Blood pressure and nutrient intake in the United States. *Science* 224:1392–98

159. McCracken, R. D. 1971. Lactase deficiency: an example of dietary evolution. *Curr. Anthropol.* 12:479–517

160. McDaniel, E. G., Hundley, J. M. 1958. Alkali-treated corn and niacin deficiency. *Fed. Proc.* 17:484 (Abstr.)

161. McNair, A., Gudmand-Hoyer, E., Jarnum, S., Orrild, L. 1972. Sucrose malabsorption in Greenland. *Br. Med. J.* 2:19–21

162. McNamara, D. J., Lowell, A. E., Sabb, J. E. 1989. Effect of yogurt intake on plasma lipid and lipoprotein levels of normolipidemic males. *Atherosclerosis* 79:167–71

163. McNeill, G., Rivers, J. P. W., Payne, P. R., de Britto, J. J., Abel, R. 1987. Basal metabolic rate of Indian men: no evidence of

metabolic adaptation to a low plane of nutrition. *Hum. Nutr. Clin. Nutr.* 41C:473–83

164. Deleted in proof

165. Messer, E. 1984. Anthropological perspectives on diet. *Annu. Rev. Anthropol.* 13:205–49

166. Messer, E. 1986. The "small but healthy" hypothesis: historical, political, and ecological influences on nutritional standards. *Hum. Ecol.* 14:57–75

167. Messer, E. 1989. Small but healthy? Some cultural considerations. *Hum. Organ.* 48:39–52

167a. Miller, J. M., Miller, J. M. 1985. Duffy antigens and hypertension in a black population. *Am. J. Public Health* 75:558–59

168. Milton, K. 1987. Primate diets and gut morphology: implications for hominid evolution. See Ref. 95, pp. 93–115

169. Minghelli, G., Schuta, Y., Charbonnier, A., Whitehead, R., Jequier, E. 1990. Twenty-four-hour energy expenditure and basal metabolic rate measured in a whole-body indirect calorimeter in Gambian men. *Am. J. Clin. Nutr.* 51:563–70

170. Mizoi, Y., Ijiri, I., Tatsuno, Y., Kijima, T., Fujiwara, S., et al. 1979. Relationship between facial flushing and blood acetaldehyde levels after alcohol intake. *Pharmacol. Biochem. Behav.* 10:303–11

171. Mizoi, Y., Tatsuno, Y., Adachi, J., Kogame, M., Fukunaga, T., et al. 1983. Alcohol sensitivity related to polymorphism of alcohol-metabolizing enzymes in Japanese. *Pharmacol. Biochem. Behav.* 18:127–33 (Suppl. 1)

172. Mohs, M. E., Leonard, T. K., Watson, R. R. 1988. Interrelationships among alcohol abuse, obesity, and type II diabetes mellitus: focus on Native Americans. *World Rev. Nutr. Diet.* 56:93–172

173. Montgomery, T. L., Pincus, I. J. 1955. A nutritional problem in pregnancy resulting from extensive resection of the small bowel. *Am. J. Obstet. Gynecol.* 69:865–68

174. Nagel, R. L., Raventos, C., Tanowitz, H. B., Wittner, M. 1980. Effect of sodium cyanate on *Plasmodium falciparum* in vitro. *J. Parasitol.* 66:483–87

175. National Diabetes Data Group. 1985. *Diabetes in America.* Washington, DC: GPO

176. Neel, J. V. 1962. Diabetes mellitus: a "thrifty" genotype rendered detrimental by "progress". *Am. J. Hum. Genet.* 14:353–62

177. Neel, J. V. 1982. The thrifty genotype revisited. See Ref. 132, pp. 283–93

178. Nei, M., Saitou, N. 1986. Genetic relationship of human populations and ethnic differences in reaction to drugs and food. See Ref. 116, pp. 21–37

179. Oomen, H. A. P. C. 1970. Interrelationship of the human intestinal flora and protein utilization. *Proc. Nutr. Soc.* 29:197–206

180. Paige, D. M., Bayless, T. M. 1981. *Lactose Digestion: Clinical and Nutritional Implications.* Baltimore: Johns Hopkins Univ. Press

181. Parizkova, J. 1987. Growth, functional capacity and physical fitness in normal and malnourished children. *World Rev. Nutr. Diet.* 51:1–44

182. Pelto, G. H., Pelto, P. J. 1987. The concept of adaptation in anthropology. Presented at Annu. Meet. Am. Anthropol. Assoc., 86th, Chicago

183. Pelto, G. H., Pelto, P. J. 1989. Small but healthy? An anthropological perspective. *Hum. Organ.* 48:11–15

184. Polednak, A. P. 1989. *Racial and Ethnic Differences in Disease.* New York: Oxford Univ. Press

185. Pollitt, E., Amante, P., eds. 1984. *Energy Intake and Activity.* New York: Alan R. Liss

186. Prema, K., Madhavapeddi, R., Ramalaskshmi, B. A. 1981. Changes in anthropometric indices of nutritional status in lactating women. *Nutr. Rep. Int.* 24:893–900

187. Prentice, A. M., Cole, T. J., Foord, F. A., Lamb, W. H., Whitehead, R. G. 1987. Increased birthweight after prenatal dietary supplementation of rural African women. *Am. J. Clin. Nutr-* 46:921–25

188. Prentice, A. M., Goldberg, G. R., Davies, H. L., Murgatroyd, P. R., Scott, W. 1989. Energy-sparing adaptations in human pregnancy assessed by whole-body calorimetry. *Br. J. Nutr.* 62:5–22

189. Prentice, A. M., Prentice, A. 1988. Energy costs of lactation. *Annu. Rev. Nutr.* 8:63–79

190. Prentice, A. M., Whitehead, R. G., Roberts, S. B., Paul, A. A. 1981. Long-term energy balance in child-bearing Gambian women. *Am. J. Clin. Nutr.* 34:2790–99

191. Rattigan, S., Ghisalberti, A. V., Hartmann, P. E. 1981. Breast-milk production in Australian women. *Br. J. Nutr.* 45:243–49

192. Reed, T. E., Kalant, H. 1977. Bias in calculated rate of alcohol metabolism due to variation in relative amounts of adipose tissue. *J. Stud. Alcohol.* 38:1773–76

193. Reed, T. E., Kalant, H., Gibbins, R. J., Kapur, B. M., Rankin, J. G. 1976. Alcohol and acetaldehyde metabolism in Caucasians, Chinese, and Amerinds. *Can. Med. Assoc. J.* 115:851–55

194. Ritenbaugh, C., Goodby, C. S. 1989. Beyond the thrifty gene: metabolic implications of prehistoric migration into the New World. *Med. Anthropol.* 11:227–36

195. Roe, D. A. 1973. *A Plague of Corn. A Social History of Pellagra.* Ithaca, NY: Cornell Univ. Press

196. Rossouw, J. E., Burger, E. M., Van der Vyver, P., Ferreira, J. J. 1981. The effect of skim milk, yoghurt and full cream milk on human serum lipids. *Am. J. Clin. Nutr.* 34:351–56

197. Rutishauser, I. H. E., Whitehead, R. G. 1972. Energy intake and expenditure in 1–3-year-old Ugandan children living in a rural environment. *Br. J. Nutr.* 28:145–52

198. Saavedra, J. M., Perman, J. A. 1989. Current concepts in lactose malabsorption and intolerance. *Annu. Rev. Nutr.* 9:475–502

199. Satyanarayana, K., Naidu, A. N., Chatterjee, B., Rao, B. S. N. 1977. Body size and work output. *Am. J. Clin. Nutr.* 30:322–25

200. Saunders, E, 1987. Hypertension in blacks. *Med. Clin. North Am.* 71:1013–29

201. Schaefer, J. M. 1981. Firewater myths revisited. *J. Stud. Alcohol Suppl.* 9:99–117

202. Schectman, G., Kaul, S., Cherayil, G. D., Lee, M., Kissebah, A. 1989. Can the hypotriglyceridemic effect of fish oil concentrate be sustained? *Ann. Intern. Med.* 110:346–52

203. Schoeninger, M. J. 1989. Reconstructing prehistoric human diet. *Homo* 39:78–99

204. Schofield, W. N. 1985. Predicting basal metabolic rate, new standards and review of previous work. *Hum. Nutr. Clin. Nutr.* 39C:5–41 (Suppl. 1)

205. Scrimshaw, N. S., Murray, E. B. 1988. The acceptability of milk and milk products in populations with a high prevalence of lactose intolerance. *Am. J. Clin. Nutr.* 48:1083–1159

206. Scrimshaw, N. S., Young, V. R. 1989. Adaptation to low protein and energy intakes. *Hum. Organ.* 48:20–30

207. Seckler, D. 1980. "Malnutrition": an intellectual odyssey. *West. J. Agric. Econ.* 5:219–27

208. Seckler, D. 1982. "Small but healthy": a basic hypothesis in the theory, measurement and policy of malnutrition. In *Newer Concepts in Nutrition and Their Implications for Policy,* ed. P. V. Sukhatme, pp. 127–37. Pune, India: Maharashtra Assoc. Cultiv. Sci. Res. Inst.

209. Seto, A., Tricomi, S., Goodwin, D. W., Kolodney, R., Sullivan, T. 1978. Biochemical correlates of ethanol-induced flushing in orientals. *J. Stud. Alcohol* 39:1–11

210. Sempos, C., Cooper, R., Kovar, M. G., Johnson, C., Drizd, T., et al. 1986. Dietary calcium and blood pressure in National Health and Nutrition Examination Surveys I and II. *Hypertension* 8:1067-74

211. Shaper, A. G., Jones, K. W., Jones, M., Kyobe, J. 1963. Serum lipids in three nomadic tribes of northern Kenya. *Am. J. Clin. Nutr.* 13:135–46

212. Shaper, A. G., Jones, M., Kyobe, J. 1961. Plasma-lipids in an African tribe living on a diet of milk and meat. *Lancet* 2:1324–27

213. Shetty, P. S. 1984. Adaptative changes in basal metabolic rate and lean body mass in chronic undernutrition. *Hum. Nutr. Clin. Nutr.* 38C:443–51

214. Shibuya, A., Yasunami, M., Yoshida, A. 1989. Genotypes of alcohol dehydrogenase and aldehyde dehydrogenase loci in Japanese alcohol flushers and nonflushers. *Hum. Genet.* 82:14–16

215. Sievers, M. L., Fisher, J. R. 1981. Diseases of North American Indians. In *Biocultural Aspects of Disease,* ed. H. Rothschild, pp. 191–252. New York: Academic

216. Sievers, M. L., Fisher, J. R. 1985. Diabetes in North American Indians. See Ref. 175, pp. XI-l-XI-20

217. Simoons, F. J. 1969. Primary adult lactose intolerance and the milking habit: a problem in biological and cultural interrelations. I. Review of the medical research. *Am. J. Digest. Dis.* 14:819–36

218. Simoons, F. J. 1970. Primary adult lactose intolerance and the milking habit: a problem in biologic and cultural interrelations. II. A culture historical hypothesis. *Am. J. Digest. Dis.* 15:695-710

219. Simoons, F. J. 1978. The geographic hypothesis and lactose malabsorption: a weighing of the evidence. *Digest. Dis.* 23:963–80

220. Deleted in proof

221. Singh, J., Prentice, A. M., Diaz, E., Coward, W. A., Ashford, J., et al. 1989. Energy expenditure of Gambian women during peak agricultural activity measured by the doubly-labelled water method. *Br. J. Nutr.* 62:315–29

222. Smedman, L., Sterky, G., Mellander, L., Wall, S. 1987. Anthropometry and subsequent mortality in groups of children aged 6–59 months in Guinea-Bissau. *Am. J. Clin. Nutr.* 46:369–73

223. Smith, M. 1986. Genetics of human alcohol and aldchyde dehydrogenases. *Adv. Hum. Genet.* 15:249–90

223a. Soares, M. J., Shetty, P. S. 1991. Basal metabolic rates and metabolic economy in chronic undernutrition. *Eur. J. Clin. Nutr.* 45:363–73

224. Spurr, G. B. 1983. Nutritional status and physical work capacity. *Yearb. Phys. Anthropol.* 26:1–35

225. Spurr, G. B. 1988. Marginal malnutrition in childhood: implications for adult work capacity and productivity. See Ref. 37, pp. 107–40

226. Spurr, G. B., Barac-Nieto, M., Maksud, M. G. 1977. Productivity and maximal oxygen consumption in sugar cane cutters. *Am. J. Clin. Nutr.* 30:316–21

227. Spurr, G. B., Barac-Nieto, M., Reina, J. C., Ramirez, R. 1984. Marginal malnutrition in school-aged Colombian boys: efficiency of treadmill walking in submaximal exercise. *Am. J. Clin. Nutr.* 39:452–59

228. Spurr, G. B., Reina, J. C. 1986. Marginal malnutrition in school-aged Colombian boys: body size and energy costs of walking and light load carrying. *Hum. Nutr. Clin. Nutr.* 40C:409–19

229. Spurr, G. B., Reina, J. C. 1988. Basal metabolic rate of normal and marginally undernourished mestizo children in Colombia. *Eur. J. Clin. Nutr.* 42:753–64

230. Spurr, G. B., Reina, J. C. 1988. Influence of dietary intervention on artificially increased activity in marginally undernourished Colombian boys. *Eur. J. Clin. Nutr.* 42:835–46

231. Spurr, G. B., Reina, J. C., Dahners, H. W., Barac-Nieto, M. 1983. Marginal malnutri-

tion in school-aged Colombian boys: functional consequences in maximum exercise. *Am. J. Clin. Nutr.* 37:834–47

232. Stamatoyannopoulos, G., Chen, S. H., Fukui, M. 1975. Liver alcohol dehydrogenase in Japanese: high population frequency of atypical form and its possible role in alcohol sensitivity. *Am. J. Hum. Genet.* 27:789–96

233. Stern, M. P. 1985. Diabetes in Hispanic Americans. See Ref. 175, pp. IX-1–IX-ll

234. Stern, M. P., Gaskill, S. P., Hazuda, H. P., Gardner, L. I., Haffner, S. M. 1983. Does obesity explain excess prevalence of diabetes among Mexican Americans? Results of the San Antonio Heart Study. *Diabetologia* 24:272–77

235. Stini, W. A. 1971. Evolutionary implications of changing nutritional patterns in human populations. *Am. Anthropol.* 73:1019–30

236. Stini, W. A. 1975. Adaptive strategies of human populations under nutritional stress. See Ref. 254, pp. 19–41

237. Strickland, S. A., Ulijaszek, S. J. 1990. Energetic cost of standard activities in Gurkha and British soldiers. *Ann. Hum. Biol.* 17:133–44

238. Deleted in proof

239. Sussman, R. W. 1987. Species-specific dietary patterns in primates and human dietary adaptations. In *The Evolution of Human Behavior: Primate Models,* ed. W. Kinzey, pp. 151–79. Albany: State Univ. New York Press

240. Szathmary, E. J. E. 1986. Diabetes in arctic and subarctic populations undergoing acculturation. *Coll. Antropol.* 10(2):145-58

241. Szathmary, E. J. E. 1990. Diabetes in Amerindian populations: the Dogrib studies. In *Disease in Populations in Transition,* ed. A. C. Swedlund, G. J. Armelagos, pp. 75–103. New York: Bergin and Garvey

242. Thomas, R. B. 1976. Energy flow at high altitude. In *Man in the Andes,* ed. P. T. Baker, M. A. Little, pp. 379–404. Stroudsburg, PA: Dowden, Hutchinson and Ross

243. Torun, B., Viteri, F. E. 1981. Energy requirements of preschool children and effects of varying energy intakes on protein metabolism. In *Protein-Energy Requirements of Developing Countries: Evaluation of New Data,* ed. B. Torun, V. R. Young, W. M. Rand, pp. 229–241. Tokyo: United Nations Univ. World Hunger Programme, *Food Nutr. Bull.* (Suppl. 5)

244. Tremaine, W. J., Newcomer, A. D., Riggs, B. L., McGill, D. B. 1986. Calcium absorption from milk in lactase-deficient and lactase-sufficient adults. *Digest. Dis. Sci.* 31:376–78

245. Tuazon, M. A. G., van Raaij, J. M. A., Hautvast, J. G. A. J., Barba, C. V. C. 1987. Energy requirements of pregnancy in the Philippines. *Lancet* 2:1129–31

246. Tyroler, H. A., James S. A. 1978. Blood pressure and skin color. *Am. J. Public Health* 68:1170–72

247. Uvnas-Moberg, K. 1989. Physiological and psychological effects of oxytocin and prolactin in connection with motherhood with special reference to food intake and the endocrine system of the gut. *Acta Physiol. Scand. Suppl.* 583:41–48

248. van Raaij, J. M. A., Vermaat-Miedema, S. H., Schonk, C. M., Peek, M. E. M., Hautvast, J. G. A. J. 1987. Energy requirements of prenancy in the Netherlands. *Lancet* 2:953–55

249. Viteri, F. E., Torun, B. 1975. Ingestión calórica y trabajo físico de obreros agrícolas en Guatemala. Efecto de la suplementación alimentaria y su lugar en los programas de salud. *Bol. Of. Sanit. Panam.* 78:58–74

250. Viteri, F. E., Torun, B. 1981. Nutrition, physical activity, and growth. In *The Biology of Normal Human Growth,* ed. M. Ritzen, A. Aperia, K. Hall, pp. 265–73. New York: Raven

251. Voors, A. W., Berenson, G. S., Dalferes, E. R., Webber, L. S., Shuler, S. E. 1979. Racial differences in blood pressure control. *Science* 204:1091–94

252. Deleted in proof

253. Waterlow, J. C. 1986. Metabolic adaptation to low intakes of energy and protein. *Annu. Rev. Nutr.* 6:495–526

254. Watts, E. S., Johnston, F. E., Lasker, G. W., eds. 1975. *Biosocial Interrelations in Population Adaptation.* The Hague: Mouton

255. Weinsier, R. L., Norris, D. 1985. Recent developments in the etiology and treatment of hypertension: dietary calcium, fat and magnesium. *Am. J. Clin. Nutr.* 42:1331–38

256. Weiss, K. M., Ferrell, R. E., Hanis, C. L. 1984. A New World Syndrome of metabolic diseases with a genetic and evolutionary basis. *Yearb. Phys. Anthropol.* 27:153–78

257. Wen, C.-P., Antonowicz, I., Tovar, E., McGandy, R. B., Gershoff, S. N. 1973. Lactose feeding in lactose-intolerant monkeys. *Am. J. Clin. Nutr.* 26:1224–28

258. Wendorf, M. 1989. Diabetes, the ice free corridor, and the Paleoindian settlement of North America. *Am. J. Phys. Anthropol.* 79:503–20

259. West, K. M. 1974. Diabetes in American Indians and other native populations of the New World. *Diabetes* 23:841–55

260. West, K. M. 1978. Diabetes in American Indians. *Adv. Metab. Disord.* 9:29–48

261. Widdowson, E. M. 1985. Responses to deficits of dietary energy. See Ref. 21, pp. 97–103

262. Wilson, T. W. 1986. History of salt supplies in West Africa and blood pressures today. *Lancet* 1:784–86

262a. Wilson, T. W., Grim, C. E. 1991. Biohistory of slavery and blood pressure differences in blacks today. A hypothesis. *Hypertension* 17:I-122–I-128 (Suppl. I)

263. Wilt, T. J., Lofgren, R. P., Nichol, K. L., Schorer, A. E., Crespin, L., et al. 1989. Fish oil supplementation does not lower plasma cholesterol in men with hypercholesterolemia. *Ann. Intern. Med.* 111:900–5

264. Wolff, P. H. 1973. Vasomotor sensitivity to alcohol in diverse Mongoloid populations. *Am. J. Hum. Genet.* 25:193–99

265. Wright, J. T. 1988. Profile of systemic hypertension in black patients. *Am. J. Cardiol.* 61:41H-45H

266. Young, T. K., Szathmary, E. J. E., Evers, S., Wheatley, B. 1990. Geographical distribution of diabetes among the native population of Canada: a national survey. *Soc. Sci. Med.* 31:129–39

267. Young, V. R. 1987. 1987 McCollum Award Lecture: Kinetics of human amino acid metabolism: nutritional implications and some lessons. *Am. J. Clin. Nutr.* 46:709–25

268. Young, V. R., Marchini, J. S. 1990. Mechanisms and nutritional significance of metabolic responses to altered intakes of protein and amino acids with reference to nutritional adaptation in humans. *Am. J. Clin. Nutr.* 51:270–89

269. Young, V. R., Moldawer, L. L., Hoerr, R., Bier, D. M. 1985. Mechanisms of adaptation to protein malnutrition. See Ref. 21, pp. 189–215

270. Zeiner, A. R., Girardot, J. M., Jones-Saumtry, D., Nichols, N. 1985. Prevalence of ALDHI isoenzyme among American Indians in Oklahoma. *Jpn. J. Alcohol Stud. Drug Dependency* 20:359–66

271. Zeiner, A. R., Paredes, A., Christensen, H. D. 1979. The role of acetaldehyde in mediating reactivity to an acute dose of ethanol among different racial groups. *Alcohol. Clin. Exp. Res.* 3:11–18

272. Zimmet, P., King, H., Serjeantson, S., Kirk, R. 1986. The genetics of diabetes mellitus. *Aust. N. Z. Med. J.* 16:419–24

273. Zimmet, P., Kirk, R., Serjeantson, S., Whitehouse, S., Taylor, R. 1982. Diabetes in Pacific populations—genetic and environmental interactions. In *Genetic Environmental Interactions in Diabetes Mellitus,* ed. J. S. Melish, J. Hanna, S. Baba, pp. 9–17. Amsterdam: Excerpta Medica

274. Zimmet, P., Taft, P., Guinea, A., Guthrie, W., Thoma, K. 1977. The high prevalence of diabetes mellitus on a Central Pacific island. *Diabetologia* 13:111–15

Annu. Rev. Anthropol. 1992. 21:171–204

INFANT FEEDING PRACTICES AND GROWTH

Katherine A. Dettwyler

Department of Anthropology, Texas A&M University, College Station, Texas 77843-4352

Claudia Fishman[1]

International Division, Porter/Novelli, 1001 30th Avenue NW, Washington, DC 20007

KEYWORDS: nutrition, anthropometry, auxology, breastfeeding, formula, biocultural anthropology

INTRODUCTION

In this review we focus on the relationship between infant feeding practices and the growth of children around the world. Children's growth is often used as an index of the overall health of a population. Because growth is affected by a variety of adverse environmental conditions, it is a sensitive indicator of children's health, and a population with healthy children is generally considered to be well adapted to its environment. However, this very sensitivity to the environment makes it difficult for researchers to disentangle the many factors that affect growth, including genetic differences in growth potential

1

Dr. Fishman's contribution was made possible through support provided by the Office of Nutrition, Bureau for Research and Development, U.S. Agency for International Development, under the terms of Contract No. DAN-5113-Z-00-7031-00. The opinions expressed herein are those of the authors and do not necessarily reflect the views of the U.S. Agency for International Development.

0084-6570/92/1015-0171$02.00

between populations (now thought to be relatively small), nutrition, disease, altitude, temperature, and psychological factors, to name only the most important. Here we are concerned primarily with nutritional factors that have an immediate and direct impact on growth.

One major research focus has been on worldwide patterns of breastfeeding, determinants of breastfeeding, the effects of using breast milk versus various artificial formulas, and the effects of the timing of the introduction of nonmilk fluids and foods on the morbidity, mortality, and growth patterns of children in Third World (and, to a lesser degree, in Western) contexts. Another, more limited, literature focuses on the cultural beliefs surrounding infant feeding, different infant feeding styles, and maternal "competence" (education, experience, attitudes, etc), and their effects on child growth.

Problems with the Literature

The two main problems with the literature on infant feeding and growth, which limit its usefulness and render comparisons between studies difficult, are a lack of consistency in the use of terminology and a lack of methodological rigor in defining clear-cut feeding groups for growth comparisons (see below). In addition, bioanthropologists question the accuracy of anthropometric measurements taken by personnel with little or no training, and/or using homemade or jury-rigged equipment. At the same time, cultural anthropologists may dismiss data on infant feeding practices collected by bioanthropologists, especially if they are based on maternal recall, which may be inaccurate (156), or report only cultural norms without also documenting behavior.

Much of the non-anthropological literature suffers from either ethnocentrism or a curiously acultural perspective. The implicit (and sometimes explicit) ethnocentrism that underlies much of the pediatric, nutritional, and psychological literature on infant feeding results in findings that apply only to middle-class Anglo-Americans and yet are written as though they refer to "human development" or "human behavior." They make bizarre reading for anthropologists used to contextualizing their findings within specific cultural milieus. In addition, much of this literature focuses on maternal behaviors as though they were not influenced by cultural belief systems. For example, one study reports that mothers in the United States are prompted to introduce solid foods to their infants based primarily on cues from the infants themselves. Another claims that "supplemental feedings are given when the infant is ready to take them," as though cultural and individual beliefs, and medical advice, play no role in structuring maternal behavior. Many clinical researchers studying infant feeding and growth among US children seem unaware of the vast Third World literature on this topic, and fail to appreciate that the effects of bottle/formula use in the United States cannot be extrapolated to Third World contexts.

Finally, although the literature seems overwhelming, it is standard practice in many disciplines (much less so within anthropology) to publish the results of one study in multiple outlets. This broadcasts the research results to a wider audience but erroneously suggests that each publication presents new data or insights.

Issues of Terminology and Methodology

As several others have lamented (15, 46, 171), inconsistencies in terminology make it nearly impossible to derive conclusions from most studies relating infant-feeding choices to morbidity, mortality, and growth.

In 1988, the Interagency Group for Action on Breastfeeding (IGAB), composed of the United States Agency for International Development (A.I.D.), the Swedish International Development Agency, the World Health Organization (WHO), and UNICEF, proposed standardized terminology for the collection and description of data on breastfeeding behavior (14, 113). Categories of "exclusive," "almost exclusive" (which together constituted "full"), "partial," and "token" breastfeeding were adopted (113). However, in 1991, the WHO proposed modifications to these definitions, and it is widely assumed that the new terminology (190) will supersede the IGAB categories. In the WHO modifications, "predominant" has replaced "almost exclusive"; infants who receive medicinal "drops or syrups" may still be classified as "exclusively" breastfed, and limited amounts of certain fluids (notably nonnutritive) are allowed in the "predominantly breastfed" category. The WHO categories and criteria are summarized in Table 1 (190:3). Another problem arises from the fact that breast milk and formula come in very different packages. Van Esterik (179) was the first to distinguish clearly between breast milk as a product and breastfeeding as a process; much of the literature (especially the biomedical literature) reads as though the only difference between breast milk and formula is in its nutrient composition, when in fact, the "packaging" and the "process

Table 1   Summary of WHO breastfeeding terminology (after 190:3)

Category of infant feeding	Requires that the infant receive	Allows the infant to receive	Does not allow the infant to receive
Exclusive breastfeeding	Breast milk (including milk expressed or from wet nurse)	Drops, syrups, (vitamins, minerals, medicines)	Anything else
Predominant breast-feeding	Breast milk (including milk expressed or from wet nurse) as the predominant source of nourishment	Liquids (water, and water-based drinks, fruit, juice, ORS), ritual fluids, and drops or syrups (vitamins, minerals, medicines)	Anything else (in particular non-human milk, food-based fluids)
Complementary feeding	Breast milk and solid or semi-solid foods	Any food or liquid including nonhuman milk	
Breastfeeding	Breast milk	Any food or liquid including nonhuman milk	
Bottle-feeding	Any liquid or semi-solid food from a bottle with nipple/teat	Any food or liquid including nonhuman milk; also allows breast milk by bottle	

of delivery" are also critical. Few studies can separate the effects on infant health of the different products from the effects of the different modes of delivery.

The terminology applied to nonbreast-milk fluids causes further confusion. In Anglo-American culture, infant feeding bottles usually contain formulas manufactured by one of the leading infant formula companies which are based on cow's milk or soy beans. However, they may contain fruit juice, flavored sugar water, colas, or tea. In many Third World contexts, bottles may contain infant formula, but often they contain whole-fat cow's milk (reconstituted from powdered form) or heavily diluted cereal porridges. Most studies do not specify what the bottle-fed infants are actually consuming. Additionally, many researchers object to the use of the term "breast milk substitute." There really is no substitute for human breast milk. It has been suggested that "artificial feeding" or even "rice water substitute" might be more appropriate when referring to the use of infant formula.

Another problematic phrase is "prolonged" or "extended" breastfeeding. "Prolonged" and "extended" are relative terms. In pediatric parlance they are often used to refer to breastfeeding beyond 6 months. In other contexts (La Leche League, Third World) prolonged breastfeeding might be interpreted as anything beyond 3 or 4 years. Discussions of whether or not prolonged breastfeeding contributes to malnutrition, as some authors have suggested, are meaningless if "prolonged" is not defined.

Uses of the terms supplementary and complementary are not consistent in the literature. Some authors use them interchangeably. Others use complementary to refer to foods given in addition to breast milk and supplementary to refer to foods that replace breast milk (172). The WHO recommends the latter distinction (113), with complementary foods being those introduced to the diet relatively late that do not affect breast milk consumption. In contrast, supplements would refer to water, cow's milk, formula, semi-solid or solid foods, or any other substances introduced to the diet relatively early that are thought to replace breast milk.

The term *beikost* was originally introduced (73) to refer to any nonmilk food (neither breast milk, formula, nor any other milk-based product) given to the infant for nutritive purposes. The term eliminates such cumbersome phrasing as "the first introduction of food/semi-solid food/solid food" while acknowledging that in many cultures infants receive token amounts of nonnutritive liquids (glucose water, plain water, teas, animal milks, medicinal drops) in the first few days of life. The term beikost was introduced to the anthropological literature by Quandt (153) and is used by a number of researchers.

No studies have adequately addressed the problems introduced by variation in what, how much, and how often beikost is given to the child. Thus, for many Anglo-American mothers, beikost is introduced according to a doctor's recommendations, and once begun, the infant receives the same (or gradually increasing) amounts every day, or even several times a day. In other cultures, the introduction of solids is a much more haphazard affair. A child may "start solids" one week, then not receive any more for several months; the quantity or quality of beikost may vary widely from day to day. Few studies differentiate feeding groups on the basis of what, how much, or how often infants are receiving beikost; rather, infants receiving "any" or "significant" amounts of solids may be lumped together in one category. Rarely are feeding-group categories adequately specified (see 94 for an exception).

The term "weaning" has two distinct uses. Many researchers use it to denote the gradual process of introducing beikost to accustom the infant to eating foods other than breast milk or formula. However, the final cessation of breastfeeding is sometimes also called "weaning." These two distinct usages are usually, but not always, apparent from the context. Problems arise when informants use the term to denote cessation of breastfeeding, while researchers assume they mean the switch from breastfeeding to an adult diet. Because of these linguistic misunderstandings, one finds reports that in some societies children are exclusively breastfed until the age of 1 or 2 years, then "abruptly weaned" onto an adult diet.

Differences in terminology and lack of a world-wide perspective also lead to erroneous interpretations of the cross-cultural literature. For example, Barness searches in vain for an "original" pattern of weaning. He completely dismisses the cross-cultural literature as confusing and contradictory because anthropologists have reported that in some cultures food or liquid other than breast milk is introduced in the first few days of life, while in others "exclusive" breastfeeding prevails for many months (19:84). Barness does not realize that both statements can be correct, even for the same culture. In addition to a lack of rigor in defining infant feeding, different measurement and analysis techniques complicate data comparison and interpretation (89, 90, 97).

BREASTFEEDING ISSUES

Forces Shaping the Biocultural Literature on Breastfeeding

The breastfeeding literature contains thousands of articles published in the past five years alone dealing with the macro- and microscopic forces affecting and affected by infant feeding choices. Anthropologists will find much relevant literature in the fields of lactation management and counseling (15, 16, 44, 138, 161) and in those of general nursing, pediatrics, nutrition, and public health. In addition, breastfeeding advocacy (103, 145), women's studies (116, 131, 136, 181), environmental issues (158, 181), economic and structural adjustment (118), and teaching and parents' manuals (63, 115, 132) constitute vast bodies of literature ripe for anthropological scrutiny.

The anthropological literature on breastfeeding per se is fairly applied, as it has been ever since Margaret Mead (126) instructed her students to "find a way that we can go from the peasant and working class breastfeeder to the elite, well-educated breastfeeder without a generation of bottles in between" (see 159:146). Van Esterik (179) notes that "ethnographic fieldwork and attention to cultural factors can enrich our understanding of infant feeding and potentially improve the health and nutritional status of infants ... ." There are several additional important collections in the cultural/descriptive genre (99, 146, 159, 187).

The multi-disciplinary breastfeeding literature of relevance to this review chiefly answers questions asked by the international aid community (e.g. UNICEF, WHO, US A.I.D., and other bi- or multilateral agencies) in its effort to define "optimal" infant feeding and develop international policy in support of it. The epidemiological concept of "relative risk" is central to the definition of "optimal," based as it is on international demographic and health surveys reporting that some 2 million children under 1 year of age die every year from diarrhea and acute respiratory infection (41). Reviewing the relative risk of death associated with various forms of infant feeding (27, 42, 43, 67, 182, 183), and speaking with one voice, many researchers suggest that these deaths could be averted if children were exclusively breastfed through 4–6 months of age, thereby reducing their exposure to contamination while also conferring the nutritional and immunological protection of breast milk through this period (12, 58, 98). Thereafter, children should continue to be breastfed, while receiving appropriate and adequate uncontaminated complementary foods, till 2 years of age or beyond. This combination of early exclusive breastfeeding with timely introduction of complementary foods, which together create "optimal infant feeding," will also benefit the mother, primarily by prolonging her period of lactational amenorrhea (81), allowing her a longer interval to rebuild some of her nutritional stores depleted though pregnancy and lactation (127).

One difficulty with implementation of the concept of "optimal infant feeding" cross-culturally is that in some cultures, solid foods are not normally introduced to the diet until well beyond 4–6 months. Very different strategies and messages will need to be developed to convince people to introduce solids at an earlier age than traditional cultural practices dictate (50, 53, 55). In some cultures, "optimal infant feeding" will mean both a discontinuation of the practice of giving newborns ritual or medicinal drops and an earlier introduction of solid foods on a regular basis.

From an Interagency Group for Action on Breastfeeding (IGAB) meeting in 1990 came the Innocenti Declaration on the Protection, Promotion and Support of Breastfeeding. The declaration recommends global optimal infant feeding policy and action steps intended to reduce the population-level risk factors described above. Some researchers concerned with maternal health are not comfortable with the Innocenti Declaration. As described by Koniz-Booher et al (111), many women in developing countries experience marginal nutritional status as a result of inadequate dietary intake, high energy expenditures in physical activity, and still higher energy and nutrient demands of pregnancy and lactation for 35–48% of their reproductive years. It is widely believed that poorly nourished women produce an insufficient quantity of breast milk or breast milk lacking in energy or other critical nutrients, although evidence suggests that women must experience severe nutritional stress before the quantity and overall quality of breast milk output are affected (28). Although water-soluble vitamins may be limited, other nutrients in human milk may be maintained at a satisfactory level at the expense of maternal stores (137).

The mother may well benefit from increased dietary intake during pregnancy and lactation. However, concerns about the infant's well-being, and recommendations to begin complementary foods before 4 months to prevent growth faltering, are not well founded. Foods available in most developing countries will not be nutritionally superior to the breast milk they replace in the infant's diet, and are likely to carry a pathogenic load that contributes to infant morbidity and death (see below.) As Rowland et al note, "It is very dubious whether we are entitled to make the value judgement that a period of malnutrition due to delayed weaning (supplementation) is preferable to the infective and immunological dangers of early supplementation. We should, however, keep growth standards in the first year of life under constant critical review, with the aim of acquiring a much more accurate notion of what is normal, or, more difficult, optimal growth in breastfed infants in different environments and of different ethnic groups. Without this quite basic knowledge the subject of weaning will be bedeviled by disagreement and polemic" (162:82).

The international aid community hopes to promote an environment in which women can feed their children optimally, which should include ways to increase women's dietary intake and/or reduce their workload. In the short run, aid workers are attempting to gain the support of developing-country health planners with studies proving that "optimal infant feeding" is probably best for most infants and mothers under all but the most extreme conditions. The extent of the change proposed is on the order of 85%, as on a worldwide basis only 8–15% of women interviewed in recent surveys practice exclusive breastfeeding for 4–6 months (170). Top-down programming is more or less guaranteed when "Global Policy" is applied to country-specific situations; however, alternatives to top-down programming have been suggested (30, 37, 71).

Getting into the Breastfeeding Literature Quickly

With the interagency support described above, it is logistically simple to access much of the breastfeeding literature. The A.I.D. Center for Development Information and Evaluation,[2] the American Public Health Association

---

[2]
Written requests for information may be addressed to PPC/CDIE/DI, Rm. 209, SA-18, Washington DC 20523-1801.

Clearinghouse on Infant Feeding and Maternal Nutrition (Washington, DC), La Leche League International (Chicago), and the Wellstart Program (San Diego and Washington) all have extensive collections, which are accessible through "Medline" and "Popline" searches.

BIOMEDICAL RESEARCH   Akre (7) synthesizes the literature on the physiological basis of infant feeding, emphasizing international research. This work should be complemented by the National Academy of Sciences's Subcommittee on Nutrition During Lactation's (137) more comprehensive volume, which focuses on maternal factors and breastfeeding in the United States. Cunningham (46) provides an update of his annotated bibliography (prepared in 1981) on breast- and bottle-feeding, current through 1986. Feachem & Koblinsky (67) lay the groundwork for the relationship between choice of infant feeding method and diarrheal disease. Cunningham et al (47) review the protective effects of breastfeeding against nongastrointestinal pediatric illnesses, stressing that breastfeeding provides significant health benefits even in Western, industrialized societies.

APPLIED BIOCULTURAL RESEARCH   In the applied/biocultural area Popkin et al's (149) seminal review emphasizes the biomedical well-being of the mother and infant, how the household supports or hinders breastfeeding, and the impact on the household of the choice of infant feeding method (although the literature is thin in this last area). A number of edited volumes offer a range of regional and research foci (117, 122, 159, 187). Beasley (20) critiqued some of this literature, which she faulted for over-emphasizing biological processes, under-emphasizing cultural interpretation, and providing few new insights. Many of the articles Beasley reviewed are considered classic applied studies, which strive to bring cultural factors to the attention of biomedically oriented decision makers. The insights are critical to their specific policy or program context, and their potential contribution to anthropological theory has not yet been tested. A recent and indispensable entry in this field is that of Brownlee (30), who reviewed for A.I.D. the behavioral issues affecting breastfeeding, weaning, and nutrition.

HISTORICAL AND SOCIAL TRENDS   Major works with particular historical or social emphases include that of Jelliffe et al (104), which presents an evolutionary and cross-cultural perspective on human milk, updated from their first edition. Detailed histories of infant feeding in Europe (69) and the United States (13) complement shorter reviews of trends in the United States during the last few decades (74). Dobbing (60) dissects the infant formula industry "controversy" (1973–1984), and Van Esterik (181) uses this period as a springboard to discuss poverty and shifts of control both towards and away from women, the medical community, and international corporations. Van Esterik (181) and Leslie & Paolisso (117) contribute anthropological voices to the breastfeeding advocacy literature.

PREVALENCE AND DURATION STATISTICS WORLDWIDE   What we can say, in general, is that nearly all women in the Third World initiate breastfeeding, and for most cultures the average duration of breastfeeding is over 1 year. Most women begin adding to the infant's diet within a few weeks or months: first liquids, then mashed foods, then semi-solids, then cooked solids.

Program efforts to promote breastfeeding clearly have an impact on breast-feeding rates. The American Public Health Association report (11) summarizes government legislation and policies to support breastfeeding, improve maternal and infant nutrition, and implement a code of marketing of breast milk substitutes. A number of good programmatic reviews are available (30, 86, 103, 114, 157), although the rapidly changing development picture limits their shelf life. The US Agency for International Development's report to Congress on A.I.D.-funded programs (4) and its *Breastfeeding for Child Survival Strategy* (5) are available from the Agency.

In the late 1960s and during the 1970s, public debate focused on the marketing practices of companies like Nestlé, which were seen as discouraging breastfeeding in Third World countries. Such promotional activity amplifies the trend among educated and urban populations to choose to limit breastfeeding practices, given the perception that bottle-feeding is more elite, white, and modern (148). Ironically, the reverse trend was occurring simultaneously in the developed world. The principal sources of information in the United States are the National Center for Health Statistics (NCHS) Surveys of Family Growth, and the Ross Laboratories Mothers Surveys. Despite methodological differences, both surveys document similar trends between 1955 and 1987. Averaging the data, breastfeeding initiation rates climbed from approximately 30% in 1955 to 55% in 1987, with 19.6% still breastfeeding at 5–6 months. As classified by the surveys, the increase in initiation is primarily accounted for by white (non-Hispanic) women over age 25 with some college education living in the western region of the United States or in cities, with normal-birth-weight infants. Black (non-Hispanic), younger women residing in rural and southern regions of the country, with less than a college education and an infant of low birth weight, were least likely to breastfeed (24% of "black" respondents reported breastfeeding at one week of age) (163). Since 1984, however, breastfeeding rates in the United States have been declining again (163a).

The World Health Organization maintains an accessible data base of international indicators on prevalence and duration of breastfeeding; the most recent publication appeared in the WHO *Weekly Epidemiological Record* (189) for over 1000 surveys carried out in 130 countries between 1980 and 1989. Demographic and Health Survey Data (170) most likely provide the raw numbers for 60 countries in this data set. Additional recent references include Millman (130) and Williamson (186). WHO's earlier collaborative study (188) is still widely quoted in the international literature, although most figures need to be updated.

FACTORS AFFECTING CHOICE OF INFANT FEEDING METHOD   While   Bostock
(26) once described the young infant as an "external fetus," in the sense that the
newborn still needs the mother's body for nourishment, immunological protection, and shelter, humans have evolved to offer the mother a choice. As Van
Esterik framed the question (180), "can we distinguish between mothers who
want to breastfeed and cannot, and mothers who do not want to breastfeed and
do not?" While the former group is assumed to have the knowledge and attitudes
to support breastfeeding, they may be constrained by a lack of social or economic
support, inadequate medical care or advice, or excessive urging (by family,
physicians, or advertising) not to breastfeed. As Van Esterik notes, "the difference between these two categories of women lies not only in their demographic
characteristics, but also in their heads—the ideas, beliefs, and assumptions about
infant feeding that make up the cognitive and affective dimensions of human
behavior" (180:189). Since values and choice are involved, social scientists have
contributed abundantly in this domain, often finding culturally relevant reasons
for women to choose not to breastfeed (see e.g. 23, 72). Forman (76) and
Brownlee (30) review much of this literature. Two theoretical orientations stand
out as particularly important.

Biocultural: the insufficient milk syndrome   While primarily determined by
the infant's sucking intensity, frequency, and duration, the woman's ability to
perform the act of breastfeeding can be influenced by "how she feels about
things"; both the breast milk letdown reflex and maintenance of breast milk
production are susceptible to cultural modeling and interpretation. Since Gussler
& Briesemeister (88) published their initial paper on the "Insufficient Milk
Syndrome," many researchers have used a biocultural explanatory model to
interpret the decision to begin, continue, supplement, or terminate breastfeeding.
The perception of insufficient breast milk has been associated with many social
and cultural factors, as well as with physiological variables. Several recent
examinations of this "syndrome" summarize and extend the earlier studies (94,
155, 177, 181). A mother's perception of insufficient milk may come from her
lack of understanding of "normal" infant breastfeeding patterns (the expectation
that the infant will only want to nurse every 3–4 hours, based on the advice of
doctors or the experience of formula-feeding friends). Millard (129a) provides
a thorough review of how pediatric advice can lead to decreased milk production.

   Additional reports of "insufficient milk" may be attributable to women
using it as a culturally acceptable explanation for using formula, beginning
solids, or even weaning the child from the breast for personal reasons (the
woman doesn't enjoy breastfeeding, finds it too tiring or constraining, or her
husband objects, etc). Moving away from the "syndrome," but retaining the
research question, several authors (8, 154, 181) have noted that disentangling
the mother-infant bio-behavioral feedback aspects of this phenomenon from
such socioeconomic markers as education, income, and returning to work

might enable us to examine the mother's concept of how specific feeding events are regulated, including her own participation in governing the feeding. Maternal confidence and competence have also been discussed by Scrimshaw et al (169), who emphasized the role of health-care providers and hospital policies in affecting subsequent infant-feeding choices. The ability of unsupportive or untrained medical staff to undermine breastfeeding efforts has been observed many times over (see 30 for multiple international references) and can be seen as the rationale for educating medical personnel in lactation management and counseling (129a, 138).

Cultural constructions of breastfeeding   Characterizations of mothering as "appropriate," "optimal," or "poor" are obviously culturally constructed, and both the perceived ability of a mother to feed her child and her choice of infant-feeding method contribute to this characterization. In some cases, women believe their breast milk is of poor quality, owing to humoral imbalance caused by diet, maternal mood, or subsequent pregnancies (51, 72, 184). In these cases, by local norms, a "good" mother finds another source of food for her infant. More often, however, choice of feeding method is determined by rules and behaviors that demonstrate participation in a particular social group rather than by perceptions about the feeding method's nutritional value (52, 107, 135).

The literature on women's employment indicates that the social construction of women's roles has placed many obstacles in the paths of women who wish to breastfeed and work away from home (17, 118, 141, 146, 181, 193). Most studies find that in urban settings, few employed women breastfeed exclusively for 4–6 months, but breastfeeding duration is at least as long as for unemployed women. In developing countries, virtually all women in rural settings work and breastfeed their children simultaneously, seemingly oblivious to breastfeeding as an activity that requires time or attention. Urban Third World women are constrained by obstacles similar to those in the United States: lack of childcare, work environments that do not facilitate pumping or storing breast milk, restrictive employer policies for maternity leave, and social attitudes of employers and coworkers toward breastfeeding that result in disapproval and harassment (137).

THE TWO-WAY RELATIONSHIP BETWEEN BREASTFEEDING AND MATERNAL NUTRITION AND HEALTH   The biomedical literature turns on several intricately linked questions: What does a human infant really need to "thrive" (survive, keep warm, fight off illness, grow, play)? Which of the 200 known constituents in human milk produces these effects (energy, specific nutrients, other factors)? What is the impact of breastfeeding on the mother? And what do these thresholds of need suggest about supplementing mothers' diets or complementing breastfeeding?

What does the infant need? What does it get?   Exclusively or predominantly breastfed infants have been found to consume between approximately 525 grams (38, 45, 139) and 1200 grams (160) of breast milk per day, or, in volume terms, roughly 600–1000 ml/day (191). The most common measurement methods are test-weighing (which disrupts feeding) and the doubly labeled water dose to the mother, which is less invasive (35).

Breastmilk is a nutritionally complete food for human infants, the result of millions of years of evolution. Estimates of the nutrient requirements of the full-term infant during the first 6 months of life are largely based on the composition of human milk (119).

Some researchers worry about the relatively low levels of vitamin D in human breast milk in societies where mothers and infants are kept from exposure to sunlight (because of purdah, pollution, high latitude, etc). Vitamin K stores in the infant are low at birth, and, except for colostrum, low in breast milk. A deficiency of vitamin B_{12} may be a problem among infants who are exclusively breastfed by vegetarian mothers for more than 6 months (120).

Iron deficiency anemia is prevalent among women worldwide and is a particular risk factor for low-birth-weight infants. Though the concentration of iron in breast milk is low, its bioavailability is much higher than in complementary food sources. Additional foods consumed by breastfed infants can interact with breast milk in the infants' digestive tract, dramatically reducing iron bioavailability (142, 164). However, new perspectives on iron metabolism argue convincingly that the low iron content of breast milk is an adaptive/protective response to infectious disease stress (108).

What does the mother need to produce breast milk?   This literature has been synthesized recently (1, 137); Butte et al's recent work contributes substantially to our understanding of energy needs during lactation (32–34). As Parker et al (146) concluded, there are many gaps in knowledge about maternal nutrition, even on basic issues that involve measuring nutritional status of adult women during times of rapid tissue change, such as pregnancy and lactation; assessing prevalence of undernutrition in women; and measuring the functional outcomes of chronic undernutrition. One attempt to fill the gap is A.I.D.'s report (6) on maternal anthropometric indicators. Merchant & Martorell (127) have modeled the factors influencing maternal nutritional status; high energy expenditure, frequent reproductive cycling, and lactation seriously compromise dietary intake in many cases, which may lead to a state of nutritional depletion (128, 129). On average, maternal dietary needs increase to approximately 700 kcal of extra energy per day while lactating to produce 700 grams of breast milk (150). Although mothers' resting metabolic rates start to decrease postpartum, their overall energy intake needs continue to increase during lactation. Women's bodies respond to this demand by reducing the basal metabolic rate to a small degree, catabolizing fat reserves, and metabolizing food more efficiently. In addition, where possible, women may reduce work expenditure and increase consumption. The weight gain of pregnancy provides food stores that are drawn on during late pregnancy and lactation. Because representative energy expenditures are hard to measure accurately for normal time use (not just per activity) in natural situations, we know little about this element of homeostasis. Most women seem able to produce enough breast milk to nourish their infants.

A number of studies have shown that women continue to produce breast milk of adequate quantity and high quality even when their own diets are marginal (104). The fatty acid composition of breast milk is affected by maternal diet, including the type of dietary fat and dietary carbohydrates (70), but overall fat concentrations appear similar in women on varying diets. Prentice et al (151, 152) found that among Gambian women, total dietary energy intake did not affect total fat levels in breast milk. Kneebone et al (110) found that among women of three different ethnic groups in Malaysia (Malay, Chinese, and Indian), dietary differences corresponded to different proportions of saturated and unsaturated fats, and different levels of linoleic acid in breast milk. In general, fatty acid levels were comparable to those reported for well-nourished Western women. A study of vegetarians (70) found that breast milk of vegetarian mothers had the same overall levels of fat as that from nonvegetarians, but "contained a lower proportion of fatty acids derived from animal fat and a higher proportion of polyunsaturated fatty acids derived from dietary vegetable fat" (70:787). The question of the effects of the differences in specific fatty acids in breast milk composition on the growth and health of infants has not been answered.

It has been argued that humankind's ability to survive droughts and ice ages, and to take advantage of different ecosystems, is related to our ability to consume opportunistically yet produce breast milk of relatively unvarying quantity and quality (104). According to Prentice & Prentice (150), adipose tissue (fat) stores of mothers are not usually catabolized for breast milk production but serve primarily as a buffer for lean times.

From a maternal-health perspective, perhaps the most striking consideration is the fact that exclusive breastfeeding, especially during the early months postpartum, causes a hormonal suppression of ovulation and menstruation. This suppression contributes to improved iron status by delaying the blood loss of menstruation. It can also effectively extend the recuperative period between pregnancies and thus enhance the opportunity for adequate repletion of maternal nutrient stores (127). Although our present understanding of the long-term nutritional impact of frequent reproductive cycling is limited, the available scientific evidence supports the conclusion that women should be encouraged to breastfeed exclusively for the first 6 months and to continue breastfeeding thereafter, since the best strategy for replenishing fat and nutrient stores is to delay the next pregnancy (111).

CONTAMINATION FROM THE EARLY INTRODUCTION OF OTHER SUBSTANCES   Exclusive breastfeeding for the first 4–6 months of a child's life is what transforms the "womanly art of breastfeeding" into "one of the most cost-effective means of insuring child survival" (4). Postponing the introduction of nonbreast-milk foods and liquids until at least 4–6 months of age dramatically reduces infants' risk of exposure to environmental contamination while assuring the nutritional and immunological benefits of breast milk through this period (12, 58, 98, 148). The evidence overwhelmingly indicates that on a population level, breastfeeding is positively correlated with lower morbidity and mortality rates, and with shorter and milder illness (47, 61, 83); exclusive breastfeeding is associated with the lowest mortality rates (82, 125, 144, 192). The protective effects of breastfeeding are largest for disadvantaged, rural, and illiterate populations. Most studies have not addressed how risk changes with increments of supplementation (see 182 for an exception). It is unclear how much of the protective effect of breastfeeding is due to the nutrients in human milk, how much to immunoprotection, and how much to the absence of the contaminants often present in supplementary foods. For whatever combination of reasons, breastfed infants have fewer and less severe infections and lower morality rates. Even water can compromise the health of the infant. The common practice of giving infants water may expose them to the environmental pathogens that breastfeeding precludes. In addition, extra water displaces infant demand for human milk, which may cause the mother to produce less breast milk. Thus giving water may indirectly lower the infant's long-term total fluid intake. Breast milk contains adequate levels of necessary electrolytes. As a result, infants do not require extra sources of electrolytes, nor do they require any extra water for hydration or excretion (165)—findings confirmed by recent studies of infant health in hot (9), dry (84), and humid (29) climates.

Offering high-calorie liquids such as juices, cereal-based beverages, and artificial formulas generally reduces the infant's intake of breast milk, with negative impacts on the infant's nutritional status and growth. High-calorie liquids may satisfy the infant's caloric needs and hunger without providing protein, fat, and other nutrients required for proper mental and physical growth and development. In addition, a decrease in demand for breast milk by the infant results in a decrease in maternal supply and a shortening of the period of lactational amenorrhea (81). Thus, giving the infant anything other than breast milk for the first 4–6 months of life is generally contraindicated.

GROWTH ISSUES

Effects of Breastfeeding Frequency on Breast milk Composition

Cross-cultural studies have documented many different styles and patterns of breastfeeding. Breastfeeding frequency, for example, is determined partly by the mother (through cultural beliefs, organization of maternal workload, etc, and individual decisions) and partly by the infant's temperament (56).

The literature often divides breastfeeding frequency into two extreme camps (155). The first is true demand feeding (also called ad libitum, "unrestricted," or "continuous feeding"): The infant is nursed whenever the mother thinks s/he wants to nurse. Researchers assume this results in very frequent feeding. The second is scheduled feeding (also called "regimented," or "restricted"), with long intervals between feedings, coupled with a concerted effort to get the infant to sleep through the night at an early age. The restricted pattern, common in the United States (155), is based on recommendations developed for formula-fed infants, with feeding restricted to every 3–4 hours during the day, with one longer interval of 6–7 hours at night. Although some cultures can be categorized as showing either demand feeding or scheduled feeding, breastfeeding frequency actually varies from culture to culture, from child to child, from mother to mother, with the age and health of the child, and with the season.

Breastfeeding frequency data from a number of cultures exhibit great variation, ranging from the four nursing bouts per daytime hour reported for the San !Kung (112), to the 5–6 feeds in 24 hours for breastfed babies in Northern Europe (14). Other studies have found intermediate values, with average frequencies declining from 15 to 10 per 24 hours as lactation proceeds in Gambia (151, 152), and from 21 to 10 per 24 hours as lactation proceeds in Thailand (100). A study of US La Leche League mothers found an average of 15 feedings per day (36). A study of non-League US mothers (155) found relatively low breastfeeding frequencies, with an average of 7.2 per 24 hours at four weeks and 7.1 at eight weeks. An unknown amount of the variation reported in the literature is due to the way separate feeds are defined, but there is nevertheless great variation in how often infants are breastfed, whether mothers perceive themselves as feeding "on demand" or according to a schedule (129a, 155).

The literature suggests that frequency of breastfeeding may have profound effects on the composition of breast milk, which, in turn, could greatly affect growth rates (92, 153a, 155). One of the continuing methodological problems in studies of energy intake in breastfed infants is that fat is both the major source of energy in human breast milk and the most variable constituent of breast milk. The fat content of human milk rises from the beginning to the end of a feeding, varies according to time of day or night, from day to day, from season to season, and from woman to woman. As a result of millions of years of natural selection, the composition of breast milk changes as the infant gets older, providing an adaptive mix of protein, energy, vitamins, and minerals at each age. Studies of short- and long-term variation in breast milk composition among rural Gambian women (151, 152) associated shorter intervals between feeds both with higher fat concentration of the next feed and with smaller fat decrease between the end of one feed and the beginning of the next. Fat concentrations were lower during the rainy season (a time of decreased intake and increased workload), which coincided with falling breast milk volumes, "magnifying the nutritional problem faced by the breastfed child" (152:501). Fat concentration declined as the infant got older. Differences between mothers were greater than those within mothers. Average fat concentrations decreased with each succeeding pregnancy until leveling off at parities greater than four. Fat concentrations were found to be related to mother's triceps skinfolds but to neither her energy intake nor the volume of milk produced.

Studies of breast milk composition among rural Thai women (100, 101) confirmed these findings: the shorter the interval between feeds, the higher the fat concentration of the next feed. They also found that the greater the milk intake (volume) at a feed, the greater the increase in fat content during the feed. Fat concentration decreased with infant age. Older infants consumed more breast milk at night than younger ones, owing to separation of mother and baby during the day by maternal workload (daytime feedings as few as 0–2). Since nighttime milk had lower fat concentrations, older infants were taking in much less fat than younger infants (100).

Several studies have reported on circadian rhythms of fat concentration. For Gambian women, fat concentrations are highest in the early morning and lowest in the late afternoon (151). Exactly the opposite obtains for Thai women: Concentrations are lowest in the early morning and highest in the late afternoon and early evening (101). Various patterns have been reported for women in Western countries.

The mechanism for how breastfeeding frequency affects fat composition of milk has been clearly explained by Quandt (153a). At the beginning of each breastfeeding episode, in response to the infant's suckling, the mother's pituitary releases a surge of the hormone prolactin. High levels of prolactin suppress lipoprotein lipase action in adipose tissue, preventing the uptake of dietary lipids into maternal fat stores. At the same time, high levels of prolactin enhance lipoprotein lipase action in breast tissue, so that serum lipids (from maternal fat stores as well as dietary fat) are diverted into breast milk production. Thus, frequent nursing leads to frequent prolactin release and elevated serum prolactin concentrations, resulting in higher levels of fat in the breast milk (153a).

Differences in patterns of breastfeeding frequency between populations and between women will result in variation in breast milk fat concentration at both the population and individual levels. Likewise, differences in circadian rhythms of fat concentration are probably related to differences in circadian rhythms of nursing frequency (153a).

Another effect of frequent nursing is a reduction in serum bilirubin levels during the perinatal period, which results in less serious cases of neonatal jaundice, perhaps through the mechanism of more frequent stooling, which moves meconium out of the gut more quickly (49). Other effects of nursing frequency on the infant are unknown.

Infants consume different quantities of breast milk, depending on their age, temperament, activity level, and maternal production. If nursing frequency affects the energy content of milk, then even infants who consume the same overall quantity of breast milk may have very different energy intakes depending on their nursing frequency. Different breastfed infants may consume different quantities and qualities of breast milk, and the same is true among bottle-fed infants. These differences mean that most comparisons of the growth patterns of "breastfed" and "bottle-fed" infants are suspect, because they obscure the variation within each of these groups.

Comparing the Growth of Breastfed and Bottle-fed Infants

The literature that compares the growth of breastfed infants with that of bottle-fed infants can be divided into two groups. First, a number of studies have been conducted in Third World settings, where traditional practices of breast-feeding have been increasingly replaced by the use of infant formula or other artificial products. These studies have consistently found that exclusively breastfed infants grow better than supplemented or bottle-fed infants (77, 106, 121, 124, 178). However, it has been difficult to determine whether the better growth of breastfed infants under these conditions is due to the nutritional superiority of breast milk; the anti-infective and immunological constituents of breast milk, which protect the infant against infections; the fact that breast milk cannot be over- or under-diluted, or contaminated by environmental pathogens, the way formula and bottles can be; some unidentified effects associated with the process of breastfeeding itself; or some combination of these factors. Despite claims to the contrary (149, 159), most researchers agree that infant growth is negatively affected by the use of formula and bottles in Third World contexts. One potentially confounding factor in all of the comparative growth studies is that infants who are not thriving on breast milk may be switched to formula, while infants who do not thrive on formula usually cannot be switched to breast milk. Thus, the bottle-fed group may include infants who were not growing well for reasons unrelated to the mode of feeding.

Second, a number of studies conducted in Western, industrialized settings compare the growth of breastfed infants to that of formula-fed infants (or to the NCHS standards; see 91) in the relative absence of the problems with water quality, environmental sanitation, and over-dilution that confound studies in Third World settings. Some of these studies report comparable growth in breastfed infants (3, 32, 94, 153, 185). Other studies report just the opposite, finding that breastfed infants have slower growth rates than formula-fed infants (or NCHS standards) during the first year of life (33, 38, 39, 48, 57, 62, 78, 79, 140, 143). Some report better growth in breastfed infants during the first few months of life, followed by poorer growth during the rest of the first year (3, 39, 80, 109, 162, 185). Some have characterized breastfed infants as "faltering" relative to the NCHS standards (93), even when weight-for-age and length-for-age z-scores remain positive throughout the first year of life.

The literature comparing exclusively breastfed infants to breastfed infants also receiving solids likewise reveals conflicting results. Some studies report better growth in exclusively breastfed infants (2, 153), while others report poorer growth in this group (22, 77, 95, 96, 166). Detailed comparisons among these studies are made difficult by definitional and methodological differences. Many studies do not control for the type and/or quantity of formula consumed, or for the type and/or quantity of beikost received by infants in their "supplemented" groups. "Solid foods" are not uniform; it makes a difference if the first foods introduced are sterilized, fortified cereals, fruits, vegetables, meats, etc (manufactured by baby food companies) or if they are high-bulk, low-calorie/low-protein cereal-based porridges, made with contaminated water and left to sit around in the heat, uncovered, for hours before consumption. It also makes a difference whether solids are given several times a day, once a day, once or twice a week as the mood strikes the mother, or in some other pattern.

Additionally, human breast milk affects the infant's gastrointestinal environment, resulting in differences in digestion and absorption, with potential effects on growth. Auerbach et al (16) conclude: "partial breastfeeding that derives from mixed feedings involving human milk should be distinguished from mixed feedings involving artificial formulas or nonhuman species–derived substances. Again, the mode of feeding needs to be specified to account for their different possible effects. Thus, although a breastfed baby is receiving solid foods, it should be assumed *until proven otherwise* that such an infant is receiving a different kind of nutrition with a potentially different outcome than an infant receiving artificial formula and the same solid foods" (16:66, emphasis in the original).

On the basis of the studies claiming that breastfed infants do not grow as well as formula-fed infants, some authors have concluded that breast milk is inadequate to support the growth of infants beyond the first few months of life, and recommend the early introduction of solids or supplementary formula to augment nutrient intake.

A more typical conclusion, however, has been that the NCHS standards are too high for infants who are breastfed (34, 39, 79, 143). NCHS standards for the period from birth to 2 years are based in large part upon the Fels Research Institute data, which came from children who were mostly formula-fed and introduced to solid foods at a very early age (often as young as 2–3 weeks) in accord with prevailing medical and cultural beliefs in the United States at the time. Based on these findings, some researchers have called for the development of alternative, presumably lower, standards for breastfed infants. However, a close examination of the literature reveals that the trend toward slower growth in breastfed infants is neither as uniform nor as pervasive as has been reported; in addition, differences in maternal health, birth weights, and breastfeeding styles might account for the slower growth in those cases where breastfed infants do grow more slowly than formula-fed infants in First World contexts.

An Alternative Explanation for "Poor Growth" in Breastfed Infants

In Western, industrialized nations, the recent resurgence in breastfeeding has occurred mainly among middle- and upper-class, well-educated women. Well-educated, middle- and upper-class women are more likely than the average woman to take good care of themselves during pregnancy by not smoking, drinking, or using drugs, by seeking good prenatal health care, by taking prenatal vitamins, and by maintaining better nutrition. Anglo-American women who breastfeed are thus not a random sample of all mothers. These factors contribute to higher birth weights and lengths and may explain the relatively high birth weights and lengths of breastfed infants found in most of the growth studies comparing breastfed infants to either bottle-fed infants or the NCHS standards (3, 31, 32, 57, 79, 80, 94, 153, 155). If this is the case, why don't these large babies maintain their positions relative to the NCHS standards after birth?

At least two factors can be identified that might contribute to slower growth in these infants: (*a*) the phenomenon of "catching-down" (174), in which greater than average intra-uterine growth is offset by slower than average growth during infancy, and (*b*) breastfeeding frequency.

Tanner (174) explains the concept of catch-down growth: "[Thus] during infancy a reassortment of relative sizes among children comes about: those who are larger at birth grow less, and those who are smaller grow more ... . In the series studied by Smith et al (1976 [171a]), not only did many small babies catch up to higher centiles, but many large babies sank back to lower ones. These were the large babies born to medium-size parents ... [and] the sinking down, or dawdling, on average lasted ... some 13–14 months. *Catch-down,* originally suggested as a linguistic joke, seems to have caught on. *Catch-down is as normal a phenomenon in infancy as catch-up*" (174:173-74, emphasis added). If breastfed infants from First World populations tend, as a group, to have above-average birth weights and lengths, their slower growth rates during the first year of life would reflect, in part, the normal phenomenon of catch-down growth.

The phenomena of "catch-up" and "catch-down" growth are clearly observable in the data of Butte et al (32). At 1 month of age, breastfed infants have weight-for-age z-scores (WAZ) of 0.54, compared to bottle-fed infants with 0.26. By 4 months, the breastfed infants have "caught-down" to 0.42, while the bottle-fed infants have "caught-up" to 0.46. At 1 month, breastfed infants have length-for-age z-scores (LAZ) of 0.47, compared to bottle-fed infants with 0.12. By 4 months, the breastfed infants have "caught-down" to 0.23, while the bottle-fed infants have "caught-up" to 0.25. All of the z-scores for both groups of infants are positive (i.e. above the NCHS standards).

The second factor that might explain "poor growth" in breastfed infants is related to breastfeeding frequency (see the discussion above of the effects of breastfeeding frequency on breast milk content). With the exception of the La Leche League mothers, it is probable that most of the mothers in the studies reviewed above breastfed their infants relatively infrequently, according to a typical "Western" schedule of every 4 hours during the day, and encouraged them to sleep apart from the mother, and to sleep through the night at an early age (in Quandt's 1986 study some of the infants were sleeping through the night as early as eight weeks after birth). Nursing frequency is not reported in the La Leche League study (3), but official League advice is for mothers to expect young infants to want to nurse only every 2–3 hours, including during the night. Although this is more frequent than a 4-hour schedule, it is still not as often as the frequencies reported for Gambia (151, 152) or Thailand (100, 101). Quandt (155) provides a thorough and well-written discussion of breast-feeding variation in US mothers; Millard analyzes the impact of American pediatric advice on maternal styles of breastfeeding according to a schedule (129a).

None of the studies to date has been based on samples of mothers in First World contexts feeding their infants using a true "on demand" or "continuous feeding" style. Relatively long daytime intervals, coupled with a cultural value placed on sleeping apart from the mother and sleeping through the night, result in relatively long inter-feed intervals and therefore lower fat content in the breast milk in Anglo-American mothers. If these mothers nursed using a true "on demand" pattern of very frequent feedings, including at night, facilitated by co-sleeping of mother and child, the energy content of the breast milk would presumably be much higher, and the infants might well grow faster.

Thus, we have three types of data: 1. growth patterns of infants breastfed "on demand" under conditions of chronic infections, 2. growth patterns of infants fed formula and early solids under conditions of good health, and 3. growth patterns of infants breastfed according to a schedule. As of this writing, we do not have the fourth type: growth patterns of infants breastfed "on demand" under conditions of good health. Such a study would have to be based on a sample of well-nourished, healthy mothers, with safe water supplies, good sanitation, and good maternal-child health care, who breastfeed their children using a true "on demand" or "continuous" breastfeeding style. Until these studies have been carried out, we won't know how breastfed children grow under good environmental conditions. The NCHS standards may be set too high for most Third World children, but standards based on US samples of high-birth-weight breastfed children, fed according to a schedule, would probably be set too low.

These two factors—the normal biological pattern of catch-down growth observed in large babies, and the cultural practice of breastfeeding according to a schedule—may account for most, if not all, of the apparent "growth faltering" of breastfed infants in Western populations. The existence of a single set of weight and length standards (NCHS) facilitates the kinds of detailed and precise comparisons of growth attainment that we see throughout the literature. Calls for the development of revised standards based on breast-fed infants are therefore premature, and should await further research.

Effects of the Timing of the Introduction of Solid Foods

A critical question concerns the timing of the introduction of solid foods to the diet of the child who has previously been exclusively breast- or formula-fed. Like all other aspects of infant feeding, the introduction of solid foods (beikost) to the infant's diet is heavily influenced by cultural beliefs: about children, about food, and about health and growth. It is also influenced by the environment and the culture's cuisine. A number of studies describe typical infant feeding practices in cultures around the world (50, 51, 99, 149, 159, 172, 176, 187), including beliefs and practices related to the introduction of solids. Reasons for introducing solids at a particular age range from purely symbolic cultural guidelines, to decisions based on chronological or developmental criteria or the infant's own interest in or demand for food, to conflicts with the mother's other responsibilities (work, school, etc). Cultural beliefs, the opinions of friends and relatives, medical advice, and idiosyncratic beliefs all influence the decision to begin feeding solid foods.

In the United States, many factors influence this decision, ranging from misinformation (e.g. the claim that introducing solids will help the baby sleep through the night, a notion shown repeatedly to be incorrect; 65) to recommendations from doctors to introduce iron-fortified cereal because of the low iron content of breast milk. During the period from the 1950s (when proprietary infant foods were first sold) until the mid-to-late 1980s in the United States, many mothers introduced solid foods very early, even as early as two weeks post-partum, often at the urging of their pediatricians. Medical recommendations are constantly being revised but they currently suggest that human milk or infant formula should be the primary source of nutrients during the first year of life and that the introduction of solid food should be delayed until about 4–6 months of age (10, 65, 75).

Recent guidelines recommending the introduction of solid foods at 4–6 months of age are based on several considerations. First, most infants grow satisfactorily for the first 4–6 months of life, whether breastfed or bottle-fed. Second, the early introduction of solids tends to substitute less nutritious foods for breast milk or formula. Third, the young infant's gut absorbs whole proteins; delaying the introduction of solid foods until the infant's intestinal tract matures lowers the risk of developing food allergies. Fourth, much of the solid food fed to young infants passes through the body undigested and unabsorbed.

In addition to cultural beliefs and medical advice, the introduction of solid foods also depends on maternal perceptions of infant needs. We are not aware of any studies that address the effects of infant size (and maternal perception of infant size) on the timing of the breastfeeding mother's decision to begin solids. However, the distribution may be bimodal, with both small- and large-for-chronological-age infants being supplemented earlier than "average" children. The mother of a small child may become concerned that she doesn't have enough breast milk and decide to begin solids at an early age in the hope that eating solid food will increase the child's overall intake, leading to better weight gain.

Several US studies have found that earlier supplementation either has no effect on intake or growth (79) or leads to poorer growth (2, 65, 153). Others have suggested that early supplementation results in greater growth and may even lead to obesity (140), and many mothers seem to subscribe to this view. On the other hand, the mother of a large infant may also fear that she can't support adequate growth of a big baby on breast milk alone, or she may begin solids at an early age simply to reduce the infant's demands to nurse. Quandt's study (153) showed that the early introduction of beikost did, in fact, reduce nursing frequency.

Such a relationship between infant size and introduction of solid foods would confound the interpretation of studies on the effects of beikost on growth, as both smaller- and larger-than-average children might start solid foods earlier than average children because of their prior growth patterns.

INFANT FEEDING STYLES, MATERNAL COMPETENCE, AND GROWTH

Much of the research on nutritional factors affecting children's growth has focused on the question of the availability of food, and on what happens when food quantity or quality is low. In much of this research, the population or the household was the unit of study, and it was generally assumed that as long as food was available to the population/household, children would receive adequate amounts to support normal growth.

In recent years, the focus has shifted to more proximate causes of child malnutrition, including, for example, the intra-household distribution of food (147), age and sex-linked inequalities, the contribution of fathers' and mothers' incomes to food-purchasing power (64), and maternal factors such as education, competence, and attitude. A number of ethnographic studies start from an "infant feeding beliefs and practices" perspective and argue on logical grounds that certain patterns of infant feeding contribute either to malnutrition or to good nutrition (24, 25, 51, 55, 99, 176). These studies often use anthropometric measurements of growth status as a confirming variable. Other studies start from an "infant growth patterns" perspective and look for differences in infant feeding practices that would explain these patterns (50, 105, 173, 194). Researchers using either or both of these approaches have found it difficult to determine how much infant feeding practices contribute to the observed growth patterns; but as evidence accumulates, it is becoming clear that providing adequate food to the community or adequate income for the household does not necessarily enhance the nutritional status and growth of children.

A number of early studies provided ethnographic descriptions of beliefs surrounding infant feeding cross-culturally (122, 149, 159, 187)—beliefs about whether to breastfeed or use artificial formula, when to begin solid foods, which foods from the local cuisine are appropriate vs taboo for young children, and when children should cease breastfeeding. In a review of the literature in the late 1980s, Dettwyler observed that few such studies treated specifically how food is given to the infant, or who decides what foods the infant should eat, how often, and, perhaps most importantly, how much (53, 54).

A number of recent studies have focused on maternal behaviors surrounding infant feeding interactions. Researchers have attributed differences in infant feeding styles to both inter- and intra-cultural variation in maternal "attitude" (50), maternal "experience" (173), or maternal "competence" (194). Despite terminological differences, all of these researchers are attempting to capture the essence, and the underlying causes, of maternal-infant feeding interaction styles. For example, Swenson found better growth among higher-birth-order children and among children whose mothers had experienced more than two previous fetal/infant deaths in Bangladesh. She concludes: "The results suggest that child care practices, particularly with regard to nutrition, may actually improve among women who have experienced previous fetal or child losses ... (who) may exercise greater caution and effort to provide adequate nutrition for their children ... . The lower proportions of malnourished children in pregnancy orders equal to or greater than 5 compared to first and second order births suggest that the experience a mother gains in child care may tend to diminish any potential adverse biological effects that have been attributed to higher pregnancy orders in infancy" (173:192). Dettwyler (50) also found better growth among higher-birth-order children in Mali and attributed it to maternal experience and attitude. McKenna reports the same findings in studies of parenting among nonhuman primates as well (118a).

A few researchers have pointed out that not all cultures share the Western emphasis on "child survival" and child health. This point has been made most eloquently by Cassidy (37), in her comparison of "adaptor" and "activist" positions. Scheper-Hughes coined the phrase "selective neglect" to refer to mothers who choose, for culturally sanctioned reasons, to allow some of their children to die, most often through nutritional deprivation (167, 168). Culturally sanctioned reasons include sex of the child, illegitimacy, physical and mental defects, too many children, children spaced too close together, and children who do not possess sufficient strength or "spirit" to survive in adverse circumstances (167, 168). What appear to Western researchers to be "maladaptive" infant feeding practices may result from ignorance of the relationship between food and health, but they may also be deliberate, though seldom articulated, choices of mothers to invest less time and fewer resources in certain children.

A number of other approaches can be found in the literature. Bledsoe and colleagues, working among the Mende of Sierra Leone, find that foster children have less access to the food resources in the family, and poorer growth, than "born" children in the same family (24, 25). In Peru, Bentley and colleagues have described "active" feeding behaviors of mothers during episodes of diarrheal illness in their infants. Although these mothers are usually relatively passive, they actively encourage their children to eat when illness has reduced the child's appetite (21). The roles of anorexia and maternal response to anorexia in affecting dietary intake and growth (21, 54) remain a rich area for further research. Gray (85) reports that Turkana children are buffered from seasonal food shortages because adults give children's nutritional needs higher priority at these times, a practice also reported for the Nuer (66). Dettwyler (55), on the other hand, finds that in rural southern Mali, adults, especially men, claim the best food for themselves, arguing that young children don't need, don't deserve, and can't appreciate good food. Engle provides a recent review of the literature on child care, including infant feeding, and its potential impact on child health (64a). Much work remains to be done on these and related topics.

The final body of literature to be reviewed here is that of Zeitlin and colleagues. Zeitlin's early work drew attention to the role of place and method of early infant feeding in the potential bacterial contamination of food (87, 195). More recently, Zeitlin and colleagues have been influential in focusing on the mothers of "positive deviants" (also known as "invulnerable" or "invincible" children)—children who are growing well in conditions that often lead to malnutrition and disease. This literature has been thoroughly reviewed in Zeitlin et al's survey (194).

The positive deviance approach has identified a wide range of social and psychological variables that affect maternal ability and motivation to provide the high quality of child care that leads to positive deviance in growth. This research aims to develop culture-specific intervention strategies that build on "positive deviance" behaviors already present rather than simply import Western beliefs and practices.

A potential criticism of the positive deviance approach is that it relies on several theoretical perspectives that most anthropologists reject and that may detract from an appreciation of the valuable insights offered by this approach. Zeitlin and colleagues interpet the mothers of "positive deviants" as unusual members of their culture. They assume that traditional infant feeding practices, which most mothers follow, must have adaptive value, in the evolutionary sense, even if they result in high rates of childhood mortality and large numbers of malnourished children who fail to grow properly. They argue that infant feeding practices that lead to malnutrition in early childhood represent adaptation at three levels.

First, Zeitlin et al claim that traditional infant feeding practices act as agents of natural selection, allowing only the hardiest to survive to become adults.

Here Zeitlin et al are employing a group selection argument. Most evolutionary biologists and human behavioral ecologists reject the group selection argument (see 45a for a review of this literature).

Second, they claim that traditional infant feeding practices produce adults with small body size who require less food. This position is known as the "small but healthy" hypothesis, and most anthropologists reject it as well. Small adult body size due to malnutrition in childhood results in functional impairments that outweigh any advantage accruing to lower nutrient requirements (123).

Third, they argue that rural societies "socialize young children not to expect favoured foods or special treatment because of their low position in the family" (194:6). "[P]arental goals," they claim, "are to produce an undemanding, compliant worker, starting work from 3–5 years of age. Once past the dangers of early infancy, the child must accept its lowly rank as the least productive and youngest member of the production team. As a symbol of his entry-level status, he may receive the poorest quality and the smallest portions of food, and must not question this" (194:7). Zeitlin et al (194) cite the work of Chavez & Martinez (40), who have argued that only people malnourished as children, who grow up with less than optimal cognitive capacities, would be able to endure the monotony of rural village life.

This third theoretical orientation, is flawed in two major ways. First, there is no evidence that traditional infant feeding practices that lead to child malnutrition (and its consequent long-term functional impairments) are "adaptive" in any way. Indeed anthropologists sometimes refer to such practices as "maladaptive," in the sense that a system in which women must go through multiple pregnancies and suffer high infant losses to produce an average of two surviving children is inefficient (in the biological sense) and painful (in the emotional sense). This is not to claim that such systems are either "maladaptive" or "adaptive" in an evolutionary sense (indeed, cultural evolution and biological evolution may not be governed by the same laws); but any cultural system that, on average, enables two or more children to survive for each adult couple qualifies as sufficiently "adaptive" in an evolutionary sense.

It may be difficult for researchers who work primarily in the United States, accustomed to the pervasive acceptance in US culture of the relationship between food and health, to appreciate that this biomedical knowledge is relatively new even to US culture, and is not part of the basic knowledge of many of the world's peoples. In cultures where this knowledge is not available, traditional infant feeding practices are based on other beliefs about food, about children, and about religion, for example, as the ethnographic literature on infant feeding amply demonstrates. The fact that these beliefs result in malnutrition does not make the beliefs themselves "maladaptive" in the evolutionary sense as long as the population is able to replace itself each generation; nor must we find ways in which they might be "adaptive" in order to explain their existence.

Second, the "rural village monotony" is ethnocentric and rather condescending. Like a New Yorker ruling out the possibility of happiness in Dime Box, Texas, Zeitlin and colleagues (194), along with Chavez & Martinez (40), don't understand a willingness to live in a rural village where, they imply, life must be stultifying. Such arguments are both insulting to the villagers and incorrect. Rural village life may appear monotonous to the outsider, but village residents have an emphatically different perspective. "From a European's point of view," wrote Evans-Pritchard, "Nuerland has no favourable qualities, unless its severity be counted as such, for its endless marshes and wide savannah plains have an austere, monotonous charm ... . But Nuer think that they live in the finest country on earth ..." (66:51).

Despite these problems, anthropological readers should resist the urge to dismiss the positive deviance literature, as it offers many interesting insights.

NON-ANTHROPOMETRIC OUTCOMES

As the quest continues for a breast milk equivalent, more and more constituents of human breast milk are identified that affect growth in subtle ways but cannot (so far) be duplicated in formula. At the same time, additional effects of breast milk and breastfeeding on the infant are being recognized. For example, recent studies have shown that formulas and "weaning foods" cannot duplicate breast milk as sources of long-chain polyunsaturated fatty acids, which are necessary for proper growth and development of the brain and of retinal and erythrocytic membranes (102). Use of formula can adversely affect the growth and development of many tissues in the body, not just those measurable through standard anthropometric techniques, and not just in Third World contexts (47).

Differences in feeding practices also affect the basic physiology of the infant. Several long-term studies by Dewey, Garza and colleagues have found that breastfed infants have significantly lower nutrient intakes than bottle-fed infants, both before and after solid foods are introduced (57, 79). Over the first 8 months of life, formula-fed infants take in about twice as much formula as breastfed infants do breast milk (1200 ml/day compared to 600 ml/day), which results in a "deficit" of 30,000 kcal in breastfed infants (79), or an excess in the formula-fed infants, depending on one's perspective. Breastfed infants have lower minimal rates of energy expenditure, lower rectal temperatures, lower heart rates, lower sleeping metabolic rates, and lower daily energy expenditures than formula-fed infants, all of which suggest significant differences in body composition (79).

Breastfed infants spend much less time fussing and crying than formula-fed infants, and, since they are more often in contact with the mother's body, they may spend less energy maintaining body temperature. These factors may account for the lower energy expenditures observed. A difference between breastfed and formula-fed infants that has not been studied in detail is that of fecal volume (for a mention of the topic in passing see 32). Among the lay breastfeeding population in the United States, it is believed that breastfed infants have a much lower volume of feces than formula-fed infants owing to the increased digestibility and absorption of breast milk. Thus, some of the increased nutrient intake documented for formula-fed babies probably passes through the infant's gastrointestinal tract undigested and unabsorbed, and will be reflected in greater fecal volume. As far as we know, this area of research has not been explored.

Infant feeding patterns also affect infant cognitive and motor development. Follow-up studies of both breastfed and formula-fed children have been conducted at 2 years (134), at 5 years (175), and at 7 years (68, 133). In each case, after adjustment for social and behavioral variables, the breastfed infants demonstrated greater cognitive development, to statistically significant levels. As a final example, Martorell & O'Gara (124) report faster motor development among breastfed than among bottle-fed infants.

CONCLUSIONS

The study of infant- and child-feeding practices and their effects on infant growth is an active interdisciplinary field, with a voluminous literature. Anthropologists have drawn attention to the fact that cultural values and beliefs affect infant feeding practices (although the medical and nutritional research community has been slow to realize this), and to the effects of such beliefs on growth.

It is well established that breastfed infants have lower mortality and morbidity, and better growth, than bottle-fed infants in Third World populations. The evidence continues to mount that breastfeeding also provides better health and growth for infants in Western populations. It has been difficult to determine whether the better growth and health of breastfed infants are due to the nutritional superiority of breast milk; the anti-infective and immunological constituents of breast milk, which protect the infant against infections; the fact that breast milk cannot be over- or under-diluted, or contaminated by environmental pathogens or toxins the way formula and bottles can be; some unidentified effects associated with the process of breastfeeding itself; the subtle effects of the underlying maternal attitudes and patterns of mother-infant interaction that accompany the decision to breastfeed; or (most likely) some combination of these factors.

Defining "normal" growth in infants is problematic, as even physiological processes such as breastfeeding can be altered by cultural practices. Future comparative studies must be precise in defining distinctive feeding groups, so that different growth patterns can be interpreted accurately. The reporting of growth data using z-scores based on the NCHS standards (91), already widely used in the growth and development literature, would facilitate comparisons among studies.

Mother-child interactions during infant feeding provide an important topic for future research. The concepts of maternal "attitude" and "competence" are critical but poorly understood; further study of maternal/caretaker behaviors will contribute to an understanding of the proximate determinants of child nutritional status and growth. Cultural beliefs about infant feeding have only been explored thoroughly in a few cultures. The relationships among infant feeding beliefs and practices and other aspects of culture also remain fruitful areas for further research.

ACKNOWLEDGMENTS

Claudia Fishman was the primary author for the section on "Breastfeeding Issues." Katherine Dettwyler was the primary author for the other sections. Claudia Fishman's participation was made possible through support provided by the Bureau for Research and Development, US Agency for International Development, through the Nutrition Communication Project of the Academy for Educational Development, Washington DC, Contract No. DAN-5113-Z-00-7031-00. Bibliographic and research assistance, as well as valuable perspectives, were provided by Sue Kolodin, PhD, under the same contract, and by Steven Hansch, MPH, out of the goodness of his heart. Their help is gratefully acknowledged. Katherine Dettwyler wishes to acknowledge the help and advice of Drs. Steven P. Dettwyler, Paul L. Jamison, and Lee Cronk, and La Leche League leader Cathy Liles; the support of Melissa Cuthbert; and the technical assistance provided by Alexander Dettwyler. Both authors are grateful to Dr. Patrice L. Engle and Dr. Sara A. Quandt for helpful comments on an earlier draft. The opinions expressed herein are those of the authors, and do not necessarily reflect the views of the US Agency for International Development. The authors acknowledge responsibility for any errors.

Literature Cited

1. Adair, L. 1987. Nutrition in the reproductive years. In *Nutritional Anthropology,* ed. F. E. Johnston, pp. 119–54. New York: Alan R. Liss, Inc.
2. Agras, W. S., Kraemer, H. C., Berkowitz, R. I., Hammer, L. D. 1990. Influence of early feeding style on adiposity at 6 years of age. *J. Pediatr.* 116(5):805–9
3. Ahn, C. H., MacLean, W. C. Jr. 1980. Growth of the exclusively breast-fed infant. *Am. J. Clin. Nutr.* 33:183–92
4. A. I. D. 1990. Breastfeeding: a report on A. I. D. Programs. Washington, DC: Agency Int. Dev.
5. A. I. D. 1990. *Breastfeeding for Child Survival Strategy.* Washington, DC: Agency Int. Dev.
6. A. I. D. 1991. Anthropometric indicators for measuring pregnancy outcomes. A report of the working group: mothercare, A. I. D., UNICEF and WHO. Washington DC: Agency Int. Dev.
7. Akre, J., ed. 1989. Infant feeding: the physiological basis. *Bull. World Health Org.* 67:1–108 (Suppl.)
8. Allen, L., Pelto, G. 1985. Research on determinants of breastfeeding duration: suggestions for biocultural studies. *Med. Anthropol.* 9:97–105
9. Almroth, S., Bidinger, P. 1990. No need for water supplementation for exclusively breast-fed infants under hot and arid conditions. *Trans. Roy. Soc. Trop. Med. Hyg.* 84:602–4
10. American Academy of Pediatrics. 1980. On the feeding of supplemental foods to infants. Committee on nutrition. *Pediatrics* 65a:1178–81
11. American Public Health Association. 1988. Government legislation and policies to support breastfeeding, improve maternal and infant nutrition and implement a code of marketing of Breast milk substitutes. Rep. 5, Washington, DC: APHA

12. Anderson, M. A. 1991. Impact of breast-feeding on infant and child morbidity and mortality. Presented at the Workshop on Child Health Priorities in the 1990s, June 20–22. Johns Hopkins Univ., Baltimore, Maryland

13. Apple, R. D. 1987. *Mothers and Medicine: A Social History of Infant Feeding, 1890–1950.* Madison: Univ. Wisconsin

14. Armstrong, H. C. 1991. International recommendations for consistent breastfeeding definitions. *J. Hum. Lact.* 7(2):51–54

15. Auerbach, K. G. 1985. *Lactation Consultant Series (17 units).* New York: Avery Publishing Group

16. Auerbach, K. G., Renfrew, M. J., Minchin, M. 1991. Infant feeding comparisons: a hazard to infant health? *J. Hum. Lact.* 7(2):63–71

17. Barber-Madden, R., Petschek, M., Pakter, J. 1987. Breastfeeding and the working mother: barriers and intervention strategies. *J. Publ. Health Pol.* Winter:531–41

18. Barness, L. A., ed. 1990. Dietary patterns and nutrient intake of U. S. infants. *J. Pediatr.* 117(2, Pt. 2, Suppl.)

19. Barness, L. A. 1990. Bases of weaning recommendations. See Ref. 18, pp. 84–85

20. Beasley, A. 1991. Breastfeeding studies: culture, biomedicine, and methodology. *J. Hum. Lact.* 7:7–13

21. Bentley, M. E., Stallings, R. Y., Fukumoto, M., Elder, J. A. 1991. Maternal feeding behavior and child acceptance of food during diarrhea, convalescence, and health in the Central Sierra of Peru. *Am. J. Publ. Health* 81(1):43–47

22. Bindon, J. 1985. The influence of infant feeding patterns on growth of children in American Samoa. *Med. Anthropol.* 9:183–95

23. Bledsoe, C. H. 1992. Side-stepping the postpartum sex taboo: Mende cultural perceptions of tinned milk in Sierra Leone. In *The Cultural Roots of African Fertility,* ed. E. van de Walle. Berkeley: Univ. Calif. Press. In press

24. Bledsoe, C. H. 1991. The trickle-down model within households: foster children and the phenomenon of scrounging. In *The Health Transition: Methods and Measures,* ed. J. Cleland, A. G. Hill, pp. 115–31. Canberra: Aust. Natl. Univ. Press

25. Bledsoe, C. H., Ewbank, D. C., Isiugo-Abanihe, U. C. 1988. The effect of child fostering on feeding practices and access to health services in rural Sierra Leone. *Soc. Sci. Med.* 27(6):627–36

26. Bostock, J. 1962. Evolutionary approaches to infant care. *Lancet* i:1033–35

27. Briend, A., Wojtyniak, B., Rowland, M. G. 1988. Breastfeeding, nutritional state and child survival in rural Bangladesh. *Brit. Med. J.* 296:879–82

28. Brown, K. H., Akhtar, N. A., Robertson, A., Ahmed, G. 1986. Lactational capacity of marginally nourished mothers: relationships between maternal nutritional status and quantity and proximate composition of milk. *Pediatrics* 78:909–18

29. Brown, K. H., de Kanashiro, H. C., del Aguila, R., de Romana, G. L., Black, R. E. 1986. Milk consumption and hydration status of exclusively breast-fed infants in a warm climate. *J. Pediatr.* 108:677–80

30. Brownlee, A. 1990. *Breastfeeding, Weaning and Nutrition:* Monogr. 4: *The Behavioral Issues;* Monogr. 5: *Expanded Bibliography.* Washington DC: Int. Health & Dev. Assocs.

31. Butte, N. F., Garza, C., Smith, E. O., Nichols, B. L. 1984. Human milk intake and growth in exclusively breast-fed infants. *J. Pediatr.* 104:187–95

32. Butte, N. F., Smith, E. O., Garza, C. 1990. Energy utilization of breast-fed and formula-fed infants. *Am. J. Clin. Nutr.* 51:350–58

33. Butte, N. F., Smith, E. O., Garza, C. 1991. Heart rates of breast-fed and formula-fed infants. *J. Pediatr. Gastroenterol. Nutr.* 13:391–96

34. Butte, N. F., Villapando, S., Wong, W. W., Flores-Huerta, S., Hernandez-Beltran, M. J., et al. 1992. Human milk intake and growth faltering of rural Mesoamerindian infants. *Am. J. Clin. Nutr.* In press

35. Butte, N. F., Wong, W., Patterson, B., Garza, C., Klein, P. 1988. Human-milk intake measured by administration of deuterium oxide to the mother: a comparison with the test-weighing technique. *Am. J. Clin. Nutr.* 47:815–21

36. Cable, T. A., Rothenberger, L. A. 1984. Breastfeeding behavioral patterns among La Leche League mothers: a descriptive survey. *Pediatrics* 73:830–35

37. Cassidy, C. M. 1987. World-view conflict and toddler malnutrition: change agent dilemmas. See Ref. 167, pp. 293–324

38. Chandra, R. K. 1981. Breast feeding, growth, and morbidity. *Nutr. Res.* 1:25–31

39. Chandra, R. K. 1982. Physical growth of exclusively breast fed-infants. *Nutr. Res.* 2:275–76

40. Chavez, A., Martinez, C. 1982. *Growing Up in a Developing Community. A Bioecologic Study of the Development of Children of Poor Peasant Families in Mexico.* Mexico City: Inst. Nac. Nutr. (English version published by the Institute of Nutrition of Central America and Panama. Cited in Ref. 194)

41. Claeson, M., Merson, M. H. 1990. Global progress in the control of diarrheal disease. *Pediatr. Infect. Dis. J.* 9:345–55

42. Clemens, J. D., Stanton, B., Stoll, B., Shahid, N. S., Banu, H., et al. 1986. Breastfeeding as a determinant of severity in shigellosis. Evidence for protection throughout the first three years of life in Bangladeshi children. *Am. J. Epidemiol.* 123:710–20

43. Clemens, J. D., Sack, D. A., Harris, J. R.,

Khan, M. R., Chakraborty, J. et al. 1990. Breastfeeding and the risk of severe cholera in rural Bangladeshi children. *Am. J. Epidemiol.* 131:400–11

44. Coates, M. M. 1990. *The Lactation Consultant's Topical Review and Bibliography of the Literature on Breastfeeding.* Chicago: Le Leche League Int.

45. Creed de Kanashiro, H., Brown, K. H., Lopez de Romana, G., Lopez, T., Black, R. E. 1990. Consumption of food and nutrients by infants in Huascar, Peru. *Am. J. Clin. Nutr.* 52:995–1004

45a. Cronk, L. 1991. Human behavioral ecology. *Annu. Rev. Anthropol.* 20:25–53

46. Cunningham, A. S. 1988. Breastfeeding, bottle-feeding, and illness: an annotated bibliography. See Ref. 103, pp. 448–80

47. Cunningham, A. S., Jelliffe, D. B., Jelliffe, E. F. P. 1991. Breastfeeding and health in the 1980s: a global epidemiologic review. *J. Pediatr.* 118:659–66

48. Czajka-Narins, D. M., Jung, E. 1986. Physical growth of breast-fed and formula-fed infants from birth to age two years. *Nutr. Res.* 6:753–62

49. DeCarvalho, M., Klaus, M. H., Merkatz, R. B. 1982. Frequency of Breastfeeding and serum bilirubin concentration. *Am. J. Dis. Child* 136:737–38

50. Dettwyler, K. A. 1986. Infant feeding in Mali, West Africa: variations in belief and practice. *Soc. Sci. Med.* 23(7):651 64

51. Dettwyler, K. A. 1987. Breastfeeding and weaning in Mali: cultural context and hard data. *Soc. Sci. Med.* 24(8):633–44

52. Dettwyler, K. A. 1988. More than nutrition: breastfeeding in urban Mali. *Med. Anthropol. Q.* 2(2):172–83

53. Dettwyler, K. A. 1989. Styles of infant feeding: parental/caretaker control of food consumption in young children. *Am. Anthropol.* 91(3):696–703

54. Dettwyler, K. A. 1989. The interaction of anorexia and cultural beliefs in infant malnutrition in Mali. *Am. J. Hum. Biol.* 1(6):683–95

55. Dettwyler, K. A. 1991. Growth status of children in rural Mali: implications for nutrition education programs. *Am. J. Hum. Biol.* 3(5):447–62

56. de Vries, M. W. 1987. Cry babies, culture, and catastrophe: infant temperament among the Masai. See Ref. 167, pp. 165–85

57. Dewey, K. G., Heinig, M. J., Nommsen, L. A., Lonnerdal, B. 1990. Growth patterns of breast-fed infants during the first year of life: the DARLING study. In *Human Lactation IV: Breastfeeding, Nutrition, Infection and Infant Growth in Developed and Emerging Countries,* ed. S. A. Atkinson, L. Hanson, R. Chandra, pp. 269–82. St. Johns, Newfoundland: ARTS Biomed.

58. De Zoysa, I., Rea, M., Martines, J. 1991. Breastfeeding promotion in diarrhoeal disease control programmes. *Health Pol. Plan.* 6:371–79

59. Dobbing, J., ed. 1985. *Maternal Nutrition and Lactational Infertility.* New York: Raven Press

60. Dobbing, J. 1987. Medical and scientific commentary on charges made against the infant food industry. In *Infant Feeding: Anatomy of a Controversy 1973–1984,* ed. J. Dobbing, pp. 9–27. London: Springer-Verlag

61. Duffy, L. C., Ripenhoff-Talty, M., Byers, T. E., La Scolea, L. J., Zielezny, M. A. et al. 1986. Modulation of rotavirus enteritis during breastfeeding. *Am. J. Dis. Child.* 140:1164–68

62. Duncan, B., Schaefer, C., Sibley, B., Fonseca, N. M. 1984. Reduced growth velocity in exclusively breast-fed infants. *Am. J. Dis. Child.* 138:309–13

63. Eisenberg, A., Murkoff, H. E., Hathaway, S. E. 1989. *What to Expect the First Year.* New York: Workman. 671 pp.

64. Engle, P. L., Pedersen, M. E. 1989. Maternal work for earnings and childrens nutritional status in urban Guatemala. *Ecol. Food Nutr.* 22:211–23

64a. Engle, P. L. 1992. Care and child nutrition. Paper presented at Int. Conf. Nutr., Rome; available from Senior Nutr. Advis. Off., UNICEF, 3 United Nations Plaza, New York, NY 10017

65. Ernst, J. A., Bull, M. J., Rickard, K. A., Brady, M. S., Lemons, J. A. 1990. Growth outcome and feeding practices of the very low birth weight infant (less than 1500 grams) within the first year of life. See Ref. 18, pp. 156–66

66. Evans-Pritchard, E. E. 1940. *The Nuer.* New York/Oxford: Oxford Univ. Press

67. Feachem, R. G., Koblinsky, M. A. 1984. Interventions for the control of diarrhoeal diseases among young children: promotion of Breastfeeding. *Bull. World Health Org.* 62:271–92

68. Fergusson, D. M., Beautrais, A. L., Silva, P. A. 1982. Breastfeeding and cognitive development in the first seven years of life. *Soc. Sci. Med.* 16:1705–8

69. Fildes, V. A. 1986. *Breasts, Bottles and Babies: a History of Infant Feeding.* Edinburgh: Edinburgh Univ. Press

70. Finley, D. A., Lonnerdal, B., Dewey, K. G., Grivetti, L. E. 1985. Breast milk composition: fat content and fatty acid composition in vegetarians and non-vegetarians. *Am. J. Clin. Nutr.* 41:787–800

71. Fishman, C. 1991. Optimal infant feeding: a West African response to global policy. Paper presented at the Annu. Meet., Am. Anthropol. Assoc., Chicago

72. Fishman, C., Evans, R., Jenks, E. 1988. Conflicts in post partum food choice for Indochinese women in California. *Soc. Sci. Med.* 26:1125–32

73. Fomon, S. J. 1974. *Infant Nutrition.* Philadelphia: W. B. Saunders Co. 2nd ed.
74. Fomon, S. J. 1987. Reflections on infant feeding in the 1970s and 1980s. *Am. J. Clin. Nutr. Suppl.* 46:171–82
75. Fomon, S. J., Filer, L. J., Anerdon, T. A., Ziegler, E. E. 1979. Recommendations for feeding normal infants. *Pediatrics* 63:52–59
76. Forman, M. R. 1984. Review of research on the factors associated with choice and duration of infant feeding in less-developed countries. *Pediatrics* 74:667–94
77. Forman, M. R., Guptill, K. S., Chang, D. N., Sarov, B., Berendes, H. W., et al. 1990. Undernutrition among Bedouin Arab infants: the Bedouin Infant Feeding Study. *Am. J. Clin. Nutr.* 51:343–49
78. Forsum, E., Sadurskis, A. 1986. Growth, body composition and breast milk intake of Swedish infants during early life. *Early Hum. Dev.* 14:121–29
79. Garza, C., Butte, N. F. 1990. Energy intakes of human milk-fed infants during the first year. See Ref. 18, pp. 124–31
80. Garza, C., Stuff, J., Butte, N. 1989. Growth of the breast-fed infant. In *Human Lactation,* ed. A. S. Goldman, S. A. Atkinson, L. A. Hanson, 3:109–21. New York: Plenum
81. Georgetown Univ. Int. Inst. Reprod. Health. 1990. *Breastfeeding: Protecting a Natural Resource.* Washington, DC: Georgetown Univ.
82. Glass, R. I., Stoll, B. J. 1989. The protective effect of human milk against diarrhea: a review of studies from Bangladesh. *Acta Paediatr. Scand. Suppl.* 351:131–36
83. Glass, R. I., Svennerholm, A. M., Stoll, B. J., Khan, M. R., Huq, M. I., Holmgren, J. 1983. Protection against cholera in breast-fed children by antibodies in breast milk. *N. Engl. J. Med.* 308:1389–92
84. Goldberg, N. M., Adams, E. 1983. Supplementary water for breast-fed babies in a hot and dry climate—not really a necessity. *Arch. Dis. Childhood* 58:73–74
85. Gray, S. J. 1988. *Growth of settled Turkana schoolchildren.* MA thesis, State Univ. New York, Binghamton. 131 pp.
86. Green, C. 1990. *Media Promotion of Breastfeeding, a Decade's Experience.* Washington, DC: Acad. Educ. Dev.
87. Guldan, G. S. 1988. *Maternal education and child caretaking practices in rural Bangladesh. Part 1: child feeding practices; Part 2: food and personal hygiene.* PhD thesis, Sch. Nutr., Tufts Univ.
88. Gussler, J., Briesemeister, L. 1980. The insufficient milk syndrome: a biocultural explanation. *Med. Anthropol.* 4:1–24
89. Habicht, J.-P., Da Canzo, J., Butz, W. P. 1985. Does breastfeeding really save lives? —or are apparent benefits due to biases? *Am. J. Epidemiol.* 123:279–90
90. Habicht, J.-P., Rasmussen, K. M. 1985.

Model for analysis of the relationship between breastfeeding data and postpartum anovulation data. See Ref. 59, pp. 119–27
91. Hamill, P. V. V., Drizd, T. A., Johnson, C. L., Reed, R. B., Roche, A. F., Moore, W. M. 1979. Physical growth: National Center for Health Statistics percentiles. *Am. J. Clin. Nutr.* 32:607–29
92. Hamosh, M. 1980. Breast milk fat: origin and digestion. In *Human Milk: Its Biological and Social Value,* ed. S. Freier, A. I. Eidelman. Amsterdam: Excerpta Medica. [Cited in Ref. 153]
93. Hijazi, S. S., Abulaban, A., Waterlow, J. C. 1989. The duration for which exclusive breastfeeding is adequate. *Acta Paediatr. Scand.* 78:23–28
94. Hillervik-Lindquist, C., Hofvander, Y., Sjolin, S. 1991. Studies on perceived breast milk insufficiency. *Acta Paediatr. Scand.* 80:297–303
95. Hitchcock, N. E., Gracey, M., Gilmour, A. I. 1985. The growth of breast fed and artificially fed infants from birth to twelve months. *Acta Paediatr. Scand.* 74:240–45
96. Hitchcock, N. E., Owles, E. N., Gracey, M. 1982. Dietary energy and nutrient intakes and growth of healthy Australian infants in the first year of life. *Nutr. Res.* 2:13–19
97. Holland, B. 1987. The validity of retrospective Breastfeeding duration data: an illustrative analysis of data quality in the Malaysian Family Life Survey. *Hum. Biol.* 59:477–87
98. Huffman, S., Yeager, B. A. C., Levine, R. E., Shelton, J., Labbok, M. 1991. *Breastfeeding Saves Lives: An Estimate of the Impact of Breastfeeding on Infant Mortality in Developing Countries.* Bethesda, MD: Cent. Prevent Childhood Malnutr.
99. Hull, V., Simpson, M., eds. 1985. *Breastfeeding, Child Health, and Child Spacing: Cross-cultural Perspectives.* London: Croom Helm
100. Jackson, D. A., Imong, S. M., Silprasert, A., Preunglumpoo, S., Leelapat, P., et al. 1988a. Estimation of 24 h breast-milk fat concentration and fat intake in rural northern Thailand. *Br. J. Nutr.* 59:365–71
101. Jackson, D. A., Imong, S. M., Silprasert, A., Ruckphaopunt, S., Woolridge, M. W., et al. 1988b. Circadian variation in fat concentration of breast-milk in a rural northern Thai population. *Br. J. Nutr.* 59:349–63
102. Jackson, K. A., Gibson, R. A. 1989. Weaning foods cannot replace breast milk as sources of long-chain polyunsaturated fatty acids. *Am. J. Clin. Nutr.* 50:980–82
103. Jelliffe, D. B., Jelliffe, E. F. P., ed. 1988. *Programs to Promote Breastfeeding.* Oxford: Oxford Univ. Press. 490 pp.
104. Jelliffe, D. B., Jelliffe, E. F. P., Kersey, L. 1989. *Human Milk in the Modern World.* Oxford: Oxford Univ. Press. 2nd ed.
105. Jenkins, C. L., Orr-Ewing, A. K., Hey-

wood, P. F. 1985. Cultural aspects of early childhood growth and nutrition among the Amele of lowland Papua New Guinea. See Ref. 122, pp. 29–50

106. Jumaan, A. O., Serdula, M. K., Williamson, D. F. et al. 1989. Feeding practices and growth in Yemeni children. *J. Trop. Pediatr.* 35:82–86

107. Katz, M. M. 1985. Infant care in a group of outer Fiji Islands. See Ref. 122, pp. 269–92

108. Kent, S., Weinberg, E. D., Stuart-Macadam, P. 1990. Dietary and prophylactic iron supplements: helpful or harmful? *Hum. Nature* 1:55–79

109. Kim, I., Pollitt, E. 1987. Differences in the pattern of weight growth of nutritionally at-risk and well-nourished infants. *Am. J. Clin. Nutr.* 46:31–35

110. Kneebone, G. M., Kneebone, R., Gibson, R. A. 1985. Fatty acid composition of breast milk from three racial groups from Penang, Malaysia. *Am. J. Clin. Nutr.* 41:765–69

111. Koniz-Booher, P., Fishman, C., Parlato, M., Roberts, A. 1991. Recommendations from the expert meeting on optimal infant feeding practices, Sept. 24–25, 1990. Washington, DC: Acad. Educ. Dev.

112. Konner, M., Worthman, C. 1980. Nursing frequency, gonadal function, and birth spacing among the !Kung hunter-gatherers. *Science* 207:788–91

113. Labbok, M., Krasovec, K. 1990. Toward consistency in breastfeeding definitions. *Stud. Fam. Plan.* 21:226–30

114. Labbok, M., McDonald, M., ed. 1990. Proceedings of the interagency workshop on health care practices related to breastfeeding of Dec 7–9, 1988. *Int. J. Gynecol. Obstet.* 31 (Suppl.)

115. La Leche League. 1991. *The Womanly Art of Breastfeeding.* Chicago: La Leche League. 5th ed.

116. Leslie, J. 1989. Women's nutrition: the key to improving family health in developing countries? *Health Pol. Plan.* 6:1–19

117. Leslie, J., Paolisso, M. 1989. *Women, Work and Child Welfare in the Third World.* Boulder, CO: Westview Press

118. McGuire, J., Popkin, B. 1990. Helping women to improve nutrition in the developing world. Beating the zero sum game. World Bank Tech. Pap. No. 114

118a. McKenna, J. J. 1987. Parental supplements and surrogates among primates: cross-species and cross-cultural comparisons. In *Parenting Across the Lifespan: Biosocial Dimensions*, ed. J. B. Lancaster, J. Altmann, A. S. Rossi, L. R. Sherrod, pp. 143–84. New York: Aldine de Gruyter.

119. MacLean, W. 1984. *Nutrition in Infancy. Present Knowledge in Nutrition.* Washington, DC: Nutr. Found.

120. McPhee, A. J., Davidson, G. P., Leahy, M., Beare, T. 1988. Vitamin B_{12} deficiency in a breast fed infant. *Arch. Dis. Child.* 63:921–23

121. Mahmoud, D. A., Feachem, R. G. 1987. Feeding and nutritional status among infants in Basrah City, Iraq: a cross-sectional study. *Hum. Nutr. Clin. Nutr.* 41C:373–81

122. Marshall, L., ed. 1985. *Infant Care and Feeding in the South Pacific.* New York: Gordon & Breach. 355 pp.

123. Martorell, R. 1989. Body size, adaptation and function. *Hum. Org.* 48:15–20

124. Martorell, R., O'Gara, C. 1985. Breastfeeding, infant health, and socioeconomic status. *Med. Anthropol.* 9:173–81

125. Mata, L. J., Urrutia, J. J., Gordon, J. E. 1967. Diarrheal disease in a cohort of Guatemalan village children observed from birth to age two years. *Trop. Geogr. Med.* 19:247–57

126. Mead, M. 1943. *The Problem of Changing Food Habits.* Washington, DC: Natl. Acad. Sci.

127. Merchant, K., Martorell, R. 1988. Frequent reproductive cycling: Does it lead to nutritional depletion of mothers? *Progr. Food Nutr. Sci.* 12:339–69

128. Merchant, K., Martorell, R., Haas, J. 1990. Maternal and fetal responses to the stresses of lactation concurrent with pregnancy and of short recuperative intervals. *Am. J. Clin. Nutr.* 52:280–88

129. Merchant, K., Martorell, R., Haas, J. 1990. Consequences for maternal nutrition of reproductive stress across consecutive pregnancies. *Am. J. Clin. Nutr.* 52:616–20

129a. Millard, A. V. 1990. The place of the clock in pediatric advice: rationales, cultural themes, and impediments to breastfeeding. *Soc. Sci. Med.* 31:211–21

130. Millman, S. 1986. Trends in breastfeeding in a dozen developing countries. *Int. Fam. Plan. Persp.* 12:91–95

131. Minchin, M. 1985. *Breastfeeding Matters.* Australia: Alma Publ./George Allen and Unwin

132. Mohrbacher, N., Stock, J. 1991. *The Breastfeeding Answer Book.* Chicago: La Leche League. 480 pp.

133. Morley, R., Cole, T. J., Powell, R., Lucas, A. 1988. Mother's choice to provide breast milk and developmental outcome. *Arch. Dis. Child.* 63:1382–85

134. Morrow-Tlucak, M., Haude, R. H., Ernhart, D. B. 1988. Breastfeeding and cognitive development in the first two years of life. *Soc. Sci. Med.* 26:635–39

135. Morse, J. M. 1985. The cultural context of infant feeding in Fiji. See Ref. 122, pp. 255–68

136. Mukhopadhyay, C., Higgins, P. 1988. Anthropological studies of women's status revisited: 1977–1987. *Annu. Rev. Anthropol.* 17:461–95

137. National Academy of Sciences, Institute of Medicine Subcommittee on Nutrition During Lactation. 1991. *Nutrition During Lactation.* Washington, DC: Natl. Acad. Press

138. Naylor, D., Wester, R. A. 1988. Health professional education: a key to successful

breastfeeding promotion programs. See Ref. 103, pp. 321–23

139. Neville, M. C., Keller, R., Seacat, J., Lutes, V., Neifert, M. et al. 1988. Studies in human lactation: milk volumes in lactating women during the onset of lactation and full lactation. *Am. J. Clin. Nutr.* 48:1375–86

140. Newmann, C. G., Alpaugh, M. 1976. Birthweight doubling time: a fresh look. *Pediatrics* 57:469–73

141. O'Gara, C. 1989. Breastfeeding and maternal employment in urban Honduras. See Ref. 117, pp. 113–30

142. Oski, F. A., Landow, S. A. 1980. Inhibition of iron absorption from human milk by baby foods. *Am. J. Dis. Child.* 134:459–60

143. Owen, G. M., Garry, P. J., Hooper, E. M. 1984. Feeding and growth of infants. *Nutr. Res.* 4:727–31

144. Pali, H., Mansbach, I., Pridan, H., Adler, B., Palti, Z. 1984. Episode of illness in breastfed and bottlefed infants in Jerusalem. *Isr. J. Med. Sci.* 20:395–99

145. Palmer, G. 1988. *The Politics of Breastfeeding.* London: Pandora Press

146. Parker, L. N., Gupta, G. R., Kurz, K. M., Merchant, K. M. 1990. *Better Health for Women: Research Results from the Maternal Nutrition and Health Care Program.* Washington, DC: Int. Cent. Res. Women

147. Piwoz, E., Viteri, F. 1985. Study health and nutrition behaviour by examining household decision-making, intra-household resource distribution, and the role of women in these processes. *Food Nutr. Bull.* 7(4):1–31

148. Popkin, B., Akin, J., Flieger, W., Wong, E. 1989. The effects of women's work on breastfeeding in the Philippines, 1973–1983. See Ref. 117, pp. 85–112

149. Popkin, B., Lasky, T., Litvin, J., Spicer, D., Yamamoto, M. 1986. *The Infant-Feeding Triad: Infant, Mother, and Household.* New York: Gordon and Breach

150. Prentice, A. M., Prentice, A. 1988. Energy costs of lactation. *Annu. Rev. Nutr.* 8:63–79

151. Prentice, A., Prentice, A. M., Whitehead, R. G. 1981. Breast-milk fat concentration of rural African women. 1. Short-term variations within individuals. *Br. J. Nutr.* 45:483–94

152. Prentice, A., Prentice, A. M., Whitehead, R. G. 1981. Breast-milk fat concentration of rural African women. 2. Long-term variations within a community. *Br. J. Nutr.* 45:495–503

153. Quandt, S. A. 1984. The effect of beikost on the diet of breast-fed infants. *J. Am. Diet. Assoc.* 84(1):47–51

153a. Quandt, S. A. 1984. Nutritional thriftiness and human reproduction: beyond the critical body composition hypothesis. *Soc. Sci. Med.* 19:117–82

154. Quandt, S. A. 1985. Biological and behavioral predictors of exclusive breast feeding duration. *Med. Anthropol.* 9:139–51

155. Quandt, S. A. 1986. Patterns of variation in breastfeeding behaviors. *Soc. Sci. Med.* 23(5):445–53

156. Quandt, S. A. 1987. Maternal recall accuracy for dates of infant feeding transitions. *Hum. Org.* 46:152–60

157. Queenan, J. T., Labbok, M., Krasovec, K. 1990. *Breastfeeding Policy: The Role of U. S. Based International Organizations.* Inst. Issues Rep. No. 5. Washington, DC: Inst. Reprod. Health, Georgetown Univ.

158. Radford, A. 1991. *The Ecological Impact of Bottle Feeding.* Cambridge: Baby Milk Action

159. Raphael, D., Davis, F. 1985. *Only Mothers Know: Patterns of Infant Feeding in Traditional Cultures.* Westport, CT: Greenwood Press

160. Rattigan, S., Ghisalberti, A. V., Hartmann, P. E. 1981. Breast-milk production in Australian women. *Br. J. Nutr.* 45:243–49

161. Rodriguez-Garcia, R., Schaefer, L., Yunes, J. 1990. *Lactation Education for Health Professionals.* Washington, DC: Pan American Health Org.

162. Rowland, M. G. M., Paul, A. A., Whitehead, R. G. 1981. Lactation and infant nutrition. *Br. Med. Bull.* 37(1):77–82

163. Ryan, A., Pratt, W., Wysong, J., Lewandowski, G., McNally, J., Krieger, F. 1991. A comparison of Breastfeeding data from the national surveys of family growth and the Ross Laboratories mothers surveys. *Am. J. Publ. Health* 81:1049–52

163a. Ryan, A. S., Rush, D., Krieger, F. W., Lewandowski, G. 1991. Recent declines in Breastfeeding in the United States, 1984 through 1989. *Pediatrics,* 88(4):719–27

164. Saarinen, U. M., Siimes, M. A. 1979. Iron absorption from breast milk, cow's milk and iron-supplemented formula. *Pediatr. Res.* 13:143–47

165. Sachdev, H. P., Krishna, J., Puri, R., Satyanarayana, L., Kumar, S. 1991. Water supplementation in exclusively breastfed infants during summer in the tropics. *Lancet* 337:929–33

166. Salmenpera, L., Perheentupa, J., Siimes, M. 1985. Exclusively breast-fed healthy infants grow slower than reference infants. *Pediatr. Res.* 19:307–12

167. Scheper-Hughes, N., ed. 1987. *Child Survival: Anthropological Perspectives on the Treatment and Maltreatment of Children.* Dordrecht/Boston: D. Reidel

168. Scheper-Hughes, N. 1992. *Death Without Weeping: the Violence of Everyday Life in Brazil.* Berkeley: Univ. Calif. Press

169. Scrimshaw, S., Engle, P., Arnold, L., Haynes, K. 1987. Factors affecting breastfeeding among women of Mexican origin or descent in Los Angeles. *Am. J. Publ. Health* 77(4):467–70

170. Sharma, R., Rutstein, S. O., Labbok, M., Ramos, G., Effendi, S. 1990. A comparative analysis of trends and differentials in breastfeeding: findings from DHS surveys.

Presented at the Popul. Assoc. Meet., Toronto, May 3

171. Simopoulos, A. P., Grave, G. D. 1984. Factors associated with the choice and duration of infant-feeding practice. *Pediatrics (Suppl.)* 74:603–14

171a. Smith, D. W., Truog, W., Rogers, J. E. Greitzer, L. J., Skinner, A. L. et al. 1976. Shifting linear growth during infancy— illustration of genetic factors in growth from fetal life through infancy. *J. Pediatr.* 89:225–30

172. Soysa, P. 1988. The introduction of semisolid and solid foods to feeding infants. *Food Nutr. Bull.* 10(1):49–51

173. Swenson, I. 1984. The relationship between selected maternal factors and the nutritional status of two and three year old children in rural Bangladesh. *J. Trop. Pediatr.* 30:189–92

174. Tanner, J. M. 1986. Growth as a target-seeking function: catch-up and catch-down growth in man. In *Human Growth*, ed. F. Falkner, J. M. Tanner, 1:167–79. New York/London: Plenum. 2nd ed.

175. Taylor, B., Wadsworth, J. 1984. Breast feeding and child development at five years. *Dev. Med. Child Neurol.* 26:73–80

176. Thomason, J. A., Jenkins, C. L., Heywood, P. F. 1986. Child feeding patterns amongst the Au of the West Sepik, Papua New Guinea. *J. Trop. Pediatr.* 32:90–92

177. Tully, J., Dewey, K. 1985. Private fears, global loss: a cross-cultural study of the insufficient milk syndrome. *Med. Anthropol.* 9:225–44

178. Unni, J., Richard, J. 1988. Growth and morbidity of breast-fed and artificially-fed infants in urban south Indian families. *J. Trop. Pediatr.* 34:179–81

179. Van Esterik, P. 1985. Commentary: an anthropological perspective on infant feeding in Oceania. See Ref. 122, pp. 331–43

180. Van Esterik, P. 1988. The cultural context of infant feeding. See Ref. 187, pp. 187–201

181. Van Esterik, P. 1989. *Beyond the Breast-Bottle Controversy.* New Brunswick, NJ: Rutgers Univ. Press

182. Victora, C. G., Smith, P. G., Vaughan, J. P., Nobre, L. C., Lombardi, C., et al. 1987. Evidence for protection by breastfeeding against infant deaths from infectious diseases in Brazil. *Lancet* 2:319–21

183. Victora, C. G., Smith, P. G., Vaughan, J. P., Nobre, L. C., Lombardi, C., et al. 1989. Infant feeding and deaths due to diarrhea. A case-control study. *Am. J. Epidemiol.* 129(5):1032–41

184. Weller, S., Dungy, C. 1986. Personal preferences and ethnic variations among Anglo and Hispanic breast and bottle feeders. *Soc. Sci. Med.* 23:539–48

185. Whitehead, R. G., Paul, A. A. 1981. Infant growth and human milk requirements: a fresh approach. *Lancet* 2:161–63

186. Williamson, N. E. 1989. Breastfeeding trends and patterns. *Int. J. Gynecol. Obstet.* 1(Suppl.):145–52

187. Winikoff, B., Castle, M. A., Laukaran, V. H., eds. 1988. *Feeding Infants in Four Societies: Causes and Consequences of Mothers' Choices.* New York/Westport: Greenwood Press

188. World Health Organization. 1981. *Contemporary Patterns of Breastfeeding. Report on the WHO Collaborative Study on Breastfeeding.* Geneva: WHO. 211 pp.

189. World Health Organization. 1989. The prevalence and duration of Breastfeeding, updated information, 1980–1989. *WHO Wkly. Epidemiol. Rec.* 42:321–35

190. World Health Organization. 1991. Indicators for assessing breastfeeding practices. Rep. Informal Meet., June 11–12, Geneva

191. Worthington-Roberts, B. S., Vermeersch, J., Williams, S. R. 1985. *Nutrition in Pregnancy and Lactation.* St. Louis: Times Mirror. 3rd ed.

192. Wray, J. D. 1990 Breastfeeding: an international and historical perspective. In *Infant and Child Nutrition,* ed. F. Falkner. Caldwell, NJ: Telford Press

193. Wright, A., Bauer, M. 1991. Maternal employment and the decline of breastfeeding: a red herring? Paper presented at the Annu. Meet., Am. Anthropol. Assoc., Chicago

194. Zeitlin, M. F., Ghassemi, H., Mansour, M. 1990. *Positive Deviance in Child Nutrition (with Emphasis on Psychosocial and Behavioural Aspects and Implications for Development).* Tokyo: United Nations Univ. 153 pp.

195. Zeitlin, M. F., Guldan, G. S. 1988. Appendix IIC: Bangladesh infant feeding observations. See Ref. 87, pp. 106–31

Annu. Rev. Anthropol. 1992. 21:205-229

ETHNOGRAPHIC WRITING ABOUT AMERICAN CULTURE[1]

Michael Moffatt

Department of Anthropology, Rutgers University, New Brunswick, New Jersey 08903

KEYWORDS: United States, native ethnography, participant-observation, cultural research

Anthropologists have done more research in the United States in the last dozen years than in the entire previous history of the discipline—far more, perhaps twice as much. Some reasons for this boom may be paradigmatic: heightened interdisciplinarity and genre-blurring all through the social sciences and humanities, postcolonial critiques of First-World/Third-World distinctions foundational to an older anthropology, new forms of older concerns about relevance and application. At least as important, however, are more down-to-earth disciplinary pragmatics: growing numbers of anthropologists in a period of declining transnational access and funding.

Anthropologists worked "at home" in the past, of course, and by 1980, a considerable body of work had slowly accumulated.[2] The pace has tremendously accelerated more recently, however. Sociologists have also continued to produce the domestic case studies they have written since the early 20th century, and researchers in American studies, linguistics, folklore, ethnomusicology, education, political science, and so on have joined the domestic ethnographic project. The outcome has been over 160 research-based monographs about the United States written in the last dozen years, plus many articles—

---

[1] American in this article means "of the continental United States [excluding native American peoples]"; apologies to American Indians, Alaskans, Hawaiians, Puerto Ricans, Canadians, Latin American, and so on. "Culture" is written in the singular loosely and for convenience. Current notions of cultural hegemony, in any case (see note 11, below), blur simplistic distinctions between one and many culture(s) in the nation-state known as the United States.

[2] Including (non-exhaustively) 2a, 19, 32a, 32b, 50, 75a, 79a, 88, 90, 94a, 111, 120a, 149, 154, 155a, 156a, 158a, 162, 167, 168, 185a, 191, 202a, 203, 205, 225, 231a, 233, 235a, 242, plus a number of Holt-Rinehart "case studies" (see 201:72-73)

0084-6570/92/1015-0205$02.00

about half by anthropologists, a third by sociologists, and the rest by everyone else.

This review is about all this recent domestic research,[3] focusing on full-length ethnographies based on long-term participant-observation or interpretively sophisticated interviewing. Who has done what research, and how, and how have these recent ethnographies been written up? What aspects of American belief and practice do they highlight, or neglect? What descriptions or interpretations of culture in the United States emerge from reading them all?

ETHNOGRAPHERS AND SUBJECTS

Aguilar sketched the pros and cons of domestic research a decade ago, in a collection that accurately predicted this recent boom (4; see also 91, 207, 245). Studying subjects relatively "like themselves," local ethnographers may be more attuned to cultural nuance than far-from-home anthropologists, better able to draw on experiential understandings. They can often "blend in" more completely—verbally, behaviorally, physically—possibly making for better rapport, possibly affecting who and what they are studying less by their presence. But how can insider-ethnographers perceive in the first place the cultural assumptions they share with subjects like themselves? How do they get at tacit culture without contrast and "difference" to attune them to it—a conventional justification for cross-cultural research?

Many of these ethnographers don't, and apparently aren't interested in doing so. Others do, some perhaps for cross-cultural reasons—being foreign-born (24, 26, 83, 125, 166, 196, 227); having done traditional far-from-home anthropological research prior to the present ethnography (3, 68, 79, 92, 93, 115, 122, 140, 147, 149, 151, 161, 176, 177, 206); or building cross-cultural research directly into their domestic monographs (67, 217). Cross-cultural experience or research sometimes plays no known role, on the other hand: Bell (17), Bluebond-Langner (19), Curran (38), di Leonardo (42), Ginsberg (74), Harper (89), Hochschild (95), Merry (143), Radway (175), Sacks (187), and Weston (237) have apparently arrived at their variously impressive or subtle understandings in different ways—imagination, cultural or historical scholarship, or attending to lesser but real differences between self and subject that are almost always part of local research as well.

For, as Aguilar has also noted, "likeness" is rarely complete, and varies in often cross-cutting ways. Nor does the ethnographer's achieved or ascribed

---

[3] One hundred sixty-nine monographs are surveyed here, including seven outstanding or neglected books from the late-1970s. In the bibliography, each of these core ethnographies is marked with an initial asterisk, and with the discipline of the ethnographer at the end of the citation (a few of these identifications are guesses; apologies for mistakes): anth = anthropology (87 are by anthropologists); soc = sociology (49 are by sociologists); ams = American studies (4 ethnographies); eds = educational studies (5); flk = folklore (5); ling = linguistics (8); other affiliations unabbreviated (4: 2 ethnomusicology, 2 political science); and unk = unknown (7).

identification with particular subjects necessarily make for a research relationship less problematic than in exotic ethnography. Identifying with "them" does not necessarily mean you are like them, or that they are all like one another, or that they all trust or identify with you, or that they want to be studied by you. Some "native" ethnographers never clearly arrive at this awareness, usually to the detriment of their interpretations. At least a half-dozen do, however; Weston and Sacks write about it perceptively, for co-lesbian subjects in northern California (237) and women workers in North Carolina (187).

Only four of these recent ethnographies are strictly autoethnographic, written directly out of the experiences of being French-American, an ex-nun, a professional poker player, and a medical student, respectively (26, 38, 92, 115). Everyone else studies someone else, variously mixed and matched with themselves. Most of the many identified studies of gender focus on women (10, 20, 38, 41, 42, 58, 59, 74, 95, 96, 98, 110, 116, 117, 122, 126, 131, 140, 144, 145, 156, 158, 160, 175, 182, 187, 220, 244) and are virtually all by women ethnographers. A few others treat men in particular, however (56, 57, 176, 189); a few treat male and female gender about equally (96, 237), or in passing, or implicitly (12, 17, 26, 45, 61a, 63, 79, 92, 133, 147, 149, 155, 161)—including those whose main topic is male-dominated professions (21, 28, 75, 104, 115, 123, 177, 234), working-class occupations (1, 3, 24, 55, 89, 139, 215), or other ways of getting a living (92, 241).

"Studies-up" (41, 104, 155, and 158) and "studies-down" (7, 55, 60, 63, 76, 83, 93, 133, 140, 143, 153, 159, 182, 187, 235, 244, plus the working-class occupational studies just cited) usually involve middle-class investigators trying to grasp persons of different class status. And, at a finer level, any academic professional (virtually all these ethnographers) not studying other academic professionals (none does) is dealing with persons with attitudes toward career, work, and lived-in culture distinctly different from their own.

Ethnographers of the young (19, 20, 49, 56, 57, 63, 77, 87, 98, 133, 147, 165, 189, 197, 210, 217, 222a, 227, 231, 235, 241) and the old (16, 48, 67, 105, 106, 149, 186, 195, 214, 224, 230) all differ from their subjects in age, though all were either once like the former or anticipate (or fear) becoming like the latter. (They always differ from these subjects in historical cohort or generation.) Ethnics study their own groups less often than other ethnic groups (42, 119, 121, 149, 196, 222, 231, 243, 244 versus 22, 43, 63, 68, 73, 81, 100, 105, 106, 122, 165, 206, 210, 212, 215, 241); cross-racial research is much more common than in-racial investigation (17, 22, 43, 62, 76, 77, 87, 93, 98, 114, 133, 140, 142, 147, 165, 183, 187, 194, 210 versus 7, 82, 112). And, perhaps distinguishing which commitments really matter to urban intellectuals in the late 20th century from which ones don't, only a few of the ethnographers of religion (5, 6, 22, 27, 38, 64, 69, 76, 79, 83, 126, 141, 152, 161, 164, 170, 184, 185, 198, 232, 238) apparently identify with the belief system they study [Prell with a Jewish prayer group (170) and Curran with a Catholic convent (38)].

Finally, reaggregating these researchers and subjects according to discipline, it's no longer the case that domestic anthropologists, faithful to their far-from-home proclivities, deemphasize the American mainstream and focus on the marginal and culturally exotic (8:xiii–xiv; 129:373). Among these ethnographers, more anthropologists than sociologists have studied social class (60, 63, 76, 79, 93, 98, 122, 140, 143, 151, 153, 159, 187, 237 versus 7, 24, 41, 55, 83, 133, 158, 182); and more anthropologists than sociologists have analyzed aspects of middle-class culture in some depth (19, 74, 79, 98, 147, 153, 163, 200, 217, 227-229, 237, versus 2, 13, 18, 57, 95, 96, 141, 156).

Domestic anthropologists do still disproportionately study culturally distinctive groups. Fifteen of the recent ethnographers of ethnicity are anthropologists (31, 42, 43, 63, 68, 73, 105, 106, 119, 121, 149, 196, 212, 231, 243, 244); only five are sociologists (100, 109, 210, 215, 222). This suggests that, in an ethnically complex nation, anthropologists have collectively happened upon the more balanced research program ("mainstream" + "diversity"); it's the sociologists who are now the more one-sided domestic ethnographers.

RESEARCH

The research for all these books was based on observing, talking with, and listening to small numbers of subjects, personally known, for months or years; but it varied widely in intensity and duration, and in type of ethnographer's relation to subjects. The ethnographers-as-authors also differ in how much they tell us about these things, in how clearly they describe what Sanjek has usefully termed "the ethnographer's path" (190:398–400). A few say almost nothing, apparently trusting their results to speak for themselves (13, 15, 29, 192). Others are vague about key details. Foster, evidently reflexively "open," tells us that he was in his Appalachian site "from August to 1975 through the remainder of the research period, which ended in 1976" (65:39), which could mean anything from 5 to 17 months. Many of the large number of ethnographers who evidently did their research part time indicate the overall period but make no useful effort to estimate what portion they actually spent in contact with their subjects.

Most at least sketch their fieldwork fundamentals. Most conducted their research close to home. Occasionally they studied their own local communities, work places, or places of leisure (7, 17, 44, 147, 176, 240); more often they did research in separate sites in the same city or region.[4] A few studied

---

[4] The most intensively researched regions of the United States are therefore those with the most social scientists in them: the northeast (especially the New York and Philadelphia areas), parts of the south, the urban midwest, and the west coast (especially California). The least-studied areas are the rural midwest, the Rockies, the northwest, and the interior southwest. See 202 for the argument that an ethnography of the "hinterland" is badly needed.

farther afield, but all choosing less cosmopolitan parts of the United States (the northern Rockies: 5, 27; the far midwest: 74; the southwest: 63; the south: 43, 112; the southeast: 64, 76, 79; Appalachia: 23, 65). Odendahl carried out her depth interviews with the philanthropic elite trans-regionally (155). Shokeid reversed the usual flow of overseas anthropology and came from Israel to study Israeli emigrants in the New York area (196). And Staub, American-Jewish by upbringing, first conducted fieldwork among Yemeni Jews in Israel, learning Arabic, and then investigated Islamic Yemenis in greater New York (206).

Simple access to subjects was not a problem for most of these fieldworkers, thanks in part to professional status and the luxury of operating in contexts in which "research" itself was a common and culturally legitimate activity. Investigators of the deviant or resistent had to proceed more cautiously, however (2, 241), sometimes mobilizing insider-status (82, 237), sometimes never obtaining much access (5, 27). On the evidence of these monographs, powerful subjects continue to fend off ethnographers successfully. Significantly, three of the four "studies-up" (150) (still a rare type) focus on women and philanthropy—i.e. on the less powerful gender and on the most image-building activity among the elite. The author of the fourth, Jackall, apparently obtained access to corporate management thanks to the old-boy connections of the prestigious little-Ivy college where he teaches (104). None of the four lived full time with their elite subjects; none dealt intensively with their subjects' private lives (for a forthcoming study-up, see 137).

About a fifth of these monographs draw their evidence almost entirely from interviews, life-histories, self-reports, or the linguistic analysis of relatively decontextualized stories and other native texts [5, 18, 20, 41, 59, 67, 68, 82, 97, 98, 105, 106, 107, 110, 123, 131, 140, 144, 152, 153, 155, 156, 158, 163, 166, 171, 172, 186, 189, 192, 198, 200, 214, 238, 243; Carbaugh uses his own viewing of TV (25)]. Curran operated through memory, her own and that of other Catholic women, to write a retrospective ethnography of American convent culture 30 years ago (38). Everyone else variously combines material from participant-observation and interviews—and some from historical research[5]—following one or more of four basic strategies in their participant-observation. A few participated in the lives of separately contacted subjects not known to one another (96, 182, 204). A larger number traced networks of interacting subjects not usually together in one place, and participated in their lives individually or in families (16, 42, 54, 83, 117, 175, 196, 206, 237); di Leonardo (42), Shokeid (196), and Weston (237) describe particularly well the

---

[5] References 43, 122 and 151 are each about half based on primary-document research; 18, 74, 161, 198, and 200 include significant chunks of secondary-source historical writing; 58, 78, 101, 152, 187, 198, 222, and 243 use oral history; 79 relates folk ahistoricism to individualism; and 65 gives a thinly contextualized account of recent historical invention in Appalachia (for a much thicker analysis of the cultural construction of history, see 71).

difficulties of this time-consuming method of what might be called "dispersed participant-observation." Some studied settings in which persons unknown to one another interacted or didn't—the public behavior of strangers (7, 29, 45, 51, 142); the marginal personal relations of alienated suburbanites (163); and (the most original topic in all these books) the imaginary personal relations in private daydreams and fantasies (30).

Most of these participant-observers, however, like anthropologists elsewhere in the world, looked for "villages"—relevant groups or collectivities of some sort—and moved in, or visited regularly: urban neighborhoods (7, 14, 100, 119, 133, 142, 143, 183, 194, 211, 222, 230, 240); small cities (151, 159) and suburbs (13, 44, 79, 83, 101, 141); rural towns and regions (15, 23, 58, 60, 64, 65, 84, 89, 93, 112, 224); occupational groups (1, 3, 139, 160, 187, 215), factories (24, 55, 83, 122, 244), and corporate settings (75, 95, 104, 120); courts (143), prisons (59, 61a), and other legal institutions (80, 136); political party organizations (188, 192, 234); preschools (217), schools (49, 63, 73, 78, 81, 87, 93, 164, 165, 184, 210, 227, 235), colleges (147), and professional schools (21, 113, 115); science labs (125, 132, 221) and academic presses (169); churches (6, 76, 83, 126, 161, 232), synagogues (69), and other religious groups (22, 27, 170, 185); hospitals (19, 21, 28, 115, 187), other health institutions (74, 141, 236)—including mental (54, 177, 193)—and homes or centers for the aged (49, 67, 149, 195, 214, 230); cliques (133), gangs (100, 231), and drug-dealing groups (2, 241); voluntary associations (57, 149, 196), hobbyist and leisure groups (10, 12, 56, 92, 175), and Disney World (61); garages (89), stores (171, 172) and restaurants (100, 160, 206); bars, straight (17, 83) and gay (176, 237); and bathing beaches for the clothed (51) and the naked (45).

These domestic ethnographers undoubtedly did part-time fieldwork much more often than far-from-home anthropologists do, though usually they also had the elementary linguistic and cultural skills that exotic researchers often have to spend time acquiring in the field; and these domestic ethnographers may have made a virtue of convenience—a nearby "field"—and conducted longer-term projects more often than overseas researchers do. Nine to twelve months is the most commonly mentioned period for domestic fieldwork; multi-year investigations include: 2–5 years, Cassell (28), di Leonardo (42), Dominquez (43), Greenhouse (79), Horowitz (100), Konner (115), Kugelmass (119), Latour & Woolgar (125), Merry (143), Myerhoff (149), Peacock & Tyson (161), T. Williams (241), and Yanagisako (243); and 6–10 years, Achenson (1), Adler (2), Anderson (7), Brown (22), Halle (83), Harper (89), Heath (93), Moffatt (147), Odendahl (155), Sacks (187) and B. Williams (240). (Reflecting the leisurely pace of academic writing, the ethnographic present for at least a third of these books published in the 1980s and early 1990s is the 1970s—for at least a dozen, the early 1970s.)

Except for the autoethnographers, virtually all suggest they usually operated as known researchers, though Adler, Moffatt, Rollins, and perhaps Lamphere[6] played covert roles part-time as a borderline drug-dealer (2), an under-graduate (147), a cleaning woman (182), and a textile worker (122), respec-tively; and MacLeod conducted his participant-observation in two mid-adolescent male cliques as a senior in college (and wrote his book as a graduate student) (133). Despite their best efforts at candid self-representation, however, those domestic ethnographers who could "pass" probably did so regularly by accident. To paraphrase Luhrmann in her splendid study of Brit-ish middle-class witches, they told their subjects carefully who they were, but then did their best research when their subjects forgot (130:17) (though re-searcher status, at home as abroad, can also give access to settings or mentali-ties ordinary folk might not be allowed).

Some, as known researchers, also took on working roles in the institutions they studied, as a childrens' ward volunteer (19), a surgical-unit gofer (21), a factory worker (55), a Little League coach (57), a prison guard (61a), a handyman (89), a social worker (133), a political organizer (187), and an agricultural laborer (215). Myerhoff simulated physical impairments to mimic the difficulties of functioning when very old (149); Estroff bravely took strong antipsychotic medication for six weeks, to share its heavy side-effects with her psychiatric out-patient subjects (54).

Van Willigen combined extensive network analysis with somewhat thinner participant-observation in his study of aged Kentuckians (224). Moffatt taught preliminary analyses of student culture to large undergraduate classes for two years, and rewrote (and collected extensive new self-reports for further analy-sis) from what the students wrote in response (147). Grant and Heath similarly used teaching to generate new cultural texts in the educational institutions they studied (83, 93), as did Myerhoff through the "Living History" classes she initiated in a Jewish senior center (149). And Sacks, Tobin et al, and Stacey shared drafts of their books with subjects—the first two making minor revi-sions in response to their critiques (187, 217), the last printing their remarks verbatim as an epilogue (204).

Only two of these books are based on ethnographic research inside the United States and out—Francis's well-structured comparison of Jewish retir-ees in Britain versus Cleveland, Ohio (67); and Tobin et al's *Preschool in Three Cultures,* the most methodologically innovative of all these mono-graphs. Preschools were studied and videotaped in the United States, Japan, and China; all the tapes were shown to preschool specialists in each nation; and nuanced interpretations of American culture (among other things) were generated from the ensuing transcultural commentary (among other evidence) (217).

6
    Another example of a vaguely described ethnographer's path—Lamphere tells us only that she "took a job" for several months as an "apprentice sewer," without making it clear whether anyone knew she was an anthropologist, or how else she might have presented herself (details suggest she was undercover, at least to one supervisor) (122).

WRITING

Despite the great interest in textual experimentalism in anthropology in the last decade (33, 36, 138), most of these domestic monographs are conventionally written. Ethnographer and relation-to-subjects is confined to the beginning or end of a book; the bulk of the text consists of impersonally written, monologic descriptions variously mixed with various theories, interpretations, or styles of analysis—tacit cultural (23, 25, 26, 79, 147, 166, 217, 237, 243), symbolic (15, 38, 149, 152, 238), performative (12, 17, 149), constructionist (43, 65, 76, 80, 125, 136, 227, 237), cognitive (3, 98), Durkheimian/Weberian (161), Tocquevillian (18, 78, 79), cultural reproductive (49, 63, 98, 133; 235 argues against it), political-economic (24, 42, 55, 95, 96, 122, 151, 187, 215), phenomenological (2, 45, 69, 132), ethnomethodological (7, 19, 51, 77), ethnography of speaking (12, 17, 77, 93, 114, 197), and postmodern (204).

Sociologists tend to produce tidy texts suggesting that separately conceptualized theory has been applied to carefully chosen case studies, for elucidation, proof, or disproof (13, 21, 24, 95, 210, 215). Anthropologists, often equally theoretical, also feature the serendipitity and creativity of the field encounter, and the complexities of their subjects' mentalities and behaviors (42, 54, 63, 64, 74, 79, 93, 143, 147, 149, 187, 196, 227, 237) (on the different relation of "case-study" research to the sociological and the anthropological traditions, see 223). Anthropologist Agar's ethnography of independent truckers, on the other hand, is as theoretically centered and methodologically precise as the neatest sociological monograph (3). And sociologist Halle's study of skilled chemical workers in New Jersey may be the single most impressive "thick description" (72) in all these ethnographies—most like classical anthropological "total ethnographies" in its rich, well-ordered, context-specific detail and organization (83) [anthropologist Heath's rich ethnography of speaking from the rural Carolinas is a close second (93)].

Bluebond-Langner's serene write-up of her heroic study of a dying-children's ward is one of the best (and, in anthropology, least known) of the far fewer experimentally written domestic monographs. Case-study material is distilled into a long illustrative "play," identified as fiction, followed by five briefer chapters about the subtle ethnomethodology of pretence among dying children, family members, and hospital staff (19). Sacks's account of the long-term contingencies of gender, race, class, and occupation in hospital-union organizing is also exemplary for the care with which it positions its author-as-researcher-and-political organizer (187). So too is Weston's ethnography of California gay and lesbian culture—quietly reflexive, unique among domestic ethnographies to date for its balance between its interpretive theme of cultural construction and its equally insightful analyses of continuities in tacit culture (237).

Tobin et al have written an unpretentious but subtle book in which a play of interpretive voices is intentionally present (local, cross-cultural, and their own); but the overall effect is more authorial than they had evidently hoped, with their "polyvocal" ambitions (217).[7] Carter gives us a quirky, readable, textually conscious meditation on the difficulties—without much access—of reconstructing what really happened at the Raj Neesh ashram in eastern Oregon (27). Latour & Woolgar, and Weatherford, use the imagery of "anthropologist," "tribe," "ritual," etc, as distancing tropes—Latour & Woolgar to bracket the truth-claims of science (125); Weatherford, Nacirema-like, to satirize Washington politicians(234).[8]

Horwitz uses photos and fluent language to evoke an American "place" rarely celebrated, a tacky suburban strip (101). Estroff writes messily but vividly about psychiatric outpatients, not entirely effectively bifurcating description and interpretation into separate chunks of her book (54). Rhodes promises Foucauldian and deconstructive complexity but delivers a generally straightforward story of psychiatric professionals handling contradictory or impossible job demands—with bravado, irony, a sense of the absurd, and shortcut techniques (177). Krieger experiments naively with ways of eliciting and writing "pure" subject "voices" among midwestern lesbians (117); Dorst buries a potentially fascinating case study of a self-conscious suburb and art center under opaque postmodern prose (44); and Rose ignores most anthropological, sociological, and historical scholarship on race and urban poverty to write a jejune, choppy, allegedly postmodern set of notes on his research among poor blacks in Philadelphia in the early 1970s (183).

Myerhoff's *Number Our Days* is, of course, among the most important and appealing of all the reflexive ethnographies in anthropology. The ethnographer is apparently always positioned in the account; her aged Jewish subjects evidently have as much voice and textual authority as herself (149). A new study of Myerhoff's writing practices, however, raises disturbing questions about the book's accuracy on certain points—and, more generally, about acceptable limits of fictionalization in ethnographic experimentation. Comparisons between the final text and early drafts suggest that (without ever indicating she was doing so) Myerhoff added background information and her own thoughts to words spoken by subjects, and shifted reported statements and actions between various persons so as to make ethnographically featured characters more central and coherent than they evidently were in the actual dynamics of the center (108).

---

[7] On the limits of polyvocality, and the tricky ethics of offering to share textual authority, see also 218; for the alternate proposition that, even given varying authorial control, polyvocal voices often "leak through" ethnographic texts, see Manganaro (135).

[8] In a Canadian ethnography, Handler experiments with a much more embedded instance of "anthropology in the text," attempting the cultural analysis of cultural nationalists who have themselves appropriated notions of cultural holism from anthropology and other social sciences (85). Moffatt tries the same technique more restrictedly for American undergraduates' use of "culture" and "relativism" in an interracial context (146).

READINGS

What, then, do these more than a hundred-and-a-half ethnographies add up to? What do they tell us about the culture or cultures of persons living in the continental United States in the 1970s and 1980s?

American Culture?

A very new constructionist approach to American culture asks how concepts of "America" are constituted, communicated, contested, and changed—how the "national unit, a geopolitical space, is transformed into a nationwide cultural space" (129:371). Applied to American culture in general, this constructionist perspective hasn't yet reached these published ethnographies[9]; but some of these ethnographers do use it in important ways to analyze the contestation of particular American cultural categories, especially "nature/culture."

Thus Ginsberg's pro-choice women chose to control their own natural reproduction; given the fundamental axes of American culture, her pro-lifers almost have to "choose" the "natural" way in reaction (74). Weston's lesbian mothers wonder if natural parentage can be conceptually confined to women, males being relevant only as sperm-donors (237). Sperling's animal-rights activists, drawing on pop anthropology, have fuzzed the animal/human distinction to the point where animals are the new Noble Savages (200). And Dominguez's Louisianans have been rewriting the different racial "natures" of Creoles, blacks, and whites for centuries (43).

Two more essentialist approaches to general American culture, on the other hand, are articulated by a few of these ethnographies, and are implicit in many more. One is explicitly Tocquevillian [18, 79; Varenne's older *Americans Together* (225)[10]]; closely related are a few monographs that include ethnic or cross-cultural comparisons, contrasting generalized "Americans" to French (26), Israelis (196), Japanese and Chinese (217), Japanese-Americans (243), etc. Both highlight an "American culture" associated with some sort of middle-class "mainstream,"[11] features of which can be outlined as follows.

---

[9] But for a splendid, in-progress example, see the work of Handler and associates on how museumologists at Williamsburg, Virginia are reconstituting mainstream and minority history (71, 86).

[10] *Americans Together* precociously emphasized the fluidity and mutual negotiation involved in "American culture" at a time when these interpretive themes were far less well developed in social science. Compared to some current work, on the other hand, it was also relatively "essentialist," boiling the culture of its midwest town down to "individualism," "community," "love," etc. For an example of Varenne's very different current orientation—simultaneously microanalytic, ethnomethodological, hyperconstructionist, and linguistically based—see his forthcoming *Ambiguous Harmony: Family Talk in America* (Ablex).

[11] None of these ethnographers deals extensively with current notions of cultural hegemony as a solution to—or a productive way of restating—old debates about *an* American culture versus "pluralism" or "multiculturalism." For this perspective, see 66 and 127.

The Tocquevillian Mainstream

In *Habits of the Heart,* Bellah et al—consciously updating Tocqueville (219)—locate "utilitarian" and "expressive" individualism at the heart of American middle-class values in the 1980s, with the complementary Tocquevillian value, "community," much more peripheral than it has been in the past. [Contrary to Lasch's "narcissistic" interpretation (124), however, they consider other-oriented community values to be deeply embedded in American consciousness, and revivable (18).] Anthropologists and others have previously reached similar conclusions about the saliency of a distinctively American individualism (9, 102, 178, 201; see also 239); a number of the present ethnographers further delineate its nuances.

THE INDIVIDUALISTIC PERSON   Thus Curran detects person-concepts shifting toward contemporary expressive individualism at a likely time but in an unlikely place—in the 1950s and 1960s, among young Catholic nuns in convents (38). Weston posits the notion of a "core self" beneath the more fluid personal transformations articulated in gay and lesbian "coming out stories" (237); and Moffatt proposes that undergraduates assume a similar distinction between an authentic inner "true self" and a manipulative outer "social self"—the latter the domain of the mandatory American self-presentation, the "friendly self" (147).

Factoring in gender, Hochschild depicts an airline requiring its stewardesses to transmute their presumably authentic, inner female emotions into aspects of their public selves, for corporate presentation ("friendly," smiling, caring, sexy, etc) (95). And Maltz & Borker's older article on male and female speech—adumbrating Tannen's current pop linguistics on the topic (213)—implies, among other things, that American male selves talk more competitively while female selves talk more interactively (134).

Cross-culturally, Tobin et al's Japanese commentators find Americans peculiarly interested in verbal expressiveness and natural idiosyncrasies in tiny children; the same comentators think Americans overcontrol small childrens' peer-group behavior (217). Shokeid's recent Israeli immigrants consider American "friendliness" constrained and formal compared to their own aggressive personalism (considered hopelessly "rude" by "American" standards in response) (196). And Carroll's middle-class French are similarly mystified by the unpredictable entailments of "openness," continual negotiation, expressiveness, tedious earnestness, and "sincerity"—and other aspects of the American self—as revealed in French-American misunderstandings in daily life (26).

CLASS   Consistent with Tocqueville's observations about American egalitarianism, consistent with the aversion of individualists to personal categorization, few Americans described in these monographs consider themselves "class-determined"[12]; consistent with sociological research, when they do think about class, most associate themselves with the broad middle. Halle's chemical workers consider their manual labor duller and lower-status than the mentally skilled occupations of the engineers and managers running their factories; they attribute their inferior occupations to educational deficiencies when young (83) (for recent cognitive analyses of working-class ideology, see also 208, 209). At home, however, they point to their mixed-class neighborhoods, incomes, consumer purchases, and childrens' chances for mobility to assert they're nevertheless just as good as anyone else. Odendahl's upper-class philanthropists make the same claim in the opposite direction: Despite their wealth, they assure the ethnographer, they live simply, just like the middle classes (155).

Odendahl's subjects live simply with original art on their walls, however, and in simple one-of-a-kind architect-designed homes (plural, not singular), while Halle's workers own tract houses and perhaps a homemade cottage at the beach. And despite their subjects' avoidance of overt status distinctions, many of these ethnographers study the impact of something like class on those they write about. [For an insightful sketch of the unspoken semiotics of American class, including a "living room test" to estimate one's own class pretensions, see satirist Fussell (70).]

Thus three ethnographers of schooling attempt with mixed success to apply British-derived cultural reproduction theory to what sociologists have known for a generation—that there's some relation between adolescent cliques and social class (49, 63, 133) (for a nuanced interpretation of the ambivalence of most American adolescents toward clique membership, see 226). More adequately, Heath contrasts richly described rural white working-class conventions of language use (strict literalism) with those of the middle class (first accurate, then more flexible and "creative") (93); and Martin finds that middle-class women accept medical models of their bodies while working-class women resist them (140) (on working-class resistance to expert systems, see also 11). Rollin's black cleaning women resist their women employers' condescension by gossiping about the dirty undersides of their respectable white lives (182) (on working women's resistance, see also 160). Agar's truckers dream pop-cultural dreams of heroic independence while leading actual work lives full of regulation (3); Halle's even-more-regulated factory workers wish they could be truckers, or policemen, or tavern-owners, all relatively more independent (83); given some workplace autonomy, plus peer-competition, Burawoy's factory workers produce more than is in their own class interest, according to Burawoy (24).

---

[12] For an analysis of American middle-class career-choice narratives that never once refer to class causation, see Linde (128). On social class and American culture, see also Ortner (157), preliminary remarks toward interesting new research about a high-school graduating class in middle age, current working title "Jews, the Middle Class, and 'American Culture.'"

Halle's workers invest less sense of self in their routine jobs than many middle-class men (83), such as Jackall's driven middle-managers, who [like Newman's same (153)] tend to lose everything in career failure (104). Bell's middle-class black men use leisurely bar talk to (among other things) mediate the "contradictions" of being both black and somewhat successful in a white world (17). And some of Odendahl's nouveau riche feel comfortable about their elevated status because they "made it themselves," while some of her Old Money wonder if they're personally worthy, given the American value creed (155).

COMMUNITY   As good individualists should, the Americans in these ethnographies articulate "community" much more happily than class; but figuring out what the term really means in American common culture in the 1970s and 1980s is not easy. B. Williams writes hopefully about a mixed urban neighborhood attempting to create richer community connections (to counteract the "weightlessness" of modern culture) through newly invented "rituals"—street festivals (240) (64 and 159 also experiment with the analysis of community secular rituals; see also 52). Beaver (15), Forrest (64), Heath (93), and Peacock & Tyson (161) gesture toward local connectedness in poor rural parts of the near-south, and Harper tenderly describes and photographs the non-alienated world of "Willie," a capable rural handyman-bricoleur in upstate New York (89). Otherwise, other ethnographers of American locality sketch citizens more interested in leading privatized lives undisturbed by their neighbors than in having substantial relationships with them.

Thus Anderson (7), Merry (142), and Edgerton (51) treat ad hoc tactics for living alongside strangers in urban America—detecting and reducing danger, dealing with proximity, etc. In safer middle-class suburbs, Perin "semiotically" probes elaborate strategies for dealing with barely known neighbors and thinking about feared outsiders (163); Baumgartner's "moral minimalism" (13) and Greenhouse's "avoidance of conflict" summarize similar suburban sensibilities (79). And though Merry finds more disputing among working-class urbanites than in the suburbs—more use of courts—the sociological motives are the same: "coexistence without contact"; "search for an impersonal moral authority [rather than] ... control [by] local political authorities and [by] local gossip" (143:83).

If many contemporary Americans don't really live in "community" with their immediate neighbors in space, on the other hand, many of them do "build" it in other directions. Community in this sense is more dynamic and agentive than anything fully evoked by these ethnographies; correctly grasped, it implies choice, seriousness of purpose [it's a sacred term, as Varenne has suggested (229)], and some personally connected group (not necessarily localized) often standing metonymically for some larger hypothetical entity [a town, a university, an ethnic community; di Leonardo's savvy remarks about Italian-American "community" point in the right direction (42:131–39)]. None of these monographs treats this sort of "community" in many of the places it's known to exist: the plentiful volunteer organizations in working-class and middle-class towns (most fire departments and rescue squads outside urban America are voluntary, for instance) and the relatively new, ubiquitous American "groups-of-the-self," "self-help groups."

When Americans connect personally for less serious purposes, they don't call what they're doing "community"; they call it something like "fun" or "relaxation." Moffatt (147) found that undergraduate dorm-floor collectivities— "residence hall communities" in the deans' fantasies—were "friendly groups of kids" in the students' experience. Adults often modify the rigors of work with similar sociability—the domestically based food exchanges and networking skills Sacks' women bring to their hospital jobs (187); and male joking-and-insult humor described by Halle for factory workers (83) and by other ethnographers for other male-centered occupations. Other ethnographic descriptions of hedonism, pleasure, or play include, for adults, Bacon-Smith's new study of television fan groups (10); Adler on fast-track, southern California, middle-class drug-users (2); Hayano on poker-players (92); Bell (17) and Read (176) on bars; Halle on working-class leisure (83); Bauman on male storytellers in Texas (12); Douglas et al on nude beaches (45); and for youths and adolescents, Moffatt on undergraduate sexuality and friendliness (147) and Fine on male Little League and Dungeon-and-Dragon-type gaming groups (56, 57).

RELIGION   When Americans become most serious, on the other hand, they call it "religion"—or, drawing on secularized religious language, "commitment" to "values" etc. [Cultural analyses of contemporary American pop psychology are absent from these ethnographies; but see D'Andrade (39) on folk models of the mind.] Among Baptists in her virtually all-white southern suburb, Greenhouse meticulously unpacks contemporary forms of Tocquevillian connections among denominational Protestantism, individualism, egalitarianism, and ahistoricism (79). Peacock & Tyson lovingly describe an even more basic American Protestant folk: a tiny, patriarchal but otherwise nonhierarchical sect in Appalachia so fundamentalist that its members consider John Calvin suspiciously liberal; strict predeterminists, they do not evangelize (what's the point?). The tale is almost too good to believe: Max Weber was related to these Appalachian fundamentalists, and visited the authors' grandfathers just before writing *The Protestant Ethic and the Spirit of Capitalism* (161).

Several other ethnographies variously explore the cultural style and relation to right-wing politics of Protestant fundamentalists (5, 6, 164, 184, 185). Halle finds a weak, "flattened" Protestantism among his New Jersey workers (83). Prell thickly describes a liberalizing Jewish prayer group (170); Furman suggests that a liberal, socially conscious synagogue has lost touch with the essential values of Judaic ritualism (69). And, back in New Jersey, McGuire categorizes middle-class ritual healing practices as they tail off into New Age religion (141). [See Luhrmann's ethnography of British witches and other New Age believers, however, for the best available ethnography of this undoubtedly transatlantic middle-class "religious" mentality (130).]

YOUTH, GENDER, FAMILY, AGE   "Kinship," once at the heart of anthropology, has faded as a topic of domestic research just as it has cross-culturally; meanwhile, however, "gender" has boomed.[13] Goodwin writes meticulously about language interactions within and between genders among black children (77). Microsociologist Fine's two detailed accounts of boys' play-groups document the development of predatory heterosexual attitudes (56, 57)—which crop up even more darkly among college-age males in Sanday's strident but sometimes insightful *Fraternity Gang Rape* (189) (on ritual expressions of older male gender mentalities, see 53).

Among college women, Holland & Eisenhart detect the importance of "romance" and ensuing commitments to husbands and traditional family roles rather than to career success (98). [Radway studies the same cultural fantasy among romance-reading housewives (175)]. Moffatt discerns a wider range of sex-and-gender attitudes among male and female undergraduates than either Holland & Eisenhart, or Sanday—including "male romantics," "female experimentalists," and extensive cross-gender friendships—but agrees with them about central tendencies (147). Weston treats adolescent homosexual experience in retrospect, in many of her gay "coming out" stories (237) (for more good recent gay ethnography, also see 94).

Compared to the "traditional," multigenerational, duty-impregnated kinship systems characterized similarly by Johnson and Yanagisako for Italian-Americans and Japanese-Americans, respectively (105, 106, 243), mainstream "American" marriage-and-family is individualistic, based on rational calculation and assessments of emotional authenticity (on middle-class marriage, see also 173, 174). Halle describes gender-segregated working-class marriages but argues that his affluent workers are converging toward a more companionate middle-class model, especially as they age (83).

Lamphere and Zavella treat work-and-family interactions for women factory workers of diverse ethnicities in New England (122) and California (244). Fink shows how farm wives' labor was devalued in the early 20th century and is now alienated by major corporations (58). And Fishman documents the can't-win status of prisoner's wives—good women who "wait," with little social support; or "not-so-good" women with even less (59).

Stacey argues vigorously but unconvincingly that two large mixed-class, gender-experimental extended families among whom she did participant-ob-

---

[13] Women were among the least-studied subjects in the anthropology of American culture a decade ago (201:67); now, about one sixth of all these ethnographies are about gender, many of the researchers intentionally cutting across older analytic categories—making women visible in work, for instance, and work visible in marriage and family. Owing to its boundary-blurring tendencies, gender research is reviewed throughout this article (as cited), not in this section alone.

servation in California represent a widespread new phenomenon, the "post-modern family" (204). Hochschild delineates the "stalled revolution" of gender equality in middle-class, dual-career marriages (96). And Daniels and Ostrander document how much unrecognized work "nonworking" upper-class wives actually do philanthropically, and in maintaining key institutions associated with their families' elite status (the arts, private schools, etc) (41, 158).

Neville's mostly oral-historical account of family "pilgrimages" in white southern Protestant culture deals with extended kin networks (152), as do Johnson's interview-based books on the Italian-American family (105, 106).[14] Most of the ethnographies of age suggest how weak these intergenerational family ties are—also documenting especially clearly a general property of American society, top to bottom, rarely analyzed as such in these monographs: its ever-more-layered age-segregation.

Thus Francis's elderly American Jews have much less daily contact with mobile junior family members than do the elderly British Jews she compares them to (67). Vesperi's non-affluent, far-from-home retirees suffer as a Florida city redefines itself as a place for younger yuppies (230). Shield's nursing-home patients lead sad lives of alienation and unritualized liminality between life and death (195). Myerhoff's Jewish aged—similarly poor and far from kin—fight bravely to create meaning and "community" among themselves, drawing on idiosyncratic strengths from their cultures of youth (eastern European *shtetl* life) (149). Becker's aging deaf are similarly preadapted to the travails of American age: Shunted to special institutions when young, disadvantaged when mature, they have long since developed skills for dealing with loneliness and finding others of their kind (16).

Only Van Willigen's rural Kentuckians still grow old surrounded by friends and family (though Van Willigen pre-selected for old subjects not living separately). In early old-age, their social networks actually expand from the average for middle-aged adults, from about 25 to 30 other persons met with or talked to regularly (then progressively declining in late old age, but still averaging about 19 "alters" for subjects over 80) (224).

Variations

Regional variations in American culture are evoked by a number of these books, especially those about Appalachia and the south; but they are dealt with directly only in a few, and then in simple opposition to the northeast or California. Greenberg's Georgian suburbanites associate their essence with being Baptist, local, and southern, versus urban and northern; Ginsberg's Dakotan women activists construct a "midwest feminism" more family and community sensitive than "coastal feminism" (74).

14

So too will Carol Stack's forthcoming ethnography of black return-migration to the south, analyzing extended kin ties and long-term family strategies—current working title, *Call to Home: African Americans Reclaim the Rural South.*

Two grim studies remind us of the continued exclusion of many blacks from the American mainstream: Boone's analysis of causes of high rates of black infant death in Washington, DC (20), and Anderson's sketch of a drug-disintegrated black ghetto in Philadelphia (and of poignant ethnomethodological tactics used by nonghetto black males to signal "I'm safe/middle-class") (7). Among the other ethnographies of race, Gwaltney and Heath evoke distinctively black cultures best—Gwaltney through lightly interpreted life histories (82), Heath through rich description of contextual and metaphorically elaborate language use in a rural black community (93).

Three recent ethnographies present the extreme cultural diversity of newly arrived American ethnic populations, as well their typically non-assimilative first-generation mentalities: Brown on Haitian voodoo in Brooklyn (detailed about the religion, less so about the American context; 22); Staub about New York-area Yemenis, inventing generalized "middle Eastern restaurants" for an American clientele, while determined to return to family, village, and tribe (and less to "nation") in Yemen (206); and Gibson about Sikhs in rural northern California, equally determined not to assimilate, also intent that their children succeed in American schools (they do, thanks to the Sikh work ethic; 73).

Shokeid's New York–area Israelis (196), on the other hand, aren't all that different from people in the mainstream, except in their novel ethnic strategy. Ashamed of leaving Israel, stigmatized by American Jews, qualified enough to get decent jobs without connections, they've evolved a non-self-presentation that Shokeid calls "low-profile ethnicity." Alienated from Americans by their ruder etiquette, on the other hand, they do collect sporadically and surreptitiously for boisterous Israeli songfests in community centers, Shokeid discovers, and then virtually deny these connections the rest of the time. In the kinkiest and most original analogy in all these books, Skokeid compares their need for this disconnected ethnic *communitas* to the homoerotic "impersonal sexuality" described in Humphreys' controversial *Tearoom Trade* (103).

Studying an older and more assimilated ethnic population, Tricarico writes a concise history based on his third-generation return to his grandparents' Italian neighborhood in New York City, deciding that contemporary Italian-Americans are "situationally ethnic" (222). Di Leonardo reaches related but more complex conclusions in her theoretically sophisticated unpacking of the "varieties of ethnic experience" among Italian-Americans in northern California—influenced by media stereotypes, varying by class, occupation, gender and political purpose, etc (42). [On "ironic" contemporary American attitudes toward such ethnic identities, see Chock (32).] And Kugelmass and Myerhoff write variously about aging Jewish populations hanging on in deteriorating urban neighborhoods in New York (119) and southern California (149).

A number of ethnographers treat aspects of Latin American or Caribbean ethnicity in the United States (63, 121, 165, 210, 215, 231, 241), with only Horowitz's study of mixed values in a Mexican-American neighborhood in Chicago approaching thick description (100; but see also the forthcoming

109). With the exception of Yanagisako (243), richly analyzed Asian-Americans are similarly conspicuous by their absence from these book-length ethnographies (only 68 and 81 are in print; but, forthcoming, see 31).

CONCLUDING REMARKS

Some aspects of this diverse ethnographic writing have inevitably been neglected here: some innovative, nonparticipatory methods[15]; applied interests; the specific findings of the many ethnographies of schooling; linguistic dimensions; research on organizations, bureaucracies, and a few professions; and smaller literatures on pop and media culture, and on science and technology [for important in-progress work on the last, see Downey (46, 47).] Little attention has been given to ethics or to epistomology. What, for instance, are social scientists doing when they're analyzing a culture in which folk forms of their own concepts are often part of the culture; or, alternatively, in which their "concepts" turn out to be drawn from the common culture?

There are also striking absences in this recent American ethnography, not mentioned above but worth reviewing in closing. Why is there no work on such organized entities as sports teams, the police, and the military? Why so little ethnographic research on formal politics? Why so many studies of medical doctors and so few of other professions? Why so many about factory workers and so few about the much bigger service sector?

Local conceptions of regional identities might be worth deeper investigation, especially in alliance with new thinking in cultural geography (see 199 and the subsequent debate in the same journal); new ways might also be developed to follow and represent Americans in motion as well as Americans rooted in particular places—for the limits of what can be studied using intensive participatory methods have not yet been established. For instance, many Americans relate personally but not face-to-face through computer networks and other forms of new technology. New studies of how ordinary folk actually think of and use mass and media culture—and possibly of how its makers are themselves culturally influenced—are also crying out to be done; Radway's research on readers of romance still stands in lonely contrast to an expanding flood of text-based, academy-based pronouncements on the meaning of pop culture (175) (see 148 for a comment on the limits of the latter).

Despite recent deconstructions of holism as ethnographic rhetoric (216), the value of thick descriptions like Halle's and Heath's suggests that the richer and more intensively researched the "partial truth" (34), the better. One possible traditional area of application might be renovated community studies, as wide-

---

15
   Robinson's long-term research on American use of time (180, 181), for instance; Csikszentmihalyi & Rochberg-Halton's methods for tapping definitions of ordinary but meaningful things (37); and Kubey & Csikszentmihalyi's beeper-driven technique for sampling the experiential states of people while they are watching television (118).

ranging in particular localities as possible, delineating contemporary meanings of "community" rather than nostalgically deploring the loss of past ones.

Finally, ethnographic innovators might follow Handler and others in looking for where "America" and its various bits and pieces are formulated and reformulated—and in looking at the ethnic boundaries of the nation more carefully and in new ways. Many more studies of the full range and mix of cultures among diverse newly arrived Americans would be valuable, possibly including home-and-abroad research on "part-time Americans" [the sociologists' "return migrants," James Clifford's "cosmopolitan workers" (35, see also 179)]—especially timely for a nation newly reinterested in, and worried about, its historically ever-remixing "multiculturalism."

ACKNOWLEDGMENTS

Special thanks to Roger Sanjek, Susan Gal, and Herve Varenne. Thanks also to Don Brenneis, Roy D'Andrade, Richard Handler, Gary Kulik, George Levine, Catherine Lutz, Marc Manganaro, Sherry Ortner, Naomi Quinn, Bruce Robbins, David Riesman, George Spindler, and Claudia Strauss.

Literature Cited

1. *Achenson, J. M. 1988. *The Lobster Gangs of Maine*. Hanover: Univ. Press New England [anth]
2. *Adler, P. A. 1985. *Wheeling and Dealing: An Ethnography of an Upper-level Drug Dealing and Smuggling Community*. NY: Columbia Univ. Press [soc]
2a. Agar, M. 1973. *Ripping and Running: a Formal Ethnography of Urban Heroin Addicts*. NY: Seminar Press
3. *Agar, M. 1986. *Independents Declared: The Dilemmas of Independent Trucking*. Washington: Smithsonian [anth]
4. Aguilar, J. 1981. On anthropology "at home." In *Anthropologists at Home in North America*, ed. D. Messerschmidt, pp. 15–28. NY: Cambridge Univ. Press
5. *Aho, J. A. 1990. *The Politics of Righteousness: Idaho Christian Patriotism*. Seattle: Univ. Washington Press [soc]
6. *Ammerman, N. T. 1988. *Bible Believers: Fundamentalists in the Modern World*. New Brunswick, NJ: Rutgers Univ. Press [soc]
7. *Anderson, E. 1990. *Streetwise: Race, Class and Change in an Urban Community*. Chicago: Univ. Chicago Press [soc]
8. Arens, W., Montague, S. P. 1976. *The American Dimension: Cultural Myths and Social Realities*. Port Washington, NY: Alfred Publishing
9. Arensberg, C. M., Niehoff, A. H. 1971. American cultural values. In *The Nacirema: Readings on American Culture*, ed. J. P. Spradley, M. A. Rynkiewich, pp. 363–78. Boston: Little, Brown
10. *Bacon-Smith, C. 1991. *Enterprising Women: Television Fandom and the Creation of Popular Myth*. Philadelphia: Univ. Pennsylvania Press [unk]
11. Balshem, M. 1991. Cancer, control, and causality: talking about cancer in a working-class community. *Am. Ethnol.* 18:152–72
12. *Bauman, R. 1986. *Story, Performance and Event: Contextual Studies of Oral Narrative*. NY: Cambridge Univ. Press [flk]
13. *Baumgartner, M. P. 1988. *The Moral Order of the Suburb*. NY: Oxford Univ. Press [soc]
14. *Baxter, E., Hopper, K. 1980. *Private Lives/Public Spaces: Mentally Disabled Adults on the Streets of NY City*. NY: Community Service Society [anth]
15. *Beaver, P. D. 1986. *Rural Community in the Appalachian South*. Lexington: Univ. Press Kentucky [anth].
16. *Becker, G. 1980. *Growing Old in Silence*. Berkeley: Univ. Calif. Press [anth]
17. *Bell, M. J. 1983. *The World from Brown's Lounge: An Ethnography of Black Middle-Class Play*. Urbana: Univ. Illinois Press [flk]
18. *Bellah, R. N., Madsen, R., Sullivan, W. M., Swindler, A., Tipton, S. M. 1985. *Habits of the Heart: Individualism and Commitment in American Life*. Berkeley: Univ. Calif. Press [soc]
19. *Bluebond-Langner, M. 1978. *The Private World of Dying Children*. Princeton: Princeton Univ. Press [anth]
20. *Boone, M. S. 1989. *Capital Crime: Black Infant Mortality in America*. Newbury Park: Sage [anth]

21. *Bosk, C. 1979. *Forgive and Remember: Managing Medical Failure.* Chicago: Univ. Chicago Press [soc]
22. *Brown, K. M. 1991. *Mama Lola: a Vodou Priestess in Brooklyn.* Berkeley: Univ. Calif. Press [anth]
23. *Bryant, F. C. 1981. *We're All Kin: a Cultural Study of a Mountain Neighborhood.* Knoxville: Univ. Tennessee Press [anth]
24. *Burawoy, M. 1979. *Manufacturing Consent: Change in the Labor Process Under Monopoly Capitalism.* Chicago: Univ. Chicago Press [soc]
25. *Carbaugh, D. 1988. *Talking American: Cultural Discourses on Donahue.* Norwood, NJ: Ablex Publishing [ling]
26. *Carroll, R. 1987. *Cultural Misunderstandings: The French-American Experience.* Chicago: Univ. Chicago Press [unk]
27. *Carter, L. 1990. *Charisma and Control in Rajneeshpuram: The Role of Shared Values in the Creation of a Community.* Cambridge: Cambridge Univ. Press [soc]
28. *Cassell, J. 1991. *Expected Miracles: Surgeons at Work.* Philadelphia: Temple Univ. Press [anth]
29. *Castleman, C. 1982. *Getting Up: Subway Graffiti in New York.* Cambridge: MIT Press [unk]
30. *Caughey, J. 1984. *Imaginary Social Worlds: a Cultural Approach.* Lincoln: Univ. Nebraska Press [ams]
31. *Chen, Hsiang-shui. 1992. *Chinatown No More: Taiwan Immigrants in Contemporary New York.* Ithaca: Cornell Univ. Press [anth]
32. Chock, P. 1987. The irony of stereotypes: toward an anthropology of ethnicity. *Cult. Anthropol.* 2(3):347–68
32a. Clark, M. 1959. *Health in the Mexican-American Culture: a Community Study.* Berkeley: Univ. Calif. Press
32b. Clark, M. et al. 1967. *Culture and Aging: an Anthropological Study of Older Americans.* San Francisco: Langley Porter
33. Clifford, J. 1983. On ethnographic authority. Reprinted in *The Predicament of Culture,* ed. J. Clifford, 1988, pp. 21–54. Cambridge: Harvard Univ. Press
34. Clifford, J. 1986. Partial truths. See Ref. 36, pp. 1-26
35. Clifford, J. 1992. Travelling cultures. In *Cultural Studies,* ed. L. Grossberg, C. Nelson, P. Treichler. NY: Routledge
36. Clifford, J., Marcus, G., ed. 1986. *Writing Culture.* Berkeley: Univ. Calif. Press
37. Csikszentmihalyi, M., Rochberg-Halton, E. 1981. *The Meaning of Things.* NY: Cambridge Univ. Press
38. *Curran, P. 1989. *Grace before Meals: Food Ritual and Body Discipline in Convent Culture.* Urbana: Univ. Illinois Press [anth]
39. D'Andrade, R. 1987. A folk model of the mind. See Ref. 99, pp. 112–50
40. D'Andrade, R., Strauss, C., ed. 1992. *Human Motives and Cultural Models.* Cambridge: Cambridge Univ. Press
41. *Daniels, A. K. 1988. *Invisible Careers: Women Civic Leaders from the Volunteer World.* Chicago: Univ. Chicago Press [soc]
42. *di Leonardo, M. 1984. *The Varieties of Ethnic Experience: Kinship, Class, and Gender among Italian-Americans.* Ithaca: Cornell Univ. Press [anth]
43. *Dominguez, V. 1986. *White by Definition: Social Classification in Creole Louisiana.* New Brunswick, NJ: Rutgers Univ. Press [anth]
44. *Dorst, J. D. 1989. *The Written Suburb: an American Site, an Ethnographic Dilemma.* Philadelphia: Univ. Pennsylvania Press [ams]
45. *Douglas, J. D., Rasmussen, P. K., Flanagan, C. A. 1977. *The Nude Beach.* Beverly Hills: Sage [soc]
46. Downey, G. 1992. Steering technology toward computer-aided design. In *Managing Technology in Society: New Forms for the Control of Technology,* ed. A. Rip, T. Misa, J. Schot. NY: Cambridge Univ. Press. In press
47. Downey, G. 1992. CAD/CAM saves the nation: toward an anthropology of technology. *Knowl. Soc.* 9: In press
48. *Eckert, J. K. 1980. *The Unseen Elderly: A Study of Marginally Subsistent Hotel Dwellers.* San Diego: Univ. San Diego Press [anth]
49. *Eckert, P. 1989. *Jocks and Burnouts: Social Categories and Identity in the High School.* NY: Teachers College Press [ling]
50. Edgerton, R. B. 1967. *The Cloak of Competence: Stigma in the Lives of the Mentally Retarded.* Berkeley: Univ. Calif. Press
51. *Edgerton, R. B. 1979. *Alone Together: Social Order on an Urban Beach.* Los Angeles: Univ. Calif. Press [anth]
52. Errington, F. 1987. Reflexivity deflected: The festival of nations as an American cultural performance. *Am. Ethnol.* 14:654–67
53. Errington, F. 1990. The Rock Creek rodeo: excess and constraint in men's lives. *Am. Ethnol.* 17:628–45
54. *Estroff, S. E. 1981. *Making It Crazy: An Ethnography of Psychiatric Clients in an American Community.* Berkeley: Univ. Calif. Press [anth]
55. *Fantasia, R. 1988. *Cultures of Solidarity: Consciousness, Action, and Contemporary Workers.* Berkeley: Univ. Calif. Press [soc]
56. *Fine, G. A. 1983. *Shared Fantasy: Role-Playing Games as Social Worlds.* Chicago: Univ. Chicago Press [soc]
57. *Fine, G. A. 1987. *With the Boys: Little League Baseball and Pre-Adolescent Culture.* Chicago: Univ. Chicago Press [soc]
58. *Fink, D. 1986. *Open Country, Iowa: Rural Women, Tradition and Change.* Albany: State Univ. NY Press [unk]

59. *Fishman, L. T. 1990. *Women at the Wall: A Study of Prisoners' Wives Doing Time on the Outside.* Albany: State Univ. NY Press [soc]

60. *Fitchen, J. M. 1981. *Poverty in Rural America: A Case Study.* Boulder: Westview [anth]

61. *Fjellman, S. J. 1992. *Vinyl Leaves: Walt Disney World and America.* Boulder: Westview. In press [anth]

61a.*Fleisher, M. S. 1989. *Warehousing Violence.* Newbury Park: Sage [anth]

62. *Folb, E. 1980. *Runnin' Down Some Lines: The Language and Culture of Black Teenagers.* Cambridge: Harvard Univ. Press [ling]

63. *Foley, D. E. 1990. *Learning Capitalist Culture: Deep in the Heart of Tejas.* Philadelphia: Univ. Pennsylvania Press [anth]

64. *Forrest, J. 1988. *Lord I'm Coming Home: Everyday Aesthetics in Tidewater, North Carolina.* Ithaca: Cornell Univ. Press [anth]

65. *Foster, S. W. 1989. *The Past is Another Country: Representation, Historical Consciousness and Resistance in the Blue Ridge.* Berkeley: Univ. Calif. Press [anth]

66. Fox-Genovese, E. 1990. Between individualism and fragmentation: American culture and the new literary studies of race and gender. *Am. Q.* 42:7–35

67. *Francis, D. 1984. *Will You Still Need Me, Will You Still Feed Me, When I'm 84?* Bloomington: Univ. Indiana Press [anth]

68. *Freeman, J., ed. 1989. *Hearts of Sorrow: Vietnamese-American Lives.* Stanford: Stanford Univ. Press [anth]

69. *Furman, F. 1987. *Beyond Yiddishkeit: The Struggle for Jewish Identity in a Reform Synagogue.* Albany: State Univ. NY Press [anth]

70. Fussell, P. 1983. *Class: A Guide Through the American Status System.* NY: Summit

71. Gable, E., Handler, R., Lawson, A. 1992. On the uses of relativism: fact, conjecture, and black and white histories at Colonial Williamsburg. *Am. Ethnol.* 15 (forthcoming)

72. Geertz, C. 1973. Thick description: toward an interpretive theory of culture. In *The Interpretation of Cultures,* ed. C. Geertz, pp. 3–30. NY: Basic Books

73. *Gibson, M. A. 1988. *Accommodation without Assimilation: Sikh Immigrants in an American High School.* Ithaca: Cornell Univ. Press [anth]

74. *Ginsberg, F. 1989. *Contested Lives: The Abortion Debate in an American Community.* Berkeley: Univ. Calif. Press [anth]

75. *Gitlin, T. 1983. *Inside Prime Time.* NY: Pantheon [soc]

75a. Goldschmidt, W. R. 1947. *As You Sow.* Glencoe: Free Press

76. *Goldsmith, P. D. 1989. *When I Rise Cryin' Holy: African-American Denominationalism on the Georgia Coast.* NY: AMS Press [anth]

77. *Goodwin, M. H. 1990. *He-Said-She-Said: Talk as Social Organization among Black Children.* Bloomington: Indiana Univ. Press [ling]

78. *Grant, G. 1988. *The World We Created at Hamilton High.* Cambridge: Harvard Univ. Press [eds]

79. *Greenhouse, C. 1986. *Praying for Justice: Faith, Order, and Community in an American Town.* Ithaca: Cornell Univ. Press [anth]

79a. Grimes, R. L. 1976. *Symbol and Conquest: Public Ritual and Drama in Santa Fe, New Mexico.* Ithaca: Cornell Univ. Press

80. *Gusfield, J. 1981. *The Culture of Public Problems.* Chicago: Univ. Chicago Press [soc]

81. *Guthrie, G. 1985. *A School Divided: An Ethnography of Bilingual Education in a Chinese Community.* Hillsdale, NJ: Lawrence Erlbaum [eds]

82. *Gwaltney, J. L. 1980. *Drylongso: A Self-Portrait of Black America.* NY: Random House [anth]

83. *Halle, D. 1984. *America's Working Man: Work, Home and Politics among Blue-Collar Property Owners.* Chicago: Univ. Chicago Press [soc]

84. *Halperin, R. 1990. *The Livelihood of Kin: Making Ends Meet "The Kentucky Way".* Austin: Univ. Texas Press [anth]

85. Handler, R. 1988. *Nationalism and the Politics of Culture in Quebec.* Madison: Univ. Wisconsin Press

86. Handler, R. 1991. "Imagine being the millionth anything": creating commemorative events at colonial Williamsburg. Presented at Annu. Meet. Am. Anthropol. Assoc., 90th, Chicago

87. *Hanna, J. L. 1988. *Disruptive School Behavior: Class, Race and Culture.* NY: Holmes and Meier [anth]

88. Hannerz, U. 1969. *Soulside: Inquiries into Ghetto Culture and Community.* NY: Columbia Univ. Press

89. *Harper, D. 1987. *Working Knowledge: Skill and Community in a Small Shop.* Chicago: Univ. Chicago Press [soc]

90. Hatch, E. 1979. *Biography of a Small Town.* NY: Columbia

91. Hayano, D. M. 1979. Auto-ethnography: paradigms, problems and prospects. *Hum. Org.* 38:99–104

92. *Hayano, D. M. 1982. *Poker Faces: The Life and Work of Professional Card Players.* Berkeley: Univ. Calif. Press [anth]

93. *Heath, S. B. 1983. *Ways with Words: Language, Life and Work in Communities and Classrooms.* NY: Cambridge Univ. Press [anth]

94. Herdt, G, ed. 1992. *Gay Culture in America: Essays from the Field.* Boston: Beacon

94a. Hippler, A. E. 1974. *Hunter's Point: a Black Ghetto.* NY: Basic Books

95. *Hochschild, A. R. 1983. *The Managed Heart: The Commercialization of Human Feeling.* Berkeley: Univ. Calif. Press [soc]

96. *Hochschild, A. R. 1989. *The Second Shift*. NY: Viking [soc]

97. *Hochschild, J. L. 1981. *What's Fair: American Beliefs about Distributive Justice*. Cambridge: Harvard Univ. Press [political science]

98. *Holland, D. C., Eisenhart, M. A. 1990. *Educated in Romance: Women, Achievement, and College Culture*. Chicago: Univ. Chicago Press [anth]

99. Holland, D., Quinn, N., ed. 1987. *Cultural Models in Language and Thought*. NY: Cambridge Univ. Press

100. *Horowitz, R. 1983. *Honor and the American Dream: Culture and Identity in a Chicano Community*. New Brunswick, NJ: Rutgers Univ. Press [soc]

101. *Horwitz, R. P. 1985. *The Strip: An American Place*. Lincoln: Univ. Nebraska Press [ams]

102. Hsu, F. 1972. American core values and national character. In *Psychological Anthropology*, ed. F. Hsu. Cambridge, Mass: Schenkman

103. Humphreys, Laud. 1975. *Tearoom Trade: Impersonal Sex in Public Places*. Chicago: Aldine

104. *Jackall, R. 1988. *Moral Mazes: The World of Corporate Managers*. NY: Oxford Univ. Press [soc]

105. *Johnson, C. L. 1985. *Growing Up and Growing Old in Italian-American Families*. New Brunswick, NJ: Rutgers Univ. Press [anth]

106. *Johnson, C. L. 1988. *Ex Familia: Grandparents, Parents, and Children Adjust to Divorce*. New Brunswick, NJ: Rutgers Univ. Press [anth]

107. *Johnstone, B. 1990. *Stories, Community, and Place: Narratives from Middle America*. Bloomington: Indiana Univ. Press [ling]

108. Kaminsky, M. 1992. Myerhoff's "third voice": ideology and genre in ethnographic narrative. *Social Text* 33. In press

109. *Kasinitz, P. 1992. *Caribbean New York: Black Immigrants and the Politics of Race*. Ithaca: Cornell Univ. Press [soc].

110. *Katch, R. 1987. *Women of the New Right*. Philadelphia: Temple Univ. Press [soc]

111. Keil, C. 1966. *Urban Blues*. Chicago: Univ. Chicago Press

112. *Kennedy, T. R. 1980. *You Gotta Deal with It: Black Family Relations in a Southern Community*. NY: Oxford [anth]

113. *Kingsbury, H. 1988. *Music, Talent and Performance: A Conservatory Cultural System*. Philadelphia: Temple Univ. Press [ethnomusicology]

114. *Kochman, T. 1981. *Black and White Styles in Conflict*. Chicago: Univ. Chicago Press [ling]

115. *Konner, M. 1987. *Becoming a Doctor*. NY: Viking [anth]

116. *Krasniewicz, L. 1992. *Nuclear Summer: The Clash of Communities at the Seneca*

Women's Peace Encampment. Ithaca: Cornell Univ. Press. In press [anth]

117. *Krieger, S. 1983. *The Mirror Dance: Identity in a Woman's Community*. Philadelphia: Temple Univ. Press [soc]

118. Kubey, R., Csikszentmihalyi, M. 1990. *Television and the Quality of Life: How Viewing Shapes Everyday Experience*. Hillsdale, NY: Lawrence Erlbaum Assoc.

119. *Kugelmass, J. 1986. *The Miracle of Intervale Avenue: The Story of a Jewish Congregation in the South Bronx*. NY: Schoken [anth]

120. *Kunda, G. 1991. *Engineering Culture: Control and Commitment in a High-Tech Corporation*. Philadelphia: Temple Univ. Press [soc]

120a. La Barre, W. 1969. *They Shall Take up Serpents: Psychology of the Southern Snake-Handling Cult*. NY: Schoken

121. *Laguerre, M. S. 1984. *American Odyssey: Haitians in New York City*. Ithaca: Cornell Univ. Press [anth]

122. *Lamphere, L. 1987. *From Working Daughters to Working Mothers: Immigrant Women in a New England Industrial Community*. Ithaca: Cornell Univ. Press [anth]

123. *Landon, D. D. 1990. *Country Lawyers: The Impact of Context on Professional Practice*. NY: Praeger [soc]

124. Lasch, C. 1978. *Culture as Narcissism: American Life in an Age of Diminishing Expectations*. NY: Norton

125. *Latour, B., Woolgar, S. 1979. *Laboratory Life: The Social Construction of Scientific Facts*; reissued 1986 with minor changes as *Laboratory Life: The Construction of Scientific Facts*. Princeton: Princeton Univ. Press [soc]

126. *Lawless, E. J. 1988. *God's Peculiar People: Women's Voices and Folk Tradition in a Pentecostal Church*. Lexington: Univ. Press Kentucky [flk]

127. Lears, T. J. J. 1985. The concept of cultural hegemony: problems and prospects. *Am. Hist. Rev.* 90:567–93

128. Linde, C. 1987. Explanatory systems in oral life stories. See Ref. 99, pp. 343–68

129. Lofgren, O. 1989. Anthropologizing America. *Am. Ethnol.* 16:366–74

130. Luhrmann, T. M. 1989. *Persuasions of the Witch's Craft: Ritual Magic in Contemporary England*. Cambridge: Harvard Univ. Press

131. *Luker, K. 1984. *Abortion and the Politics of Motherhood*. Berkeley: Univ. Calif. Press [soc]

132. *Lynch, M. 1985. *Art and Artifact in Laboratory Science*. Boston: Routledge Kegan Paul [soc]

133. *MacLeod, J. 1987. *Ain't No Makin' It: Level Aspirations in a Low Income Neighborhood*. Boulder: Westview [soc]

134. Maltz, D. N., Borker, R. A. 1982. A cultural approach to male-female miscommunication. In *Language and Social Identity*, ed.

John Gumperz, pp. 195–216. Cambridge: Cambridge Univ. Press
135. Manganaro, M. 1989. 'The tangled bank' revisited: Anthropological authority in Frazer's *The Golden Bough. Yale J. Crit.* 3(1):107–26
136. *Manning, P. 1980. *The Narc's Game: Organizations and Informational Limits on Drug Law Enforcement.* Cambridge: MIT Press [soc]
137. *Marcus, G. 1992. *Lives in Trust: The Fortunes of Dynastic Families in Late Twentieth Century America.* Boulder: Westview [anth]. In press
138. Marcus, G., Cushman, D. 1982. Ethnographies as texts. *Annu. Rev. Anthropol.* 11:25–69
139. *Maril, R. L. 1983. *Texas Shrimpers: Community, Capitalism and the Sea.* Texas A and M Press [soc]
140. *Martin, E. 1987. *The Woman in the Body: A Cultural Analysis of Reproduction.* Boston: Beacon Press [anth]
141. *McGuire, M. 1988. *Ritual Healing in Suburban America.* New Brunswick, NJ: Rutgers Univ. Press [soc]
142. *Merry, S. E. 1981. *Urban Danger: Life in a Neighborhood of Strangers.* Philadelphia: Temple [anth]
143. *Merry, S. E. 1990. *Getting Justice and Getting Even: Legal Consciousness Among Working-Class Americans.* Chicago: Univ. Chicago Press [anth]
144. *Miller, E. M. 1986. *Street Woman.* Philadelphia: Temple Univ. Press [soc]
145. *Miller, P. J. 1982. *Amy, Wendy and Beth: Learning Language in South Baltimore.* Austin: Univ. Texas Press [eds]
146. Moffatt, M. 1986. The discourse of the dorm: race, friendship, and "culture" among college youth. See Ref. 228, pp. 159–77
147. *Moffatt, M. 1989. *Coming of Age in New Jersey: College and American Culture.* New Brunswick, NJ: Rutgers Univ. Press [anth]
148. Moffatt, M. 1990. Do we really need "Post-Modernism" to understand Ferris Bueller's Day Off? — a Comment on Traube. *Cult. Anthropol.* 5:367–73
149. *Myerhoff, B. 1979. *Number Our Days.* NY: Simon and Schuster [anth]
150. Nader, L. 1974. Up the anthropologist: perspectives gained from studying up. In *Reinventing Anthropology,* ed. D. Hymes, pp. 284–311. NY: Random House
151. *Nash, J. C. 1989. *From Tank Town to High Tech: The Clash of Community and Industrial Cycles.* Albany: State Univ. NY Press [anth]
152. *Neville, G. K. 1987. *Kinship and Pilgrimage: Rituals of Reunion in American Protestant Culture.* NY: Oxford Univ. Press [anth]
153. *Newman, K. 1988. *Falling from Grace:*

The Experience of Downward Mobility in the American Middle Class. NY: Free Press [anth]
154. Newton, E. 1972. *Mother Camp: Female Impersonators in America.* NJ: Prentice-Hall
155. *Odendahl, T. 1990. *Charity Begins at Home: Generosity and Self-Interest among the Philanthropic Elite.* NY: Basic Books [independent]
155a. Ogbu, J. 1974. *The Next Generation: an Ethnography of Education in an Urban Neighborhood.* NY: Academic Press
156. *Oliker, S. J. 1989. *Best Friends and Marriage: Exchange among Women.* Berkeley: Univ. Calif. [soc]
156a. Orbach, M. K. 1977. *Hunters, Seamen, and Entrepreneurs: the Tuna Seinerman of San Diego.* Berkeley: Univ. Calif. Press
157. Ortner, S. B. 1991. Reading America: preliminary notes on class and culture. In *Recapturing Anthropology: Working in the Present,* ed. R. G. Fox, pp. 163–90. Santa Fe: School of American Research Press
158. *Ostrander, S. 1984. *Women of the Upper Class.* Philadelphia: Temple Univ. Press [soc]
158a. Padfield, H., Martin, W. E. 1965. *Farmers, Workers and Machines: Technological and Social Change in Farm Industries of Arizona.* Tucson: Univ. Arizona Press
159. *Pappas, G. 1989. *The Magic City: Unemployment in a Working Class Community.* Ithaca: Cornell Univ. Press [anth]
160. *Paules, G. F. 1992. *Dishing It Out: Power and Resistance among Waitresses in a New Jersey Restaurant.* Philadelpia: Temple Univ. Press. In press [anth]
161. *Peacock, J. L., Tyson, R. W. Jr. 1989. *Pilgrims of Paradox: Calvinism and Experience among the Primitive Baptists of the Blue Ridge.* Washington: Smithsonian Inst. Press [anth]
162. Perin, C. 1977. *Everything in Its Place: Social Order and Land Use in America.* Princeton: Princeton Univ. Press
163. *Perin, C. 1988. *Belonging in America: Reading Between the Lines.* Wisconsin: Univ. Wisconsin Press [anth]
164. *Peshkin, A. 1986. *God's Choice: The Total World of a Fundamentalist Christian School.* Chicago: Univ. Chicago Press [eds]
165. *Peshkin, A. 1991. *The Color of Strangers, The Color of Friends: The Play of Ethnicity in School and Community.* Chicago: Univ. Chicago Press [eds]
166. *Polanyi, L. 1989. *Telling the American Story: A Structural and Cultural Analysis of Conversational Storytelling.* Norwood, NJ: Ablex Publishers [ling]
167. Powdermaker, H. 1939. *After Freedom: A Cultural Study in the Deep South.* NY: Viking
168. Powdermaker, H. 1951. *Hollywood: The*

Dream Factory. London: Secker and Warburg

169. *Powell, W. W. 1985. *Getting into Print: The Decision-Making Process in Scholarly Publishing.* Chicago: Univ. Chicago Press [ling]

170. *Prell, R.-E. 1989. *Prayer and Community: The Havurah in American Judaism.* Detroit: Wayne State Univ. Press [anth]

171. *Prus, R. 1989. *Pursuing Customers: An Ethnography of Marketing Activities.* Newbury Park, CA: Sage [soc]

172. *Prus, R. 1989. *Making Sales: Influence as Interpersonal Accomplishment.* Newbury Park, CA: Sage [soc]

173. Quinn, N. 1987. Convergent evidence for a cultural model of American Marriage. See Ref. 99, pp. 343–68

174. Quinn, N. 1992. The motivational force of self-understanding: evidence from wives' inner conflicts. See Ref. 40, pp. 89–124

175. *Radway, J. 1984. *Reading the Romance: Women, Patriarchy, and Popular Literature.* Chapel Hill: Univ. North Carolina Press [ams]

176. *Read, K. E. 1980. *Other Voices: The Style of a Male Homosexual Tavern.* Novato, CA: Chandler and Sharp Publishers [anth]

177. *Rhodes, L. A. 1991. *Emptying Beds: The Work of an Emergency Psychiatric Unit.* Berkeley: Univ. Calif. Press [anth]

178. Riesman, D. 1961. *The Lonely Crowd: A Study of Changing American Character.* New Haven: Yale Univ. Press

179. Robbins, B. 1992. Comparative cosmopolitanism. *Social Text.* 31/32

180. Robinson, J. P. 1977. *How Americans Use Time: A Social-Psychological Analysis of Everyday Behavior.* NY: Praeger

181. Robinson, J. P., Andreyenkov, V. G., Patrushev, V. D. 1988. *The Rhythm of Everyday Life: How Society and American Citizens Use Time.* Boulder, CO: Westview Press

182. *Rollins, J. 1985. *Between Women: Domestics and Their Employers.* Philadelphia: Temple [soc]

183. *Rose, D. 1987. *Black American Street Life: South Philadelphia 1969–1971.* Philadelphia: Univ. Pennsylvania Press [anth]

184. *Rose, S. 1988. *Keeping Them Out of the Hands of Satan: Evangelical Schooling in America.* NY: Routledge [soc]

185. *Rosenberg, E. M. 1989. *The Southern Baptists: A Subculture in Transition.* Knoxville: Univ. Tennessee Press [anth]

185a. Rubel, A. J. 1966. *Across the Tracks: Mexican-Americans in a Texas City.* Austin: Univ. Texas Press

186. *Rubinstein, R. 1986. *Singular Paths: Old Men Living Alone.* NY: Columbia Univ. Press [unk]

187. *Sacks, K. 1988. *Caring by the Hour: Women, Work and Organizing at Duke Medical Center.* Urbana: Univ. Illinois Press [anth]

188. *Sady, R. 1990. *District Leaders: A Political Ethnography.* Boulder: Westview [anth]

189. *Sanday, P. R. 1990. *Fraternity Gang Rape: Sex, Brotherhood and Privilege on Campus.* NY: NY Univ. Press [anth]

190. Sanjek, R. 1990. On ethnographic validity. In *Fieldnotes: The Makings of Anthropology,* ed. R. Sanjek, pp. 385–418. Ithaca: Cornell Univ. Press

191. Schneider, D. 1968. *American Kinship: A Cultural Account.* Englewood Cliffs, NY: Prentice-Hall

192. *Schwartz, M. A. 1990. *The Party Network: The Robust Organization of Illinois Republicans.* Madison: Univ. Wisconsin Press [political science]

193. *Schwartzman, H. 1989. *The Meeting: Gatherings in Organizations and Communities.* NY: Plenum [anth]

194. *Sheehan, B. J. 1984. *The Boston Integration Dispute: Social Change and Legal Maneuvers.* NY: Columbia Univ. Press [anth]

195. *Shield, R. R. 1988. *Uneasy Endings: Daily Life in an American Nursing Home.* Ithaca: Cornell Univ. Press [anth]

196. *Shokeid, M. 1988. *Children of Circumstances: Israeli Emigrants in New York.* Ithaca: Cornell Univ. Press [anth]

197. *Shuman, A. 1986. *Storytelling Rights: The Uses of Oral and Written Texts by Urban Adolescents.* NY: Cambridge Univ. Press [flk]

198. *Slobin, M. 1989. *Chosen Voices: The Story of the American Cantorate.* Urbana: Univ. Illinois Press [ethnomusicology]

199. Smith, N. 1987. Dangers of the empirical turn: some comments on the CURS initiative. *Antipode* 19:59–68

200. *Sperling, S. 1988. *Animal Liberators: Research and Morality.* Berkeley: Univ. Calif. Press [anth]

201. Spindler, G., Spindler, L. 1983. Anthropologists view American culture. *Annu. Rev. Anthropol.* 12:49–78

202. Spindler, G., Spindler, L., Williams, M. D. 1991. *The American Cultural Dialogue and Its Transmission.* Bristol, PA: Falmer

202a. Spradley, J. P. 1970. *You Owe Yourself a Drunk: an Ethnography of Urban Nomads.* Boston: Little, Brown

203. Spradley, J. P., Mann, B. 1975. *The Cocktail Waitress: Women's Work in Man's World.* NY: Wiley

204. *Stacey, J. 1990. *Brave New Families: Stories of Domestic Upheaval in Late Twentieth Century America.* NY: Basic Books [soc]

205. Stack, C. 1974. *All Our Kin: Strategies for Survival in a Black Community.* NY: Harper and Row

206. *Staub, S. 1989. *Yemenis in New York City: The Folklore of Ethnicity.* Philadelphia: Balch Inst. Press [flk]

207. Strathern, M. 1987. The limits of auto-anthropology. In *Anthropology at Home*, ed. A. Jackson, pp. 16–37. London: Tavistock
208. Strauss, C. 1990. Who gets ahead? Cognitive responses to heteroglossia in American political culture. *Am. Ethnol.* 17:312–28
209. Strauss, C. 1992. What makes Tony run? Schemas as motives reconsidered. See Ref. 40, pp. 197–224
210. *Sullivan, M. L. 1989. *Getting Paid: Youth, Crime and Work in the Inner City*. Ithaca: Cornell Univ. Press [anth]
211. *Susser, I. 1982. *Norman Street: Poverty and Politics in an Urban Neighborhood*. NY: Oxford Univ. Press [anth]
212. *Swiderski, R. M. 1987. *Voices: An Anthropologist's Dialogue with an Italian-American Festival*. Bowling Green: Bowling Green State Univ. Popular Press [anth]
213. Tannen, D. 1990. *You Don't Understand*. NY: Ballantine Books
214. *Teski, M. 1981. *Living Together: An Ethnography of a Retirement Hotel*. Washington: Univ. Press of America [anth]
215. *Thomas, R. J. 1985. *Citizenship, Gender and Work: Social Organization of Industrial Agriculture*. Berkeley: Univ. Calif. Press [soc]
216. Thornton, R. 1988. The rhetoric of ethnographic holism. *Cult. Anthropol.* 3:285–303
217. *Tobin, J. J., Wu, D., Davidson, D. H., 1989. *Preschool in Three Cultures: Japan, China and The United States*. New Haven: Yale Univ. Press [anth]
218. Tobin, J., Davidson, D. 1990. The ethics of polyvocal ethnography: empowering vs. textualizing children and teachers. *Qual. Stud. Educ.* 3:271–83
219. Tocqueville, A. de. 1966 [1835, 1842]. *Democracy in America*. NY: Harper and Row
220. *Todd, A. D. 1989. *Intimate Adversaries: Cultural Conflict between Doctors and Women Patients*. Philadelphia: Univ. Pennsylvania Press [soc]
221. *Traweek, S. 1988. *Beamtimes and Lifetimes; the World of High Energy Physics*. Cambridge: Harvard Univ. Press [anth]
222. *Tricarico, D. 1984. *The Italians of Greenwich Village: The Social Structure and Transformation of an Ethnic Community*. NY: Center Migrat. Stud. [soc]
222a. *Unruh, D. R. 1983. *Invisible Lives: Social Worlds of the Aged*. Beverly Hills: Sage
223. Van Maanen, J. 1988. *Tales of the Field: On Writing Ethnography*. Chicago: Univ. Chicago Press
224. *Van Willigen, J. 1989. *Gettin' Some Age on Me: Social Organization of Older People In a Rural American Community*. Lexington: Univ. Kentucky Press [anth]
225. Varenne, H. 1977. *Americans Together: Structured Diversity in a Midwestern Town*. NY: Teachers College Press
226. Varenne, H. 1982. Jocks and freaks: the symbolic structure of the expression of social interaction among American senior high school students. In *Doing the Ethnography of Schooling*, ed. G. Spindler, pp. 210–35. NY: Holt, Rinehart
227. *Varenne, H. 1983. *American School Language: Culturally Patterned Conflicts in a Suburban High School*. NY: Irvington Publishers [anth]
228. Varenne, H., ed. 1986. *Symbolizing America*. Lincoln: Univ. Nebraska Press
229. Varenne, H. 1986. "Drop in anytime": community and authenticity in American everyday life. See Ref. 228, pp. 209–28
230. *Vesperi, M. D. 1985. *City of Green Benches: Growing Old in a New Downtown*. Ithaca: Cornell [anth]
231. *Vigil, J. 1988. *Barrio Gangs: Street Life and Identity in Southern California*. Austin: Univ. Texas Press [anth]
231a. Vogt, E. Z. 1955. *Modern Homesteaders: The Life of a 20th Century Frontier Community*. Cambridqe: Belknap Press
232. *Warner, R. S. 1988. *New Wine in Old Wineskins: Evangelicals and Liberals in a Smalltown Church*. Berkeley: Univ. Calif. Press [soc]
233. Warner, W. L. 1963. *Yankee City*. New Haven: Yale Univ. Press
234. *Weatherford, J. M. 1981. *Tribes on the Hill: The U.S. Congress Rituals and Realities*. NY: Rawson, Wade [anth]
235. *Weis, L. 1990. *Working Class without Work: High School Students in a Deindustrializing Economy*. NY: Routledge [unk]
235a. Weiss, M. S. 1974. *Valley City: a Chinese Community in America*. Cambridge: Schenkman
236. *West, C. 1984. *Routine Complications: Troubles between Doctors and Patients*. Bloomington: Indiana Univ. Press [soc]
237. *Weston, K. 1991. *Families We Chose: Lesbians, Gays, Kinship*. NY: Columbia Univ. Press [anth]
238. *Whitehead, H. 1987. *Renunciation and Reformation: A Study of Conversion in an American Sect*. Ithaca: Cornell [anth]
239. Wilkinson, R. 1989. *The Pursuit of American Character*. NY: Harper and Row
240. *Williams, B. 1988. *Upscaling Downtown: Stalled Gentrification in Washington, DC*. Ithaca: Cornell Univ. Press [anth]
241. *Williams, T. 1989. *The Cocaine Kids: The Inside Story of a Teenage Drug Ring*. Reading, PA: Addison-Wesley [soc]
242. Withers, C. ("James West"). 1945. *Plainville, U. S. A.* NY: Columbia Univ. Press
243. *Yanagisako, S. 1985. *Transforming the Past: Tradition and Kinship among Japanese Americans*. Stanford: Stanford Univ. Press [anth]
244. *Zavella, P. 1987. *Women's Work and Chicano Families: Cannery Workers of the Santa Clara Valley*. Ithaca: Cornell Univ. Press [anth]
245. Zinn, M. B. 1979. Field research in minority communities: ethical, methodological and political observations by an insider. *Soc. Problems* 27:209–19

Annu. Rev. Anthropol. 1992. 21:231-55

TAKING STOCK OF QUANTITATIVE ARCHAEOLOGY

Albert J. Ammerman

Department of Sociology and Anthropology, Colgate University, Hamilton, New York 13346

KEYWORDS: classification, spatial analysis, history of archaeology

> The doctors, certain that I would draw my last breath at midnight, came back in the morning, thinking perhaps to attend my funeral, and found me busy writing.
>
> *Petrarch*

INTRODUCTION

As the 20th century draws to a close, it is normal for those who do research in the human sciences to put faith in the Pythagorean creed (42): that in numbers comes certainty. There is a strong tendency, at least in our own culture, for numbers and quantification to rule the world. In the field of economics, as Simon (90) notes in his recent autobiography, it was still difficult in 1950 to get an article published in the *American Economic Review* if it contained equations. Two decades later, the situation had entirely changed. "I think that it could be said that by 1970 mathematics had taken over economics (for better or worse); the simplest theory had to be clothed in mathematical garb before it could receive any serious attention." Thus, the archaeologist's desire to make arguments in quantitative form, like those put forward in other disciplines, is fully understandable. As Aldenderfer (4) observes in the case of anthropological archaeology in the United States, "most of us believe that by the proper manipulation of numbers, we can obtain significant insight into the past."

But a surprise awaits us in the more recent literature. Indeed, just when adherence to a quantitative approach has become widely established in archaeology as a whole, a note of caution is being voiced by specialists in such matters. A sense of disappointment, even of failure, seems to mark the special-

231

0084-6570/92/1015-0231$02.00

ist literature. Quantitative archaeology, some of its longstanding proponents appear to be saying, has not met its own high expectations. Thus, after years of enthusiasm and optimism, it is time for careful self-evaluation. In the words of Cowgill (26), a leading figure in the field, "both the number and sophistication of archaeological publications that are concerned with mathematics or formal methods are greater than they were a few years ago. However there are still very few, if any, mathematical or formal techniques that are applied by archaeologists both frequently and also in ways that are simultaneously technically correct, appropriate to data and problems, and highly useful. In that sense, the art is still in a weakly developed state." More seems to have been promised than has so far been delivered.

How might we explain in historical terms this unexpected turn of events? To what extent did the ambitions of those such as Spaulding who were advocates of the quantitative movement—who aspired not only to solve specific problems but also to redefine archaeology in more scientific terms—contribute to this state of affairs? And what does this more recent inversion imply for the future of the field? I address these issues here.

The time is right for undertaking such a review for two reasons. First, quantitative archaeology, after two boisterous decades, has entered the doldrums. Second, in several major publications scholars have recently attempted to take stock of quantitative archaeology. In my approach to this stock-taking I emphasize broad trends in the field, writing principally with the practicing archaeologist, the nonspecialist, in mind. Thus I would like to trace the history of the ambitions, the working assumptions, the frustrations, and the basic attitudes of the field.

In the remainder of this section, I comment on some of the main trends in the field of quantitative archaeology between 1950 and 1980. I then review two recent volumes of collected papers: *Quantitative Research in Archaeology: Progress and Prospects,* edited by Aldenderfer (2), which appeared in 1987, and *Mathematics and Information Science in Archaeology: A Flexible Framework,* edited by Voorrips (102), which came out at the end of 1990. The various contributions in these two books, in combination with the review articles written by Cowgill (26, 27) and Read (78) that appeared separately, offer a wide spectrum of thought on the current state of quantitative archaeology in the New World and to a lesser extent in Europe. In order to gain historical depth, I then look more closely at two topics that have been the subject of active discussion and debate: application of quantitative approaches to artifact typologies or classification in archaeology, and the spatial analysis of the artifact distributions that occur on so-called occupation floors at sites. As a means of reflecting the attitude and tone of the arguments being advanced, I attempt to let each writer speak in his or her own words. In the final section, I try to draw general conclusions and to offer some suggestions about the future development of the field.

In 1953, in a seminal *American Antiquity* article (93), Spaulding proposed the use of the chi-square statistic as a new approach to the discovery of artifact types. The article opened with the claim "that certain statistical techniques offer economical methods of extracting information of cultural significance from archaeological data." In effect, Spaulding wanted archaeological types to become more "natural": They should reside in the physical properties of the objects under study and not be artificial constructs of the analyst. In his own words, "classification into types is a process of discovery of combinations of attributes favored by the makers of the artifacts, not an arbitrary procedure of the classifier." He went on to claim that a type, properly established in the new way, "cannot fail to have historical meaning." Spaulding's tone was confident and optimistic, but a fundamental question remained: How was the archaeologist to come up with the right touchstone, the statistical technique needed? Spaulding provided a brief and revealing answer: "There seems little doubt that the best approach to these problems involves a search of statistical literature for appropriate methods." Two implicit assumptions are made here: First, that the statistical literature already contained the required method and second, that research problems in archaeology are analogous, in formal terms, to those in other disciplines. In short, the quantitative archaeologist was fully licensed to borrow.

By the end of the 1950s, the use of statistics in archaeology was still a novelty. The proceedings of the Wenner-Gren conference on the application of quantitative methods in archaeology (45) provide an index of the slow early development of the field. In a pointed exchange between Howells and Spaulding, the former thought "it would be a rash man who would apply statistics of a really sophisticated kind." To which Spaulding replied: "It seems that statistics is a naughty word." In his own contribution to the meeting, again on his quantitative approach to classification, Spaulding (94) was emboldened to close with the following statement. "It is not an exaggeration, I think, to predict that the future of archaeology is in large measure bound up with the success or failure of this effort." The destiny of archaeology itself had thus been linked with a research program striving for a more objective approach to typology—an approach in which quantitative analysis would play the key role. Spaulding had raised the stakes in the game.

Interest in quantitative archaeology increased during the 1960s, a fact reflected, for instance, by the proceedings of the international conference on mathematics in the archaeological and historical sciences (50) held in 1969. As the pioneer and senior spokesman of the quantitative movement, Spaulding (95) gave the opening address. Once again he used simplified examples in making the argument for his own quantitative approach to classification. He emphasized the promise of the methodology, and not any substantive gains that had resulted from its use. Spaulding sought to move beyond intuition, common sense, and implicit reasoning toward a more rigorous and explicit approach to archaeology. "We do not concede," he wrote, "that common human knowledge of common human properties exhausts the theoretical possibilities of prehistoric studies." At the end of his address, Spaulding urged upon his listeners the need, above all, to "convince the pre- and nonmathematical archaeologist that these techniques merely make explicit and extend the implicit mathematical reasoning that all archaeologists use." Beyond its missionary rhetoric, Spaulding's claim had profound implications. If archaeologists had been using mathematical reasoning implicitly and informally all along, then the explicit logic of the field was to be sought in the realm of mathematics and statistics. If the logic of archaeological thinking and the logic of mathematical reasoning were indeed one and the same, as Spaulding seemed to imply, then there would be no need to tailor new quantitative methods specifically to archaeological problem solving; one had simply to use the formal machinery already at hand in the mathematical and statistical literature.

The 1970s witnessed the takeoff of quantitative archaeology. Under the influence of the New Archaeology, with its commitment to an explicitly scientific orientation, more and more archaeologists in the United States jumped on the bandwagon. In Britain, there was a parallel growth in quantitative archaeology at this time, although there the pathway from David Clarke (23) through Doran & Hodson (35) to Shennan (82) would take a course different from the one in North America.

Perhaps the most direct statement of the aims of the New Archaeology is that found in *Explanation in Archaeology,* which appeared in 1971. Here Watson and coauthors (104) argue, for example, that "a scientific approach to archaeological data requires the use of various statistical techniques." One could no longer do archaeology without using statistics. Indeed, at all levels of the new research program, quantitative methods were required: from the formulation of research questions to sampling designs in the field, from artifactual analysis to the testing of hypotheses. Again, following Spaulding, a deeper rationale was offered—namely, that "the logic of these techniques further illustrates the logical framework of the discipline." Statistics would help to reveal the foundations of reasoning in the field. As we know, the New Archaeology sought law-like generalizations, a quest that it regarded as the real business of science; its advocacy of quantitative methods then was a means to this end—that is, a lesser part of the program.

In retrospect, few meaningful law-like generalizations have been discovered by the new archaeologists over the last 20 years, notwithstanding considerable effort, and their approach to mathematics and statistics has been rather mechanical. As Read (78) has noted, the competence of the analyst and the understanding of formal methods were not stressed. In its challenge to the authority structure of the old archaeology, the new program encouraged everyone to use the statistical packages available at the nearest computer center. The consequences were innumerable studies of uneven quality. While these problems of competence did not go entirely unnoticed at the time (99), the limitations of much of this work would become more evident in time. As Aldender-fer (3), in his assessment of this period, was to observe in the mid 1980s: "Most of the archaeologists who jumped on the bandwagon had little formal training in mathematics, statistics, and quantitative analysis and were thus prone to make basic mistakes. Those archaeologists who did not jump on the bandwagon were similarly ill-prepared to identify the mistakes being made. To many, statistical analysis became an end in itself."

By the end of the 1970s, a few in the quantitative movement had begun to realize that the task they faced was more complex and difficult than they had originally thought. Perhaps it was not enough simply to count and measure the objects that happened to come forward in the archaeological record. What was really needed were measurements chosen carefully to suit the concepts and constructs of a particular research problem. Thus, according to Whallon (108), more attention had to be paid to the identification of underlying dimensions and measurements along them. For him, this was now "the critical stage, because it is in the degree to which we can or cannot directly measure along these underlying dimensions of variation that the choice of all further analytical methods and techniques ultimately must be based." A shift in priorities was thus announced. The analysis of data does not immediately follow from the mere availability of a statistical technique. Instead, the choice of technique must respond to what one was trying to measure. Whallon's statement also left open the possibility that we might not always be able to achieve what we wanted.

But if the attitude was more prudent, the mood of the quantitative literature in general was still buoyant as the 1970s ended. Progress, one believed, was being made. "It is obvious that advances in computer technology and applications of this technology to theoretically sophisticated quantitative methods [have] given the practice of typology in archaeology a tremendous boost. The chapters in this volume testify to the crucial contribution that these technical and methodological advances have made toward improving the practice of classification in archaeology." So Brown (12) wrote in the concluding chapter of *Essays on Archaeological Typology* (111). It is of interest to contrast this statement with one made by Dunnell (37) only a few years later. At issue was the growing gulf between everyday classificatory practice of the working archaeologist and the approach espoused in theory by the quantitative archae-ologist. "Nowhere in the Americas is the archaeological record organized and understood in terms supplied by the means debated in the contemporary pro-grammatic literature. The 'theoretical' literature has diverged from practice to such a degree that the two are now unrelated." I discuss this divergence further below.

The tension between theory and practice in contemporary archaeology, as identified by Dunnell, is much like that in medieval medicine. Dressed in red gowns and tall hats, the physicians of the Middle Ages would gather round a sick person, discuss the patient's case in philosophical terms, and then turn the individual over to a lowly assistant, perhaps a barber, who would administer a cure. The physician was supposed to be interested in theory, not practice. The doctors directed their thoughts to the programmatic rationale of their science and only to a lesser extent to the treatment of the sick. They were prepared to discourse at length over what Hippocrates, the father of medicine, may have meant centuries before when he pronounced that "Whoever wishes to pursue properly the science of medicine must proceed thus."

One of the more striking episodes in the annals of medieval medicine, as described by Iris Origo in *The Merchant of Prato,* was a time when the poet Petrarch was laid low by a fever. As Petrarch recounts in one of his letters,

> the physicians gathered at once round my bed, as is their custom. Having disputed at length, they declared that by midnight I would be dead. A quarter of the night had already passed … . They said that the only remedy by which I might prolong my life would be to draw some little cords tightly round me, to keep me from sleep, and so I might perhaps live to see the dawn. No one heeded their prescriptions, for I have always besought my friends and bidden my servants that nothing should ever be carried out on my person of what physicians had ordered, but that, if indeed something must be done, it should be just the opposite.

The next morning, to their surprise, the doctors found Petrarch busy writing at his desk. Is this not just what Dunnell sees the practicing archaeologist doing in the face of the advice of the good doctors of *Essays on Archaeological Typology*?

Indeed, if we seek a parallel for archaeology in the sciences, an applied science such as medicine may be more appropriate than a pure one such as physics. Illness can take many different forms. No single unified theory exists for the causation of ill health; explanation is rich in its diversity. At any given time, much remains unknown. In medical science, complex interactions often occur among factors such as physiology, immunology, genetics, nutrition, and environmental hazards. The situation with archaeology is much the same. One of the turning points in the history of medicine came in the 16th century when Vesalius and others decided to turn to dissection actively to close the gap between theory and practice (73). For centuries, physicians had spoken of the *rete mirabile,* a structure central to Galen's conception of the circulatory system; the dissection knife now demonstrated the absence of such a structure in human anatomy.

TWO RECENT BOOKS

The chapters of *Quantitative Research in Archaeology* represent a moment of self-reflection, of soul searching, by those in the quantitative movement. A central theme of the volume is that things have not gone as planned over the last 20 years. The results obtained to date have fallen short of what was promised. Accordingly, it is now time to correct course. "How should we place quantitative thinking into the research process?" This was Aldenderfer's original charge to those contributing to the symposium in 1985. Most of the chapters, in response, still emphasize broad programmatic concerns. Voorrips (101), for example, reexamines the relationship among three different conceptions of a model in archaeology (as a causal narrative, as a formal abstraction, and as a form of statistical analysis). Only Aldenderfer, in his opening chapter (3), takes a more historical approach, pointedly disapproving of the bandwagon phenomenon of the 1970s. In only two contributions, those by Read (76) and Whallon (110), are concrete examples developed at some length. The discourse in the field, following Spaulding's lead, remains, for the most part, on an abstract plane.

But the mood of the chapters is now more cautious. As Aldenderfer (4) frankly admits, "most of us would agree quantitative methods have yet to fulfill the promise we thought they offered." Much the same sentiment is voiced by Brown (13), when he asks rhetorically at the start of his chapter: "Given the emphasis on quantitative analysis that has become standard in the computerized world of contemporary science, has such analysis in archaeology lived up to expectation?" This assessment is reiterated by Doran (33), who notes "the disappointing performance of formal techniques as they have been applied over the last two decades." And Kintigh (55) is of much the same mind as Aldenderfer, Brown, and Doran when he remarks that "many archaeological problems are just inherently difficult." In its early days, the quantitative movement made the overconfident assumption that problem solving in archaeology, once one adopted a more scientific approach, would be a comparatively easy business. Instead of setting up an opposition or antagonism between new quantitative methods and more traditional approaches to archaeology, Kintigh is prepared to recognize that archaeologists over the years have developed sophisticated intuitive problem-solving strategies and to recommend a rapprochement. By translating tried-and-true methods into a quantitative framework, it may be possible to combine the best of two worlds.

A second theme of the volume is the need for greater creativity on the part of the quantitative archaeologist. It is not enough simply to borrow statistical techniques and apply them mechanically, as advocated by proponents of the New Archaeology in the 1970s. Clark (21) had touched on the issue of creativity in an earlier review article; he returns to it here in the context of the design of archaeological research (22). As stated by Aldenderfer (4), "we must look more deeply into the creative act of how we assign meaning to data." He observes that the archaeologist tends to want to study or measure what he refers to as "indirect observables." For him, activity areas and tool kits would be examples of things that are not directly observable in the archaeological record (4). "Tool kits certainly cannot be observed but are instead inferred through the covariation of artifact types as found in archaeological assemblages." Recall Whallon's remark, cited above, of the challenge of measuring along underlying dimensions of variation. Nance (68) concurs that in archaeology one often has to measure indirectly the variable that one really wishes to study. "Often the phenomenon is really an abstract concept which can never be measured directly, as is the case in the social sciences generally." For Carr (18), "a data set's relevant structure, particularly for archaeological data, usually will not have a physical correlate in a specific set of data items." However it is stated, this problem has deep implications for the field of quantitative archaeology. Let us hope that our constructs—whether we call them "indirect observables" or "relevant structure"—do not prove in the long run to have the status of Galen's *rete mirabile*.

Carr's "Removing discordance from quantitative analysis" is a condensed version of his edited book, *For Concordance in Archaeological Analysis,* an ambitious attempt to push formalism to new heights (17). In both, Carr is determined to find tool kits and activity areas by means of the spatial analysis of the distributions of artifacts on the surface of a site such as Pincevent, an open-air site near Paris, dating to the late Upper Palaeolithic (65). Carr wants to avoid inconsistency in how an analysis is conceived (16). "Yet it is precisely this concordance between theory, technique, data, and phenomenon that is required for analysis, theory building, and technical development to be relevant, accurate, meaningful, and effecient." Carr is ready to swing, as it were, for the fences. In spatial analysis, one normally develops what is called a form-to-process argument (24, 72). One starts with a spatial distribution, the pattern or form, and seeks to infer the process that generated it. Most methods of analysis assume that a single process is responsible for the spatial distribution. As others have noted (57), however, several processes may contribute to the formation of the patterns seen at a site such as Pincevent. Recognizing this, Carr builds an elaborate analytical edifice; but his effort does not achieve commensurate results. As we shall see in the section on spatial analysis, below, Carr (17) is not able in the end to find meaningful tool kits and activity areas at Pincevent.

Among the contributions to *Quantitative Research in Archaeology,* those of greatest interest to me are Read's (76) and Whallon's (110). Especially at the start of an analysis, the archaeologist is placed in a double bind. At the start the researcher has only the data; little may be known about the data's relevant structure. In the words of Carr (18), "He cannot choose an appropriate technique of analysis and an appropriate subset of the data for analysis without some knowledge about the data set's structure; at the same time, he cannot obtain this knowledge without applying some pattern-searching technique to summarize the data's structure in a simpler form that is comprehendable [sic] by the human mind." This is essentially a problem of formalism; most practicing archaeologists who have spent years assembling a data set are likely to have a dense network of ideas, albeit imperfect and incomplete, about their data. In any event, Read (75, 76) offers a formal way to circumvent the double bind by introducing what he calls "preanalysis." Read works his way step-by-step through an example of a set of data on projectile points from one of Gould's sites in Australia, showing us how preanalysis is motivated and undertaken. This gives us a chance to see how quantitative thinking is applied in a sustained way to the research process. Whallon (110) also works by means of an example, the Gravette points at Abri Pataud. He begins by urging archaeologists to pay more attention to how they display their data. His approach is in the spirit of Tukey's concept and practice of Exploratory Data Analysis (51, 100). Whallon then goes on to argue that theories and models in archaeology should not be guided by statistical methods and techniques. "The reason is simple: the basic principles in terms of which these methods and techniques have been developed and in terms of which they operate have little or nothing to do with the principles in terms of which we have reason to believe human cultural systems, prehistoric as well as historic or contemporary, are organized and operate." This is a complete reversal of the position held by Spaulding (95) and Watson et al (104) in 1971. The logic of the archaeological past is no longer something to be discovered or made explicit in terms of the logic of statistics and mathematics. We should not allow our quantitative methods, our "hammers" as Moore & Keene call them (67), to drive our questions. Rather, it should be the other way around.

In retrospect, we can see that the quantitative movement got off on the wrong foot when it made the initial assumptions that archaeological problems were easy to solve, that statistical techniques could simply be borrowed from the statistical literature, and that statistics and archaeology shared a logic of problem solving. Somehow it took more than 20 years to realize that the movement was on the wrong track. Given such a misguided start, may we not have the answer, at least in part, to the important question raised by Clark (22): "Why is there such a schism between the archaeologist as theoretician and the archaeologist as practitioner"?

Mathematics and Information Science in Archaeology, the second book under review here, is organized in a more topical fashion (102). Each contributor was asked for a state-of-the-art overview of a given subject, and the book has more coherence than the usual conference volume. It is comprehensive in its coverage of the field. One of the few omissions would be recent work on *Quantifying Diversity in Archaeology,* an edited volume that I have reviewed elsewhere (6).

If there is less soul searching here than one finds in the volume edited by Aldenderfer, *Mathematics and Information Science in Archaeology* is nevertheless likely to prove a more valuable handbook for the student in the 1990s. After a short introductory chapter by editor Voorrips (103), in which the years before 1975 are referred to as a "learning phase" and a "crude affair" and the promise of the future continues to be the ever-increasing capacity for information processing on a new generation of computers, one passes to what is no doubt the most original contribution to the book. In "The structure of archaeological theories," Gardin (41) adopts "a bottom-up strategy, beginning with the study of archaeological theories found in the literature and leading to an assessment of their structural features." Gardin uses "theories" in a loose sense "to include all kinds of interpretations of archaeological remains, whatever their substance or form." He attempts to look at what practicing archaeologists do when they make interpretations or draw conclusions, and to represent the common elements of such arguments in formal terms. To appreciate fully the elegance of Gardin's account the reader needs some background in expert systems and cognitive science. He draws particular attention to the role of analogies in the "theories" put forward by the archaeologist.

The volume contains sound reviews of such standard topics in quantitative archaeology as sampling (69), multivariate techniques (32), and computer-based simulation (34). There are few surprises to be encountered in these chapters. In the case of sampling, for example, we still find much the same tension between the justification of the use of sampling techniques in abstract terms and the difficulty of putting them into practice that I observed in these pages a decade ago (5). In the case of seriation methods, Djindjian has made a major contribution in bringing the various methods under a single mathematical formulation, but no new techniques are proposed. Doran provides a useful service in outlining the objectives, strategy, and outcome of 13 different case studies in which simulation has been employed in archaeology; he then discusses some of the theoretical issues raised by the studies. The volume includes two chapters in which methods from other fields are now being applied to archaeological problems: one by Scollar (81) on the numerical treatment of air photos and the other by Kvamme (63) on the predictive modeling of site location on a regional level. The latter draws upon Geographic Information Systems for its characterization of the environment of the region under study (62). An important issue in studies of this kind is site visibility on the land surface, since the data used in any regional archaeological analysis will derive in large part from surveys. In order to control for surface visibility, one must possess detailed information—not always immediately available—on the long-term history of patterns of erosion and deposition on the respective landforms of the region.

Chapters by Ihm (52) and Read (79) cover less familiar ground. Both are concerned with models—in particular, with the development of a new generation of models appropriate to the nature of archaeological problems. For Ihm, this means a shift to stochastic treatments of data analysis. He argues that "analytical methods cannot be applied efficiently without assumptions about the probability distribution of the variables under study." A variable is considered to be stochastic whenever "the quantities under study are obscured by error components with probability distributions." After introducing some of the models of probability distribution one might use, Ihm works through several examples—the grave goods of a group of Neolithic burials at a site near Aldenhoven in Germany, and the analysis of the shape of Mycenaean tholoi.

Read wants to see mathematics used to a much greater extent as a tool for thinking in archaeology: that is, not just for the analysis of data but for the formal representation of ideas and theories. This chapter should be read in conjunction with a review by the same author (78). Read calls for first the symbolic representation of the relationship, structure, process, or system that one would like to study and then the derivation of expectations or implications on the basis of mathematical reasoning. Read surveys cases in the literature where formal representations of this kind have been attempted and concludes that the efforts at model building to date have often been limited in scope; they have not taken enough account of the capacity for self-modification or re-flexiveness, the role of intentionality, in human systems of thought and action. "It is not so much laws of behavior that we need," argues Read but "models of how complex, information processing, self-reflective, self-restructuring systems operate, develop and change." Obviously, this is a tall order. Read is aware that model building of this kind will not be easy, but he believes that it constitutes a legitimate aspiration for archaeology and that mathematical reasoning can play a creative and constructive role in such explorations.

The two chapters in *Mathematics and Information Science in Archaeology* that are most relevant here are those on classification (28) and intrasite spatial analysis (56). The former is largely a response to the criticisms of the formal approach to classification recently put forward by Dunnell (37) and Adams (1). The chapter's tone is conciliatory. Cowgill begins by patiently delineating the main disparities between customary and formal approaches to the subject. For the first time in the formal literature, an author acknowledges the role of "sensitivity," the knack for classification that one acquires from having sorted boxes of pottery or stone tools in a given region for years. As Cowgill admits, "formal analysts have been too ready to overlook these skills altogether, to depreciate them as 'trial and error'. To clarify our ideas about archaeological classification we cannot leave out logic, but we also cannot leave out hard-to-articulate pattern-recognition abilities." The two opposing sides in this debate are now beginning to talk to one another again. For Cowgill, the central notion of classification involves the establishment of groups such that "the objects in each group are all decidedly more similar to one another than they are to any objects in other groups. This concept of 'type' is expressed by the phrase 'internal cohesion and external isolation'." Of course, there are many different ways to operationalize internal cohesion and external isolation, and much of the discussion in the quantitative literature is naturally concerned with trying to establish the best way.

Cowgill next turns to the issue—one again raised by both Dunnell and Adams—of research purposes and classification. Cowgill recognizes three main purposes of classification—chronology, the behavioral uniformities of artifact makers, and the transmission of ideas in time and space—and comments on some of the formal considerations that arise in each case. For all of the balance and intelligence of his commentary, however, no significant attention is paid to the issue of substance. After more than 30 years, what do formal methods of classification have to offer us in terms of meaning and substance?

By this point, the archaeologist as practitioner has a right to expect more. To return to the analogy of medieval medicine, the cure of the actual patient still seems to be secondary to the logic of how the patient will be treated. Or to put it another way, the proof of the pudding, for the formal analyst, is not in the eating but still in how one reads the recipe.

Kintigh (56) takes a more practical tack. He applies each major method of spatial analysis to the spatial distributions found at a given site and then comments on the strengths and weaknesses of each method in terms of their respective results. The reader can compare the methods directly. The site selected to illustrate the methods is the Mask site, where Binford (10) conducted well-known studies in ethno-archaeology. [In a related study along comparative lines, Djindjian (31) notes that the Mask site may be somewhat too easy to analyze; he suggests that a site such as Pincevent would be more typical of the challenge of Palaeolithic sites.] Kintigh compares nearest neighbor analysis; Hodder and Okell's A index (47); local density analysis (53); pure locational clustering, which was originally called k-means analysis (57); and unconstrained clustering (109). The first three are what he terms "indices of spatial patterning," in that they all reduce a spatial distribution to a summary measure and offer a global characterization of the pattern. On the other hand, pure locational clustering and unconstrained clustering, both developed specifically for spatial analysis in archaeology (as we shall see below), are much less reductive. As Kintigh indicates, these two methods should be seen as complementary. "Whereas pure locational clustering focuses on artifact density and location, unconstrained clustering focuses on class composition of areas of a site without regard to density." Instead of striving for a single best method of spatial analysis, the emphasis now is on using several techniques together as a package. The best example in the literature (44) of the combined use of these two methods is a recent reexamination of sites of the San originally studied by Yellen (112)

CLASSIFICATION

Let us now take a closer look at several issues connected with a quantitative approach to classification in archaeology. The first concerns technical problems with the analytical machinery. As we have already seen, in his pioneering study Spaulding (93) borrowed a method based upon two-way contingency tables and the use of the chi-square statistic as a test of association. This was an imperfect piece of machinery for the task at hand. As Doran & Hodson (34) observed in 1975, "Here was the real difficulty: no 'appropriate statistical methods' existed. Probably the only paper of real value to Spaulding at this time would have been T. Sørensen's in the Danish journal *Biologiske Skrifter* for 1948. But this would have required an immense search." [Doran & Hodson, in their turn, would pin their hopes on the machinery to be found in Sokal & Sneath's *Numerical Taxonomy* (92), but the results here would likewise prove disappointing in most archaeological cases (77).] As he tells us in his paper on Owasco ceramics in 1976, Spaulding was himself uneasy about what he had proposed (96): "but I have not been able to repress a certain sense of insecurity, a feeling that we are not quite solid at the base—that we are not solving the problem of describing assemblages in a clear, straightforward way. This insecurity was caused by the absence of an adequate statistical technique for analysis of multiple contingency tables." A method for dealing with contingency tables that contain three or more dimensions at a time had appeared in the literature of quantitative ecology in 1970 (40); the log-linear model, used for the analysis of such tables, had already been applied to archaeological examples by Read (74) in 1974. However, the log-linear model itself is not without its complications and problems, and the actual results obtained from case studies in archaeology so far have been mixed at best (66, 78). Thus, the promise of a new and improved machinery for classification, as envisioned by Spaulding in 1976, has failed again to match expectations over the long haul. Whatever merits this strategy for the discovery of types may have in the abstract, it is still not user friendly in practical terms; the archaeologist with an interest in tangible results will have to look elsewhere.

One of the points debated by Hodson (49) and Spaulding (97) in *Essays on Archaeological Typology,* centered on the kinds of variables that should be used. Hodson held that no special priority should be given to variables of any one kind: that is, variables on an interval, ratio, ordinal, or nominal scale could all be used for purposes of analysis. Spaulding, on the other hand, maintained that nominal variables should have a privileged position. An example of a nominal scale would be color, where the variable takes a discrete, qualitative value such as red or brown. Clearly, if one intends to use contingency tables, the move made by Spaulding is a positive one, since it enables one to avoid the awkward and often arbitrary step of having to split a continuous variable into two or more discrete state values. Recall that from the start Spaulding objected to the arbitrary character of traditional approaches to typology (93). Thus the last thing Spaulding wants is for his own method to be vulnerable to the same criticism. In *Essays on Archaeological Typology* he makes a substantive argument—rather than a strictly technical one—for nominal variables. They are fundamentally important in his view, "because of the close connection between nominal variables and cultural patterning of human behavior." Others may argue the truth of this proposition. Of interest here are its implications for quantitative analysis in archaeology. In effect, this strong assumption, by stressing the qualitative aspect of objects, places the study of variability in a straitjacket. For example, in the case of a ceramic assemblage, it rules against the study of variability between vessels in terms of their sizes and shapes, as measured respectively along interval and ratio scales. At the same time, the stress here on nominal variables sets up a fundamental tension between two competing rationales—a *qualitative* one for the choice of variables and a *quantitative* one for manipulating the cell counts in the contingency tables.

A third issue concerns the substantive gains or lack of them achieved by the new methods, especially in comparison with traditional ones. Not everyone involved in quantitative archaeology believed that traditional methods had failed. Thus, according to Thomas (99), "to propose a computer technique for deriving morphological types presumes that traditional methods have failed, and nobody has demonstrated that yet." Aldenderfer (2), voicing his own heterodoxy, sides with Thomas: "Traditional methods of type building, especially for morphological types with presumed temporal and cultural meaning, seem to work just fine." This opening in the ranks of archaeologists with a quantitative orientation, in combination with Dunnell's sharp reproach in 1986 (cited above; 37), now encouraged Adams (1), a nonquantitative archaeologist, to argue anew the merits of a more traditional approach to classification and to put forward his own perspective on the gap between theory and practice. He wrote in 1988, "I simply want to see the 'typological debate' returned to the arena where it rightly belongs: to the realm of the field archaeologist who has not only to make classifications but to use them, day in and day out, year in and year out." Adams thinks that the potential of statistics and computers has been exaggerated; he recommends the use of procedures that are responsive to the various purposes of classification and that are "do-able." For him, the bottom line is practicality.

Dunnell's criticism (37) is both deeper and more challenging. Dunnel has had a long-term interest in systematics in prehistory (36) and a more recent one in the application of evolutionary theory to archaeology (38). In his review article on classification, he regards Spaulding's approach as "the initial emic method." He asks what a positive nonrandom association means, if and when an analyst finds such a combination of variables in a contingency table. As he puts it, "if the pattern of nonrandom association is inherent in the data and the data are the product of behavior, then the pattern of behavior is a behavior pattern, but one can go no further." This may be why the cultural or historical meaning of the results obtained from this kind of analysis often seem to be flat. Dunnell also draws attention to a distinction between essentialism, which he links with typological thinking, and materialism, which he connects with population thinking and evolutionary theory. He goes on to equate Spaulding's approach with an essentialist position, in the sense that it ultimately ascribes reality to essences embodied in things perceptible to the senses. And he concludes, much as I did above with regard to variables restricted to a nominal scale, that such an approach is not really favorable to the study of patterns of variation within an assemblage. In contrast, a materialist position, one with an etic cast, would place more emphasis on the study of variation, according to Dunnell. The complex issue of the extent to which types in archaeology should be given an emic cast is also taken up by Read (77) in 1989. Read is critical of Dunnell's position, placing himself squarely in the emic camp. Although he admits that objects from prehistory are unfit for emic study in the linguistic sense of the term, since one has no names and no overt cognitive categories to work with, Read holds that emic studies are possible in the looser sense of an attempt to understand behavioral phenomena in terms of the internal structure or functional elements of a particular system. Only time will tell whether such an approach to prehistory will prove productive or not. At present Read defines the challenge in the following terms: "So the same problem keeps rearising; how to form homogeneous groups from heterogeneous data when dealing with incompletely understood structuring processes." The path of his reasoning leads Read to propose a rather surprising opening move for a quantitative archaeologist: to wit, "the collection of material should be sorted initially by qualitative criteria." But perhaps this move is not so surprising after all. It may be only the logical extension of Spaulding's strong assumption in *Essays on Archaeological Typology*. For Read goes on to say, "While these are etically stated criteria, the assumption is that both qualitative differences and breaks in what would otherwise be a continuum of values reflect underlying emically salient distinctions." Who would have imagined, in the early days of the quantitative movement, such an involution, such a return to Rouse and the ideas of half a century ago?

A recent development of interest concerns the issue of the unit of analysis to be used in the discovery of types (6, 91). In the case of pottery, in particular, this means a shift from sherds to vessels as the focus of analysis. In behavioral terms, it clearly makes more sense to speak in terms of vessels—the objects that people made and used. But traditionally, even within quantitative archaeology, studies of ceramic classification have been conducted at the level of sherds. What do the counts of sherds in a contingency table, for example, really represent as numbers? This is an obvious question to ask but one that has seldom been taken seriously until quite recently. Different pots at a site break into different numbers of sherds; the sherds of a broken vessel, as noted by Ihm (52), represent a contagious distribution. To my knowledge, no formal calculus for the relationship between parts and wholes, for purposes of the discovery of pottery types, has yet to be worked out in archaeology.

This question was probably not raised before for two reasons. For one thing, it may take days, even weeks, of hand sorting to translate an assemblage of sherds into an assemblage of vessels. For another, with some sets of ceramic remains it may not be possible to accomplish a successful translation. My own experience in the study of ceramic assemblages from Neolithic sites in Italy (7) nevertheless suggests that the translation effort is worthwhile. It highlights the variability present in the ceramic assemblage—variability even within a single vessel. Conversely, much of the variability within and between ceramic assemblages is simply masked by the study of sherds. In any event, those in future who wish to base classification on a quantitative idiom will have to pay greater attention to fundamental questions of this kind, as part of their exploration of new directions.

INTRASITE SPATIAL ANALYSIS

The quantitative analysis of spatial data in archaeology has had a much shorter history than that of classification. Only in 1973 did Whallon (106) publish his first article on the subject, an examination of patterns of spatial aggregation among the artifacts distributed on the occupation floor at the cave site of Guila Naquitz in Mexico. In the same year, Dacey (30), a geographer, contributed an article on statistical tests of spatial association to *American Antiquity*. The method that Whallon first used, the dimensional analysis of variance, was borrowed directly from quantitative ecology. The basic strategy adopted in work of this kind is inductive. As noted by the ecologist Pielou (72), "customarily, work begins with the contemplation of, and collection of data from, some part of the biosphere itself; the ecologist then tries to argue back, inductively, from observed effects to hidden causes." The researcher attempts to make a form-to-process argument—the form here being the spatial distribution of points on a map.

Until 1973, archaeologists had relied on informal methods. In the words of Whallon (106), "virtually all archaeological examples of analysis of such spatial patterns have been based upon inspection and impressionistic interpretation." Thus, one of Whallon's immediate aims, reflecting the spirit of the time, was to put such analysis on a more objective footing. The first step in Whallon's analysis is to determine whether the distribution of items in each class (flint debitage and plant and animal remains) shows a pattern of aggregation or concentration. The ultimate goal is to compare the spatial patterns of different classes and to establish groups of classes that exhibit similar patterns of aggregation over the site. In 1974, Whallon (107) applied the method of nearest neighbor analysis, again borrowed from ecology and geography, to spatial distributions occurring at the site of Abri Pataud in France. Each of the two methods has both advantages and limitations. For example, the dimensional analysis of variance permits data in the form of counts per grid square, as opposed to point proveniences; but its spatial format, a nested series of blocks of sequentially smaller scale (which works well in the case of experimental designs in ecology), is ill adapted to the irregular shapes of archaeological sites. On the other hand, while nearest neighbor analysis is more sensitive in detectiing nonrandom spatial patterns than dimensional analysis of variance, it is weak in defining artifact clusters themselves on the map and comparing the patterns of different artifact types. The latter consideration significantly affects the wider motivation for the analyses, the discovery of tool kits on occupation floors at Palaeolithic sites. As Whallon (106) indicates at the start of his first contribution, "it is hoped that inferences concerning patterns of prehistoric human activity can be made by interpreting these 'tool kits' in terms of their contents and their position on the occupation floors. Spatial analysis would thus be of direct relevance to many of the current questions in prehistory."

It may be useful to digress briefly here and say a few words about the history of the functional argument, as it is called. In 1966, the Binfords (11) published a landmark paper in which they applied factor analysis to a group of Middle Palaeolithic assemblages from various sites and claimed that the differences among the assemblages could be explained by differences in the activities performed at the respective sites. Previously, the differences among the assemblages, as described in terms of their percentages of tool types, had been used to identify different cultural traditions or facies. The Binfords, basing their analysis on the same data (that is, tool types defined in the traditional morphological way) now argued that tool kits were associated with specific activities and that the differences in the activities performed at the respective sites generated the variability observed. This innovative and much-debated proposal was to set the agenda for Palaeolithic archaeology in North America for the next two decades. The key assumption was that the percentages of tool types in an assemblage were determined, in effect, by activities and their associated tool kits. In 1974, it was possible to show, however, that other factors—the dropping or discard rates associated with the tool types and the "mapping relations" between the tool types and the activities—help to determine the percentages (8). A formal model was developed of the process by which stone tools enter the archaeological record—of how an assemblage is *made*. Because the implications of the model for the application of a multivariate statistical technique such as factor analysis made the original approach to the functional argument problematic, spatial analysis became the more promising analytic arena. Again, in the words of Whallon (105), "we would therefore expect that the various tool types in Palaeolithic sites will be differentially distributed over the area of occupation and that groups of tool types will be mutually correlated in terms of their patterns of distribution, particularly in the larger and richer sites. These groups should represent functionally associated tools, or 'tool kits,' which were used in the same activity or activities." In other words, intrasite spatial analysis now became a matter of life and death for the functional argument.

From the mid-1970s onwards, there was a steady stream of publications on the topic of intrasite spatial analysis. An active, parallel interest was taken in the application of point pattern analysis to settlement patterns on a regional scale (39, 48). Several useful contributions appeared in *Intrasite Spatial Analysis,* a volume edited by Hietala, which, after many years of delay, finally appeared in 1984 (29, 46, 53, 59, 98, 109). The studies in this volume for the most part use indices of spatial patterning. They summarize the distribution of points on a map by only one or a few values. Not only are they highly reductive, but they usually emphasize global patterning at the expense of local patterning.

By the late 1970s, some of us had begun to realize that the methods we were borrowing from ecology and geography did not really serve the purposes of archaeology. Whallon was one of the first to try to develop a method tailored specifically to the study of the class composition of zones within an occupation floor. His new method, called unconstrained clustering, involves three main steps. One first transforms the artifact distribution map into a vector of smooth densities; Kintigh (56) describes alternative ways of accomplishing this. Next, one converts the vector of absolute densities at each artifact location to a vector of proportional densities (that is, class composition at each locality). Finally, one subjects these vectors to a cluster analysis. As noted by Kintigh (56), unconstrained clustering is more an analytical strategy than a specific method, since a variety of analytical decisions can be made with respect to the treatment employed at each step. As in the case of pure locational clustering, most archaeologists will understand this strategy best from practical examples. Hence the value of Kintigh's recent review (56). Whallon makes only a modest claim for unconstrained clustering. For him (109) it is "hardly more than an elaborate approach to a descriptive summary or display of the data, or a series of such summaries and displays."

Another new approach developed in the early 1980s was pure locational clustering (56, 57), which makes use of the k-means procedure, a form of nonhierarchical cluster analysis that tries to minimize the intracluster variances while maximizing the intercluster distances. In fact, only after Kintigh and I had clearly outlined what we would like spatial analysis to do for the archaeologist did we realize that k-means analysis, with some additions and modifications, offered the needed machinery (9). The method followed from the definition of a problem; it was not the more common case in archaeology of a method in search of a problem (67). We attempted to put location and configurational patterning—things of interest to the archaeologist that were often lost in the course of the classical methods of point pattern analysis—back in spatial analysis. We took as a starting point that the processes that generated the distribution maps were probably complex (57). In addition, we thought there might not be a single, simple analytical solution. Patterns of interest and the processes structuring them might occur on a given map at more than one scale of spatial resolution. Moreover, we wanted the procedure to be display oriented, so that the skilled human analyst's ability at pattern matching could be brought into play and context could be used in the evaluation of the results. What we advocated was in the spirit of Herbert Simon's strategy for solving problems in the human sciences—a more heuristic approach to spatial analysis. In 1982, this marked a sharp departure from previous attitudes toward quantitative archaeology in North America, namely the tradition of Spaulding and the New Archaeology. In 1983, pure locational clustering was applied to the site of Pincevent by Simek & Larick (89), who found no clear indication of activity areas at the site and suggested instead that its spatial patterns had more to do with the discard of items into depositional zones, in line with the original interpretation of the excavators (86–88). The method has also been used by Simek (85) in his detailed study of the site of Le Flageolet in the Dordogne. Koetje (58), in his study of Magdalenian open air sites in the Isle Valley, made a significant improvement in how comparisons between artifact classes are handled in the analysis. Pure locational clustering has also been productively applied to an ethnoarchaeological study of the Shipbo (84) as well as to Yellen's San sites, as mentioned earlier, where it was used in combination with unconstrained clustering (44).

One of the more prolix and less fortunate chapters in the recent history of intrasite spatial analysis was written by Carr (17), who made a last-ditch effort to save the research program of the functional argument. Determined to identify tool kits and activity areas at a site such as Pincevent, he chose to take the high road of formalism. Carr (14) got off to a good enough start in a long review article on intrasite spatial analysis, which was comprehensive and informed. But in order to deal with the complication that spatial patterns result from multiple processes rather than a single one—in order to remove discordance from spatial analysis—he constructed an elaborate conceptual edifice (15). The high ambitions of the analysis and their justification seem to have received more attention than implementation; the results obtained from Carr's own analysis of Pincevent are disappointing. This is not the place to describe the five main steps in Carr's analysis of the site. [Incidentally, his first step is an inductive one; on the basis of artifact density contours, 15 "natural" areas or strata of the site are distinguished. In a later paper (19), Carr proposes a Fourier-based method, similar to the one used by Graham (43), for initially dissecting artifact palimpsests that may occur at a site. It is unclear whether such preanalysis, a re-description of the original data to be undertaken prior to the first step, is practical or useful in most archaeological cases (56, 78).] In any event, after the fifth step in Carr's analysis, no well-defined activity areas appear to have been found at Pincevent. Strangely, Carr does not plot the results of the fifth step (those of a cluster analysis performed on the matrix of distance values among 10 artifact classes obtained from multidimensional scaling in the fourth step) back onto the map of the site. Such a step is needed, if only as a check on what has transpired as one reduction is piled upon the next in this case study. Nor does Carr compare his results for Pincevent with those of others already in the literature (89). In a more recent contribution on the subject in 1991, Carr (20) seems to pull back from his previous work. He now recommends a greater use of context (in line with the approach of pure locational clustering) as well as the use of several different analytical approaches in combination with one another.

Kroll & Price (61) express the current consensus that well-defined activity areas and tool kits are seldom found in the spatial analysis of the occupation floors at Palaeolithic sites. This seems to be no less the case at contemporary ethno-archaeological sites. In his study of the Alyawara site, for example, O'Connell (70) found that different activities were performed at the same place while the same activity was performed at different locations over the site. He and his coauthors now argue in a study on the Hadza (71) that "Instead of continuing to look for activity areas and tool kits, we must begin to ask how and why behavior is organized as it is within sites, how that organization is reflected in the distribution of refuse, and whether our knowledge of the relationship can be applied in archaeological context." Rigaud & Simek (80) make the further point that spatial distributions can be influenced by natural processes occurring at a site as well as by human behavior. In a study of tool use and spatial patterning at Verberie, a site on the Oise river much like Pincevent (54), Keeley does not undertake an intrasite spatial analysis as such but partitions the site into seven areas and examines the sub-assemblage from each area in terms of the microscopic use wear observed on the edges of stone tools. Keeley claims that only about one half of the tools in any one area were used and discarded in situ. The life histories of the other half of the tools, in terms of their discard rates, are taken to be more complicated. Without perhaps being fully aware of it, Keeley here takes us back to the formal model discussed above (8, 33); he begins to estimate the values for rates of discard, one of the key variables in the making of an assemblage of stone tools. Accordingly, it now becomes much easier to understand the complexity present in the spatial patterns of a site such as Pincevent or Verberie. In this context, I would agree with Kroll & Price (61) when they say that "we are beginning to know what we do not know about the meaning of the distribution of prehistoric material at stone age sites." On the other hand, I would completely disagree with their claim that the methods and techniques required for intrasite spatial analysis are presently at hand. While we may have some methods or strategies that now seem to work, such as pure locational clustering and unconstrained clustering, these analytical techniques are still in their infancy.

CONCLUSIONS

In retrospect, quantitative archaeology in North America, under Spaulding's early guidance, started off on the wrong foot. The field, instead of developing new methods tailored to its own problems, was not well served by those who urged it simply to go ahead and borrow methods and techniques from the statistical literature. High programmatic aspirations ought not to have been divorced to such a degree from practice. Nor was it in the field's best interest to assume that the arguments to be made in archaeology entailed the same logic as the methods of statistics. But it was perhaps in the choice of classification as the field upon which the new quantitative archaeology would do ritual battle with traditional archaeology that one finds the greatest mistake in judgment. As Adams (1) and Dunnell (37) hold, this approach has simply not panned out. Fortunately, in their practice archaeologists have chosen to follow the example of Petrarch; they have more or less ignored the theoretical prescriptions delivered ex cathedra by the good doctors of classification. Cowgill (25) himself suggested in 1982, "it seems to be the kind of situation in which old-fashioned intuitive pattern recognition may work better (less badly) than anything more formal." We should avoid the impulse to ignore or gloss over the misguided early history of quantitative archaeology, since it may help explain some of the later frustrations and tensions of the field. Given the propensity of our age to count things, quantitative archaeology was bound to emerge, in one form or another, during the last four decades. Of the many early pathways it might have taken, it apparently chose one of the least rewarding.

The situation did not improve in the early 1970s, under the commanding influence of the New Archaeology. We now look back at this time as one of scientism and the mechanical application of quantitative techniques still borrowed from others. The fledgling analyst often lacked training in the use of such methods; the result, as noted by Aldenderfer (3), was often misapplication and error. The notion still reigned, following Spaulding (95), that the logic of the discipline was to be discovered in the logic of quantitative methods. Only much later, in the 1980s, was this idea finally put to rest. Enthusiasm for the information processing capacity of the computer swept through the quantitative movement in the 1970s, and the price of this infatuation was both unanticipated and cruel. Not enough attention was paid to placing quantitative thinking on a solid foundation. Instead of merely learning how to manage data on the computer, the archaeologist should have acquired more background in how to represent a research problem and how to explore it in formal terms. More training of this kind would have given the analyses of data eventually performed more focus and meaning. Read (78, 79) has correctly recognized the field's weakness with regard to model building—a weakness that persists to the present day. While the bandwagon of the quantitative movement rushed ahead, graduate students in archaeology were not being educated in the fundamentals of the subject. A major opportunity, at a time when resources were available, was thus lost.

In the mid-1980s, when attempts were made to take stock, the mood was often a heavy-hearted and unsettled one. The soul searching in the volume edited by Aldenderfer (2) exemplifies this malaise. The clearest expression of disappointment, however, is found in Cowgill's address to the 50th annual meeting of the Society for American Archaeology (26). Cowgill was duly tired of the many errors and misapplications of quantitative methods that he found in the literature; he was frustrated by the slow pace of progress in the field. Yet neither his attempt at stocktaking nor those of others delved deeply enough into the historical roots of the problem. Consequently they did not come to grips with the deep sources of tension and contradiction that have accumulated in the field over the years. Moreover, their reading of the situation—their response to disappointment and frustration—may lead them to take positions that are counterproductive at times. Cowgill, for example, whose counsel is usually balanced and sensible, would assert in 1985 that the real problem faced by quantitative archaeology concerns not methods and techniques but rather the state of socio-cultural theory and the quality of our data (26). Now, the former is largely beyond the pale of the archaeologist; theories of culture and society are, for the most part, the domain of others in anthropology. Moreover, such theories (like those of modern medicine) are diverse, not unified, and subject to change from one generation to the next. Unless one consciously decides to join in the fray—as Doran (33) has recently chosen to do—the archaeologist can only hold on for the roller coaster ride. And although there will always be room for improvement in data, our best data (sites like Pincevent and Verberie) are currently far ahead of our best methods. We still need methods that are better tailored to the nature of archaeological problems. It is too early for the quantitative archaeologist to find another vocation or to go on vacation.

In a 1989 paper Cowgill (27) returns to a more positive outlook. He sees brighter prospects on the horizon—such as the recent developments in spatial analysis. Thus it seems to be time for the quantitative archaeologist to stop ruminating and go back to work. If from the short history of quantitative archaeology we have learned one thing it is to distrust high-sounding programmatic statements not backed up by practice. We have learned as well the need for patience, an old virtue. Our view, all along, has had too short a range.

Literature Cited

1. Adams, W. Y. 1988. Archaeological classification: theory versus practice. *Antiquity* 61:40–56
1a. Adams, W. Y., Adames, E. W. 1991. *Archaeological Typology and Practical Reality.* Cambridge: Cambridge Univ. Press
2. Aldenderfer, M. S., ed. 1987. *Quantitative Research in Archaeology: Progress and Prospects.* Newbury Park, CA: Sage. 312 pp.
3. Aldenderfer, M. S. 1987. Assessing the impact of quantitative thinking on archaeological research. See Ref. 2, pp. 9–29
4. Aldenderfer, M. S. 1987. On the structure of archaeological data. See Ref. 2, pp. 89–113
5. Ammerman, A. J. 1981. Surveys and archaeological research. *Annu. Rev. Anthropol.* 10:63–88
6. Ammerman, A. J. 1991. Review of *Quantifying Diversity in Archaeology. Am. J. Archaeol.* 95:341–42
7. Ammerman, A. J., Bonardi, S. 1985–1986. Ceramica stentinelliana di una struttura a Piana di Curinga (Catanzaro). *Riv. Sci. Preist.* 40:201–24
8. Ammerman, A. J., Feldman, M. W. 1974. On the "making" of an assemblage of stone tools. *Am. Antiq.* 39:610–16
9. Ammerman, A. J., Kintigh, K., Simek, J. 1987. Recent developments in the application of the K-means approach to spatial analysis. In *The Human Uses of Flint and Chert,* ed. G. Sieveking, M. Newcomer, pp. 211–16. Cambridge: Cambridge Univ. Press. 263 pp.
10. Binford, L. R. 1978. Dimensional analysis of behavior and site structure: learning

from an Eskimo hunting stand. *Am. Antiq.* 43:330–61
11. Binford, S., Binford, L. 1966. A preliminary analysis of functional variability in the Mousterian of Levallois facies. *Am. Anthropol.* 68:238–95
11a. Blankholm, H. P. 1991. *Intrasite Spatial Analysis in Theory and Practice.* Aarhus: Aarhus Univ. Press. 406 pp.
12. Brown, J. A. 1982. On the structure of artifact typologies. See Ref. 111, pp. 176–89
13. Brown, J. A. 1987. Quantitative burial analyses as interassemblage comparison. See Ref. 2, pp. 294–308
14. Carr, C. 1984. The nature of organization of intrasite archaeological records and spatial analytic approaches to their investigation. In *Advances in Archaeological Method and Theory,* ed. M. B. Schiffer, 7:103–22. New York: Academic. 462 pp.
15. Carr, C., ed. 1985. *For Concordance in Archaeological Analysis.* Kansas City: Westport Publishers. 662 pp.
16. Carr, C. 1985. Perspective and basic definitions. See Ref. 15, pp. 1–17
17. Carr, C. 1985. Alternative models, alternative techniques: variable approaches to intrasite spatial analysis. See Ref. 15, pp. 302–473
18. Carr, C. 1987. Removing discordance from quantitative analysis. See Ref. 2, pp. 185–243
19. Carr, C. 1987. Dissecting intrasite artifact palimpsests using Fourier methods. In *Method and Theory for Activity Area Research,* ed. S. Kent, pp. 236–91. New York: Columbia Univ. Press. 643 pp.
20. Carr, C. 1991. Left in the dust: contextual

ples of Numerical Taxonomy. San Francisco: Freeman. 359 pp.

93. Spaulding, A. C. 1953. Statistical techniques for the discovery of artifact types. *Am. Antiq.* 18:305–14

94. Spaulding, A. C. 1960. Statistical description and comparison of artifact assemblages. See Ref. 45, pp. 60–83

95. Spaulding, A. C. 1971. Some elements of quantitative archaeology. See Ref. 50, pp. 3–16

96. Spaulding, A. C. 1976. Multifactorial analysis of association: an application to Owasco ceramics. In *Culture Change and Continuity: Essays in Honor of James Bennett Griffin,* ed. C. E. Cleland, pp. 59–68. New York: Academic. 378 pp.

97. Spaulding, A. C. 1982. Structure in archaeological data: nominal variables. See Ref. 111, pp. 1–20

98. Spurling, B., Hayden, B. 1984. Ethnoarchaeology and intrasite spatial analysis: a case study from the Australian Western Desert. See Ref. 46, pp. 224–41

99. Thomas, D. H. 1978. The awful truth about statistics in archaeology. *Am. Antiq.* 43:231–44

100. Tukey, J. W. 1977. *Exploratory Data Analysis.* Reading, MA: Addison-Wesley. 506 pp.

101. Voorrips, A. 1987. Formal and statistical models in archaeology. See Ref. 2, pp. 61–72

102. Voorrips, A., ed. 1990. *Mathematics and Information Science in Archaeology: a Flexible Framework.* Bonn: Holos. 295 pp.

103. Voorrips, A. 1990. The evolution of a flex-

ible framework for archaeological analysis. See Ref. 102, pp. 1–6

104. Watson, P. J., LeBlanc, S. A., Redman, C. L. 1971. *Explanation in Archaeology. An Explicitly Scientific Approach.* New York: Columbia Univ. Press. 191 pp.

105. Whallon, R. E. 1973. Spatial analysis of palaeolithic occupation areas. The present problem and the "functional argument." In *The Explanation of Culture Change,* ed. C. Renfrew, pp. 115–29. London: Duckworth. 788 pp.

106. Whallon, R. E. 1973. Spatial analysis of occupation floors I: application of dimensional analysis of variance. *Am. Antiq.* 38:266–78

107. Whallon, R. E. 1974. Spatial analysis of occupation floors II: the application of nearest-neighbor analysis. *Am. Antiq.* 39:16–34

108. Whallon, R. E. 1982. Variables and dimensions: the critical step in quantitative typology. See Ref. 111, pp. 127–61

109. Whallon, R. E. 1984. Unconstrained clustering for the analysis of spatial distributions in archaeology. See Ref. 46, pp. 242–77

110. Whallon, R. E. 1987. Simple statistics. See Ref. 2, pp. 135–50

111. Whallon, R. E., Brown, J. A., eds. 1982. *Essays on Archaeological Typology.* Evanston, IL: Cent. Am. Archaeol. 200 pp.

112. Yellen, J. E. 1977. *Archaeological Approaches to the Present: Models for Reconstructing the Past.* New York: Academic. 259 pp.

Annu. Rev. Anthropol. 1992. 21:257-82

COMING OF AGE IN BIRMINGHAM:
Cultural Studies and Conceptions of Subjectivity

Jean Lave, Paul Duguid, and Nadine Fernandez

University of California, Berkeley, California 94720

Erik Axel

Copenhagen University, Copenhagen, Denmark

KEYWORDS: subculture, social practice, subjectivity, class, culture, gender

INTRODUCTION

In the past, anthropological discussions that gave central place to socialization did so on the assumption that socialization provided the social glue, the sources of continuity and uniformity of shared culture across generations. But theoretical conceptions of social formations have undergone deep transformations, emphasizing their historical, changing, conflictual, and partial character. Unitary accounts of "the person" have also become deeply problematic. Nonetheless, questions about how subjectivities are forged and about how persons emerge and change through engagement in social practice, in particular historical epochs and in particular social formations, still need to be addressed.

It seems worth trying to explore these questions in the light of a theory of social practice. Such a theory assumes that in order to comprehend either subjects or social orders one must begin with the relations between them. This project might be thought of as the investigation of the "creation of the historical person in historical process" (6; see also 28, 103). A theory of social practice should be able to account for the varied, problematic, partial, and unintentional production of persons through historical and biographical time, in a multiplicity of identities constructed and reconstructed through participation in social practice. Work from the Centre for Contemporary Cultural

0084-6570/92/1015-0257$02.00

257

Studies (CCCS) at the University of Birmingham—especially that focused on youth, subcultures, and subjective transitions into adult working-class lives—grapples intensively with some of these questions. This work addresses the production in practice of diverse working-class identities, lives, styles, cultures, and their modes of appropriation and transformation. It develops a theoretical position that takes class as a central assumption. The CCCS takes as its task the exploration of class-culture(s), seeking to account for cultural production in practice without reducing it to a simple epiphenomenon of class. As a consequence, CCCS scholars were led to confrontations between social class, on the one hand, and other aspects of social identity that proved both irreducible and inseparable. In pitching their problematic at the level of the cultural forms that mediate between structure and subjectivity, CCCS researchers produced work that, at its best, allows discussion of the creation of persons in terms that are variously dialectical, mediated, social-historical, and practice based.

Nonetheless, we draw attention to this work with a certain amount of caution. We are aware, of course, that there is currently a great deal of interest in cultural studies broadly construed. We are also aware that the basic aspect of early cultural studies we intend to explore—its class-culture problematic—is not central to the current fashion in cultural studies. In recent years, students of culture, including several from the CCCS (e.g. 32, 67, 93), have determinedly uprooted themselves from the class-cultural theoretic and argued instead towards a less materialist, more discourse-based position. While the latter approach has undoubtedly made a forceful contribution to cultural studies, particularly in its insistence on the decentering of the subject, we suggest that it is now time to look back, with all the benefits of hindsight, to cultivate some of the more deeply rooted initial insights that current fashion is in danger of obscuring. Looking for resources to address the challenge of a complex and historical account of the production of persons, we still find this earlier strand of cultural studies powerful, both in its proclamations and in its silences.

Peculiarities of the Birmingham Route

In attempting to describe the development of the Centre, we take heed of Stuart Hall's (55) warning against the "polemic search for an impossible retrospective consistency." Yet the history of the CCCS has been presented with surprising consistency by its directors, Hall and Johnson (53, 54, 57, 79, 80). Although these accounts are important and insightful, it is useful also to bear in mind histories of the Centre "from below" (e.g. 23, 42)—in particular the strong dissenting voices heard in *Women Take Issue* (15) and *The Empire Strikes Back* (14). Critiques of the Centre's genesis by knowledgeable outsiders are also helpful. We note the historian E. P. Thompson's (123) castigation of Hall and Johnson for producing a "sloppy and impressionistic history" of the "moment of culture"—the moment in which it is plausible to trace the beginnings of the CCCS.

This moment does not so much date the birth of the CCCS as stretch across its gestation, spanning the publication of the *Ur*-texts of British cultural studies: Richard Hoggart's *Uses of Literacy* [1956 (70)], Raymond Williams's *Culture and Society 1780–1950* [1958 (134)] and *Long Revolution* [1962 (131)], and Thompson's *Making of the English Working Class* [1963 (121)]. These three authors, though far from speaking with a single voice (see 73, 117, 123), challenged the conventional cultural authorities and galvanized British cultural theorizing from the left, making possible the formation of a center for radical cultural study.

Initially the three were, to use the resonant British term, extra-mural, outside the high-walled institutions of cultural and academic authority. (They taught adults, mostly from the working class, in night schools.) In a traditional response to dissent, the institutions moved to immure the dissenters. Each was given a university post: Hoggart at Birmingham, Williams at Cambridge, Thompson at Warwick. The three were, however, barely more compliant inside the walls than they had been outside [for example, see Thompson (122)]. To the dismay of his colleagues in the Birmingham English department, Hoggart established the CCCS there in 1964 to pursue his challenge to the complacent cultural consensus at which he takes aim in the opening of his *Uses of Literacy:*

> It is often said that there are no working-classes in England now, that a "bloodless revolution" has taken place which has so reduced social differences that already most of us inhabit an almost flat plain, the plain of the lower-middle- to middle-classes. … [T]his book discusses some ways in which a change, towards a culturally "classless" society, is being brought about (70:1).

Using a mix of autobiographical and literary-critical arguments, Hoggart disputes accounts of this "bloodless revolution"—said to have been brought about by the increasing affluence of the British working classes—by questioning the quality of the changes being introduced. [In *The Making of the English Working Class* (121), Thompson uses a similar approach to challenge historical arguments about the "improvements" provided by the industrial revolution.] Against the "embourgeoisement" thesis, Hoggart's book recognizes the culture of the working classes and insists that the members of these classes cannot be thought of simply as impoverished aspirants to a middle-class or "national culture" to which they do not contribute. Rather, Hoggart argues, the working classes are becoming victims of an impoverished culture foisted upon them for commercial reasons.

Though the idea of national culture was central to the "acceptable" literary criticism of, for example, T. S. Eliot, social classes, class cultures, and the causes and effects of social change were still considered thoroughly unacceptable topics for discussion in most English departments. Hoggart's project [outlined in "Schools of English and contemporary society" (72), the Centre's inaugural lecture given in 1963] was greeted as a vulgar solecism. His plan to build a relationship between English literature and sociology led only to fierce denunciations from both departments. Almost 30 years later, it is hard to find cause for the antipathetic response in Hoggart's extremely modest proposal. But the attempt to start the CCCS should be seen in the context of both the rigid disciplinary boundaries prevailing in British universities at the time and similar contemporary pressures for change such as the History Workshop at Ruskin College, Oxford [established partly as a consequence of Thompson's work (110)]. Such pressures represented a significant political, cultural, and intellectual challenge to academic comfort and departmental hegemony, and all were fiercely opposed.

Despite the antipathy it aroused, Hoggart's CCCS was more a harbinger of change than a particularly radical departure in itself. He planned to use "close reading" techniques of Leavisite literary study and to build connections from literary studies to other disciplines—including sociology, linguistics, history, and social anthropology—in order to explore what he loosely (but presciently) called "all sorts of interrelations." These unspecified connections Hall (57) later describes boldly as a "series of raids on other disciplinary terrain," but before guerrilla war the CCCS tried appeasement. This is clear from one of the Centre's first pieces of work, *Paper Voices* (113), an analysis of change in British newspapers between 1935 and 1965. For this, Hoggart hoped to recruit sociologists to pick up whatever fell outside close readings of the text. No sociologists applied. This fortunate refusal made it increasingly clear that the CCCS would have to construct cultural studies for itself rather than through alliances with other departments.

Paper Voices reveals a set of recognizable and recurrent CCCS preoccupations. First, it initiated, if only because their hand was forced, CCCS direct engagement in other disciplines. Second, like so much of the Centre's later work, it was based on a collaborative research project. This is not an incidental point. It is difficult to imagine how they could have undertaken such a broad agenda of class-cultural analysis if they had not been committed to working collectively. Third, like Hoggart's *Uses*, it introduces, somewhat unreflectively, the complex interrelations of "high culture" (the usual terrain of close reading) with forms of "mass art, pop art, folk art, urban art and the rest" (72:255). And consequently, fourth, it continued Hoggart's investigation of class-culture.

To make progress in what, despite its unquestionably insightful beginnings, was nevertheless a technically impoverished and dramatically undertheorized project, the CCCS clearly needed a more solid theoretical foundation. This was developed under the direction of Stuart Hall, who had been Hoggart's research fellow from the inception of the CCCS and who ran the Centre after Hoggart took a position at UNESCO in 1970. Under Hall's tenure the Centre profoundly altered its concept of cultural studies. The extent of the changes

can be read not only in the filial rejection of many of Hoggart's assumptions
(e.g. 114), but also between the lines of Willis's *Profane Culture* (138). This
began as one of a set of predominantly literary analyses of "popular song" (71;
see also 37, 66, 70, 83, 135), but after the fieldwork Willis conducted in the
late 1960s and the dissertation he produced in 1972, the book emerged [after
Learning to Labor (140)] as a close, quasi-ethnographic analysis of two subcultures. (For the Centre's ideas on ethnography and what Willis has called the
"ethnographic moment," see 49, 75, 139, 138.)

During this period of transition, Hall tried to maintain the strong collective
nature of the early Centre. But as its membership grew and as interests diversi-
fied, the Centre settled for a weaker collectivity, splitting into overlapping
working groups—including at various times a Subculture Group, Women's
Studies Group, Media Group, History Group, Education Group, Popular Memory Group, and Work Group. Collectivity was maintained, however, by joint
projects within groups and by a shared, Centre-wide theory seminar. Fragmentation helped turn the gentlemanly interdisciplinary consultations initiated by
Hoggart into Hall's more predatory "raids." The separate groups explored an
enormous intellectual territory. Ideas, discoveries, and developments were
rapidly summarized, circulated, and critiqued in collective summer sessions
and a bewildering array of "Working Papers," "Occasional Papers," and "Stencilled Occasional Papers." [1]

Cross-disciplinary raids on theories and theoreticians run significant risks.
Occasionally CCCS "borrowings" look a little naive; but in general the Centre
emerged from its raids unscathed. This is not a matter of pure chance. CCCS
scholars were far more conscious of the risks involved than are many "interdisciplinary" students of today. Not all theories are compatible, they knew;
and evidence cannot be extracted unquestioningly from conflicting theoretical
analyses. Thus the Work Group's admirable critique of community studies, for
example, aims also to model the theoretical work involved in "a principled
attempt to borrow data and evidence from differently constituted academic
regions" (116:1).

Struggles over compatibility bear directly on the interdisciplinary relationships required for an adequate account of the historical creation of persons in
practice. Enthusiasts for interdisciplinary crossfertilization should first heed
Comaroff's (29) admonition to be aware of precisely what kind of anthropology and what kind of history they bring together. CCCS work provides a
particularly good locus for theorizing the social creation of persons because of

---

[1]
We must note how extraordinarily productive the CCCS was at this time, producing over 10
years some 60 stencilled papers [for a list of these see 24, pp. 302–3], 10 editions of the journal
Working Papers in Cultural Studies, and much of the work that contributed to the major collected
books: *Resistance through Rituals* (58), *On Ideology* (10), *Women Take Issue* (15), *Policing the
Crisis* (60), *Working Class Culture* (24), *Culture, Media, Language* (11), *The Empire Strikes
Back* (14), *Unpopular Education* (12), and *Making Histories* (82).

the critical attention they paid to what sorts of work, from what sorts of background, they brought together.

In establishing compatibility, CCCS scholars were undoubtedly aided by the inherent theoretical reflexivity of Marxism, which formed the central theoretical pillar developed under Hall's tenure and whose contribution we now trace (see 50, 77, 78, 81, 89). The most influential strains of Marxism were undoubtedly what has come to be called British "Cultural Marxism"[2] and its distinctive but initially estranged continental cousins. Historically, British Marxism's cultural analyses had existed on an extremely narrow diet of base-superstructure. Indeed, it was to this as much as to the dominant liberal ideology that Williams and Thompson had responded.

As Williams noted in 1971 (132, see also 34, 54, 117), the British Cultural Marxists began their work in almost total isolation from similarly premised work being carried out elsewhere in Europe. The class-culture concept is central (though distinct) in each of the *Ur*-texts of cultural studies. Its increasingly rich problematization, however, awaited the arrival in Britain of continental Marxism. The continental array of analytical tools allowed CCCS scholars, in particular, to develop views of social totalities far more complex than large and converging "slabs of culture" and class (79). Fortunately, the Centre's development coincided with increasing availability of what would become seminal "New Left" texts, including English translations of Marx's early, humanist work (in particular the 1844 manuscripts) as well as his later, monumental *Grundrisse* (88; see 50). Simultaneously, *The New Left Review* began to make available key explorations of "Western Marxism" (including works by Lukàcs, Goldman, the Frankfurt School, Habermas, Marcuse, Althusser, and Sartre). And in 1971 selections from Gramsci's *Prison Notebooks* were first translated into English.

For a crucial period the most influential of the first wave of contemporary continental theorists in Britain was Althusser. His was the last and most elaborate of the Marxist "structuralisms" (53)—one that spread through British left-intellectual life as wildly as a new subcultural fashion. The history of Althusserian structuralism in Britain is more complex than Thompson's famous denunciation, "The poverty of theory," might suggest (120; see also 10, 36, 50, 77, 90, 123). As the History Group notes, "the choices exemplified by the opposition between Althusser and Thompson are too stark and unproductive" (82:8). Whatever the poverty of his theory and the debits of processes of abstraction, Althusser added or enriched concepts such as "ideology," "structure," "overdetermination," and "relative autonomy" that had been either

---

2

We should note that Hoggart was not a Marxist, either politically or theoretically, while for a long time Williams did not describe himself as a Marxist. Thompson, on the other hand, an unashamed former member of the Communist Party Historians (112), denounced the confusion of his work with cultural studies (123). Nonetheless, given Williams's theoretical orientation [from which *Marxism and Literature* (133) eventually emerged] and the importance of cultural institutions in Thompson's work (e.g. 119), the term seems apt.

wholly absent or significantly undertheorized in the British tradition—and all of which helped move work at the Centre decisively beyond what have been called "the merely empiricist or phenomenological methods" of Hoggart (34:34).

The Althusserian intervention was followed by the more enduring influence of Gramsci (53, 58, 87, 79). His work showed how static, indeed how ahistorical Althusser's work could be, for all its complexity. Gramsci's analysis offered instead a sense of dynamism, productive agency, and struggle, highlighting the continuous work, and particularly cultural work, necessary to establish, overthrow, and importantly even to maintain hegemony.

Under these various influences, the Centre developed its own accounts of culture and class. For Hoggart, culture primarily retained its historical sense of an essentially unitary literary-aesthetic category. Crudely, his mission was to expand its catchment to include the culture of the working classes and what Williams (130), with a similar viewpoint, termed the "ordinary." Thompson always had a more complex, less monolithic, and less literary-aesthetic view of culture, its creation, and its role in social formation. Over time, both Williams and scholars at the CCCS moved towards a more recognizably anthropological, though ultimately distinct, approach to culture. [In his stern review of *The Long Revolution,* Thompson (117) reprimands Williams for not consulting anthropologists, sociologists, and archaeologists.] [3] Thompson argued crucially that culture was not unitary, not "common," nor was it Williams's "whole way of life." At the very least, under capitalism it was "a whole way of struggle," a process, as we shall see with regard to the subcultures, of the production of meaning and interpretation that was inevitably implicated in the capitalist struggle over domination and subordination. Furthermore, Thompson insisted that in a materialist account, culture cannot subsume everything—there must be some residue, something other than or beyond culture. Drawing on these accounts, members of the CCCS sought, in Hall's words,

> a more historical definition of cultural practices: questioning the anthropological meaning [of culture] and interrogating its universality by means of the concepts of social formation, cultural power, domination and regulation, resistance and struggle ... [and questioning] the relation between cultural practices and other practices in definite social formations. Here we posed the issue of the relation of the "cultural" to what we may call ... the economic, political, and ideological instances ... to develop a materialist definition of culture (53:27).

If the increasingly complex account of culture developed at the Centre owed much to both the British and the European traditions, so too did the related concept of class. Here again, the intellectual tradition preceding CCCS work provides important context. Non-Marxist sociology tended to claim that,

---

3

Elsewhere, however, Thompson (118) is less friendly towards anthropologists. In fact, CCCS scholars rarely seem to have raided (or even consulted) social anthropology, except for an important and long-running engagement with the work of Lévi-Strauss (see 98, 71, 53).

as a consequence of embourgeoisement, the term lacked currency. Even some Marxist theorists (e.g. Marcuse and other progeny of the Frankfurt school) had, as Giddens (40) has argued, equally denied the salience of class analysis. More traditional Marxists still (e.g. 106) built solidly on the restrictive—almost elitist (42)—basis of "productive" labor alone. In contrast to such accounts the CCCS work in this area retains class as a central concept in the analysis of the production and reproduction of social formations but undermines assumptions about its monolithic unity by addressing its elaborate internal divisions, conflicts, and contradictions; its hegemonic alliances and tensions; and its cultural forms, cultural production, and cultural consumption.

Unfortunately, while it was developing and making available these theoretical insights the CCCS (as we discuss below) was simultaneously failing to encompass notions of gender adequately within the analysis of class-culture.[4] While feminism became a personal, political, and intellectual force during these formative years, the extent of the challenge to the personal, political, and intellectual practice of the CCCS members was only slowly absorbed. (For accounts of reactions see 15, 125.) Despite ample warnings (15, 94, 95, 107) ethnographic and theoretical opportunities to investigate gender relations were missed (65, 138, 140). It is only in retrospect that Hall can note with conviction how the "impact of the feminisms ... displaced forever any exclusive reference to class contradictions as the stable point of reference for cultural analysis" (53:38).

Yet other factors challenged the dominance of class analysis at the Centre. The "posts" (poststructuralism, postmodernism, postcapitalism, etc) in particular questioned its salience. Furthermore, the growing fashion for what falls under the general heading of "discourse theory" incited an atavistic yearning at the Centre for its literary-textual roots. In general, however, scholars at the CCCS managed to distinguish what was valuable from what was vapid in this diversion (e.g. 56:157). Where, for example, for many exponents of the posts the subject disappears altogether, for Hall at least, discourse theory valuably identified "empty spaces" in Marxist theory, but instead of losing either the subject or the theory entirely, this, "restore[d] the *decentered* subject, the contradictory subject" (54:34; emphasis in the original). As we have argued, the CCCS had earlier insisted on the significance of multiple social divisions, cultural regions, and their interrelations within a given class and in the fabric across classes. Attempts like Hall's to recognize a restored though decentered subject further contribute to establishing a base from which to theorize the complex character of situated subjectivity. In the end we suspect that the solidity of this base owes a great deal not only to the interrogation of Marxisms by feminism and the posts, but also, as a result of the CCCS's peculiar

---

4
    Clearly, a similar argument could be made about race. The CCCS did, however, confront relations of class and race directly (if, at first, inadequately; see 14, 41, 42, and the later race critiques, 8, 86, 105) in *Policing the Crisis*.

route (and roots), to the core materialist history and theory of the CCCS, which survived that interrogation (see, in particular, 23). The building of this core and its relation to theories of subjectivity and social practice are clearest in the CCCS subculture work.

The Making of the English Class Subcultures

It is often hard, occasionally impossible, and usually unimportant to determine where work from the Subculture Group ends and where that of other overlapping CCCS groups, such as the Work Group, the Women's Studies Group, or the Mugging Group, begins. Thus we do not observe the CCCS internal boundaries meticulously here. We see coherent groups of questions first about historical and cultural local collectivities that mediate between social forms and forces, and second about the processes through which persons are historically constituted. These arise in such central, subculture-related CCCS writings as *Resistance through Ritual* (58), *Policing the Crisis* (60), *Women Take Issue* (15), *Subculture: The Meaning of Style* (65), *Profane Culture* (138), and *Learning to Labour* (140).

At the heart of most of this work lies the apparently simple concept of youth. Contemporary sociology and popular wisdom had used youth and intergenerational tensions to explain social conflict (102). Social analysts of the 1950s, as the quotation from Hoggart's *Uses* above notes, claimed that class had disappeared as a result of embourgeoisement. (Ideological claims about the end of class provide eloquent testimony for its endurance.) Youth became a "powerful but concealed image of social change." So, as Hall et al later pointed out

> the restlessness, visibility, and anti-authority attitudes of youth came to stand, in the public consciousness, as a metaphor for social change; but even more, for all the things wrong with social change … . A genuine sense of cultural dislocation, then, came to focus not on structural causes but on symbolic expressions of social disorganization, e.g. the string of working-class youth sub-cultures (60:48).

The "generation gap" obfuscated larger issues. It was not, however, simply illusory. The prewar depression, the war, the postwar austerity, the rise of the welfare state, the expansion and rehabilitation of the public housing stock (and the ensuing dislocation of working-class communities), and the increasing consumer options and power of young adults marked a real and deeply felt intergenerational gap. Given the apparently contradictory affluence yet resentfulness of the young, there was much that needed explanation.

Mainstream sociology, particularly British sociology, and even Hoggart (70) to some extent in his disdainful analysis of the "jukebox boys," had little more to offer in explanation of the "sense of cultural dislocation" than thoroughly inadequate accounts of deviancy and delinquency. In contesting these explanations (e.g. 51), CCCS researchers first found insightful analyses in the work of symbolic interactionists and in particular in Becker's use of labelling theory. But while their initial encounter with this work is described as exhilarating, they came to see that "these accounts, whilst containing many important, new insights were not comprehensive enough" and to develop "a feeling, particularly, that deviant behavior had other origins besides public labelling" (58). "This sense of unease," they continue, "was given a concrete and empirical substance by our reading of Phil Cohen's seminal paper on youth subcultures and their genesis."

Cohen, himself not a member of the CCCS, insisted that debate had to focus on how "certain community structures generate or mediate cultural or subcultural diversity" (26:6). Thus in a way highly congenial to CCCS researchers he brought to the analysis questions of class (and class fractions), of culture (and subcultures), of community (and territory), and of intergenerational conflict, uniting them in a "dynamic historical framework" (58:35).

Cohen's intricate explanation of the emergence of British youth subcultures (such as the Teds, Mods, Rockers, Skinheads, Crombies, Rudies, and Rastas) is built around the dislocation of working-class communities in the 1950s as the needs of economic expansion disrupted and destroyed extended kinship relations and local communities. In these conditions, fundamental contradictions of production and consumption confronted one another in new forms across generations. The traditional ideology of production confronted both the new ideology of indulgent consumption and new, less skilled and less classically productive jobs. Identities constructed around old ideas of work and virtue confronted new identities built around leisure and indulgence. Furthermore, class solidarity confronted the increasingly varied trajectories of different class fractions. Youth subcultures, in Cohen's analysis, were "magically displaced," "restrictively coded" expressions of parent culture (class fraction) contradictions. The displacement results from the unsustainable conflict between generations in families whose former broad kin networks have been reduced to nuclear families. Cohen's work replaced arguments about "the disappearance of class as a whole" with "the far more complex and differentiated picture of how the different sectors and strata of class are driven into different courses and different options by their determining socio-economic circumstances" (58:31).

The essays in *Resistance through Ritual,* the CCCS's central collective work on subculture, explore and expand Cohen's argument. The book comprises a long and powerful introductory essay, a series of brief and unsatisfying "studies" of particular subcultures, and a group of essays that survey the limitations of their own analysis and investigation. (It thus neatly exemplifies the profound strengths and weaknesses of CCCS work in general: long and strong on theoretical analysis, short and inadequate on empirical study, and extraordinarily aware of its own shortcomings.) The CCCS subcultures researchers wanted to reconstruct subcultures in terms of their relation, first, to "parent" cultures, and through that, to the dominant culture, or better, to the struggle between dominant and subordinate cultures .... By trying to set up these intermediary levels in place of the immediate catch-all of 'youth culture,' we try to show how youth subcultures are related to class relations, to the division of labor and to the productive relations of the society, without destroying what is specific to their content and position (58: xx).

Subcultures are not themselves viewed as major structuring principles of the social formation. Rather, they are sites at which the major forces of society are experienced and lived. Subcultural practices are responses to the felt contradictions of working-class structures and processes. Subcultures are not reducible to structures or to individual lives, but mediate each in its relation to the other, and they do so in complex ways.

The earlier subculture work at the CCCS had, in the scholars' own words, simply engaged in "filling in" gaps within Cohen's framework (see 17–20, 52, 63, 64, 76, 108). *Resistance,* however, takes four significant steps beyond [see Clarke et al (25)]. First, their most significant addition to Cohen's work was the Gramscian concept of hegemony. *Resistance* reexamines Cohen's historical period in terms of the change from the hegemonic domination of the 1950s to the hegemonic struggle of the 1960s and 1970s, with successive but unsuccessful attempts to dissipate resistance by dividing the working classes against themselves (see also 60, 109).

Second, *Resistance* redefines Cohen's levels of analysis. Cohen suggests three levels: historical analysis "which isolates the specific problematic of a particular class fraction"; semiotic analysis "of the subsystems and the way they are articulated and the actual transformations which those subsystems undergo from one subcultural moment to another"; and phenomenological analysis "of the way the subculture is actually lived out by those who are the bearers and supports of the subculture" (26:23–24). The response in *Resistance* takes a significant step forward. It sets as a goal to "explain both social action and social reaction structurally and historically in a way that attempts to do justice to all the levels of analysis from the dynamics of 'face-to-face' interactions ... to the wider more mediated questions ... of the relations of these activities to shifts in class and power relations, consciousness, ideology, and hegemony." Accounts like Cohen's, *Resistance* argues, took too little notice of "the material, economic, and social conditions specific to the 'subcultural solution.'" Thus the three levels they suggest are the structural level, the "socially organized positions and experiences of the class in relation to the major institutions and structures"; the cultural level, the "range of socially organized and patterned responses to these basic material and social conditions"; and biographies, "the 'careers' of particular individuals through these structures and cultures ... the means by which individual identities and life-histories are constructed out of collective experiences." Here the "structural" rather than "historical" turns attention to economic forces and relations outside the community (Cohen's "community structures" seems to place it within); the cultural expands the semiotic, becoming more like praxis than merely expressive behavior; and the biographical is connected more closely to contributions from the other two levels than the merely phenomenological suggests. Thus, *Resistance* concludes, "we insist that biographies only make sense in terms of the structures and cultures through which the individual constructs himself or herself" (58:57).

Third, *Resistance* contests Cohen's notion that subculture activity is merely "magical displacement." It argues that "by concentrating on the imaginary, ideological relation in which subcultures stand to the life of a class, [Cohen's] analysis may now have gone too far in the direction of reading subcultures ideologically" (58:33) The CCCS analysis holds instead that subcultures are "not simply 'ideological' constructs. They too win space for the young … [whose] concerns, activities, relationships, materials become embodied in rituals of relationship and occasion and movement." These may have been only "*one* strategy for negotiating their collective existence." (And as they acknowledge, a strategy for one class stratum and one gender only.) Nevertheless, "their highly ritualised and stylised form suggests that they were also *attempts at a solution* to that larger problematic experience" (58:45–47; italics in the original; see also 140:138).

Fourth, *Resistance* simply ignores Cohen's psychological argument, moving the debate decisively away from psychoanalysis and situating it firmly, instead, at the level of social analysis. Unfortunately, although this should have allowed them to undertake a more adequate social and political analysis of the internal structuring of the family, in fact the work of most CCCS scholars does not progress much further in this direction than that of Cohen (124). Yet for an adequate account of the creation of subjectivities, the internal relations of both need examination. This failure to examine internal relations is more general in CCCS work (as we shall see), and so is the point: Where subjectivity is not conceived as constitutive of structure or culture, but is only construed as an additional—even residual—level of analysis, old theories of socialization are reproduced and agency and resistance are (only) responses to societal forms no matter what specific claims are advanced to the contrary.

Two important and diverging strands of cultural studies come out of the *Resistance* work and the opposition between Cohen's "semiotic" and the CCCS's own "cultural" studies. On the one hand there is the more semiotic analysis of cultural ritual, and on the other, more political analysis of the ramifications of cultural resistance. Hebdige's enormously influential book *Subculture: The Meaning of Style* (65) focuses mainly on the semiotic, reluctant in its own way, as McRobbie (92) points out, to insist on class resistance as a central category in subcultural analysis. Style, for Hebdige, "signals a Refusal," a "symbolic violation of the social order." Hebdige "would like to think that this Refusal is worth making," but he remains primarily agnostic. But even if the Refusal is politically inconsequential, he continues, style still "can make fascinating reading" (65, p.3). Thus Hebdige, in a manner that has in some spheres become the dominant mode in cultural studies, pursues semiotic "readings" of spectacular subcultural activities, to notice, as his later (67) title puts it, the way young people, under the glare of adult surveillance, are capable, through their highly visible participation in "revolting subcultures," of "Hiding in the Light." Hebdige's work, like Willis's (138, 142), is particularly valuable for its emphasis on how young people appropriate and transform standard cultural artefacts "obscurely re-present[ing] the very contradictions [the artefacts] are designed to conceal" (65:18). We suspect, however, that such "retrospective" readings (see 16) take subjects as products only. They fail to catch subjectivities in the process of development. Hall captures this distinction well (though in another context): "Instead of thinking of identity as an already accomplished fact, which the new cultural practices then represent, we should think ... of identity as 'production,' which is never complete, always in process" (55a:222).

The value of the other strand of cultural studies, which focused more on cultural resistance than on ritual, lies in its questioning of the unitary category of resistance, as it attempts to reveal the intersecting and conflicting trajectories of cultural responses. The work has been accused of being incurably romantic, seeing class rebellion where, presumably, it should only have seen style (32,38). In fact, this work, like Cohen's before it, takes a generally pessimistic view of the political potential of subcultural activity and refuses to valorize it.

In *Policing the Crisis* (60), an analysis of the ideological use of race and mugging in framing political consensus, valorization and demonization are opposite sides of the same debased political coin. Modifying both Stan Cohen's (27) notion of the ideological production of "folk devils" in times of "moral panic," and Becker's (3a) notion of labelling, *Policing* argues that mugging groups (and by inference, violent subcultures) are as much ideological products of the press as products of members' cultural production. *Policing* points to the role that the identification of a particular folk devil ("youth," "foreigners," "women taking your jobs") plays in distracting from structural explanations of social dislocation and discontent. As a result, some forms of resistance (e.g. mugging, but equally intersubculture violence) endlessly mediate domination and consequently dissipate politically efficacious resistance. The various groups and class fractions are thereby deflected from identifying causes and taking political action. Groups and factions identify each other as "folk devils" and direct their actions against each other instead of against the structural causes of their oppression, the working class fatally fragments. The "lads" direct their aggression against women. The black muggers direct theirs against the white proletariat, the Mods attack the Rockers, and so on. Territory—physical location—displaces social location. Working-class force is exerted horizontally, not vertically through the class system. Meanwhile the broad acceptance of the "folk devil" identification provides a pretext for state repression (22).

This cold-eyed analysis of subcultural "resistance," of its intraclass violence and ideological deflection, is explored with almost equal pessimism from *Resistance* (58) to *Profane Culture* (138) and summed up in *Policing* in an unsettling but "necessary warning" against "any strategy which is based simply on favouring current modes of resistance, in the hope that, in and of themselves, by natural evolution rather than by break and transformation, they could become spontaneously another thing" (60:397).

The analysis, in *Policing,* of racial conflicts generated by class cultural production pushes the cultural debate further towards questions of the relations among race and class, but the subculture-related work nonetheless tends to remain firmly on male terrain (94, 107). The continued refusal to include gender relations structurally in the debate ["the emphasis ... has remained consistently on male youth cultural forms," McRobbie noted in 1980 (92:37)], along with the evidently strained gender relations within the Centre as a whole, precipitated the formation of the Women's Studies Group in the mid-1970s (15). As McRobbie (92) points out, the male bias devalues "the real political commitment behind the work and ignor[es] its many theoretical achievements" (p. 40).

The Women's Studies Group's critique of the subculture work had two distinct phases. The first involved direct engagement with subculture theory as it applied (or failed to apply) to young women's experiences. McRobbie & Garber (94) begin this critique in *Resistance,* exploring the virtual silence about the nonmale half of "youth," gender relations, and sexism, indicating the invisibility of young women in the analysis of subcultures, and asking how the dimension of gender reshapes subcultural analysis as a whole. McRobbie & Garber (94) and McRobbie (91) argue that young women are central, but in subordinate activities, based in the family. They are thus excluded from the relatively more affluent, public, deviant, publicity-drawing, and leisure activities of young men, and thus from the highly selective attention of the public and the media. It is exactly this sort of selection that CCCS researchers should have challenged but did not. The Women's Studies Group concludes that the private leisure activities of young women offer "a different resistance, in a different cultural space." Young women's subculture is limited, private, and commercially structured, and is thus more to be consumed than produced. They play out their subcultural involvement in subordinated institutions (particularly the home) that prepare them for subordination to men in their adult lives. (For contrasting views see 44, 45, 47, 92, 107.)

The initial critique prescribes segregated work on the lives of men and women and ignores the mutually constitutive character of gender relations. Undoubtedly, this phase involved a certain amount of ahistorical essentializing and valorizing. And these practices inevitably put the Women's Studies Group at odds with the a-gendered historicizing going on elsewhere at the Centre (4).

But the valorizing of women merely echoed ways in which, for instance, Thompson had valorized 19th-century working-class vanguards in order to save them from "the condescension of history," or Hoggart had productively valorized the prewar working class in order to have it recognized; or, indeed, echoed the ways the subculture work, going on simultaneously in the Centre, valorized its subjects in order to rescue them from the condescension and even oblivion of the present. If the Women's Studies Group was to be accused of separatism, essentialism, or vanguardism then the force of those accusations had to be allowed to run throughout the Centre and its major influences.

Later critiques, reflecting advances in feminist theory in general, turned to rethinking the very theoretical paradigms they were using—paradigms that were inherently male centered. It is in this work that the feminists at the CCCS helped to alter the project of the Centre, playing a crucial role in dismantling the subculture work in favor of a focus on everyday activities (but see also 58:14–16) in a "desire to expose the ways in which commonplace relations, experiences and representations of youth are quite crucially related to questions of the masculine and the feminine" (96:ix). This move presaged a more general realization in the CCCS that analysis must include the less-spectacular members of the working classes—the readers of *Jackie* (91, 93), the boy scouts (48), the wearers of "ski-jumpers" (16), and less egregious interpreters of popular ideology (13).

Thus the Women's Studies Group called into question the elitist appeal of the subcultures and revealed with regard to gender, as *Policing* had with regard to race, the subcultures' limitations as sites for theorizing or producing political resistance. Together the *Policing* work and the feminist critiques led to a realization that there was no universal working-class experience, nor class-wide resistance, nor any universal sisterhood that transcends class, culture, and racial boundaries. The goal for the CCCS gradually became one of understanding how differences of race, class, and gender transform the ways each is experienced. Thus *Policing* indicates how race

> is the principal modality in which the black members of that class 'live' their experience—make sense of and thus come to a consciousness of their structured subordination. It is through the modality of race that blacks comprehend, handle, and then begin to resist the exploitation which is an objective feature of their class situation (60:346).

Furthermore, *Policing* pointed out the role schooling played as a "cultural battleground," positioning people, based on their class, race, and gender, in the social hierarchy. It was to school and to the transition from school to work that Willis turned in his examination (140; see also 136, 137; for a critique see 92, particularly p. 41) of the roles class and gender play in the comprehension or penetration of the objective features of the class situation of working-class "lads."

The Subject of Learning to Labor

The CCCS research on subcultures delineated in historical and theoretical terms multiple levels and relations of class-cultural struggles; it opened up possibilities for elaborating conceptions of cultural production; and yet it never quite succeeded in getting to the intersubjective production of subjectivity in subcultural practices. This issue remained consistently residual. Such an analytic impasse could not change so long as the CCCS viewed "biographies" as only responses to structural conditions, and not as also constitutive of them. Willis certainly recognized the importance (and difficulty) of multilevel analysis for investigating the subjective preparation of labor in social practice:

> I am indebted here to the work in Marxist psychoanalysis of the Tel Quel group, Barthes and Kristeva in Paris ... [but] in my view they move too quickly from structural considerations to the subject without attention to the mediations of the state, institutions, class cultures and human groups (140:140n).

He could well have had the subculture research in mind as an antidote, given its delineation in historical and structural terms of cascades of conflictual social relations between classes, within classes, between parent cultures and subcultures, between subcultures themselves, and even between local cohorts of a single subculture. Together these locate subcultural practices with respect to class and generational relations more broadly. They undoubtedly served to prevent anyone from moving "too quickly" to the subject. On the other hand, they may have prevented some CCCS researchers from moving there at all. Willis's *Learning to Labour,* an essay on the subjective preparation of labor power through a study of a group of "lads" in an English working-class high school, goes some way toward addressing this problem.

Like many of his CCCS colleagues, Willis is critical of mainstream sociology with its almost lifeless "notion of socialisation, and its implication of passive transmission." But Willis makes three distinctive moves that cumulatively take his work significantly beyond other CCCS work.[5]

First, Willis roots his analysis of changing subjectivity in lived, sensuous practice. Thus he conceives of cultural production as activity, as the lived edge of praxis (141). To this end, Willis insists that "the cultural level" is never epiphenomenal. The "lads" have real possibilities for partially understanding the real conditions of their existence. Their subjectivity is not an ideologically determined imaginary relation to the relations of production. He is directly critical of Althusserian structuralists on this point (140:175). For example:

> It is unfortunate that in their justified conviction to discredit the simple ideological optimism of humanism the structuralists should also scotch the human. The point is not to write off the subjective as any believable force for penetration and

---

5

    Parkhurst (104) points out that Willis also differs from most of his colleagues by attempting (in Gramscian terms) "organic" rather than "conjunctural" analysis. This, as Parkhurst goes on to argue, problematizes relations between Willis's work and the subculture work.

objective analysis, but to reject its over-centred, undialectical, intended nature as outlined in a certain kind of marxism (140:138)

Similarly, he argues that subjective formation is accomplished in practice. Deep underlying political-economic relations are experienced deeply by the "lads"; it is the living out of their lives that holds both penetrations and limitations for their understanding of them:

> Membership of the informal group sensitises the individual to the unseen informal dimension of life in general. Whole hinterlands open up of what lies behind the official definition of things. A kind of double capacity develops to register public descriptions and objectives on the one hand, and to look behind them, consider their implications, and work out what will actually happen, on the other. This interpretative ability is felt very often as a kind of maturation (140:25)

What the "lads" are coming to know and not know about their conditions of existence is a part of who they are becoming. The argument is thus basically social-ontological first and epistemological second (see 84, 85).

Furthermore, the practices and the processes of subjective preparation are profoundly social:

> Class identity is not truly reproduced until it has properly passed through the individual and the group, until it has been recreated in the context of what appears to be personal and collective volition. The point at which people live, not borrow, their class destiny is when what is given is re-formed, strengthened and applied to new purposes. Labour power is an important pivot of all this because it is the main mode of active connection with the world: the way *par excellence* of articulating the innermost self with external reality. It is in fact the dialectic of the self to the self through the concrete world (140:2).

In his second distinctive move, Willis's commitment to understanding social practice also commits him to some form of ethnographic study. It is important to note that while it is in many ways inextricable from ongoing CCCS work in the 1970s, in its pursuit of a quasi-ethnographic method, *Learning to Labour* is unfortunately not representative. There seems to be a tension, throughout the history of the Centre, between analysis of historical and ideological *representations* of social practice and more ethnographic approaches. After their anathematization of sociological methods, their critiques of "community studies" (116), and their rejection of phenomenological sociology, CCCS researchers sometimes seem to forget their earlier critiques of their own literary-critical heritage and resources, replacing Hoggartian "close readings" with Althusserian "symptomatic" ones. We see the CCCS's "ethnographic moment" as crucially important in moving beyond the text. Undoubtedly it helps to explain why *Learning to Labour* is one of the best-known pieces of CCCS work.

Third, Willis focuses on the social creation of subjectivity *across* a multiplicity of historically and practically interconnected settings. [He set out to investigate the transition from school to work (136, 137).] He explores the decentered character of the construction of subjectivities by tracing the inter-connectedness between sites of their construction (resonances among shop floor, neighborhood, and counterschool culture; their double articulation, as they make different meanings and connections in different sites) and, of course, in examining the unintended consequences of the production of working-class "lads" as subjects. His argument about the "lads'" deeply flawed understanding of the conditions of their existence hinges at every step on such cross-contextual articulations and resonances. Reworking Cohen's argument (26) that subcultures are only possible in a subordinated class, Willis argues that no counterculture is possible without these cross-contextual articulations framed outside the dominant class. Middle-class children may rebel, he argues, but they cannot form countercultures.

The "lads" achieve certain penetrations of their circumstances as they draw on shop floor, street, and pub (and working-class culture more generally) for the cultural resources they rework into their countercultural trajectories through the school. In the process, they come to see that the notion of mobility for the working class as a whole is absurd and consequently that the individualism underlying school urgings that the "lads" obtain school qualifications for (perhaps) upwardly mobile jobs is a trap. They reject this school ideology of individual advancement by creating a division between manual and mental labor (140:145–46):

> Although "the lads" stand together, they do so on this side of the line with individualism and mental activity on the other .... Individualism is penetrated by the counter-school culture but it actually [thereby] produces division (140:147).

And, most crucially, they come to see that all work is alike and that they are engaged in preparation for the giving of abstract labor power, and that in doing so they separate themselves as selves from the doing of work. These penetrations are, however, only partial, distorted and confusing (though not imaginary), and fundamentally related to the production of limitations. In the end it is the dialectical relations between penetrations and their limitations that bind the "lads" to their class location and working-class lives.

The primary divisions that generate limitations on their understanding are divisions between mental and manual labor, on the one hand, and divisions of gender, on the other. It is the fusion and cross-valorization of these two kinds of division that insures the reproduction of the "lads'" class location and futures; for if mental labor is clearly valued over manual labor, masculinity is valued over femininity; fused, mental labor is rejected as feminine, manual labor celebrated. The ability to endure the miseries of hard wage labor under capital is seen as the essence of masculinity: "[T]he machismo of manual work, the will to finish a job, the will to really work, is posited as a masculine logic and not as the logic of exploitation"(140:150–51). Conversely, the mental/manual division strengthens and helps to reproduce modern forms of sexual division and oppression. It is precisely because there are divisions at school and work which operate objectively to their disfavour but which can be understood and inverted in patriarchal terms that those gender terms must themselves be continuously reproduced and legitimated. If the currency of femininity were revalued then that of mental work would have to be too (140:149).

The "lads" come to penetrate the meaninglessness of abstract labor in part because the informal group offers an alternative basis for self valuation. They "subjectively appropriate" a way of giving labor based on the "withholding" of self and the "giving" of abstract labor power. Willis then argues that if such labor is meaningless, it must be the medium of expression of other parts of culture if it is to have value (pp. 102–4). If labor power were not divided from itself, cross-valorization of the mental/manual labor division with divisions of gender would not occur. It is the forms of labor under capitalism that are the condition for the valuation of labor in gendered terms:

> Where the principle of general abstract labor has emptied work of significance from the inside, a transformed patriarchy has filled it with significance from the outside. Discontent with work is hinged away from a political discontent and confused in its proper logic by a huge detour into the symbolic sexual realm (140:150).

Willis's argument so far is an exploration of subjectivities in the making.

There are, however, two significant places concerning the subjective preparation of the "lads" where his argument falls short. First, he establishes the informal group (the site of creative cultural penetrations) in universalistic, ahistorical terms that rely on a Freudian mythology and (equally mythical) social psychology to establish its irreducible character (see p. 140). Yet the informal group requires analysis in terms of the subjectivities that it comprises—the "lads'" entrances, exits, and ways of participating in the ongoing activities of the informal group are important facets of the constitution of both the group and members' subjectivities. He might have addressed these issues in Chapter 3, where he takes as a central question how working-class boys become "lads." But just at the point where he has dismissed both the "lads'" account of this process and the teachers', and said that there needs to be a better sociological explanation, he drops the question, or rather transforms it into a different one: How do the formal and informal cultures create each other, through processes of differentiation and integration. (See 35 and 74 for similar analyses that nonetheless take relations among peer-group members as a central aspect of their arguments.)

Second, in the specific context in which Willis establishes the key importance of sexism to the "lads," he does so simply by attribution: The "lads" are sexist, as are their parents, shop floor culture, and working-class culture in general. In contrast to the subtle way he derives the mental/manual division, his derivation of gender divisions falls back on an uncharacteristic appeal to unmediated processes of "passive transmission" such as those Willis himself

276 LAVE ET AL

criticizes. We cannot follow the processes of their subjective preparation as sexual and sexist subjects, given that Willis did not pursue the "lads'" relations with women; nor even their sexism in any great detail. Once the assumption is made, however, he goes on to wield it, in fusion with other limitations, in a complex account of its effects on labor and masculinity.

In sum, though, claims that the work is deeply sexist in nature have been common (e.g., 92, 94). Such accusations seem to us partly unfair, for the book does make an acute analysis of relations between gender inequalities and the workings of capital as these intersect in the subjective preparation of masculine labor. Nevertheless, certain complaints of sexism are appropriate, for Willis does not investigate the very relations of gender that he claims to be central to understanding the "lads'" lives (140:43) and that he later argues to be one of two central limitations on their understanding of the conditions of their existence.

Willis's argument about relations between capitalism and patriarchy are usefully provocative (see particularly 140:155). It is ironic then, that in focusing on the sexism of his practice, the feminist critique of his work overlooked this analytic argument concerning the fused cross-valorization of the mental/manual division with the division of gender. And Willis, in his turn, has not yet (142) taken up feminist analyses of the class- and race-differentiated character of gender relations, nor the rich studies in the 1980s of the constitution of gender, race, and class identities in the workplace produced or inspired by Centre researchers and their work (e.g. 41, 44–47, 105, 128, 129; see 111). However, along with other CCCS scholars he helps to broaden the scope of working-class cultural studies, opening them up to the inclusion of the everyday lives of women and men of various racial and ethnic identities. Together they throw into the confusion and turmoil of fused and cross-cutting subjectivities and identity politics the multi-level class-cultural relations that made it possible to specify the social locations of even informal groups of "lads." Willis sums up his views in *Learning to Labour* thus:

> As ethnography reminds us it is not a theoretical capacity but an empirical imperative that there must be a conjunction of systems. The secret of the continuation of both sets of divisions in labor and gender lies, at least partly, in their lived profane conjunction under the class system of capitalism, and not in their own pure logics (140:149).

That is, the divisions are given together in social practice. This argument has the familiarity of contemporary debates focused on the intersection of race, gender, and class—not, of course accidentally: We turned to the CCCS work on subculture in the first place because of a broad concern with the ramifications of social practice theory for the social creation of persons in practice, knowing, or at least suspecting, strong commonalities between the CCCS theoretical arena and that of social practice theory more generally.

CONCLUSION

The Centre's successes fall into four groups. First, CCCS researchers developed an internally differentiated and complex view of social formations, which they explore in terms of class locations, class cultures, and intra- as well as interclass struggles. Investigations of the production of interrelated subjectivities need to be able to locate varied settings, activities, identities, and relations of membership and nonmembership as part of such a differentiated social landscape. Second, the research connects the internal workings of institutions whose official mission is to regulate and channel subjective preparation for adult lives to other sites of production of subjectivities, official or not. Young people's actions in school, for instance, are only fully understood in terms of their understanding (some penetrating, some thoroughly limiting) of their possible trajectories into, through, and beyond that institution. Consequently, third, CCCS work makes notions of cultural transmission historically and theoretically complex. Culture is something to be produced, to be struggled over, not to be received sacramentally like ordination. Moreover, cultural forms are not like empty school hallways, to be occupied anew by each generation. They are dialectically generated in practice. The subculture work makes this argument as well as any we know. Fourth, as a result of the three previous strengths, and developing out of the Centre's theoretical roots in class-culture analysis, the CCCS work begins to pose fundamental questions about the intersection and irreducibility of class, race, and gender in the social-historical constitution of persons, and it suggests promising avenues of inquiry into how these are created and recreated.

Nevertheless, from our point of view, the work inevitably has its limitations. Specifically, as we have argued above, in addressing the relations of structure and subjectivity, it fails to encompass the latter adequately. Though from the start (e.g. 58, 76) the subculture researchers sought to capture the "authentic experience" of subculture members, Gary Clarke (16) could rightly protest eight years later that it still eluded them. [Experience and its authenticity, we must note, are highly loaded terms in these circles. Compare, for instance, Hoggart's (70) unexamined uses of experience in the *Uses*—and the unreflective role of autobiography in CCCS work.[6] Steedman (114a), for instance, challenges preoccupations with the "scholarship boy" (26, 58, 70, 134a) in these and related works.] Further, they rarely explored the interrelations of the "lads," or of subculture participants, or of family members. Perhaps they feared sinking simply to methodological individualism. This fear betrays a lack of conviction that subjectivity enters into the constitution of

---

[6] Thompson (123) acknowledges that he uses *experience* in (at least) two ways. Eagleton expresses almost comical outrage at Williams's rather innocent remarks about the way in which base-superstructure relations are felt: "[N]o one, surely, ever took the base-superstructure distinction to be a matter of *experience*" (34:22; italics in original).

class-culture and social order in a reciprocal relation. Had they grappled with this conviction, it might in fact have transformed their conception of structure as well.

As Johnson's (79) critique argues, *Resistance through Rituals* (58) and *Policing the Crisis* (60) examine the subcultures from the viewpoint of production, but neglect to look at them from the viewpoint of consumption (see also 50). The argument is complicated because, as Hebdige's (65, 67) and Willis's work (138, 140, 142) consistently suggests, consumption is itself a form of cultural production. What Johnson's insight makes clear is the CCCS work's preoccupation—perhaps because of the Centre's historic media interests (see, for instance, 7, 11, 10, 21, 51, 59, 68, 99, 100, 113)—with the production of subculture identities not in persons, but in the media, in texts. It is undoubtedly important to analyze cultural forms in terms of their ideological representation, but the work too readily assumes that researchers could impute the nature of consumption from that standpoint alone. In fact, they needed to look beyond this high level of inherently ideological representation to the level of cultural-production-in-consumption itself. In conclusion, we think the work of the CCCS, in both its successes and failings, provides rich ideas that should continue to infuse theoretically informed enthnographic projects investigating the historical creation of persons in practice.

ACKNOWLEDGMENTS

We are grateful to friends and colleagues who provided invaluable help during the two years we took to write this paper. In particular, we are indebted to Carol Stack, Martin Packer, Dorothy Holland, Shawn Parkhurst, Ole Dreier and Etienne Wenger, whose patient readings of earlier versions helped us to discover what we wanted to say. We are also grateful to fellow members of a seminar at UC Berkeley on the work of the CCCS, including Michael Black, Angela Gallegos, Lindy Hough, Jeremy Howell, Cathy Kessel, Gita Steiner-Khamsi, Joanne Lieberman, Jeff Maxson, Martin Packer, Shawn Parkhurst, Amy Scharf, Alissa Shethar, and Etienne Wenger. We are grateful for financial support kindly provided by Nelson Polsby, director of the Institute for Government Studies at UC Berkeley. We also wish to thank the Spencer Foundation for their generous support. Finally, we acknowledge our admiration for the members of the CCCS itself. Their collaborative work inspired our collaboration.

Literature Cited

1. Althusser, L. 1976. *Essays in Self-Criticism*. London: New Left Books
2. Amos, V., Parmar, P. 1981. Resistance and responses: the experiences of black girls in Britain. See Ref. 95, pp. 129–48
3. Aronowitz, S. 1981. Preface to the Morningside edition. In *Learning to Labour,* ed. P. Willis. New York: Columbia Univ. Press
3a. Becker, H. S. 1966. *Outsiders: Studies in the Sociology of Deviance.* New York: Free Press/Macmillan
4. Bland, L., Brundson, C., Hobson, D., Winship, J. 1978. Women "inside and outside"

the relations of production. See Ref. 15, pp. 35–78

5. Bloch, M. 1977. The past and the present in the present. *Man* 12(3):278–92

6. Bloch, M. 1989. "Anthropology since the sixties" seen from across the Atlantic. In *Author Meets Critics,* ed. S. Ortner, pp. 1–14. Ann Arbor, MI: CSST Work. Pap.

7. Butcher, H., et al. 1974. Images of women in the media. Cent. Contemp. Cult. Stud., Birmingham. SP no. 31, Women Ser.

8. Carby, H. 1979. Multicultural fictions. Cent. Contemp. Cult. Stud., Birmingham. SP no. 58

9. Carby, H. 1982. White woman listen! Black feminism and the boundaries of sisterhood. See Ref. 14, pp. 212–35

10. CCCS. 1978. *On Ideology.* London: Hutchinson

11. CCCS. 1980. *Culture, Media, Language: Working Papers in Cultural Studies, 1972–1979.* London: Hutchinson

12. CCCS (Education Group). 1981. *Unpopular Education: Schooling and Social Democracy in England since 1944.* London: Hutchinson

13. CCCS (Popular Memory Group). 1982. Popular memory: theory, politics, method. See Ref. 82, pp. 205–52

14. CCCS (Race and Politics Group). 1982. *The Empire Strikes Back: Race and Racism in 70s Britain.* London: Hutchinson

15. CCCS (Women's Studies Group). 1978. *Women Take Issue: Aspects of Women's Subordination.* London: Hutchinson

16. Clarke, G. 1982. Defending ski-jumpers: a critique of theories of youth sub-cultures. Cent. Contemp. Cult. Stud., Birmingham. SP no. 71

17. Clarke, J. 1973. The politics of popular culture: culture and sub-culture. Cent. Contemp. Cult. Stud., Birmingham. SP no. 14, Sub. Pop. Cult. Ser.

18. Clarke, J. 1973. Working class youth cultures. Cent. Contemp. Cult. Stud., Birmingham. SP no. 18. Sub- Pop. Cult. Ser.

19. Clarke, J. 1973. The skinheads and the study of youth culture. Cent. Contemp. Cult. Stud., Birmingham. SP no. 23. Sub-Pop. Cult. Ser.

20. Clarke, J. 1973. Football hooliganism and the skinheads. Cent. Contemp. Cult. Stud., Birmingham. SP no. 42. Sub- Pop. Cult. Ser.

21. Clarke, J. 1974. Framing the arts: the role of cultural institutions. Cent. Contemp. Cult. Stud., Birmingham. SP no. 32

22. Clarke, J. 1976. The three Rs, repression, rescue and rehabilitation: ideologies of control for working class youth. Cent. Contemp. Cult. Stud., Birmingham. SP no. 41. Sub- Pop. Cult. Ser.

23. Clarke, J. 1991. *New Times and Old Enemies.* London: Harper Collins

24. Clarke, J., Critcher, C., Johnson, R., eds. 1979. *Working Class Culture: Studies in History and Theory.* London: Hutchinson

25. Clarke, J., Hall, S., Jefferson, T., Roberts, B. 1975. Subcultures, cultures, and class. See Ref. 58, pp. 9–79

26. Cohen, P. 1972. Subcultural conflict and the working-class community. *Work. Pap. Cult. Stud.* 2(Spring): 5–51

27. Cohen, S. 1972. *Folk Devils and Moral Panics: The Creation of the Mods and the Rockers.* London: MacGibbon & Kee

28. Collier, J., Yanigasako, S. 1989. Theory in anthropology since feminist practice. See Ref. 6, pp. 15–31

29. Comaroff, J. L. 1982. Dialectical systems, history and anthropology: units of study and questions of theory. *J. Southern African Stud.* 8:143–72

30. Connell, R. W. 1983. *Which Way Is Up? Essays on Sex, Class and Culture.* Boston: Allen & Unwin

31. Corrigan, P., Frith, S. 1975. The politics of youth culture. See Ref. 58, pp. 231–39

32. Coward, R. 1977. Class, "culture," and the social formation. *Screen* 18(1):27–41

33. Davis, T., Durham, M., Hall, C., Langan, M., Sutton, D. 1982. 'The Public Face of Feminism': early twentieth-century writings on women's suffrage. See Ref. 82, pp. 205–52

34. Eagleton, T. 1976. Mutations of critical ideology. In *Criticism and Ideology: A Study in Marxist Literary Theory.* London: Verso

35. Eckert, P. 1989. *Jocks and Burnouts: Social Categories and Identity in the High School.* New York: Teachers' College Press

36. Eliot, G. 1987. *Althusser: The Detour of Theory.* London: Verso

37. Flood-Page, M., Fowler, P. 1974. Writing about rock. *Work. Pap. Cult. Stud.* 2(Spring): 139–52

38. Foley, D. E. 1989. Does the working class have a culture in the anthropological sense? *Cult. Anthropol.* 4(2):137–62

39. Gaventas, J. 1980. *Power and Powerlessness.* Chicago: Univ. Illinois Press

40. Giddens, A. 1980. *The Class Structure of Advanced Societies.* London: Hutchinson

41. Gilroy, P. 1982. Steppin' out of Babylon—race, class, and autonomy. See Ref. 14, pp. 276–314

42. Gilroy, P. 1991. *There Ain't No Black in the Union Jack.* Chicago: Univ. Chicago Press

43. Gramsci, A. 1971. *Selections from the Prison Notebooks,* ed. and transl. Q. Hoare, G. Nowell Smith. London: Lawrence & Wishart

44. Griffin, C. 1982. Cultures of femininity: romance revisited. Cent. Contemp. Cult. Stud., Birmingham. SP no. 69. Women Ser.

45. Griffin, C. 1982. The good the bad and the ugly: images of young women in the labour market. Cent. Contemp. Cult. Stud., Birmingham. SP no. 70. Women Ser.

46. Griffin, C. 1984. Young women and work: the transition from school to the labour market. Cent. Contemp. Cult. Stud., Birmingham. SP no. 76. Women Ser.

47. Griffin, C. 1985. *Typical Girls?: Young*

Women from School to the Job Market.
London: Routledge & Kegan Paul
48. Grimshaw, R. 1980. Green farm scout camp. See Ref. 11, pp. 105–15
49. Grimshaw, R., Hobson, D., Willis, P. 1980. Introduction to ethnography at the Centre. See Ref. 11, pp. 73–75
50. Hall, S. 1973. A "reading" of Marx's 1957 introduction to the Grundrisse. Cent. Contemp. Cult. Stud., Birmingham. SP no. 1
51. Hall, S. 1974. Deviancy, politics and the media. Cent. Contemp. Cult. Stud., Birmingham. SP no. 11. Media Ser.
52. Hall, S. 1974. The hippies: an American moment. Cent. Contemp. Cult. Stud., Birmingham. SP no. 16. Sub- Pop. Cult. Ser.
53. Hall, S. 1980. Cultural studies and the centre: some problematics and problems. See Ref. 11, pp. 15–47
54. Hall, S. 1981. Cultural studies: two paradigms. In *Culture, Ideology, and Social Process,* ed. T. Bennett, pp. 19–37. London: Batsford with the Open Univ.
55. Hall, S. 1984. The Williams' interviews. *Screen Educ.* 34(Spring):94–104
55a. Hall, S. 1990. Cultural identity and diaspora. In *Identity, Community, Culture, Difference,* ed. J. Rutherford, pp. 222–37. London: Lawrence & Wishart
56. Hall, S., Jacques, M. 1988. *The Hard Road to Renewal: Thatcherism and the Crisis of the Left.* London: Lawrence & Wishart
57. Hall, S. 1990. The emergence of cultural studies and the crisis of the humanities. *October* 53(Summer):11–23
58. Hall, S., Jefferson, T., eds. 1975. *Resistance through Rituals.* London: Hutchinson
59. Hall, S., Clarke, J., Critcher, C., Jefferson, T., Roberts, B. 1975. Newsmaking and crime. Cent. Contemp. Cult. Stud., Birmingham. SP no. 37. Sub- Pop. Cult. Ser.
60. Hall, S., Critcher, C., Jefferson, T., Clarke, J., Roberts, B., 1978. *Policing the Crisis: Mugging, The State, and Law and Order.* New York: Holmes & Meier
61. Hall, S., Whannel, P. 1964. *The Popular Arts: A Critical Guide to the Mass Media.* London: Hutchinson
62. Hargreaves, A. 1982. Resistance and relative autonomy theories: problems of distortion and incoherence in recent Marxist analyses of education. *Brit. J. Sociol. Educ.* 3(2):
63. Hebdige, D. 1973. Reggae, rastas, and rudies. Cent. Contemp. Cult. Stud., Birmingham. SP no. 25. Sub- Pop. Cult. Ser.
64. Hebdige, D. 1974. The style of the Mods. Cent. Contemp. Cult. Stud., Birmingham. SP no. 20. Sub- Pop. Cult. Ser.
65. Hebdige, D. 1979. *Subculture: The Meaning of Style.* London: Routledge, Kegan Paul
66. Hebdige, D. 1987. *Cut 'n' Mix: Culture, Identity, and Caribbean Music.* London: Methuen
67. Hebdige, D. 1988. *Hiding in the Light.* London: Comedia/Routledge, Kegan Paul

68. Heck, M. C. 1974. The ideological dimension of media messages. Cent. Contemp. Cult. Stud., Birmingham. SP no. 10. Media Ser.
69. Hobsbawm, E. 1981. Primitive rebels: Studies in archaic forms of social movement in the 19th and 20th centuries. New York: W. W. Norton
70. Hoggart, R. 1958. *Uses of Literacy: Aspects of Working-Class Life with Special Reference to Publications and Entertainments.* Harmondsworth, Middlesex: Penguin. [First published 1957.]
71. Hoggart, R. 1969. Contemporary cultural studies: an approach to the study of literature and society. Occas. Pap. Cent. Contemp. Cult. Stud., Birmingham
72. Hoggart, R. 1970. Schools of English and Contemporary Society. In *Speaking to Each Other,* 2:246–59. London: Chatto & Windus
73. Hoggart, R. 1990. *A Sort of Clowning: Life and Times.* London: Chatto & Windus
74. Holland, D., Eisenhart, M. 1990. *Educated in Romance: Women, Achievement, and College Culture.* Chicago: Univ. Chicago Press
75. Hollands, R. G. 1985. Working for the best ethnography. Cent. Contemp. Cult. Stud., Birmingham. SP no. 79. Theor. Meth. Ser.
76. Jefferson, T. 1973. The Teds: a political resurrection. Cent. Contemp. Cult. Stud., Birmingham. SP no. 22. Sub- Pop. Cult. Ser.
77. Johnson, R. 1979. Three problematics: elements of a theory of working class culture. In *Working Class Culture,* ed. J. Clarke et al, pp. 201–38. New York: St. Martin's Press
78. Johnson, R. 1982. Reading for the best Marx: history-writing and historical abstraction. See Ref. 82, pp. 153–210
79. Johnson, R. 1983. What is cultural studies anyway? Cent. Contemp. Cult. Stud., Birmingham. SP no. 74
80. Johnson, R. 1986. The story so far: and further transformations. In *Introduction to Contemporary Cultural Studies,* ed. D. Punter, pp. 277–313. London: Longman
81. Johnson, R., McLennan, G., Schwarz, B. 1977. Economy, culture and concept: three approaches to Marxist history. Cent. Contemp. Cult. Stud., Birmingham. SP no. 50. Hist. Ser.
82. Johnson, R., McLennan, G., Schwarz, B., Sutton, B. 1982. *Making Histories: Studies in History Writing and Politics.* London: Hutchinson
83. Jones, B. 1974. A bibliography of rock. *Work. Pap. Cult. Stud.* 2(Spring):129–38
84. Lave, J., Packer, M. 1991. Toward a social ontology of learning. Presented at Wenner-Gren Conf. Rethinking Linguistic Relativity, April, 1991
85. Lave, J., Wenger, E. 1991. *Situated Learn-*

ing: Legitimate Peripheral Participation.
New York: Cambridge Univ. Press
86. Lawrence, E. 1981. Common sense, racism, and the sociology of race relations. Cent. Contemp. Cult. Stud., Birmingham. SP no. 66
87. Lumley, B. 1977. Gramsci's writings on the state and hegemony, 1916–1935: A critical analysis. Cent. Contemp. Cult. Stud., Birmingham
88. Marx, K. 1973. *Grundrisse,* transl. M. Niclaus. Harmondsworth, Middlesex: Penguin
89. McLennan, G. 1976. "Ideology" and "consciousness": some problems in Marxist historiography. Cent. Contemp. Cult. Stud., Birmingham. SP no. 45. History Ser.
90. McLennan, G. 1982. E. P. Thompson and the discipline of historical context. See Ref. 82, pp. 96–130
91. McRobbie, A. 1978. Jackie: an ideology of adolescent femininity. Cent. Contemp. Cult. Stud., Birmingham. SP no. 53
92. McRobbie, A. 1980. Settling accounts with subcultures: a feminist critique. *Screen* 34(Spring):37–49
93. McRobbie, A. 1991. *Jackie* and *Just Seventeen:* girls' comics and magazines in the 1980s. In *Feminism and Youth Culture,* ed. A. McRobbie, pp. 138–88. London: Unwin Hyman
94. McRobbie, A., Garber, J. 1975. Girls and subcultures: an exploration. See Ref. 58, pp. 209–23
95. McRobbie, A., McCabe, T. eds. 1981. *Feminism for Girls: An Adventure Story.* London: Routledge & Kegan Paul
96. Deleted in proof
97. Millum, T. 1975. *Images of Women: Advertising in Women's Magazine's.* London: Chatto & Windus
98. Moore, T. 1968. Lévi-Strauss and the cultural sciences. Occas. Pap. Cent. Contemp. Cult. Stud., Birmingham
99. Morin, E. 1968. New trends in the study of mass communications. Occas. Pap. Cent. Contemp. Cult. Stud., Birmingham,
100. Morley, D. 1973. Industrial conflict and the mass media. Cent. Contemp. Cult. Stud., Birmingham. SP no. 8. Media Ser.
101. Morley, D. 1974. Reconceptualising the media audience: towards an ethnography of audiences. Cent. Contemp. Cult. Stud., Birmingham. SP no. 9. Media Ser.
102. Murdock, G., McCron, R. 1975. Consciousness of class and consciousness of generation. See Ref. 58, pp. 192–208
103. Ortner, S. 1984. Theory in anthropology since the sixties. *Comp. Stud. Soc. Hist.* 26:126–66
104. Parkhurst, S. 1991. *Working through culture historically: a critique of* Learning to Labour *and* Subculture. M. A. thesis, Univ. Calif., Berkeley, Sch. Educ.
105. Parmar, P. 1982. Gender, race, and class: Asian women in resistance. See Ref. 14, pp. 236–75
106. Poulantzas, N. 1974. *Classes in Contemporary Society.* London: New Left Books
107. Powell, R., Clarke, J. 1975. A note on marginality. See Ref. 58, pp. 223–31
108. Roberts, B. 1973. Parent and youth cultures: alternative views. Cent. Contemp. Cult. Stud., Birmingham. SP no. 28. Sub-Pop. Cult. Ser.
109. Robins, D., Cohen, P. 1978. *Knuckle Sandwich: Growing Up in the Working-Class City.* Harmondsworth, Middlesex: Penguin
110. Samuels, R., ed. 1981. *People's History and Socialist Theory.* London: Routledge & Kegan Paul
111. Scharf, A. 1991. *Roots of reproduction, seeds of resistance.* M. A. thesis, Univ. Calif., Berkeley, Sch. Educ.
112. Schwartz, B. 1982. "The People" in history: the Communist Party Historians' Group, 1946–56. See Ref. 82, pp. 44–95
113. Smith, A., Immirzi, E., Blackwell, T. 1975. *Paper Voices. The Popular Press and Social Change, 1935–1965,* intro. Stuart Hall. Totowa, NJ: Rowman and Littlefield
114. Sparks, G. 1974. The abuses of literacy. *Work. Pap. Cult. Stud.* 6:96–124
114a. Steedman, C. 1985. *Landscape for a Good Woman.* London: Virago
115. Taylor, P. 1976. Women domestic servants, 1919–1939: a study of a hidden army, illustrated by servants' own recollected experiences. Cent. Contemp. Cult. Stud., Birmingham. SP no. 40. History Ser.
116. Taylor, P., Brookes, E., Finn, D., Tolson, A., Willis, P., Powell, R. 1976. A critique of "community studies" and its relation to social thought. Cent. Contemp. Cult. Stud., Birmingham. SP no. 40. History Ser.
117. Thompson, E. P. 1961. [Review of] *The Long Revolution. New Left Rev.* 9:24–33; 10:34–39
118. Thompson, E. P. 1971. Anthropology and the discipline of historical context. *Midland Hist.* 1(3):41–55
119. Thompson, E. P. 1975. *Whigs and Hunters: The Origin of the Black Act.* New York: Random House
120. Thompson, E. P. 1978. *The Poverty of Theory & Other Essays.* New York: Monthly Review Press
121. Thompson, E. P. 1980. *The Making of the English Working Class.* Harmondsworth, Middlesex: Penguin. [First published 1963]
122. Thompson, E. P. 1980. *Writings by Candlelight.* London: Merlin Press
123. Thompson, E. P. 1981. The politics of theory. In *People's History and Socialist Theory,* ed. R. Samuels, pp 396–408. London: Routledge & Kegan Paul
124. Tolson, A. 1975. The family in a "permissive society." Cent. Contemp. Cult. Stud., Birmingham. SP no. 30. Women Ser.
125. Tolson, A. 1977. *The Limits of Masculinity.* London: Tavistock
126. Deleted in proof
127. Deleted in proof

128. Westwood, S. 1984. *All Day, Every Day: Factory and Family in the Making of Women's Lives.* Chicago: Univ. Illinois Press
129. Westwood, S., Bachu, P., eds. 1988. *Enterprising Women: Ethnicity, Economy, and Gender Relations.* London: Routledge & Kegan Paul
130. Williams, R. 1989. Culture is ordinary. In *Resources of Hope,* ed. R. Gable, pp. 3–18 London: Verso. [First published 1958.]
131. Williams, R. 1962. *Long Revolution: An Analysis of the Democratic, Industrial, and Cultural Changes Transforming our Society.* New York: Columbia Univ. Press. [First published, 1961]
132. Williams, R. 1980. Literature and sociology. In *Problems* and *Materialism and Culture,* pp. 11–30. London: Verso [First published 1971]
133. Williams, R. 1977. *Marxism and Literature.* Oxford: Oxford Univ. Press
134. Williams, R. 1983. *Culture and Society 1780–1950.* New York: Columbia Univ. Press. [First published 1958]
134a. Williams, R. 1988. *Second Generation.* London: Hogarth
135. Willis, P. E. 1974. Symbolism and practice: a theory for the social meaning of pop music. Cent. Contemp. Cult. Stud., Birmingham. SP no. 13. Sub- Pop. Cult. Ser.
136. Willis, P. E. 1975. How working class kids get working class jobs. Cent. Contemp. Cult. Stud., Birmingham. SP no. 43. Work Ser.
137. Willis, P. E. 1975. Human experience and material production: the culture of the shop floor. Cent. Contemp. Cult. Stud., Birmingham. SP no. 33. Work Ser.
138. Willis, P. E. 1978. *Profane Culture.* London: Routledge & Kegan Paul
139. Willis, P. E. 1980. Notes on method. See Ref. 11, pp. 196–204
140. Willis, P. E. 1981. *Learning to Labour: How Working Class Kids Get Working Class Jobs.* Morningside ed. NY: Columbia Univ. Press. [First published 1977]
141. Willis, P. E. 1981. Cultural production is different from cultural reproduction is different from social reproduction is different from reproduction. *Interchange* 12(2–3):48–68
142. Willis, P. E. 1990. *Common Culture.* London: Open Univ. Press
143. Winship, J. 1981. Woman becomes an "individual": femininity and consumption in women's magazines 1954–69. Cent. Contemp. Cult. Stud., Birmingham. SP no. 65. Women Ser.

Annu. Rev. Anthropol. 1992. 21:283–305

ADVANCES IN ANTHROPOLOGICAL MORPHOMETRICS

Joan T. Richtsmeier

Department of Cell Biology and Anatomy, The Johns Hopkins University School of Medicine, Baltimore, Maryland 21205

James M. Cheverud

Department of Anatomy and Neurobiology, Washington University School of Medicine, St. Louis, Missouri 63110

Subhash Lele

Department of Biostatistics, The Johns Hopkins University School of Hygiene and Public Health, Baltimore, Maryland 21205

KEYWORDS: size and shape, landmark data, coordinate based, coordinate free, hypothetical geometries

INTRODUCTION

The past two decades have witnessed explosive development of morphometric theory and method and novel application of these techniques to biological data sets. Since a thorough review of developments in morphometric methods has recently been provided by Rohlf (5), we limit the review portion of this paper to a brief evaluation of methods we find important to anthropological morphometrics. Our choice of focus is prejudiced by our research orientations and experience, highlighting methods for analyzing three-dimensional landmark

283

0084-6570/92/1015-0283$02.00

coordinate data. In the second half of the paper, we emphasize future developments in the field, outlining exciting goals in anthropological morphometrics
and current approaches to their fulfillment.

MORPHOMETRICS: SOME PRELIMINARIES

We find Bookstein's (11) definition of morphometrics fitting: "morphometrics
is the empirical fusion of geometry with biology." A true merger of geometry
and biology requires that the biological form can be unambiguously reconstructed from the data collected to represent that form. Traditional multivariate
approaches to morphometrics rarely analyze a set of linear distances that
enables reconstruction of the form. Instead, linear distances are chosen that are
thought a priori to best distinguish between forms (see 64 for a broad survey of
multivariate approaches to the analysis of linear distance data). Such a decision usually results in a series of traits that describe particular features but do
not define the geometry of form.

Landmark coordinate data provide a repeatable, geometric representation of
homologous structures. Landmark data have limitations, however, in that curvature and other features of surfaces between landmarks are lost in analysis *no
matter what morphometric method is used*. Boundary-outline data summarize
surface features but impose other limitations (see 57, 58, 70, and 86:Pt. II,
Sect. B for morphometric approaches that use boundary-outline data). That
geometry is preserved only up to a point when landmark data are used must be
recognized and accepted (see 73).

THE STATISTICS OF MORPHOMETRICS

In traditional morphometrics, a set of metrics, usually linear distances, describe features of the object. Standard statistical models used in the analysis of
such data typically assume normal or gamma distributions (74). These distributions have proved useful in the analysis of traditional anthropological measurements.

A natural choice of models for analysis of coordinate data is the class of
distributions for matrix-valued random variables. The models chosen should
be capable of representing the effect of translation (moving the object within a
given coordinate system) and rotation (spinning the object on an axis) on form.
A perturbation model for two-dimensional landmark data was first proposed
by Bookstein (13). This model assumes that each landmark is moved independently in the X and Y directions around the mean location of the landmark
according to a bivariate normal distribution. Goodall (32) provided a generalized version of this model in three dimensions that allows for correlations
among landmarks.

When the forms considered are composed of K landmarks and D dimensions, the mean form, **M**, is a K × D matrix representing the landmark coordi-

nates of the mean form in some arbitrary coordinate system. To statistically study $\mathbf{M}$, each of the mean landmark coordinates is perturbed according to a Gaussian distribution designated by $\mathbf{E}$, which allows for correlations among the landmarks. This allowance for correlation is important statistically but also biologically because within any form, the location of a single landmark is likely related to and/or determined by the location of other biological structures. We assume that $\mathbf{E}_i$ is a $K \times D$ matrix randomly generated from a matrix normal distribution with mean 0 and variance covariance matrix Σ (with dimension $KD \times KD$) that characterizes variability among coordinate values along each axis for each landmark (see 4 for details on matrix valued random variables). These assumptions imply certain properties about the way landmarks are related to one another within a form. If our sample consisted of forms corresponding with predictable perturbations of $\mathbf{M}$, the statistics of landmark data would be straightforward. Arnold (4) offers a statistical model for landmark data with normal perturbations at each landmark. However, we observe data sets that are arbitrarily and unpredictably rotated and translated versions of $\mathbf{M}$. The specific rotation and translation of each form with relation to the mean form cannot be known by the observer; they must be estimated.

For the statistically oriented morphometrician the important problem is the estimation of the mean form $\mathbf{M}$ and the variance covariance matrices among landmarks (Σ_K) and among dimensions (Σ_D). Unfortunately, the total number of parameters that need to be estimated greatly exceeds the number of observations (50), making estimation difficult. This dilemma, which can result in variance parameters that cannot be estimated, was first considered by Neyman & Scott (68).

Bookstein (14), Bookstein & Sampson (18), and Goodall (32) suggest estimation of the parameters $\mathbf{M}$, Σ_K, and Σ_D using superimposition methods. Although using superimposition to estimate the mean and variance parameters is practical, the estimators possess certain statistically undesirable and biologically fictitious properties (49, 50, 52). Estimators obtained through superimposition methods are inconsistent, meaning that even with large samples the mean form, $\mathbf{M}$, cannot be estimated correctly. Lele (49) suggests an alternative, consistent estimator based on Euclidean distance matrices (see following section) that estimates $\mathbf{M}$, correctly when sample size is large. Properties of this estimator for small samples require further investigation. The biological advantage of Lele's (50) estimator lies in its ability to handle missing data and partial specimens effectively.

In summary, estimation of $\mathbf{M}$, Σ_K, and Σ_D remains statistically inadequate. However, for practical purposes, the various estimators available may be equally acceptable. Bookstein's (14) and Lele's (49) estimators are computationally simpler than that offered by Goodall (32), but we believe that the Procrustes estimator (32, 75, 87) is conceivably more robust and better behaved. A large simulation study is needed to further define properties of the various estimators of $\mathbf{M}$, Σ_K, and Σ_D.

SOME CURRENT MORPHOMETRIC TECHNIQUES

Several different morphometric algorithms are available for analyzing landmark data. All of these methods utilize the same raw data: coordinate values of landmarks in two or three dimensions. This information is reorganized in different ways by different algorithms; in some methods ancillary input, in the form of a smoothing function, a homology function, or a loss function (minimization criterion), is part of the analytical procedure. Different aspects of the morphological contrasts are consequently highlighted by different methods. Use of alternate methods on the same data affects biological interpretation. We believe that the scientific question posed determines data requirements and narrows the choice of appropriate analytical techniques. However the specific choice of analytical method should not be based on comparison of the results obtained by various related techniques.

Two general classes of morphometric methods can be used to analyze landmark coordinate data: *coordinate-based methods* and *coordinate-free methods*. In coordinate-based methods, the choice of coordinate system is arbitrary: results can be rotated to any coordinate system without change in or loss of information, and a coordinate system is a necessary part of the analytical machinery. Coordinate-based methods measure form difference as a deformation from a reference to a target form, or as the fit resulting from the superimposition of two forms. Coordinate-free methods analyze form difference without reference to a coordinate system. The last method we discuss, Euclidean distance matrix analysis, is to our knowledge the only 3D morphometric method that is coordinate free. The difference between coordinate-based and coordinate-free methods is subtle. The distinction becomes apparent in the analysis of specific problems, especially in the comparison of comparisons—e.g. comparisons of patterns of form-change through time.

Finite-Element Scaling Analysis

Finite-element scaling analysis (FESA) is a form of finite-element analysis widely used in engineering to model strain in materials under loads (60, 92). FESA is a method of comparisons, so at least two forms are required: a reference form representing the initial configuration of a set of landmarks on an object, and a target form representing the final configuration of the same set of landmarks on another object. Biological landmarks are connected to make a series of discrete finite elements that unite to model the forms being considered. In three dimensions, elements can be configured as tetrahedrons (4 landmarks), wedges (6 landmarks), or hexahedrons (8 landmarks). These elements provide a model of the forms under study (Figure 1), and the analysis proceeds by measuring the amount of morphometric strain required to produce

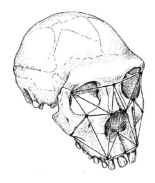
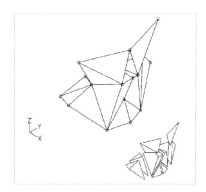

Figure 1   Oblique view of a finite-element model of the facial skeleton of KNM-WT 15000 based on the location of 18 landmarks superimposed over the *Homo erectus* fossil. Also shown is an exploded version of the finite-element design to aid visualization of the three-dimensional nature of the finite-element model. The computer generated oblique view (*right*) distorts objects so that landmarks and/or surfaces that actually exist behind other surfaces are visible. The view of the finite-element model superimposed over KNM-WT 15000 is more realistic. This figure is reproduced following Ref. 80.

the target form from the reference form. Morphometric strain is simply the ratio of the difference between homologous linear distances in the two forms under study divided by that linear distance in the reference form (60). FESA maps the deformation of the reference into the target form. This is done exactly for landmark coordinates because their reference and target positions are known. Mapping of points internal to the element is accomplished by the homology function (see 21). Homology functions can theoretically be designed to model material properties or other relevant parameters but are usually chosen for mathematical convenience. This is not necessarily a negative aspect of the method, but a single choice may not be equally appropriate for all data sets. Lewis et al (60) successfully tested the precision of the homology function in FESA using landmarks internal to the elements that were not used as nodes (see also 61). However, checking the accuracy of the interpolation is not a standard part of most FESA analyses.

Numerical results of a three-dimensional finite-element scaling analysis are produced for each landmark and consists of a 3×3 symmetric matrix referred to as the form tensor (21). The three diagonal elements of the form tensor measure the strain at each landmark along the X, Y, and Z axes of the arbitrary coordinate system in which the objects are described. The three off-diagonal elements measure the change in angle required for the observed transformation between the X and Y, X and Z, and Y and Z axes. This numerical description can be rotated to any coordinate system without changing the result; in this sense it is invariant relative to the coordinate system used but is coordinate based.

The form tensor is the numerical description of an ellipsoid, mathematically similar to a variance-covariance or correlation matrix in multivariate statistical analysis (see 60). The form tensor identifies orthogonal directions (eigenvectors) of maximum, intermediate, and minimum difference between the forms at each landmark. These principal directions of strain designate the axes of the ellipsoid (Figure 2). A value (eigenvalue) associated with each direction specifies the length of each axis and thereby defines local magnitudes of morphological differences along the principal directions.

Three basic types of information concerning localized morphological differences can be extracted from the form tensor. The size difference, s, measures the increase or decrease in volume required at each landmark to produce the target from the reference form. It is calculated as the average of the tensor's eigenvalues, after transformation to a linear scale. Shape difference is composed of two parts. The *magnitude* of shape difference, t, measures the extent of variation in size increase across the anatomical directions (how much the ellipsoid deviates from a sphere) as the standard deviation of the linearly transformed eigenvalues. The *pattern* of shape difference is given by the directions of change of the form tensor.

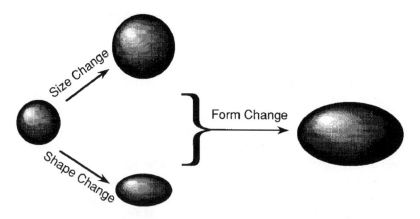

Figure 2   Geometric representation of change in form as calculated by finite-element scaling analysis. The sphere at the left represents the area surrounding a landmark in the reference form. Local differences in form between reference and target configurations are presented as changing dimensions of this sphere along three principal directions. When the sphere changes in equal magnitude along all directions, size change has occurred local to the landmark. When the sphere undergoes differential change in magnitude along various axes and becomes an ellipsoid but maintains the same volume, shape change has occurred. When differential change in magnitude occurs along various axes and there is a difference in volume between the sphere surrounding the landmark in the reference form and the ellipsoid surrounding the landmark in the target form, form change has occurred.

FESA has been used in several kinds of contrasts to shed new light on morphological differences among groups including within-species allometry and morphological integration (20, 22, 48), between-species similarity (47), craniofacial growth (12, 21, 26, 38, 43, 62, 66, 67, 77), craniofacial abnormality (15, 27, 75, 76, 82), and artificial cranial modification (24, 44, 95). The numerical and especially the graphical results available through the program FIESCA (65) provide an interpretable description of pairwise comparisons of individual or mean forms. FESA's ability to localize morphological differences between forms to the regions surrounding specific anatomical landmarks is a unique and valuable asset of this approach. Ability to identify the specific anatomical dimensions along which two forms differ most or least is another feature unique to FESA of obvious benefit to the researcher.

Problems associated with this method relate to the statistical analysis of FESA results. In comparing two populations, the nonparametric bootstrap procedures of Lele & Richtsmeier (53) have been used (24). Statistical testing of difference between samples of forms is important because the particular pattern of shape difference between population means (as described by the eigenvalues and eigenvectors of the form tensor) are not necessarily meaningful unless the amount of local shape difference (t) between groups is statistically significant (13). If local shape difference is not statistically significant, change along a particular anatomical dimension cannot be considered as contributing disproportionately to the difference between forms at a given landmark.

Statistical studies of within-group variation or differences among multiple groups using FESA are also problematic (20, 22, 23, 48). In this case, an arbitrary single standard reference form must be chosen, typically the mean of a population. However, the optimal anatomical dimensions for distinguishing this reference form from each individual target form is different for each individual and at each landmark. Thus, a compromise is necessary: choosing anatomical dimensions that are "optimal" for the population as a whole, though suboptimal for each individual. The best measurements for contrasting Group A with Group B may not be useful in describing the differences between Groups A and C, for example. The choice of anatomical dimensions becomes increasingly arbitrary as the number of individuals or groups increases. Thus, one of the major intuitive advantages of FESA, the description of the anatomical dimensions that best distinguish between forms, is lost in statistical analysis of multiple individual and group comparisons.

The influence of element design on results is now better understood (81). New element types in various geometric shapes are now available (65), but care must still be taken when partitioning forms for study. Elements cannot be too narrow along any given dimension or the strain tensor will contain values thousands of times those usually found. This occurs because a matrix involved in the calculation of extremely narrow elements has a very small determinant and thus an undefined inverse (60).

All landmarks must be present on all forms in order to perform FESA, so individuals with missing data must be excluded, or the missing data imputed. Given new methods for the imputation of missing landmarks (see the section below on future developments), forms with missing data can be included in future FESA.

FESA remains extremely useful, especially for the characterization of differences between pairs of forms. Its ability to localize changes between forms to the areas surrounding particular landmarks is a particularly valuable feature, especially when graphically presented. The biological interpretability of this method makes it an attractive choice for anthropologists.

Thin-Plate Splines

The theory of thin-plate splines (TPS) originated in the mathematical field of approximations theory. TPS are widely used in fields outside anthropology. The basic ideas behind TPS may best be explained using an example from geography. Suppose one is observing elevation data at various stations within a county. Let (x,y) be the spatial coordinates of a given station and z be the altitude measured at that location. The data then consist of triplets (x,y,z). Now suppose we want to predict elevation at a location that lies between these stations. This could be done using regression, by regressing z on (x,y). TPS are regression functions chosen in such a manner that: 1. they predict the observed elevation exactly at each station, and 2. they satisfy a certain smoothness criterion, namely that a certain quantity called *bending energy* is minimized. Graphically one can think of a plate corresponding to the plane on which these stations are situated. We want to "bend" this plate in such a manner that by using the least amount of "energy," the plate has a height equal to the measured altitude at the stations. Since the regression function is based on the choice of the energy function that is minimized, it follows that graphical presentation of the results is affected by the choice of the energy function. TPS have been generalized to include three (or higher) dimensional spatial coordinates (e.g. latitude, longitude, and altitude) and more than one quantity of interest at each location (e.g. rainfall and temperature). Wahba (94) provides mathematical details and references to various applications of TPS in geology and the atmospheric sciences.

Bookstein (16, 17) has considered the application of TPS in morphometrics. In the comparison of two two-dimensional objects, let (x,y) denote the landmark coordinates of form A and (z,w) denote the landmark coordinates of form B. Following our earlier example, (x,y) can be equated to the spatial locations of the measuring stations and (z,w) can be equated to rainfall and temperature measurements taken at those locations. TPS are applied to the comparison of forms in a straightforward fashion. The intent is to regress (x,y) on (z,w) in a manner that fulfills the following requirements: 1. the value of the function, f, at (x_i, y_i) is exactly (z_i, w_i); and 2. the chosen "energy" function is minimized. This description and the one we provided for FESA in the previous section are similar. In both TPS and FESA homologous data points are matched exactly between forms according to a specified function. In TPS however, objects are not discretized into smaller elements for study and a homology function is chosen explicitly to minimize bending energy.

Bookstein's (16) idea is to study the approximation function, f, since it gives information pertaining to how the reference figure is deformed to fit the target figure. He suggests that this deformation be decomposed into several orthogonal parts. One part corresponds to the affine (uniform) change required to take the reference into the target form. Affine transformations correspond to global or uniform changes that keep parallel lines parallel within a transformation and do not involve any bending. The rest of the deformation corresponds to the non-affine (non-uniform) changes [TPS of weighted sums of the principal warps (85)] required for the deformation. Descriptions of local deformations are given by the non-affine changes. If the objects are two dimensional, these non-affine changes can be inspected visually for biological interpretations (see 16).

Since applications of TPS to problems in anthropology are not yet numerous (but see 2, 3), the impact of this method on the discipline cannot yet be evaluated. There are, however, certain observations that can be made about this coordinate-based method. Bending energy is a nonsymmetric function. This means that the bending energy required to deform object A into object B is not the same as the bending energy required to deform object B into object A. The biological implications of this observation are insignificant when the direction of the deformations is based on a known sequence (e.g. younger compared to older individuals in the case of growth comparisons). However, when members of different groups (e.g. sexes, species) are being compared, the biological implications of this nonsymmetry must be carefully considered. The biological meaning of the coefficients produced in analysis must also be fully defined. Graphic displays of these coefficients appear biologically interpretable, but will they remain interpretable when forms are three dimensional? Since graphical representation of decompositions of these deformations in three dimensions would consist of four dimensions, how can they be usefully displayed? Finally, the biological significance of bending energy, and of affine and non-affine transforms, should be clarified if we are to appreciate fully the potential of this method in the study of anthropological data.

These problems are not insurmountable. The use of TPS in morphometric research appears promising. The graphics are attractive and interpretable, and inexpensive software has been made available (86). Future application of this method to anthropological data sets may bring new understanding to important research problems.

Procrustes Analysis

Procrustes analysis (PA) (41, 93) compares forms by superimposing them according to a specified minimization criterion. The method attempts to match landmark coordinates on two forms as closely as possible by scaling, rotating, and translating one object with reference to another such that all landmark coordinates of the second form fit the first form as closely as possible. Gower (37) developed an algorithm enabling the comparison of multiple forms to a single representative form.

Generalized Procrustes analysis (36) attempts to fit two forms as closely as possible by minimizing the sum of the squared distances between homologous landmarks on the two forms after translation, rotation, and scaling. The difference in shape between two forms is measured as the landmark-wise, coordinate-wise difference between them (34, 32). The scaling factor is a measure of size difference between the forms (34), while shape change is measured as the lack of fit among the landmarks. This minimization criterion, however, tends to spread the morphological differences evenly across the form, biologically implying that all landmarks contribute equally to the lack of fit. Noting this, Siegel & Benson (90) proposed a robust approach to the superimposition of forms. *Resistant-fit theta rho analysis* superimposes forms under an alternate minimization criterion based on robust regression using repeated medians (87). The difference between two forms is measured by the lack of fit of the landmarks that cannot be matched exactly. Rohlf & Slice (87) extend this resistant-fit method so that a large number of forms can be superimposed. Additionally, Rohlf & Slice (87) generalize least squares and resistant-fit approaches to allow for uniform shape change (affine transformations).

Resistant-fit Procrustean approaches work well when the difference between forms is due to the position of only a few landmarks (90, 87). This means that the relative ability of either minimization criterion to describe the difference between forms accurately depends upon the nature of the morphological difference. Since the goal of most morphometric analyses is to determine and characterize this difference, the researcher rarely has prior knowledge of which Procrustes algorithm is best suited to the data. Rohlf & Slice (87) suggest using least squares and resistant-fit methods with both affine and orthogonal transformations and then comparing results. Choosing which method provides the most accurate result based on the analytic outcome seems unwise, especially when the researcher has certain expectations of the data based on a theoretical orientation. More importantly, since differences in loss functions produce different results in the analysis of the same data sets (compare Figures 1 and 2 in 90, and 87), biological interpretations of differing analytical outcomes of the same data sets will most likely differ. Lele (49) discusses the importance of the effect of the choice of loss function on the biological interpretation of analytical results.

PA has been applied to the study of the evolution of form in fossil ostracods (e.g. 8, 9), the interrelationship of egg size with life history variables in marine benthic invertebrates (91), and the study of cell growth (33). Many applications have appeared in the form of examples presented within more methodologically oriented papers (e.g. 19, 32, 33, 34, 90). One advantage to the method is that results can be plotted directly onto geometric forms, providing an easily interpretable graphic of the difference in forms. PA may be most useful in comparing forms when a specific hypothesis about localized morphological differences is being tested. Statistics for the method are well developed and the method calculates what we consider is a robust estimator of the mean. Finally, PA explicitly limits itself to landmark data and makes no assumptions about the area between landmarks (87). It therefore provides a summary of the differences between forms based exclusively on physical data.

Euclidean Distance Matrix Analysis

In Euclidean distance matrix analysis, or EDMA (49, 53, 55), *form* is defined as the geometrical representation of the object by the landmarks which remains *invariant* when you move the object within a given coordinate system (translate the object), when coordinates of landmarks are changed by mathematically spinning the object on an axis within a given coordinate system (rotate the object), and when coordinates of bilateral landmarks are switched (reflect the object) (49). *Shape* is defined as that characteristic which remains *invariant* under these conditions as well as under scaling of the object. Since definition of size is ambiguous (49), meaning simply that there is no single, orthodox size measure, EDMA studies morphology in terms of *form* and *form change*. The merits of the *invariance principle* in the study of form (49) are summarized below.

Briefly, if the measure of form difference changes when forms are translated, rotated, or reflected, form difference has not been described optimally. Since the form of an object is invariant under translation, rotation, and reflection, it follows that an approach for comparing forms should start with a representation of the forms that is invariant under these operations. For landmark data, one such optimal method (a maximal invariant) is based on the analysis of Euclidean distance matrices that are *coordinate-free* representations of forms. Advantages of such a representation are most apparent in comparative analyses of growth patterns (see 54 and the section below on future directions).

Suppose the forms considered are represented by recording the K landmark coordinates as a matrix with K rows and D columns (where D = the number of dimensions). Starting with landmark coordinates, objects can be equivalently represented by the Euclidean distance matrix of all possible distances between the landmarks (see Figure 3; also reference 28). There are $K(K-1)/2$ such distances. We denote the Euclidean distance matrix or *form matrix* (FM) of object X by F(X). Each element of the matrix corresponds to a particular linear distance. For example, the distance between landmarks i and j is the (i,j)th element of the matrix and is denoted as $F_{ij}(X)$.

Using the FM, we say that two objects, X and Y, have the same form if and only if all linear distances are of equal length in X and Y. X and Y are said to have the same shape if all corresponding distances in X and Y are proportional to one another; that is, if the ratio of all like linear distances $F_{ij}(X)/F_{ij}(Y)$ is the same. In this case, objects would differ only in size. The *form difference matrix (FDM)*, denoted as $D_{ij}(X,Y)$, is used to compare forms X and Y, and is composed of the ratios of corresponding distances:

$$D_{ij}(X,Y) = F_{ij}(X)/F_{ij}(Y)$$

When comparing samples of forms, an average form is calculated for each sample using a generalized Procrustes algorithm (37). A FM representing the average form of sample X is compared to the FM for the average form of sample Y by computing a matrix of ratios of like linear distances, the FDM. A bootstrap approach to the statistical testing of differences between mean forms based on EDMA is available (53).

The strength of EDMA lies in its ability to maintain geometric integrity of forms while retaining information on individual dimensions. This is done by analyzing all linear distances simultaneously. This does not mean that all linear distances are equally relevant to the difference between forms. As in any morphometric technique, the researcher determines the set of landmarks that adequately represents the biological form, but beyond that initial decision he/she makes no prior judgments concerning which subset of landmarks, linear distances, or regions contributes most significantly to form difference. From the complete set of data, EDMA identifies those inter-landmark distances that are most influential in discriminating between the forms under consideration (55). Once identified, these linear distances can be analyzed separately, or as units based on structural/functional hypotheses.

Manual inspection of an entire FDM can be laborious when the number of landmarks is large, since there are $K(K-1)/2$ linear distances for a form consisting of K landmarks. In the past, this problem has been avoided by analyzing anatomic regions separately (25–27, 38). It is possible that a large proportion of the morphological information included in the landmark data could be accessed with a much smaller number of biologically informative linear dimensions. This smaller number of dimensions would be statistically desirable and might simplify interpretation. Special subsets consisting of $3(K-2)$ linear distances in two dimensions, and $4K-10$ linear distances in three dimensions, could be chosen precisely to enable reconstruction of the form. Unfortunately, if these subsets are chosen to ensure reconstruction, they may not be biologically informative. Currently, we have no way of judging the proportion of morphological information contained within an arbitrary subset of linear dimensions. Such a judgment would be helpful in choosing measurement sets in morphological analysis. The solution to this problem would reduce the number of distances analyzed. This might result in the choice of a subset that does not preserve the geometry of the form but that provides solid biological inferences.

It is imperative to have models, pictures, or images of the forms, or the actual forms on hand when interpreting results. This enables the researcher to optically superimpose the results onto the three-dimensional morphology and visually to localize the information contained in the FDMs. Currently there is no elegant graphical method available for display of EDMA results. This is partially due to the coordinate-free nature of the method. Richtsmeier & Lele (78) adopted an arbitrary coordinate system to display analytical results, but most other EDMA analyses have been accompanied by FESA graphics drawn by FIESCA (65) or graphics that are not based on the geometry of the forms (84).

The statistics of EDMA have been formally developed (49, 53), and EDMA results are biologically interpretable. EDMA has been used successfully in analyzing growth patterns within primate species (25–27, 84), among craniofacial patients affected with craniofacial abnormalities (79, 82), and within experimental populations (95). More recently, methods for the comparative analysis of growth patterns based on EDMA have emerged (73, 83, 84). The ability to compare growth patterns statistically is probably the most significant aspect of this coordinate-free technique. A method for the proper estimation of confidence intervals for the statistical comparison of FDMs has been developed (56) and can be applied directly to the comparison of growth patterns.

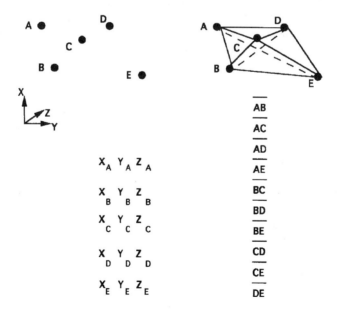

Figure 3   Equivalent ways of representing an object using landmark data. A matrix of three-dimensional coordinates of landmarks A through E is shown at the left. This representation is coordinate based. On the right are all possible linear distances among these landmarks. This representation is coordinate free. Both the coordinate-free and the coordinate-based depictions maintain geometric integrity of the form. Figure reproduced with permission following Ref. 38.

Summary

We have briefly described and evaluated selected morphometric techniques. The focus on these methods and the exclusion of others is not meant to suggest that alternate methods for the study of shape and size are without merit. Alternate recent reviews and compilations of morphometric techniques (59, 69, 85, 86) should be consulted for this information.

ANTHROPOLOGICAL MORPHOMETRICS: FUTURE DIRECTIONS

Developmental and Evolutionary Trajectories

Morphology changes through evolutionary and ontogenetic time. The ability to characterize differences among forms using morphometric techniques provides the tools for the study of change in form due to growth. Atchley (6) suggested that the manner in which complex morphological structures are produced during ontogeny and how they evolve are among the most important problems in modern biology. Atchley & Hall's (7) most recent work stresses the importance of determining the developmental mechanism responsible for morphology and how the mechanisms generate variability during ontogeny. It is from this variability that evolutionary change is produced. In order to determine how developmental patterns contribute to the maintenance of given forms, the production of morphological variation, and the evolution of novel morphologies, a method is needed that enables the comparison of developmental patterns.

It seems judicious to propose an hypothesis of a developmental trajectory [see for example (1) and (5)] and then see how closely available data fit that trajectory. All of the methods for the analysis of form change in three dimensions discussed above can provide a quantitative description of growth patterns. Problems arise when the goal is the *comparison* of growth patterns. Imagine, for example, that we want to compare growth from age 1 to 2 in species A with that in species B. Using a coordinate-based approach, growth in species A is defined in the coordinate system of A1 while growth in species B is defined in the coordinate system of B1. Comparison of the two descriptions of growth is problematic due to the lack of correspondence between the coordinate systems. Coordinate-free approaches avoid this problem and are therefore well suited to the comparison of growth patterns (see 25–27, 54, 80, 83, 84).

We define *growth pattern* as the physical interpretation of the changing arrangement of biological structures through time. We define *growth trajectory* as the path that a form traverses through time as it changes in morphology. Growth trajectories and growth patterns are different expressions of the same phenomenon: *trajectories* summarize growth using abstract mathematical terms in n-dimensional space (n depending upon the number of metrics

GROWTH

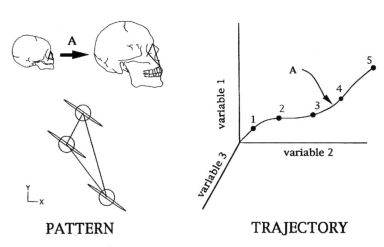

PATTERN   TRAJECTORY

Figure 4   The process of growth modeled as a pattern and as a trajectory. Growth pattern is the physical description of a changing geometry due to growth in form space. Ellipses produced by finite-element scaling analysis denoting the direction and magnitude of change due to growth at each landmark are one way to depict growth patterns graphically. A *growth trajectory* models the path of a biological object (in our example the triangle of three biological landmarks) as it changes form due to growth over time. Each point on the trajectory locates the object in terms of variables 1, 2, and 3. In our example the axes might represent the linear distances that make up the triangle, but alternate variables such as size and shape could also define these axes.

used in analysis), while *patterns* summarize the physical (biological) aspects of growth in three-dimensional space (see Figure 4). Because trajectories and patterns are different expressions of the same growth data, the distinction between the two is transparent: With the proper methods one can go from trajectory to pattern and back again.

Growth patterns are more tangible than trajectories because they map the geometric rearrangement of parts in real space. The study of time-dependent processes (e.g. growth, evolution) can be reduced to studying properties of trajectories, or one-dimensional curves through high-dimensional space (see 1). When growth is described as a trajectory, biological problems concerning differences among curves can be precisely formulated as mathematical properties of these curves. Such comparisons could be made for growth trajectories defined for two groups since trajectories can be manipulated mathematically in hyperspace. A projection of a trajectory onto two-dimensional or three-dimensional space (Figure 4) enables us to visualize a trajectory. However, these graphics cannot tell us of the structural differences between growth patterns (e.g. differences in how one bone changes with relation to another) that cause trajectories to deviate from one another. The relationship between trajectories and patterns and the ability to go from trajectory to pattern and back again are meaningful because they ensure that statistical rigor and biological meaning are components of the same approach.

Methods that enable the simultaneous study of growth pattern and trajectories could be used to test ideas concerning changes in morphology due to changes in growth pattern; i.e. heterochrony. Hypotheses of rate or time hypermorphosis (*sensu* 88) could be rigorously tested once these terms are modeled as properties of curves. Simultaneous examination of changes in patterns of growth would provide a mapping of the geometric consequences of a heterochronic process. Use of this method for the study of allometric relationships (35, 42, 89) might also prove worthwhile. Allometric relationships could be defined as properties of curves while a concurrent study of growth pattern would define the structural differences in growth that cause trajectories to maintain a relationship or to deviate from one another.

Hypothetical Geometries

An interesting but as yet little utilized aspect of morphometrics is the production of hypothetical forms based on data from other areas of inquiry. Informa-

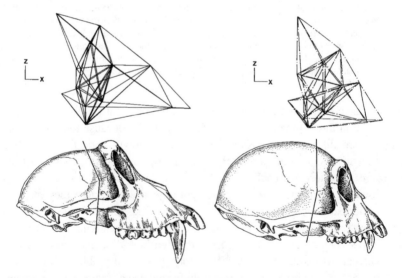

Figure 5   Drawing of real *(left)* facial morphology of adult male *M. fascicularis* and a hypothetical monkey face *(right)* scaled to be of equal volume. Drawings at the top of the figure are finite-element scaling analysis representations of facial morphologies based on data from 20 landmarks. The landmarks are located at the vertices of tetrahedra and wedge-shaped elements. Landmark coordinates for the real *M. fascicularis* form represent the average coordinate locations of landmarks collected from 50 adult male individuals. Landmark coordinates for the simulated form were calculated by applying the *Cebus apella* growth pattern to the immature *M. fascicularis* face. Statistical test for differences in morphology show the real and simulated forms to be significantly different. The *M. fascicularis* facial skeleton is shown at bottom left. An artist's reconstruction of the hypothetical form's facial skeleton based on landmark locations is shown at bottom right.

tion from ecology, biology, biomechanics, genetics, phylogeny, and/or onto-geny can be used to build hypothetical geometries that can be tested against real forms using morphometric techniques. This requires translating different sorts of information into metric variables useful for predicting morphology. We have begun work in this area but have barely scratched the surface. We provide the following example in the hope that it will stimulate others to propose additional approaches.

Description of a given form in FM format and a known growth pattern expressed as a FDM can be combined to produce hypothetical adult forms (80). For example, the growth pattern of *Cebus apella* is determined by com-paring the infant form (Ya) with the adult form (YA) using the ratio of all pairwise distances ($D_{ij} = YA_{ij}/Ya_{ij}$). This growth pattern is applied to an infant *M. fascicularis* expressed as an FM (Xa) producing a hypothetical variant skull representing what a *M. fascicularis* would look like if it grew like a *C. apella* ($HXA_{ij} = Xa_{ij} * D_{ij}$). This hypothetical adult form can then be com-pared to the real *M. fascicularis* adult form to test the hypothesis that *M. fascicularis* and *C. apella* grow in the same manner (Figure 5). Depending upon the hypothesis being tested, it may be desirable to scale the hypothetical form so that it is the same size as the adult form to which it is being compared.

Most of the methods discussed thus far require landmark coordinates to compare forms. The method just described produces a hypothetical form ex-pressed as a FM. To calculate three-dimensional coordinates from the matrix of all pairwise inter-landmark distances, the centered inner product matrix of the FM representing the hypothetical form is calculated. The spectral decom-position of the centered inner product matrix consists of K eigenvectors and K eigenvalues, but if the distances represent a real form, only the first three eigenvalues corresponding to the X, Y, and Z axes are nonzero. If the fourth and higher eigenvalues are nonzero, the process modeled is not biologically consistent (real) and the simulated form is not a physical object [i.e. it exists in four (or higher) dimensional space]. Since the first three eigenvalues are used with the eigenvectors to calculate the three-dimensional coordinate locations of the landmarks for the hypothetical form, solutions should perhaps be con-strained to those matrices with nonzero entries existing exclusively for the first three eigenvalues. Such a method could be used to determine the physical boundaries of ontogenetic and evolutionary change and answer questions con-cerning constraints on physical systems.

Quantitative genetic data and approaches (29) could be joined with methods for making hypothetical forms to produce a physical structure that reflects a hypothesized response to natural selection. The expected response of the popu-lation mean (Δz) to selection is given by:

$$\Delta \bar{z} = G\beta$$

where **G** is the genetic variance/covariance matrix describing the patterns of genetic inheritance for the characters considered, and β is the selection gradient measuring the direct selection acting on each character [calculated by the partial regression coefficient of relative fitness on each character (45, 46)]. Using this equation and measurements of the patterns of genetic variance and covariance, the expected morphological response to hypothetical selection pressures could be calculated for a series of inter-landmark distances. If the particular set of inter-landmark distances allows reconstruction of three-dimensional landmark coordinates as with the form matrices of EDMA, the morphological results of this hypothetical selection could be assembled and compared to the results of realized evolution. This method could also be used to construct the results of evolutionary "what if" scenarios.

Data from other areas of study (e.g. biomechanics, physiology, life history) could be operationalized in such a way as to produce hypothetical forms (see 71). Allometry might also benefit from this approach. For example, investigation of the structural validity of a form created on the basis of an allometric equation could add an important component to allometric studies.

Statistical Approaches to the Reconstruction of Forms when Landmarks Are Missing

Paleontological and anthropological specimens are notoriously fragmentary. Frequently, a sample of specimens is available that are for the most part complete, but certain individuals have missing landmarks. Rohlf (85) indicates that current methods for treatment of missing data are unsatisfactory. Howells (39) has summarized the anthropologist's predicament nicely: "since imperfections from damage permeate any typical collection of skulls, multivariate treatment calls for striking a balance between excluding a specimen entirely even though it may contain a lot of useable information, and finding some cosmetic treatment to restore missing bits of information acceptably, i.e. restoring the original total shape within narrow limits of possible errors ... The missing measurements must be supplied by estimation."

The problem of handling missing data has a long history in statistics (e.g. 63). The usual solution is to impute missing observations using regression analysis. Let us suppose that individuals within a sample are represented by a discrete set of *linear measurements,* numbering 20. Now suppose that there is one individual, Q, in the sample on which only 19 measurements are available. We could replace the missing measurement on Q by the mean of this measurement among individuals for which we have all 20 measurements. Owing to individual variability within the sample, this is not always the best approach. If Q is smaller than the average, the procedure described above would replace the missing measurement by too large a metric. In order to provide estimates for missing metrics that more accurately fit the actual form, metrics present on Q should be used in the imputation of the missing measurement(s). In statistical terminology, we should impute the 20th measurement using the sample mean for measurement 20 conditional on the other 19 measurements taken on Q.

Lele (51) addresses the problem of missing landmarks on a form conditional on existing data for that form. There are two possible approaches: coordinate-based and coordinate-free. Both approaches can be generalized to situations in which more than one landmark is missing on a single form.

A COORDINATE-FREE APPROACH   Suppose there are n individuals, each with K landmarks in D dimensions. Suppose one of these individuals has a single landmark missing. The form matrix representing this individual consists of only $(K - 1)(K - 2)/2$ distances instead of $K(K - 1)/2$ distances. The missing $K - 1$ distances must be computed from the distances available. Technically one needs to impute only three (in two dimensions) or four (in three dimensions) distances. Lele (51) proposes imputing these distances by applying the modern technique of Projection Pursuit Regression (PPR) (31,40). PPR is used instead of multiple regression because the linear distances considered in the form matrix are highly linearly related. PPR effectively incorporates the linear relatedness of the linear distances by using linear combinations of the distances as explanatory variables, instead of isolated distances themselves. If a nonlinear function fits the data best, PPR chooses a nonlinear function naturally.

A COORDINATE-BASED APPROACH   In this approach, coordinates of the missing landmarks must be imputed based on the coordinates of the landmarks that are present. To do this all individuals (even those with missing data) are translated and rotated in such a manner that landmark 1 is at the origin [i.e. has coordinates (0,0,0)], landmark 2 lies along the x axis [i.e. has coordinates (a,0,0) with a > 0], and landmark 3 lies on the (X,Y) plane [i.e. has coordinates (b,c,0) with c > 0]. There is no particular biological significance to the choice of landmarks 1, 2, and 3, but they must be present on all forms under consideration. After this procedure, regression analysis or PPR can be performed on the translated and rotated landmark coordinates to impute the missing landmark—that is, to predict the landmark coordinates of the missing landmark for a particular individual.

Simulations done (51) using both approaches have been encouraging. Such methods could be especially useful in anthropology, since we are often plagued by incomplete data. Currently, artistic ability and expertise are used in the reconstruction of fossils. Such a reconstruction was done for a morphometric comparison of *Aegyptopithecus* with *Afropithecus* cranial fossils (47). It would be an informative and useful exercise to check the reconstruction of those landmarks missing from the various *Aegyptopithecus* faces against placement of those landmarks as calculated by the methods described above. In modern species where one or two landmarks are missing from a large sample of forms, an automated method for reconstruction of the missing landmark coordinates would enable inclusion of the entire sample in analysis, diminish the amount of time required for reconstruction, and increase the accuracy of the reconstructions. Finally, there are several primate species, paleontological and neontological, for which morphometric data are rare. A future challenge is to determine how data from better known species might be used to gain knowledge about the morphology of poorly known, or only partially complete specimens.

CONCLUSIONS

There are still scientists among us who ask, "Why bother with quantification when I can *see* the difference between forms?" First, the precision gained through quantification is important. Second, although differences between forms may appear obvious, the *significance* of the difference cannot be ascertained by the naked eye. This is because variability within a group cannot be discerned through visual observation alone. A seemingly small morphological difference can be significant when within-group variability is low. Third, some of our most interesting questions entail comparison of comparisons in the form of ontogenetic and phylogenetic sequences. A comparison of comparisons is not possible without morphometric analysis.

Technological advancements of the past four or five years bring within reach the solution of many practical problems associated with data collection (see 30, 85) and the study of three-dimensional form. Several currently available methods *describe* differences between forms well, and improvement of these methods will continue. The main purpose of descriptive studies is to define accurately and systematically what is observed. Analytical studies, on the other hand, attempt to *explain* by determining relationships or causality among variables. Quantitative manipulation of variables (and of geometric forms) is the anthropologist's answer to the usual lack of control over most influential variables and the absence of laboratory conditions under which scientific experimentation can take place.

To this date, anthropological morphometrics have generally been concerned with description (though quantitative). It is now time for morphometric techniques to go beyond the quantitative description of form and become part of a research design that studies relationships, causal or otherwise, among variables. This is done most efficiently through the formulation of testable, explanatory hypotheses. We have suggested a method for formulating hypotheses as three-dimensional forms. Existing data can be fit to these structural hypotheses to test the feasibility of a particular configuration. Morphometric methods that maintain the geometric integrity of three-dimensional forms and hypotheses that test the validity of geometrically possible morphologies are our best resources for investigating scientific questions.

Morphometrics provides tools. Ingenuity of research design will determine the role of morphometrics in the future of anthropological inquiry. Implemented in the manner suggested, or made part of other novel research designs, morphometric methods will provide a clearer understanding of the relationship of morphology to other biologically relevant variables.

ACKNOWLEDGMENTS

This chapter summarizes work that was supported in part by Whitaker Foundation Biomedical Research Grants to JTR and JMC, a March of Dimes Birth Defects Foundation Basil O'Connor award to JTR, and NSF grant BSR 8906041 to JMC. We thank Dr. Luci Kohn, Dr. Hannah Grausz, and Kathy Rafferty for reading and commenting on previous versions of this manuscript. Elaine Kasmer drafted parts of Figures 1 and 5 and Hannah Grausz created Figure 2.

Literature Cited

1. Alberch, P., Gould, S. J., Oster, G. F., Wake, D. B. 1979. Size and shape in ontogeny and phylogeny. *Paleobiology* 5(3):296–317
2. Albrecht, G. H. 1990. Landmarks, thin-plate splines, and comparative anatomy of the primate scapula. *Am. Zool.* 30:73A (Abstr.)
3. Albrecht, G. H. 1991. Thin-plate splines and the primate scapula. *Am. J. Phys. Anthropol. Suppl.* 12:42–43 (Abstr.)
4. Arnold, S. F. 1981. *Theory of Linear Models and Multivariate Analysis.* New York: John Wiley and Sons
5. Atchley, W. R. 1987. Developmental quantitative genetics and the evolution of ontogenies. *Evolution* 41(2):316–30
6. Atchley, W. R. 1990. Heterochrony and morphological change: a quantitative genetic perspective. *Dev. Biol.* 1:289–97
7. Atchley, W. R., Hall, B. K. 1991. A model for development and evolution of complex morphological structures. *Biol. Rev.* 66:101–57
8. Benson, R. H. 1982. Comparative transformation of shape in a rapidly evolving series of structural morphotypes of the ostracode *Bradleya.* In *Fossil and Recent Ostracodes,* ed. R. H. Batre, E. Robinson, L. M. Sheppard, pp. 147–64. New York: Halstead. 350 pp.
9. Benson, R. H., Chapman, R. E., Deck, L. T. 1984. Paleoceanographic events and deep-sea Ostracodes. *Science* 224:1334–36
10. Deleted in proof
11. Bookstein, F. L. 1982. Foundations of morphometrics. *Annu. Rev. Ecol. Syst.* 13:451–70
12. Bookstein, F. L. 1983. The geometry of craniofacial growth invariants. *Am. J. Orthod.* 83:221–34
13. Bookstein, F. L. 1984. A statistical method for biological shape change. *J. Theor. Biol.* 107:475–520
14. Bookstein, F. L. 1986. Size and shape spaces for landmark data. *Stat. Sci.* 1:181–242
15. Bookstein, F. L. 1987. Describing a craniofacial anomaly: finite elements and the biometrics of landmark locations. *Am. J. Phys. Anthropol.* 74:495–510

16. Bookstein, F. L. 1989. Principal warps: thin-plate splines and the decomposition of deformations. *IEEE Trans. Patt. Anal. Mach. Intell.* 11:567–85
17. Bookstein, F. L. 1990. Higher order features of shape. See Ref. 86, pp. 237–50
18. Bookstein, F. L., Sampson, P. D. 1990. Statistical methods for the geometric components of shape change. *Commun. Stat. Theory Methods* 19:1939–72
19. Chapman, R. E. 1990. Conventional Procrustes approaches. See Ref 86, pp. 251–68
20. Cheverud, J. M. 1989. A comparative analysis of morphological variation patterns in the papionins. *Evolution* 42:958–68
21. Cheverud, J. M., Richtsmeier, J. T. 1986. Finite-element scaling applied to sexual dimorphism in rhesus macaque (*Macaca mulatta*) facial growth. *Syst. Zool.* 35:381–99
22. Cheverud, J. M., Lewis, J. L., Bachrach, W., Lew, W. B. 1983. The measurement of form and variation in form: an application of three-dimensional quantitative morphology by finite-element methods. *Am. J. Phys. Anthropol.* 62:151–65
23. Cheverud, J. M., Hartman, S., Richtsmeier, J., Atchley, W. 1991. A quantitative genetic analysis of localized morphology in mandibles of inbred mice using finite element scaling analysis. *J. Craniofac. Genet. Dev. Biol.* 11:122–37
24. Cheverud, J. M., Kohn, L. A. P., Konigsberg. L. W., Leigh, S. 1992. The effects of fronto-occipital artificial cranial vault modification on the cranial base and face. *Am. J. Phys. Anthropol.* In press
25. Corner, B. D., Richtsmeier, J. T. 1991. Morphometric analysis of craniofacial growth in *Cebus apella. Am. J. Phys. Anthropol.* 84:323–42
26. Corner, B. D. and J. T. Richtsmeier 1992a. Cranial growth in *Ateles geoffroyi* and growth dimorphism. *Am. J. Phys. Anthropol.* In press
27. Corner, B. D., Richtsmeier, J. T. 1992b. Experiments in nature: premature unicoronal synostosis in the mantled howler monkey (*Alouatta palliata*). *Cleft Palate Craniofac. J.* 29:143–51

28. Corruccini, R. S. 1988. Morphometric replicability using chords and cartesian coordinates of the same landmarks. *J. Zool., Lond.* 215: 389–394
29. Falconer, D. S. 1981. Introduction to quantitative genetics. Second edition, Longman, New York. 340 pp
30. Fink, W. 1991. Data acquisition in systematic biology. See Ref 86, pp. 251–268
31. Friedman, J. H., Stuetzel, W. 1981. Projection pursuit regression. *J. Am. Stat. Assoc.* 76:817–23
32. Goodall, C. 1991. Procrustes methods in the statistical analysis of shape. *J. Roy. Statist. Soc. Ser. B* 53:285–339
33. Goodall, C. R., Green, P. B. 1986. Quantitative analysis of surface growth. *Bot. Gaz.* 147(1):1–15
34. Goodall, C. R., Bose, A. 1987. Models and Procrustes methods for the analysis of shape differences. Proc. 19th Symp. Interface between Computer Science and Statistics, Philadelphia, pp. 86–92
35. Gould, S. J. 1966. Allometry and size in ontogeny and phylogeny. *Biol. Rev.* 41:587–640
36. Gower, J. C. 1971. Statistical methods of comparing different multivariate analyses of the same data. In *Mathematics in the Archaeological and Historical Sciences,* ed. F. R. Hodson, D. G. Kendall, P. Tautu, pp. 138–49. Edinburgh: Edinburgh Univ. Press. 565 pp.
37. Gower, J. 1975. Generalized Procrustes analysis. *Psychometrika* 40:33–50
38. Grausz, H. M. 1992. *Growth of the human perinatal craniofacial skeleton characterized in three dimensions.* PhD thesis. The Johns Hopkins Unive. 278 pp.
39. Howells, W. W. 1973. Cranial variation in man: a study by multivariate analysis of patterns of difference among recent human populations. *Pap. Peabody Mus. Archaeol. Ethnol. Harvard Univ.* 67:1–259
40. Huber, P. J. 1985. Projection pursuit. *Ann. Statist.* 13:435–529
41. Hurley, J. R., Cattell, R. B. 1962. The Procrustes program: producing direct rotation to test an hypothesized factor structure. *Behav. Sci.* 7:258–62
42. Huxley, J. S. 1932. *Problems of Relative Growth.* London: Methuen
43. Kohn, L. A. P., Moorrees, C. F. A., Kent, R. L. 1992. Differential growth in the human craniofacial complex between 6 and 16. Unpublished manuscript
44. Kohn, L. A. P., Leigh, S., Jacobs, S., Cheverud, J. M. 1992. Effects of annular cranial vault modification on the cranial base and face. *Am. J. Phys. Anthropol.* In press
45. Lande, R. 1979. Quantitative genetic analysis of multivariate evolution, applied to brain:body size allometry. *Evolution* 33:402–16
46. Lande, R. , Arnold, S. J. 1983. The measurement of selection on correlated characters. *Evolution* 37:1210–36
47. Leakey, M. G., Leakey, R. E., Richtsmeier, J. T., Simons, E. L., Walker, A. C. 1991. Morphological similarities in *Aegyptopithecus,* and *Afropithecus. Fol. Primatol.* 56:65–85
48. Leigh, S., Cheverud, J. M. 1991. Sexual dimorphism in the baboon facial skeleton. *Am. J. Phys. Anthropol.* 84:193–208
49. Lele, S. 1991. Some comments on coordinate free and scale invariant methods in morphometrics. *Am. J. Phys. Anthropol.* 85:407–18
50. Lele, S. 1992. Analysis of-landmark, data: estimation of mean form and form difference. Unpublished manuscript
51. Lele, S. 1992. The imputation of missing landmarks on biological forms. Unpublished manuscript
52. Lele, S., Richtsmeier, J. T. 1990. Statistical models in morphometrics: are they realistic? *Syst. Zool.* 39(1):60–69
53. Lele, S., Richtsmeier, J. T. 1991. Euclidean distance matrix analysis: a coordinate free approach for comparing biological shapes using landmark data. *Am. J. Phys. Anthropol.* 86(3):415–28
54. Lele, S., Richtsmeier, J. T. 1992. Quantitative analysis of growth: theoretical considerations. Unpublished ms
55. Lele, S., Richtsmeier, J. T. 1992. On comparing biological shapes: detection of influential landmarks. *Am. J. Phys. Anthropol.* 87(1):49–66
56. Lele, S., Richtsmeier, J. T. 1992. Estimating confidence intervals for the comparison of forms. Unpublished manuscript
57. Lestrel, P. E. 1974. Some problems in the assessment of morphological size and shape differences. *Yrbk. Phys. Anthropol.* 18:140–62
58. Lestrel, P. E. 1989. A method for analyzing complex two-dimensional forms: elliptical Fourier functions. *Am. J. Hum. Biol.* 1:149–64
59. Lestrel, P. E. 1989. Some approaches toward the mathematical modeling of the craniofacial complex. *J. Craniofac. Genet. Dev. Biol.* 9(1):77–92
60. Lewis, J. L., Lew, W. B., Zimmerman, J. L. 1980. A nonhomogeneous anthropometric scaling method based on finite element principles. *J. Biomech.* 13:815–24
61. Lozanoff, S. 1990. Comparison between two finite-element modelling methods for measuring change in craniofacial form. *Anat. Rec.* 227:380–86
62. Lozanoff, S., V. Diewert 1986. Measuring histological form change with finite element methods: an application using diazo-oxo-norleucine (DON) treated rats. *Am. J. Anat.* 177:187–201
63. Madow, W. G., Nisselson, H., Olkin, I. 1983. Incomplete data in sample surveys. Academic Press, NY

64. Marcus, L. 1990. Traditional morphometrics. See Ref 86, Pp. 77–122
65. Morris, G. R. 1989. FIESCA: graphic and analytic software for finite element scaling analysis in biological research. The Johns Hopkins University, Department of Civil Engineering
66. Moss, M. L. 1988. Finite element method comparison of murine mandibular form differences. J. Cranio. Gen. and Dev. Biol. 8: 3–20
67. Moss, M. L., Skalak, R., Patel, H., Sen, K., Moss-Salentijn, L., Shinozuka, M., Vilmann, H. 1985. Finite element method modeling of craniofacial growth. Am. J. Orthod. 87:453–72
68. Neyman,J., Scott, E. 1948. Consistent estimates based on partially consistent observations. Econometrics, 16:1–32
69. O'Higgins, P. 1989. Developments in cranial morphometrics. Folia Primatologica 53(1):101- 124
70. O'Higgins, P., Williams, N. W. 1987. An investigation into the use of Fourier coefficients in characterizing cranial shape in primates. J. Zool. Lond. 211:409–30
71. Oxnard, C. 1991. Anatomies and lifestyles, morphometrics and niche metrics: tools for studying primate evolution. Human Evol. 5(2):97–115
72. Deleted in proof
73. Read, D. W., Lestrel, P. 1986. Comments on the uses of homologous-point measures in systematics: a reply to Bookstein et al. Sys. Zool. 35:241–53
74. Reyment, R. A., Blackith, R. E., Campbell, N. A. 1984. Multivariate morphometrics. New York: Academic. 233pp. 2nd ed
75. Richtsmeier, J. T. 1987. A comparative study of normal, Crouzon and Apert craniofacial morphology using finite- element scaling analysis. Am. J. Phys. Anthropol. 74:473–93
76. Richtsmeier, J. T. 1988. Craniofacial growth in Apert syndrome as quantified by finite-element scaling analysis. Acta Anatomica 133:50–56
77. Richtsmeier, J. T., Cheverud, J. M. 1986. Finite element scaling analysis of human craniofacial growth. J. Craniofacial Genet. Dev. Biol. 6:289–323
78. Richtsmeier, J. T., S. R. Lele 1990. Analysis of morphological variation within neontological and paleontological species. Am. J. of Phys. Anthropol. 81(2):286 (Abstr.)
79. Richtsmeier, J. T., S. Lele 1990. Analysis of craniofacial growth in Crouzon syndrome using landmark data. J. Craniofac. Genet. Dev. Biol. 10(1): 39–62
80. Richtsmeier, J. T., Walker, A. 1992. Morphometric analysis of facial growth in Homo erectus. In The Nariokotome Homo

erectus skeleton, ed. A. Walker, R. E. Leakey. Cambridge: Harvard Univ. Press. In press
81. Richtsmeier, J.T., Morris, G. R., Marsh, J. L., Vannier, M. W. 1990. The biological implications of varying element design in finite-element scaling analyses of growth. Annu. Int. Conf. IEEE Eng. Med. Biol. Soc. 12(1):387–88
82. Richtsmeier, J. T., Grausz, H. M., Morris, G. R., Marsh, J. L., Vannier, M. W. 1991. Growth of the cranial base in craniosynostosis. Cleft Palate Craniofac. J. (28)1:55–67
83. Richtsmeier, J. T., Cheverud, J. M., Corner, B. C., Danahey, S. M., Lele, S. 1992. Sexual dimorphism of ontogeny in the crab eating macaque (Macaca fascicularis). Unpublished manuscript
84. Richtsmeier, J. T., Corner, B. D., Grausz, H. M., Cheverud, J. M. 1992. The role of postnatal growth pattern in the production of facial morphology. Unpublished manuscript
85. Rohlf, J. 1991. Morphometrics. Annu. Rev. Ecol. Syst. 21:299–316
86. Rohlf, J., Bookstein, F. L., eds. 1990. Proc. Michigan Morphomet. Work. Spec. Publ. No. 2, Univ. Michigan Mus. Zool. 380 pp.
87. Rohlf, F. J., Slice, D. 1990. Extensions of the Procrustes method for the optimal superimposition of landmarks. Syst. Zool. 39(1):40–59
88. Shea, B. T. 1983. Allometry and heterochrony in the African apes. Am. J. Phys. Anthropol. 62 (3):275–90
89. Shea, B. T. 1989. Heterochrony in human evolution: the case for neoteny reconsidered. Yrbk. Phys Anthropol. 32:69–101
90. Siegel, A. F., Benson, R. H. 1982. A robust comparison of biological shapes. Biometrics 38:341–50
91. Sinervo, B., McEdward, L. R. 1988. Developmental consequences of an evolutionary change in egg size: an experimental test. Evolution 42(5):885–99
92. Skalak, R., Dasgupta, G., Moss, M. L., Otten, E., Dullemeijer, P., Vilmann, H. 1982. Analytical description of growth. J. Theor. Biol. 94:555–77
93. Sneath, P. H. A. 1967. Trend-surface analysis of transformation grids. J. Zool. 151:65–122
94. Wahba, G. 1990. Spline Models for Observational Data. Philadelphia: SIAM
95. Wong, L., Dufresne, C. R., Richtsmeier, J. T., Manson, P. M. 1991. The effect of rigid fixation on the growing craniofacial skeleton: periosteal elevation, coronal suture plating, and frontal bone plating. Plast. Reconstruc. Surg. 88(3):395–403

Annu. Rev. Anthropol. 1992. 21:307-30

SHAMANISMS TODAY

Jane Monnig Atkinson

Department of Sociology/Anthropology, Lewis and Clark College, Portland, Oregon 97219

KEYWORDS: gender, ritual performance, ritual and politics, altered states of consciousness, ritual and healing

Just a few decades ago, shamanism appeared to be a dead issue in American anthropology. Geertz (75) deemed it one of those "desiccated" and "insipid" categories by means of which ethnographers of religion devitalize their data." Spencer (230) consigned it to a disciplinary "dustbin." More recently, Taussig (236) declared that "shamanism is ... a made-up, modern, Western category, an artful reification of disparate practices, snatches of folklore and overarching folklorizations, residues of long-established myths intermingled with the politics of academic departments, curricula, conferences, journal juries and articles, [and] funding agencies." Despite such dismissals, the topic of shamanism has proved remarkably resilient (102, 146). Indeed, the 1980s witnessed a resurgence—some call it a renaissance—in scholarship on shamanism (167:214; 40:17).

Once risking extinction through association with outmoded schools of evolution and culture history, the study of shamanism has been revitalized by multidisciplinary interest in states of consciousness and mechanisms of therapy, and by popular interest in alternative forms of spirituality. This reawakening has not been a function of internal developments in anthropology, but then shamanism has never been the exclusive purview of anthropology. Flaherty (67–70) depicts 18th century European fascination with shamanism, which then, as now, influenced scholars across a range of disciplines. Philosophers, theologians, physicians, archaeologists, philologists, aestheticians, dramatists—as well as ethnographers—all figured among those who thought and wrote about shamanism two centuries ago. The list today is similar, with the addition of modern psychologists, the deletion of the old-style philologists, and the relative absence of philosophers (but see 249).

307

0084-6570/92/1015-0307$02.00

As the category of shamanism is being reconstituted and revitalized by academic and popular interest, it is being deconstructed within the field of anthropology. Among cultural anthropologists there is widespread distrust of general theories about shamanism, which run aground in their efforts to generalize. The category simply does not exist in a unitary and homogeneous form, even within Siberia and Central Asia—the putative homeland of "classical shamanism" (224). Holmberg (102:144) claims that "shamanism remains intractable as a general field of study, in part because disparate practices have been disassociated from larger cultural contexts and linked to universal motivations." Likening the illusion of shamanism to the illusion of totemism that Lévi-Strauss brilliantly dismantled, Holmberg himself speaks of a plurality of "shamanisms," thus disrupting temptations to universalize (101).

At present, most general theorizing about shamanism appears outside the anthropological literature. Among anthropologists one finds widespread resistance not necessarily to the use of transcultural categories for purposes of analysis (cf 189a), but to the reification of such categories at the expense of history, culture, and social context. Kendall (133) critiques the tendency in the literature on shamanism to stress the difference between shamans and their consociates and the likeness among shamans from different times and places. Pursuing "common themes in the experiences of a contemporary Korean shaman seated in front of her television set and a Chuckchee shaman on the Siberian steppe at the turn of the century" diverts our attention from the shared worlds of shamans and their clients (133:446). Nevertheless, there are "common themes" and general patterns that appear among widely dispersed populations, some attributable to historical connection (82, 214), others not. Recent work on psychological states has offered ways to explain these recurring likenesses in terms of universal human proclivities instead of historical diffusions and cultural survivals, thereby fueling renewed scholarly interest in shamanism writ large and peripheralizing ethnographic studies of local traditions.

The contemporary literature reflects the patterns described here. Dominating the topic of shamanism in bibliographical indexes and abstracts are general and comparative works, especially in the fields of psychology and religious studies, along with a wide array of popular writings on self-actualization and New Age spirituality. In the latter, one increasingly finds contributions by internationally recognized scholars such as Ake Hultkrantz and Michael Harner (e.g. 51). With the exception of contributions in psychological anthropology and cross-cultural survey work, most items by anthropologists are ethnographic and focused on single cultural traditions. Much valuable ethnographic work on shamans is not billed as such but is contained in monographs with titles that give no hint of a shamanic focus except perhaps to an area specialist (e.g. 107a, 198, 199, 239a, 242). Such scholarship has had insufficient impact on the wider field of shamanic studies, which features general theorizing, model-building, and self-actualization. A central aim of this review is to interject contemporary ethnographic research into the literature on shamanism writ large. Without an ethnographic counterweight this literature slips quickly into unwarranted reductionism and romantic exoticizing of a homogeneous non-Western Other. Newer ethnographic writings offer an important corrective by underscoring the connections of shamanic practices to local, regional, national, and transnational contexts. They also call attention to some of the culture-bound assumptions Euroamerican scholars and their audiences have brought to the study of shamanic traditions.

In what follows I first examine two dominant preoccupations of recent multidisciplinary work on shamanism—the psychological state of shamans and the therapeutic value of shamanic healing. Both reveal a quest on the part of behavioral scientists to find some rational basis—physiological, psychological, or medical—to explain the existence and continuance of shamanic practices. Both emphasize primarily the states of individual shamans and patients. By contrast, recent ethnographic research has explored the connections of shamanic practices to wider social processes. Doing so entails the use of what the religious scholar Ake Hultkranz (114) has criticized as a "dismembered concept of religion." In such work, "shamanism" does not figure as a problem to be solved. [One recent monograph eschews the term entirely except in reference to a body of scholarly literature (6).] Instead, shamanism is used as a gloss for certain discourses and practices that operate in local, regional, national, and transnational contexts. Extracting shamanism from such contexts to be studied as a detachable and self-contained problem is at odds with the goals of such research, which is aimed at understanding historically situated and culturally mediated social practice.

THE PSYCHOLOGIZING OF SHAMANISM

Preoccupation with the mental health of shamans dominated the literature on shamanism for most of this century, with some scholars arguing that shamanic behavior was the result of a mental disorder (21, 41, 48, 226) and others arguing for the sanity of shamanic practitioners (26–29, 87, 165). At this point, the argument that shamanism is not a function of mental illness appears to have prevailed. Whereas earlier work assumed shamans represented extreme personality types, more recent scholarship argues that the shifts in psychological states that characterize shamanic behavior are within the behavioral repertoire of normal human beings (24, 148, 149, 165, 221), although some propose that shamans are likely to be "fantasy-prone" individuals (140). Psychological abnormalities are still occasionally mentioned in connection with shamanism, particularly in writings by certain Soviet scholars (11). Recently Perrin (184) explored the overlap of a cultural model of hysteria, "a penchant for shamanery," and individual pathology among an Amazonian population. Ohnuki-Tierney (173) has identified an overlap between Ainu shamanism and *imu,* a culture-bound syndrome. She suggests that in larger, more complex societies in which shamanism is marginalized, it may not be unusual to find individuals with psychological problems availing themselves of the expressive outlet offered by trance. By and large, however, shamanic behavior has been moved from the category of abnormal psychology to the category of universal psychobiological capacities.

This major shift in thought about shamanic behavior was effected by changing scholarly and popular understandings of consciousness in the 1960s. Contributing to the recognition that shamanic states were within the capacity of ordinary people was widespread societal experimentation with drugs. Within anthropology, a generation of fieldworkers—especially in South America where drugs play a key role in shamanic traditions—found that by "jumpstarting" their consciousness with hallucinogens it was possible to experience firsthand the visions and sensations of shamanic seances (74, 91, 233, 234). Scholarly interest in shamanic use of hallucinogens continues (30, 50, 122, 250). But studies of "psychedelic shamanism" now constitute a minor part of a wider literature on altered states of consciousness.

ASC, the ubiquitous acronym for "altered states of consciousness," has been the buzzword in interdisciplinary studies of shamanism over the last decade. Whereas earlier scholars of religion had defined shamanism in ways that incorporated cultural understandings of shamans and their followers (63, 110), behavioral scientists skeptical about the ontological basis of spirit worlds have found epistemological bedrock in the concept of altered psychological states (e.g. 247; see 39:13 on the translation of "spirit idiomata" into Western psychological terms). Shying away from the flamboyance of Eliade's term "ecstasy," they have favored the more behavioristic connotations of trance (225). But the term "trance" has its own problems. The rubric could apply to a vast range of cultural practices, including possession states, the relation of which to shamanism has been the focus of considerable debate (24, 25, 42, 62, 63, 146, 205). Researchers have sought to clarify what is distinctive about the state or states of consciousness employed by shamans. Peters & Price-Williams (189) framed shamanic ecstasy as a particular form of ASC. Harner (88) characterized a single "shamanic state of consciousness," or SSC. Winkelman (253) argued that a single kind of trance state was characteristic not only of shamans but of all kinds of magico-religious practitioners. Goodman (77, 78, 80, 81) goes even further to define one "religious or ritual state of consciousness" resembling a Chomskian deep structure and to posit that surface differences in the experience of that state are produced by differences in bodily posture. By contrast, Walsh (246, 248) offers a "phenomenological mapping" of various states and levels of consciousness involved in the practices of shamanism, Buddhism, and yoga. He demonstrates the variety of psychological states that each entails, and highlights the considerable differences among them.

The identification of shamanism with altered states of consciousness has become so strong that indeed the two terms are sometimes used interchangeably. One definition cited by Ridington (199:125) characterizes shamanism as "an institutionalization of a transformation from the ordinary waking phase to a nonordinary one, in which internally generated information comes to dominate and override the ordinary decision-making and orientation function of the waking phase." Muted here are social and cultural dimensions; the emphasis is purely psychological. A similar emphasis is seen in the work of Lewis-Williams and his collaborators (146a, 147, 251), who have interpreted rock paintings of Southern Africa, the Great Basin, and Upper Paleolithic Europe as the products of shamanic ritual and altered states of consciousness. Lewis-Williams & Dowson (147:204) assert that in using the term shaman they "do not thereby imply anything about the social position of the person, his or her mental health, or indeed, many of the other characteristics often associated with the very heterogeneous phenomenon called shamanism." Rather they intend to highlight "the most important and overriding feature of shamanism" which they regard as its defining state of consciousness (see 17, 37). Indeed such reductionism is widespread now in the variegated literature on shamanism.

Interest in ASCs has prompted interest in their neurophysiological bases. For anthropologists, one of the major developments in this regard was the publication in 1982 of a special issue of *Ethos* entitled "Shamans and Endorphins" (191a). Inspired by the discovery of endorphins, opiate-like compounds the brain releases in response to certain stimuli, contributors considered relations among chemical balances, emotional states, and ritual. Both shamanic states of consciousness and therapeutic responses of patients have been addressed as functions of chemically induced euphoria. Neher's (158, 159) work on the induction of ASCs through acoustical driving has received both consideration (see 118) and criticism on philosophical (205) and experimental grounds (1, 2). Little systematic neurophysiological research has been conducted on practicing shamans (248), although a recent article reports physiological differences between a "shamanic state of consciousness" and possession trance states (258). Speculation about the neurophysiology and psychobiology of ritual (see 178) has predictably prompted a reaction against a "neuromythological stance" (170) that systematically reduces social, cultural, and psychological phenomena to biochemical and neurological terms.

Much of the work on altered states and shamanism has been offputting to sociocultural anthropologists as it has emphasized psychological processes over social dynamics (see 40) and in some cases implied a reduction of symbolism and ritual to psychobiological functions. Certainly shifts in consciousness are a key part of shamanic practice. But to analyze shamanism primarily as a trance phenomenon is akin to analyzing marriage solely as a function of reproductive biology. Understanding the neurophysiology of trance is valuable, but it does not explain the associated structures of ritual, knowledge, and society that have been the focus of so much research over the past decade. In an important essay on consciousness and structures of knowledge among the Dunne-za of Canada, Ridington (194) offers a valuable corrective to scholarly and popular preoccupation with psychological states. Altered states of consciousness are revelatory, he argues, not in and of themselves but because of their place in cultural systems of knowledge. For example, the oral tradition of the Dunne-za (formerly, an ecologically stable hunting and gathering society) offered templates relevant to every conceivable individual experience over the course of a lifetime. Such templates, supplying information essential for personal and societal well-being, could be engaged through transformations of consciousness. It is not the case, he argues, that contemporary Euroamericans are denied access to such revelatory information by a "repressive phenomenology," as some would have it (e.g. 126). Owing to the nature, development, and organization of its culturally central knowledge, Western society places a premium on the transformation of society and history, rather than transformations in individual consciousness, and assigns the latter idiosyncratic significance rather than cultural centrality. More work of this sort is needed to redress the imbalance in the current literature emphasizing psychological states to the exclusion of their social, cultural, and historical dimensions.

Nevertheless, as Porterfield (190) argues, embodiment of social and psychological problems is fundamental to shamanic practice. In Rouget's (205:319) words, "to shamanize ... is as much a corporeal technique as a spiritual exercise." For this reason, a comparative understanding of the physiological and psychological processes employed by shamans in different traditions can be useful, but only insofar as they are taken to be elements of shamanic practice and not shamanism itself. A number of models have been proposed to integrate the insights from the psychological and physiological work on ASC with anthropological and sociological approaches (e.g. 151). The most comprehensive and systematic of these is the pioneering work of Siikala (221), who takes a social psychological approach to ritual performance. Her premise is that "the technique of communication used by the shaman as a creator of a state of interaction between this world and the other world is fundamentally an ecstatic role-taking technique" (p. 28). It is a shaman's role-taking vis-à-vis spirit "counter roles," in her view, that distinguishes shamanism from other ecstatic endeavors. The psychic process of this shamanic technique, she argues, is the same as that used in hypnosis, which Sarbin defined as one form of role-taking (see also 12, 189). Drawing on role theory in both psychology and sociology, Siikala presents a model of the interactions among shaman, spirits, and human audience that lead to altered states of consciousness. Particularly interesting is her discussion of depth of trance as it is shaped by the dynamics of a shaman's role-taking with spirit and human alters. Siikala places great emphasis on the diversity of shamanic traditions, yet her model offers ways of thinking about the commonalities among traditions, especially in regard to the significance of spirit helpers who play a key part in the dynamics of shamanic role-playing.

Also of interest is Noll's (166) argument that shamans use a "controlled visionary state" that can be distinguished from other states by its "active engagement" of visions. The goal of shamanism is not, he argues, the achievement of an altered state of consciousness; the latter is simply a means to promote enhanced mental imagery. Noll's commentators have scaled back the claims of his approach (e.g. 103, 113, 224, 228). Nevertheless, Noll's work is significant for tempering the exclusive focus on ASCs—which fieldworkers often find is more the preoccupation of social scientists than of practicing shamans and their audiences—and for addressing the theme of "shamanic vision" featured in many cultural traditions. A related topic, that of dreams—decidedly undertheorized in the century since E. B. Tylor's work (138)—is now receiving scholarly attention (236a,b,c)

SHAMANISM AS THERAPY

Before altered states of consciousness had offered behavioral scientists a scientific foundation for shamanism, therapeutic efficacy was already established as a rationally comprehensible justification for shamanic rituals. If the spiritual grounds for the practice made Western social scientists uneasy, its purported medical and psychological functions rendered it intelligible and subject to rational explanation. Likening shamans to physicians and psychotherapists was a move that elevates the former and jocularly taunts the latter with the reminder that Western biomedicine too makes use of rituals, impression management, and faith (237). The expansion of Western biomedicine into regions with traditions of shamanic therapy has invited consideration of the ways shamanic practice is shaped and modified by access to biomedical care (e.g. 8, 9, 43, 135) and the interdependence of shamanic and biomedical systems (e.g. 155, 163). Furthermore, growing interest since the 1960s in alternative medicine has prompted efforts to integrate shamanic techniques into Western health care (e.g. 3, 51, 139).

The presumed therapeutic effects of shamanic ritual have been explained in terms of everything from metaphors to endorphins—from "experiential mosaics" in the poetry of Nepali shamans (47), to the transfer of secreted opioid peptides from !Kung trancers to the patients whom they rub with sweat (71). Interest continues in the mechanisms of placebo and symbolic healing (53, 54, 153, 207, 219) as well as in the psychotherapeutic dimensions of shamanic practice (141, 185, 186, 188).

The parallels between shamanic therapy and Western psychotherapies have been a continuing concern. Jung himself took a deep interest in shamanism, and his own form of therapy has been likened to shamanic transformation of healer and patient (55, 82, 84, 215). Jung's influence is clear in a number of influential general works on shamanism (e.g. 85, 142). Recently Laderman (141) has offered an ethnographic consideration of Jungian thought in her insightful comparison of a Malaysian theory of temperament and Jung's notions of archetypes. Central to Malay shamanism, Laderman argues, is a non-projective system of psychotherapy, which calls upon patients to address the internal sources of their own problems. She challenges the assumption that there is less "truth value" in shamanic systems than in Western psychotherapy, claiming that one is not more rational or empirically justified than the other. Rather both have merit as theoretical frameworks and clinical practices. Variations of this argument appear in the work of a number of analysts and physicians including Jilek (98, 119, 120, 121), a psychiatrist with anthropological training, who has published accounts of his research and collaboration with Northwest Coast Indian healers. Of interest too are the reflections of Kakar (125), an India-born psychoanalyst, trained in the West, who writes on his three years of fieldwork exploring indigenous forms of Indian healing.

Lévi-Strauss's (143) famous article comparing a Cuna healing text to psychoanalysis continues to draw attention and comment. Criticized for its structuralism, its functionalism, its textual rather than contextual focus, and even for situational details of Cuna ethnography, this article remains a starting point for many discussions of shamanism and ritual healing because of the key questions it raises about therapy and symbolic efficacy (e.g. 5, 9, 32, 140a, 102, 105a, 161, 162, 236).

Some have taken issue with the idea that shamanic practices are principally directed at healing. Arguing that Tamang shamanism deals with the "preconditions" of affliction, rather than the illness, Holmberg (102) analyzes a Tamang shamanic "sounding" that does not have healing as its focus (cf 185). I have shown how considerations other than the therapeutic may dominate a shaman's performance (5, 6). And Porterfield (190:734) notes that by emphasizing the therapeutic functions of shamanism, scholars have glossed over shamanic practices of manipulation, deception, and, in some cases, outright destruction (see 33). As in the case of Lévi-Strauss's Cuna analysis, general models prove helpful for sorting out what is going on in particular cases; analyses of the latter offer checks and corrections to the model-building. To this point, I have considered two dominant themes in the general literature of shamanism—namely the psychological states of shamans and the therapeutic value of shamanic healing. These themes center on the physical and psychological conditions of shaman and patient. In what follows I highlight recent work that has emphasized instead the place of shamanic discourses and practices in wider cultural frameworks and social processes.

SHAMANISMS IN CONTEXT

Politics and Shamanisms

New anthropological work, following a wider trend in the discipline, has grounded shamanic traditions in the history and political economy of particular regions and explored the relations between culture and politics, locally and in relation to state formations. Reacting against the phenomenological strain in writings on shamanism since Eliade (63), Taussig (233:221) criticizes the "romantic nostalgia and misty exultation" found in portrayals of shamanic mediation between mundane and spirit worlds. Although shamanic discourse may feature the alienation of human and spirit realms, shamans, he argues, mediate divisions of caste and class relations as well. Shamans of the Pumomayo region of Colombia do so not as etherealized visionaries but as Rabelaisian characters, exercising a "solid, earthy practicality ..., spiced with humor and all too human passions" (233:268). Taussig (234) presents shamanic responses to colonial and neocolonial domination in multi-ethnic Colombia as a regional discourse rather than the function of a unique "culture." In similar fashion, Tsing (239) examines Meratus practices of healing and sorcery as they have been shaped by the wider context of interethnic dialog in South Kalimantan. Holmberg's (102) exploration of the systemic relations among Tamang shamanic, sacrificial, and lamaic rituals, and Mumford's Bakhtinian analysis (154) of Tibetan lamaic ritual and shamanic tradition highlight the dialogic interplay of opposing and fused discourses in Nepal. These studies underscore that "shamanisms" never occur in isolation but always are embedded in wider systems of thought and practice.

Shamanic traditions have long been the target of institutionalized religion and state powers. Echoing Weber, Lewis (146:34) writes, "If certain exotic religions thus allow ecstasy to rule most aspects of their adherents' lives, all the evidence indicates that the more strongly-based and entrenched religious authority becomes, the more hostile it is toward haphazard inspiration." Such hostility is not limited to religious authority, as seen in recent studies of political struggles involving shamanic practices and state formations. Salomon (206), for example, uses court records to explore the transformation and operation of "shamanic politics" on the peripheries of Spanish colonial rule in southern Colombia and Ecuador. Taussig (234) has explored the imaginings of shamanism in the terror and healing of colonists in the Putomayo region of Colombia. Both Salomon and Taussig note that the projection of colonial fear and fantasies onto Indian magic enhances the power and value of the latter.

In the 20th century two powerful states in particular have made war on shamanism in the interests of scientific atheism. Balzer's (11) recent collection of Soviet work contains lengthy accounts of Soviet efforts to eradicate shamans and their pernicious effects on the Soviet population. Anagnost (4) analyzes the Chinese government's campaign against "feudal superstition" and healers who would exploit others for their own "economic self-interest."

Strong stances by states toward shamanism invite both ingenious political responses and rich scholarly analysis. Korean shamanism (for recent reviews see 34, 130, 243), subjected to control and persecution by state authorities for centuries, is experiencing a startling revival. Long disparaged as superstition and negatively associated with women, Korean shamanism has paradoxically become the target of government efforts to preserve Korean culture under the

Cultural Conservation Law (35, 107). In a counter-hegemonic move, Korean students and intellectuals have adopted shamanism as a weapon for anti-government protest. Shamanic performances, led by shamanizing academics, have become an established form of mass demonstration (136). How the politics of this Korean form of neo-shamanism will feed back upon village shamanism will be as interesting to track as the relations between neo-shamanism in the United States and Native American communities.

Whereas US scholarship has been preoccupied with the psychology of shamanism, Soviet scholarship, with its tradition of historical materialism, has maintained a steady bead on political economy, emphasizing the fact that shamanic traditions are dynamic and inextricable parts of changing social systems. Soviet scholars regard shamanism as a form of religious practice in pre-class societies. Some posit an early collective stage in which shamanic practice was open to anyone, followed by the development of professional specialization. As specialists who demanded payments and sacrifices from clients, shamans served to promote and legitimate growing economic inequality and the rise of feudal society. With increasing societal complexity and the emergence of the state with monarchies and priestly hierarchies, shamans were "pushed ever farther from the stage of social existence into the dark corners of daily life" (Basilov in 11:34). Resurgences of shamanism have been regarded as the death throes of a dying institution. Basilov (11:46) does, however, grant that there may be a revival in response to "an infatuation with mysticism:" "The motley mystical teachings that are proliferating in capitalist countries, especially the United States, eagerly use information about shamans to convince the average person of the existence of otherworldly forces." Such are the general outlines of the historical materialist framework, but they do not do credit to the highly detailed ethnological research on Siberian and Central Asian shamanism conducted for decades by Soviet and European scholars, only some of which is available in English (11, 13, 14, 104, 105, 115, 191). Trained as it is upon the history and cultures of a single area of the world, this scholarship has avoided the excesses of more scattershot attempts to generalize about shamanism.

A number of recent works offer detailed analyses of the political dynamics of shamanism within small-scale noncentralized societies elsewhere in the world. Challenging Lewis's (145) generalizations about a single Inuit example, Sonne (229) undertakes a comparative examination of the relationship between Inuit shamanism and political leadership in a review of the literature from Alaska to Greenland. Santos-Granero (208–210) explores the moral basis of authority among the Amuesha of Central Peru with a focus on the respective ritual and political roles of priests and shamans. By probing deeply into questions of power and legitimacy in Amuesha society, which is shaped by both Amazonian and Andean influences, he demonstrates the importance of fine-grained ethnographic analysis for intelligent comparative thinking. Overing's (179–181) work on knowledge and power among the Piaroa of the Orinoco

river area of Venezuela is likewise valuable for the study of shamanic authority in noncentralized societies. Half a world away in Indonesia, I have analyzed the culture and politics of shamanic practice with attention to local and
regional political processes and the changing nature of authority from precolonial times to the present (6).

Shamanisms and Gender

Scholarly constructions of the category of shaman reveal highly gendered
assumptions. One of the long-standing debates in the literature on shamanism
hinges on an issue of gender that has been inadequately explored. The classic
shaman defined by Eliade and portrayed in Siberian and Central Asiatic literature is the master of spirits, not their puppet. Eliade, who defined shamanism
in terms of "magical flight," out-of-body visionary quests, flatly excluded
"possession" from the complex he called shamanism, as did de Heusch (42)
and Rouget (205). Lewis (146), however, located in Shirokogoroff's (220)
classic work on Tungusic shamanism all the ecstatic forms that Eliade and
others excluded from their definition (see 25, 187, 189). Anagnost (4) proposes that Eliade's distinction between the "true shaman" and East Asian
"spirit mediums" is the product of the rise of the state and the corresponding
loss of charismatic authority on the part of shamans. Shamanic practices
continued, she argues, but with their "image realm" transformed, thereby
rendering shamans passive receptacles for spirits. Korean shamans may not be
passive, but Walraven (243:243) comments on their placatory attitude in contrast to the agonistic heroism of the now classic Siberian shamans. The former
undertakes no journeys; the latter sets off on spiritual travels fraught with
dangers. The former are women whose site of activity is the household; the
latter are men in a traditionally nomadic society.

Basic to the distinction between possession and shamanism is the issue of
control (192). Male practitioners predominate in the traditions to which Eliade
assigns the label shamanism, whereas women are conspicuously present in
traditions relying on possession (25, 254, 256). Lewis (145) has attributed this
pattern to women's peripheralization and deprivation. His argument has been
challenged as mechanistic and inapplicable in certain cases (101, 130). Nevertheless where women dominate in the shamanic ranks, it is often the case that
shamanic prowess has been edged out or subsumed by political and religious
centralization (cf 173). Balzer (11) describes such a process for the Khanty,
where an upsurge in female shamans has accompanied a decline in shamanic
prestige due to modernizing pressures from the Soviet State. In contrast to
shamanic traditions in much of the world, East Asian shamanism is often (and
in some cases almost always) in the hands of women. Significantly, East Asia
is a region in which shamanic authority was long ago displaced by state
authority and where the label "spirit medium" is often used in place of shaman
for ritual healers who do not match the classic model of the shaman in nonstate
societies—charismatic, masterful, and male. The richest contemporary ac-

counts of female shamans come from Korea, where, according to Covell (38), over 95% of shamans are women and the remainder are men who perform in women's dress (see 93, 94, 116, 131, 132, 134, 137, 252). Kendall (130:176) characterizes the Korean shaman as "a woman among women, a ritual expert of and for housewives"—certainly not a description that would have provoked the fascination the prototypical (male) tribal shaman holds for Western audiences.

Intrigued by questions of gender and shamanic practice, Wolf (257) draws on the work of Chodorow and Gilligan to elucidate the case of one Taiwanese woman, Mrs. Chen, who failed to gain recognition as a shaman. As an outsider in her community, without a respected family network intact, Mrs. Chen may have lacked the significant human alters essential for a Chinese woman to construct a self. Lacking such, she attempted to construct herself through interactions with spirits. But "the self that spoke with the gods could not be used to construct a self that could survive in a social world constructed by strangers" (p. 429).

Several recent works examine the gendered dimensions of shamanic traditions in which men predominate as shamans. Holmberg (101, 102) finds that Tamang shamans are typically men, but the shamanic complex is heavily associated with women and addresses contradictions in the Tamang system of cross-cousin marriage. I have explored how Wana women (Sulawesi, Indonesia) are discouraged from becoming shamans in the Wana system—not by explicit rules but by gendered practice—and yet, as patients and audience, play a key role in shaping shamans' careers and reputations (6, 7).

Oosten (174) raises a significant question about gender and shamanism. Observing that both women and men performed with no formal distinction as Inuit *angakkut*, Oosten asks whether, in performing the same role, they do the same thing? For example, Inuit male shamans engaged in competitive rivalries. Did women as well? Male shamans held major seances. Did their women counterparts? In other words, where no cultural distinction is articulated between women's and men's performances, do differences emerge in practice?

The gendered dimensions of shamanism bring us to the subject of transvestism. Flaherty (68) has explored Enlightenment assumptions that sex was fundamental to shamanism; that women in primitive societies were degraded but envied by men for having special power and mystery; and that shamanic transvestism was a means whereby men attempted to tap these special female qualities. Ethnography has not borne out a universal or intrinsic connection between these two "isms." In certain regional traditions, however, transvestite shamans have been significant, though not ubiquitous. Graham (81a) offers a perceptive cultural analysis of the Iban *manang bali* in light of Iban constructions of gender and what Ortner & Whitehead (177) would call the "prestige structures" of Iban society. Williams's (251a) study of the American Indian berdache contains useful information on berdache shamans (see also 95, 152).

There is much to be done in reconsidering the relationship of gender and shamanic power. For any given case both need to be understood as parts of wider sets of discourses and practices specific to particular regions and histories, instead of predictable outcroppings of a general physiological and psychological substratum. It is instructive to consider Taussig's (236:73; see also 235) recent critique of Lévi-Strauss's famous reading of the Cuna shaman's text as a phallologocentric explanation that "amounts to a man amidst magically empowering smoke, singing an unintelligible text into the birth canal of the world, forever chaotic and female, so as to reproduce 'structure.'" Taussig argues that Lévi-Strauss's structuralism, by ignoring the political dimensions of such an image, in fact adopts those dimensions as its own. Taussig's own take on shamans emphasizes their disruptive decenterings rather than their efforts at sustaining and maintaining order (127). In his account, the image of the male sustainer of structure and order is the product of colonial and neo-colonial imaginings. Thus we are left simply to speculate about the sexual politics of Cuna healing apart from the European gaze. As Holmberg (102) and Taussig (234) argue, shamans certainly engage in the disruption of order (conceptual, psychic, social), but shamans create and sustain order as well—the coherence and viability of their patient's beings, the continuity of a community (5, 6), or the well-being of a household (130). Their assertions of control through rhetorics of order are as significant as their flirtations with chaos and anarchy. Exploring the dialectics of shamanic power in relation to gender must take into account the ambiguities and multivalences of shamanic power and anticipate related complexities in gendered ideas and practice. Tsing's (239a) new book on the Meratus of Indonesia demonstrates the theoretical leverage afforded by such an approach.

Shamanic Texts and Performances

New work has stressed the performative dimensions of shamanic ritual, both verbal and nonverbal. Transcribing shaman's words is the most common way of "fixing" a shamanic performance for subsequent analysis, and shamanic language itself has become a focus of study. Recent publications on shamanism in several disciplines show a range of cultural, historical, religious, and literary approaches to such materials (e.g. 56, 223, 244, 245). Presentation and analysis of shamans' chants and attention to the challenges of translation have been featured in recent anthropological work (6, 141, 181). Shamanic texts found in the publications and fieldnotes of earlier ethnographers have been reanalyzed as well. Graham (81a), for example, uses a series of chants collected by ethnographers over the last century to reinterpret Iban shamanism. Using different versions of an 18th-century Inuit seance, Rollman (201) argues that in order to identify shifts in meaning and interpretation introduced by translation one must consider an entire corpus of textual material.

Interesting use is being made of textual materials of a nonritual sort as well. To represent a Mexican shamanic tradition, Dow (53) pairs an Otomi shaman's account of "what a shaman knows and does" with his own account of the social and cultural context of Otomi thought and practice. Novik (171) applies a structuralist approach to the relation between narratives about shamans and shamanic rituals themselves, arguing contra Propp (191b) that the connection is not "genetic" but is dictated by the relations between shamans and others. Durrant (61) explores contradictions between a woman's shamanic power and her social inferiority in a 17th-century Manchurian folktale (172). Takiguchi (231) analyzes a diary kept by a Miyako shaman during and after his initiation that intersperses "divine messages" in an account of daily events and thoughts. Ethnographers' notes and diaries have been subject to scrutiny as well (176). Particularly interesting is Rice's (193) analysis of the relationship between the Lakota shaman Black Elk and his interviewer John G. Niehardt during the 1930s and 1940s (31, 43a, 46, 160). Rice attempts to disentangle the voices of Black Elk and his interlocuter and to interpret them in their social-historical context. Also valuable for its insights into structures of shamanic thought is a recent experimental ethnography by Ridington (198) that examines his own engagement with Dunne-za associates through the use of Dunne-za narrative conventions.

Finally, widespread popular interest in shamanism and multiculturalism has created a market for anthologies and recordings of shamans' narratives, songs, and other verbal genres (e.g. 86, 204). The appropriation of shamanic traditions by contemporary performance artists is addressed in Noel's (164) treatment of the relation between US poet Anne Waldman's poem "Fast Speaking Woman" and its inspiration—the Wassons' 1956 recording of a *velada* performed by Mexican shaman Maria Sabrina (cf 204, pp. 62–65, 492–94).

Recent scholarship, however, has not been entirely logocentric or textbound. The nonverbal dimensions of shamanic ritual, especially music, are receiving attention (49, 141, 205). Roseman's (202, 203) study of Temiar healing rituals offers a particularly powerful demonstration of music's centrality in the creation of cultural meaning and ritual effectiveness.

Perhaps the most important development in studies of shamanic ritual has been the increasing attention paid to the conditions and dynamics of shamanic performance. Important here has been the legacy of Victor Turner, whose influence both in and beyond the field of anthropology continues. Together with Turner, Richard Schechner (211–213) has sought to build bridges between anthropology and theater. Schechner finds in shamanic ritual what he takes to be a goal in postmodern theater—namely an emphasis on performance not as a finished product but as a process of religious self-expression. Just as experimentation with drugs and altered states of consciousness offered new insights into shamanic practice, so theatrical experiments, as Turner (240) suggested, may reveal new dimensions of shamanic performance.

Whereas relations between shaman and patient have been stressed in therapeutic models of shamanism, and relations between shamans and the spirit world in phenomenological ones, dynamics involving shamans and their human audiences are featured in new work on ritual performance (e.g. 126a). Brown (32) contrasts the impression drawn solely from reading a performing shaman's speech alone to the understanding derived from an analysis of its polyvocal and highly political context. His analysis of the agonistic exchanges of an Amazonian shaman and his clients reveals the contested nature of the shaman's attempts to define the patient's condition and understanding. In an analysis of Wana "shamanship"—a term that invokes associations with both leadership and showmanship—I have (5, 6) treated an Indonesian shamanic seance as an arena for creating and sustaining shamanic authority and examined how audiences serve as arbiters of shamanic reputations. Joralemon (124) argues that the differences between a Peruvian shaman's performances in rural and urban settings are dictated not by the performer nor by eroding tradition but by clients' different desires and definitions of the scene. Such work underscores the point that ritual meaning and efficacy, success, and failure are negotiated jointly by performer and audiences.

SUMMARY

Of the recent research reviewed here, most addresses local shamanisms rather than shamanism writ large. Much of this work is directed at theoretical and topical concerns other than shamanism per se—such as politics in small-scale societies, the rise of the state, colonialism, gender and power, and ritual and language. Eschewing nomothetic formulations in favor of close scrutiny of local practices embedded in particular historical, cultural, and social contexts, many of the works reviewed here are antithetical to the universalizing aims that characterize many shamanistic studies. And yet, these close-grained analyses of shamanic practices contain important information and valuable correctives for the wider field of shamanic studies.

For their part, ethnographers would do well to consider their disciplinary voice in broader conversations about shamanism. Local knowledge from distant cultures does not always carry great weight in interdisciplinary dialogs, especially those involving psychology, the natural sciences, and medicine. The qualifying and deconstructive skeptical notes sounded by ethnographers in current discussions of shamanism are often drowned out by proponents of models and theories that address universal and broadly comparative issues. Furthermore, given the current place of shamans and shamanisms in spiritual movements and cultural commentary, it is incumbent upon ethnographers to attend to the wider conversations both popular and academic, not only to devise new ways of being heard but also to engage reflexively these contemporary inventions.

POSTSCRIPT: NEO-SHAMANISM AND ANTHROPOLOGY

By far the most significant recent development for the field is the blossoming of a new shamanism in the United States and Europe, spawned by the drug culture of the 1960s and 1970s, the human potential movement, environmentalism, interests in non-Western religions, and by popular anthropology, especially the Castaneda books. [Reference 59 offers an update on the Castaneda debates, including commentary on the work of Castaneda's dauntless critic, Richard De Mille (44, 45).] A "veritable cottage industry" has developed to promote and support shamanic practice in the United States (247:1). Michael Harner, an established authority on shamanism, left his academic position to teach shamanic techniques to urban Americans and Europeans through The Foundation for Shamanic Studies (92), to promote The Harner Method of Shamanic Counseling by which clients heal themselves through shamanic experience (89), and to teach shamanism to populations who have lost their shamanic traditions as a result of missionization (59).

"Neo-shamanism" or "urban shamanism" offers a form of spiritual endeavor that aligns its adherents at once with Nature and the primordial Other, in opposition to institutionalized Western religions and indeed Western political and economic orders. It presents in the 1980s and 1990s what Buddhism and Hinduism provided in the preceding decades, namely a spiritual alternative for Westerners estranged from major Western religious traditions. Particularly appealing for its "democratic" qualities that bypass institutionalized religious hierarchies (106), the new shamanism is compatible with contemporary emphases on self-help, self-actualization, and—not incidentally—rapid results (see 88). According to reports, it takes far less time for people to learn to achieve altered states of consciousness through shamanic techniques than through spiritual practices such as yoga and meditation (248)—as indeed might be expected of spiritual techniques developed first in societies with minimal specialization and no full-time religious specialists.

Neo-shamanists share a serious concern about precedent and symbolic content, and some defensiveness about charges of "playing Indian" (59a, 90a). Efforts are made to identify as precursors of neo-shamanism in Western history such phenomena as witchcraft, spiritualism, and mysticism. Drury (57), for example, looks back into occult practices in 19th- and early 20th-century Western Europe and America to claim an "easily accessible" shamanic heritage into which Westerners can tap. Whether neo-shamanism will be sustained beyond the next decade or two is, of course, an open question (238). The reworking of shamanic traditions from around the world in terms of American and European cultural idioms and concerns is a significant development that anthropologists would do well to study (cf 108).

Anthropologists' stance toward this "invention of tradition" is likely to be ambivalent. It is easy to be amused by Clifton's (36) critique of the "book-shamans of modern North America" and their promotion of "psychic aerobics."

The romanticization of shamanism by its current Euroamerican promoters is also unsettling for anthropologists (despite—or perhaps because of—their own familiarity with romantic tropes). One recent writer, for example, likened shamans ("these elusive and shy professionals") to "our most endangered species" (152a: xii). Salvationary hopes are placed on shamanism to overcome everything from environmental degradation to AIDS. Such depictions not uncommonly set standards for the ideal shamans and dismiss ethnographic accounts of shamans who do not meet them. Drury, for example, opens his 1982 book by relating Freeman's (72) discovery that the Iban shaman Manang Bungai used monkey blood to fake a battle with an "incubus." He then comments, "The case of Bungai represents the shaman-who-is-not. True shamanism is characterized by access to other realms of consciousness." That certainly would be news to many practicing shamans worldwide. Flaherty (67) traces Enlightenment Europe's fascination with shamanism and "its self-induced cure for a self-induced fit" (p. 528) and makes the case that European notions of genius and creativity drew inspiration from Enlightenment accounts of shamanic performance long before the appropriation of shamanism as the hallmark of the postmodern age (15). Useful as such correctives might be for scholars of shamanism, they have little effect on the burgeoning popular literature on shamanism. Such literature is fashioned to assist its readers in the cultivation of their own spirituality—an effort anthropologists are better trained to appreciate in tribes other than their own (cf 123).

Nevertheless, a measure of reflexivity is in order because anthropologists are deeply implicated in these developments. Cast as villains for their work by some (e.g. 126), anthropologists, through their writings and teachings, are a key source for this new tradition. Anthropologists and the new urban shamanists have different and potentially conflicting aims—the former seek to document and understand local traditions, whereas questing neo-shamans seek to develop their own spirituality with help from eclectically borrowed wisdom from "older" cultures (see 33, 123). In the process, shamanic traditions are reconfigured to fit Western notions of self-actualization (170). As "gatekeepers" to knowledge and experience of shamanic traditions, anthropologists may feel threatened by nonscholarly opportunities for Westerners to encounter such traditions. Joralemon (123) explores this point in an article about Eduardo Calderon Palomino, the Peruvian shaman who worked with Douglas Sharon (216, 218) and subsequently collaborated with psychologist Alberto Villoldo, a promoter of international tours of shamanic cultures. (For a stunning criticism of Calderon by his one-time collaborator, see 241:246). In short, the romantic engagement of shamans in popular culture forces anthropologists to rethink their own roles and discursive stances vis-à-vis shamanic practice—one manifestation of what Clifford (35a) has deemed the "predicament" facing contemporary ethnography.

ACKNOWLEDGMENTS

Robert Goldman, David Holmberg, Carol Laderman, and Anna Tsing provided candid and constructive criticism on an earlier draft and did so on short notice. I am grateful to them and to others as well who have furnished useful bibliographical leads. The title of this review is on loan from David Holmberg. I thank Elaine Heras and Beverly Stafford for essential bibliographic support, and Beth Pratt, Pam Schaefer, and Amy Wolf for technical assistance in preparing the manuscript.

Literature Cited

1. Achterberg, J. 1985. *Imagery in Healing: Shamanism and Modern Medicine.* Boston: New Science Library/Shambala
2. Achterberg, J. 1987. The shaman: master healer in the imaginary realm. See 162a, pp. 103–24
3. Achterberg, J. 1988. The wounded healer: transformational journeys in modern medicine. See Ref. 51, pp. 115–25
4. Anagnost, A. S. 1987. Politics and magic in contemporary China. *Mod. China* 13(1):40–61
5. Atkinson, J. M. 1987. The effectiveness of shamans in an Indonesian ritual. *Am. Anthropol.* 89:342–55
6. Atkinson, J. M. 1989. *The Art and Politics of Wana Shamanship.* Berkeley, CA: Univ. Calif. Press
7. Atkinson, J. M. 1990. How gender makes a difference in Wana society. In *Power and Difference: Gender in Island Southeast Asia,* ed. J. M. Atkinson, S. Errington, pp. 59–93. Stanford: Stanford Univ. Press
8. Atkinson, J. M. 1992. Review of *Taming the Winds of Desire* by Carol Laderman. *Am. Ethnol.* In press
9. Balzer, M. M. 1983. Doctors or deceivers? The Siberian Khanty shaman and Soviet medicine. In *The Anthropology of Medicine,* ed. L. Romanucci-Ross, D. Moerman, L. Tancredi, pp. 54–76. South Hadley, MA: Bergin/Praeger
10. Balzer, M. M. 1987. Behind shamanism: changing voices of Siberian Khanty cosmology and politics. *Soc. Sci. Med.* 24(12):1085–93
11. Balzer, M. M. 1990. *Shamanism: Soviet Studies of Traditional Religion in Siberia and Central Asia.* London: M. E. Sharp, Inc.
12. Banyai, E. L. 1984. On the technique of hypnosis and ecstasy: an experimental psychophysiological approach. See Ref. 105, pp. 174–79
13. Basilov, V. 1976. Shamanism in Central Asia. See Ref. 18, pp. 149–57
14. Basilov, V. N. 1984. The study of shamanism in Soviet ethnography. See Ref. 105, p. 4.
15. Benamou, M. 1977. Presence and play. In *Performance in Postmodern Culture,* ed. M. Benamou, C. Caramello. Madison: Coda
16. Deleted in proof
17. Benarik, R. G., Lewis-Williams, J. D., Dowson, T. A. 1990. On neuropsychology and shamanism in rock art. *Curr. Anthropol.* 31(1):77–84
18. Bharati, A. 1976. *The Realm of the Extra-Human: Agents and Audiences.* The Hague: Mouton
19. Black Elk, W. H., Lyon, W. S. 1990. *Black Elk: The Sacred Ways of a Lakota.* San Francisco: Harper and Row
20. Deleted in proof
21. Bogoras, W. 1907. *The Chukchee.* Part II. The Jessup North Pacific Expedition, Vol. 7. Mem. Am. Mus. Nat. Hist. New York: G. E. Techert
22. Deleted in proof
23. Deleted in proof
24. Bourguignon, E. 1976. *Possession.* San Francisco: Chandler and Sharp
25. Bourguignon, E. 1989. Trance and shamanism: What's in a name? *J. Psychoact. Drugs.* 21(1):9–15
26. Boyer, L. B. 1962. Remarks on the personality of shamans, with special reference to the Apache of the Mescalero Indian Reservation. *PYSSB* 2:233–54
27. Boyer, L. B. 1964. Further remarks concerning shamans and shamanism. *Isr. Ann. Psychiatr.* 2(3):235–57
28. Boyer, L. B. 1969. Shamans: to set the record straight. *Am. Anthropol.* 71:307–9
29. Boyer, L. B., Klopfer, B., Brawer, F. B., Kawai, H. 1964. Comparisons of the shamans and pseudoshamans of the Apaches of the Mescalero Indian Reservation: a Rorschach study. *JPTEA* 28:173–80
30. Browman, D. L., Schwartz, R. A. 1979. *Spirits, Shamans, and Stars: Perspectives from South America.* The Hague: Mouton
31. Brown, J. E. 1953. *The Sacred Pipe: Black Elk's Account of the Seven Rites of the Oglala Sioux.* Norman, OK: Univ. Oklahoma Press
32. Brown, M. F. 1988. Shamanism and its discontents. *Med. Anthropol. Q.* 2(2):102–20

33. Brown, M. F. 1989. Dark side of the shaman. *Nat. Hist.* November:8–10
34. Cho Hung-youn. 1984. Problems in the study of Korean shamanism. *Korea J.* 25(5):18–30
35. Choi, C. 1991. Nami, Ch'ae and Oksun: superstar shamans in Korea. See Ref. 95a, p. 5
35a. Clifford, J. 1988. *The Predicament of Culture. Cambridge: Harvard Univ. Press*
36. Clifton, C. 1989. Armchair shamanism: a Yankee way of knowledge. In *The Fringes of Reason, A Whole Earth Cat,* ed. T. Schultz, pp. 43–49. New York: Harmony Books
37. Consens, M. 1988. Comment. *Curr. Anthropol.* 29(2):221–22
38. Covell, A. 1983. *Ecstasy: Shamanism in Korea.* Elizabeth, NJ: Hollym International Corporation
39. Crapanzano, V. 1977. Introduction. In *Case Studies in Spirit Possession,* ed. V. Crapanzano, V. Garrison, pp. 1–40. New York: John Wiley and Sons
40. Crocker, J. C. 1985. *Vital Souls: Bororo Cosmology, Natural Symbolism, and Shamanism.* Tucson: Univ. Arizona Press
41. Czaplika, M. A. 1914. *Aboriginal Siberia.* London: Oxford Univ. Press
42. de Heusch, L. 1971. *Why Marry Her?: Society and Symbolic Structures.* Cambridge: Cambridge Univ. Press
43. de Laguna, F. 1987. Atna and Tlingkit shamanism: witchcraft on the Northwest Coast. *Arctic Anthropol.* 24(1):84–100
43a. Deloria, V. 1984. *A Sender of Words: Essays in Memory of John G. Neihardt.* Salt Lake City: Howe Brothers
44. De Mille, R. 1976. *Castaneda's Journey: The Power and the Allegory.* Santa Barbara, CA: Capra Press
45. De Mille, R. 1980. *The Don Juan Papers: Further Castaneda Controversies.* Santa Barbara: Ross-Erikson
46. DeMallie, R. J. 1984. *The Sixth Grandfather.* Lincoln: Univ. Nebraska Press
47. Desjarlais, R. R. 1989. Healing through images: the magical flight and healing geography of Nepali shamans. *Ethos* 17(3):289–307
48. Devereux, G. 1961. Shamans as neurotics. *Am. Anthropol.* 63:1088–90
49. Dobkin di Rios, M., Katz, F. 1975. Some relationships between music and hallucinogenic ritual: the 'Jungle Gym' in consciousness. *Ethos* 3(1): 64–76
50. Dobkin di Rios, M., Winkelman, M. 1989. Shamanism and altered states of consciousness. *J. Psychoact. Drugs* 21(1)
51. Doore, G. 1988. *The Shaman's Path.* Boston: Shambhala
52. Deleted in proof
53. Dow, J. 1986. *The Shaman's Touch: Otomi Indian Symbolic Healing.* Salt Lake City: Univ. Utah Press
54. Dow, J. 1986. Universal aspects of symbolic healing: a theoretical synthesis. *Am. Anthropol.* 88(1):56–69
55. Downton, J. 1989. Individuation and shamanism. *J. Anal. Psychol.* 34:73–88
56. Drake, C. 1990. A separate perspective: shamanistic songs of the Ryukyu Kingdom: review article. *Harvard J. Asiatic Stud.* 50(1):283–333
57. Drury, N. 1978. *Don Juan, Mescalito and Modern Magic: The Mythology of Inner Space.* London: Arkana
58. Drury, N. 1982. *The Shaman and the Magician: Journeys Between the Worlds.* London: Routledge and Kegan Paul
59. Drury, N. 1989. *The Elements of Shamanism.* Longmead: Element Books Ltd.
59a. Dubin, V. S. 1991. Elizabeth Cogburn, A Caucasian Shaman. See 95a, pp. 70–85
60. Deleted in proof
61. Durrant, S. 1979. The Nisan shaman complex in cultural contradiction. *Signs* 5:338–47
62. Eliade, M. 1961. Recent works on shamanism. *Hist. Relig.* 1(1):152–86
63. Eliade, M. 1964. *Shamanism: Archaic Techniques of Ecstasy.* Princeton: Princeton Univ. Press
64. Deleted in proof
65. Deleted in proof
66. Deleted in proof
67. Flaherty, G. 1988. The performing artist as the shaman of higher civilization. *Mod. Lang. Notes* 103(3):519–39
68. Flaherty, G. 1988. Sex and shamanism in the eighteenth century. In *Sexual Underworlds of the Enlightenment,* ed. R. Porter, G. Rousseau. Chapel Hill: Univ. N. Carolina Press
69. Flaherty, G. 1989. Goethe and shamanism. *Mod. Lang.* 104(3):580–96
70. Flaherty, G. 1992. *Shamanism and the Eighteenth Century.* Princeton: Princeton Univ. Press
71. Frecska, E., Kulcsar, Z. 1989. Social bonding in the modulation of the physiology of ritual trance. *Ethos* 17(1):70–87
72. Freeman, D. 1964. Shaman and incubus. *Psychoanal. Stud. Soc.* 4:315–44
73. Deleted in proof
74. Furst, P. T. 1972. *Flesh of the Gods: The Ritual Use of Hallucinogens.* New York: Praeger
75. Geertz, C. 1966. Religion as a cultural system. In *Anthropological Approaches to the Study of Religion,* ed. M. Banton. London: Tavistock
76. Deleted in proof
77. Goodman, F. D. 1988. Shamanic trance postures. See Ref. 51, pp. 53–61
78. Goodman, F. D. 1986. Body posture and the religious altered states of consciousness: an experimental investigation. *J. Humanist. Psychol.* 26(3):81–118
79. Deleted in proof
80. Goodman, F. D. 1990. *Where the Spirits Ride the Wind: Trance Journey and Other*

Ecstatic Experiences. Bloomington: Indiana Univ. Press
81. Goodman, F. D. 1988. Shamanic trance postures. See Ref. 51, p. 5
81a. Graham, P. 1987. *Iban Shamanism: An Analysis of the Ethnographic Literature. Occasional Paper of the Research School of Pacific Studies.* Canberra: Australian National University
82. Grim, J. 1984. *The Shaman: Patterns of Siberian and Ojibway Healing.* Tulsa: Univ. Oklahoma
83. Deleted in proof
84. Groesbeck, C. J. 1989. C. G. Jung and the shaman's vision. *J. Anal. Psychol.* 34(3):255–75
85. Halifax, J. 1982. *The Wounded Healer.* New York: Crossroad
86. Halifax, J. E. 1979. *Shamanic Voices: A Survey of Visionary Narratives.* New York: E. P. Dutton
87. Handelman, D. 1967. The development of a Washo shaman. *Ethnology* 6(4):444–64
88. Harner, M. 1982. *The Way of the Shaman.* New York: Bantam
89. Harner, M. 1988. Shamanic counseling. See Ref. 51, pp. 179–87
90. Deleted in proof
90a. Harner, M. 1988. Core Shamanism defended. *Shaman's Drum.* Spring issue:65–67
91. Harner, M. J. 1973. *Hallucinogens and Shamanism.* London: Oxford Univ. Press
92. Harner, M. J. 1990. *Journeys Outside of Time: The Way to Knowledge and Wisdom.* London: Unwin Paperbacks
93. Harvey, Y. S. 1979. *Six Korean Women: The Socialization of Shamans.* St. Paul: West
94. Harvey, Y. S. 1980. Possession sickness and women shamans in Korea. In *Unspoken Worlds: Women's Religious Lives in Non-Western Cultures,* ed. N. Falk, R. Gross, pp. 41–52. New York: Harper and Row
95. Hauser, R. E. 1990. The berdache and the Illinois Indian tribe during the last half of the seventeenth century. *Ethnohistory* 37(1):45–65
95a. Heinze, R. I. 1991. *Shamans of the Twentieth Century.* New York: Irvington
96. Deleted in proof
97. Deleted in proof
98. Hippler, A. 1980. Review of "The Psychiatrist and His Shaman Colleague" by W. Jilek and L. Jilek-Aall. *Transcult. Psychiatr. Res.* 17:189–93
99. Deleted in proof
100. Holm, N. G. 1982. Ecstasy research in the 20th century—an introduction." In *Religious Ecstasy,* ed. N. G. Holm. Stockholm: Almqvist and Wiksell International
101. Holmberg, D. 1983. Shamanic soundings: femaleness in the Tamang ritual structure. *Signs: J. Women Cult. Soc.* 9(1):40–58
102. Holmberg, D. H. 1989. *Order in Paradox: Myth, Ritual, and Exchange Among Nepal's Tamang.* Ithaca: Cornell Univ. Press

103. Honko, L. 1985. Commentary. See Ref. 166, pp. 452–53
104. Hoppál, M. 1987. Shamanism: an archaic and/or recent belief system. See Ref. 162a, pp. 76–100
105. Hoppál, M., ed. 1984. *Shamanism in Eurasia.* Göttingen: Edition Herodot
105a. Hoskins, J. 1988. The drum is the shaman, the spear guides his voice. *Soc. Sci. Med.* 27(8):819–28
106. Houston, J. 1987. Foreword: the mind and soul of the shaman. See Ref 162a, pp. vi–xiii
107. Howard, K. 1989. *Bands, Songs and Shamanistic Rituals.* Seoul: Royal Asiatic Soc., Korea Branch
107a. Hugh-Jones, C. 1979. *From the Milk River: Spatial and Temporal Processes in Northwest Amazonia.* Cambridge: Cambridge Univ. Press
108. Hughes, D. J. 1991. Blending with an other: an analysis of trance channeling in the United States. *Ethos* 19(2):161–84
109. Deleted in proof
110. Hultkrantz, A. 1973. A definition of shamanism. *Temenos* 9:25–37
111. Deleted in proof
112. Hultkrantz, A. 1985. The shaman and the medicine-man. *Soc. Sci. Med.* 20(5):511–15
113. Hultkrantz, A. 1985. Commentary. See Ref. 166, p. 453
114. Hultkrantz, A. 1988. Shamanism: a religious phenomenon? See Ref. 51, pp. 33–41
115. Humphrey, C. 1980. Theories of North Asian shamanism. In *Soviet and Western Anthropology,* ed. E. Gellner, pp. 243–54. New York: Columbia Univ. Press
116. Iida Takafumi. 1988. Folk religion among the Koreans in Japan: the shamanism of the 'Korean Temples'. *Jpn. J. Relig.* 15(2–3)
117. Jilek, W. G. 1982. Altered states of consciousness in North American Indian ceremonials. *Ethos* 10(4):409–23
118. Jilek, W. 1982. *Indian Healing: Shamanic Ceremonialism in the Pacific Northwest Today.* Surrey, British Columbia: Hancock House
119. Jilek, W. G. 1971. From crazy witch doctor to auxiliary psychotherapist: the changing image of the medicine man. *Psychiatr. Clin.* 4:200–20
120. Jilek, W., Jilek-Aall, L. 1978. The psychiatrist and his shaman colleague: cross-cultural collaboration with traditional Amerindian therapists. *J. Operat. Psychiatr.* 9:32–39
121. Jilek, W., Todd, N. 1974. Witchdoctors succeed where doctors fail: psychotherapy among Coast Salish Indians. *Can. Psychiatr. Assoc. J. 1* 9:351–56
122. Joralemon, D. 1984. The role of hallucinogenic drugs and sensory stimuli in Peruvian ritual healing. *Cult. Med. Psychol.* 8:399–430
123. Joralemon, D. 1990. The selling of the sha-

man and the problem of informant legitimacy. *J. Anthropol. Res.* 46(2):105–18

124. Joralemon, D. 1986. The performing patient in ritual healing. *Soc. Sci. Med.* 23(9):841–45

125. Kakar, S. 1982. *Shamans, Mystics, and Doctors: A Psychological Inquiry into India and its Healing Traditions.* New York: Knopf

126. Kalweit, H. 1988. *Dreamtime and Inner Space: The World of the Shaman.* Boston: Shambhala

126a. Kapferer, B. 1983. *A Celebration of Demons: Exorcism and the Aesthetics of Healing in Sri Lanka.* Bloomington: Indiana University Press

127. Kapferer, B. 1988. The anthropologist as hero: three exponents of post-modernist anthropology (review article). *Crit. Anthropol.* 8(2):77–104

128. Deleted in proof

129. Deleted in proof

130. Kendall, L. 1981. Supernatural traffic: East Asian shamanism. *Cult. Med. Psychol.* 5:171–91

131. Kendall, L. 1984. Korean shamanism: women's rites and a Chinese comparison. In *Religion and the Family in East Asia,* ed. T. Sofue, G. Devos. Osaka: Natl. Mus. Ethnol.

132. Kendall, L. 1985. *Shamans, Housewives, and Other Restless Spirits: Women in Korean Ritual Life.* Honolulu: Univ. Hawaii Press

133. Kendall, L. 1988. Healing thyself: a Korean shaman's afflictions. *Soc. Sci. Med.* 27(15):445–50

134. Kendall, L. 1988. *The Life and Hard Times of a Korean Shaman.* Honolulu: Univ. Hawaii Press

135. Kessler, C. S. 1977. Conflict and sovereignty in Kelantanese Malay spirit seances. See Ref. 39, pp. 295–331

136. Kim, K. 1992. Rituals of resistance: the manipulation of shamanism in contemporary Korea. In *Religion and the Modern States of East and Southeast Asia,* ed. C. Keyes, L. Kendall, H. Hardacre. Honolulu: Univ. of Hawaii Press. In press

137. Kim-Harvey, Y. 1979. *Six Korean Women: The Socialization of Shamans.* St. Paul: West Publishing Co.

138. Kracke, W. H. 1987. 'Everyone who dreams has a bit of shaman': cultural and personal meanings of dreams—evidence from the Amazon. *Psychiatr. J. Univ. Ottawa* 12(2):65–72

139. Krippner, S. 1987. Shamanism, personal mythology, and behavior changes. *Int. J. Psychosom.* 34(4):22–27

140. Krippner, S. 1991. Foreword. See Ref. 95a

140a. Laderman, C. 1987. The ambiguity of symbols in the structure of healing. *Soc. Sci. Med.* 24(4):293–301

141. Laderman, C. 1991. *Taming the Wind of Desire: Psychology, Medicine, and Aesthetics in Malay Shamanistic Performance.* Berkeley: Univ. Calif. Press

142. Larsen, S. 1988. *The Shaman's Doorway: Opening Imagination to Power and Myth.* Barrytown, NY: Station Hill Press

143. Lévi-Strauss, C. 1963. The effectiveness of symbols. In *Structural Anthropology,* C. Lévi-Strauss, pp. 181–200. New York: Basic Books

144. Deleted in proof

145. Lewis, I. M. 1989. *Ecstatic Religion: An Anthropological Study of Spirit Possession and Shamanism.* London: Routledge. 2nd ed.

146. Lewis, I. M. 1981. What is a shaman? *Folk* 23:25–35 (reprinted in 105)

146a. Lewis-Williams, J. D. 1987. A dream of eland: An unexplored component of San shamanism and rock art. *World Archaeol.* 19(2):165–77

147. Lewis-Williams, J. D., Dowson, T. A. 1988. The signs of all times: entoptic phenomena in Upper Paleolithic art. *Curr. Anthropol.* 29(2):201–45

148. Lex, B. 1979. The neurobiology of ritual trance. In *The Spectrum of Ritual: A Biogenetic Structural Analysis,* ed. E. d'Aquili. New York: Columbia Univ. Press

149. Lex, B. 1976. Altered states of consciousness in Northern Iroquoian ritual. See Ref. 18, pp. 277–300

150. Deleted in proof

151. Locke, R. G., Kelly, E. F. 1985. A preliminary model for the cross-cultural analysis of altered states of consciousness. *Ethos* 13(1):3–55

152. Lynch, R. 1985. Seeing twice: shamanism, berdache, and homoeroticism in American Indian culture. *South. Expos.* 13(6):90–93

152a. Lyon, W. S. 1990. Introduction. See Ref. 19

153. Moerman, D. E. 1982. Physiology and symbols: the anthropological implications of the placebo effect. In *The Anthropology of Medicine: From Culture to Method,* ed. L. E. Romanucci-Ross, pp. 156–67. New York: Praeger

154. Mumford, S. R. 1989. *Himalayan Dialogue: Tibetan Lamas and Gurung Shamans.* Madison: Univ. Wisconsin Press

155. Naka, K., et al. 1985. Yuta (shaman) and community mental health on Okinawa. *Int. J. Soc. Psychiatr.* 31(4):267–74

156. Deleted in proof

157. Deleted in proof

158. Neher, A. 1961. Auditory driving observed with scalp electrodes in normal subjects. *Electroencephalogr. Clin. Neurophysiol.* 13(3):449–51

159. Neher, A. 1962. A physiological explanation of unusual behavior in ceremonies involving drums. *Hum. Biol.* 34:151–60

160. Neihardt, J. G. 1972. *Black Elk Speaks.* New York: Pocket Books

161. Neu, J. 1975. Lévi-Strauss on shamanism. *Man* 10(2):285–92

162. Neu, J. 1977. *Emotion, Thought and Therapy.* Berkeley: Univ. Calif. Press
162a. Nicholson, S., ed. 1987. *Shamanism: An Expanded View of Reality.* Wheaton, IL: Quest Books
163. Nishimura, K. 1987. Shamanism and medical cures. *Curr. Anthropol.* 28(4, Suppl.):S59-S64
164. Noel, D. C. 1987. Shamanic ritual as poetic model: the case of Maria Sabina and Anne Waldman. *J. Ritual Stud.* 1:57–71
165. Noll, R. 1983. Shamanism and schizophrenia: a state specific approach to the "schizophrenia metaphor" of shamanic states. *Am. Ethnol.* 10:443–59
166. Noll, R. 1985. Mental imagery cultivation as a cultural phenomenon: the role of visions in shamanism. *Curr. Anthropol.* 26:443–61
167. Noll, R. 1990. Comment on individuation and shamanism. *J. Anal. Psychol.* 35(2):213–17
168. Noll, R. 1985. Mental imagery cultivation as a cultural phenomenon: the role of visions in shamanism. *Curr. Anthropol.* 26(4):443–61
169. Deleted in proof
170. Noll, R. 1989. What has really been learned about shamanism? *J. Psychoact. Drugs* 21:47–50
171. Novik, E. S. 1989. Ritual and folklore in Siberian shamanism: experiment in a comparison of structures. *Sov. Anthropol. Archaeol.* 28(2):20–84
172. Nowak, M., Durrant, S. 1977. *The Tale of the Nisan Shamaness: A Manchu Folk Epic.* Seattle: Univ. Washington
173. Ohnuki-Tierney, E. 1980. Shamans and Imu: among two Ainu groups: toward a cross-cultural model of interpretations. *Ethos* 8(3):204–28
174. Oosten, J. 1986. Male and female in Inuit shamanism. *Etudes Inuit.* 10(1–2):115–31
175. Deleted in proof
176. Oosten, J. G. 1984. The diary of Therkel Mathiassen: an examination of the practice of Inuit shamanism on Southampton Island (1922–1923). See Ref. 105, pp. 377–90
177. Ortner, S. B., Whitehead, H. 1981. *Sexual Meanings: The Cultural Construction of Gender and Sexuality.* Cambridge: Cambridge Univ. Press
178. Oubre, A. 1986. Shamanic trance and the placebo effect: the case for a study in psychobiological anthropology. *PSI Res.* 5(1–2):116-44
179. Overing, J. 1985. Images of cannibalism, death, and domination in a 'non-violent' society. In *The Anthropology of Violence,* ed. D. Riches. Oxford: Basil Blackwell
180. Overing, J. 1985. There is no end of evil: the guilty innocents and their faillible god. In *The Anthropology of Evil,* ed. D. Parkin. Oxford: Basil Blackwell
181. Overing, J. 1990. The shaman as a maker of worlds—Nelson Goodman in the Amazon. *Man* 25(4):602–19
182. Overing, J. 1988. Personal autonomy and the domestication of the self in Pioroa Society. In *Acquiring Culture: Cross-Cultural Studies in Child Development,* ed. G. Jahoda, I. M. Lewis, pp. 169–92. London: Croom Helm
183. Palmer, R. 1977. Toward a postmodern hermeneutics of performance. In *Performance in Postmodern Culture,* ed. M. Benamou, C. Caramello, pp. 19–32. Madison, WI: Coda Press
184. Perrin, M. 1987. Shamanist symptoms or symbols? A case of indetermination (the body of the Guajiro shaman). *Anthropos* 82:567–80
185. Peters, L. 1978. Psychotherapy in Tamang shamanism. *Ethos* 6(2):63–91
186. Peters, L. 1981. *Ecstasy and Healing in Nepal: An Ethnopsychiatric Study of Tamang Shamanism.* Malibu, CA: Undena Publications
187. Peters, L. G. 1981. An experiential study of Nepalese shamanism. *J. Transperson. Psychol.* 13(1):1–26
188. Peters, L. G. 1982. Trance, initiation, and psychotherapy in Tamang shamanism. *Am. Ethnol.* 9:21–46
189. Peters, L. G., Price-Williams, D. 1980. Towards an experiential analysis of shamanism. *Am. Ethnol.* 7:398–418
189a. Poole, F. J. P. 1986. Metaphors and maps: towards comparison in the anthropology of religion. *J. Am. Acad. Rel.* 54:411–58
190. Porterfield, A. 1987. Shamanism: a psychosocial definition. *J. Am. Acad. Rel.* 55(4):721–39
191. Potapov, L. P. 1976. Certain aspects of the study of Siberian shamanism. See Ref. 18, pp. 335–44
191a. Prince, R. 1982. Shamans and endorphins. *Ethos* 10(4): Special Issue
191b. Propp, V. 1968. *Morphology of the Folktale.* Austin: Univ. of Texas Press. 2nd ed.
192. Reinhard, J. 1976. Shamanism and spirit possession: the definition problem. In *Spirit Possession in the Nepal Himalayas,* ed. J. T. Hitchcock, R. L. Jones, pp. 12–20. New Delhi: Vikas Publishing House PVT Ltd.
193. Rice, J. 1991. *Black Elk's Song: Distinguishing Its Lakota Purpose.* Albuquerque: Univ. New Mexico Press
194. Ridington, R. 1979. Sequence and hierarchy in cultural experience: phases and the moment of transformation. *Anthropol. Hum. Q.* 4(4):2–10. Reprinted in Ref. 199
195. Deleted in proof
196. Deleted in proof
197. Deleted in proof
198. Ridington, R. 1988. *Trail to Heaven: Knowledge and Narrative in a Northern Native Community.* Iowa City: Univ. Iowa Press
199. Ridington, R. 1990. *Little Bit Know Something: Stories in the Language of Anthropology.* Iowa City: Univ. Iowa Press
200. Deleted in proof
201. Rollman, H. 1984. Inuit shamanism and the

Moravian missionaries of Labrador: a textual agenda for the study of native Inuit religion. *Etudes Inuit.* 8(2):131–38
202. Roseman, M. 1988. The pragmatics of aesthetics: the performance of healing among Senoi Temiar. *Soc. Sci. Med.* 27(8):811–18
203. Roseman, M. 1991. *Healing Sounds from the Malaysian Rainforest: Temiar Music and Medicine.* Berkeley: Univ. Calif.
204. Rothenberg, J. 1985. *Technicians of the Sacred: A Range of Poetries from Africa, America, Asia, Europe, and Oceania.* Berkeley: Univ. Calif. Press
205. Rouget, G. 1985. *Music and Trance.* Chicago: Univ. Chicago Press.
206. Salomon, F. 1983. Shamanism and politics in late-colonial Ecuador. *Am. Ethnol.* 10(3):413–28
207. Sandner, D. 1979. *Navaho Symbols of Healing.* New York: Harcourt Brace Jovanovich
208. Santos-Granero, F. 1986. The moral and social aspects of equality amongst the Amuesha of Central Peru. *J. Soc. Ames.* 72:107–31
209. Santos-Granero, F. 1986. Power, ideology and the ritual of production in lowland South America. *Man* 21(4):657–79
210. Santos-Granero, F. 1991. *The Power of Love: The Moral Use of Knowledge amongst the Amuesha of Central Peru.* London: The Athlone Press
211. Schechner, R. 1977. Towards a poetics of performance. In *Essays on Performance Theory 1970–1976.* New York: Drama Book Specialists
212. Schechner, R. 1985. *Between Theatre and Anthropology.* Philadelphia: Univ. Pennsylvania Press
213. Schechner, R., Appel, W. 1990. *By Means of Performance: Intercultural Studies of Theatre and Ritual.* Cambridge: Cambridge Univ. Press
214. Schlesier, K. H. 1987. *The Wolves of Heaven: Cheyenne Shamanism, Ceremonies, and Prehistoric Origins.* Norman, OK: Univ. Oklahoma Press
215. Senn, H. 1989. Jungian shamanism. *J. Psychoact. Drugs* 21(1):113–21
216. Sharon, D. 1978. *Wizard of the Four Winds: A Shaman's Story.* London: The Free Press
217. Deleted in proof
218. Sharon, D. 1976. A Peruvian Curandero's seance: power and balance. See Ref. 18, pp. 371–81
219. Shipley, T. E. 1988. Opponent-processes, stress and attributions: some implications for shamanism and the initiation of healing relationships. *Psychotherapy* 25(4):593–603
220. Shirokogoroff, S. 1935. *The Psychomental Complex of the Tungus.* London: Kegan, Paul, Tranch and Trubner
221. Siikala, A. 1978. The rite technique of the Siberian shaman. *Folklore Commun.* 220
222. Deleted in proof
223. Siikala, A. 1980. Two types of shamanizing and categories of shamanistic songs: a Chukchi case. In *Genre, Structure and Reproduction in Oral Literature,* ed. L. Honko, V. Voigt. Budapest: Akademiai Kiado
224. Siikala, A. 1985. Commentary. See Ref. 166, p. 455–56
225. Siikala, A. 1982. The Siberian shaman's technique of ecstasy. See Ref. 100, p. 1
226. Silverman, J. 1967. Shamanism and acute schizophrenia. *Am. Anthropol.* 69:21–31
227. Deleted in proof
228. Skultans, V. 1986. On mental imagery and healing. *Curr. Anthropol.* 27(3):262
229. Sonne, B. 1982. The Professional Ecstatic in His Social and Ritual Position. In *Religious Ecstasy,* ed. N. G. Holm, pp. 146–50. Uppsala/Stockholm: Almqvist and Wiksell Int.
230. Spencer, R. F. 1968. Review of studies in shamanism edited by Carl-Martin Edsman. *Am. Anthropol.* 70(2):396–97
231. Takiguchi, N. 1990. Liminal experiences of Miyako shamans: reading a shaman's diary. *Asian Folk Stud.* 49(1):1–38
232. Deleted in proof
233. Taussig, M. 1980. Folk healing and the structure of conquest in the Southwest Columbian Andes. *J. Latin. Am. Lore.* 6(2):217–78
234. Taussig, M. 1987. *Shamanism, Colonialism, and the Wild Man: A Study in Terror and Healing.* Chicago: Univ. Chicago Press
235. Taussig, M. 1991. *The Nervous System.* New York: Routledge
236. Taussig, M. 1989. The nervous system: homesickness and Dada. *Stanford Human. Rev.* 1.1:44–81
236a. Tedlock, B. 1981. Quiche Maya dream interpretation. *Ethos* 9(4):313–30
236b. Tedlock, B. 1987. *Dreaming: Anthropological and Psychological Interpretations.* Cambridge: Cambridge Univ. Press
236c. Tedlock, B. 1991. The new anthropology of dreaming. *Dreaming* 1(2):161–78
237. Torrey, E. F. 1972. *The Mind Game: Witchdoctors and Psychiatrists.* New York: Bantam Books
238. Townsend, J. B. 1988. Neo-shamanism and the modern mystical movement. See Ref. 51, pp. 73–83
239. Tsing, A. L. 1988. Healing boundaries in South Kalimantan. *Soc. Sci. Med.* 27(8):829–39
239a. Tsing, A. L. 1992. *In the Realm of the Diamond Queen: Gender, Marginality, and State Rule in an Out-of-the-Way Place in Indonesia.* Princeton: Princeton Univ. Press. In press
240. Turner, V. 1985. Preface. See Ref. 212
241. Villoldo, A., Jendresen, E. 1990. *The Four Winds: A Shaman's Odyssey into the Amazon.* New York: Harper and Row
242. Walens, S. 1981. *Feasting with Cannibals: An Essay on Kwakiutl Cosmology.* Princeton: Princeton Univ. Press

243. Walraven, B. C. A. 1983. Korean shamanism (review article). *Numen* 30(2):240–64
244. Walraven, B. C. A. 1985. *Muga. The Songs of Korean Shamanism.* Dordrecht: ICG Printing
245. Walraven, B. 1991. *Songs of the Shaman: Shamanism in Korea.* London: Kegan Paul International
246. Walsh, R. 1989. Mapping states of consciousness: comparing shamanic, schizophrenic, insight meditation, and yogic states. In *Proceedings of the Fifth International Conference on the Study of Shamanism and Alternate Modes of Healing, 1988,* ed. R. Heinze, Berkeley: Independ. Scholars Asia, Inc.
247. Walsh, R. 1989. What is a shaman? Definition, origin, and distribution. *J. Transperson. Psychol.* 21(1):1–11
248. Walsh, R. N. 1990. *The Spirit of Shamanism.* Los Angeles: Tarcher, Inc.
249. Wautischer, H. 1989. A philosophical inquiry to include trance in epistemology. *J. Psychoact. Drugs* 21(1):35–46
250. Wilbert, J. 1987. *Tobacco and Shamanism in South America.* New Haven: Yale Univ. Press
251. Willcox, A. R., Layton, R., Lewis-Williams, J. D. 1987. The cultural context of hunter-gatherer rock art. *Man* 22(1):171–75
251a. Williams, W. L. 1986. *The Spirit and the Flesh: Sexual Diversity in American Indian Culture.* Boston: Beacon
252. Wilson, B. 1983. The Korean shaman: image and reality. In *Korean Women: A View from the Inner Room,* ed. L. Kendall, M., pp. 113–28. New Haven, CT: East Rock Press
253. Winkelman, M. 1986. Trance states: a theoretical model and cross-cultural analysis. *Ethos* 14:174–204
254. Winkelman, M. J. 1990. Shamans and other magicoreligious healers—a cross-cultural study of their origins, nature, and social transformations. *Ethos* 18(3):308–52
255. Deleted in proof
256. Winkelman, M. 1989. A cross-cultural study of shamanistic healers. *J. Psychoact. Drugs* 21(1):17–24
257. Wolf, M. 1990. The woman who didn't become a shaman. *Am. Ethnol.* 17(3):419–30
258. Wright, P. A. 1989. The nature of the shamanic state of consciousness: a review. *J. Psychoact. Drugs* 21(1):25–33

Annu. Rev. Anthropol. 1992. 21:331–55

APPLICATIONS OF EVOLUTIONARY CULTURE THEORY

William H. Durham

Department of Anthropology and Program in Human Biology, Stanford University, Stanford, California 94305-2145

KEYWORDS: cultural evolution, descent, homology, transformation, cultural selection

INTRODUCTION

Evolutionary culture theory (ECT) is a growing corpus of principles and arguments that attempt to explain the "descent with modification" of human cultural systems. Although it encompasses diverse viewpoints (see comparisons in 24:158–66; 52; 53:Ch. 4), ECT is united by three underlying propositions: (*a*) that the socially transmitted information systems we call "cultures" provide human populations with an important second source of heritable variation; (*b*) that these cultural systems are historically interrelated by a branching, hierarchical pattern of descent; and (*c*) that this "cultural phylogeny" is itself a product of two basic kinds of processes—transformation (that is, sequential change within any given culture) and diversification (the branching of one culture into two or more descendants). It bears emphasizing that evolutionary culture theory differs substantially from earlier views of cultural evolution (such as those of classical evolutionary anthropology, neoevolutionism, and sociobiology; see 52) and that it refers not to any one position or line of argument today, but rather to the diverse collection of efforts to elucidate the patterns and processes of descent with modification in cultures.

331

0084-6570/92/1015-0331$02.00

In this chapter, I review recent attempts to use evolutionary culture theory to analyze stasis and change in human cultural systems. Among the many reasons why a review of these attempts is useful today, three seem particularly compelling. First, ECT is still to some degree isolated from mainstream concerns in anthropology and related social sciences. One reason for this is simply the field's youth: Its first important theory papers were published only in 1973 (32, 33). Another reason is the notoriety of earlier kinds of cultural inquiry that called themselves "evolutionary"—a notoriety vigorously renewed during the sociobiology debate (e.g. 30, 144). But perhaps a more important reason is that applications, especially thorough empirical analyses of phenomena of wider interest to social scientists, have to date received less attention than theoretical arguments and mathematical models. I hope a review of existing applications will both demonstrate the value of ECT and encourage new and more extensive empirical studies.

Second, evolutionary culture theory does not require an impoverished conceptualization of culture as is often believed. Although early arguments did give that impression (e.g. 35, 50, 51, 106, 171), the problem was one of oversimplification, not incompatibility. A review of applications can make clear that this shortcoming resulted more from the novelty of this line of inquiry than from an inherent weakness in the evolutionary approach. Finally, I believe that ECT has itself evolved without adequate attention to the social structure of human populations. In most formulations, for example, cultural change is modeled as the statistical outcome of simple decision-making by individuals; as one author noted (151:6), this reduces cultural evolution to "the product of choices made in the marketplace of cultural possibilities" (for an explicit case in point, see 106:176). A review of applications illustrates why this is at best a caricature of cultural evolution, and can suggest steps to correct it.

With these goals in mind, I address empirical work bearing on two main areas of ECT, conveniently summarized by Darwin's aphorism: namely, "descent" (i.e. cultural uses of the descent relationship) and "modification" (i.e. studies of the processes causing sequential transformation within cultural systems). I have taken the liberty of including a number of works that were not undertaken as applications of evolutionary theory by their authors, but that do provide useful empirical examples of cultural descent and modification. Because ECT is still a relatively new endeavor, I focus largely on its application to culturally homogeneous societies or "ethnolinguistic populations." This body of theory can make many useful contributions to the study of culture in more complicated, heterogeneous settings, including the modern nation-state; for now, however, the arguments and issues are best illustrated in less complex contexts. For other reviews of ECT, or "dual inheritance theory" as it is often called in comparisons with genetic evolution, see 16, 45, 52, 53:Ch. 4. For recent reviews of other, often complementary, approaches see 6, 26, 158 on evolutionary psychology; 22, 42, 153 on human behavioral ecology; 21, 77 on human sociobiology; 86, 103, 104 on "biocultural" evolution; and 95, 149 on social evolution.

DESCENT

A principal assumption in ECT is that new cultures generally originate from pre-existing "parental cultures" via a splitting or branching process called "diversification" or "culture birth." The assumption holds that diversification is normally a process of uniparental fissioning; although the so-called "daughter cultures" produced in this way may certainly go on to acquire many of their features by subsequent diffusion, in most cases they still begin as offshoots from a single parental stock. In principle, of course, new cultures can also originate through a simultaneous "fusion" or merger of different parental cultures, giving rise to descendants that are thoroughly hybrid or "mixed" from the start [as implied, e.g., by Kroeber's "tree of culture" (93:260–61)]. Surely bi-parental, tri-parental, or even multi-parental culture births are possible; indeed this has sometimes been the goal of attempts in the last few centuries to build synthetic "national cultures" (see 59 for a pertinent example). The implicit assumption of most ECT, however, is that genuine cultural hybrids have been rare, special cases in human history, at least until very recently—much as are the so-called "mixed languages" (pidgins, creoles, and "products of extreme borrowing"; see 84a, 164a) in the universe of human languages [e.g. Ruhlen's global inventory (142) lists only 37 pidgins and creoles]. Supporting this assumption are the arguments: (a) that there is neither a logical requirement nor a routine mechanism for bi-, tri-, or multi-parental inheritance in culture (in other words, successful culture birth requires the equivalent of neither sex nor syngamy); and (b) that there exist a number of effective barriers to hybridization—ecological, psychological, linguistic, and cultural (see 170)—that act as transmission isolating mechanisms (TRIMs), by analogy to the reproductive isolating mechanisms (RIMs) of speciation theory in biology. Although the strength of these and other barriers surely must vary from context to context, it is revealing that languages of mixed origin—not to mention whole cultures of mixed origin—seem to have formed only rarely, and then only under coercive conditions (see 15:108; also 110, 164a).

The Family-Tree Hypothesis

For these reasons, the "cultural phylogeny" behind most cultures—that is, the pattern of relationships generated by culture birth—is believed to form a systematic hierarchy of successive splits. Let me call this argument the "family-tree hypothesis" after its counterparts in linguistics (see e.g. 82:27–35; 142:Ch. 1) and evolutionary biology (see e.g. 77a, 78, 136, 154 on cladistic classification). Again, I emphasize that the family-tree hypothesis applies only to ties of descent (i.e. to links created by the actual birth of new cultures); it surely does not apply to ties of diffusion, which tend to be more clinal than tree-like (142:257) and are better described by "wave theory" (see 82:32–33). It will therefore be useful to distinguish between the bona fide phylogenies of cultures related by birth and the phylogeny-like mix of horizontal transfer and descent that may characterize the evolutionary history of any given technology, tradition, or social institution; my focus here is on the former.

Where TRIMs are strong and diversification consistently uniparental, there will be no mixed ancestries in a group of related cultures, and the corresponding family tree will specify a "unique and unambiguous" phylogeny, much as assumed by cladistic classification in biology (136:51). Such "unmixed" trees, or unmixed portions of trees, have a special importance in the study of cultural evolution because they provide a kind of "general reference system" for the group of related cultures (after 78), containing useful information about their historical ties. Where TRIMs are less effective and fusion occasional or intermittent, the resulting "mixed" family tree will still contain useful information and implications about cultural history. However, it will also be more difficult to infer parental relationships and thus to piece together an accurate phylogeny.

In organic evolution, the descent relationship has special importance because it creates what Darwin (44:206) called a "unity of type" among descendants: that "fundamental agreement in structure, which we see in organic beings of the same class, which is quite independent of their habits of life." In cultural evolution, one can speak of an analogous "unity" consisting of the cultural similarities among societies of a given region and period that are, likewise, independent of current circumstances and ecological exigencies. Any particular instance of such similarity can be called a cultural homology (that is, a similarity by descent) to distinguish it from other kinds of similarity among cultural systems (see 52:191) including: analogy (similarity by convergence or by parallel change), synology (similarity by diffusion or borrowing), "icology" or iconic similarity (similarity by intrinsic association; see example below), and mere coincidence (similarity by chance or accident). The family-tree hypothesis posits a large and generally unappreciated amount of similarity by descent among human cultural systems. Although some homologies are surely universal in their distribution (see discussion in 52:188–89), similarities by descent will generally be more specific, more detectable, and more abundant in instances of relatively recent cultural divergence—within language families or subfamilies, for example (see 1, 2). For convenience, I refer to this generalization as the "descent principle."

Putting Cultural Descent to Work

The analytical value and utility of the descent relationship among human cultures have been suggested many times by scholars in all four main subfields of anthropology (see e.g. 92, 102, 141, 143, 159, 169). Yet descent has rarely been given its due, in part because of the difficulty of obtaining the necessary data, comparative and/or diachronic, but also because of a prejudice widely held since Boas (see e.g. 19:211–25; and discussion in 52, 160) that diffusion reliably "swamps" all traces of phylogeny. The advent of evolutionary culture theory, together with studies like those described below, suggests that descent deserves a new hearing.

HISTORICAL LINGUISTICS   Since the pioneering arguments of Sir William Jones in 1786 (see 140:134), the descent relationship has played a prominent role in historical and comparative linguistics (5, 27, 82), where it has been used in two related ways. First, descent has served as the basis for the so-called "genetic classification" of languages into a structured taxonomy of phyla, stocks, families, subfamilies, and the like (75, 142, 143). Here the idea is that ties of descent have created a hierarchy of differential similarity among related languages, a hierarchy that can be detected through systematic comparative analysis. One of the more successful, though still controversial, techniques for doing this is Greenberg's method of "multilateral comparison" (71, 72, 142, 143): the study of basic word lists from an array of languages in an effort to distinguish probable "genetic cognates" from similarities caused by diffusion, sound symbolism (i.e. the iconic similarity between sound and its meaning, as in onomatopoeic words), and chance. A substantial list of suspected cognates is taken as prima facie evidence that two or more languages have probably descended with modification from a common ancestor. This follows from the "relatedness hypothesis" (82:17), which holds that descent from common origins is the most likely explanation for systematic similarities of sound and meaning in the basic vocabularies of a group of languages (see also 160). By themselves, of course, suspected cognates do not "prove" a descent relationship, particularly in situations where language contact has occurred (a point emphasized in 164a); still, they are useful for identifying similarities that warrant further study (see 72).

Once this first step is completed, the search continues within the group of hypothetical descendants for "exclusively shared innovations" (142:14), whether lexical, phonological, semantic, or syntactic. The presence of such innovations can both confirm suspected descent relationships and reveal more detailed similarities among certain subgroupings, allowing one to reconstruct a model of phylogenetic relationships. Here, as in Hennigian classification in biology (where the focus is similarly on "shared, derived characters" among related species; see 136:Ch.4), the assumption is that convergent evolution is relatively rare, and thus that exclusively shared innovations will appear only among the descendants of the parental language they first appeared in. This technique has been used intermittently since the time of Sapir (150; see review in 143) but perhaps nowhere more productively than in the major linguistic classifications of Greenberg (70, 71, 73).

The second use of descent within historical linguistics works the other way around. In this instance, homologous aspects of descent-related languages are used to reconstruct basic features of the common ancestor or "protolanguage" of the group (163). Aided by the "regularity hypothesis" (82:17)—that is, the hypothesis that linguistic evolution produces a characteristic series of sound changes through time within each language family (e.g. "Grimm's law" for Indo-European languages)—linguists have used sound correspondences among related languages to infer the historical pattern of sound shifts and thereby to reconstruct original words and expressions of the protolanguage. This procedure, too, has been widely applied, generating word lists and associated cultural inferences for many ancestral languages, including Proto-Athapaskan (55, 80), Proto-Indo-European (e.g. 63; see also 107, 128–130), Nostratic (85), Austronesian (12, 17, 18), and Proto-Polynesian (124–126), to name a few. In addition, comparative reconstruction has an important, more general role to play in the study of cultural evolution as described below.

BIOLOGICAL ANTHROPOLOGY   Paradoxically, one of the early studies to put the principle of cultural descent to good use was Livingstone's (102) pioneering work in human genetics. In an attempt to test the "malaria hypothesis" for the distribution of the sickle cell gene (S) in West Africa, Livingstone found a striking correlation between the linguistic affiliation of local populations and frequencies of the S gene. The comparison allowed him to attribute genetic differences between language groups to salient cultural differences, such as subsistence strategies, settlement patterns, and migration habits, but only because these properties were more or less consistent within language families. The success of the analysis, in other words, both in early tests and in later confirmations (see 53:Ch. 3), depended directly upon cultural similarities produced by descent.

Livingstone's analysis paved the way for other comparisons between the biological and linguistic phylogenies of human populations. Among other things, these studies add up to a striking confirmation of the validity of the procedures used to infer descent relationships in historical linguistics. One recent study by Greenberg et al (74), for example, compared linguistic, dental, and genetic evidence among broad samples of indigenous New World populations, and found three closely matched subdivisions. The correspondence suggested "that the Americas were settled by three separate population movements whose identity can be most precisely expressed in linguistic terms as Amerind, Na-Dene, and Aleut-Eskimo" (74:477). The finding raised no small controversy (see e.g. 43, 112), but subsequent genetic analysis (see 23, 31) has only strengthened the claim for the three-way split. Meanwhile, other researchers working on more or less analogous comparisons in Africa, Europe, and Oceania have confirmed the first study's most basic finding: "genetic differentiation clearly parallels the clustering of major linguistic families" (58:151; also 79a, 88, 155). It takes little imagination to predict that the search for other correlated phylogenies will continue to shed new light on the genetic and cultural histories of regional populations.

Meanwhile, the descent principle has reached a kind of ultimate expression for both historical linguistics and biological anthropology in recent comparisons of the global phylogenies of gene pools and languages. Consider the linguistic side first: There are new arguments and evidence for the monogenesis of human language—that is, for the existence, long postulated (161, 168; see discussion in 131), of a single common ancestor to all known human languages. Thus Greenberg's recent work with multilateral comparisons suggests that human languages form "what is very likely a single language family," all related by a branching hierarchy of descent (71:337; 73; and J. H. Greenberg, personal communication). To this, Bengtson and Ruhlen have added an impressive, growing list of global cognates and supporting etymologies (13). But the single most convincing piece of evidence comes again from correlated phylogenies—this time on a global scale, as documented by Cavalli-Sforza and colleagues (23, 31, 37, 39). Using, on the one hand, genetic data (from both "classical" protein analysis and nuclear DNA polymorphisms) and, on the other hand, linguistic data [from Ruhlen's (142) impressive world-scale compilation], these researchers find that the genetic family tree of human populations correlates "suprisingly well" with its (still somewhat incomplete) linguistic counterpart (31:76). This analysis, too, has drawn much criticism, some of it inevitable for a project of this scale (see e.g. 9, 120, 121, 173; see also replies in 38, 72). But the fact remains that not even a rough and approximate correlation would be found were the descent relationship important only to the genes, and not the cultures, of human populations.

ARCHEOLOGY   The descent relationship has also played a visible role within archeology, although its analytical importance has often been overshadowed by unilinear stage models and "essentialist," typological thinking (47–49, 95, 152). Prominent archeological studies with a "phylogenetic theme" include works by Bellwood (11), Childe (40, 41), Ehret (57), Flannery & Marcus (61), and Linares & Ranere (96). But surely the most comprehensive of such undertakings are recent works on (a) "the puzzle of Indo-European origins" by Renfrew and Mallory (e.g. 107, 128–131) and (b) "the evolution of the Polynesian chiefdoms" by Kirch (89–91) and Kirch & Green (92). In both cases the expanding archeological data base is supplemented by a wealth of independent information from historical linguistics (see sources above) and comparative ethnography. In the interest of brevity, and because the Indo-European case has been thoroughly reviewed elsewhere (see e.g. 107, 129), let me focus on the Polynesian work, which also draws upon the lessons of earlier phylogenetic studies by Goldman (64, 65; reviewed in 164) and Sahlins (145, 146; reviewed in 68). As Kirch has pointed out, Polynesia is almost an ideal setting for this kind of investigation: The more than 40 ethnographically described societies "can be likened to a set of historical, cultural 'experiments', in which the founding ancestor was identical, but where certain variables—ecological, demographic, technologic, and so on—differed from case to case" (90:2–3; see also 11a, 67, 162).

Results from Polynesia bode well for the future of cultural descent studies in archeology and anthropology more generally. First, drawing upon comparative archeological data and lexical reconstructions, Kirch (90:Ch. 3) is able to reconstruct significant features of "Ancestral Polynesian Society" (APS), and its internal variability, as these existed between about 500 BC and 300 AD. The characterization includes key aspects of technology, agriculture, animal husbandry, marine exploitation, settlement pattern, kinship, and social relations. Among other things, the reconstruction shows that "Colonizing Polynesians in every case carried with them concepts of pyramidal social structure, of first fruits and tribute as obligatory to the chiefs, of chiefs as earthly representatives of ancestral dieties ... [and] of domination by the chiefs over labor and the means of production" (90:281). In all, it adds up to one of the more complete cultural reconstructions available, confirming by example the value of the descent principle for archeology.

From this common base, Kirch argues, the cultural/ideational systems of Polynesia differentiated and transformed, as did the interrelated systems of social relations (a distinction I would emphasize more than Kirch, for reasons outlined in 53), giving rise to the "myriad cultural and social variations" that characterized the region at the time of contact (90:2). By then, variations on the ancestral theme ranged from relatively egalitarian societies, most commonly on atolls, all the way to highly stratified polities, most commonly on high islands, "where the chiefly class claimed descent independent from commoners, ranked themselves internally into seven or eight grades, practiced sibling marriage to maintain those grades, mobilized corvée labor and organized production on a grand scale, and most notably, alienated land from ownership by commoners" (90:4).

What forces guided the evolution of such differences? Here again Kirch draws upon the relationship of descent to infer a "synthetic explanation" with varied roles played by many factors (90:283; 92). The main argument can be summarized as follows: (a) Culturally sanctioned, politically motivated demands by the chiefs for surplus production, plus (b) natural population increases, operating within (c) the constraints of technology and varying local environments, propelled (d) various forms of expansion and intensification in agriculture and other production systems (90:281–82). Sooner or later (or not at all), depending on local conditions, expansion led to (e) competition and warfare between lineages, which (f) increased the power and wealth of successful chiefs, allowing them (g) to consolidate polities and restructure the social hierarchy, which in turn permitted them (h) to impose changes in local culture, including changes in the rules governing landholding, first-fruits ceremonies, and the tribute they were owed, which then (i) fueled further demands for surplus, leading back to item a above and creating, under suitable circumstances, a positive feedback loop.

The processes are clearly delineated, the causal links plausible, and the overall model reasonably well supported by selected cases (especially Hawai'i; see 90:Ch. 10). Moreover, by basing the APS reconstruction largely upon independent linguistic data, Kirch & Green avoid the potential for circularity in their inferences (as would result, for example, if APS were reconstructed by running the model backward, so to speak). There remain large gaps in the data, however, and many more cases beg to be tested (as in 91a), including atolls; in addition, much would be gained if the analysis were extended into the early post-contact period and explicitly linked up with studies of more recent Polynesian culture history (e.g. 147, 148; see also 164). Nevertheless, the study is a benchmark in the annals of descent research. Indeed, it is almost a paradigm of the historical interplay between cultural evolution and social change. Here one sees particularly clearly how power differentials can, through the mechanism of imposition (see below), give particular direction to cultural change. But one also sees how directional change in culture translates back into further increases in the social asymmetry that allowed the imposition in the first place. The result—a reciprocally interactive "coevolution" of culture and social structure—is certainly not unique to Polynesia, but it does seem especially accessible there to further study.

CULTURAL ANTHROPOLOGY   Descent-based analyses have a similar history, if not yet an equivalent apogee, in works of various authors in cultural anthropology (see especially 1, 2; 99:Ch. 21; 113–116, and an early review in 56). At times, the descent relationship even shows up in studies that are self-avowedly anti-evolutionary and/or anti-Darwinian in their approach. A classic example is Hallpike's argument, on the one hand, that it is "impossible to apply Darwinian principles ... to socio-cultural systems" (76:32) and, on the other hand, that "a number of those basic institutional and ideological forms which we regard as characteristic of Western European [society] ... can be traced to [a common ancestral] Indo-European origin" (76:329ff).

In the interest of brevity, let me offer examples of the use of the decent relationship in cultural anthropology according to the kind of inference that has been made, thus illustrating something of the greater potential for this kind of work. Descent has been used:

1. *To construct phylogenies and branching tree diagrams from comparative ethnographic data for groups of closely related cultures.* A good example is Marshall's (108) analysis of structural patterns of sibling classification in island Oceania, which generated a new "synopsis of Oceanic prehistory." The ensuing debate over the ancestral prototype, however (see 108:626–29), underscores an important procedural point: Some technique such as "outgroup comparison" (see 136:60ff) is essential for distinguishing ancestral from derived forms. Although building cultural phylogenies in this way is a perfectly legitimate use of the descent principle, the methodological challenges of assembling a comparative data base (as e.g. in 109) and carrying out multivariate statistics (as e.g. in 84) may limit its appeal; fortunately, in most instances, historical linguistics already provides an independent phylogenetic model—as in Ruhlen's classification (142; although the fine-grained categories should be approached with caution)—against which more selective ethnographic data

may then be compared (for examples of this more limited application, see 53:520–24; 54).

2. *To establish the relative age of certain traditions, or to make sense of their geographical distributions.* Such was the use of "genetic heritage" among cultures by Driver (46; see also 83), who sought to understand patterns of in-law avoidances among North American Indians; and by Murdock et al (118:459), who sought to comprehend regional patterns in the global distribution of theories of illness. As reviewed by Goodenough (68a:Ch. 4), descent was also "a major interest" to some American anthropologists, notably Wissler and Kroeber, and to German scholars of the *Kulturkreislehre* in the early decades of this century, "as they tried to trace the origin and diffusion of particular traditions" (p. 127). In my own work, I have used the descent relationship to infer the time depth of particular customs—a valuable aid where more direct historical information is lacking (e.g. see 53:474; 54).

3. *To reconstruct key features of ancestral cultural systems.* A prominent example here is Dumézil's reconstructed "tripartition" of Proto-Indo-European (PIE) society into the classes of priests, warriors, and herder-cultivators (see 98, 100, 101, and reviews in 98a:Chs. 19–21 and 107:Ch. 5). A related example is Lincoln's reconstruction of the PIE "myth of the first sacrifice" and its correspondences across Indo-European mythologies (97, 98:Ch. 4). The analysis allows Lincoln to infer subtle differences among prehistoric Indo-European cultures, as between the value of cattle to agriculturalists vs pastorialists (97:143), which in turn have shed light on the history of dairying and adult lactose absorption (see 53:269–73, 505–10). Lincoln's recent self-criticism (98a)—provoked by certain new insights into Dumézil's political life (explained in Ch. 19)—is a useful reminder that, in order to argue convincingly for cultural homology, one must always rule out convergence and coincidence (see p. xvi). In addition, it is an appropriate call for greater attention "to the multiple competing voices that find expression in differing variants [of myths], and to the struggles they wage in and through mythic discourse" (98a:124).

4. *To infer key processes guiding the differentiation of descendant cultures from the common ancestor.* Vogt (169:35–45) uses the descent principle in this way, much as do Kirch & Green in the example discussed above, to formulate a number of hypotheses about the radiation of "the Maya genetic unit" as affected by ecological setting, contacts with other groups, and internal cultural dynamics. Again, it is important to guard against the potential circularity of arguing, from the same data, both up the family tree and back down again. But where that can be avoided, this use of descent helps to show that "societies are not simply bundles of adaptations to the here-and-now ... [but] can inherit certain basic institutional and ideological principles from a remote and primitive antiquity ... [that] are often of vital significance" to their ongoing evolution (76:370).

MODIFICATION

So given the premises (*a*) that existing cultural systems are all related by descent, but (*b*) that homologies are most apparent where divergence is relatively recent, it becomes important to ask about transformation. What are the main processes that have guided the cumulative, sequential change of diverging cultures? Here the goals of ECT coincide nicely with recent efforts to "historicize anthropology" (e.g. 122, 123).

On the subject of transformation, ECT proposes a general "selective retention" framework (after 28, 29) within which different authors or schools of thought argue for different versions. The basic idea is that transformation is caused by changes through time in the social distribution of alternative cultural forms or "variants" within a given population or subpopulation. The focus is on "who believes what" (or at least who seems to) and "why" within a given group of people, and on how the answers to these questions change through time. The problem is obviously complicated by social structure, and particularly by differences in the social distribution of options, consequences, and power within a given population. To a considerable extent, social structure can be accommodated by identifying relatively homogeneous "reference groups" within the whole, and then by analyzing cultural dynamics within and between them (see also 53:210–11); however, this area of ECT deserves far more work and attention than it has thus far received.

Nevertheless, the basic idea of selective retention models is that the culture of a given reference group evolves as some variants gain in frequency among its members and others lose. ECT now hosts a whole range of propositions about how this happens. To date, the most promising involve "conveyance forces," that is, processes ("forces" in a metaphorical sense) causing differential rates of social transmission among the existing variants (see 52). Moreover, all such propositions assume that conveyance forces have a cumulative "recursive nature"; that is, the forces discussed below are viewed as acting repeatedly, over and over with the passage of time, such that trends (or stasis, as the case may be) emerge as a cumulative product of sequential, incremental change. Much in the way that individual frames relate to a movie, the forces at play in one "time step" relate to the eventual outcome of the cultural evolutionary process. In mathematical models of cultural change, this relationship is represented by so-called "recursion equations" or "recursion systems" (see e.g. 24, 35).

Transmission Forces

The first of three kinds of conveyance force can be called transmission forces. These arise from patterns of transmission—that is, from regularities in the social setting of the conveyance process. There are two central arguments here: One, from contextual studies, holds that the social organization and "style" of transmission have profound, cumulative effects on the aggregate properties of knowledge and culture; the second, from formal models, proposes that regularities in the simple structure of transmission greatly influence the direction and rates of cultural change (or stasis).

Consider the formal models first, particularly those developed by Cavalli-Sforza and Feldman (see especially 35). These investigators have identified 10 "major modes" of cultural transmission (e.g. from parent to child, among age peers, from teacher to pupil, from social leader to follower, etc), each with distinctive kinetic properties and different effects on the evolutionary persistence of variants (34). These 10 modes have been further distilled to four "major mechanisms" of cultural transmission: 1. one-to-one "vertical" transmission (i.e. parent-to-child); 2. one-to-one transmission between nonrelatives, either "horizontal" (between two members of the same generation) or "oblique" (between a member of one generation and a nonrelated member of the next); 3. "one-to-many" transmission (one sender to many receivers), and 4. "many-to-one" transmission (or "concordant pressure" from many senders). The general evolutionary implications of each mode have been worked out using recursion mathematics. In the case of one-to-many transmission, for example, "cultural change is expected to be rapid and within-population variation low"; in the case of many-to-one, on the other hand, transmission will be conservative and evolution slow, as fits intuitive expectations (36:20).

These predictions have been tested in a number of quantitative assessments. One study examined "trait similarity" (e.g. religious and political affiliation, sports preferences, miscellaneous personal habits and beliefs) between students at Stanford University, considered "recipients," and their parents and friends, considered "transmitters" (36). The average correlation coefficients for vertical transmission ($r = 0.22$) were almost double those for horizontal transmission ($r = 0.13$) and were especially high for political and religious affiliation. Another study examined key contributors to the social transmission of subsistence, maintenance, and child-care skills among a sample of Aka pygmies of the Central African Republic (79). If anything, vertical transmission was even stronger in this context, with parents being significant teachers/models for 80.7% of all skills examined. In contrast, one-to-many transmission "seems very rarely if ever found" among the Aka, suggesting that "the high similarity of pygmy cultural traits across a vast area in central Africa" is, in part, "a consequence of the prevalent transmission mechanisms" that tend to favor conservation of cultural forms (p. 933). In short, the models have solid heuristic value and generate testable, if not always surprising, predictions. Already drawing inspiration from epidemiology, the models could surely be improved by heeding Sperber's advice and striving more explicitly for "an epidemiology of representations ... rooted in cognitive psychology" (156:73; 157).

The second, more contextual argument about transmission forces comes from recent work by Barth. His argument, nicely summarized in a 1990 paper (8:640), is that "Differences between traditions of knowledge are illuminated by comparing the transactions in knowledge by which they are reproduced." For example, Barth compares the role of "the Conjurer" in Melanesian initiation rites (especially those of the Mountain Ok of western Papua New Guinea)—in which the transmission of knowledge to initiates is actually less important than a brief, "spell-binding performance" of mysterious procedures and secret rites—with the role of the Guru of Southeast Asia (e.g. a Balinese Muslim teacher), where the pressures are not for secrecy and performance but for the clarity, elaboration, and duration of instruction. Barth argues that the differences in these modes of transmission "generate deep differences in the form, scale and distribution of knowledge ... with profound historic effects on their cultures, even where similar substantive ideas are embraced" (p. 640). The arguments are a logical, comparative extension of the theme of an earlier monograph (7), which showed how "processes of codification, transmission, and creativity in Ok cosmology generate the [impressive] pattern of variation" manifest among different Ok groups today. In both works, Barth takes his cue from Darwin (see 7:Ch. 4), attempting to identify a specific mechanism of cumulative, incremental change within the "informational economy" of communities and regions. And in both cases, the argument provides a reasonably convincing account for observed variation, whether within or between traditions. Now it would be useful for the formal and contextual treatments of transmission to meet each other halfway and thus to generate models and simulations of the long-term, aggregate effects on culture of different "modes of managing knowledge" (8).

Natural Selection

The second of the three kinds of conveyance force is simply Darwinian natural selection acting on cultural variation, whether at the level of individuals, reference groups, or entire societies. In its most general form, natural selection may be said to occur whenever heritable variants, cultural or otherwise, differ in "fitness"—that is, whenever they differ in ways that affect the number of copies of each in the next generation. As Braun (25:79) puts it, "Natural selection for Darwin referred to the multiplicity of processes that together blindly shape the transmission of heritable characteristics in natural populations without artificial interference."

On this reading of Darwin, the natural selection of a variant refers to the preservation of that variant in a population by virtue of any replication advantage it has over alternative variants. This meaning of natural selection has been championed by Boyd and Richerson in an important series of publications (24, 133–135). They argue that natural selection on cultural variation can produce both cultural adaptations (as judged by the standard biological criterion of reproductive success) and cultural maladaptations, depending upon whether cultural transmission is "symmetric" to that of the genes, and thus directed from parents to offspring, or "asymmetric," and thus includes input from persons other than parents. The symmetric case is straightforward and relatively intuitive. As Richerson & Boyd note (135), a pronatalist religion will spread through a population by natural selection at the expense of an "abstemious" one whenever parents both adhere to one creed or the other and successfully pass it on to their children. Another example might be natural selection for fava bean consumption in malaria prone regions (see 24:178; 86, 87).

The asymmetric case is both more provocative and potentially more important. As Boyd & Richerson note (24:178), "Selection will act on asymmetrically transmitted cultural variation if (1) there is competition to occupy the roles that are effective in such transmission and (2) individuals characterized by some cultural variants are more often winners in this competition than individuals characterized by other variants." This argument is applied, albeit in a preliminary way (24:200; also 133), "to explain the demographic transition ... . [People] like teachers and managers are disproportionately important in horizontal and oblique transmission in modernizing societies. In these circumstances, natural selection should act to increase the freqency of norms and values that stress the importance and value of these roles. Conflict with [reproductive] fitness will occur if one's success ... in professional roles is negatively correlated with family size. This is plausible since individuals with small families will have more time, money, and other resources to devote to the attainment of these social roles."

The argument is logical, consistent with findings from numerous demographic studies, and loaded with implications; clearly a detailed longitudinal study is warranted. The same logic has been applied to the evolution of unilineal kinship systems (see 132) where, again, careful empirical analysis is sorely needed; and to the evolution of celibate religious traditions where, "by avoiding the costs of bearing or supporting children, celibates could devote more time and resources to spreading their beliefs horizontally" (24:202). The latter case underscores the importance of empirical substantiation: Despite its plausibility, the argument runs up against fairly convincing alternative explanations for at least a few of the world's major celibacy traditions (see 69:77–81 and 20 on Christian religious celibacy; 66:69–70 on celibacy in Tibet). These alternative explanations all entail another force—imposition—which brings us to the third and final category of conveyance force.

Cultural Selection

My own reading of Darwin convinces me that he normally used "natural selection" in the more specific sense of preservation by survival and reproduction advantage (i.e. preservation by actual biological propagation). To avoid confusion, I find it helpful (a) to think of Boyd & Richerson's "asymmetric" kind of selection as a transmission force (the first kind of conveyance force, discussed above), and thus (b) to distinguish it from both natural selection (kind 2) and a third kind, the differential social transmission of cultural variants as a function of human decision-making (see 53). Generally called "cultural selection" (after 4, 35, 50, 53, 138, 139, and others; called "biased transmission" in 24), this force arises from the value-guided preferences of culture carriers, whether exerted while they are adopting, sustaining, or conveying an aspect of a cultural system. The term is a deliberate parallel to "natural selection," but it refers to preservation by *preference advantage,* not survival and reproduction advantage.

Although there are as many forms of cultural selection as there are kinds of decision-making (individual and collective, formal and informal, conscious and unconscious, etc), I find it conceptually and analytically useful to distinguish two pairs of intergraded categories. First, following Pugh (127), decisions can be subdivided according to the types of value most influential to the outcome. Primary value selection thus refers to decisions in which 'primary' or 'developmental' values hold sway (these are the values that develop within each individual out of his or her own experience and the interplay of 'nature and nurture'; by definition they contain no significant, decision-altering information from social transmission). Such decisions form a continuum with those resulting from secondary value selection, that is, with decisions in which secondary values play the governing role ("secondary" refers to their derived character, not their importance; a value is secondary if it includes significant socially transmitted information). By these definitions, a decision can be influenced simultaneously by both primary and secondary values; the value that predominates in a given case specifies the form of selection. A decision qualifies as secondary value selection whenever the outcome is governed by socially transmitted information, either because the decision is different from what it would have been according to primary values (the clearest and strongest case) or because what makes it convincing to the deciders is socially transmitted information (an example is given below; compare with 172:643–46). In these terms, the decision-making procedures called "direct bias," "frequency dependent bias," and "indirect bias" by Boyd & Richerson (24) are particular forms of cultural selection; the latter two qualify as important, special cases of secondary value selection.

Another useful pair of intergraded categories ranges from choice to imposition, or more precisely, from autonomous election (autonomous within the constraints of technology, worldview, and actually existing variation) through to total compliance with the decisions of others. In instances of relatively unrestrained choice, the "carriers" of a given cultural variant are also its "selectors:" They decide whether to sustain one variant rather than another. Where choice predominates, the variants kept alive, so to speak, in a given cultural system reflect the local, endogenous preferences of the carriers. Such variants are likely to have the stable and enduring qualities often associated with "cultural tradition."

In imposition, on the other hand, the selectors and carriers are different groups of people. The selectors decide according to their own value systems and then find ways to induce compliance among the carriers. This compliance can be achieved by limiting the number and/or kinds of options, by changing or threatening to change the perceived consequences of options, or indeed by influencing the secondary values that will be used by the carriers. Either way, the variants kept "alive" by imposition will reflect the endogenous preferences of the selectors, not those of the carriers. To be sure, imposition is a decision process; however, the social locus of decision-making in imposition is different from that in choice, and implementation is here achieved through the exercise of power. Indeed, the very fact that power is generally required for effective imposition (see e.g. 105) suggests that the human "decision system" may well have been designed during its organic evolution to detect and resist such efforts. If so, then impositions are likely to be inherently unstable: Their persistence should then vary as a function of power asymmetries, the degree of imposed hardship, and awareness of potential options, among other things.

As noted elsewhere (52:199–200; 53:202), these two pairs of intergraded categories—choice to imposition, and primary to secondary value selection—can be viewed as the orthogonal axes of a Cartesian reference system for describing different forms of cultural selection. It should be emphasized that both axes represent continua rather than dichotomous categories, and thus that "choice" and "imposition" indicate relative, not absolute, positions on a spectrum. Nevertheless, I consider the contrast between them to be crucial with respect to both theory and empirical applications. The following sections illustrate this point while documenting the evolutionary efficacy of cultural selection in a fitting context: the cultural evolution of incest taboos. For other examples of the role of decision-making processes in cultural evolution, see 60, 62, 111, 137.

SELECTION BY CHOICE   A striking example of cultural selection by choice is offered in the recent analysis of "changing concepts of incest" among the Eastern Nuer by Hutchinson (81). As a by-product of social and economic change, the eastern Nuer today are questioning the limits of *rual* (incest) in their traditional incest prohibition, using a method that Hutchinson terms "pragmatic 'fecundity testing'" (p. 637). Locally called "feuding," the method entails the elopement of a young couple whose relationship has been declared *rual* by local courts. "If the union then proves fruitful and the child thrives, the couple can later return to their families confident that some sort of marriage arrangement will be made. If not, the lovers usually separate voluntarily ... . It is the fortune or misfortune of such couples, closely watched and commented upon by all, that is later cited as evidence for or against the validity of a particular [incest] prohibition" (81:630). The reason this process is so effective, continues Hutchinson, is that the Nuer believe that any union that bears healthy children is "divinely blessed" and is thus free of *rual*. In contrast, "'incest children' are expected to reveal their dangerous [divinely disapproved] origins through illness, abnormality, and early death" (p. 630). Hutchinson notes that because feuding reveals the limits of "divine tolerance" in this way it is "more powerful" than official court decrees in shaping local beliefs.

In this example, the Nuer conception of incest is evolving by choice. No external elite or political authority defines *rual* and imposes it upon the Nuer, and not even the local courts can effectively stem the tide of public opinion. Instead, the limits of *rual* are a matter of open discussion and autonomous election: Selected variants reflect the endogenous preferences of the carriers. (For a second, equally clear example, see 119:58–64.) An important exception in Nuerland tests the rule: the prohibition of incest between a man and his father's sister's daughter (FZD), which is considered worse than incest with his own daughter or sister (p. 625). Hutchinson shows that this one facet of the Eastern taboo reflects an enduring, internal power asymmetry between older men and their own sons (pp. 635–38). As befits imposition rather than choice, this facet is not subject to fecundity testing but is instead set aside, "insulated from the public rethinking and questioning of *rual* limits" (p. 639).

Note that the whole process, including both choice and imposition, also exemplifies secondary value selection. As a result of feuding, decisions among alternative definitions of incest are governed by an explicit value—that unions producing healthy children are divinely blessed—which itself requires social transmission. In addition, socially transmitted cultural notions of "shared blood," "shared cattle," and sacrifice (pp. 630–32) come into play; for example, "the ritual splitting of an ox by a Nuer earth priest is believed effective in tempering, if not neutralizing, the misfortunes" of some forms of incest (p. 626). Secondary values are also crucial in the case of imposition. Says Hutchinson, Eastern Nuer share "the conviction that no sacrifice is powerful enough to counter the negative effects of FZD incest" (p. 637).

SELECTION BY IMPOSITION   A contrasting example of cultural selection by imposition is provided by Goody's analysis (69:Ch. 3) of historical change in the marriage prohibitions of Western Europe. Beginning with the "Letter of [Pope] Gregory" in the 6th century AD, which forbade the marriage of first cousins, the prohibition of marriage between close kin in Europe became a matter of "prime significance" for the Church and its missionaries (p. 56). In subsequent centuries, the Church extended the ban first to second cousins, then third cousins, and eventually, by the 11th century, to sixth cousins. Reports Goody, "Not only were these enormously extended prohibitions attached to blood or consanguineal ties, but they were assigned to affinal and spiritual kinship as well," including the levirate and sororate (p. 56). Morover, they were joined by new prohibitions against adoption, concubinage, and divorce, all of which were imposed by the Church. "Why," Goody then asks, "should the Christian Church institute a whole set of new [rules] in the sphere of kinship and marriage, when these ran contrary to the customs of the inhabitants they had come to convert, contrary to the Roman heritage upon which they drew, and contrary to the teaching of their [own] sacred texts" (p. 42.)?

The answer, says Goody, lies in the economic interests of the Church. "By setting itself against [pre-existing local] 'strategies of heirship' that would assist a family line to continue—namely adoption, cousin marriage, [and so on] ... the Church brought about the [rapid] alienation of family holdings" (p. 123) and became, in short order, the single largest landowner in most European countries. As Goody notes, the view of the Church as an "accumulator of property" does not deny or contradict its other roles and functions (for example, as guardian of the poor), "for property it had to have in order to look after the faithful and provide a home [for the priesthood]" (p. 46). Yet its cultural impositions in the realm of marriage and the family bore the unmistakable signature of the selectors' own values and priorities, not those of the affected populations. That there was "continual resistance" from below, even before the Reformation, matches the expectation, mentioned above, about the instability of imposed decisions (see 69:Chs. 7, 8).

CROSS CULTURAL TESTS   As convincing as the Nuer and European examples may be, the question remains, Do these processes generalize? Has cultural selection played a major role in the descent with modification of incest taboos in other human societies? If so, what have been the relative roles of choice and imposition? Under what circumstances has choice been more influential, and under what circumstances imposition?

Although no single study yet focuses precisely on these questions, preliminary answers are available from a reasonably "matched" pair of analyses, one by Thornhill (165–167), which focuses on the effects of imposition, and one by myself (53:Ch. 6), which focuses largely on choice. Consider the Thornhill study first, which uses data from 129 of the societies in the Standard Cross Cultural Sample (SCCS) (117) to analyze variation not in "incest rules" per se but rather in rules of exogamy—that is, in "rules that regulate the mating and marriage of less closely related consanguineal kin and of affinal kin (kin by marriage)" (165:15). Several interrelated hypotheses are included in the full analysis (see 167), one of which is particularly germane here: "that rules of mating and marriage are made in order to prevent families from concentrating wealth and/or power within lineages by intermarriage because such concentration may [threaten] the social status of leaders in society" (165:15).

On the assumption (from 3) that "powerful men" generally make the rules of mating and marriage, Thornhill tests three specific predictions that follow from this hypothesis. She finds, first, that "in highly stratified societies the rules of mating and marriage [are] more extensive ... than in societies with little stratification" (165:15). The association is particularly striking in the case of "maximally extensive" rules (i.e. those applying to all patrilateral and matrilateral relatives), which are found only in societies with three or more hierarchical classes. Second, she finds that "highly stratified societies [have] harsher punishment for infraction of mating and marriage rules than societies with little stratification" (165:16), a finding consonant with Betzig's earlier analyis of despotism (14). Finally, Thornhill also finds that "as stratification increases, rules [tend to be] less equitably applied" (165:17), such that "rulers in stratified societies are rarely expected to observe the marriage rules and frequently marry their own relatives" (167:253).

Thornhill's analysis leaves little doubt that imposition has been a major force in the cultural evolution of marriage rules. By the same token, Thornhill's definition of "mating and marriage rules"—which explicitly requires "the behavior ruled against [to have an effect] on the evolved interests of those who make the rules" (167:249)—builds in a certain guarantee of such results. Moreover, this definition must surely explain why "only 44%" of the sample had nuclear family incest rules—a finding contrary to almost every published report since Murdock's (114)—and thus why it seems "that people (rulers in particular) are much more concerned about ... the mating and marriage of distant relatives and nonrelatives than they are about incest" (167:252).

My own, independent analysis (53:Ch. 6) uses the smaller "Sixty Cultures" world probability sample (see 94) to investigate variation in incest taboos per se—that is, variation in the breadth of prohibitions against sexual activity between kin. First, for each population in the sample, I define the breadth or extension of the taboo to refer to the most distant consanguineous relative, *not including* those covered by rules of exogamy, with whom ego is forbidden to have sexual relations (and therefore to marry; for details, see 53:352–53, 511–15). By excluding the strictures of exogamy, this procedure effectively factors out much of the influence of imposition documented by Thornhill. Second, I then propose a model, based on Bateson's "optimal outbreeding theory" (10), for the cultural evolution by choice of incest taboos. The model predicts that the incest taboos of local populations will evolve toward extensions that minimize the total average "costs" of inbreeding and outbreeding. (Here "costs" include all adverse consequences—genetic, social, and psychological—of sexual relations with a given category of relative.) More specifically, the model predicts that incest taboos will be more extensive in the case of large communities that also promote geographical out-marriage, compared to small communities that also promote local in-marriage—a prediction directly opposite to that expected by the well-known Westermarck hypothesis (53:345–46). My prediction is based on the argument that, other things being equal, the costs of outbreeding will tend to be higher in small, endogamous communities, and inbreeding costs may be lower there as well.

The test of these predictions against data from the "Sixty Cultures" sample produced a statistically significant association between the extension of incest prohibitions and the degree of community exogamy: generally speaking, a greater range of kin are prohibited as sex partners within exogamous communities, as compared with agamous and endogamous ones. Moreover, the association is stronger in the subset of societies (N = 30) with a small average community size (i.e. fewer than 400 members). In short, the test favors the optimal outbreeding theory and suggests that selection by choice has played an important, general role in the cultural evolution of existing incest taboos. On the other hand, the associations, though statistically significant, are not particularly strong (nonparametric Kendall's tau was 0.37 for the full sample and 0.48 for a subsample with small community size). And the study does not control for differences in social structure and hierarchy among the sample societies. It therefore seems likely that much of the unexplained variation reflects the evolutionary influence of imposition; further work on this topic is certainly called for.

CONCLUSION

In this chapter, I have reviewed recent efforts to apply tools of evolutionary analysis to the study of cultural change. From studies of "descent" and studies of "modification" the following lessons, among others, can be drawn:

1. The hypothesis that existing cultural systems are all historically related in a branching hierarchical pattern of descent is worthy of more attention in anthropology and other social sciences than it has received to date.

2. Although some consequences of shared descent may well be visible in broad cross-cultural comparisons, cultural homologies are best seen and appreciated in closely related (or recently diverged) groups of cultures, such as those of the same language family or subfamily.

3. Cultural homologies and ties of descent have been explored in specific studies from all main subfields of anthropology; however, they have not yet been integrated by methods or conclusions into a unified, general approach.

4. Historical and comparative linguistics already provide an important general reference system for many of the cultures and societies known to anthropology; comparisons between linguistic and genetic family trees may soon provide a global phylogenetic model of the descent relationships among human populations.

5. The study of descent relations among human cultures would benefit from further empirical and theoretical work, particularly in regard to appropriate methodology and the perennial problem of disentangling diffusion from descent.

6. New headway is also being made in the study of "transformation," or sequential change within a given cultural system, particularly in regard to major processes or "forces" of change. "Diversification," or the branching of one culture into two or more descendants, warrants much more attention than it now receives.

7. Transmission forces, the natural selection of cultural variation, and various forms of cultural selection have all yielded provocative results in specific individual studies. New applications of evolutionary culture theory, and new and better refinements of the theory, are bound to be insightful and productive.

8. Also needed are new and stronger links between evolutionary culture theory and other kinds of culture theory (interpretive, political economic, etc) on the one hand, and among evolutionary culture theory, evolutionary psychology, and human behavioral ecology on the other hand.

ACKNOWLEDGMENTS

In recognition of his role in the evolution of the *Annual Review of Anthropology*, Volumes 1 to 21, this paper is respectfully dedicated to Dr. Bernard J. Siegel.

Portions of this review were presented in October 1991 at the opening meeting of the Research Group on "The Biological Foundations of Human Culture" at the Center for Interdisciplinary Research (ZiF) in Bielefeld, Germany. I thank the Director of that group, Dr. Peter Weingart, and its members for many interesting and stimulating discussions of the topics and issues reviewed here. Particular thanks go to ZiF Fellows Monique Borgerhoff Mulder, Walter Goldschmidt, Peter Hejl, Alexandra Maryanski, Peter Richerson, Nancy Thornhill, and Jonathan Turner for specific comments or suggestions. In addition, I appreciate the timely input and advice of John Beatty, John Rick, Merritt Ruhlen, and Stephen Shennan.

Literature Cited

1. Aberle, D. F. 1974. Historical reconstruction and its explanatory role in comparative ethnology. See Ref. 83, pp. 63–79
2. Aberle, D. F. 1984. The language family as a field for historical reconstruction. *J. Anthropol. Res.* 40:129–36
3. Alexander, R. D. 1977. Natural selection and the analysis of human sociality. In *Changing Scenes in Natural Sciences,* ed. C. E. Goulden, pp. 283–337. Philadelphia: Philadelphia Acad. Nat. Sci.
4. Alland, A. 1970. *Adaptation in Cultural Evolution: An Approach to Medical Anthropology.* New York: Columbia Univ. Press
5. Anttila, R. 1989. *Historical and Comparative Linguistics.* Amsterdam: John Benjamins
6. Barkow, J., Cosmides, L., Tooby, J., eds. 1992. *The Adapted Mind: Evolutionary Psychology and the Generation of Culture.* New York: Oxford Univ. Press. In press
7. Barth, F. 1987. *Cosmologies in the Making: A Generative Approach to Cultural Variation in Inner New Guinea.* Cambridge: Cambridge Univ. Press
8. Barth, F. 1990. The guru and the conjurer: transactions in knowledge and the shaping of culture in Southeast Asia and Melanesia. *Man (NS)* 25:640–53
9. Bateman, R., Goddard, I., O'Grady, R., Funk, V. A., Mooi, R., et al. 1990. Speaking of forked tongues: the feasibility of reconciling human phylogeny and the history of language. *Curr. Anthropol.* 31(1):1–24
10. Bateson, P. P. G. 1983. Optimal outbreeding. In *Mate Choice,* ed. P. P. G. Bateson. Cambridge: Cambridge Univ. Press
11. Bellwood, P. 1985. *Prehistory of the Indo-Malaysian Archipelago.* New York: Academic
11a. Bellwood, P. S. 1987. The prehistory of

Island Southeast Asia: a multidisciplinary review of recent research. *J. World Prehist.* 1:171-224
12. Bellwood, P. 1991. The Austronesian dispersal and the origin of languages. *Sci. Am.* 265(1):88–93
13. Bengtson, J. D., Ruhlen, M. 1992. Global etymologies. In *On the Origin of Languages: Studies in Linguistic Taxonomy,* ed. M. Ruhlen. In press
14. Betzig, L. L. 1986. *Despotism and Differential Reproduction: A Darwinian View of History.* New York: Aldine
15. Bickerton, D. 1983. Creole languages. *Sci. Am.* 249(1):108–15
16. Blurton Jones, N. G. 1990. Three sensible paradigms for research on evolution and human behavior? *Ethol. Sociobiol.* 11:353–59
17. Blust, R. 1980. Early Austronesian social organization: the evidence of language. *Curr. Anthropol.* 21(2):205–47
18. Blust, R. 1988. The Austronesian homeland: a linguistic perspective. *Asian Perspect.* 26(1):45–67
19. Boas, F. 1940. *Race, Language, and Culture.* Chicago: Univ. Chicago Press
20. Boone, J. L. 1986. Parental investment and elite family structure in preindustrial societies: a case study of late medieval-early modern Portuguese genealogies. *Am. Anthropol.* 88:859–78
21. Borgerhoff Mulder, M. 1987. Progress in human sociobiology. *Anthropol. Today* 3:5–8
22. Borgerhoff Mulder, M. 1991. Human behavioral ecology. In *Behavioral Ecology: An Evolutionary Approach,* ed. J. R. Krebs, N. B. Davies, pp. 69–98. Oxford: Blackwell Scientific
23. Bowcock, A. M., Kidd, J. R., Mountain, J. L., Hebert, J. M., Carotenuto, L., et al. 1991.

Drift, admixture and selection in human evolution: a study with DNA polymorphisms. *Proc. Natl. Acad. Sci. USA* 88:839–43

24. Boyd, R., Richerson, P. J. 1985. *Culture and the Evolutionary Process.* Chicago: Univ. Chicago Press

25. Braun, D. P. 1990. Selection and evolution in nonhierarchical organization. In *The Evolution of Political Systems: Sociopolitics in Small-Scale Sedentary Societies,* ed. S. Upham, pp. 62–86. Cambridge: Cambridge Univ. Press

26. Buss, D. M. 1991. Evolutionary personality psychology. *Annu. Rev. Psychol.* 42:459–91

27. Bynon, T. 1983. *Historical Linguistics.* Cambridge: Cambridge Univ. Press

28. Campbell, D. T. 1960. Blind variation and selective retention in creative thought as in other knowledge processes. *Psychol. Rev.* 67(6):380–400

29. Campbell, D. T. 1965. Variation and selective retention in socio-cultural evolution. In *Social Change in Developing Areas: A Reinterpretation of Evolutionary Theory,* ed. H. R. Barringer, G. I. Blanksten, R. W. Mack, pp. 19–49. Cambridge, MA: Schenkman

30. Caplan, A. L., ed. 1978. *The Sociobiology Debate: Readings on Ethical and Scientific Issues.* New York: Harper and Row

31. Cavalli-Sforza, L. L. 1991. Genes, peoples and languages. *Sci. Am.* 265(5):72–78

32. Cavalli-Sforza, L. L., Feldman, M. 1973. Cultural versus biological inheritance: phenotypic transmission from parents to children. *Am. J. Hum. Genet.* 25:618–37

33. Cavalli-Sforza, L. L., Feldman, M. 1973. Models for cultural inheritance. I: Group mean and within group variation. *Theor. Popul. Biol.* 4:42–55

34. Cavalli-Sforza, L. L., Feldman, M. W. 1978. Towards a theory of cultural evolution. *Interdiscip. Sci. Rev.* 3(2):99–107

35. Cavalli-Sforza, L., Feldman, M. 1981. *Cultural Transmission and Evolution: A Quantitative Approach.* Princeton: Princeton Univ. Press

36. Cavalli-Sforza, L. L., Feldman, M. W., Chen, K. H., Dornbusch, S. M. 1982. Theory and observation in cultural transmission. *Science* 218:19–27

37. Cavalli-Sforza, L. L., Piazza, A., Menozzi, P., Mountain, J. 1988. Reconstruction of human evolution: bringing together genetic, archaeological, and linguistic data. *Proc. Natl. Acad. Sci. USA* 85:6002–6

38. Cavalli-Sforza, L. L., Piazza, A., Menozzi, P., Mountain, J. 1989. Genetic and linguistic evolution. *Science* 244:1128–29

39. Cavalli-Sforza, L. L., Menozzi, P., Piazza, A. 1992. *History and Geography of Human Genes.* Princeton: Princeton Univ. Press. In press

40. Childe, V. G. 1926. *The Aryans: A Study of Indo-European Origins.* New York: Alfred A. Knopf

41. Childe, V. G. 1951. *Social Evolution.* London: Watts

42. Cronk, L. 1991. Human behavioral ecology. *Annu. Rev. Anthropol.* 20:25–53

43. Custer, J. F., Ruhlen, M., Shimkin, D. B. 1990. Linguistics and the earliest Americans. *Science* 248:345–46

44. Darwin, C. 1964 [1859]. *On the Origin of Species.* A facsimile of the first edition. Cambridge, MA: Harvard Univ. Press

45. Dietz, T., Burns, T. R., Buttel, F. H. 1990. Evolutionary theory in sociology: an examination of current thinking. *Sociol. Forum* 5(2):155–71

46. Driver, H. E. 1966. Geographical-historical versus psycho-functional explanations of kin avoidances. *Curr. Anthropol.* 7(2):131–82

47. Dunnell, R. C. 1980. Evolutionary theory and archaeology. *Adv. Archaeol. Method Theory* 3:35–99

48. Dunnell, R. C. 1985. Methodological issues in Americanist artifact classification. *Adv. Archeol. Method Theory* 9:149–207

49. Dunnell, R. C. 1990. Aspects of the application of evolutionary theory in archeology. In *Archeological Thought in America,* ed. C. C. Lamberg-Karlovsky, pp. 35–49. Cambridge: Cambridge Univ. Press

50. Durham, W. H. 1976. The adaptive significance of cultural behavior. *Hum. Ecol.* 4(2):89–121

51. Durham, W. H. 1979. Toward a coevolutionary theory of human biology and culture. In *Evolutionary Biology and Human Social Behavior: An Anthropological Perspective,* ed. N. A. Chagnon, W. Irons, pp. 39–59. North Scituate, MA: Duxbury

52. Durham, W. H. 1990. Advances in evolutionary culture theory. *Annu. Rev. Anthropol.* 19:187–210

53. Durham, W. H. 1991. *Coevolution: Genes, Culture, and Human Diversity.* Stanford: Stanford Univ. Press

54. Durham, W. H., Nassif, R. C. 1991. Managing the competition: a Tupi adaptation in Amazonia. Presented at UNESCO Conf. Food and Nutrition in the Tropical Forest, Paris

55. Dyen, I., Aberle, D. F. 1974. *Lexical Reconstruction: The Case of the Proto-Athapaskan Kinship System.* Cambridge: Cambridge Univ. Press

56. Eggan, F. 1954. Social anthropology and the method of controlled comparison. *Am. Anthropol.* 56:743–63

57. Ehret, C. 1976. Linguistic evidence and its correlation with archaeology. *World Archaeol.* 8(1):5–18

58. Excoffier, L., Pellegrini, B., Sanchez-Mazas, A., Simon, C., Langaney, A. 1987. Genetics and history of sub-Saharan Africa. *Yearb. Phys. Anthropol.* 30:151–94

59. Fischer, D. H. 1989. *Albion's Seed: Four*

British Folkways in America. New York: Oxford Univ. Press

60. Flannery, K. V., ed. 1986. *Guila Naquitz: Archaic Foraging and Early Agriculture in Oaxaca, Mexico.* Orlando, FL: Academic

61. Flannery, K. V., Marcus, J., eds. 1983. *The Cloud People: Divergent Evolution of the Zapotec and Mixtec Civilizations.* New York: Academic

62. Flannery, K. V., Marcus, J., Reynolds, R. G. 1989. *The Flocks of the Wamani: A Study of Llama Herders on the Punas of Ayacucho, Peru.* San Diego: Academic

63. Gamkrelidze, T. V., Ivanov, V. V. 1990. The early history of Indo-European languages. *Sci. Am.* 262(3):110–16

64. Goldman, I. 1955. Status rivalry and cultural evolution in Polynesia. *Am. Anthropol.* 57:680–97

65. Goldman, I. 1970. *Ancient Polynesian Society.* Chicago: Univ. Chicago Press

66. Goldstein, M. C. 1971. Stratification, polyandry and family structure in central Tibet. *Southwest. J. Anthropol.* 27:64–74

67. Goodenough, W. 1957. Oceania and the problem of controls in the study of cultural and human evolution. *J. Polynes. Soc.* 66:146–55

68. Goodenough, W. 1959. Book review of *Social Stratification in Polynesia* by M. D. Sahlins. *J. Polynes. Soc.* 68:255–58

68a. Goodenough, W. 1970. *Description and Comparison in Cultural Anthropology.* Cambridge: Cambridge Univ. Press

69. Goody, J. 1983. *The Development of the Family and Marriage in Europe.* Cambridge: Cambridge Univ. Press

70. Greenberg, J. H. 1963. *The Languages of Africa.* Bloomington: Indiana Univ.

71. Greenberg, J. H. 1987. *Language in the Americas.* Stanford: Stanford Univ. Press

72. Greenberg, J. H. 1990. The American Indian language controversy. *Rev. Archeol.* 11(2):5–14

73. Greenberg, J. H. 1992. *Indo-European and Its Closest Relatives: The Eurasiatic Language Family.* Stanford: Stanford Univ. Press. In press

74. Greenberg, J. H., Turner, C. G., Zegura, S. L. 1986. The settlement of the Americas: a comparison of the linguistic, dental, and genetic evidence. *Curr. Anthropol.* 27(5):477–97

75. Haas, M. R. 1966. Historical linguistics and the genetic relationship of languages. In *Current Trends in Linguistics,* ed. T. A. Sebeok, 3:113–53. The Hague: Mouton

76. Hallpike, C. 1986. *The Principles of Social Evolution.* Oxford: Clarendon

77. Harpending, H., Rogers, A., Draper, P. 1987. Human sociobiology. *Yearb. Phys. Anthropol.* 30:127–50

77a. Harvey, P. H., Pagel, M. D. 1991. *The Comparative Method in Evolutionary Biology.* Oxford: Oxford Univ. Press

78. Hennig, W. 1966. *Phylogenetic Systematics.* Urbana: Univ. Illinois Press

79. Hewlett, B. S., Cavalli-Sforza, L. L. 1986. Cultural transmission among Aka pygmies. *Am. Anthropol.* 88(4):922–34

79a. Hill, A. V. S., Serjeantson, S. W. 1989. *The Colonization of the Pacific: A Genetic Trail.* Oxford: Clarendon

80. Hoijer, H. 1956. Athapaskan kinship systems. *Am. Anthropol.* 58:309–33

81. Hutchinson, S. 1985. Changing concepts of incest among the Nuer. *Am. Ethnol.* 12(4):625–41

82. Jeffers, R. J., Lehiste, I. 1979. *Principles and Methods for Historical Linguistics.* Cambridge, MA: MIT Press

83. Jorgensen, J. G., ed. 1974. *Comparative Studies by Harold E. Driver and Essays in His Honor.* New Haven: HRAF Press

84. Jorgensen, J. G. 1983. Comparative traditional economics and ecological adaptations. In *Handbook of North American Indians,* ed. A. Ortiz, 10:684–710. Washington DC: Smithsonian Inst.

84a. Jourdain, C. 1991, Pidgins and creoles: the blurring of categories. *Annu. Rev. Anthropol.* 20:187-209

85. Kaiser, M., Shevoroshkin, V. 1988. Nostratic. *Annu. Rev. Anthropol.* 17:309–29

86. Katz, S. H. 1982. Food, behavior, and biocultural evolution. In *The Psychobiology of Human Food Selection,* ed. L. M. Barker, pp. 171–88. Westport, CT: AVI

87. Katz, S. H. 1987. Fava bean consumption: a case for the coevolution of genes and culture. In *Food and Evolution,* ed. M. Harris, E. B. Ross, pp. 133–59. Philadelphia: Temple Univ. Press

88. Kelly, K. M. 1990. Gm polymorphisms, linguistic affinities, and natural selection in Melanesia. *Curr. Anthropol.* 31(2):201–19

89. Kirch, P. V. 1980. Polynesian prehistory: cultural adaptation in island ecosystems. *Am. Sci.* 68:39–48

90. Kirch, P. V. 1984. *The Evolution of the Polynesian Chiefdoms.* Cambridge: Cambridge Univ. Press

91. Kirch, P. V. 1986. Rethinking east Polynesian prehistory. *J. Polynes. Soc.* 95:9–40

91a. Kirch, P. V. 1991. Chiefship and competitive involution: the Marquesas Islands of eastern Polynesia. In *Chiefdoms: Power, Economy, and Ideology,* ed. T, Earle, pp. 119–45. Cambridge: Cambridge Univ. Press

92. Kirch, P. V., Green, R. C. 1987. History, phylogeny, and evolution in Polynesia. *Curr. Anthropol.* 28(4):431–56

93. Kroeber, A. L. 1948. *Anthropology.* New York: Harcourt, Brace

94. Lagacé, R. O., ed. 1977. *Sixty Cultures: A Guide to the HRAF Probability Sample Files. New Haven: HRAF Press*

95. Leonard, R. D., Jones, G. T. 1987. Elements of an inclusive evolutionary model for archeology. *J. Anthropol. Archaeol.* 6:199–219

96. Linares, O. F., Ranere, A. J., eds. 1980.

Adaptive Radiations in Prehistoric Panama. Cambridge, MA: Harvard Univ. Press

97. Lincoln, B. 1975. The Indo-European myth of creation. *Hist. Relig.* 15:121–45

98. Lincoln, B. 1981. *Priests, Warriors, and Cattle: A Study in the Ecology of Religions.* Berkeley: Univ. Calif. Press

98a. Lincoln, B. 1991. *Death, War, and Sacrifice: Studies in Ideology and Practice.* Chicago: Univ. Chicago Press

99. Linton, R. 1936. *The Study of Man: An Introduction.* New York: D. Appleton-Century

100. Littleton, C. S. 1974. Georges Dumézil and the rebirth of the genetic model: an anthropological appreciation. In *Myth in Indo-European Antiquity,* ed. G. J. Larson, pp. 169–79. Berkeley: Univ. Calif. Press

101. Littleton, C. S. 1982. *The New Comparative Mythology: An Anthropological Assessment of the Theories of Georges Dumézil.* Berkeley: Univ. Calif. Press

102. Livingstone, F. B. 1958. Antropological implications of sickle-cell distribution in West Africa. *Am. Anthropol.* 60:533–62

103. Lopreato, J. 1984. *Human Nature and Biocultural Evolution.* Boston: Allen and Unwin

104. Lopreato, J. 1990. From social evolutionism to biocultural evolutionism. *Sociol. Forum* 5(2):187–212

105. Lukes, S. 1974. *Power: A Radical View.* London: Macmillan

106. Lumsden, C. J., Wilson, E. O. 1981. *Genes, Mind and Culture: The Coevolutionary Process.* Cambridge, MA: Harvard Univ. Press

107. Mallory, J. P. 1989. *In Search of the Indo-Europeans: Language, Archaeology and Myth.* London: Thames and Hudson

108. Marshall, M. 1984. Structural patterns of sibling classification in island Oceania: implications for culture history. *Curr. Anthropol.* 25(5):597–637

109. Métraux, A. 1928. *La Civilisation Materielle Des Tribus Tupi-Guaraní.* Paris: P. Geuthner

110. Mintz, S. W. 1971. The socio-historical background to pidginization and creolization. In *Pidginization and Creolization of Languages,* ed. D. Hymes, pp. 481–96. Cambridge: Cambridge Univ. Press

111. Mithen, S. J. 1990. *Thoughtful Foragers: A Study of Prehistoric Decision Making.* Cambridge: Cambridge Univ. Press

112. Morell, V. 1990. Confusion in earliest America. *Science* 248:439–41

113. Murdock, G. P. 1948. Anthropology in Micronesia. *Trans. NY Acad. Sci.* 2(1):9–16

114. Murdock, G. P. 1949. *Social Structure.* New York: Macmillan

115. Murdock, G. P. 1968. Patterns of sibling terminology. *Ethnology* 7(1):1–24

116. Murdock, G. P. 1970. Kin term patterns and their distribution. *Ethnology* 9(2):165–81

117. Murdock, G. P., White, D. R. 1980. The standard cross-cultural sample and its codes. In *Cross-Cultural Samples and Codes,* ed. H. Barry, A. Schlegel, pp. 3–44. Pittsburgh: Univ. Pittsburgh Press

118. Murdock, G. P., Wilson, S. F., Frederick, V. 1978. World distribution of theories of illness. *Ethnology* 17:449–70

119. Netting, R. M. 1981. *Balancing on an Alp: Ecological Change and Continuity in a Swiss Mountain Community.* Cambridge: Cambridge Univ. Press

120. Nichols, J., Wiley, E. O., Comuzzie, A., Bamshad, M., Bateman, R. M., et al. 1990. More on human phylogeny and linguistic history. *Curr. Anthropol.* 31(3):313–16

121. O'Grady, R. T., Goddard, I., Bateman, R. M., Dimichele, W. A., Funk, V. A., et al. 1989. Genes and tongues. *Science* 243:1651–52

122. Ohnuki-Tierney, E. 1990. Introduction: the historicization of anthropology. In *Culture Through Time: Anthropological Approaches,* ed. E. Ohnuki-Tierney, pp. 1–25. Stanford: Stanford Univ. Press

123. Ortner, S. B. 1984. Theory in anthropology since the sixties. *Comp. Stud. Soc. Hist.* 26:126–66

124. Pawley, A. 1966. Polynesian languages: a subgrouping based on shared innovations in morphology. *J. Polynes. Soc.* 75:39–64

125. Pawley, A., Green, K. 1971. Lexical evidence for the Proto-Polynesian homeland. *Te Reo* 14:1–36

126. Pawley, A., Green, K. 1984. The Proto-Oceanic language community. *J. Pac. Hist.* 19:123–46

127. Pugh, G. E. 1977. *The Biological Origin of Human Values.* New York: Basic Books

128. Renfrew, C. 1987. *Archaeology and Language: The Puzzle of Indo-European Origins.* London: Jonathan Cape

129. Renfrew, C. 1988. Archaeology and language: the puzzle of Indo-European origins. *Curr. Anthropol.* 29(3):437–68

130. Renfrew, C. 1989. The origins of Indo-European languages. *Sci. Am.* 261(4):106–14

131. Renfrew, C. 1991. Before Babel: speculations on the origins of linguistic diversity. *Cambridge Archaeol. J.* 1(1):3-23

132. Richerson, P. J., Boyd, R. 1978. A dual inheritance model of the human evolutionary process. I: Basic postulates and a simple model. *J. Social Biol. Struct.* 1:127–54

133. Richerson, P. J., Boyd, R. 1984. Natural selection and culture. *Bioscience* 34(7):430–34

134. Richerson, P. J., Boyd, R. 1989. A Darwinian theory for the evolution of symbolic cultural traits. In *The Relevance of Culture,* ed. M. Freilich, pp. 120–42. New York: Bergin and Garvey

135. Richerson, P. J., Boyd, R. 1992. Cultural inheritance and evolutionary ecology. In *Evolutionary Ecology and Human Behavior,* ed. E. A. Smith, B. Winterhalder. New York: Aldine de Gruyter. In press

136. Ridley, M. 1986. *Evolution and Classification: The Reformation of Cladism.* London: Longman

137. Rindos, D. 1984. *The Origins of Agriculture: An Evolutionary Perspective.* New York: Academic
138. Rindos, D. 1985. Darwinian selection, symbolic variation, and the evolution of culture. *Curr. Anthropol.* 26(1):65–88
139. Rindos, D. 1986. The evolution of the capacity for culture: sociobiology, structuralism, and cultural selectionism. *Curr. Anthropol.* 27(4):315–32
140. Robbins, R. H. 1968. *A Short History of Linguistics.* Bloomington: Univ. Indiana Press
141. Romney, A. K. 1957. The genetic model and Uto-Aztecan time perspective. *Davidson J. Anthropol.* 3(2):35–41
142. Ruhlen, M. 1987. *A Guide to the World's Languages,* Vol. 1: *Classification.* Stanford, CA: Stanford Univ. Press
143. Ruhlen, M. 1992. An overview of genetic classification. In *The Evolution of Human Languages,* ed. J. A. Hawkins, M. Gell-Mann, pp. 1–27. Reading, MA: Addison-Wesley
144. Ruse, M. 1979. *Sociobiology: Sense or Nonsense?* Dordrecht: D. Reidel
145. Sahlins, M. D. 1957. Differentiation by adaptation in Polynesian societies. *J. Polynes. Soc.* 66:291–300
146. Sahlins, M. D. 1958. *Social Stratification in Polynesia.* Seattle: Univ. Washington Press
147. Sahlins, M. 1981. *Historical Metaphors and Mythical Realities: Structure in the Early History of the Sandwich Islands Kingdom.* Ann Arbor: Univ. Michigan Press
148. Sahlins, M. 1985. *Islands of History.* Chicago: Univ. Chicago Press
149. Sanderson, S. K. 1990. *Social Evolutionism: A Critical History.* Oxford: Basil Blackwell
150. Sapir, E. 1968 [1916]. Time perspective in aboriginal American culture: a study in method. In *Selected Writings of Edward Sapir in Language, Culture, and Personality,* ed. D. G. Mandelbaum, pp. 389–462. Berkeley: Univ. Calif. Press
151. Schmookler, A. B. 1984. *The Parable of the Tribes.* Boston: Houghton Mifflin
152. Shennan, S. J. 1992. After social evolution: a new archaeological agenda? Bielefeld, Germany: Cent. Interdiscip. Res. (ZiF), Preprint Ser. 2/92
153. Smith, E. A., Winterhalder, B. 1992. *Evolutionary Ecology and Human Behavior.* New York: Aldine de Gruyter. In press
154. Sober, E. 1988. *Reconstructing the Past: Parsimony, Evolution, and Inference.* Cambridge, MA: MIT Press
155. Sokal, R. R., Oden, N. L., Legendre, P., Fortin, M.-J., Kim, J., et al. 1990. Genetics and language in European populations. *Am. Nat.* 135(2):157–75
156. Sperber, D. 1985. Anthropology and psychology: towards an epidemiology of representations. *Man (NS)* 20:73–89
157. Sperber, D. 1990. The epidemiology of beliefs. In *The Social Psychological Study of Widespread Beliefs,* ed. C. Fraser, G. Gaskell, pp. 25–44. Oxford: Clarendon
158. Steklis, H. D., Walter, A. 1991. Culture, biology, and human behavior: a mechanistic approach. *Hum. Nat.* 2(2):137–69
159. Swadesh, M. 1964. Linguistics as an instrument of prehistory. In *Language in Culture and Society,* ed. D. Hymes, pp. 575–84. New York: Harper & Row
160. Swadesh, M. 1964. Diffusional cumulation and archaic residue as historical explanations. In *Language in Culture and Society,* ed. D. Hymes, pp. 624–37. New York: Harper & Row
161. Swadesh, M. 1971. *The Origin and Diversification of Language.* Chicago: Aldine-Atherton
162. Terrell, J. 1986. Causal pathways and causal processes: studying the evolutionary prehistory of human diversity in biology, language and customs. *J. Anthropol. Archaeol.* 5:187–98
163. Thieme, P. 1964. The comparative method for reconstruction in linguistics. In *Language in Culture and Society,* ed. D. Hymes, pp. 585–99. New York: Harper & Row
164. Thomas, N. 1989. *Out of Time: History and Evolution in Anthropological Discourse.* Cambridge: Cambridge Univ. Press
164a. Thomason, S. G., Kaufman, T. 1988. *Language Contact, Creolization, and Genetic Linguistics.* Berkeley: Univ. Calif. Press
165. Thornhill, N. W. 1990. The comparative method of evolutionary biology in the study of societies of history. *Int. J. Contemp. Sociol.* 27(1–2):7–27
166. Thornhill, N. W. 1990. The evolutionary significance of incest rules. *Ethol. Sociobiol.* 11:113–29
167. Thornhill, N. W. 1991. An evolutionary analysis of rules regulating human inbreeding and marriage. *Behav. Brain Sci.* 14(2):247–93
168. Trombetti, A. 1905. *L'Unita d'Origine del Linguaggio.* Bologna: Luigi Beltrami
169. Vogt, E. Z. 1964. The genetic model and Maya cultural development. In *Desarrollo Cultural de los Mayas,* ed. E. Z. Vogt, A. Ruz L., pp. 9–48. Mexico, DF: Univ. Nac. Autonoma de Mexico
170. Whinnom, K. 1971. Linguisitic hybridization and the 'special case' of pidgins and creoles. In *Pidginization and Creolization of Languages,* ed. D. Hymes, pp. 91–115. Cambridge: Cambridge Univ. Press
171. Wilson, E. O. 1978. *On Human Nature.* Cambridge, MA: Harvard Univ. Press
172. Wolfe, A. 1990. Social theory and the second biological revolution. *Soc. Res.* 57(3):615–48
173. Zegura, S. L., Walker, W. H., Stout, K. K., Diamond, J. D. 1990. More on genes, language, and human phylogeny. *Curr. Anthropol.* 31(4):420–26

Annu. Rev. Anthropol. 1992. 21:357–79

ANTHROPOLOGY, LAW, AND TRANSNATIONAL PROCESSES

Sally Engle Merry

Department of Anthropology, Wellesley College, Wellesley, Massachusetts 02181

KEY WORDS: legal anthropology, colonialism, dispute processing, popular justice, consciousness

In the past, anthropologists looking at legal phenomena tended to restrict the context of analysis to the local situation. Now, however, national and international contexts are increasingly important in developing theoretical understandings of local situations, particularly as research demonstrates how the law of the nation-state and even international regulations have penetrated and shaped local social arenas. World system theory (164, 276), theories of domination and resistance (5, 57, 59, 225), and a renewed emphasis on the historicity of social organization (59, 211, 246, 247) have focused attention on the impact of transnational processes on legal arenas. In this review I argue that transnational processes are becoming increasingly important in theorizing about the nature of local legal phenomena.

Transnational processes shape local legal situations in a variety of ways. Colonialism pulled entire legal systems across national borders and imposed them on very different sociocultural systems. Pockets of formerly autonomous indigenous peoples have become incorporated within nation-states as a result of European expansion in the last three centuries. The processes of nation-state formation have produced multi-ethnic societies in which local groups struggle to maintain autonomous legal systems while national interests endeavor to unify and standardize these diverse systems. Some nations have voluntarily

357

imported entire law codes or legal procedures from other nations and applied them to culturally different communities. Innovations in policing, judging, punishing, and settling disputes have been borrowed among postcolonial nations and former colonizers. International institutions and regulations exercise an increasingly important influence over local legal orders.

In the past, the coexistence of local, national, and transnational legal systems was described as legal pluralism. Critics point out that past usage often produced static analyses of plurality that failed to explore the interactions between the systems or the implications of power inequalities among them (107, 108, 246). More recently, however, studies of legal pluralism have focused on the mutually constitutive nature of these systems rather than their separateness (12, 23, 81, 108, 109, 119, 120, 122, 220, 258). Moreover, definitions of the constituent orders have expanded to include a range of informal ordering systems, sometimes called private governance, which are found in societies with pervasive state law (such as the United States) as well as in postcolonial nations (90, 121, 142, 153). Consequently, plurality of legal systems now appears to be a fundamental characteristic of all societies, not only those with colonial histories (108, 153). One or more of these systems is often the product of transnational processes.

A focus on the dialectic, mutually constitutive relations between state law and other normative orders emphasizes the interconnectedness of social orders and the vulnerability of local places to structures of domination far outside their immediate worlds. This theoretical position considers how state law penetrates and restructures other normative orders and how nonstate normative orders resist and circumvent penetration or how they even capture and appropriate state law. It also examines how, in turn, informal normative orders or systems of private governance affect state law (120, 175, 241).

Indeed, legal pluralism can be seen as the key concept in a postmodern view of law (220). In making this argument, Santos suggests that law is a system of signs that, like a map, represents/distorts reality through the mechanisms of scale, projection, and symbolization (220: 297). Different legal orders, like maps, have different scales, different forms of projection and centering, different systems of symbolization (see also 216–218).

A theory of unequal but mutually constitutive legal orders leads to new questions: How do these systems interact and reshape one another? To what extent is the dominant system able to control the subordinate? How do subordinate systems subvert or evade the dominant system? Are there ways in which the disputing strategies of subordinate users reshape the dominant system? To what extent do contests among plural legal systems explain historical change?

Here I explore literature that looks at local legal processes within a national and a transnational context and examine the possibilities of a revived theory of legal pluralism closely linked to questions of culture and power. The review is restricted to literature published since 1975, the date of Jane Collier's excellent review of legal processes in this series (52). I briefly trace significant shifts within legal anthropology since then, focusing in particular on the emergence of cultural and historical approaches.[1]

DEVELOPMENTS IN ANTHROPOLOGY ON LAW

Anthropological work on law has changed significantly since the mid-1970s. The dispute-processing theory of the 1970s pioneered by Laura Nader produced a florescence of studies of village law using a choice-making model of action, a focus on local places, and a processual mode of analysis (178). This perspective reestablished the centrality of ethnographies of law to studies of sociocultural organization. Disputing was examined in its sociocultural framework, but there was no explicit focus on national or transnational contexts. Nevertheless, many of the case studies on local disputing provided rich accounts of the importance of these contexts to the local scene. Parnell writes of the relationship of village and national courts in Mexico (192, 193), themes that appear as well in articles and books by Canter (44), Collier (55), Lowy (141), Nader (176, 177), Rothenberger (209), Ruffini (210), Starr (242, 243, 245), Witty (274, 275), and Yngvesson (277, 278). During the 1970s and 1980s, however, critics noted the turn toward an overly narrow context and overemphasis on rational choice-making models of behavior taken by some dispute-processing research (42, 136, 156, 246, 238). Starr & Collier's important collection also criticizes micro-level disputing studies and shows how the framework of dispute analysis can be expanded to historical time and the world system (247).

The processual model of law, of which dispute processing was a part, was derived from extended case analysis and Malinowskian notions of social action. It challenged older rule-centered approaches and generated acrimonious debate during the 1960s. In the 1970s, some scholars endeavored to synthesize the rule-centered approach and the processual approach instead of accepting them as mutually exclusive. In a series of sophisticated papers, Moore showed how rules could be incorporated into a processual model of law (169), an approach she applied to her historical study of changing Chagga law (171). This study shows how "traditional" law changed in the context of major political and economic changes while at the same time it remained in some ways continuous with the past (171). Comaroff & Roberts, examining the cultural logic of Tswana disputing, found that rules were negotiated in dispute processes; at the same time, social life was governed by normative repertoires and involved more than mere manipulation of the rules by individuals (61:18–

---

[1]
    This review covers, as completely as possible, *American Anthropologist, American Ethnologist, Law and Society Review, Journal of Legal Pluralism,* and *Man* since 1975. I have attempted to be as comprehensive as possible in including materials from other journals and books. There will inevitably be important works I have missed, but I hope the literature cited here will guide the reader to further materials. I have not tried to include works in languages other than English.

19; see also 29, 201). For these authors, rules governing conflict behavior were not internally consistent codes of action analogous to Western written law but were instead negotiable and internally contradictory repertoires that were applied with discretion.

Dispute processing continues to serve as a core methodological approach to understanding legal phenomena in the 1990s, but it is joined by a greater concern with meaning and power. To examinations of the processes of dispute in social context have been added studies of how legal institutions and actors create and transform meanings. Considerable recent work on disputing has analyzed it as a process of making and transforming meanings in which both disputants and third parties exercise roles of unequal power (31, 61, 77, 144, 221, 222, 230, 277, 278). Barbara Yngvesson analyzes the shifting definitions of disputes, focusing on the way their meanings are constructed in interactions among litigants and lower court officials (277, 278). Jane Collier shows how processes for managing conflicts are linked to forms of marriage and social stratification in societies without classes (55a).

I see four new ingredients in the contemporary anthropology of law. The first is a shift to a national and transnational context (discussed here). The second is a greater interest in cultural analysis: in the ways legal institutions and actors create meanings, the impact of these meanings on surrounding social relationships, and the effect of the cultural framework on the nature of legal procedures themselves. The third is a renewed interest in legal pluralism, freed of its static heritage but used as a way of talking about the multiplicity of coexisting legal systems and their interconnections. As the linkage between law and culture becomes more central, situations of legal pluralism are redefined as relations between different sets of cultural practices and discourses.

The fourth is increased attention to power and to the ways law constructs and deconstructs power relations. Law is no longer only a mode of social control; it is also a constitutive system that creates conceptions of order and enforces them. Moreover, law as an ideology contributes to the social construction of the world as fair and just and at the same time provides a language and forums for resisting that order (35, 40, 133, 251, 253). Law, of course, as Hoebel argued, is more than a system of meanings; it is also a form of violence endowed with the legitimacy of a constituted authority (see also 231).

These new ingredients result in part from a shift of focus from law among tribal and peasant peoples to law among urban sophisticates (and some who are less sophisticated) (12, 14, 37, 62, 73–75, 91, 104, 105, 112, 113, 149, 152, 154, 174, 197, 221–223, 228, 250, 261, 277, 278). As legal anthropologists started to work more extensively in the United States, Britain, and other industrialized nations, their analytic frameworks were enriched and expanded by the theoretical orientations of related disciplines in the social sciences and law, particularly those of law and society and critical legal studies. The new research setting, in which national and transnational processes are inescapably present, has challenged earlier theories that focused only on local places. The extended case study, the dispute-processing paradigm shorn of its wider social context, and theories of order maintenance and social control growing out of the structural-functional paradigm have gradually given way to theoretical models more appropriate to a world in which transnational processes exercise enormous power. This is a world occupied by tribal and peasant peoples as well as members of advanced capitalist nations.

Culture and Power

Law is closely linked to culture, to the representation as well as regulation of social life. Clifford Geertz suggests that law is a species of social imagination (99). He advocates the comparative analysis of law parallel to the comparative analysis of myth, ritual, ideology, art, or classification systems focused on structures of meaning, especially on the symbols and systems of symbols through whose agency such structures are formed, communicated, and imposed (99:182). Lawrence Rosen develops this cultural analysis of courts in his study of *qadi* courts in Morocco (204, 207, 208). He demonstrates that they are closely linked to surrounding cultural processes rather than isolated and arcane institutions. Richard O'Connor argues that law is an indigenous social theory, using Thai ethnography (185), while Arno explores the range of messages communicated by court proceedings (11).

The practices of legislators, judges, attorneys, court officials, police officers, and litigants can all be viewed as productive of meaning. Following this approach, Carter Bentley explores the culturally constructive role of law in his analysis of disputing among the Maranao in the Philippines, a legally plural society that joins custom (*adat*), Islamic law, and Philippine civil and criminal law (25). Disputants manipulate the various legal systems in an effort to construct an interpretation of truth in the world that others will accept. Peter Just explores the way disputants manipulate the meanings of rules and evidence among the Dou Donggo in Indonesia (130, 131). Outside the court setting, Laura Nader develops the provocative argument that ideologies such as harmony are used by local peoples to exclude state law and to promote settlement of conflicts (176, 177). Her book is an important theoretical advance in the way it joins the study of disputing with the analysis of ideology. Carol Greenhouse explores the meaning of conflict to a community of Southern Baptists, finding that it is inextricably intertwined with religion and with the way people see their past (105, 106). I have examined legal consciousness—the ways ordinary people understand the legal system and their rights to use it—as a way of assessing the domination exercised by the legal system over working-class white Americans (152, 154; see also 255).

A prominent movement within legal scholarship, that of critical legal studies, has adopted the concept of culture to describe the ways law maintains power relationships (66, 132, 133; but see 9). Instead of looking simply at the role law plays in enforcing rules, it examines how law creates images of social relationships that seem natural and fair because they are endowed with the authority and legitimacy of the law. This perspective focuses on the culturally productive role of law rather than on its sanctioning and limiting role. Given the Marxian origins of this work, it is interested in the ways legal ideology and legal consciousness maintain and support existing power relations (40, 132, 251, 253). Several ethnographic studies have used this theoretical frame to examine legal consciousness and legal process in local contexts (35, 154, 228, 277). Work in this vein argues that law maintains power relations by defining categories and systems of meaning. When these categories and systems shape consciousness, they can be seen as hegemonic.

Because legal conceptions and principles are powerful and potentially hegemonic, they have been mobilized by revolutionary movements as well as by those challenging state law and attempting to construct an alternative justice. The discussion of popular justice below describes situations in which governments and/or local people construct alternative judicial forums in an effort to resist state law, to rejuvenate local communities, or to increase the efficiency of the existing legal system. Groups that demand ethnic or cultural sovereignty often seek an autonomous judicial system as well. Because of the symbolic link between judicial autonomy and sovereignty, demands for self-determination and land rights often include legal autonomy.

Law, Language, and Discourse

Associated with an increased interest in the cultural meanings constructed by law is work that examines the way language is used in legal settings such as courts and lawyers' offices. The concept of discourse, adopted from Foucault (88), has provided an important bridge between the sociolinguistic analysis of talk in legal settings and theories linking prevailing modes of talk with power (64, 127, 130, 157, 161, 183, 184, 221, 268). Much work has been done on US language and law (16, 24, 26, 101, 106, 117, 144, 147, 148, 222, 230, 278). Other studies look more broadly at a range of social arenas that handle conflict, examining varieties of conflict discourse and their linkage to modes of conflict (15). Brenneis, for example, links genres of talk to conflict management in Fiji (30–33), Bilmes analyzes the details of mediation discourse in Thailand (27), and Watson-Gegeo & White explore varieties of conflict discourse in the Pacific (265).

Some consider situations of legal pluralism in which the talk of litigants differs from that of the court, undermining the capacity of litigants to speak effectively in the court and to prevail in their cases (26, 62, 184). These and related studies look at the link between linguistic competence and various legal forums as a way of understanding the relative power litigants exercise in these forums (24, 26, 62, 116, 117, 152, 183, 184). Brenneis has recently reviewed the literature on language and disputing, some of which is located in court contexts and some in more informal arenas (34).

LAW AND TRANSNATIONAL PROCESSES

Colonial and Postcolonial Situations

Colonialism is a transnational legal process taking place on a vast scale. During the European and American imperialism of the 18th and 19th centuries, European legal systems were superimposed on large regions of Africa, Asia, and the Pacific, as Spanish and Portuguese law had been imposed on Latin America two centuries earlier. European law was typically expected to "civilize" colonized peoples: to reshape their family lives, work habits, land ownership practices, and ways of handling conflicts (45–47, 63–65, 81–83). As the Comaroffs point out, along with other institutions of the colonial state, European law contributed to the colonial reformulation of culture and consciousness, creating new conceptions of time, space, work, property, marriage, and the family (57–59). The result was a legal pluralism in which culturally very different legal systems coexisted that were vastly unequal in power. Postcolonial countries are now grappling with this legacy as they debate how to fashion a unified legal system out of this duality and how to resurrect and implement the remnants of indigenous, precolonial law. Ghai et al provide a valuable overview of this literature from a Marxist perspective (100), while Hooker offers a legal scholar's global perspective (124).

A great deal of early anthropological work on law took place under such conditions (see 110, 111, 201). More recently, many ethnographic studies of law in postcolonial settings have explored the implications of the heritage of imposed colonial law for local peoples (38, 135, 247). I cannot begin to do justice to the vast literature on the interaction of colonial and local legal systems found in comparative legal scholarship, legal history, and colonial history or to the literature in languages other than English. Here I indicate the literature available in some of the regions most intensively studied and written about in English: on the legal relations of the colonial aftermath in various nations in Africa (1, 6, 45, 46, 56, 58, 61, 63, 64, 70, 86, 114, 128, 137, 141, 150, 168, 171, 172, 186, 212, 213, 215, 236, 237, 239, 256, 259, 260, 264, 271), India (7, 10, 50, 51, 94, 116, 134, 167, 263), Papua New Guinea (71, 78–82, 85, 103, 126, 179, 188–190, 195, 196, 266, 267, 270), Mexico (53, 55, 176, 177, 192, 193), Brazil (216), Southeast Asia, including Indonesia (17, 20–22, 109, 130, 131, 235), Thailand (72) and the Philippines (25, 232), the Pacific (31, 129, 202, 203, 224, 229), and the Middle East (28, 146, 163, 165, 204, 206, 209, 244, 245, 274, 275); broader comparative studies are also available (8, 18, 38, 124, 170, 178, 182, 247, 249). In comparison to work on the British colonies, there has been relatively little work on the American colonies (but see 67, 87, 138, 145, 180, 191).

Although colonizing nations' interests in political takeover were narrowly economic, they typically sought to reform family life and work habits as well. Colonial law was used to create a wage labor force available to the plantation, mine, and factory out of peasant and subsistence producers (58, 59, 63, 64, 80,

82). Much early legal regulation of colonized peoples forced them to become a capitalistic work force by requiring regular hours, punishing failure to work, outlawing festivals and other entertainments (such as cockfighting) that distracted from work, prohibiting alcoholic beverages, controlling vagabondage, and defining criminality (46, 63–65, 82, 84). Colonial powers often outlawed polygamy and other customary practices of family life. Chatterjee argues that some of these assaults on family customs, such as the British critique of the Indian practice of *suttee,* were efforts to denigrate the customs of colonized peoples in the name of protecting women (48).

On the other hand, the law also provided a way for the colonial state to restrain the more brutal aspects of settlers' exploitation of land and labor (58, 60, 82). In Papua New Guinea, for example, some regulations limited the power of masters over servants, although these were relatively mild and not often enforced (82). In colonial society, traditional leaders, educated elites among the colonized population, colonial officials, missionaries, and settlers all struggled to control the legal arena (58, 60, 65, 103). This was an unequal contest in which colonial officials and settler populations exerted far greater power than colonized groups.

Many colonies tried to convert communal land into individual property ownership, a transition supported by Europeans' conceptions of progress and individual proprietary rights. Law facilitated the commodification of land and its extraction from precolonial users by redefining property rights (81, 186). In South Africa, for example, conceptions of wealth in things were introduced in place of conceptions of wealth in persons (47). It is now clear, of course, that the legacy of these enterprises has been the massive dispossession of lands and subsistence rights of colonized peoples.

Colonial governments, especially the British, typically ruled their subjugated populations through what they considered traditional or indigenous law, which they labeled "customary law." One of the major insights garnered by work on law in colonial situations is that the customary law implemented in "native courts" was not a relic of a timeless precolonial past but instead an historical construct of the colonial period. Several careful historical and anthropological studies demonstrate that the so-called "customary law" of the colonial period was forged in particular historical struggles between the colonial power and colonized groups. Francis Snyder shows how modernizing elites often took a central role in defining "indigenous law" in the native courts in Senegal (236, 237, 239). Moore challenges the illusion that custom was static and essentially obsolete while innovation was linked to the national political leadership and the top of the political system; she demonstrates the capacity of the Chagga to reformulate and reshape their tradition to live in a constantly changing world, retaining some of the past while reforming it (171). She shows that a high proportion of the cases handled by the Chagga in customary law courts concerned loans and cash transactions for which there was no precolonial Chagga law (171:190). Judges relied on their own understanding of the principles of buying, selling, lending, and hiring in making their "customary law" decisions.

As colonizers developed a "customary law" system in various parts of Africa, India, the Middle East, and the Pacific, law was commonly transformed from a subtle, adaptable, and situational code to a system of fixed and formal rules (46, 47, 81, 82, 94, 163, 213). Even when the laws were ostensibly based on traditional codes, in practice they were usually derived from European interpretations of these codes or in accordance with European approaches to defining law. Bernard Cohn shows how the British effort to "find" Hindu law assumed that Hindu law developed through methods (like those of British common law) of deduction from precedent and cases (51). Brinkley Messick analyzes the transformation of laws and courts in Yemen from the Ottoman colonial period to the present from an embodied system carried in the minds of the judges to an abstract and disembodied system incorporated into a bureaucratic structure (160, 163).

The legal transformations accompanying colonialism, including the codification of "customary law," were paralleled by changes in forms of knowledge and representation (165). These transformations were central to the processes by which the colonizing power attempted to learn about and to order the very different legal systems of the colonized. They are part of the construction of a bureaucratic legality compatible with the organization of the expanding capitalist economy of the West (100, 163, 165). They reveal a subtle form of power that exists alongside more overt, coercive forms: one based on control over knowledge and representation. A key ingredient was the colonial transformation of law from the embodied, spoken, and interpreted text into a fixed, abstracted, and disembodied one that was written (159, 160, 162).

One of the recurring themes in the expansion of European colonial control through law was the surveillance exerted over sexual relationships (65). Mixed-union children challenged the boundaries drawn between colonizer and colonized and were frequently discouraged by anti-miscegenation laws (249). In order to control a subordinate group, it was essential to control women as well. Indeed, fear of sexual assault on the women of the dominant group by subordinated men was often mobilized to restrict the activities of these women and to justify policing the men (36, 98, 249). The judicial/policing apparatus was therefore a critical institution for constructing and maintaining the boundary between the colonial overlords and their subjects and was used to control sexuality and its disruptive influences. As Cooper & Stoler point out, imperial thinkers were preoccupied with the relations between subversion and sex (65:614).

One contemporary manifestation of neo-colonialism is tourism, in which formerly colonial nationals reconstitute their formerly colonized subjects as "primitive" or "exotic" objects of investigation (165). The tourist's gaze constructs a world that the tourist imagines (262). This is a transnational phenomenon of increasing significance economically, culturally, and legally. The vast transfer between rich and poor nations of resources and persons accompanying international tourism will undoubtedly increase the demand for international legal regulation of tourist destinations.

Local/National/Transnational Struggles among Plural Legal Orders

Local legal institutions have a porous quality. Local legal arenas, well described by Moore's term, the "semi-autonomous social field (169)," are to some extent structured by national and transnational legal orders and to some extent autonomous places for the creation of cultural meanings and imposition of local rules (90, 153). Governments establish local courts in order to produce uniform and consistent results, while local people frequently develop their own distinctive practices and ways of using the courts. Expansionist states, often aided by lawyers who feel that they are contributing to modernization, development, or rights-consciousness, may seek to become more closely involved in local affairs (3, 28, 96). Even village people who consider state law remote and alien will occasionally use it (44, 55, 177, 192, 193, 209, 210, 274, 275).

However, many peasant and village peoples resist the expansion of state law, preferring informal alternatives more subject to their control (e.g. 2, 28:166–67; 103, 177). Or they may usurp control of local courts by taking over management positions, reinterpreting rules, controlling access, and resisting supervision (78, 171, 190). In Gordon & Meggitt's study of Papua New Guinea, the village court in Enga country became an arena for Big Men to practice local politics by providing favors and services (103).

Nation states are increasingly entwined in a host of international economic arrangements and international laws, many of which affect local places. New international regulations and institutions established in recent decades to provide a more orderly framework for the maintenance of the international capitalist system include transnational corporations, the World Bank, systems of patents, copyrights, and trademarks, and the International Monetary Fund, among others (100:275). The implications of the expanding international legal order for local legal orders are highly diverse. I mention only two examples. One is the legal side of mass disasters with international implications. The 1984 leakage of poisonous gas into a sleeping squatter settlement in Bhopal, India from a factory partially owned by an American corporation is one of the best-known incidents of this type. It set off an enormous legal wrangle concerning which nation's courts should hear the case and according to whose laws it should be decided (92, 93, 95). As Galanter points out, one consequence was that some American tort law was transplanted to India, whose tort law system had been rudimentary (92).

A second example illustrates how the world economic system can affect the capacity of a postcolonial nation to revive its indigenous law. Papua New Guinea's revival of precolonial law included permitting payback killing of sorcerers, but international business leaders complained about doing business in a country that allowed payback killings. Because of the country's situation of economic dependency, it had to abandon this policy (79, 80).

Popular Justice

Popular justice too has a transnational aspect. Popular justice tribunals are local courts characterized by a strong tie to local communities, but they are often inspired by transnational ideologies (41, 89, 155). Traditions of popular justice are borrowed among various nations from the core to the periphery and back to the core. Many socialist nations, including Cuba and China, created workers' courts modeled after Soviet Comrades' Courts, while current innovations endeavoring to reform Anglo-American law (e.g. community mediation) are spreading from the United States to Europe and the Third World (125, 126, 129, 139, 158, 166, 190, 194, 214, 215, 217, 219, 226, 233, 240, 254, 257). Community justice institutions in the United States were originally modeled on prototypes from Africa, Mexico, and Asia (3, 140, 151, 175, 275).

Popular justice institutions, or people's courts, are legal institutions located between state law and local ordering. Popular justice often envisages a system of justice under the control of local communities enforcing local or customary law and following amicable, consensual processes instead of the adversarial procedures of state law. But in practice popular justice mediates between plural legal orders, tugged by both but constructing a relatively autonomous order of its own. Through informality in procedure, nonprofessionalism in personnel and rules, and limited authority to impose penalties, it mimics local orders. Yet through reference to a system of rules, adoption of the costumes and procedures of the judge and the court, and claims to represent the legitimate authority of the state, it follows formal state law (89). Popular justice tribunals are often named after indigenous forms of dispute resolution (sometimes imagined), such as *katarungang pambarangay* in the Philippines (194, 233), Conciliation Boards in Sri Lanka (254), or Neighborhood Justice Centers in the United States (112, 113); but they are typically under the supervision, control, and funding of the state legal system.

Sometimes people's courts are created by governments in order to make justice more accessible to ordinary people and to decrease the demands on the formal courts, a reform ideology widespread in the West that has been transplanted in parts of Asia and Africa (54, 94, 158, 166, 171, 190, 194, 205, 254; S. E. Merry, unpublished). Or they are created to revive "traditional" law (179, 188). In India, the government encouragement of village *panchayats* was part of an effort to free Indian villages from the expensive and corrupt courts and to restore conciliation processes to these villages (94:40, 134, 158, 166). Governments also create popular justice tribunals to promote a new social order after a revolution following prototypes established in similar revolutionary situations. Examples can be found in China (125, 139), Cuba (214), Mozambique (128), Chile in 1973 (240), and Portugal in 1974 (219).

Some popular justice tribunals develop in opposition to a hostile or alien state (39, 97, 127). Those seeking to gain power attempt to attract followers by creating new courts independent of a discredited state, as in South Africa (39). South African youth brigade courts, for example, were created by young African activists in opposition to the apartheid state in Cape Town in 1985 during the political turmoil accompanying struggles against apartheid (39:722). Like many other instances of popular justice, however, these tribunals changed over time, shifting from being a popular mode of resistance to state power to a harsh, punitive tribunal that challenged adult authority. As punishments became more severe and violent, the tribunals lost community support (see also 226).

There are often struggles between local authorities and national authorities for control of these tribunals (103, 190, 270). Autonomous tribunals are typically opposed by the state (2, 97, 241). It is not unusual for popular justice tribunals developed by the state either to become moribund because plaintiffs refuse to use them or to become more formalized and more closely connected with state law (155, 158). For example, Hayden describes informal workers' courts in Yugoslavia that are heavily used, in contrast to those of many other socialist countries, because they have become relatively formal and closely connected with the authority of the state (115, 118).

Indigenous Rights, Human Rights, and Sovereignty

Indigenous peoples who find themselves minorities in larger nation states, particularly in liberal democracies such as the United States, Canada, Australia, and New Zealand, often use legal claims framed in a transnational discourse of human rights, treaty rights, or self-determination to reassert land and subsistence rights (7, 43, 49, 68, 187, 198, 200, 227, 234, 252, 269, 272, 273). The United Nations declaration on human rights of 1948 and declarations on self-determination and decolonization have substantially shaped the discourse and the politics of indigenous groups (187, 198). In addition, international law and the experiences of other groups in comparable situations in other nations structure local political struggles concerning land, subsistence, and sovereignty in many parts of the world (13:126; 7, 138, 181, 198, 227, 234, 269, 272, 273). Ironically, as aboriginal peoples living in developed industrial nations governed by people of European ancestry make claims for land and its products, they must argue these claims in the terms provided by the legal systems of these European nations (273:viii). On the other hand, there are some situations in which native peoples have used these legal systems to modify, if not block, development efforts on their lands (76:72). Thus, national and transnational contexts are of critical importance to indigenous groups seeking to preserve or reclaim land, resources, and sovereignty.

Groups typically file legal claims on the basis of past treaties or communal tenure of the land. Lawyers and anthropologists often work closely together in land claim cases (43, 49, 143, 273). Legal proceedings surrounding land rights and sovereignty, along with new anthropological research, have helped to develop new conceptions of the dynamic, interactive, and historically formed relations between indigenous peoples and land in place of formalistic ahistorical models derived from structural/functionalism and ecological theory (123, 138, 191). For example, Edwin Wilmsen's edited volume on land tenure among aboriginal peoples challenges the common assumption that hunter/foragers have no sense of land ownership (273). The collected essays document the complex relations between hunter/foragers and land among Australian aborigines (123, 143, 173), Kalahari San (102, 273), and native peoples in Canada (13, 76). These relations are mediated through social ties among people who share ownership to land. Wilmsen points out that reexamining aboriginal land tenure is critically important for political as well as theoretical reasons since many foragers have lost their lands because their systems of land tenure were not understood (273:4–5).

Comparative work within similar countries reveals recurring patterns, such as processes by which indigenous peoples are dispossessed of their collective lands through the transition from communal to private landholding (252). In 19th-century Hawaii, Anglo-American land tenure law was imposed upon peoples with previous communal rights (138), a pattern similar to that described in Australia, the Kalahari, and Canada (273). Parker compares the history of the American appropriation of lands, fishing, and water rights from the Native American Indians and Native Hawaiians (191). For both Native Americans and Hawaiians, the products of the land and the right to these products were often of greater importance than the possession of the land itself.

Anthropologists have also explored the possibilities of a culturally sensitive conception of universal human rights to support the claims of these and similar subordinated groups. Human rights can be understood as a discourse with multiple political uses as well as a rhetorical strategy for subordinated peoples to assert claims to such diverse rights as freedom from child labor and wife battering, rights that resonate with globally recognized moral systems (198). Some advocates link land rights to human rights discourse, claiming that aboriginal land rights are also human rights (13:122). Although the notion of a universal, transnational standard for human rights appears to pose a fundamental challenge to the traditional anthropological stance of cultural relativism, Renteln argues that this apparent challenge is based on an inadequate understanding of the meaning of cultural relativity (199).

Incorporation into the Administrative State

Several studies examine ways local places are entangled in the regulations and benefits of the administrative state. One examines the impact of importing the welfare state into postcolonial nations from Europe or North America. This includes the extension of systems of social security to urban workers and rural farmers in Third World countries. A recent collection on social security and folk law indicates that the model for forms of social security ranging from unemployment compensation to old-age pensions comes from the industrial economies of Europe and is far too costly for more agrarian societies that have in the past relied on informal systems of kin relations (19). The latter systems are breaking down under the pressure of migration to the city for work and the extension of the cash economy.

A second area of research concerns the extension of new courts into regions previously lacking formal courts. Here I refer to courts that are part of the state legal system rather than the more informal courts described above as popular justice. There has been considerable research into the interaction between new courts and preexisting systems of ordering, some of which takes an historical perspective (1, 38, 46, 51, 53–56, 78, 94, 103, 145, 172, 179, 188, 190, 193, 232, 239, 256). When a nation adopts a new legal code from another nation, the extension of local courts takes on a particularly important cultural role (124, 248). Starr provides a valuable study of how the secular law, introduced into the Islamic society of Turkey in the 1920s, penetrated to village life and constructed a new social order (243–245). In order to understand why secular law predominated over Islamic law in village life during the 1960s, she found it necessary to expand her study context from the local and regional one of her previous work (242) to include national political and legal changes and historical transformations. Other studies explore the Ottoman introduction of French codes in the 19th century (28, 163).

However, the regulations and legal procedures of the modern administrative state impinge on local places in significant areas that have received little anthropological attention. One of the most fundamental is that of tax policies. A second is policing. Considerable work has been done on local courts, but much less on policing strategies. An enormous body of research on police in the United States indicates that policing is a highly discretionary activity shaped by the cultural categories and assumptions of police officers, yet it is regarded as a background phenomenon rather than a central problem in most ethnographic accounts of law (178, 242; but see 103). Police techniques and training materials clearly cross national borders. For example, the policing strategies of Central American nations were inspired by US models.

A third area of research given short shrift concerns punishment strategies, including prisons, fines, and supervision. Following Foucault's innovative analysis of modern forms of discipline and surveillance (88), a focus on such changes as the use of confinement in place of corporal punishment suggests enormously important social transformations. Studies of colonial and postcolonial societies occasionally mention the use of prisons and describe their significance in passing, but this has not been the central concern of much ethnographic research. In an intriguing illustration of the meaning of these shifts in forms of power and discipline, Pospisil describes the dismay of the Kapauku Papuans at the use of jail as a punishment, one that to them seems extraordinarily severe since it separates the individual from the essential cooperation of soul and body, the linkage between one's actions and one's own free decisions (195:141). In their words, in jail "The man's vital substance deteriorates and the man dies (195:142)." Indeed, the Dutch colonial administrators found that Kapauku tended to pine and die if imprisoned long, despite the administrators' conviction that prison had a positive, "civilizing" effect.

Power, in Foucault's theory, is not based simply on prohibition but also on the positive formation of norms and shaping of individuals to fit these norms (88). Law gives shape to institutions that supervise rather than contain; it creates new technologies of discipline that stretch from the prison to the factory to the military to the school. If the nature of law that has emerged in the wake of capitalism is fundamentally different from that of precapitalist societies in what Foucault refers to as its "disciplinary technologies"—productive forms of power such as the timetable, the cell, and the panopticon—the encounter between these forms of power and discipline and those of noncapitalist societies takes on new meaning.

A fourth area given relatively little attention in ethnographic research is the role of the legal profession. Scholars have frequently studied lawyers in European, North American, and Third World countries and the transnational law and development movement (4, 69, 96, 134), but relatively few such studies are detailed ethnographies of lawyers in a local place. Bisharat's study of Palestinian lawyers on the West Bank is one exception (28). His study shows how the legal profession, originally a transnational import from the West into Palestine in the 19th century with shallow roots in civil society, flourished under the British Mandate, then languished under Israeli occupation, suffering wide swings in social prestige and power during the 20th century in response to the political turmoil engulfing the West Bank.

Anthropological work appears to focus on law in areas of local social life that seem more indigenous and "traditional"—particularly disputing processes, informal forums, and local courts. They have neglected precisely those legal institutions that are largely transnational in inspiration: police, prisons, lawyers, administrative regulations, taxes, social security systems. While local courts may predate substantial contact with the world system, these other institutions in Third World countries are often the result of transnational processes.

CONCLUSION

The literature reviewed here indicates that an anthropology of law in the 1990s will increasingly need to take transnational processes into account in understanding local places. This means considering the legacy of foreign legal systems imposed along with colonial takeovers, the persistence of remnants of a previously autonomous society in a larger state, the impact of international regulations or declarations, and the effect of borrowed legal procedures (e.g. popular justice tribunals) and entire legal codes on local communities. Moreover, it is likely that in multi-ethnic states, legal systems will play critical symbolic roles in defining collective identity. The demand for sovereignty will include the desire for an autonomous legal system that represents the peoplehood of the collectivity. National and transnational processes are critical to understanding these situations as we move further toward a multi-national legal order with global communication about rules and processes.

Under these conditions, a model of mutually constitutive legal orders that includes national and transnational orders provides, in my opinion, the most effective theoretical framework for understanding the role of law in local places. The analysis of relations among normative orders as mutually constitutive provides a framework for examining the relationship between dominant and subordinate groups or classes in situations of legal pluralism. It offers a way of thinking about the possibilities of domination through law and of the limits to this domination, pointing to areas in which individuals and groups can and do resist. Attention to plural orders examines limits to the ideological power of state law and alerts us to the existence of areas where state law does not penetrate and alternative forms of ordering persist.

Literature Cited

1. Abel, R. L. 1979. Western courts in non-Western settings: patterns of court use in colonial and neo-colonial Africa. See Ref. 38, pp. 167–200
2. Abel, R. L. 1982. The contradictions of informal justice. See Ref. 3, 1:267–321
3. Abel, R. L., ed. 1982. The Politics of Informal Justice, Vols. 1, 2. New York: Academic
4. Abel, R. L., Lewis, P. S. C., eds. 1988. Lawyers in Society, Vols. 1, 2, 3. Berkeley: Univ. Calif. Press
5. Abu-Lughod, L. 1990. The romance of resistance: tracing transformations of power through Bedouin women. Am. Ethnol. 17:41–56
6. Adewoye, O. 1986. Legal practice in Ibadan, 1904–1960. J. Legal Plural. 24:57–76
7. Agarwal, B. 1988. Who sows? Who reaps? Women and land rights in India. J. Peasant Stud. 15:531–81
8. Allott, A. N., Woodman, G. R., eds. 1985. People's Law and State Law: The Bellagio Papers. Dordrecht, Netherlands: Foris
9. Altman, A. 1990. Critical Legal Studies: A Liberal Critique. Princeton, NJ: Princeton Univ. Press
10. Appadurai, A. 1981. Worship and Conflict Under Colonial Rule: A South Indian Case. Cambridge: Cambridge Univ. Press
11. Arno, A. 1985. Structural communication and control communication: an interactionist perspective on legal and customary procedures for conflict management. Am. Anthropol. 87:40–55
12. Arthurs, H. W. 1985. Without the Law:

Administrative Justice and Legal Pluralism in Mid 19th-Century England. Toronto: Univ. Toronto Press
13. Asch, M. 1989. To negotiate into confederation: Canadian aboriginal views on their political rights. See Ref. 273a, pp. 118–38
14. Auerbach, J. 1983. Justice Without Law? New York: Oxford Univ. Press
15. Avruch, K., Black, P. W., Scimecca, J. A., eds. 1991. Conflict Resolution: Cross-Cultural Perspectives. New York: Greenwood
16. Beer, J. E. 1986. Peacemaking in Your Neighborhood: Reflections on an Experiment in Community Mediation. Philadelphia: New Society Publ.
17. Benda-Beckmann, F. von. 1979. Property in Social Continuity: Continuity and Change in the Maintenance of Property Relationships through Time in Minangkabau, West Sumatra. The Hague: Nijhoff
18. Benda-Beckmann, F. von. 1981. Some comments on the problems of comparing the relationship between traditional and state systems of administration of justice in Africa and Indonesia. J. Legal Plural. 19:165–75
19. Benda-Beckmann, F. von, Benda-Beckmann, K. von, Casino, E., Hirtz, F., Woodman, G. R., Zacher, H. F., eds. 1988. Between Kinship and the State: Social Security and Law in Developing Countries. Dordrecht, Netherlands: Foris
20. Benda-Beckmann, K. von. 1981. Forum shopping and shopping forums: dispute processing in a Minangkabau village in West Sumatra. J. Legal Plural. 19:117–59
21. Benda-Beckmann, K. von. 1984. The Bro-

ken Stairways to Consensus: Village Justice and State Courts in Minangkabau. Dordrecht, Netherlands: Foris
22. Benda-Beckmann, K. von. 1985. The social significance of Minangkabau state court decisions. J. Legal Plural. 23:1–68
23. Benda-Beckmann, K. von, Strijbosch, F., eds. 1986. Anthropology of Law in the Netherlands: Essays in Legal Pluralism. Dordrecht/Cinnaminson: Foris
24. Bennett, W. L., Feldman, M. S. 1981. Reconstructing Reality in the Courtroom. New Brunswick: Rutgers Univ. Press
25. Bentley, G. C. 1984. Hermeneutics and world construction in Maranao disputing. Am. Ethnol. 11:642–55
26. Berk-Seligson, S. 1990. The Bilingual Courtroom: Court Interpreters in the Judicial Process. Chicago: Univ. Chicago Press
27. Bilmes, J. 1989. A Northern Thai Mediation. Work. Pap., Progr. Conflict Resolution. Honolulu, HI: Univ. Hawaii
28. Bisharat, G. E. 1989. Palestinian Lawyers and Israeli Rule: Law and Disorder in the West Bank. Austin, TX: Univ. Texas Press
29. Bossy, J., ed. 1983. Disputes and Settlements: Law and Human Relations in the West. Cambridge: Cambridge Univ. Press
30. Brenneis, D. 1984. Grog and gossip in Bhatgaon: style and substance in Fiji Indian conversation. Am. Ethnol. 14:236–50
31. Brenneis, D. 1984. Straight talk and sweet talk: political discourse in an occasionally egalitarian community. In Dangerous Words: Language and Politics in the Pacific, ed. D. Brenneis, F. Myers, pp. 69–84. New York: NY Univ. Press
32. Brenneis, D. 1987. Performing passions: aesthetics and politics in an occasionally egalitarian community. Am. Ethnol. 14:236–51
33. Brenneis, D. 1987. Dramatic gestures: the Fiji Indian pancayat as therapeutic discourse. Pap. Pragmat. 1:55–78
34. Brenneis, D. 1988. Language and disputing. Annu. Rev. Anthropol. 17:221–37
35. Brigham, J. 1987. Right, rage, and remedy: forms of law in political discourse. Studies in American Political Development. New Haven: Yale Univ. Press
36. Brownfoot, J. N. 1984. Memsahibs in colonial Malaya: a study of European wives in a British colony and protectorate 1900–1940. In The Incorporated Wife, ed. H. Callan, S. Ardener, pp. 186–210. London: Croom Helm
37. Buckle, L., Thomas-Buckle, S. R. 1982. Doing unto others: dispute and dispute-processing in an urban American neighborhood. In Neighborhood Justice, ed. R. Tomasic, M. Feeley, pp. 78–90. New York: Longman
38. Burman, S. B., Harrell-Bond, B. E., eds. 1979. The Imposition of Law. New York: Academic

39. Burman, S., Schaerf, W. 1990. Creating people's justice: street committees and people's courts in a South African city. Law & Soc. Rev. 24:693–745
40. Cain, M. 1983. Gramsci, the state, and the place of law. In Legality, Ideology, and the State, ed. D. Sugarman, pp. 95–118. London: Academic
41. Cain, M. 1985. Beyond informal justice. Contemp. Crises 9:335–73
42. Cain, M., Kulcsar, K. 1981–1982. Thinking disputes: an essay on the origins of the dispute industry. Law & Soc. Rev. 16:375–403
43. Campisi, J. 1991. The Mashpee Indians: Tribe on Trial. Syracuse, NY: Syracuse Univ. Press
44. Canter, R. 1978. Dispute settlement and dispute processing in Zambia: individual choice versus societal constraints. See Ref. 178, pp. 247–80
45. Chanock, M. 1982. Making customary law: men, women, and courts in colonial Northern Rhodesia. See Ref. 114, pp. 53–67
46. Chanock, M. 1985. Law, Custom, and Social Order: The Colonial Experience in Malawi and Zambia. Cambridge: Cambridge Univ. Press
47. Chanock, M. 1991. A peculiar sharpness: an essay on property in the history of customary law in colonial Africa. J. Afr. Hist. 32:65–88
48. Chatterjee, P. 1989. Colonialism, nationalism, and colonized women: the contest in India. Am. Ethnol. 16:622–33
49. Clifford, J. 1988. Identity in Mashpee. In The Predicament of Culture: Twentieth Century Ethnography, Literature, and Art, pp. 277–46. Cambridge, MA: Harvard Univ. Press
50. Cohn, B. S. 1985. The command of language and the language of command. In Subaltern Studies IV: Writings on South Asian History and Society, ed. R. Guha, pp. 276–330. Delhi: Oxford Univ. Press
51. Cohn, B. S. 1989. Law and the colonial state in India. See Ref. 247, pp. 131–52
52. Collier, J. F. 1975. Legal processes. Annu. Rev. Anthropol. 4:121–44
53. Collier, J. F. 1976. Political leadership and legal change in Zinacantan. Law & Soc. Rev. 11:131–63
54. Collier, J. F. 1977. Popular justice in Zinacantan. Verfass. Recht Übersee: Sonderdruck 3:431–40
55a. Collier, J. F. 1988. Marriage and Inequality in Classless Societies. Stanford: Stanford Univ. Press
55. Collier, J. F. 1979. Stratification and dispute handling in two highland Chiapas communities. Am. Ethnol. 6:305–28
56. Colson, E. 1976. From chief's court to local court: the evolution of local courts in Southern Zambia. In Freedom and Constraint, ed. M. J. Aronoff, pp. 15–29. Amsterdam: Van Gorcum
57. Comaroff, J. 1985. Body of Power: Spirit

of Resistance: Culture and History of a South African People. Chicago: Univ. Chicago Press

58. Comaroff, J., Comaroff, J. L. 1986. Christianity and colonialism in South Africa. Am. Ethnol. 13:1–22

59. Comaroff, J., Comaroff, J. L. 1991. Of Revelation and Revolution: Christianity, Colonialism, and Consciousness in South Africa, Vol. 1. Chicago: Univ. Chicago Press

60. Comaroff, J. L. 1989. Images of empire, contests of conscience: models of colonial domination in South Africa. Am. Ethnol. 16:661–85

61. Comaroff, J. L., Roberts, S. 1981. Rules and Processes: The Cultural Logic of Dispute in an African Context. Chicago: Univ. Chicago Press

62. Conley, J. M., O'Barr, W. M. 1990. Rules versus Relationships: The Ethnography of Legal Discourse. Chicago: Univ. Chicago Press

63. Cooper, F. 1987. Contracts, crime, and agrarian conflict: From slave to wage labour on the East African coast. See Ref. 235a, pp. 228–53

64. Cooper, F. 1989. From free labor to family allowances: labor and African society in colonial discourse. Am. Ethnol. 16:745–65

65. Cooper, F., Stoler, A. L. 1989. Tensions of empire: colonial control and visions of rule. Am. Ethnol. 16:609–21

66. Critical Legal Studies Symp. 1984. Stanford Law Rev. 36(Jan.):1, 2

67. Deloria, V., Lytle, C. M. 1983. American Indians, American Justice. Austin, TX: Univ. Texas Press

68. Denhez, M. 1985. The role of "folk law" as evidence of historic title in international boundary claims. J. Legal Plural. 23:69–101

69. Dias, C. J., Luckham, R., Lynch, D. O., Paul, J. C. N., eds. 1981. Lawyers in the Third World: Comparative and Developmental Perspectives. Uppsala: Scand. Inst. Afr. Stud./New York: Int. Cent. Law Dev.

70. Dillon, R. G. 1980. Violent conflict in Meta' society. Am. Ethnol. 7:658–73

71. Dinnen, S. 1988. Sentencing, custom, and the rule of law in Papua New Guinea. J. Legal Plural. 27:19–54

72. Engel, D. M. 1978. Code and Custom in a Thai Provincial Court: The Interactions of Formal and Informal Systems of Justice. Tucson: Univ. Ariz. Press

73. Engel, D. M. 1980. Legal pluralism in an American community: perspectives on a civil trial court. Am. Bar Found. Res. J. 3:425–54

74. Engel, D. M. 1987. Law, time, and community. Law & Soc. Rev. 21:605–38

75. Engel, D. M. 1984. The oven bird's song: insiders, outsiders, and personal injuries in an American community. Law & Soc. Rev. 18:549–82

76. Feit, H. A. 1989. James Bay Cree self-governance and land management. See Ref. 273a, pp. 68–99

77. Felstiner, W., Abel, R., Sarat, A. 1980–1981. The emergence and transformation of disputes: naming, blaming, and claiming… . Law & Soc. Rev. 15:631–55

78. Fitzpatrick, P. 1980. Law and State in Papua New Guinea. London: Academic

79. Fitzpatrick, P. 1981. The political economy of dispute settlement in Papua New Guinea. In Crime, Justice, and Underdevelopment, ed. C. Sumner, pp. 228–47. London: Heinemann

80. Fitzpatrick, P. 1982. The political economy of law in the post-colonial period. See Ref. 267a, pp. 25–59

81. Fitzpatrick, P. 1983. Law, plurality, and underdevelopment. In Legality, Ideology, and the State, ed. D. Sugarman, pp. 159–83. London: Academic

82. Fitzpatrick, P. 1987. Transformations of law and labour in Papua New Guinea. See Ref. 235a, pp. 253–99

83. Fitzpatrick, P. 1989. Custom as imperialism. In Law and Identity in Africa, ed. J. M. Abun-Nasr, U. Spellenberg.

84. Fitzpatrick, P. 1989. Crime as resistance: the colonial situation. The Howard J. 28:272–74

85. Fitzpatrick, P., Blaxter, L. 1979. Imposed law in the containment of Papua New Guinea economic ventures. See Ref. 38, pp. 115–27

86. Fluehr-Lobban, C. 1987. Islamic Law and Society in the Sudan. London: Cass

87. Forer, N. 1979. The imposed wardship of American Indian tribes: a case study of the Prairie Band Potawatomi. See Ref. 38, pp. 89–114

88. Foucault, M. 1979. Discipline and Punish: The Birth of the Prison. New York: Vintage

89. Foucault, M. 1980. On popular justice: a discussion with Maoists. In Power/Knowledge: Selected Interviews and Other Writings 1972–1977, ed. C. Gordon, pp. 1–37. transl. C. Gordon, L. Marshall, J. Mepham, K. Soper. New York: Pantheon

90. Galanter, M. 1981. Justice in many rooms: courts, private ordering, and indigenous law. J. Legal Plural. 19:1–48

91. Galanter, M. 1983. Reading the landscape of disputes: What we know and don't know (and think we know) about our allegedly contentious and litigious society. UCLA Law Rev. 31:4–71

92. Galanter, M. 1986. The day after the litigation explosion. Maryland Law Rev. 46:3–39

93. Galanter, M. 1986. When legal worlds collide: reflections on Bhopal, the good lawyer, and the American law school. J. Legal Educ. 36:292–310

94. Galanter, M. 1989. *Law and Society in Modern India,* ed. R. Dhavan. Delhi: Oxford Univ. Press
95. Galanter, M. 1990. Bhopals, past and present: the changing legal response to mass disaster. *Windsor Yearb. Access Justice* 10:151–70
96. Gardner, J. A. 1980. *Legal Imperialism: American Lawyers and Foreign Aid in Latin America.* Madison, WI: Univ. Wis. Press
97. Garlock, J. 1982. The knights of labor courts: a case study of popular justice. See Ref. 3, pp. 17–34
98. Gartrell, B. 1984. Colonial wives: villains or victims? In *The Incorporated Wife,* ed. H. Callan, S. Ardener, pp. 165–86. London: Croom Helm
99. Geertz, C. 1983. Local knowledge: Fact and law in comparative perspective. In *Local Knowledge,* pp. 167–234. New York: Basic Books
100. Ghai, Y., Luckham, R., Snyder, F., eds. 1987. *The Political Economy of Law: A Third World Reader.* New Delhi: Oxford Univ. Press
101. Goodwin, M. H. 1982. Processes of dispute management among urban black children. *Am. Ethnol.* 9:76–97
102. Gordon, R. 1989. Can Namibian San stop dispossession of their land? See Ref. 273a, pp. 138–55
103. Gordon, R. J., Meggitt, M. J. 1985. *Law and Order in the New Guinea Highlands: Encounters with Enga.* Hanover\London: University Press of New England
104. Greenhouse, C. 1982. Nature is to culture as praying is to suing: legal pluralism in an American suburb. *J. Legal Plural.* 20:17–37
105. Greenhouse, C. 1986. *Praying for Justice: Faith, Order, and Community in an American Town.* Ithaca, NY: Cornell Univ. Press
106. Greenhouse, C. 1988. Courting difference: issues of interpretation and comparison in the study of legal ideologies. *Law & Soc. Rev.* 22:687–709
107. Griffiths, J. 1985. Introduction. See Ref. 8, pp. 13–20
108. Griffiths, J. 1986. What is legal pluralism? *J. Legal Plural.* 24:1–56
109. Griffiths, J. 1986. Recent anthropology of law in the Netherlands and its historical background. See Ref. 23, pp. 11–66
110. Gulliver, P. H., ed. 1978. *Cross-Examinations: Essays in Memory of Max Gluckman.* Leiden: Brill
111. Hamnett, I., ed. 1977. *Social Anthropology and Law.* Assoc. Soc. Anthropol. Monogr. 14. London: Academic
112. Harrington, C. 1985. *Shadow Justice: The Ideology and Institutionalization of Alternatives to Court.* Westport, CT: Greenwood Press
113. Harrington, C., Merry, S. E. 1989. Ideological production: the making of community mediation. *Law & Soc. Rev.* 22:709–37
114. Hay, M. J., Wright, M., eds. 1982. *African Women and the Law: Historical Perspectives.* Boston: Boston Univ. Pap. Afr., VII
115. Hayden, R. M. 1984. Popular use of Yugoslav labor courts and the contradiction of social courts. *Law & Soc. Rev.* 20:229–51
116. Hayden, R. M. 1984. A note on caste panchayats and government courts in India: different kinds of stages for different kinds of performances. *J. Legal Plural.* 22:43–52
117. Hayden, R. M. 1987. Turn-taking, overlap, and the task at hand: ordering speaking turns in legal settings. *Am. Ethnol.* 14:251–70
118. Hayden, R. M. 1990. *Social Courts in Yugoslavia.* Philadelphia, PA: Univ. Penn. Press
119. Henry, S. 1983. *Private Justice.* Boston: Routledge & Kegan Paul
120. Henry, S. 1985. Community justice, capitalist society, and human agency: the dialectics of collective law in the cooperative. *Law & Soc. Rev.* 19:303–27
121. Henry, S. 1987. Private justice and the policing of labor: the dialectics of industrial discipline. In *Private Policing,* ed. C. Shearing, P. Stenning. Beverly Hills, CA: Sage
122. Henry, S. 1987. The construction and deconstruction of social control: thoughts on the discursive production of state law and private justice. In *Transcarceration: Essays in the Sociology of Social Control,* ed. J. Lowman, R. J. Menzies, T. S. Palys, pp. 89–108. Aldershot: Gower
123. Hiatt, L. R. 1989. Aboriginal land tenure and contemporary claims in Australia. See Ref. 273a, pp. 99–118
124. Hooker, M. B. 1975. *Legal Pluralism: An Introduction to Colonial and Neo-Colonial Laws.* Oxford: Clarendon Press
125. Hsia, T. 1978. Legal developments since the purge of the gang of four. *Issues & Stud.* 14:1–26
126. Huber, B. 1981. A note on village courts in Papua-New Guinea. *J. Legal Plural.* 19:161–63
127. Ietswaart, H. F. P. 1982. The discourse of summary justice and the discourse of popular justice: an analysis of legal rhetoric in Argentina. See Ref. 3, 2:149–83
128. Isaacman, B., Isaacman, A. 1982. A socialist legal system in the making: Mozambique before and after independence. See Ref. 2:281–324
129. Johnny, N. 1987. The relationship between traditional and institutionalized dispute resolution in the Federated States of Micronesia. Progr. Conflict Resolution Occas. Pap. 1987-3. Honolulu: Univ. Hawaii at Manoa

130. Just, P. 1986. Let the evidence fit the crime: evidence, law, and "sociological truth" among the Dou Donggo. *Am. Ethnol.* 13:43–61

131. Just, P. 1990. Dead goats and broken betrothals: liability and equity in Dou Donggo law. *Am. Ethnol.* 17:75–90

132. Kairys, D., ed. 1982. *The Politics of Law.* New York: Pantheon Books

133. Kennedy, D. 1982. Antonio Gramsci and the legal system. *Am. Legal Stud. Assoc. Forum* 6:32–37

134. Kidder, R. L. 1974. Formal litigation and professional insecurity: legal entrepreneurship in South India. *Law & Soc. Rev.* 9:11–37

135. Kidder, R. L. 1979. Toward an integrated theory of imposed law. See Ref. 38, pp. 289–306

136. Kidder, R. L. 1981. The end of the road? Problems in the analysis of disputes. *Law & Soc. Rev.* 15:717–27

137. Konings, P. 1984. Capitalist rice-farming and land allocation in Northern Ghana. *J. Legal Plural.* 22:89–119

138. Lam, M. 1985. The imposition of Anglo-American land tenure law on Hawaiians. *J. Legal Plural.* 23:103–28

139. Leng, S. 1977. The role of law in the People's Republic of China as reflecting Mao Tse-Tung's influence. *J. Crim. Law Criminol.* 68:356–73

140. Li, V. H. 1978. *Law without Lawyers: A Comparative View of Law in China and the United States.* Boulder, CO: Westview

141. Lowy, M. 1978. A good name is worth more than money: strategies of court use in urban Ghana. See Ref. 178, pp. 181–208

142. Macaulay, S. 1986. In *Law and the Social Sciences,* ed. L. Lipson, S. Wheeler. New York: Russell Sage Found.

143. Maddock, K. 1989. Involved anthropologists. See Ref. 273a, pp. 155–77

144. Mather, L., Yngvesson, B. 1980–1981. Language, audience, and the transformation of disputes. *Law & Soc. Rev.* 15:775–822

145. Matsuda, M. J. 1988. Law and culture in the District Court of Honolulu, 1844–1845: a case study of the rise of legal consciousness. *Am. J. Legal Hist.* 32:16–41

146. Mayer, A., ed. 1985. *Property, Social Structure, and Law in the Modern Middle East.* Albany: State Univ. NY Press

147. Maynard, D. W. 1984. The structure of discourse in misdemeanor plea bargaining. *Law & Soc. Rev.* 18:75–104

148. Maynard, D. W. 1984. *Inside Plea Bargaining: The Language of Negotiation.* New York: Plenum

149. Merry, S. E. 1979. Going to court: strategies of dispute management in an American urban neighborhood. *Law & Soc. Rev.* 13:891–925

150. Merry, S. E. 1982. The articulation of legal spheres. See Ref. 114, pp. 68–89

151. Merry, S. E. 1982. The social organization of mediation in nonindustrial societies: implications for informal community justice in America. See Ref. 3, 2:17–47

152. Merry, S. E. 1986. Everyday understandings of the law in working-class America. *Am. Ethnol.* 13:253–70

153. Merry, S. E. 1988. Legal pluralism. *Law & Soc. Rev.* 22:869–96

154. Merry, S. E. 1990. *Getting Justice and Getting Even: Legal Consciousness among Working-Class Americans.* Chicago: Univ. Chicago Press

155. Merry, S. E. 1993. Sorting out popular justice. In *The Possibility of Popular Justice: A Case Study of American Community Mediation,* ed. S. E. Merry, N. Milner. Ann Arbor: Univ. Michigan Press

156. Merry, S. E., Silbey, S. S. 1984. What do plaintiffs want?: Reexamining the concept of dispute. *Justice Syst. J.* 9:151–79.(Spec. Issue Alternative Dispute Resolution)

157. Mertz, E. 1988. The uses of history: language, ideology, and law in the United States and South Africa. *Law & Soc. Rev.* 22:661–87

158. Meschievitz, C. S., Galanter, G. 1982. In search of Nyaya Panchayats: the politics of a moribund institution. See Ref. 3, 2:47–81

159. Messick, B. 1983. Legal documents and the concept of "Restricted Literacy." *Int. J. Sociol. Lang.* 4:41–52

160. Messick, B. 1986. The Mufti, the text, and the world: legal interpretation in Yemen. *Man* (NS) 21:102–19

161. Messick, B. 1988. Kissing hands and knees: hegemony and hierarchy in Shari'a discourse. *Law & Soc. Rev.* 22:637–61

162. Messick, B. 1988. Literacy and the law: documents and document specialists in Yemen. In *Law and Islam in the Middle East,* ed. D. Hilse Dwyer, pp. 61–76. South Hadley, MA: Bergen & Garvey

163. Messick, B. 1992. *The Calligraphic State: Textual Domination and History in a Muslim Society.* Berkeley: Univ. Calif. Press

164. Mintz, S. 1985. *Sweetness and Power.* New York: Viking

165. Mitchell, T. 1988. *Colonising Egypt.* Cambridge: Cambridge Univ. Press

166. Moog, R. S. 1991. Conflict and compromise: the politics of Lok Adalats in Varanasi District. *Law & Soc. Rev.* 25:545–70

167. Moore, E. 1985. *Conflict and Compromise: Justice in an Indian Village.* Monogr. Ser. 26, Cent. South and Southeast Asia Stud., Univ. Calif., Berkeley, CA. Lanham, MD: Univ. Press America

168. Moore, S. F. 1977. Individual interests and organizational structures: dispute settlements as "events of articulation." In *Social Anthropology and Law,* ed. I. Hamnett, pp. 159–89. New York: Academic

169. Moore, S. F. 1978. *Law as Process: An Anthropological Approach.* London: Routledge & Kegan Paul

170. Moore, S. F. 1986. Legal systems of the world: an introductory guide to classifications, typological interpretations, and bibliographic resources. In *Law and the Social Sciences*, ed. L. Lipson, S. Wheeler, pp. 11–62. New York: Russell Sage Found.

171. Moore, S. F. 1986. *Social Facts and Fabrications: Customary Law on Kilimanjaro, 1880–1980.* Cambridge: Cambridge Univ. Press

172. Moore, S. F. 1989. History and the redefinition of custom on Kilimanjaro. See Ref. 247, pp. 277–301

173. Myers, F. 1989. Burning the truck and holding the country: Pintupi forms of property and identity. See Ref. 273a, pp. 15–43

174. Nader, L., ed. 1980. *No Access to Law.* New York: Academic

175. Nader, L. 1984. The recurrent dialectic between legality and its alternatives. *Univ. Penn. Law Rev.* 132:621–45

176. Nader, L. 1989. The crown, the colonists, and the course of Zapotec village law. See Ref. 247, pp. 320–45

177. Nader, L. 1990. *Harmony Ideology: Justice and Control in a Zapotec Mountain Village.* Stanford: Stanford Univ. Press

178. Nader, L., Todd, H. F., eds. 1978. *The Disputing Process—Law in Ten Societies.* New York: Columbia Univ. Press

179. Narokobi, J. B. 1982. History and movement in law reform in Papua New Guinea. See Ref. 267a, pp. 13–25

180. Nelligan, P. J. 1983. *Social Change and Rape Law in Hawaii.* PhD thesis. Dept. Sociol., Univ. Hawaii

181. Nettheim, G. 1987. Australian aborigines and the law. In *Law and Anthropology*. Int. Jahrb. Rechanthropol. 2:371–403. Wien: VWGO: Hohenschaftlarn-Renner

182. Newman, K. 1983. *Law and Economic Organization: a Comparative Study of Preindustrial Societies.* New York: Cambridge Univ. Press

183. O'Barr, W. M. 1982. *Linguistic Evidence: Language, Power, and Strategy in the Courtroom.* New York: Academic

184. O'Barr, W. M., Conley, J. M. 1985. Litigant satisfaction versus legal adequacy in small claims court narratives. *Law & Soc. Rev.* 19:661–703

185. O'Connor, R. A. 1981. Law as indigenous social theory: a Siamese Thai case. *Am. Ethnol.* 8:223–37

186. Okoth-Ogendo, H. W. O. 1979. The imposition of property law in Kenya. See Ref. 38, pp. 147–66

187. Ortiz, R. D. 1985. Protection of American Indian territories in the United States: applicability of international law. In *Irredeemable America: The Indians' Estate and Land Claims*, ed. I. Sutton, pp. 247–66. Albuquerque, NM: Univ. New Mexico Press

188. Ottley, B. L., Zorn, J. G. 1983. Criminal law in Papua New Guinea: code, custom and the courts in conflict. *Am. J. Comp. Law* 31:251–300

189. Paliwala, A. 1978. Economic development and the legal system of Papua New Guinea. *Afr. Law Stud.* 16:3–79

190. Paliwala, A. 1982. Law and order in the village: the village courts. See Ref. 267a, pp. 191–219

191. Parker, L. S. 1989. *Native American Estate: The Struggle Over Indian and Hawaiian Lands.* Honolulu: Univ. Hawaii Press

192. Parnell, P. 1978. Village or state? Competitive legal systems in a Mexican judicial district. See Ref. 178, pp. 315–50

193. Parnell, P. 1989. *Escalating Disputes: Social Participation and Change in the Oaxacan Highlands.* Tucson: Univ. Ariz. Press

194. Pe, C. L., Tadiar, A. F. 1979. *Katarungang Pambarangay: Dynamics of Compulsory Conciliation.* Manila: UST Press

195. Pospisil, L. 1979. Legally induced culture change in New Guinea. See Ref. 38, pp. 127–46

196. Pospisil, L. 1981. Modern and traditional administration of justice in New Guinea. *J. Legal Plural.* 19:93–116

197. Provine, M. D. 1986. *Judging Credentials: Non-Lawyer Judges and the Politics of Professionalism.* Chicago: Univ. Chicago Press

198. Renteln, A. D. 1988. The concept of human rights. *Anthropos* 83:343–64

199. Renteln, A. D. 1988. Relativism and the search for human rights. *Am. Anthropol.* 90:56–72

200. Renteln, A. D. 1990. *International Human Rights: Universalism versus Relativism.* Newbury Park, CA: Sage

201. Roberts, S. 1979. *Order and Dispute: An Introduction to Legal Anthropology.* New York: St. Martin's Press

202. Rodman, W. L. 1977. Big men and middlemen: the politics of law in Longana. *Am. Ethnol.* 4:525–37

203. Rodman, W. L. 1985. "A law unto themselves": legal innovation in Ambae, Vanuatu. *Am. Ethnol.* 12:603–24

204. Rosen, L. 1980–1981. Equity and discretion in a modern Islamic legal system. *Law & Soc. Rev.* 15:217–45

205. Rosen, L. 1981. Making justice more accessible. *Am. Ethnol.* 8:567–71

206. Rosen, L. 1989. Responsibility and compensatory justice in Arab culture and law. In *Semiotics, Self, and Society*, ed. B. Lee, G. Urban, pp. 101–20. Berlin: Mouton

207. Rosen, L. 1989. Islamic case law and the logic of consequence. See Ref. 247, pp. 302–20

208. Rosen, L. 1989. *The Anthropology of Justice: Law as Culture in Islamic Society.* Cambridge: Cambridge Univ. Press

209. Rothenberger, J. E. 1978. The social dynamics of dispute settlement in a Sunni Muslim village in Lebanon. See Ref. 178, pp. 152–80

210. Ruffini, J. L. 1978. Disputing over livestock in Sardinia. See Ref. 178, pp. 209–46

211. Sahlins, M. 1985. *Islands of History.* Chicago: Univ. Chicago Press

212. Salamone, F. A. 1983. The clash between indigenous, Islamic, colonial, and post-colonial law in Nigeria. *J. Legal Plural.* 21:15–60

213. Salamone, F. A. 1987. The social construction of colonial reality: Yauri Emirate. *J. Legal Plural.* 25/26:47–70

214. Salas, L. 1983. The emergence and decline of the Cuban popular tribunals. *Law & Soc. Rev.* 17:587–613

215. Salman, S. M. A. 1983. Lay tribunals in the Sudan: an historical and socio-legal analysis. *J. Legal Plural.* 21:61–128

216. Santos, B. de Sousa. 1977. The law of the oppressed: the construction and reproduction of legality in Pasagarda. *Law & Soc. Rev.* 12:5–126

217. Santos, B. de Sousa. 1979. Popular justice, dual power, and socialist strategy. In *Capitalism and the Rule of Law,* ed. B. Fine, R. Kinsey, J. Lea, S. Picciotto, J. Young, pp. 151–71. London: Hutchinson

218. Santos, B. de Sousa. 1982. Law and community: the changing nature of state power in late capitalism. See Ref. 3, 1:249–67

219. Santos, B. de Sousa. 1982. Law and revolution in Portugal: the experiences of popular justice after the 25th of April, 1974. See Ref. 3, 2:251–81

220. Santos, B. de Sousa. 1987. Law: a map of misreading; toward a postmodern conception of law. *J. Law & Soc.* 14:279–302

221. Sarat, A., Felstiner, W. L. F. 1986. Law and strategy in the divorce lawyer's office. *Law & Soc. Rev.* 20:93–134

222. Sarat, A., Felstiner, W. L. F. 1988. Law and social relations: vocabularies of motive in lawyer/client interaction. *Law & Soc. Rev.* 22:737–71

223. School of Justice Studies, Ariz. State Univ., ed. 1990. *New Directions in the Study of Justice, Law, and Social Control.* New York: Plenum

224. Schwimmer, E., ed. 1977. *"The Vailala Madness" and Other Essays: Francis Edgar Williams.* Honolulu: The Univ. Press Hawaii

225. Scott, J. 1985. *Weapons of the Weak.* New Haven: Yale Univ. Press

226. Seekings, J. 1989. People's courts and popular politics. *S. Afr. Rev.* 5

227. Sevilla-Casas, E. 1977. Notes on Las Casas' ideological and political practice. In *Western Expansion and Indigenous Peoples,* ed. E. Sevilla-Casas, pp. 15–29. Hague: Mouton

228. Sheehan, B. J. 1984. *The Boston School Integration Dispute: Social Change and Legal Maneuvers.* New York: Colombia Univ. Press

229. Shore, B. 1978. Ghosts and government: a structural analysis of alternative institutions for conflict management in Samoa. *Man* 13:175–99

230. Silbey, S. S., Merry, S. E. 1986. Mediator settlement strategies. *Law & Policy* 8:7–32

231. Silbey, S. S., Sarat, A. 1987. Critical traditions in law and society research. *Law & Soc. Rev.* 21:165–74

232. Silliman, G. S. 1981–1982. Dispute processing by the Philippine agrarian court. *Law & Soc. Rev.* 16:89–115

233. Silliman, C. S. 1985. A political analysis of the Philippines' Katarungang Pambarangay system of informal justice through mediation. *Law & Soc. Rev.* 19:279–303

234. Sinclair, I. M. 1963. Treaty interpretation in the English courts. *Int. Comp. Law Q.* 12:508–51

235. Slaats, H., Portier, K. 1985. The implementation of state law through folk law: Karo Batak village elections. *J. Legal Plural.* 23:153–76

235a. Snyder, F., Hay, D., eds. 1987. *Law, Labour, and Crime: An Historical Perspective.* London/New York: Tavistock

236. Snyder, F. G. 1977. Land law and economic change in rural Senegal: Diola pledge transactions and disputes. In *Social Anthropology and Law,* ed. I. Hamnett, pp. 113–57. New York: Academic

237. Snyder, F. G. 1981. Colonialism and legal form: the creation of "customary law" in Senegal. *J. Legal Plural.* 19:49–90

238. Snyder, F. G. 1981. Anthropology, dispute processes, and law: a critical introduction. *Br. J. Law & Soc.* 8:141–80

239. Snyder, F. G. 1981. *Capitalism and Legal Change: An African Transformation.* New York: Academic

240. Spence, J. 1978. Institutionalizing neighborhood courts: two Chilean experiences. *Law & Soc. Rev.* 13:139–82

241. Spitzer, S. 1982. The dialectics of formal and informal control. See Ref. 3, 1:167–207

242. Starr, J. 1978. *Dispute and Settlement in Rural Turkey.* Leiden: Brill

243. Starr, J. 1989. The role of Turkish secular law in changing the lives of rural Muslim women, 1950–1970. *Law & Soc. Rev.* 23:497–523

244. Starr, J. 1990. Islam and the struggle over state law in Turkey. In *Law and Islam in the Middle East,* ed. D. Dwyer. Westport, CT: Bergin/Garvey

245. Starr, J. 1992. *Law as Metaphor: From Islamic Courts to the Palace of Justice.* Albany: SUNY Press

246. Starr, J., Collier, J. F. 1987. Historical studies of legal change. *Curr. Anthropol.* 28:367–72

247. Starr, J., Collier, J. F., eds. 1989. *History and Power in the Study of Law: New Directions in Legal Anthropology.* Ithaca, NY: Cornell Univ. Press

248. Starr, J., Pool, J. 1974. The impact of a legal revolution in rural Turkey. *Law & Soc. Rev.* 8:533–60

249. Stoler, A. L. 1989. Making empire respectable: the politics of race and sexual morality in 20th century colonial cultures. *Am. Ethnol.* 16:634–61

250. Strijbosch, F. 1985. The concept of pela and its social significance in the community of Moluccan immigrants in the Netherlands. *J. Legal Plural.* 23:177–208
251. Sumner, C. 1979. *Reading Ideologies: An Investigation into the Marxist Theory of Ideology and Law.* London: Academic
252. Sutton, I., ed. 1985. *Irredeemable America: The Indians' Estate and Land Claims.* Albuquerque, NM: Univ. NM Press
253. Thompson, E. P. 1982 [1975]. The rule of law. Reprinted from: Whigs and hunters: the origin of the black acts. In *Marxism and Law,* ed. P. Beirne, R. Quinney. New York: Wiley
254. Tiruchelvam, N. 1984. *The Ideology of Popular Justice in Sri Lanka: A Socio-Legal Inquiry.* New Delhi: Vikas Publ. House
255. Tyler, T. R. 1990. *Why People Obey the Law.* New Haven: Yale Univ. Press
256. Ubah, C. N. 1982. Islamic legal system and the Westernization process in the Nigerian emirates. *J. Legal Plural.* 20:69–93
257. Deleted in proof
258. Vanderlinden, J. 1989. Return to legal pluralism: twenty years later. *J. Legal Plural.* 28:149–57
259. Vincent, J. 1981. *Teso in Transformation: Peasantry and Class in Colonial Uganda.* Berkeley: Univ. Calif. Press
260. Vincent, J. 1989. Contours of change: agrarian law in colonial Uganda, 1895–1962. See Ref. 247, pp. 153–68
261. Vincent, J. 1990. *Anthropology and Politics: Visions, Traditions, and Trends.* Tucson: Univ. Ariz. Press
262. Volkman, T. A. 1990. Visions and revisions: Toraja culture and the tourist gaze. *Am. Ethnol.* 17:91–111
263. Voyce, M. B. 1986. Some observations on the relationship between the king and the Buddhist order in ancient India. *J. Legal Plural.* 24:127–50
264. Wanda, B. P. 1988. Customary family law in Malawi: adherence to tradition and adaptability to change. *J. Legal Plural.* 27:117–34
265. Watson-Gegeo, K. A., White, C. M., eds. 1990. *Disentangling: Conflict Discourse in Pacific Societies.* Stanford: Stanford Univ. Press
266. Weisbrot, D. 1982. The impact of the Papua New Guinea constitution on the recognition and application of customary law. In *Pacific Constitutions: Proc. Canberra Law Workshop VI,* ed. P. Sack, pp. 271–90. Canberra: Austr. Natl. Univ.
267. Weisbrot, D., Paliwala, A. 1982. Changing society through law: an introduction. See Ref. 267a, pp. 3–13
267a. Weisbrot, D., Paliwala, A., Sawyers, A., eds. 1982. *Law and Social Change in Papua New Guinea.* Sydney: Butterworths
268. Weissbourd, B., Mertz, E. 1985. Rule-centrism versus legal creativity: The skewing of legal ideology through language. *Law & Soc. Rev.* 19:623–61
269. Weissbrodt, D. 1988. Human rights: an historical perspective. In *Human Rights,* ed. P. Davies, pp. 1–20. London: Routledge
270. Westermark, G. D. 1986. Court is an arrow: legal pluralism in Papua New Guinea. *Ethnology* 25:131
271. Williams, D. V. 1982. State coercion against peasant farmers: the Tanzanian case. *J. Legal Plural.* 20:95–127
272. Williams, N. M. 1986. *The Yolngu and Their Land: A System of Land Tenure and the Fight for Its Recognition.* Stanford: Stanford Univ. Press
273. Wilmsen, E. N. 1989. Those who have each other: San relations to land. See Ref. 273a, pp. 43–68
273a. Wilmsen, E. N., ed. 1989. *We Are Here: Politics of Aboriginal Land Tenure.* Berkeley, CA: Univ. Calif. Press
274. Witty, C. J. 1978. Disputing issues in Shehaam, a multireligious village in Lebanon. See Ref. 178, pp. 281–314
275. Witty, C. J. 1980. *Mediation and Society: Conflict Management in Lebanon.* New York: Academic
276. Wolf, E. 1982. *Europe and the People without History.* Berkeley, CA: Univ. Calif. Press
277. Yngvesson, B. 1985. Legal ideology and community justice in the clerk's office. *Legal Stud. Forum* 9:71–89
278. Yngvesson, B. 1988. Making law at the doorway: the clerk, the court, and the construction of community in a New England town. *Law & Soc. Rev.* 22:409–48

Annu. Rev. Anthropol. 1992. 21:381–406

LANGUAGE AND WORLD VIEW

Jane H. Hill

Department of Anthropology, University of Arizona, Tucson Arizona 85721

Bruce Mannheim

Department of Anthropology, University of Michigan, Ann Arbor, Michigan 48109-1382

KEYWORDS: linguistic relativity, Whorf, Sapir, Boas, linguistic anthropology

INTRODUCTION

We open the current essay with a necessary problematization of the terms of the title assigned us by the editors of the *Annual Review of Anthropology*, which we have preserved precisely for this rhetorical purpose. On the one hand, the traditional notion of "language" dissolves as formal linguistics rarefies its object into a small set of constraints on the possibilities for autonomous syntactic structure, while semiotics and the theory of "discourse" advanced by Foucault (58) erase the privilege of specifically linguistic signifiers in a universe of mediating signs and practices. On the other hand, "world view" [Humboldt's (95) *Weltanschauung*], has served anthropology as a term for the philosophical dimensions of "cultures" seen as having a degree of coherence in time and space (174, 175; also 113a). Today, with our confidence in the coherence, integration, and political innocence of cultures long lost, a term from the high-water mark of bourgeois "German ideology" must be problematic.[1] "World view" also suggests reflection and mastery of a repertoire of forms and meanings, neglecting the way culture is shaped in everyday practices below the threshold of awareness. Today, both theoretical inclination and the ethnographic data force us to admit the fragmented and contingent nature

---

[1]
 The historical roots of Western interest in "language and world view" in the work of Vico, Herder, and Humboldt are discussed in 64:Ch.2; 107, 147, 159, and 166.

0084-6570/92/1015-0381$02.00

of human worlds, as opposed to their "wholeness" and persistence. Thus, where "world view" would once have served, "ideology" is often heard, suggesting representations that are contestable, socially positioned, and laden with political interest.

Within these new frameworks linguistic anthropologists and scholars in related disciplines are returning to classical questions about the relationships between language and other forms of knowledge and practice. (See the citations in footnote 3; also 96, 112, 167, 176, 177; and ethnographic studies: 41, 68, 69, 89, 117, 144, 149, 168, 223). Our essay first sketches some conceptual fundamentals and then aims to correct certain widespread misrepresentations of the positions of Boas, Sapir, and Whorf. We then review the revival of interest in these three scholars, highlighting several important reinterpretations of their work that are producing new research programs.[2]

"LANGUAGE" AND "NONLANGUAGE"

Problematic in the first instance is the separation of "language" and "nonlanguage" such that these can be then "related" one to another. The notion of the "linguistic" versus the "nonlinguistic" eludes contemporary cultural anthropologists. Bloch (15), for instance, argues that what is most important about cultural knowledge cannot be represented in what he takes to be the terms appropriate to the discussion of language—such as "rules." Bloch is apparently unaware that contemporary linguistics conceptualizes speech production as the exemplar par excellence of "embodied," "expert" knowledge (also see 208). In this the discipline returns to a position advocated by Sapir (186) for whom the tacit, "aesthetic" quality of the form-feeling of actors for their culture meant precisely that pattern in culture was like pattern in language.

There is no prima facie way to identify certain behaviors—or better, certain forms of social action—as linguistic and others as cultural (cf 72). Even the most formal and minute aspect of phonetics—syllable timing—completely interpenetrates the most identifiably nonlinguistic, unconscious part of behavior—the timing of body movements and gestures (see 46, 47; also 30, 114, 165, 195). Thus "language" and "culture" cannot be neatly separated by distinctions like "structure" versus "practice." Further, "meaning" can only be known in another language through social action and speech, and the relevant units for analyzing these in another culture can only be worked out through their language. The entire intricate calibration is undertaken by the ethnographer in the field, often in an intuitive way. The process finally yields a report (usually) in the ethnographer's native language. So language, culture, and

2
   Hill (87) takes a slightly different approach to these questions, emphasizing issues not treated here. The timeliness of the issues discussed here can be gauged by a recent discussion on the electronic mailing list, *Linguist,* which drew about 40 responses, including substantive discussions by N. Besnier, W. Kempton, A. Manaster-Ramer, and B. E. Nevin.

meaning have inextricably contaminated each other in the course of doing ethnography.

LINGUISTIC RELATIVITY IN THE THOUGHT OF BOAS, SAPIR, AND WHORF[3]

The stance of "linguistic relativity," a term coined for the cross-cultural episte-mology of the Boasian tradition by Sapir, is often taken to be a "hypothesis" that linguistic patterning at every level exhibits unconstrained variation, such that each language must be approached entirely on its own terms (106:96). We maintain that "linguistic relativity" as proposed by Boas, Sapir, and Whorf is not a hypothesis in the traditional sense, but an axiom, a part of the initial epistemology and methodology of the linguistic anthropologist. Boas, Sapir, and Whorf were not relativists in the extreme sense often suggested by modern critics, but assumed instead a more limited position, recognizing that linguistic and cultural particulars intersect with universals (64:9; see 204 for a nuanced discussion of Boasian ethnography as "cosmography," focusing on Sapir's intellectual style.)[4] Boas, Sapir, and Whorf all recognized that kinds of cogni-tive organization quite general to human beings might underlie the capacity for language. Thus Boas wrote that "in each language only part of the complete concept that we have in mind is expressed" (18:43), recognizing, if only implicitly, that there is a domain of conceptual organization that pre-exists language. While Sapir regarded culture as "a historically derived, shared ge-stalt of patterns" (64:11; cf 4, 204:87ff), he also sought the mechanisms by which individuals appropriated and configured such patterns, turning to the "personality psychology" of his day in the absence of a developed cognitive psychology. Whorf, almost echoing Boas, suggested that a pre-linguistic stra-tum organized linguistic and cultural experience, "a universal ... way of link-ing experiences which shows up in laboratory experiments and appears to be independent of language—basically alike for all persons" (235:267; see 134, 194:27–28; compare 28:51ff).

Scholars approaching anew the relationship between language and world view today problematize the formulation of linguistic relativity with an in-creasingly sophisticated understanding of what kinds of linguistic phenomena are likely to be universal aspects of human psychobiology, and regard this as a positive development (79). As we have noted, in doing so they do not depart radically from the Boasian tradition. And the sophistication with which they evaluate the status of proposed universals owes much to Whorf, who was

---

[3] For our summary, we are indebted to a series of recent rereadings of Boas, Sapir, and Whorf, including 1, 2, 3, 7a, 28, 31, 56, 57, 60, 64, 75, 99, 104, 129, 131, 132, 133, 194, 204; and to historical works on Boas and Sapir, including 37, 38, 81, 82, and 211.

[4] None of these scholars formulated "relativity" as a discontinuity between primitive, pre-ra-tional, or "folk" thought and "modern" thought; this distinguishes the linguistic-anthropological tradition from "relativism" in modern social philosophy (cf 91).

acutely conscious of the cultural roots of the language of science. While admitting the likelihood of such universals, most anthropological students of language insist that the epistemological and methodological foundations of the linguistic research through which putative universals are identified must be subjected to reflexive scrutiny, for—a profoundly "Whorfian" point—it is entirely possible that these foundations are artifacts of Western linguistic ideology. Thus they leave open the possibility that some "universalism" and the associated idea of biological innateness may be a product of an essentializing ontology, deriving from practices of referential objectification in European languages (13, 76, 200).[5] Becker proposes that to think of our glossing of other languages as a form of access to "pure meaning" rather than as a set of metaphors is to develop an exuberance of English: "the exuberancy of thinking of logical categories as reified 'things'" (12:142). Even the act of transcription itself is, for Becker, the political imposition of our own "language games" on the forms of life of speakers of other languages. Most linguistic anthropologists take a more moderate position, criticizing specific "universalist" programs while admitting the likelihood of dimensions of language where exuberances and deficiencies between distinct codes are minimized, such as abstract conditions on the relationships between anaphora and their antecedents (29), or the extensions of terms for living kinds (5), and where our attention should turn to similarity.

Boas, Sapir, and Whorf all limited their claims about the power language had over thought to specific, highly habituated, forms. Boas focused on the "selective power" of obligatory categories of grammar (104). Sapir emphasized unreflective, idiomatic expression (184) and wrote extensively about the alienation that might come with scholarly consciousness of pattern (88). Whorf restricts the linguistic phenomena of relevance to the habitual "fashions of speaking" (234).[6] The idea of "linguistic relativity" in the writings of Boas, Sapir, and Whorf must be contextualized historically. In their time a naive and racist universalism in grammar, and an equally vulgar evolutionism in anthropology and history, were lively intellectual forces. Boas (18) criticized grammarians for their tendency to see the system of categories of Indo-European in Native American languages, and argued that it was critical to identify grammatical patterns by criteria internal to the language. Like his contemporary,

---

[5] Compare biologist Ernst Mayr (156:41), who attributes essentialist thinking in evolutionary theory to category formation and grammatical definiteness in English.

[6] Notice that the "effability" of language (108), the possibility of translating utterances of a language into any other (194:27), is not at issue here. The translatability argument is pushed to its logical extreme by Davidson (39), who argues that were two languages so radically incommensurate that translation is impossible, speakers of one would not recognize that speakers of the other were speaking at all. Since Boas's, Sapir's, and Whorf's theses rest on habitual uses of language rather than on radical untranslatability, Davidson's contention is tangential to theirs. Hunt & Agnoli (96) propose that the translatability argument be rephrased in terms of processing effort: In principle, a statement in one language can be translated into a statement in another. Nevertheless, such a translation might render a natural, easily processed statement in the first language as a clumsy, unmanageable statement in the other.

Ferdinand de Saussure (192), Boas observed that grammatical meaning could only be understood in terms of the system of which it is part. Sapir also warned against the temptation to treat language as a set of labels on a pre-existing, noncultural (or "objective") world. Such a move would inevitably lead to treating linguistic and cultural forms as reflexes of timeless, universal meanings, which could only prevent the ethnographer or linguist from understanding formal patterns in another culture or language. The famous passage from "The status of linguistics as a science" (187) needs to be understood in this light:

> It is quite an illusion to imagine that one adjusts to reality without the use of language and that language is merely an incidental means of solving specific problems of communication or reflection. The fact of the matter is that the 'real world' is to a large extent unconsciously built up on the language habits of the group. No two languages are ever sufficiently similar to be considered as representing the same reality. The worlds in which different societies live are distinct worlds, not merely the same world with different labels attached (187:162).[7]

Sapir's phrase "real world" is an ironic reminder that the naturalized world of our everyday experience is no more culturally unmediated than that of any other culture. His insistence that it is "to a large extent unconsciously built up on the language habits of the group" prefigures Raymond Williams's (239) characterization of language as a "constitutive material practice."

By the middle of the 1950s, a scholarly folklore grew around Sapir and Whorf that hardened "linguistic relativity" into the familiar formula that treats language, thought, and meaning as three discrete, identifiable, and orthogonal phenomena (194:3–19).[8] This formula rests on a category error that identifies language, thought, and culture with the institutional fields of linguistics, psychology, and anthropology respectively. Such an error does considerable violence to the integrative thrust of the program Sapir and Whorf shared with Boas as they worked with him to create the modern disciplines of anthropology and linguistics. Boas (18), carving out an intellectual rationalization for anthropology as a science, argued for attention to the "unconscious patterning" in language as a guarantee of objectivity regarding "fundamental ethnic ideas," as a source of relatively pristine evidence of areal-geographic connections between peoples, and as evidence for the organization of categories in thought itself, in both culturally specific and universal senses. Sapir's famous "different worlds" quotation appears in a frankly polemical context, in an address in which he argued for the necessity of a linguistic component in the social sciences. Against the trend of his times, Sapir moved increasingly away from viewing language, culture, and personality as autonomous systems. In the

---

[7] Compare Antonio Gramsci (78:323), who like Sapir, was influenced by the philosopher Benedetto Croce.

[8] See Alford (2) for a lucid history of the hardening of intellectual positions on Whorf during the 1950s.

middle 1930s, during the period when he moved to Yale University to attempt the founding of a broad interdisciplinary program in the social sciences (38), he appeared rather to regard such a view as an unfortunate consequence of the intellectual immaturity of the disciplines of linguistics, anthropology, and psychology, respectively (see 190:592). Like those of his teacher Sapir, Whorf's writings cut against the grain. In an era when a leading figure suggested in the pages of the *American Anthropologist* that much could be accomplished without fluent knowledge of a field language, Whorf insisted on the continued importance of language difference—particularly difference in grammatical patterning—to ethnography.

Almost invariably, textbooks and reviews refer to a "Sapir-Whorf Hypothesis." Yet, just as the Holy Roman Empire was neither holy, nor Roman, nor an empire, the "Sapir-Whorf Hypothesis" is neither consistent with the writings of Sapir and Whorf, nor a hypothesis. As Grace (77) has pointed out, the rhetoric of "hypotheses" and "variables" makes sense only within a view of language as a map of nonlinguistic reality. From such a point of view, Grace suggests, it is impossible to understand Whorf's work as anything other than a sort of failed attempt at a hypothesis. Yet such a view of language is hardly found within linguistic anthropology, rendering mysterious the universal perpetuation of this representation.

Note, however, Schultz's caution against a monological assimilation of Whorf's work to any single modern point of view. Schultz (194) holds that positivist science and literary interpretation were in profound tension in Whorf's writings, and suggests that attempts to assign them entirely to an "interpretive," "social-constructionist," or "ethical" tradition [as in the work of Fishman (56), Alford (1,2), and Grace], is as wrong-headed as attempts to read Whorf only as a scientist. Schultz argues for a Bakhtinian interpretation of Whorf's work as a polyphonic (and even paradoxical) dialog between the voices of positivistic science and poetic interpretation.

It is wrong to believe that the idea of language, culture, and thought as separate variables is somehow validated by the well-known insistence of Boas and Sapir on the separation of race, language, and culture. Statements like Sapir's (183:218–19) that "the drifts of language and culture [are] noncomparable and nonrelated processes" have no direct relevance to any hypothetico-deductive "operationalizing" of a hypothesis of linguistic relativity. Instead they argue against a contemporary tendency to naively assign "language" and "race" to archaeological remains. Further, Whorf did not use hypothetico-deductive language; nowhere does he speak of "dependent" or "independent" "variables," although his mathematical training would have made him thoroughly familiar with such locutions. Instead, the "linguistic relativity" of Boas, Sapir, and Whorf is an axiom (cf 2:87). As with other working assumptions, such as "the arbitrariness of the sign," it can only be judged on the basis of the extent to which it leads to productive questions about talk and social action (61), not by canons of falsifiability. Yet the Boasian tradition does not preclude subcultural universals, as Boas and Sapir implicitly and Whorf explicitly recognized. Nor does it exclude cross-cultural and cross-linguistic laws of patterning. The modern debate over "linguistic relativity" has consistently confused assumptions with research findings, axiom with hypothesis.

In a narrower sense, however, a set of claims is being advanced: that grammatical categories, to the extent that they are obligatory or habitual, and relatively inaccessible to the average speaker's consciousness, will form a privileged location for transmitting and reproducing cultural and social categories. Grammatical categories will play a key role in structuring cognitive categories and social fields by constraining the ontology that is taken for granted by speakers. Such an approach is hardly unique to linguistic anthropology. It has been proposed independently of the Boasian tradition by philosopher W. V. O. Quine (169; see also 137) in his declaration that "entification begins at an arm's length," influenced by syntactic category and definiteness. A substantial body of experimental evidence supports the critical role that major syntactic categories play in the acquisition of word meanings (22, 73, 109, 141, 148, 219, 231, 232). The narrow interpretation of the Boasian tradition would also fit well with a theory of "structuration," of the sort proposed by Giddens (74:121), in which structure is at once an emergent property of social interaction and constitutive of the interaction. Grammatical categories would structure the cognitive and social fields at the same time as they are themselves the sedimented outcome of long histories of interaction (cf 45). Linguists working on the discourse basis of syntactic categories (e.g. 70, 92, 93, 94, 224) have begun to explore the process of category formation, though strategically underplaying the importance of hard cognitive constraints. Anthropologists have explored how grammatical categories project social positions and relations, especially for the pragmatics of person (48, 49, 59), and the types and hierarchy of social agents (9: Ch.4; 45, 199, 205). The processes by which grammatical categories structure cognitive and social fields, or "Whorfian effects" (112, also 96), have not been tied into an integrated theory, both because of disciplinary boundaries and because the scholarly folklore has diverted attention from the narrow interpretation of Whorfian effects proposed above. The following section illustrates Whorfian effects, using a familiar example.

WHORFIAN EFFECTS: ENGLISH GENDERED PRONOUNS

The structure of gender in the third-person pronouns of English provides a politically saturated example of a Whorfian effect. Although they make up a relatively small part of the way gender distinctions are reproduced through the language, the third-person pronouns have received disproportionate attention as the focus of conscious prescriptions since late in the 18th century. The example illustrates the complexity of interaction among the tacit structure of the categories, the cognitive prototypes associated with each category, the pragmatics of their use, grammatical prescriptions, and the tacit cultural frame-works and explicit ideologies associated with the categories. The gendered pronouns of English have been the focus of conscious prescriptions for at least 200 years, so they also illustrate the complexity of interaction between con-scious domination-and-resistance and tacit hegemony. This summary draws especially on research by Waugh (230) on the categorial hierarchy of the system, McConnell-Ginet (157) on prototype effects for incumbents of roles designated with related gendered categories, Bodine (19) on the history of prescriptive responses to the category system, and Silverstein (202) on the interactions among grammatical structure, pragmatics, and ideology. (See also 20:93–98, 32:218–24, 116, 150–152, 155, 209, 214.)

Figure 1 uses the non-object, nonpossessive forms to stand for all personal pronouns. The + value for each feature is the defining feature of the opposition and the more focused semantically. The Ø feature is systematically ambigu-ous, between an interpretation in which the + value is denied (a "–" value) and an interpretation in which it is merely not asserted. From a structural point of view, *she* has the interpretation [+FEMALE], while *he* can be understood as either [ØFEMALE], with no assertion of gender, or [–FEMALE], that is, "male." Each feature that is higher in the tree sets up a context for an obligatory choice between values of the feature that is one step lower.

A focal property of the system in Figure 1 is that *he* can be used in an indefinite sense (the default value or "Ø-interpretation") (when the sex of the referent is unknown or irrelevant), or in an inclusive, generic sense, as in *Everyone in New York State is entitled to an abortion if he wants it* (example from 230:305). The problems with setting the default value to "masculine" are well known: Each pronoun indexes a category that is associated with a cogni-tive prototype or paradigmatic instance. The paradigmatic instance of *he* (ex-

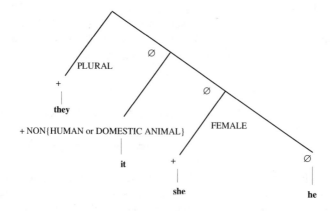

Figure 1   "Traditional" categorial distinctions in third-person pronouns, English

cept in the example above), of course, is male. Even generic uses of *he* evoke a male prototype. In addition, for pragmatic reasons, "indefinite" *he* will normally be interpreted as male. These associations are made habitually by speakers, below the threshold of consciousness. Here is a straightforward Whorfian effect, in which the structure of a system of grammatical categories affects the social ontology posited by the speakers.

Prescriptive remedies for the difficulties that these associations produce were suggested as early as the late 18th century (19, 8:190–216). No fewer than 65 neologisms have been coined for a neuter singular pronoun since the middle of the 19th century. Among other options, for political reasons many speakers adopt *they* as a neuter singular. For theoretical or political reasons, some speakers choose to use *she* in a generic interpretation, and some alternate between the *he* and *she*. The most common solution is to use *they* as a neuter singular. This has always been a pragmatic option available to speakers who were choosing to conceal the sex of the referent. Other speakers have been socialized exclusively to a pronoun system in which the default third person pronoun, singular or plural, is *they*—a system distinct from, and probably older than that in Figure 1. Use of singular *they* was attacked by prescriptive grammarians in the middle of the 19th century. [A British Act of Parliament prohibited the usage within that body, requiring use of the generic masculine instead (19:131-33)!]

Prescriptive suggestions for a neuter or gender-inclusive pronoun include using *it* to refer to humans. This proposal probably fails because the distinction between *it* and the other third person pronouns projects a more deeply ingrained cultural postulate than the distinction between plural and nonplural, a distinction between humans (and some domestic animals) as potential social agents and all other referents of nouns. To maintain a culturally more central distinction in the pronoun systems, many speakers of English are giving up (or have given up) a more peripheral distinction (cf 119:169-70).

The example shows how a system of obligatory grammatical categories has cultural implications. The system naturalizes and reproduces categories of social action. The articulation of the grammar of pronominal gender with the categories of humanness and social agency stabilizes the grammatical representation of gender by restricting possible changes of the grammatical system and, in turn, the system of cultural reproduction. The directness of the Whorfian effect is partly obscured by the tension between internal determinants and external normative pressures, both establishing and eroding the generic masculine (202). Although it is an arena of conflict, the category system continues to function in everyday contexts even for speakers who are examining and purposefully remodeling their behavior, for, even as one part of a category system is brought into conscious contention, other parts remain in place unchallenged. The category system creates a particular cultural hegemony, the unquestioned acceptance, by both men and women, of men as a normative, unmarked category of person (cf 163). The hegemonic structure is reproduced below the speaker's threshold of awareness, unconsciously, but is challenged from above the threshold of awareness, consciously. The different systems move back and forth across the threshold of consciousness, occasionally emerging into direct, purposive conflict.

RETHINKING THE "SAPIR-WHORF HYPOTHESIS"

We turn now to a review of the most recent major readings of the work of Boas, Sapir, and Whorf. Most of this scholarship deals primarily with the writings of the latter, although the work of Sapir has been of special interest for Friedrich. The main source for interpretations of Whorf is the posthumous collection by John B. Carroll (236), especially, "The relation of habitual thought and behavior to language" (234), the only essay that Whorf prepared in his lifetime for an audience of fellow linguists.[9] Before turning to the work of other scholars, we begin with a favorite emphasis of our own.

Boas, Sapir, and the Significance of Sound Patterning

Lucy states that nowhere did Boas "give detailed discussion or exhibit much enthusiasm or conviction about the possibility of language influencing thought" (131:81). This ignores one of the most penetrating discussions of such influence in the history of linguistics, Boas's 1889 article "On alternating sounds." [An important discussion of the significance of the paper is found in Stocking (211).] The relationship between sound patterning and sound categorization was also the site both of Sapir's most significant contributions to modern structuralism and his most convincing evidence for the relationship between linguistic and cognitive patterning (185, 186, 189).

Boas (17) showed that the apparent instability or alternation of sounds in American Indian language data illustrated not the imperfections of primitive languages but the fact that even trained scholars could not reliably hear a system of sound distinctions different from that in their own language. Boas thereby foreshadows one of the most profound lessons of Whorf's work: that the languages of Western scholars, as much as any others, impose their patterns on their speakers. Boas points out the embodied and habitual nature of sound production: As speakers master production and perception, they simultaneously formulate a classification to which new sound types are assimilated. Werker (233) has shown that exposure to a native language shapes phonetic discrimination early in life. While all children are born with the potential to make any kind of sound discrimination that is possible in a human language, between six and twelve months of age their ability to make discriminations that are not present in their native language is sharply reduced. This reduction

---

[9]
    Space precludes careful attention to recent reconsiderations of Whorf's analyses of Hopi. See 130, 142, 143, and 229.

is not a loss of auditory sensitivity but a "language-based reorganization of the categories of communicative sounds" (233:58), and may be related to the infant's developing comprehension of the native language. These phonological effects are instances of "categorical perception," in which linguistic categories establish thresholds that regulate perception (112; 96:381; 83a). Kuhl et al (118a) show that the phonological effects of categorical perception can be observed in infants as young as six months old.

Sapir's concept of "phonemic" pattern specified with great precision the systemic source of the categorial effects identified by Boas: the "inner configuration" of the sound system within which sounds acquired functional significance, expressed in patterns of phonotactic distribution, conditioned variation, and contrast. Sapir argued that categorization and formal patterning in phonology were aesthetic experiences for speakers, forms of "art" where the pronunciation of a sound was like the accomplishment of a step in the dance (Sapir 185:35). This recognition of an aesthetic "form-feeling" for language foreshadows a contemporary concern with sound patterning as a significant and neglected form of human experience, a concern to which we return below.

Lucy's Reformulation

John Lucy (131–133, 136) has attempted to breathe new anthropological life into the "hypothetico-deductive" reading of Whorf, thereby challenging our contention of the unlikely nature of such a project within today's linguistic anthropology. His concern is an operationalization of a "Whorf hypothesis" that is consistent with Whorf's own linguistic practice. Lucy complains that previous hypothetico-deductive work has moved from its Whorfian roots by decentering "language" in favor of "cognition," making the former a dependent variable. Lucy (131, 132) emphasizes that implementation of Whorf's analytic project requires recognition of linguistic patterning on a large scale, as in Whorf's demonstration of the habitual ways of speaking about time as an "entity" in European languages. This example shows that covert and overt principles of categorization in language may exhibit multiple unexpected linkages, and we cannot understand the impact these may have on a speaker's categorization of experience until their complexity is fully grasped. Lucy also attempts a new conceptualization of Whorf's term "reality," in order to avoid a naive realism that almost invariably turns out to be ethnocentric. Lucy (133) argues that "reality" must be explicitly "linguistic reality," defined against a universal grid, such as Silverstein's (205) referential hierarchy of types of noun phrases. Further, Lucy argues that a genuinely "Whorfian" ethnolinguistic project must be rigorously comparative, identifying the full penetration of particular linguistic patterns in at least two languages and comparing their impact on speakers.

Lucy's research, comparing Yucatec and English, focuses not on culture [although he praises Whorf for attention to the cultural resonances of grammatical patterning (131, 132)] but on thought, which he understands as an "autonomously constituted cognition" (131:83). Lucy (133) finds three major types of noun phrases in both English and Yucatec, characterized in terms of universally applicable noun-phrase features: Type A [+ANIMATE, +DISCRETE], Type B [−ANIMATE, +DISCRETE] and Type C [−ANIMATE, −DISCRETE]. English grammar requires pluralization of Type A and Type B noun phrases, while Yucatec grammar does not require pluralization at all. Instead, the grammar of Yucatec requires "unitization" (the process seen in English "a," "the," and "piece of") when noun phrases are counted. Analyzing descriptions of line drawings by speakers of the two languages, Lucy confirmed that the grammatical patterns are in fact reflected in ways of speaking, at least in the experimental context. Experiments using recall and sorting showed that English speakers were more likely to be sensitive to number than to substance, while Yucatec speakers were the opposite. Lucy argued that this result was related to linguistic patterning: English speakers presuppose unity centering on form, and find number changes interesting and noticeable, while Yucatec speakers presuppose substance and are thus somewhat indifferent to number; this is consistent with their characteristic grammatical strategy, which is not pluralization of units, but unitization of substances.

As groundwork for his own study, Lucy (132) develops a series of critiques of earlier studies of linguistic relativity (also see 96:379–81), which we exemplify with his discussion of research on color terminologies, a body of work that is often said to have accomplished a "universalist" refutation of Whorfian "linguistic relativity" (14, 111, 113, 140, to list only a few landmarks in an enormous literature).[10] Lucy's (132) important new contribution to a critical tradition (cf 84, 85, 153, 180, 238) argues that the "universalist" results of this color-terminology research are largely consequences of conceptual and methodological choices. First, researchers on color terminology equate "thought" (represented as acts of categorization and memory) with "processing potential," in contrast to Whorf's own emphasis on the actual and habitual. The operational goal of strict comparability across subjects and languages forces a reduction to decontextualized and purely denotational usage. Individual lexemes are studied without reference to their grammatical properties or structural relationships in the lexicon. Lucy argues that precisely the domain of investigation, "color," with its parameters of hue, brightness, and saturation, is constructed within the English language. Many languages in fact have no general word for "color." The imposition of this English category renders impossible the identification of other categories and parameters, for instance the Hanunóo dimension of "reflectance" or the Zuni distinction between yellow as a result of process and yellow as intrinsic. Finally, and consistent with a general tendency in cognitive psychology, cross-cultural similarities in the experimen-

---

10
    Lucy also develops a critique of the problematic work of Bloom (16) comparing Chinese and English counterfactuals. (See also 6, 7.)

tal results are referred not to possible methodological artifacts or to patterns of communication in the research task (cf 71, 135) but to biopsychology. Thus language becomes the dependent variable, and the initial "Whorfian" trajectory of color research is reversed. Lucy does credit this tradition for serious attention to methodology, and it continues to be an important site for research on categorization (cf 138, 139, 140).

Cognitive Linguistics and the Large-Scale Structure of Language

In the last decade "Cognitive Linguistics" (linked to some degree with linguistic work in "Cognitive Anthropology") has developed two dimensions of the neo-Whorfian research program recommended in Lucy's programmatic statements: exploration of the large-scale patterning of grammar in particular languages, and the development of a theory of linguistic cognition. Most so-called "cognitive linguists" see their project as emerging from contemporary theoretical linguistics, but in self-conscious opposition to a number of important assumptions of the latter (cf 36, 50, 55, 103, 120, 125–127, 164, 181, 216–218, 237).

Cognitive linguists take formal linguistic discontinuities to index underlying conceptual discontinuities. Thus, the boundaries of denotation of a linguistic element are held to coincide with the boundaries of a cognitive schema (23, 34, 54, 120, 170, 215, 242). Chafe (27) has suggested that intonation units may be surface indices of the packaging of consciousness in short-term memory (see also 240, 241). Strauss (213) suggests that syntagmatic continuities and discontinuities at the thematic level in argumentation and narration may suggest underlying continuities and discontinuities in the organization of cognitive schemas. Langacker (125, 126, 127) argues that such schemas take the form of images. G. Lakoff (120, 122–124) has argued for the pivotal role of metaphor in constituting cognitive schemas. Lakoff argues that his invariance hypothesis—"Metaphorical mappings preserve the cognitive topology [that is, the image-schema structure] of the source domain" (121:54; cf 24)—allows his metaphorical models to be linked to Langacker's grammatical images, with the latter characterizing the topology of source domains.

While cognitive linguists have admitted that their work can be linked to the Whorfian tradition, they have not emphasized cross-linguistic relativity (but see 120:304–37). Instead, Langacker (125) points out that although his grammatical theory clearly permits the possibility that the habitual ways of speaking in different languages are organized around different systems of imagery, he believes that the actual behavior of speakers reflects a constant shifting of point of view, rather than construction of a few habitual images. Kay (110) has also urged attention to the fact that a language can encode more than one point of view at a time, as with the "Fregean" implications of the English hedge "loosely speaking" (which implies that there exists a form of speech that is "exact" vis-à-vis the world), versus the "Putnamian" implications of the hedge, "technically" (which suggests a "baptism" of appropriate usage by experts).

Cognitive linguists have not been much interested in culture. Quinn (172) attacks Lakoff for neglecting the cultural locus of metaphor. She finds that eight metaphors virtually exhaust the figurative strategies used by American English speakers she interviewed about marriage. She suggests that this occurs because their choice of metaphors is motivated by a cultural scenario about marriage, not by underlying image schemas rooted in bodily experience of space. The cultural scenario, not the metaphors themselves, plays a constitutive role in representations of, and reasoning about, marriage. Quinn suggests that cultural differences are only understandable if this is the case: The knowledge of cultural scenarios is shared, but, unlike bodily image schemas of the type suggested by Johnson (105), it is not universal.

Friedrich (67, see below) and Turner (227) criticize the single-mindedness with which both cognitive linguists and interpretive anthropologists have concentrated on metaphor to the exclusion of other forms of figuration. Turner turns several classic studies on their heads by showing that the narrow focus on metaphor mystifies the semiotic figuration of social forms such as totemism. His study and Friedrich's (67) theory of interlocking master tropes have the potential of transforming the analytical apparatus of cognitive linguists into a framework of sufficient power to elucidate cultural figuration.

Slobin (206, 207) endorses a limited neo-Whorfian position that derives from explicitly comparative study. In a cross-linguistic survey of children's narrative strategies using pictures as stimuli, Slobin and his colleagues found that from an early age children who speak different languages talk about identical pictures quite differently, in a way that seems to reflect habitual ways of encoding experience in their languages. Slobin suggests that many distinctions used by speakers (such as aspect, definiteness, and voice) seem to have no function other than to be expressed in language: They are not present in experience. Slobin endorses the Whorfian position that languages are not neutral coding systems, but instead are "subjective orientations" to experience. Nevertheless, he proposes that these orientations may be limited in their impact, active only while we are "thinking for speaking."

Cognitive Linguistics is often vulnerable to the critique of "linguacentrism" (132). Rather than relating patterning in language to patterning in nonverbal cultural or cognitive practice, linguacentric research relates a pattern in one form of linguistic organization to a pattern in another. Thus in Slobin's work the independent variable is grammatical patterning, while the dependent variable is narrative strategy. These are both "linguistic" phenomena. Supposed "cultural" scenarios, as in the work of Quinn (170–172) or Sweetser (215) are based entirely on linguistic evidence, with no nonverbal attestation of these generalizations. Where "cultural" evidence for a frame or scenario is proposed, it is usually anecdotal, as in Fillmore's (53) example of children who were astonished to see an adult peel a grapefruit and eat it "like an orange."

Silverstein's Semiotic Reading of Whorf

In contrast to the tradition that organizes the study of the relationships among language, culture, and thought in hypothetico-deductive terms, the remaining "neo-Whorfian" work that we discuss is largely semiotic or interpretive. Although Silverstein (198, 200–203, 205) occasionally speaks of "science," he intends by this the conduct of linguistic analysis in rigorous comparative structuralist terms. He does not talk about "independent" versus "dependent" variables. Instead, he argues that "the total linguistic fact, the datum for a science of language, is irreducibly dialectic in nature" (202:220). Centering his work in Peircian semiotics, Silverstein places pragmatics and semantics on an equal footing, privileging the nonreferential, especially the indexical, functions of language equally with proposition and reference. Silverstein refocuses Whorf's "habitual thought and behavior" as "ideology" (also see 65, 222). "Linguistic ideology" enters into complex feedback relationships with pragmatic practice and grammatical form. In a related project, exploring the circumstances under which such feedback is especially likely or unlikely, Silverstein takes up Boas's interest in the relative "consciousness" of patterning in language and culture, developing preliminaries to a theory of sites for conscious reflection on patterning in language (201).

Silverstein (200) sees the suggestion of a systematic relationship between "the grammatical structure of the language" and an "ideology of reference, an understanding at the conceptual level of how … language represents 'nature'" (p. 202), as Whorf's most significant contribution. Silverstein argues that Whorf's insight is crucially dependent on his development of a new inventory of analytic tools (especially, the distinction between overt and covert grammatical categories) through which grammatical systems can be rigorously identified. Once identified, systems of grammatical categories can be seen to be "referentially projected" by speakers to produce "objectifications," notions like form, substance, time, and space. These are rooted in complex continuities and discontinuities in the structure of language, but are attributed by speakers to the nature of experience.

Silverstein's research goal is to generalize Whorf's insight "from the plane of reference to the whole of language function" (200:94). He argues that Western linguistics has tended to reduce all semiosis to reference. The problem is then to reverse this ideological project by developing a fully scientific and comparative theory of language function, which will recognize that indexicality, not reference alone, lies at the core of language use.

Silverstein has explored the empirical implications of his theory in several case studies: of speech act theory as a manifestation of English linguistic ideology (200), of Javanese honorifics in pragmatic and linguistic-ideological perspective (cf 48, 49), of the linguistic ideology of gender in English (202), and of the pragmatic ideology of Chinookan (203).

Rumsey (179) develops Silverstein's ideas in a particularly suggestive account of the interaction of structure, usage, and linguistic ideology. In English, he identifies at least two grammatical patterns that distinguish "wording" from meaning: the grammar of reported speech, which distinguishes direct discourse (faithful to wording) from indirect discourse (faithful to meaning); and the distinction in textual cohesion, identified by Halliday & Hasan (80) between reference, the use of discourse anaphors that implicate identical meaning (as in "Raylene told her very best friends. Then Bruce told them"), and ellipsis, a text-forming relationship that implicates identical wording (as in "Raylene told her very best friends. Then Bruce told his"). English linguistic ideology distinguishes meanings, properties of the world, from wordings, properties of talk. In contrast, in the Australian language Ungarinyin there is no distinction between direct and indirect discourse (and, in fact, the representation of "locutions" is not clearly distinguished from the representation of propositional attitudes such as wants and beliefs). Nor is there a formal distinction in Ungarinyin textual cohesion that might distinguish wording and meaning. Ngarinyin people, when discussing language, do not distinguish between talk and action, focusing instead on the social effects of words and seeing them as strongly connected with their referents. Rumsey suggests that the distinct linguistic ideologies of English speakers and speakers of Ungarinyin are closely linked to the formal patterning in these languages, mutually determining one another [although Rumsey hints that, since "a rudimentary formal opposition between direct and indirect discourse [has been present] from ancient times" (179: 357) in European languages, the linguistic pattern may be prior].

Perhaps the most probing and detailed working out of Silverstein's (202) proposal of an irreducible dialectic among structure, practice, and ideology is Hanks's (83) account of the relationship among the formal encoding of deictic elements in Yucatec, the practices of spatial reference among its speakers, and Yucatec cosmology. By characterizing reference as a form of practice, Hanks is able to develop a particularly subtle account of Yucatec usage. Hanks argues not only for the pragmatics of the referential, but also for the structure of the pragmatic, emphasizing that the effects of indexicality can be seen not as purely emergent but as schematized through the practice of speakers who repeatedly invoke indexical frameworks in accomplishing reference.

Ochs (161, 162) joins Silverstein in emphasizing the importance of the indexical functions of language: Such indexes can inculcate appropriate sociocultural dispositions in the course of language socialization (162:92; see also 193). Especially significant are indirect indexes. Ochs suggests that the contextual dimension of affect, along with the dimension of epistemological disposition (as manifested, for instance, in evidentials and hedges), are used cross-linguistically in the indirect indexical function, to constitute social identities and categories. Thus, Japanese affective usage (in the particles *zo, ze,* through which men express strong affect, and *wa,* through which women express hesitant affective disposition) indirectly constitutes gender. Samoan evidential usage indirectly indexes the realm of phenomena about which one can speculate, precisely not including the thoughts and feelings of other people. Thus Japanese children acquire a folk theory about the aggressiveness of men and the gentleness of women, and Samoan children acquire a folk epistemology that characterizes other people's minds as inaccessible and perhaps socially irrelevant entities. However, Ochs (161,162) emphasizes that children are active participants in socialization, such that indirect indexicality is not irrevocably deterministic.

Friedrich's "Poetic Imagination"

The second major neo-relativist reading of the classic sources within the interpretive and semiotic fold is that of Paul Friedrich (62–64). Friedrich argues that Whorf's neglect of the unique individual and of poetic language reflects his scientific and pragmatic roots; Sapir, with his emphasis on the aesthetic feeling for language and on the genius of poets, can inspire a new kind of linguistic relativity. In a neo-Sapirian formulation the unique individual imagination must take a central place, alongside structure and context, in a new relativism that will give as much privilege to the relatively indeterminate and chaotic dimensions of language as to the dimensions of structure and formal constraint. A relativism thus configured, Friedrich argues, is likely to give deeper insights than one focused exclusively on grammatical patterning, since poetic language is the most important locus of differences between languages (see also 10, 11, 102, 221, 240).

In operationalizing (if this is the appropriate word for the project of a scholar whose linguistic practice increasingly takes poetic form; cf 66) his understanding of the poetic and indeterminate aspects of language, Friedrich (67) has recently proposed a theory of five master tropes, arguing that overemphasis on metaphor in anthropology is impoverishing our understanding of the figurative power of language. Of special interest for our topic is his suggestion that these imply characteristic "entanglements" with extra-linguistic understandings. Thus "image tropes" resonate with primary senses of qualities, such as the sense of redness. Tropes of mood are involved in the emotional and epistemological foundations of understanding. Formal tropes resonate with the formal and statistical properties of the world, as in fractal forms. Metonymic tropes are particularly "political," engaging with part-whole relationships in nature. Analogical tropes (these include metaphor) create new relationships among language, thought, and reality.

The figuration of language extends to the iconics of sound itself. Languages vary in the degree to which they exploit sound icons. They may do so both at the systematic paradigmatic level and at relatively inchoate levels that cannot be characterized in systemic-linguistic terms, yet may have clear resonance with affective and cognitive patterning among speakers. Recent studies of such phenomena are available (e.g. 9:Ch. 4; 42–44, 52, 146:Ch.8; 160, 220). These studies, which find that sound patterning resonates intricately with conceptual patterning, evoke the early Boasian work on sound configuration and cognition (see above and 182, 188). Here the configurations are loose associational networks, rather than closed paradigms.

By studying relatively indeterminate dimensions of language and culture, they also present the sharpest challenge to date of the assumption, shared by cognitivist and interpretivist alike, that pattern consistency pervades cognitive and cultural systems. Studies like these, along with those of DeBernardi (40), showing how Malaysian Chinese religious practices fail to synthesize into a single self-consistent master discourse, and of Leavitt (128) on the emotionally charged, linguistically marginal "infralanguage" of Kuamani spirit possession, effectively rescue their ethnographic subjects from an overly focused emphasis on intellectual order and open up the possibility of exploring the more chaotic and inchoate sides of language and social life.

Sherzer's "Discourse-Centered Approach to Language and Culture"

Building on Hymes's development of Whorf's notion of "fashions of speaking" (97, 98; also 100, 101), Sherzer (196) challenges the priority of "grammar" in favor of "discourse." Sherzer suggests that a "discourse-centered approach" will move away from the virtual patterning of grammar, constituted by difference, or by large-scale patterning of covert and overt categorization, toward a more concrete and immediate domain, about which he is deliberately vague. However, among the major meanings of "discourse"—patterning beyond the level of the sentence, Foucaultian systems of rarefaction and restriction that are ideologically constituted, and emergent, immediately contextualized and contextualizing, linguistic usage—Sherzer aligns himself with the last. He argues that to center linguistic anthropology in discourse, "the broadest and most comprehensive level of linguistic form, content, and use" (Sherzer 196:305), "enables us to reconceptualize the Sapir-Whorf hypothesis, because "discourse ... is the nexus, the actual and concrete expression of the language-culture-society relationship. It is discourse which creates, recreates, modifies, and fine tunes both culture and language and their interesection ..." (Sherzer 196:296).

Sherzer finds these processes to be most vivid in artistic and poetic speech. This emphasis links the "discourse-centered approach" to the work of Friedrich, but there are also important differences: The poetic tradition elaborated by Sherzer (196, 197), Urban (228), and others such as Caton (25, 26) is the formal one, centering on Jakobson's theory of parallelism, while Friedrich emphasizes the unstructured, chaotic, and emergent. Urban (228) sharply problematizes "individuality" as a cultural phenomenon, while Friedrich gives "individualism" independent theoretical privilege as the site of "imagination."

In addition to Sherzer's own illustrations, an example of this kind of approach is Mannheim's (145) study of semantic parallelism in Southern Peruvian Quechua verbal art, which finds that verbal art plays a role essentially similar to grammatical categories in the Boasian tradition. Semantic parallelism constrains the variability of word meanings by ensuring that they are learned relationally, rather than individually. Ramanujan (172a, 173) finds an entire landscape taxonomy embedded in the classical Tamil poetic tradition, reproduced through poetic imagery, and mapped onto an affective "interior landscape." From the position of a ritual novice, Trix (226) shows how Bektashi Sufi ritual knowledge is transmitted through, and shaped by, the poetry that is its vehicle. Verbal art is thus a medium through which lexical meaning, imagery, and religious knowledge are reproduced and transmitted, sometimes by the conscious appropriation of a poetic tradition and sometimes by the unconscious appropriation of the resources of a linguistic code.

The most elaborate conceptualization and exemplification of the discourse-centered approach is developed by Urban (228). Urban argues that discourse must have priority over culture conceived as an abstract system of meaning, because discourse is public, and because it is both sensible (actually occurring and manifested in sound distributed in space and time) and abstract and intelligible (in that speakers must interpret moments of discourse based on historically specific networks of stylistic similarities and differences). In Shokleng, a language of Brazil, speakers have ideologized stylistic similarity and difference. Their ideology of historical continuity is expressed in close similarities between myth recitations by different speakers over many years. Their emphasis on similarity at the level of discourse, Urban suggests, is accompanied by a high tolerance of difference at the level of grammar and lexicon; this latter finding challenges Silverstein's (201) suggestion that ideological attention will be focused on maximally segmentable and referential linguistic elements. The Shokleng ideology of continuity and similarity contrasts with an ideology of continuity and difference in the Northwest Amazon. Pascal Boyer (21) also posits a communicative basis for cultural tradition. Both Boyer and Urban place the concrete moment of discourse at the center of analysis, but only Urban develops a sense of the intricate dialectic between what is "sensible" and what is "intelligible." Urban's emphasis on the "sensible" is related to the exploration of the concrete power of figures of sound reviewed above.

CONCLUSION

An era in which the study of the relationships between patterning in language and patterning in other dimensions of human knowledge and experience emphasized universal relationships is giving way to a more balanced distribution of scholarly attention. Now those relationships constructed within the terms of particular languages and cultural systems of usage and ideology can be approached with new sophistication. This sophistication includes increasing openness to universals among those influenced by a tradition of "axiomatic relativism," balanced by a healthy critical attention to the cultural foundations of linguistics itself. It includes careful studies of the roots of the relativist tradition by a wide range of scholars, shaping new research programs. It joins an appreciation for cultural persistence to increasingly sophisticated conceptualizations of the contested and historically contingent nature of cultural knowledge and its reproduction. It moves away from a rigid dichotomization of structure and practice, focusing instead on their complex interactions.

Sapir (184:153) stressed the "formal completeness" of language, in which "all of its expressions, from the most habitual to the merely potential, are fitted into a deft tracery of prepared forms from which there is no escape." It is because of the formal completeness of languages that they seem so compelling to their speakers and become powerful vehicles for the reproduction of cultural knowledge and social relations. No doubt we write this review prematurely. In the next few years new empirical work, framed within new syntheses of the diverse strands of neo-relativist thought, will help us understand how language shapes, and is shaped by, the nature of our knowledge.

ACKNOWLEDGMENTS

We are grateful to Susan A. Gelman for a thoughtful critique of an earlier draft and to John Lucy for furnishing us with materials.

Literature Cited

1. Alford, D. K. H. 1978. Demise of the Whorf hypothesis. *Proc. Berkeley Linguist. Soc.* 4:485–99
2. Alford, D. K. H. 1980. Demise of the Whorf hypothesis. *Phoenix* 4:85–91
3. Alford, D. K. H. 1981. Is Whorf's relativity Einstein's relativity? *Proc. Berkeley Linguist. Soc.* 7:13–26
4. Allen, R. J. 1986. The theme of the unconscious in Sapir's thought. See Ref. 33, pp. 455–77
5. Atran, S. 1990. *Cognitive Foundations of Natural History: Towards an Anthropology of Science.* Cambridge: Cambridge Univ. Press
6. Au, T. K.-F. 1983. Chinese and English counterfactuals: The Sapir-Whorf hypothesis revisited. *Cognition* 15:155–87
7. Au, T. K.-F. 1984. Counterfactuals: in reply to Alfred Bloom. *Cognition* 17:289–302
7a. Bach, E. W. 1981. On tense, time, and aspect: an essay in English metaphysics. In *Radical Pragmatics*, ed. P. Cole, pp. 63–81. New York: Academic
8. Baron, D. 1986. *Grammar and Gender.* New Haven: Yale Univ. Press
9. Basso, E. 1985. *A Musical View of the Universe.* Philadelphia: Univ. Penn. Press
10. Bauman, R. 1975. Verbal art as performance. *Am. Anthropol.* 77:290–311
11. Bauman, R., Briggs, C. 1990. Poetics and performance as critical perspectives on language and social life. *Annu. Rev. Anthropol.* 19:59–88

12. Becker, A. L. 1984. Biography of a sentence: a Burmese proverb. In *Text, Play, and Story, the Construction and Reconstruction of Self and Society*, ed. E. Bruner, pp. 136–55. Washington: AES
13. Benveniste, E. 1958. Catégories de pensée et catégories de langue. *Études philosophiques* 4:419–29. Transl. 1971 as "Categories of thought and language," in *Problems in General Linguistics*, pp. 55–64. Coral Gables: Univ. Miami Press
14. Berlin, B., Kay, P. 1969. *Basic Color Terms: Their Universality and Evolution.* Berkeley: Univ. Calif. Press
15. Bloch, M. 1991. Language, anthropology, and cognitive science. *Man* 26:183–98
16. Bloom, A. H. 1981. *The Linguistic Shaping of Thought: A Study in the Impact of Language on Thinking in China and the West.* Hillsdale, NJ: Erlbaum
17. Boas, F. 1889. On alternating sounds. *Am. Anthropol.* 2:47–53. Reprinted in *The Shaping of American Anthropology, 1883–1911: A Franz Boas Reader*, ed. G. W. Stocking, Jr., pp. 72–7. New York: Basic Books
18. Boas, F. 1911. Introduction. *Bur. Am. Ethnol. Bull.* 40(1):1–83
19. Bodine, A. 1975. Androcentrism in prescriptive grammar: singular "they", sex-indefinite "he", and "he or she." *Lang. Soc.* 4:129–46
20. Bolinger, D. 1980. *Language: The Loaded Weapon.* London: Longman

21. Boyer, P. 1991. *Tradition as Truth and Communication.* Cambridge: Cambridge Univ. Press
22. Brown, R. 1957. Linguistic determinism and parts of speech. *J. Abnorm. Soc. Psychol.* 55:1–5
23. Brugman, C. M. 1989. *The Story of Over: Polysemy, Semantics, and the Structure of the Lexicon.* New York: Garland
24. Brugman, C. M. 1990. What is the Invariance Hypothesis? *Cogn. Linguist.* 1:257–66
25. Caton, S. C. 1987. Contributions of Roman Jakobson. *Annu. Rev. Anthropol.* 16:223–60
26. Caton, S. C. 1990. *Peaks of Yemen I Summon: Poetry as Cultural Practice in a North Yemeni Tribe.* Berkeley: Univ. Calif. Press
27. Chafe, W. L. 1987. Cognitive constraints on information flow. See Ref. 225, pp. 21–51
28. Chatterjee, R. 1985. Reading Whorf through Wittgenstein. *Lingua* 67:37–63
29. Chomsky, N. 1981. *Lectures on Government and Binding.* Dordrecht: Foris
30. Condon, W. S. 1980. The relation of interactional synchrony to cognitive and emotional processes. See Ref. 115, pp. 49–65
31. Contini-Morava, E. 1986. Form in language: Sapir's theory of grammar. See Ref. 33, pp. 341–64
32. Corbett, G. G. 1991. *Gender.* Cambridge: Cambridge Univ. Press
33. Cowan, W., Foster, M. K., Koerner, K., eds. 1986. *New Perspectives in Language, Culture, and Personality: Proceedings of the Edward Sapir Centenary Conference.* Amsterdam: Benjamins
34. Craig, C. 1986. Jacaltec noun classifiers: a study in language and culture. See Ref. 35, pp. 263–93
35. Craig, C., ed. 1986. *Noun Classes and Categorization.* Amsterdam: Benjamins
36. Croft, W. 1991. *Syntactic Categories and Grammatical Relations: the Cognitive Organization of Information.* Chicago: Univ. Chicago Press
37. Darnell, R. 1986. Personality and culture: the fate of the Sapirian alternative. See Ref. 212, pp. 156–83
38. Darnell, R. 1990. *Edward Sapir: Linguist, Anthropologist, Humanist.* Berkeley: Univ. Calif. Press
39. Davidson, D. 1974. On the very idea of a conceptual scheme. *Proc. Addresses Am. Philos. Assoc.* 47. Reprinted 1984 in *Inquiries into Truth and Interpretation,* pp. 183–98. Oxford: Oxford Univ. Press
40. DeBernardi, J. E. 1986. *Heaven, earth, and man: a study of Chinese spirit mediums.* PhD thesis, Univ. Chicago
41. Denny, J. P. 1979. The "extendedness" variable in classifier semantics: universal

features and cultural variation. See Ref. 154, pp. 97–119
42. deReuse, W. 1986. The lexicalization of sound symbolism in Santiago de Estero Quechua. *IJAL* 52:54–64
43. Diffloth, G. 1972. Notes on expressive meaning. Papers from the 8th. Reg. Meet. Chicago Linguist. Soc., pp. 440–47
44. Diffloth, G. 1976. Expressives in Semai. In *Austroasiatic Studies,* ed. P. N. Jenner, L. C. Thompson, S. Starosta, Pt. 1, pp. 250–64. Honolulu: Univ. Press Hawaii
45. Duranti, A. 1990. Politics and grammar: agency in Samoan political discourse. *Am. Ethnol.* 17:646–66
46. Erickson, F. 1980. Timing and context in everyday discourse: implications for the study of referential and social meaning. In *Language and Speech in American Society,* ed. R. Bauman, J. Sherzer. Austin: Southwest Educ. Dev. Lab.
47. Erickson, F., Schultz, J. 1982. *The Counselor as Gate-Keeper.* New York: Academic
48. Errington, J. J. 1985. On the nature of the sociolinguistic sign: describing the Javanese speech levels. See Ref. 158, pp. 287–309
49. Errington, J. J. 1988. *Structure and Style in Javanese: A Semiotic View of Linguistic Etiquette.* Philadelphia: Univ. Penn. Press
50. Fauconnier, G. 1985. *Mental Spaces.* Cambridge: MIT Press
51. Fernandez, J. W., ed. 1991. *Beyond Metaphor: The Theory of Tropes in Anthropology.* Stanford: Stanford Univ. Press
52. Feld, S. 1982. *Sound and Sentiment: Birds, Weeping, Poetics, and Song in Kaluli Expression.* Philadelphia: Univ. Penn. Press
53. Fillmore, C. 1975. An alternative to checklist theories of meaning. *Proc. Berkeley Linguist. Soc.* 1:123–31
54. Fillmore, C. 1982. Frame semantics. In *Linguistics in the Morning Calm,* ed. Linguist. Soc. Korea, pp. 111–38. Seoul: Hanshin
55. Fillmore, C., Kay, P., O'Connor, M. C. 1988. Regularity and idiomaticity in grammatical constructions. *Language* 64:501–38
56. Fishman, J. A. 1980. The Whorfian hypothesis: varieties of valuation, confirmation, and disconfirmation. *Int. J. Soc. Lang.* 26:25–40
57. Fishman, J. A. 1982. Whorfianism of the third kind: ethnolinguistic diversity as a worldwide societal asset. *Lang. Soc.* 11:1–14
58. Foucault, M. 1972. *The Archaeology of Knowledge and The Discourse on Language.* New York: Pantheon
59. Friedrich, P. 1966. Structural implications of Russian pronominal usage. See Ref. 62, pp. 63–125
60. Friedrich, P. 1979a. Poetic language and the

imagination: a reformulation of the Sapir hypothesis. See Ref. 62, pp. 441–512

61. Friedrich, P. 1979b. The symbol and its relative non-arbitrariness. See Ref. 62, pp. 1–61

62. Friedrich, P. 1979. *Language, Context, and the Imagination.* Stanford: Stanford Univ. Press

63. Friedrich, P. 1985. The poetry of language in the politics of dreams. See Ref. 64, pp. 65–83

64. Friedrich, P. 1986. *The Language Parallax: Linguistic Relativism and Poetic Indeterminacy.* Austin: Univ. Texas Press

65. Friedrich, P. 1989. Language, ideology, and political economy. *Am. Anthropol.* 91:295–312

66. Friedrich, P. 1989. The Tao of language. *J. Prag.* 13:833–58

67. Friedrich, P. 1991. Polytropy. See Ref. 51, pp. 17–55

68. Galda, K. 1975. *Logical reasoning and the Yucatec Maya language.* PhD thesis, Stanford Univ.

69. Galda, K. 1979. Logic in non-Indo-European languages: Yucatec Maya, a case study. *Theor. Linguist.* 6:145–60

70. García, E. C. 1979. Discourse without syntax. In *Discourse and Syntax,* pp. 23–48. New York: Academic

71. Garro, L. C. 1986. Language, memory, and focality: a reexamination. *Am. Anthropol.* 88:128–36

72. Gatewood, J. 1983. Loose talk: linguistic competence and recognition ability. *Am. Anthropol.* 85:378–87

73. Gelman, S. A., Wilcox, S. A., Clark, E. V. 1989. Conceptual and lexical hierarchies in young children. *Cogn. Devel.* 4:309–26

74. Giddens, A. 1976. *New Rules of Sociological Method: A Positive Critique of Interpretative Sociologies.* New York: Basic

75. Gipper, H. 1979. Is there a linguistic relativity principle? *Indiana* 5:1–14

76. Gould, S. A., Lewontin, R. 1974. The spandrels of San Marco and the Panglossian paradigm: a critique of the adaptationist program. *Proc. Roy. Soc. London Ser. B* 205:581–98

77. Grace, G. W. 1987. *The Linguistic Construction of Reality.* London: Croom Helm

78. Gramsci, A. 1971. *Selections from the Prison Notebooks of Antonio Gramsci.* London: Lawrence & Wishart. [originally written 1929–1935]

79. Gumperz, J., Levinson, S. 1991. Rethinking linguistic relativity. *Curr. Anthropol.* 32:613–23

80. Halliday, M. A. K., Hasan, R. 1976. *Cohesion in English.* London: Longman

81. Handler, R. 1986. Vigorous male and aspiring female: poetry, personality, and culture in Edward Sapir and Ruth Benedict. See Ref. 212, pp. 127–55

82. Handler, R. 1986. The aesthetics of Sapir's Language. See Ref. 33, pp. 433–51

83. Hanks, W. F. 1990. *Referential Practice: Language and Lived Space among the Maya.* Chicago: Univ. Chicago Press

83a. Harnad, S., ed. 1987. *Categorical Perception: The Groundwork of Cognition.* Cambridge: Cambridge Univ. Press

84. Hickerson, N. P. 1971. Review of Ref. 14. *IJAL* 37:257–70

85. Hickerson, N. P. 1975. Two studies of color: implications for cross-cultural comparability of semantic categories. In *Linguistics and Anthropology: In Honor of C. F. Voegelin,* ed. M. D. Kinkade, K. L. Hale, O. Werner, pp. 317–30. Lisse: de Ridder

86. Hickmann, M., ed. 1987. *Social and Functional Approaches to Language.* Orlando: Academic

87. Hill, J. H. 1988. Language and world view. In *Linguistics: The Cambridge Survey,* ed. F. J. Newmeyer, 4:14–36. Cambridge: Cambridge Univ. Press

88. Hill, J. H. 1988. Language, genuine and spurious? See Ref. 118, pp. 9–53

89. Hoffman, C., Lau, I., Johnson, D. R. 1986. The linguistic relativity of person cognition: an English-Chinese comparison. *J. Pers. Soc. Psychol.* 51:1097–1105

90. Holland, D., Quinn, N., eds. 1987. *Cultural Models in Language and Thought.* Cambridge: Cambridge Univ. Press

91. Hollis, M., Lukes, S., eds. 1982, *Rationality and Relativism.* Cambridge: MIT Press

92. Hopper, P. J., ed. 1982. *Tense-Aspect: Between Semantics and Pragmatics.* Amsterdam: Benjamins

93. Hopper, P. J. 1988. Emergent grammar and the a priori grammar postulate. In *Linguistics in Context: Connecting Observation and Understanding,* ed. D. Tannen, pp. 117–34. Norwood: Ablex

94. Hopper, P. J., Thompson, S. A. 1984. The discourse basis for lexical categories in universal grammar. *Language* 60:703–52

95. Humboldt, W. von. 1836. *Über die Verschiedenheit des menschlichen Sprachbaues und ihren Einfluss auf die geistige Entwickelung des Menschengeschlechts.* Berlin: Königlichen Akademie der Wissenschaften. Transl. 1988 as *On Language: The Diversity of Human Language-Structure and its Influence on the Mental Development of Mankind,* transl. P. Heath. Cambridge: Cambridge. Univ. Press

96. Hunt, E., Agnoli, F. 1991. The Whorfian hypothesis: a cognitive psychology perspective. *Psychol. Rev.* 98:377–89

97. Hymes, D. H. 1961. On the typology of cognitive styles in language (with examples from Chinookan). *Anthropol. Linguist.* 3(1):22–54

98. Hymes, D. H. 1966. Two types of linguistic relativity. In *Sociolinguistics,* ed. W. Bright, pp. 114–57. The Hague: Mouton

99. Hymes, D. H. 1983 [1970]. Linguistic method in ethnography. In *Essays in the History of Linguistic Anthropology,* pp. 135–244. Amsterdam: Benjamins

100. Hymes, D. H. 1974. *Foundations in Socio-linguistics: An Ethnographic Approach.* Philadelphia: Univ. Penn. Press
101. Hymes, D. H. 1974. Ways of speaking. In *Explorations in the Ethnography of Speaking,* ed. R. Bauman, J. Sherzer, pp. 433–51. Cambridge: Cambridge Univ. Press
102. Hymes, D. H. 1981. *In Vain I Tried To Tell You: Essays in Native American Ethnopoetics.* Philadelphia: Univ. Penn. Press
103. Jackendoff, R. 1983. *Semantics and Cognition.* Cambridge: MIT Press
104. Jakobson, R. 1990 [1959]. Boas' view of grammatical meaning. In *On Language,* R. Jakobson; ed. L. R. Waugh, M. Monville-Burston, pp. 324–31. Cambridge: Harvard Univ. Press
105. Johnson, M. 1987. *The Body in the Mind: The Bodily Basis of Meaning, Imagination, and Reason.* Chicago: Univ. Chicago Press
106. Joos, M. 1957. Editorial matter in *Readings in Linguistics,* p. 96. New York: ACLS
107. Joseph, J. E. 1991. Review of Humboldt 1988 [1836]. *Language* 67:843–51
108. Katz, J. J. 1978. Effability and translation. In *Meaning and Translation,* ed. F. Guenthner, M. Guenthner-Reutter, pp. 191–234. New York: New York Univ. Press
109. Katz, N., Baker, E., Macnamara, J. 1974. What's in a name? A study of how children learn common and proper names. *Child Devel.* 45:469–73
110. Kay, P. 1987. Linguistic competence and folk theories of language: two English hedges. See Ref. 90, pp. 67–77
111. Kay, P., Berlin, B., Merrifield, W. 1991. Biocultural implications of systems of color naming. *J. Linguist. Anthropol.* 1:12–25
112. Kay, P., Kempton, W. 1984. What is the Sapir-Whorf hypothesis? *Am. Anthropol.* 86:65–79
113. Kay, P., McDaniel, C. K. 1978. The linguistic significance of the meanings of basic color terms. *Language* 54:610–46
113a. Kearney, M. 1984. *World View.* Novato: Chandler & Sharp
114. Kempton, W. 1980. The rhythmic basis of interactional micro-synchrony. See Ref. 115, pp. 67–76
115. Key, M. R., ed. 1980. *The Relationship of Verbal and Nonverbal Communication.* The Hague: Mouton
116. Kidd, V. 1971. A study of the images produced through the use of the male pronoun as the generic. *Mom. Cont. Rhetoric Commun.* 1:25–30
117. Khorsroshahi, F. 1989. Penguins don't care, but women do: a social identity analysis of a Whorfian problem. *Lang. Soc.* 18:505–25
118. Kroskrity, P. V., ed. 1988. *The Ethnography of Communication: the Legacy of Sapir, Essays in Honor of Harry Hoijer, 1984.* Los Angeles: Dept. Anthropol., Univ. Calif., Los Angeles
118a. Kuhl, P. K., Williams, K. A., Lacerda, F., Stevens, K. N., Lindblom, B. 1992. Linguistic experience alters phonetic perception in infants by 6 months of age. *Science* 255:606–8
119. Kuryłowicz, J. 1949. La nature des procès dits "analogiques". Reprinted 1966 in *Readings in Linguistics,* ed. E. Hamp, F. Householder, R. Austerlitz, 2:158–74. Chicago: Univ. Chicago Press
120. Lakoff, G. 1987. *Women, Fire, and Dangerous Things: What Categories Reveal about the Mind.* Chicago: Univ. Chicago Press
121. Lakoff, G. 1990. The invariance hypothesis. *Cogn. Linguist.* 1:39–74
122. Lakoff, G., Johnson, M. 1980. *Metaphors We Live By.* Chicago: Univ. Chicago Press
123. Lakoff, G., Kövesces, Z. 1987. The cognitive model of anger inherent in American thought. See Ref. 90, pp. 195–221
124. Lakoff, G., Turner, M. 1989. *More than Cool Reason.* Chicago: Univ. Chicago Press
125. Langacker, R. W. 1986. An introduction to cognitive grammar. *Cogn. Sci.* 10:1–40
126. Langacker, R. W. 1987. *Foundations of Cognitive Grammar.* Vol. 1. *Theoretical Prerequisites.* Stanford: Stanford Univ. Press
127. Langacker, R. W. 1988. An overview of cognitive grammar. See Ref. 178, pp. 3–48
128. Leavitt, J. H. 1985. *The language of the gods: discourse and experience in a Central Himalayan ritual.* PhD thesis, Univ. Chicago
129. Lee, B. 1985. Peirce, Frege, Saussure, and Whorf: the semiotic mediation of ontology. See Ref. 158, pp. 99–128
130. Lee, P. 1991. Whorf's Hopi tensors: subtle articulators in the language/thought nexus. *Cogn. Linguist.* 2:123–47
131. Lucy, J. A. 1985. Whorf's view of the linguistic mediation of thought. See Ref. 158, pp. 73–98
132. Lucy, J. A. 1992. *Language Diversity and Thought.* Cambridge: Cambridge Univ. Press
133. Lucy, J. A. 1992. *Grammatical Categories and Cognition.* Cambridge: Cambridge Univ. Press
134. Lucy, J. A., Shweder, R. A. 1979. Whorf and his critics: linguistic and non-linguistic influences on color memory. *Am. Anthropol.* 81:581–607
135. Lucy, J. A., Shweder, R. A. 1988. The effect of incidental conversation on memory for focal colors. *Am. Anthropol.* 90:923–31
136. Lucy, J. A., Wertsch, J. V. 1987. Vygotsky and Whorf: a comparative analysis. See Ref. 86, pp. 67–86
137. Lyons, J. 1989. Semantic ascent: a neglected aspect of syntactic typology. In *Essays on Grammatical Theory and Universal Grammar,* ed. D. Arnold, M. Atkinson, J. Durand, C. Grover, L. Sadler, pp. 153–86. Oxford: Oxford Univ. Press

138. MacLaury, R. E. 1991. Prototype theory. *Annu. Rev. Anthropol.* 20:55–74

139. MacLaury, R. E. 1991. Social and cognitive motivations of change: measuring variability in color semantics. *Language* 67:34–62

140. MacLaury, R. E. 1992. From brightness to hue: an explanatory model of color-category evolution. *Curr. Anthropol.* 33:137–86

141. Macnamara, J. T. 1981. *Names for Things: a Study of Human Learning.* Cambridge: MIT Press

142. Malotki, E. 1979. *Hopi-raum.* Tübingen: Gunter-Narr

143. Malotki, E. 1983. *Hopi time.* Berlin: Mouton

144. Manelis Klein, H. E. 1979. Noun classifiers in Toba. See Ref. 154, pp. 85–95

145. Mannheim, B. 1986. Popular song and popular grammar, poetry and metalanguage. *Word* 37:45–75

146. Mannheim, B. 1991. *The Language of the Inka Since the European Invasion.* Austin: Univ. Texas Press

147. Marchand, J. W. 1982. Herder, precursor of Humboldt, Whorf, and modern language philosophy. In *Johann Gottfried Herder, Innovator through the Ages,* ed. W. Koepke, S. B. Knoll. Bonn: Bouvier

148. Markman, E. M. 1987. How children constrain the possible meanings of words. In *Concepts and Conceptual Development: Ecological and Intellectual Factors in Categorization,* ed. U. Neisser, pp. 255–87. Cambridge: Cambridge Univ. Press

149. Martin, J. R. 1988. Grammatical conspiracies in Tagalog: family, face and fate with regard to Benjamin Lee Whorf. In *Linguistics in a Systemic Perspective,* ed. J. Benson, J. Cummins, W. Greaves, pp. 243–30. Amsterdam: Benjamins

150. Martyna, W. 1978. What does "he" mean? Use of the generic masculine. *J. Commun.* 28:131–38

151. Martyna, W. 1980. Beyond the "he/man" approach: the case for nonsexist language. *Signs* 5:482–93

152. Martyna, W. 1980. The psychology of the generic masculine. In *Women and Language in Literature and Society,* ed. S. McConnell-Ginet, R. Borker, N. Furman, pp. 69–78. New York: Praeger

153. Mathiot, M. 1979. Folk-definitions as a tool for the analysis of lexical meaning. See Ref. 154, pp. 121–260

154. Mathiot, M. ed., 1979. *Ethnolinguistics: Boas, Sapir, and Whorf Revisited.* The Hague: Mouton

155. Mathiot, M., Roberts, M. 1979. Sex roles as revealed through referential gender in American English. See Ref. 154, pp. 1–47

156. Mayr, E. 1991. *One Long Argument: Charles Darwin and The Genesis of Modern Evolutionary Thought.* Cambridge: Harvard Univ. Press

157. McConnell-Ginet, S. 1979. Prototypes, pronouns, and persons. See Ref. 154, pp. 63–83

158. Mertz, E., Parmentier, R. J., eds. 1985. *Semiotic Mediation: Sociocultural and Psychological Perspectives.* Orlando: Academic

159. Miller, R. L. 1968. *The Linguistic Relativity Principle and Humboldtian Ethnolinguistics: A History and Appraisal.* The Hague: Mouton

160. Nuckolls, J. B. 1990. *The grammar and images of aspect in Lowland Ecuadorian Quichua.* PhD thesis, Univ. Chicago

161. Ochs, E. 1988. *Culture and Language Development: Language Acquisition and Language Socialization in a Samoan Village.* Cambridge: Cambridge Univ. Press

162. Ochs, E. 1990. Indexicality and socialization. See Ref. 210, pp. 287–308

163. Ortner, S. B. 1990. Gender hegemonies. *Cult. Crit.* 14:35–80

164. Pawley, A. 1987. Encoding events in Kalam and English: different logics for reporting experience. See Ref. 225, pp. 229–60

165. Pelose, G. C. 1987. The functions of behavioral synchrony and speech rhythm in conversation. *Res. Lang. Soc. Interact.* 20:171–220

166. Penn, J. M. 1972. *Linguistic Relativity Versus Innate Ideas. The Origins of the Sapir-Whorf Hypothesis in German Thought.* The Hague: Mouton

167. Pinxten, R., ed. 1976. *Universalism Versus Relativism in Language and Thought.* The Hague: Mouton

168. Pinxten, R., van Dooren, I., Harvey, F. 1983. *The Anthropology of Space.* Philadelphia: Univ. Penn. Press

169. Quine, W. V. O. 1961. *Word and Object.* Cambridge: MIT Press

170. Quinn, N. 1982. "Commitment" in American marriage: a cultural analysis. *Am. Ethnol.* 9:775–98

171. Quinn, N. 1987. Convergent evidence for a cultural model of American marriage. See Ref. 90, pp. 173–92

172. Quinn, N. 1991. The cultural basis of metaphor. See Ref. 51, pp. 56–93

172a. Ramanujan, A. K. 1985. *Poems of Love and War: From the Eight Anthologies and the Ten Long Poems of Classical Tamil.* New York: Columbia Univ. Press

173. Ramanujan, A. K. 1989. On translating a Tamil poem. In *The Art of Translation,* ed. R. Warren, pp. 47–63. Boston: Northeastern Univ. Press

174. Redfield, R. 1941. *The Folk Culture of Yucatan.* Chicago: Univ. Chicago Press

175. Redfield, R. 1957. *The Primitive World and Its Transformations.* Ithaca: Cornell Univ. Press

176. Rosch, E. 1987. Linguistic relativity. *Etc.* 44:254–79

177. Rossi-Landi, F. 1973. *Ideologies of Linguistic Relativity.* The Hague: Mouton

178. Rudzka-Ostyn, B., ed. 1988. *Topics in Cognitive Linguistics.* Amsterdam: Benjamins

179. Rumsey, A. 1990. Wording, meaning, and linguistic relativity. *Am. Anthropol.* 92:346–61
180. Sahlins, M. 1976. Colors and cultures. *Semiotica* 16:1–22
181. Santambrogio, M., Violi, P. 1988. Introduction. In *Meaning and Mental Representations,* ed. U. Eco, M. Santambrogio, P. Violi, pp. 3–22. Bloomington: Indiana Univ. Press
182. Sapir, E. 1915. Abnormal types of speech in Nootka. See Ref. 191, pp. 179–96
183. Sapir, E. 1921. *Language.* New York: Harcourt, Brace & Company
184. Sapir, E. 1924. The grammarian and his language. See Ref. 191, pp. 150–59
185. Sapir, E. 1925. Sound patterns in language. *Language* 1:37–51; see Ref. 191, pp. 33–45
186. Sapir, E. 1927. The unconscious patterning of behavior in society. See Ref. 191, pp. 544–59
187. Sapir, E. 1929. The status of linguistics as a science. *Language* 5:207–14. See Ref. 191, pp. 160–66
188. Sapir, E. 1929. A study in phonetic symbolism. See Ref. 191, pp. 61–82
189. Sapir, E. 1933. La réalité psychologique des phonèmes. *J. Psychol. Norm. Pathol.* 30:247–65. English version in Sapir 1949, pp.46–60
190. Sapir, E. 1934. The emergence of the concept of personality in a study of cultures. See Ref. 191, pp. 590–97
191. Sapir, E. 1949. *Selected Writings of Edward Sapir,* ed. D. Mandelbaum. Berkeley: Univ. Calif. Press
192. Saussure, F. de. 1915. *Cours de linguistique générale.* Paris: Payot. Transl. 1959 as *Course in General Linguistics,* transl. W. Baskin. New York: McGraw-Hill
193. Schieffelin, B. B. 1990. *The Give and Take of Everyday Life: Language Socialization of Kaluli Children.* Cambridge: Cambridge Univ. Press
194. Schultz, E. A. 1990. *Dialogue at the Margins: Whorf, Bakhtin, and Linguistic Relativity.* Madison: Univ. Wisconsin Press
195. Scollon, R. 1982. The rhythmic integration of ordinary talk. In *Analyzing Discourse: Text and Talk* (Georgetown Univ. Roundtable on Lang. & Linguist. 1981), ed. D. Tannen, pp. 335–49, Washington: Georgetown Univ. Press
196. Sherzer, J. 1987. A discourse-centered approach to language and culture. *Am. Anthropol.* 89:295–309
197. Sherzer, J. 1990. *Verbal Art in San Blas: Kuna Culture Through its Discourse.* Cambridge: Cambridge Univ. Press
198. Silverstein, M. 1976. Shifters, linguistic categories and cultural description. In *Meaning in Anthropology,* ed. K. Basso, H. Selby, pp. 11–55. Albuquerque: Univ. New Mexico Press
199. Silverstein, M. 1976. Hierarchy of features and ergativity. In *Grammatical Categories in Australian Languages,* ed. R. M. W. Dixon, pp. 112–71. Canberra: Austr. Inst. Aboriginal Stud.
200. Silverstein, M. 1979. Language structure and linguistic ideology. In *The Elements: A Parasession on Linguistic Units and Levels,* ed. P. R. Clyne, W. F. Hanks, C. L. Hofbauer, pp. 193–247. Chicago: Chicago Linguist. Soc
201. Silverstein, M. 1981. The limits of awareness. *Work. Pap. Sociolinguist.* 84
202. Silverstein, M. 1985. Language and the culture of gender: at the intersection of structure, usage, and ideology. See Ref. 158, pp. 219–59
203. Silverstein, M. 1985. The culture of language in Chinookan narrative texts; or, On saying that . . . in Chinook. In *Grammar Inside and Outside the Clause,* ed. J. Nichols, A. Woodbury, pp. 132–71. Cambridge: Cambridge Univ. Press
204. Silverstein, M. 1986. Sapir's synchronic linguistics. See Ref. 33, pp. 67–106
205. Silverstein, M. 1987. Cognitive implications of a referential hierarchy. See Ref. 86, pp. 125–64
206. Slobin, D. 1990. The development from child speaker to native speaker. See Ref. 210, pp. 233–56
207. Slobin, D. 1991. Learning to think for speaking: native language, cognition, and rhetorical style. *Pragmatics* 1:7–26
208. Smolensky, P. 1988. On the proper treatment of connectionism. *Behav. Brain. Sci.* 11:1–74
209. Stanley, J. P. 1977. Gender marking in American English. In *Sexism and Language,* ed. A. P. Nilsen, H. Bosmajian, H. L. Gershuny, J. P. Stanley, pp. 43–74. Urbana: NCTE
210. Stigler, J. W., Shweder, R. A., Herdt, G., eds. 1990. *Cultural Psychology: Essays on Comparative Human Development.* Cambridge: Cambridge Univ. Press
211. Stocking, G. W. Jr. 1968. *Race, Culture, and Evolution: Essays in the History of Anthropology.* New York: Free Press
212. Stocking, G. W. Jr., ed. 1986. *Malinowski, Rivers, Benedict, and Others: Essays on Culture and Personality.* Madison: Univ. Wisconsin Press
213. Strauss, C. 1990. Who gets ahead? Cognitive responses to heteroglossia in American political culture. *Am. Ethnol.* 17:312–28
214. Sullivan, W. J. 1983. Sex, gender, and sexism in English. In *The Linguistic Connection,* ed. J. Casagrande, pp. 261–301. Lanham: Univ. Press America
215. Sweetser, E. 1987. The definition of lie: an examination of the folk models underlying a semantic prototype. See Ref. 90, pp. 43–66
216. Talmy, L. 1985. Lexicalization patterns: semantic structure in lexical form. In *Language Typology and Syntactic Description, Volume III, Grammatical Categories and*

the Lexicon, ed. T. Shopen, pp. 57–149. Cambridge: Cambridge Univ. Press

217. Talmy, L. 1988. The relation of grammar to cognition. See Ref. 178, pp. 165–206

218. Talmy, L. 1988. Force dynamics in language and cognition. *Cogn. Sci.* 12:49–100

219. Taylor, M., Gelman, S. A. 1988. Adjectives and nouns: children's strategies for learning new words. *Child Dev.* 59:411–19

220. Tedlock, B. 1982. Sound texture and metaphor in Quiché Maya ritual language. *Curr. Anthropol.* 23:269–72

221. Tedlock, D. 1983. *The Spoken Word and the Work of Interpretation.* Philadelphia: Univ. Penn. Press

222. Tedlock, D. 1988. Mayan linguistic ideology. See Ref. 118, pp. 55–108

223. Tham, S. C. 1977. *Language and Cognition: An Analysis of the Thought and Culture of the Malays.* Singapore: Chopmen

224. Thompson, S. A. 1988. A discourse approach to the cross-linguistic category "adjective." In *Explaining Language Universals,* ed. J. A. Hawkins, pp. 167–85. Oxford: Blackwell

225. Tomlin, R. S., ed. 1987. *Coherence and Grounding in Discourse.* Philadelphia: John Benjamins

226. Trix, F. 1992. *Spiritual Discourse in Islamic Mysticism: Learning with a Sufi Master.* Philadelphia: Univ. Penn. Press

227. Turner, T. S. 1991. "We are parrots," "Twins are birds": Bororo, Kayapó, and Nuer assertions of the identity of birds and humans as operational structures and as "play of tropes." See Ref. 51, pp. 121–58

228. Urban, G. 1991. *A Discourse-Centered Approach to Culture.* Austin: Univ. Texas Press

229. Voegelin, C. F., Voegelin, F., Masayesva-Jeanne, L. 1979. Hopi semantics. In *Handbook of North American Indians.* Vol. 9. *Southwest,* ed. A. Ortíz, pp. 581–86. Washington: Smithsonian Inst.

230. Waugh, L. R. 1982. Marked and unmarked:

a choice between unequals in semiotic structure. *Semiotica* 38:299–318

231. Waxman, S. 1991. Convergences between semantic and conceptual organization in the preschool years. In *Perspectives on Language and Thought,* ed. S. A. Gelman, J. P. Byrnes, pp. 107–45. Cambridge: Cambridge Univ. Press

232. Waxman, S., Gelman, R. 1986. Preschoolers' use of superordinate relations in classification and language. *Cogn. Dev.* 1:139–56

233. Werker, J. F. 1989. Becoming a native listener. *Am. Sci.* 77:54–59

234. Whorf, B. L. 1941. The relation of habitual thought and behavior to language. See Ref. 236, pp. 134–59

235. Whorf, B. L. 1942. Language, mind, and reality. See Ref. 236, pp. 246–70

236. Whorf, B. L. 1956. *Language, Thought, and Reality: Selected Writings of Benjamin Lee Whorf,* ed. J. B. Carroll. Cambridge, MA: MIT Press

237. Wierzbicka, A. 1988. *The Semantics of Grammar.* Amsterdam: Benjamins

238. Wierzbicka, A. 1990. The meaning of color terms: semantics, culture, and cognition. *Cogn. Linguist.* 1:99–150

239. Williams, R. 1977. *Marxism and Literature.* London: Oxford Univ. Press

240. Woodbury, A. C. 1987. Rhetorical structure in a Central Yupik Eskimo traditional narrative. In *Native American Discourse,* ed. J. Sherzer, A. Woodbury, pp. 176–239. Cambridge: Cambridge Univ. Press

241. Woodbury, A. C. 1989. Phrasing and intonational tonology in Central Alaskan Yupik Eskimo: some implications for linguistics in the field. In *1988 Mid-America Linguistics Conference Papers,* ed. John Dunn, pp. 3–40. Norman: Univ. Oklahoma

242. Zubin, D., Koepcke, K. M. 1986. Gender and folk taxonomy: the indexical relation between grammatical and lexical categorization. See Ref. 35, pp. 139–80

Annu. Rev. Anthropol. 1992. 21:407–33

PRIMATE LIMB BONE STRUCTURAL ADAPTATIONS

C. B. Ruff and J. A. Runestad

Department of Cell Biology and Anatomy, Johns Hopkins University School of Medicine, Baltimore, Maryland 21205

KEYWORDS: biomechanics, allometry, skeleton, locomotion

INTRODUCTION

Despite growth in other areas of biological anthropology, osteology, or skeletal biology, remains a dominant subfield in the discipline (50). Although the reasons for this are partly historical (6), continuing interest in describing and interpreting skeletal features is fueled by a practical consideration: For most extinct vertebrates, the skeleton is the only biological system preserved for study. Thus, evolutionary studies will always rely to a large extent on skeletal (including dental) material. This is particularly true for reconstructions of the past biological and behavioral characteristics of a species or individual; while molecular evidence from extant species provides complementary information on possible phylogenetic relationships, it is only through study of the fossils (bones and teeth) themselves that we are able to address such important issues as diet, body size, and locomotor/positional behavior.

A functionally oriented rather than descriptive/statistical approach to skeletal morphological variation has many advantages, including much greater explanatory potential (e.g. see 6). Biomechanics, the application of mechanics theory to biological systems, has proven fruitful in addressing several long-standing form/function issues—for example, the significance of variation in mandibular form among early hominids (16, 35) or of limb bone robusticity among extant and extinct anthropoids (42, 44, 64, 65, 73). Important to such an analysis is the identification of an appropriate mechanical model for the biological system under study. For example, it has been shown that the human lower limb during gait (walking) can be modeled reasonably accurately by a simple pendulum (55:198–203). This basic concept has been applied to esti-

0084-6570/92/1015-0433$02.00

mate the walking speed of fossil hominids from their preserved footprints (2). Finding a fairly simple mechanical model for a biological system has two major benefits: 1. the analysis can concentrate on aspects of morphology relevant to the model, thereby reducing the total morphology to a few more manageable variables; and 2. observed variation in morphological characteristics can be interpreted directly in functional terms.

One mechanical model—that of an engineering beam (33)—has been used increasingly in structural analyses of primate limb bone diaphyses, and is emphasized here. We also consider studies of articular structure, geometry of whole bones (e.g. bone curvature), and briefly, bone microstructure, all carried out within a general functional-mechanical framework. We do not review studies that were primarily descriptive and/or concerned with phylogenetic rather than functional questions. Here we emphasize applications to nonhuman primates; biomechanical studies of human skeletal samples have been reviewed recently elsewhere (68).

LEVELS OF STRUCTURAL ORGANIZATION

The structure of a bone (or functional complex of bones) may theoretically be analyzed at a number of different levels. Figure 1 illustrates one way in which structural studies of long bones may be subdivided: by size (microscopic/macroscopic) and by region (articulations/diaphyses). Microscopic structure is taken here to include the cellular organization of compact bone as well as trabecular bone architecture. Although trabecular structure is not strictly "microstructural" since it is largely visible to the naked eye, it has been categorized that way here to distinguish it from the larger external "macrostructural" features of articulations—the size and geometry of the articular surfaces and associated supporting structures (epiphyses and metaphyses).

The division between articular and diaphyseal regions and between micro- and macrostructural features of bones is not only convenient heuristically, it is also based logically on inherent functional and physiological differences. Synovial joints function to permit (or limit) particular ranges of motion between bones and to transfer mechanical loads (forces) between bones without wearing out articular cartilage. Their structure reflects these two functions—an expanded articular surface composed of thin compact bone underlain by a large area of compliant trabecular bone (which reduces articular surface stress); specific shape and size are correlated with the magnitude of forces transmitted, the customary position of the joint during loading, and the ranges of motion necessary during movement (15, 36, 65). Articular geometry is constrained physiologically by the need for close congruence between neighboring structures and the interdependence of all functioning components of a joint; a change in any one component is likely to have negative or even pathological consequences for the joint as a whole (59). Thus, the external size and shape of articulations remain relatively constant during adult life, short of pathological alterations, regardless of changes in mechanical loadings (60, 65, 71).

In contrast, long-bone diaphyses function more like engineering beams, providing rigidity (rather than compliance) to the appendicular skeleton, particularly against bending and torsional (twisting) loads. There are few physiological constraints on diaphyseal structure; thus, dramatic alterations in diaphyseal cross-sectional size and shape may occur with changes in mechanical loadings (e.g. 89). Similar adaptations in articulations appear to occur through changes in the architecture of the underlying trabecular bone (46, 61). The histological structure of bone may also reflect, in part, mechanical usage (e.g. 11), although the relationship between mechanical factors and bone cellular structure is probably fairly complex (52).

These differences in function and physiology have important implications when we interpret observed variation in articular or diaphyseal form. For example, both diaphyseal cross-sectional geometry and articular trabecular architecture appear to be much more environmentally sensitive, or "plastic," than external joint size or shape, and thus may be much more readily influenced by changes in mechanical loadings during life (65, 71). Such features may therefore reflect what an animal was *actually* doing during its lifetime, rather than what it was *capable* of doing. Considerations like these can have significant evolutionary ramifications—for example, in distinguishing "incipi-

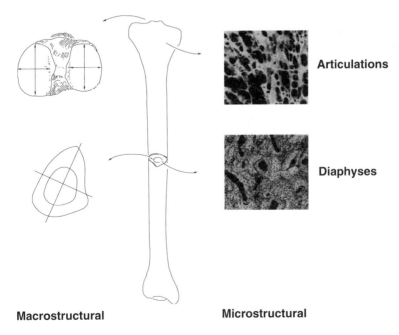

Articulations

Diaphyses

Macrostructural   **Microstructural**

Figure 1   Levels of structural organization of a long bone.

ent" functional adaptations from more conservative features present mainly as phylogenetic "baggage" (for an example, see below).

To the types of features illustrated in Figure 1 may be added measurements of the configuration of the whole bone, such as shaft curvature (81), muscle moment ("leverage") arm lengths (5, 22), and bone length proportions (39). Bone material properties—tissue density, elasticity, strength, etc—represent other mechanically significant characteristics that depend upon microstructural as well as ultrastructural and chemical properties of bone (15). However, most of these material characteristics are difficult if not impossible to determine directly in the types of specimens usually studied by anthropologists—dried museum or archaeological collections and fossils—and are not further considered here.

General Configuration

As noted above, this category includes studies of the geometry of entire bones, general proportions (both within and between bones), and nonmetric visual characteristics such as presence of tubercles, position of muscular attachments, etc.

A good example of a recent study that considered all of these types of attributes to address a specific structural/functional question is Fleagle & Meldrum's (22) comparison of the skeletons of the white-faced and bearded saki (*Pithecia pithecia* and *Chiropotes satanas*), two sympatric South American monkeys with very different positional repertoires: The former leaps frequently, while the latter is predominantly quadrupedal. Systematic differences paralleling this locomotor distinction were found in such features as inter- and intra-membral bone length proportions, articular shape, orientation, buttressing, and shaft robusticity. In many ways this study is analogous to Fleagle's earlier (21) study of the skeletons of two sympatric species of langurs (*Presbytis obscura* and *P. melalophos*), which also differed in frequency of leaping. In both studies he makes the important point that comparisons of this kind between phylogenetically closely related species help to reduce the potentially confounding effects of heritage (i.e. the phylogenetic "baggage" referred to above) and thus more clearly identify those structural adaptations related specifically to locomotor/positional differences. [Demes et al (19) make a similar point, but in this case with respect to allometric scaling, in their analysis of indriid limb bone structure, reviewed below.] Fleagle & Meldrum were able to apply their observations on living sakis to a preliminary analysis of the fossil platyrrhine *Cebupithecia sarmientoi,* concluding that it showed more structural similarities to the white-faced saki and thus probably had a similar, although not identical locomotor repertoire.

Another recent study of this general nature, but covering a wider range of species, is Anemone's (5) examination of differences in femoral structure within extant prosimians, specifically concentrating on features associated with vertical clinging and leaping. He concluded that while all living clingers and leapers exhibit some similarities in femoral structure, such as an elongated femur and anteriorly projecting patellar surface, other traits related to proximal femoral morphology are shared only by galagos and tarsiers, specifically a relatively cylindrical femoral head; short, thick, and horizontally oriented femoral neck; and posteriorly expanded articular surface of the head (see Figure 2). He suggested that these special traits of galagos and tarsiers reflect a "postural adaptation ... during vertical clinging behavior in small-bodied prosimians" (p. 386)—an adaptation that maintains appropriate femoral head articular contact with the acetabulum with strong flexion, abduction, and lateral rotation of the femur. Some of these structural adaptations may also help to buttress the femoral neck against the expected higher forces acting across hindlimb joints in small versus larger bodied leapers, due to allometric considerations (17).

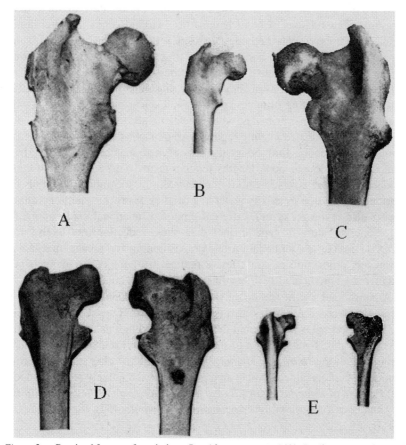

Figure 2   Proximal femora of prosimians: *Propithecus verreauxi* (A), *Lepilemur mustelinus* (B), *Lemur catta* (C)*, Galago crassicaudatus* (D), and *Tarsius spectrum* (E). Note the cylindrical head and thick, horizontally oriented neck of the *Galago* and *Tarsius* femora relative to those of other species. (Adapted from 5, copyright 1990 John Wiley and Sons, Inc.; reprinted with permission of the author and Wiley-Liss, a division of John Wiley and Sons, Inc.)

The effects of body size in general have been shown to be important to the interpretation of skeletal structural variation in a functional context (e.g. 17, 39). The choice of which size variable is most appropriate in such analyses (e.g. body mass, skeletal trunk length, etc) has been discussed at length, particularly by Jungers (38, 39). He showed that among anthropoids, skeletal trunk length (STL) is not an appropriate measure of body size against which to compare features of the appendicular skeleton, since it scales negatively allometrically with body mass. However, among prosimians body mass and STL are isometric, so that STL can be used as a body mass substitute in this group.

This same issue of how to compare different taxa spanning a large "size" range was also addressed indirectly by Swartz (81) in her analysis of limb bone curvature in anthropoid primates. Using a biomechanical (beam) model, she argued that it was the absolute deviation, or eccentricity, of a long-bone shaft from a straight line, rather than the radius of curvature or some other measure taken relative to bone length, that was important in determining mechanical stress within the bone due to axial (end-on) loading. Thus, some apparently "straight" limb bones, such as those in the gibbon forearm, only appear to be straight because they are so long—i.e. they have low radii of curvature, but average or even above average absolute shaft eccentricities. The humerus of brachiating primates (gibbons and spider monkeys) is somewhat straighter than in other primates, which she explained as a possible adaptation to its torsion-dominated loading regime during brachiation (82). Primates as a whole have straighter limb bones than nonprimate mammals, a fact perhaps related to their longer bone lengths relative to body mass (3), which could produce higher transverse bending moments during locomotion and thus necessitate a reduction in axially generated bending loads (i.e. shaft curvature). Swartz also reviewed several different proposed functional explanations for long-bone curvature in general, including stress reduction (not likely to be correct), muscle accommodation and/or positioning for greater mechanical advantage, production of strain levels optimal for bone tissue maintenance, and increased predictability of bending stresses within bones.

Among other recent studies of this general type should be mentioned in particular Gebo et al's series of investigations of the foot skeleton in extant and extinct primates (24–27) and the various contributions to the symposium "Evolution and Diversification of the Postcranium in Primates," published as Volume 17 of the *Journal of Human Evolution* (1988). Other studies stressing a more kinesiological viewpoint can be found in two relatively recent compendia: *Primate Morphophysiology, Locomotor Analyses and Human Bipedalism* (45) and *Gravity, Posture, and Locomotion in Primates* (37).

Diaphyseal Cross-Sectional Geometry

Structural analyses of long-bone diaphyses have usually been limited to qualitative assessments of general form and some simple metric indices (e.g. "robusticity"—external breadth or circumference over length) and various

Cortical Properties

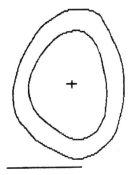

TA	:	222.16
CA	:	109.26
Xbar	:	8.77
Ybar	:	10.74
Ix	:	3827.97
Iy	:	2237.06
Theta	:	84.14
Imax	:	3844.91
Imin	:	2220.12

Figure 3   Example of SLICE output from an analysis of a tibial diaphyseal cross-section of an early Miocene hominoid, *Proconsul nyanzae* (KNM-RU 5572) (see 73). TA: total subperiosteal area; CA: cortical area; Xbar and Ybar: coordinates of section centroid; I_x and I_y: second moments of area about x and y axes; Theta: orientation of greatest bending rigidity; I_{max} and I_{min}: maximum and minimum second moments of area; J: polar second moment of area. Scale bar is 1 cm long.

"shape" indices, derived as the ratio of external breadths taken in perpendicular planes (51). Although these traits can be used effectively in functional analyses (e.g. 22; also see 63), it is possible to gain more information from long-bone shafts if whole cross-sections are analyzed using engineering beam theory. The general concepts underlying the use of beam theory can be found in any basic engineering textbook (e.g. 84) and have been described several times in the anthropological literature (e.g. see 49, 69); an excellent recent treatment of the topic can be found in Hayes (30). With the development of automated methods of analyzing cross-sectional contours (e.g. 57), the only major technical difficulty remaining involves obtaining sufficiently accurate cross-sectional images. Since most bones cannot be directly sectioned and are usually not broken at the locations of interest (although see 73), various noninvasive techniques, especially computed tomography (CT), have been increasingly used in this kind of study (see 66 for a review; also 70). For some applications simple biplanar radiographs may be sufficient, provided the correct geometric reconstruction technique is used (10, 23, 74).

Figure 3 shows a computer reconstruction of a mid-proximal tibial shaft cross-section of a specimen of *Proconsul nyanzae,* an early Miocene (17.8 MYBP) hominoid —a specimen (KNM-RU 5572) from Rusinga Island in Kenya (73). In this case cross-sectional contours were obtained from a broken section, traced on a digitizer, and analyzed using a program called SLICE (57). The associated biomechanical section properties are listed next to the section and are defined in the figure legend. They include cross-sectional area and second moments of area, or area moments of inertia. Together these properties can be used to determine the rigidity (proportional to the strength) of the bone at that section under a variety of mechanical loadings. In this particular case the properties were used to estimate the body mass (weight) of the individual, using equations developed from modern primates (64). Since support of body mass constitutes an important aspect of the total mechanical loading of a limb, this method produces smaller errors of estimate than alternative techniques such as regressions based on tooth size (see 66, 73; also 74).

In addition to improving techniques for body mass estimation, several recent studies have employed this approach to examine the effects of size (allometric scaling) and behavioral use of the limbs (locomotor repertoire) in nonhuman primates (13, 18, 19, 64, 76). Schaffler and coworkers (76) showed that among gibbons, langurs, and two species of macaques, the bending and torsional rigidity of the humerus relative to that of the femur matched behavioral observations of relative forelimb/hindlimb mechanical loadings in these species (i.e. gibbons had the highest humerus/femur rigidity ratio, and langurs, who leap frequently, had the lowest). Ruff (64) found that among great apes, orangutans had the weakest hindlimb bone diaphyses, apparently owing to their higher frequency of forelimb suspensory behavior and relative unloading of the hind limb (e.g. see 14) (Figure 4). However, in general, locomotor adaptations in the limb bones of the primates examined here (macaques, great apes, and humans) were more apparent as proportional changes in bone length to body mass than as cross-sectional properties to body mass (Figure 4). This finding affects the interpretation of observed within-bone proportions. For example, a gorilla femur looks more "robust" than a macaque femur primarily because it is shorter, and not so much because it is thicker. This same general point [presaged by Schultz in 1953 (77)] has also been made recently by Demes and coworkers (18, 19) with respect to prosimian long bones.

Three recent studies have examined variation in long-bone diaphyseal structure within groups of fairly closely related species: Burr et al's (13) study of three species of macaques, Demes & Jungers's (18) study of two Asian lorisines (with comparisons to several other prosimians), and Demes et al's (19) study of five indriid species. Burr and coworkers (13) identified a "barrel-shaped" morphology of the femur (greater bending and torsional rigidity in the midshaft region) characteristic of *Macaca fascicularis,* a highly arboreal macaque that leaps relatively frequently, and not present in the more terrestrial *M. mulatta* and *M. nemestrina.* The same general "barrel" morphology is also present in *Galago senegalensis,* a very proficient leaper. This structural feature may be a specific adaptation to leaping behavior or perhaps more specifically to relative limb bone lengthening, since both the high muscular forces involved in leaping and the relatively long hindlimb bones of leapers should increase bending (and buckling) loads in the femur, particularly near midshaft. Examination of structural variation along the shafts of other species, leaping and nonleaping, should help to clarify this issue. Ruff (66) found that changes in cross-sectional shape—relative anteroposterior (A-P) to mediolateral (M-L) bending rigidity—along the femoral diaphysis in four primate species appear to parallel changes in relative frequency of leaping, possibly owing to the increased action of the hip extensors (and thus increased A-P bending of the

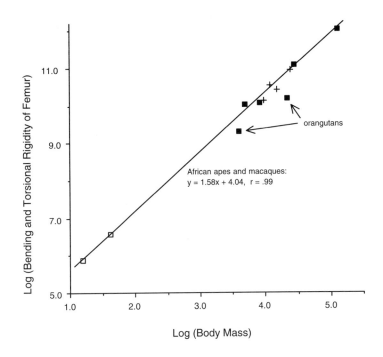

Figure 4   Bending-torsional rigidity (polar second moment of area) of the midshaft femur relative to body mass in some anthropoid species. Each point is a sex/species mean. Closed squares: apes (gorillas, orangutans, common chimpanzees); open squares: *Macaca fascicularis;* crosses: *Homo sapiens* (two populations). Least squares regression line drawn through gorillas, chimpanzees, and macaques. Note the less rigid femora of orangutans. Data are from 64.

proximal femur) in leapers. Structural modifications of this kind related to locomotor behavior may be more apparent in the hindlimb than in the fore-limb. Burr and coworkers (13) found that the humeri of the three macaque species examined showed less variation in morphology than the femur, a finding they attributed to the forelimb's use as a "multifunctional generalized limb apparatus in which simple weightbearing may play a relatively minor role in the adaptive process" (p. 364).

Demes & Jungers (18) compared long-bone structural properties of *Loris tardigradus* with that of *Nycticebus coucang,* two Asian lorisines both charac-terized by slow, cautious arboreal movement but differing in body mass by a factor of a little over three. Neither species showed any significant difference in bone rigidity of the forelimb and hindlimb, or in different planes of the bones (i.e. cross-sections were relatively round). They attributed these findings to a relatively equal distribution of mechanical load between the limbs in these species and a nonspecific (or multiple) orientation of bending loads during positional behavior, respectively. Regarding this last observation, however, it should be noted that macaques and some other primate species that are not slow climbers also have relatively cylindrical diaphyses near midshaft, at least in the femur (19, 66, 76). Consideration of more general size-related trends in long-bone cross-sectional shape, discussed further below, may help to explain this finding. Both lorisine species had much lower bending/torsional rigidity of the femur than did prosimians of comparable body mass specialized for leaping, as would be expected. However, comparisons of actual long-bone cross-sectional dimensions with those predicted from general mammalian regressions did not show consistently lower properties for the slow-moving lorisines, particularly the larger of the two, *Nycticebus*. The discrepancy from predictions here was most marked for the forelimb bones, which may be less important in locomotion per se (see above). A possible explanation for the relatively strong forelimb bones of lorisines is presented below.

Demes et al (19) examined interlimb differences and patterns of allometric scaling of bone cross-sectional properties in five indriid species ranging in body mass from 1 to 7.5 kg. These species are highly specialized for saltatory (leaping) locomotion. In all five, both rigidity and strength of the femur were much greater than those of the humerus, matching their hindlimb-dominated locomotor repertoire. The authors carried out no comparisons with more generalized mammalian scaling relationships, but our comparison of their data with those predicted from Biewener's (7) general mammalian regression equation shows indriids to have humeri close in rigidity to those of comparable-sized mammals but femora that are three to four times stronger—results again consistent with their mode of locomotion. Demes and coworkers (19) also noted a slight but significant trend for larger indriids to have more cylindrical femora than smaller indriids—i.e. to show less preferential buttressing of the shaft against anteroposterior bending. Examination of their earlier data for lorisines (18) reveals the same size-related trend in femoral cross-sectional shape. A possible explanation for this trend lies in more general size-related changes in body posture and behavior that have been proposed to explain observed allometric scaling of the musculoskeletal system among vertebrates, as follows.

Straightforward application of simple geometric principles would predict that bone cross-sectional dimensions would increase faster than body mass—i.e. show marked positive allometry—in order to maintain mechanical equivalence (e.g. see 29). However, most empirical data do not support this prediction, indicating instead only slight positive allometry of these dimensions among mammals (4, 7). Among primates, this isometry or modest positive allometry has been demonstrated for anthropoids (1, 64, 76), and indriids (19), although not for lorisines (18). In the simplest terms, these observed trends mean that larger animals appear to have bones too gracile to support themselves safely. Proposed mechanisms to explain this apparent discrepancy include modifications in behavior and limb posture in larger animals that would reduce mechanical stress, although limiting speed and maneuverability relative to smaller animals (7–9, 62; also see 17). However, the major effects of at least some of these modifications—e.g. changes in limb angulation (see 9: Figure 3)—would be to selectively reduce only *anteroposterior* bending loads in larger animals, and not mediolateral bending loads. Thus if these proposed mechanisms are in fact operative, with an increase in body size M-L bending loads within limb bones should increase faster than A-P bending loads.

Figure 5 plots the ratio of M-L/A-P bending rigidity of the midshaft femur against body mass in several primate samples, including greater and lesser apes, Old World monkeys, lorisines, and indriids (18, 19, 64, 76, and C. Ruff, unpublished data). The predicted general increase in the ratio with increasing body size is confirmed, both within the total sample (not including lorisines,

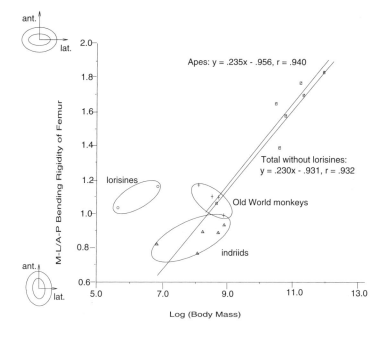

Figure 5   Mediolateral to anteroposterior bending rigidity (ratio of M-L to A-P second moments of area) of the midshaft femur relative to body mass in some primate species. Each point is a species mean, except sex/species means for great apes and *Macaca fascicularis*. Closed squares: apes [gorillas, orangutans, common chimpanzees, gibbons (lowest ape point)]; crosses: Old World monkeys (*Macaca nemestrina, M. fascicularis, Presbytis cristata*); closed triangles: indriids (*Indri indri, Propithecus diadema, P. verreauxi, P. tattersalli, Avahi laniger*); open circles: lorisines (*Loris tardigradus, Nycticebus coucang*). Least squares regression lines drawn through apes alone and through all species except for lorisines. There is a general increase in M-L/A-P bending rigidity of the femur with an increase in body size, both between and within most groups. Data are from 18, 19, 64, 76.

which are clear outliers) and within groups of animals that have broadly similar locomotor behaviors: apes, indriids, and lorisines. The only exception is among Old World monkeys (represented here by macaques and langurs), which show an opposite trend. The limited body-size range of the available species here and their rather heterogeneous locomotor repertoire may explain this partial exception. When general allometric trends are considered, the slow-moving lorisines are seen to have high M-L/A-P ratios, for their body masses, while most indriids show the opposite pattern. Thus, when scaled against body mass, diaphyseal shape differences are consistent with locomotor repertoire, with increased frequency of rapid locomotion dominated by A-P bending reflected in increased A-P/M-L (decreased M-L/A-P) bending rigidity (indriids vs lorisines).

There is some evidence of a "leveling off" of the general size-related trend in the smallest indriid, *Avahi laniger* (about 1 kg)—i.e. it shows no further decrease in the M-L/A-P bending rigidity ratio. This interpretation is strengthened by examining data available for very small bodied prosimian leapers (albeit "foot-powered" rather than, like indriids, "thigh-powered")—*Galago senegalensis* and *Galago elegantulus*—with body masses between 275 and 300 g (cited in 18: Table 6). The M-L/A-P bending rigidity ratio in these species is almost identical to that of *A. laniger,* suggesting no further change in cross-sectional shape in this lower size range. It has been hypothesized by Biewener (9) that postural adjustments to reduce increases in mechanical stress are limited to small to medium-sized mammals (in his model, about 100 g to 300 kg), with different mechanical constraints on the structural design of skeletons operative among very small mammals. While the lower size limit in this model for postural adjustments was set at 100 g, examination of the available limb angulation data (9: Figure 4) indicates that this limit could as easily be set at 1 kg, which would better match the results shown here. It should also be noted that Demes et al (19) found virtual isometry (not slight positive allometry) of cross-sectional dimensions to body mass among indriids of up to 7.5 kg, which is what Biewener's (9) model predicted for much smaller mammals under 100 g. This again suggests that hypothesized size "limits" for particular types of behavioral/structural adaptations should be interpreted loosely and may be partially dependent upon the specific group or locomotor behavior under consideration.

Another kind of analysis possible with diaphyseal cross-sectional data is the comparison of bone rigidity or strength under different types of mechanical loadings—e.g. bending, torsional, axial compression or tension. Bending and torsional rigidities are proportional to the second moments of area (SMA) of a section, while axial compressive and tensile rigidities are proportional to the cross-sectional area (see 69). Thus, in a species that emphasizes axial rather than bending/torsional loading of a limb element, cortical area should be relatively greater than second moments of area.

An example of this approach is given in Figure 6, which shows cortical area plotted against an SMA of the femoral midshaft in chimpanzees, gorillas, and orangutans (64; and C. Ruff, unpublished data). The SMA in the A-P plane is used here, since this property is the most relevant in terms of propulsive forces in the hindlimb developed during active locomotion (see above). Reduced major axis (RMA) analysis is used instead of least squares to fit regression lines because of the relatively low correlation for orangutans (approaching r = .9). As shown in the figure, orangutans tend to have increased axial rigidity to A-P bending rigidity of the femur compared to the African apes, suggesting that their lower limb is used less for active propulsion during locomotion than are the lower limbs of chimpanzees and gorillas. This prediction matches behavioral observations of these species, in which orangutans tend to move more deliberately, adopt static hanging postures, and even when moving quadrupedally on the ground load their hindlimbs less than the other great apes (14; see 64 for discussion).

Another example of this kind is shown in Figure 7, from an ongoing study of prosimian and small anthropoid limb bone structure (74). In this plot mid-distal humeral cortical area is regressed on the polar second moment of area of the same section (40% of bone length from the distal end of the humerus). The

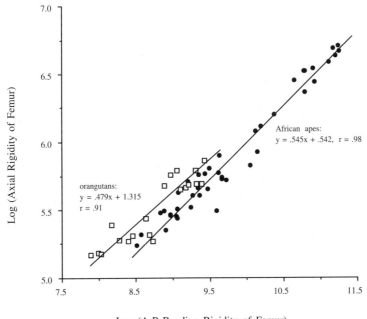

Figure 6   Axial relative to anteroposterior bending rigidity (cortical area to A-P second moment of area) of the midshaft femur in gorillas, chimpanzees, and orangutans (individuals). Closed circles: African apes; open squares: orangutans. Reduced major axis regression lines plotted through each group. Orangutans have increased axial and decreased A-P bending rigidity of the femur. Data are from 64 and C. Ruff, unpublished.

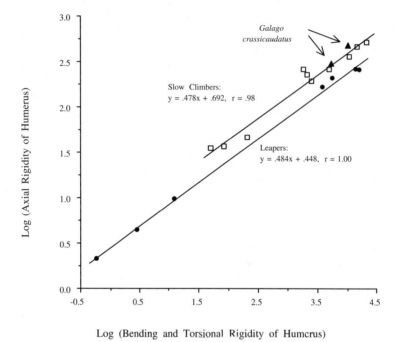

Figure 7   Axial relative to bending-torsional rigidity (cortical area to polar second moment of area) of the mid-distal humerus in some prosimians (individuals). Closed circles: leapers (*Avahi laniger, Lepilemur mustelinus, Hapalemur griseus, Tarsier syrichta, Galago demidovii*); open squares: slow climbers (*Perodicticus potto, Nycticebus coucang, Loris tardigradus*); closed triangles: *Galago crassicaudatus*. Least squares regression lines drawn through each group. Slow climbers have increased axial to bending-torsional rigidity of the humerus; *Galago crassicaudatus* falls directly with slow climbers. Data are from 74 and J. Runestad, unpublished.

polar SMA was chosen here rather than some other SMA because it reflects both torsional and average bending rigidities in all planes, which is appropriate for evaluating the multifunctional use of the forelimb (as opposed to hindlimb). Two general locomotor groups—all prosimians—are plotted: slow climbers (Asian and African lorisines) and specialized leapers (*Galago, Tarsier, Hapalemur, Lepilemur,* and *Avahi.*) Relative to body mass the slow climbers have larger cortical area (or smaller SMA) than leapers, indicating an adaptation to higher axial and/or lower bending/torsional loads on the humerus. In fact, other evidence indicates that relative to body mass, humeral cortical area is larger in slow climbers than in leapers (and generalized quadrupeds), while the polar SMA is comparable in the two groups (74). Thus, slow climbers appear to be adapted for high axial loadings of the forelimb. Behavioral and physiological studies (58, 78, 85) indicate that their typical mode of locomotion is stealthy, cautious progression accompanied by powerful gripping of supports. Such behavior would tend to produce strong isometric contraction of muscles around the limb bones, subjecting them to high axial ("balanced") loads. The cross-sectional structure of their humeri appears to match this specialized locomotor behavior. (The femur shows a similar, but less marked pattern when compared to generalized quadrupeds.)

Also shown on Figure 7 are two data points for *Galago crassicaudatus,* the largest living galago. This species leaps much less frequently than most other galagos and has been compared to the African lorisine *Perodicticus potto* (58). However, its proximal femoral articular morphology (Figure 2) is like that of other galagos (5), and its intermembral bone-length proportions are intermediate between those of specialized leapers and nonleaping forms (5, 74). The cross-sectional analysis in Figure 7 shows that *G. crassicaudatus* falls directly on the slow-climber regression line in this respect, suggesting adaptation to powerful isometric gripping and lorisine-like movement. In many other respects its cross-sectional humeral and femoral properties also ally it with slow climbers or generalized quadrupeds rather than leapers (74). Thus, in some ways the limb bone cross-sectional geometric characteristics of *G. crassicaudatus* appear to reflect behavioral field observations more accurately than either its articular morphology or intermembral length proportions. This interpretation is consistent with the greater environmental plasticity of long-bone cortices to applied mechanical loadings, and appreciation of the difference between what an animal is capable of doing and what it actually does. *G. crassicaudatus* is still capable of proficient leaping, however, given its diet and ecology, it just doesn't leap often (58). The contrast among different structural properties (cross-sectional, articular, length) with different physiological/genetic constraints clearly shows the "mixed" set of adaptations in this species, and the interplay of inheritance with actual mechanical demands on the skeleton. As Oxnard and coworkers have noted in comparing *G. crassicaudatus* with *P. potto,* "*Peridicticus*' specializations are only partially echoed in *G. crassicaudatus,* which is, of course, a galago, if a rather unusual one" (58:49). A similar approach could shed light on evolving locomotor and positional behaviors in other primates, including hominids (65, 72).

ARTICULAR SIZE

Four recent studies have examined the allometry of limb bone articular size in primates (28, 42, 44, 65, 80). The studies varied in approach, species sampled, suite of measurements, and interpretation of results.

The studies by Jungers (42, 44) and Ruff (65) focussed on hominoids, used linear measurements to estimate articular size and/or surface area, and used body mass as the "size" variable against which to compare articular dimensions. Combined results of these two studies for femoral head size (breadth) are shown in Figure 8. Apes (including gibbons, siamangs, and the great apes) have femoral head sizes isometric with body mass (log-log slope very close to

.333); that is, femoral head size and body mass increase in a geometrically similar manner. Old World monkeys have smaller femoral heads than apes of a comparable body mass, and there may be slight positive allometry of femoral head size in this group (slope somewhat greater than .333). Humans have larger femoral heads for their body masses than nonhuman primates, with very marked positive allometry (slope much greater than .333). In all groups, femoral head size is strongly correlated with body mass. As such, it can provide an excellent estimate of body mass in fossil primates, providing that the particular fossil can be placed into the appropriate taxonomic/locomotor group. Prediction equations generated by these two studies have been used to estimate body mass in *Oreopithecus*, a Late Miocene hominoid (40), giant subfossil Malagasy lemurs (43), the early hominid A. L. 288-1 ("Lucy") (41, 43), and two species of *Proconsul*, an early Miocene hominoid (73; also see above). When the locomotor/postural characteristics of an extinct species are not known with

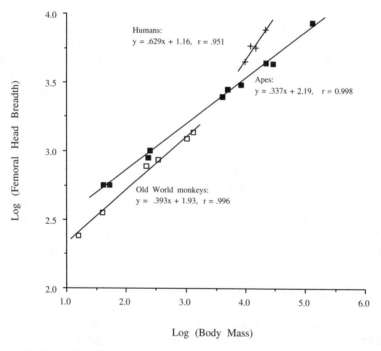

Figure 8   Femoral head breadth relative to body mass in some anthropoids. Closed squares: apes (gorillas, orangutans, common chimpanzees, siamangs, gibbons); open squares: Old World monkeys (*Papio anubis, Nasalis larvatus, Macaca fascicularis*); crosses: *Homo sapiens*. Data are sex/species means (sex/population means for *H. sapiens*) except individual data for *P. anubis* and *N. larvatus*. All regressions are least squares. Monkeys have smaller femoral heads than apes, and both are not far from isometric. Humans have the largest femoral heads but also show extreme positive allometry. Great ape, human, and *M. fascicularis* data are from 64; other data are from 44.

certainty, as is the case for some early hominids (e.g. compare 79 with 48), use of such equations can be problematic and can lead to widely differing estimates of body size depending upon the particular modern reference group chosen (e.g. for A. L. 288-1 see 41, 43, 53, 54). Owing to the marked effects of joint excursion on relative articular size (65; also see below), cross-sectional diaphyseal dimensions may provide less "taxonomically sensitive" (i.e. generally applicable) estimates of body mass in some cases (67)—for example, in *Proconsul,* which shows a mixture of ape-like and monkey-like characteristics in its postcranium (see references in 73; also 86).

The effect of joint excursion on articular size is clearly illustrated by comparing the relative position of orangutans in Figures 4 and 8. Orangutans mechanically load their hindlimbs less than other great apes and thus have less robust hindlimb diaphyses (Figure 4); but they have extremely mobile hip joints (14) for which a large femoral head is adaptive (65). Thus, orangutans fall directly with other nonhuman hominoids for femoral head size (Figure 8). Direct comparison of femoral head size or surface area with cross-sectional diaphyseal size (65: Figures 5, 6) clearly shows the deviation of orangutans from other great apes (lower hindlimb loadings combined with higher hindlimb mobility) and suggests that this kind of combined analysis could be used to further elucidate locomotor/positional behavior in fossil forms. In fact, increased femoral head size is only one part of a complex of characters around the hip joint to increase mobility in orangutans; this trait should also be examined in conjunction with femoral neck size, acetabular depth, and proportion of the head covered by articular surface (65). For example, humans also show increased femoral head size (compare Figures 4 and 8; also see 65: Figures 5, 6) but none of the other features associated with hip mobility in orangutans (65). Larger hindlimb joints in humans (also see 42, 44) are adaptations to the expected greater forces generated across joints of the lower limb in habitual bipeds, not to increased joint mobility. Why modern humans should not show the same increase in lower limb *diaphyseal* robusticity (Figure 4) has been explored in detail elsewhere (65, 72).

The same issue of force transmission versus mobility is central to Swartz's (80) examination of articular scaling in 13 species of nonhuman hominoids, Old and New World monkeys. She measured long-bone articular surface areas using a latex cast method, and ranges of motion of joints through physical manipulation of articulated skeletal specimens. In lieu of individually associated body masses, a "body size estimate"—proximal femoral shaft circumference raised to the power of 2.78—was used in allometric analyses. She found that most joints in anthropoid primates scale with positive allometry to body size; "suspensory" species (gibbons, spider monkeys) show no significant deviation from the overall scaling patterns found in "nonsuspensory" species. Primarily on the basis of this latter result, she concluded that "the diverse range of locomotor repertoires and corresponding patterns of limb loadings in primates is not reflected directly in joint surface design ... . Joint surface proportions seem to be poorly reflective even of highly specialized species-level functional adaptation" (pp. 456–57). Further, rather than indicating any particular functional adapation, large forelimb joints of suspensory animals "can be interpreted as historical remnants of a nonbrachiating period in their evolutionary history" (p. 458).

Closer examination of Swartz's data, however, indicates that her results were largely an artifact of her analytic procedure, in particular the combining of monkeys and apes in all regression analyses. In Figures 9 and 10 we have plotted humeral and femoral head surface areas, respectively, against body mass, using the data given in Tables 1–3 of Swartz's paper. (These are sex/species means, except for species monomorphic in body mass, including gibbons, where we averaged the joint surface data given by Swartz for males and females; body masses are averages obtained by Swartz from the literature—note the misprint for *Nasalis larvatus* in her Table 1.) Regression lines have been plotted through apes and monkeys separately, using reduced major axis (RMA) analysis. RMA was used rather than least squares regression because of the relatively low correlations for monkeys (r < .9) and the fact that Swartz used RMA in her original study. As shown in the figures, apes (includ-

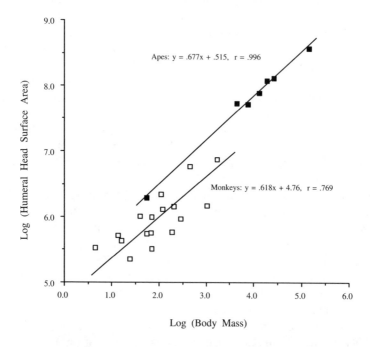

Figure 9   Swartz's (80) data for humeral head surface area and body mass in apes and monkeys (see text and original reference for explanation of data points). Reduced major axis regression lines shown for each group. When analyzed separately, apes and monkeys show almost parallel, nearly isometric changes in humeral head surface area, with apes having larger articulations.

ing lesser apes) and monkeys fall on essentially parallel but vertically displaced regression lines, with apes having larger joint surfaces, especially for the humerus. Figure 10, in fact, is similar to Figure 8, derived from data given by Ruff (65) and Jungers (42, 44), when account is taken of the different dimensions examined (linear versus surface area measurements of joints). In all analyses, apes show virtual isometry of both forelimb and hindlimb joints (close to .333 for linear dimensions, .667 for surface areas). Monkeys are a bit more variable, but still overall cluster around isometry of joint size with body mass. Neither group shows the positive allometry of joint surface areas claimed by Swartz (80), whose observation clearly resulted from combining the large-jointed and generally large-bodied apes with the small-jointed, small-bodied monkeys, an approach that increases all regression slopes. In fact, RMA lines plotted through the combined ape-monkey samples shown in Figures 9 and 10 produce regression slopes very similar to those obtained by Swartz (her Table 4): for the humeral head, .825 (ours) versus .799 (hers); for the femoral head, .756 (ours) versus .737 (hers). Swartz also claimed that positive allometry generally characterized intraspecific joint surface scaling as well (where the problem of sample composition would not be a factor). How-

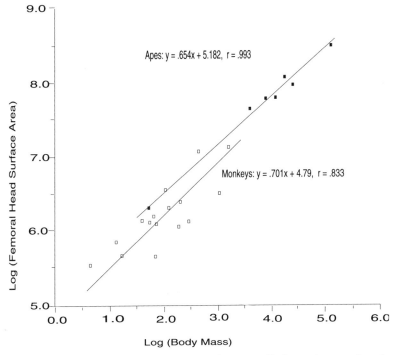

Figure 10   Swartz's (80) data for femoral head surface area and body mass in apes and monkeys, analyzed as in Figure 9. Results are similar to those shown in Figure 9 for the humeral head, although the difference between the groups is less pronounced. Also compare with Figure 8.

ever, examination of her intraspecific data (her Table 6) reveals that about half of the significant slopes calculated are below or within 1 SE above the value for isometry (.67), and almost three quarters are below or within 2 SE above (i.e. not significantly different from) isometry. This includes all of the calculated femoral head slopes and all but one of the humeral head slopes. Thus, the intraspecific results also don't argue for any general positive allometry of articular surface areas.

Figures 9 and 10 also show that gibbons, along with great apes, have larger joint-surface areas than monkeys, particularly for the humeral head. As discussed above (also see 65), the larger limb bone articulations of apes are most likely related primarily to increased joint excursion in these species relative to most nonhominoids, which in turn is probably related to more climbing/suspensory behavior among apes (e.g. 14, 20, 34). *Ateles,* the spider monkey, falls close to gibbons in Figures 9 and 10, also demonstrating relatively large joints, as predicted given its similarities to apes in locomotor mode (56). Swartz's own data (80: Figure 4a) also illustrate this clearly: Of all the species tested, the range of motion in the shoulder joint was greatest for gibbons, spider monkeys, and orangutans, with chimpanzees and gorillas also in the upper half of the range of distribution (note the downwardly misplaced duplicate data points for gibbons and spider monkeys in the original figure). Thus, contrary to Swartz's interpretations, there appears to be a clear functional association in nonhuman anthropoids among larger joints, increased joint mobility, and mode of locomotion. Her conclusion that load bearing rather than joint mobility is the "key constraint on joint surface design" (p. 450) was based on her finding of no correlation or only weak correlation between joint surface area and measured range of motion (her Table 5). However, there is no reason why absolute joint surface area should be related to range of motion, since absolute surface area will vary with body size, regardless of joint mobility (e.g. a large baboon will have larger joint surfaces than a small macaque but may have less joint mobility). When surface areas relative to body mass (our Figures 8 and 9) are compared to range of motion (80: Figure 4a), it is clear that a strong, although not perfect relationship exists between relative joint size and mobility. It is thus not necessary to invoke a special historical scenario in order to explain the large forelimb joints of living "suspensory animals"; rather, this morphology is explicable in terms of currently observable use of the limbs. This is not to say that evolutionary mosaics cannot occur as a result of changing locomotor adaptations—a possible example was given above in *Galago crassicaudatus.* But this explanation does not appear to apply to the present limb articular morphology of lesser apes.

The other potentially serious problem with Swartz's study is the use of femoral diaphyseal circumference as a body size indicator. [The same criticism applies, in part, to her study of diaphyseal curvature (81) reviewed above.] As shown above for orangutans, the relationship between body mass and shaft cross-sectional dimensions can vary depending upon locomotor mode and consequent mechanical loading of a limb. Thus, in a study of locomotor effects on articular size, use of a structural parameter that is itself influenced by locomotion to control for body size may introduce confounding biases. Additional statistical problems with this procedure have been discussed at length by Godfrey et al (28). The fact that the differences between our regressions on body mass and Swartz's regressions on femoral shaft circumference for pooled ape-monkey samples are small suggests that this parameter choice did not introduce a large systematic error; but this potential for circular reasoning should be avoided, particularly if one seeks to elucidate subtle differences in morphology and behavior.

Godfrey and coworkers (28) reached similar conclusions, by a somewhat different route, in their review and extension of Swartz's (80) study. They examined the scaling of proximal femoral and humeral articular surface areas (measured directly by latex casting or estimated from other measurements) to body mass (species averages from the literature) and femoral midshaft circumference in 73 mammalian species, including 37 primate species. They found virtual isometry (geometric similarity, slope of .67) in the scaling of joint surface areas to body mass among 15 species of carnivores and also among mammals as a whole. However, in their total primate sample they found positive allometry in both joints, more marked in the humerus [slopes of .82 (anthropoids) and .83 (anthropoids and prosimians)] than in the femur [slopes of .78 (anthropoids) and .73 (anthropoids and prosimians)]. These results are quite similar to those obtained by us and by Swartz (80) for samples that included both hominoids and nonhominoids. Godfrey et al point out that those species with the largest positive residuals from the general mammalian regression line for humeral head surface area on body mass—orangutans, gibbons, and spider monkeys—are also the species with the greatest inferred "movement potential" of the shoulder—i.e. joint mobility. The fact that these also tend to be larger-bodied species creates a spurious positively allometric scaling relationship due to "functional differences between groups of anthropoids that also happen to differ in body size" (p. 620). Although they did not carry out this particular test, examination of their graphs (their Figures 3a and b) indicates that removal of the two hominoid and four spider monkey data points would probably result in a nearly isometric relationship of joint surface area and body mass, similar to what we found here (our Figures 8–10). Their emphasis on comparisons within functionally similar groups of animals in allometric scaling studies is well taken and echoes the recommendations of Demes and coworkers (18, 19) in their studies of lorisines and indriids reviewed above.

Microstructure

Microstructural analysis is a potentially informative but currently underexplored method of studying primate limb bone adaptations. Lack of progress in this area is due in part to the difficulty of obtaining some kinds of data nondestructively. Mechanical models appropriate for microstructural analysis may also be more complex and difficult to apply than those employed in macrostructural studies—for example, the use of finite element models (FEM) in studies of trabecular architecture, which require detailed information on both geometry and material properties in the region of interest (e.g. 31).

The only relatively recent study of which we are aware that attempted to relate compact bone microstructural parameters to locomotor behavior in primates was that of Schaffler & Burr (75). They determined the percentage of osteonal bone and average osteon density of femoral midshaft sections in 20 primate species. On average, percentage of osteonal bone (i.e. percentage of the section secondarily remodeled) seemed to distinguish between several broad locomotor categories, with "arboreal quadrupeds" showing the least secondary remodeling, followed by "terrestrial quadrupeds," "suspensory" species, and bipeds (*Homo sapiens*). However, precise interpretation of these results is hampered by several limitations of the study: Almost all of the specimens were laboratory or zoo animals, a status known to cause marked changes in bone structure (e.g. see 22:236); in almost all cases only one animal per species was examined, leaving in doubt the extent of intraspecies variability and interspecies overlap; and neither age nor body size was controlled for in the analysis. This last factor is particularly important since percentage of osteonal bone increases with age in adults owing to continued bone remodeling. Also, lifespan is to some degree correlated with body size. Thus, because the largest and longest-lived species in this study were precisely those that tended to show the greatest percentage of osteonal bone (e.g. humans, chimpanzees), it is impossible to determine from these data how locomotor mode per se affected bone microstructure. For these reasons, and as noted by the original authors, this study should be viewed as exploratory rather than conclusive. It serves as a pioneering example of the kind of work that needs to be carried out if we are to better understand and utilize this aspect of skeletal adaptation. (See reference 12 for a review of earlier studies of primate cortical bone microstructure and material properties.)

The trabecular structure of primate limb bones has received even less attention. The sensitivity of trabecular architecture to applied mechanical loadings has been known for some time (e.g. see 46), and its value to inferences about mechanical function in fossil species has been demonstrated (83). However, we are aware of no comparative investigation of limb bone trabecular structure in extant or extinct nonhuman primates, apart from some earlier largely impressionistic studies (see 88, and references therein) and two brief notes regarding trabecular density differences in tarsal bones (47; 87:370, Ftn. 1). Heller (32) compared proximal femoral trabecular patterns in archaic and modern *Homo sapiens,* noting some significant differences between the two that appeared to have biomechanical implications. This is obviously an area ripe for further investigation. As noted above, trabecular and compact cortical bone structure may in some ways be analogous in terms of their responsiveness to mechanical loadings during life (unlike external articular size or shape). Thus, among other potential applications, the same issues of phylogenetic inheritance versus actual mechanical usage discussed above could be approached through comparisons of external articular size/shape with the underlying trabecular architecture of joints.

SUMMARY AND CONCLUSIONS

Recent years have seen an increase in the number of functionally oriented biomechanical studies of primate limb bone morphology. Two of the major goals of these studies were 1. to distinguish functionally significant traits through better control over phylogenetic history (i.e. morphological similarity/dissimilarity due to ancestry rather than current behavior); and 2. to elucidate the effects of size (i.e. allometry) on morphology, both directly (body mass as a mechanical load) and indirectly (behavioral modifications associated with size). The most appropriate sample composition depends upon the primary aim of the study. For example, the first goal may be addressed most effectively through comparisons between closely related species differing in locomotor/positional behavior. Conversely, the second goal may best be addressed through analysis of a set of species with similar locomotor patterns but different body sizes. It may be important in the latter type of study not to combine groups differing systematically in both body size and locomotor/positional behavior. Such studies can confound the two effects of size and behavior, leading to erroneous conclusions about both allometric scaling and the effects of behavior on morphology. The choice of which "size" parameter to use in evaluating morphological variation has been shown to be critical in several studies. The specific biomechanical relevance of such parameters should be carefully considered in evaluating these choices.

Bones exhibit several levels of structural organization—general configuration of the whole bone, macrostructure of diaphyseal cross-sections and articulations, microstructure of compact and cancellous bone—each with its own set of physiological constraints, methods of investigation, and significance for behavioral and evolutionary studies. Appreciation of the different constraints acting at each level can help to differentiate the effects of phylogenetic inheritance from actual mechanical loadings acting on the skeleton during life. While most past studies have concentrated on the general external configuration of limb bones, several recent studies have examined cross-sectional diaphyseal geometric properties and articular scaling in various primates from a biomechanical perspective. Microstructural properties of primate limb bones have received virtually no attention.

Isometry or slight positive allometry of cross-sectional and articular dimensions of primate limb bones (to body mass) have been demonstrated in several taxonomically diverse groups (although not all groups). Such scaling is consistent with general observations for mammals as a whole. Thus, despite specific adaptations such as longer limb bones, primates appear to follow the same general scaling trends in this regard as other mammals, probably owing at least in part to modifications in posture and behavior with size that have been proposed for vertebrates in general. However, these size-related modifications may have different effects on different structural properties—i.e. the effects of size may not be uniform on all aspects of morphology. For example, changes in limb posture with size probably have a greater effect on anteroposterior than on mediolateral cross-sectional dimensions of long-bone diaphyses, resulting in systematic cross-sectional shape changes as a result of change in body size. Such factors must be appreciated in any attempt to decipher the functionally significant aspects of limb bone morphological variation.

ACKNOWLEDGMENTS

Much of the present authors' work reported here was supported by research grants from the Wenner-Gren Foundation for Anthropological Research and the National Science Foundation. We thank the various museums and individuals who helped make available the specimens upon which those studies were based. We also thank Dr. Robert Anemone for providing the original photographic prints for Figure 2, and for permission to reproduce this figure here. Finally, we would like to thank Dr. Alan Walker, Dr. Erik Trinkaus, and other colleagues for stimulating discussions and suggestions relating to this work.

Literature Cited

1.Aiello, L. C. 1981. The allometry of primate body proportions. *Symp. Zool. Soc. Lond.* 48:331–58
2.Alexander, R. M. 1984. Stride length and speed for adults, children, and fossil hominids. *Am. J. Phys. Anthropol.* 63:23–27
3.Alexander, R. M. 1985. Body size and limb design in primates and other mammals. In *Size and Scaling in Primate Biology*, W. L. Jungers, pp. 337–43. New York: Plenum
4.Alexander, R. M., Jayes, A. S., Maloiy, G. M. O., Wathuta, E. M. 1979. Allometry of the limb bones of mammals from shrews (*Sorex*) to elephants (*Loxodonta*). *J. Zool. Lond.* 189:305–14
5.Anemone, R. L. 1990. The VCL hypothesis revisited: patterns of femoral morphology among quadrupedal and saltatorial prosimian primates. *Am. J. Phys. Anthropol.* 83:373–93
6.Armelagos, G. J., Carlson, D. S., VanGerven, D. P. 1982. The theoretical foundations and development of skeletal biology. In *A History of American Physical Anthropology: 1930–1980*, ed. F. Spencer, pp. 305–28. New York: Academic
7.Biewener, A. 1982. Bone strength in small mammals and bipedal birds: Do safety factors change with body size? *J. Exp. Biol.* 98:298–301

8.Biewener, A. A. 1989. Scaling body support in mammals: limb posture and muscle mechanics. *Science* 245:45–48
9.Biewener, A. A. 1990. Biomechanics of mammalian terrestrial locomotion. *Science* 250:1097–103
10.Biknevicius, A. R., Ruff, C. B. 1992. Use of biplanar radiographs for estimating cross-sectional geometric properties of mandibles. *Anat. Rec.* 232:157–63
11.Bouvier, M., Hylander, W. L. 1982. The effect of dietary consistency on morphology of the mandibular condylar cartilage in young macaques (*Macaca mulatta*). In *Factors and Mechanisms Influencing Bone Growth*, pp. 569–579 New York: Alan R. Liss, Inc.
12.Burr, D. B. 1980. The relationship among physical, geometrical and mechanical properties of bone, with a note on the properties of nonhuman primate bone. *Yrbk. Phys. Anthropol.* 23:109–46
13.Burr, D. B., Ruff, C. B., Johnson, C. 1989. Structural adaptations of the femur and humerus to arboreal and terrestrial environments in three species of macaque. *Am. J. Phys. Anthropol.* 79:357–68
14.Cant, J. G. H. 1987. Positional behavior of female Bornean orangutans (*Pongo pygmaeus*). *Am. J. Primatol.* 12:71–90
15.Currey, J. 1984. *The Mechanical Adapta-

tions of Bone. Princeton: Princeton Univ. Press

16.Daegling, D. J., Grine, F. E. 1991. Compact bone distribution and biomechanics of early hominid mandibles. *Am. J. Phys. Anthropol.* 86:321–39

17.Demes, B., Gunther, M. M. 1989. Biomechanics and allometric scaling in primate locomotion and morphology. *Folia Primatol.* 53:125–41

18.Demes, B., Jungers, W. L. 1989. Functional differentiation of long bones in lorises. *Folia Primatol.* 52:58–69

19.Demes, B., Jungers, W. L., Selpien, K. 1991. Body size, locomotion, and long bone cross-sectional geometry in indriid primates. *Am. J. Phys. Anthropol.* 86:537–47

20.Fleagle, J. G. 1976. Locomotion and posture of the Malayan siamang and implications for hominoid evolution. *Folia Primatol.* 26:245–69

21.Fleagle, J. G. 1976. Locomotor behavior and skeletal anatomy of sympatric Malaysian leaf-monkeys (*Presbytis obscura* and *Presbytis melalophos*). *Yrbk. Phys. Anthropol.* 20:440–53

22.Fleagle, J. G., Meldrum, D. J. 1988. Locomotor behavior and skeletal morphology of two sympatric Pitheciine monkeys, *Pithecia pithecia* and *Chiropotes satanas*. *Am. J. Primatol.* 16:227–49

23.Fresia, A., Ruff, C. B., Larsen, C. S. 1990. Temporal decline in bilateral asymmetry of the upper limb on the Georgia Coast. *Anthropol. Pap. Am. Mus. Nat. Hist.* 68:121–32

24.Gebo, D. L. 1988. Foot morphology and locomotor adaptation in Eocene primates. *Folia Primatol.* 50:3–41

25.Gebo, D. L. 1989. Locomotor and phylogenetic considerations in anthropoid evolution. *J. Hum. Evol.* 18:201–33

26.Gebo, D. L. 1989. Postcranial adaptation and evolution in Lorisidae. *Primates* 30:347–67

27.Gebo, D. L., Dagosto, M. 1988. Foot anatomy, climbing, and the origin of the Indriidae. *J. Hum. Evol.* 17:135–54

28.Godfrey, L., Sutherland, M., Boy, D., Gomberg, N. 1991. Scaling of limb joint surface areas in anthropoid primates and other mammals. J. Zool. Lond. 223:603–25

29.Gould, S. J. 1966. Allometry and size in ontogeny and phylogeny. *Biol. Rev.* 41:587–640

30.Hayes, W. C. 1991. Biomechanics of cortical and trabecular bone: implications for assessment of fracture risk. In *Basic Orthopaedic Biomechanics*, V. C. Mow, W. C. Hayes, pp. 93–142. New York: Raven Press

31.Hayes, W. C., Snyder, B. 1981. Toward a quantitative formulation of Wolff's Law in trabecular bone. In *Mechanical Properties of Bone*, ed. S. C. Cowin, pp. 43–68. New York: Am. Soc. Mech. Eng.

32.Heller, J. A. 1989. Stress trajectories in the proximal femur of archaic *Homo sapiens*

and modern humans. *Am. J. Phys. Anthropol.* 78:239

33.Huiskes, R. 1982. On the modelling of long bones in structural analyses. *J. Biomech.* 15:65–69

34.Hunt, K. D. 1992. Positional behavior of *Pan troglodytes* in the Mahale Mountains and Gombe Stream National Parks, Tanzania. *Am. J. Phys. Anthropol.* 87:83–105

35.Hylander, W. L. 1988. Implications of in vivo experiments for interpreting the functional significance of "robust" australopithecine jaws. In *Evolutionary History of the "Robust" Australopithecines*, ed. F. E. Grine, pp. 55–83. New York: Aldine de Gruyter

36.Jenkins, F. A., Camazine, S. M. 1977. Hip structure and locomotion in ambulatory and cursorial carnivores. *J. Zool. Lond.* 181:351–70

37.Jouffroy, F. K., Stack, M. H., Niemitz, C. 1990. *Gravity, Posture and Locomotion in Primates*. Florence: Il Sedicesimo

38.Jungers, W. L. 1984. Scaling of the hominoid locomotor skeleton with special reference to lesser apes. In *The Lesser Apes. Evolutionary and Behavioral Biology*, ed. D. J. Chivers, H. Preuschoft, W. Y. Brockelman, N. Creel, pp. 146–69. Edinburgh: Edinburgh Univ. Press

39.Jungers, W. L. 1985. Body size and scaling of limb proportions in primates. In *Size and Scaling in Primate Biology,* ed. W. L. Jungers, pp. 345–81. New York: Plenum

40.Jungers, W. L. 1988. Body size and morphometric affinities of the appendicular skeleton in *Oreopithecus bambolii* (IGF 11778). *J. Hum. Evol.* 16:445–56

41.Jungers, W. L. 1988. New estimates of body size in australopithecines. In *Evolutionary History of the "Robust" Australopithecines*, ed. F. E. Grine, pp. 115–25. New York: Aldine de Gruyter

42.Jungers, W. L. 1988. Relative joint size and hominid locomotor adaptations with implications for the evolution of hominid bipedalism. *J. Hum. Evol.* 17:247–65

43.Jungers, W. L. 1990. Problems and methods in reconstructing body size in fossil primates. In *Body Size in Mammalian Paleobiology: Estimation and Biological Implications*, ed. J. Damuth, B. J. MacFadden, pp. 103–18. Cambridge: Cambridge Univ. Press

44.Jungers, W. L. 1990. Scaling of postcranial joint size in hominoid primates. In *Gravity, Posture and Locomotion in Primates,* ed. F. K. Jouffroy, M. H. Stack, C. Niemitz, pp. 87–95. Florence: Il Sedicesimo

45.Kondo, S. 1985. *Primate Morphophysiology, Locomotor Analyses and Human Bipedalism*. Tokyo: Univ. Tokyo

46.Lanyon, L. E. 1982. Mechanical function and bone remodeling. In *Bone in Clinical Orthopaedics*, ed. G. Sumner-Smith, pp. 273–304. Philadelphia: Saunders

47.Latimer, B., Lovejoy, C. O. 1989. The calca-

432   RUFF & RUNESTAD

neus of *Australopithecus afarensis* and its implications for the evolution of bipedality. *Am. J. Phys. Anthropol.* 78:369–86

48.Lovejoy, C. O. 1988. Evolution of human walking. *Sci. Am.* 259:118–25

49.Lovejoy, C. O., Burstein, A. H., Heiple, K. G. 1976. The biomechanical analysis of bone strength: a method and its application to platycnemia. *Am. J. Phys. Anthropol.* 44:489–506

50.Lovejoy, C. O., Mensforth, R. P., Armelagos, G. J. 1982. Five decades of skeletal biology as reflected in the *American Journal of Physical Anthropology*. In *A History of American Physical Anthropology: 1930–1980*, F. Spencer, pp. 329–36. New York: Academic

51.Martin, R. 1928. *Lehrbuch der Anthropologie*. Jena: Fischer

52.Martin, R. B., Burr, D. B. 1989. *Structure, Function, and Adaptation of Compact Bone*. New York: Raven

53.McHenry, H. M. 1988. New estimates of body weight in early hominids and their significance for encephalization and megadontia in "robust" Australopithecines. In *Evolutionary History of the "Robust" Australopithecines*, ed. F. E. Grine, pp. 133–48. New York: Aldine de Gruyter

54.McHenry, H. M. 1991. Sexual dimorphism in *Australopithecus afarensis*. *J. Hum. Evol.* 20:21–32

55.McMahon, T. A. 1984. *Muscles, Reflexes, and Locomotion*. Princeton, NJ: Princeton Univ. Press

56.Mittermeier, R. A., Fleagle, J. G. 1976. The locomotor and postural repertoires of *Ateles geoffroyi* and *Colobus guereza*, and a reevaluation of the locomotor category semibrachiation. *Am. J. Phys. Anthropol.* 45:235–56

57.Nagurka, M. L., Hayes, W. C. 1980. An interactive graphics package for calculating cross-sectional properties of complex shapes. *J. Biomech.* 13:59–64

58.Oxnard, C. E., Crompton, R. H., Lieberman, S. S. 1990. *Animal Lifestyles and Anatomies: the Case of the Prosimian Primates*. Seattle: Univ. Washington Press

59.Pauwels, F. 1976. *Biomechanics of the Normal and Diseased Hip*. Berlin: Springer-Verlag

60.Poss, R. 1984. Functional adaptation of the human locomotor system to normal and abnormal loading patterns. *Calcif. Tiss. Int.* 36:151–61

61.Radin, E. L., Orr, R. B., Kelman, J. L., Paul, I. L., Rose, R. M. 1982. Effect of prolonged walking on concrete on the knees of sheep. *J. Biomech.* 15:487–92

62.Rubin, C. T. 1984. Skeletal strain and the functional significance of bone architecture. *Calcif. Tiss. Int.* 36:11–18

63.Ruff, C. B. 1987. Sexual dimorphism in human lower limb bone structure: relationship to subsistence strategy and sexual division of labor. *J. Hum. Evol.* 16:391–416

64.Ruff, C. B. 1987. Structural allometry of the femur and tibia in Hominoidea and *Macaca*. *Folia. Primatol.* 48:9–49

65.Ruff, C. B. 1988. Hindlimb articular surface allometry in Hominoidea and *Macaca*, with comparisons to diaphyseal scaling. *J. Hum. Evol.* 17:687–714

66.Ruff, C. B. 1989. New approaches to structural evolution of limb bones in primates. *Folia Primatol.* 53:142–59

67.Ruff, C. B. 1990. Body mass and hindlimb bone cross-sectional and articular dimensions in anthropoid primates. In *Body Size in Mammalian Paleobiology*, ed. J. Damuth, B. J. McFadden, ed. pp. 119–49. Cambridge: Cambridge Univ. Press

68.Ruff, C. B. 1992. Biomechanical analyses of archaeological human material. In *The Skeletal Biology of Past Peoples*, ed. S. R. Saunders, A. Katzenburg, pp. 41–62. New York: Alan R. Liss

69.Ruff, C. B., Hayes, W. C. 1983. Cross-sectional geometry of Pecos Pueblo femora and tibiae—a biomechanical investigation. I. Method and general patterns of variation. *Am. J. Phys. Anthropol.* 60:359–81

70.Ruff, C. B., Leo, F. P. 1986. Use of computed tomography in skeletal structural research. *Yrbk. Phys. Anthropol.* 29:181–95

71.Ruff, C. B., Scott, W. W., Liu, A. Y.-C. 1991. Scaling of proximal femoral dimensions to body mass in a living human sample. *Am. J. Phys. Anthropol.* 86:397–413

72.Ruff, C. B., Trinkaus, E., Walker, A., Larsen, C. S. 1992. Postcranial robusticity in *Homo*. Paper presented at Annu. Meet. Am. Assoc. Phys. Anthropol., Las Vegas

73.Ruff, C. B., Walker, A. C., Teaford, M. F. 1989. Body mass, sexual dimorphism and femoral proportions of *Proconsul* from Rusinga and Mfangano Islands, Kenya. *J. Hum. Evol.* 18:515–36

74.Runestad, J. A., Ruff, C. B., Teaford, M. F. 1992. Reconstruction of body mass and locomotor mode in primates from structural properties of limb bones. Paper presented at Annu. Meet. Am. Assoc. Phys. Anthropol., Las Vegas

75.Schaffler, M. B., Burr, D. B. 1984. Primate cortical bone microstructure: relationship to locomotion. *Am. J. Phys. Anthropol.* 65:191–97

76.Schaffler, M. B., Burr, D. B., Jungers, W. L., Ruff, C. B. 1985. Structural and mechanical indicators of limb specialization in primates. *Folia Primatol.* 45:61–75

77.Schultz, A. H. 1953. The relative thickness of the long bones and the vertebrae in primates. *Am. J. Phys. Anthropol.* 11:277–311

78.Suckling, J. A., Suckling, E. E., Walker, A. 1969. Suggested function of the vascular bundles in the limbs of *Perodicticus potto*. *Nature* 221:379–80

79.Susman, R. L., Stern, J. T. Jr., Jungers, W. L. 1984. Arboreality and bipedality in the Hadar hominids. *Folia Primatol.* 43:113–56

80.Swartz, S. M. 1989. The functional morphology of weight bearing: limb joint surface area allometry in anthropoid primates. *J. Zool. Lond.* 218:441–60

81.Swartz, S. M. 1990. Curvature of the forelimb bones of anthropoid primates: overall allometric patterns and specializations in suspensory species. *Am. J. Phys. Anthropol.* 83:477–98

82.Swartz, S. M., Bertram, J. E. A., Biewener, A. A. 1989. Telemetered in vivo strain analysis of locomotor mechanics of brachiating gibbons. *Nature* 342:270–72

83.Thomason, J. J. 1985. The relationship of trabecular architecture to inferred loading patterns in the third metacarpals of the extinct equids *Merychippus* and *Mesohippus. Paleobiol.* 11:323–35

84.Timoshenko, S. P., Gere, J. M. 1972. *Mechanics of Materials.* New York: Van Nostrand Reinhold

85.Walker, A. 1969. The locomotion of the lorises, with special reference to the potto. *E. Afr. Wildl. J.* 7:1–5

86.Ward, C. V. 1991. *Functional anatomy of the lower back and pelvis of the Miocene hominoid* Proconsul Nyanzae *from Mfangano Island, Kenya.* Phd thesis, The Johns Hopkins Univ.

87.Ward, S. C., Sussman, R. W. 1979. Correlates between locomotor anatomy and behavior in two sympatric species of lemur. *Am. J. Phys. Anthropol.* 50:575–90

88.Weidenreich, F. 1941. The extremity bones of *Sinanthropus pekinensis. Paleont. Sinica (N. S. D.)* 5:1–150

89.Woo, S. L. Y., Kuei, S. C., Amiel, D., Gomez, M. A., Hayes, W. C., et al. 1981. The effect of prolonged physical training on the properties of long bone: a study of Wolff's law. *J. Bone Joint Surg.* 63A:780–87

Annu. Rev. Anthropol. 1992. 21:435-60

IROQUOIAN ARCHAEOLOGY

Susan Bamann, Robert Kuhn, James Molnar, and Dean Snow

Department of Anthropology, University at Albany, SUNY, Albany, New York 12222
and New York State Division for Historic Preservation, Albany, New York 12238

KEYWORDS: Iroquois, settlement pattern, demography, subsistence

This selective review of Iroquois archaeology briefly summarizes the main research themes in the region today. Our inventory lists more than 1000 major Iroquoian village sites for the millennium covered by this review. The region is rich in archaeological resources relevant to research problems of both special and general interest.

"Iroquoia" identifies the province of the speakers of Northern Iroquoian languages living in northern Pennsylvania, New York, southern Ontario, and southern Quebec in the 16th and 17th centuries. These include at least nine national groups having names that are well known from documentary sources. Their aggregate population was close to 100,000 before the epidemics of the 17th century. However, several more such groups in the region did not survive into documentary history and are known only from clusters of archaeological sites. Figure 1 shows the distribution of major village clusters, providing names for those that survived into the 17th century.

The Iroquoians lived north of the southern limit of Wisconsin glaciation and south of the edge of the Canadian Shield. They did not extend eastward into what is now called New England, and to the west they enveloped only the eastern half of Lake Erie. The archaeological record shows that since at least AD 1000, Iroquoians lived in semi-sedentary villages comprised of longhouses or incipient longhouse residences. These extended family dwellings grew over time in conjunction with village growth, village nucleation, and increasing reliance on a horticultural subsistence strategy based on the major cultigens corn, beans, and squash (159, 167).

The word "Iroquois" comes from a Basque word meaning "killer people," which was later picked up by the French and given its familiar spelling (7). It later came to be applied to the Iroquois proper, the five Iroquoian nations that

0084-6570/92/1015-0435$02.00

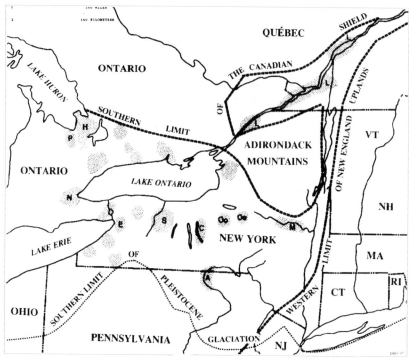

Figure 1   Northern Iroquoia from AD 900–1650. Most sites cluster in the shaded areas. Lettered clusters identify those still inhabited by nations or multinational confederacies in the 16th and 17th centuries. They were: (A) Andaste/Susquehannock, (C) Cayuga, (E) Erie, (H) Huron, (L) St. Lawrence Iroquoian, (M) Mohawk, (N) Neutral, (Oe) Oneida, (Oo) Onondaga, and (P) Petun.

made up the League of the Iroquois (Mohawk, Oneida, Onondaga, Cayuga, and Seneca). However, the Huron (actually a confederacy of five nations), Petun, Neutral, Erie, Susquehannock, St. Lawrence Iroquoians, and others unnamed were no less Iroquoian (41).

Iroquoians are well known to anthropology because of their role in colonial American history and their importance to the work of L. H. Morgan and later scholars. Because many have survived in their homeland and they retain a high cultural profile, they remain an important force in current regional affairs.

Iroquoian archaeology has been regionally active for over a century. There is some serendipity for the archaeologist in Iroquoia. The Iroquois have a prominent place in both American ethnography and modern popular consciousness. Iroquoians loom large in colonial American history, and there is undisputed historical continuity with Iroquoians still living in the region. Modern Iroquoian people have a strong interest in their own histories, and their support has been especially valuable to regional archaeologists. Urbanization and its archaeological consequences are particularly important in Ontario, where public archaeology projects have produced enormous amounts of data. Quite apart from these advantages, the region is an important laboratory for the study of processes of more general archaeological interest because of special characteristics of Iroquoian sites that are made clear below. For example, Trigger (162) has noted that systems of shifting (swidden) cultivation are of considerable general interest in anthropology, and that the Iroquoians offer one of the best known and most easily studied cases.

Iroquoianists have been returning to once settled issues in recent years. Scholars are now calling for a testing of models whose validity has long been assumed. This trend, part of a natural progression in this science, accords well with new calls for the study of variability in categories most archaeologists have assumed to be uniform. New data have forced abandonment of many comfortable old categories.

SETTLEMENT STUDIES

We consider settlement patterns at three levels of inquiry—household, village, and region (22, 157). Here we use the term "site cluster" to refer to smaller groups of related sites within a region. Iroquoian researchers have passed beyond settlement itself as an object of study, and lately have been using it as a tool or approach to answer broader questions about both prehistory and social and political organization. The settlement data available to Iroquoianists are particularly well suited to addressing these problems. Histories of Iroquoian studies including a treatment of settlement approaches can be found in Trigger (159, 160) and D. Smith (137).

Ritchie & Funk (130) compared house forms across time in the New York Iroquoian area. They excavated eight sites, generalizing their data to build a classification of habitation types and a history of changing house forms over time. Like Tuck (166), they demonstrated the variability in house morphology over the course of the Iroquoian periods. Trigger (160:69) noted that many of their excavations are too small in area to produce reliable interpretations. Snow (139:313) and Trigger (159:12) both noticed that the inferred small structures at the Sackett site were probably actually portions of longhouses. Prezzano (123) used the same plans in a computer program to support this reinterpretation.

W. Kenyon published the first Iroquoian village plan for the Miller site (81), soon followed by J. Wright's Nodwell site report (193). These, particularly Nodwell, demonstrated the data and interpretations that could be generated from large-area excavations and set the pattern for the many large-scale projects that would follow in Ontario. Grassmann (53) similarly set an early standard in New York, which Ritchie and Funk later improved. However, most of the resulting village settlement data for New York remain unpublished.

On the site-cluster level, Tuck (166) concentrated on the development of one group in a specific area, the Onondaga and their precursors. He created a sequence of relocating villages, tracing their populations from one site to another over a 300-year period, again showing what can be interpreted from a large, complete data set. Wray & Schoff (187) developed a similar sequence for the Seneca; but as with the Onondaga sequence, there is less certainty about the inferred movements of twin communities than their general acceptance by archaeologists might imply (132).

Recent Household Studies

In later household studies, Dodd (32) presented a statistical analysis of the formal attributes of 417 Ontario Iroquoian longhouses—variables such as length, width, wall post density, feature density within houses, numbers of hearths, orientation, and shapes of house ends. Dodd confirmed the expansion and later shrinkage of houses through time across the province and demonstrates the variability in house forms among contemporaneous Ontario Iroquoians. Although she could say little about lifeways inside longhouses, Dodd provided a basis for other studies of particular elements of longhouse form and function.

More specific household studies have focused on particular types of Iroquoian houses or their structural features. In general, longhouses were modular in form, composed of a series of living compartments for pairs of nuclear families. Significant variation is observed in the placement of sleeping cubicles, storage, and special work areas. Longhouses varied both in gross form and in the details. Kapches (73) has looked at cabins and anomalous small structures found in some villages. Studies of particular structural features include wall trenches (72), end storage cubicles (99), and interior sweat lodges (15, 100, 152).

Kapches (74) has also attempted to analyze longhouses in terms of active living space rather than the formal attributes of Dodd's work. She considered the areas of longhouses devoted to long-term features such as hearth areas, side wall benches, and end storage cubicles to be "variables indicative of communal social control" (74:50). Thus the amount of organized space within a house correlates with the strength of social organization of its inhabitants. This method was used to address the development of matrilineages over time and the variability in occupation of houses within single villages.

Warrick partially solved the problem of assessing site duration. He formulated a technique for determining the duration of longhouse occupation based on the amount of wall rebuilding and the average time required for posts to decay in the ground (175).

Since the early 1970s the amount of area typically uncovered on Iroquoian sites has increased dramatically. Most of this work has occurred in Ontario (34, 177). By our estimates, 82 Iroquoian sites have been excavated extensively enough to produce plots of structures or longhouses. Of these, 42 are complete community patterns, 28 are partial patterns, and a further 12 sites have had single houses excavated.

The Draper site is the largest Iroquoian village to have been fully excavated. This site has produced a new kind of Iroquoian community pattern—

that of a village that had incorporated other populations over the course of its existence. It expanded five times, its inhabitants rebuilding the palisade and adding new longhouses (42). The complete excavation of Draper has allowed a statistical appraisal of sampling techniques. Bellhouse & Finlayson (8) modeled excavations of fractions of middens, comparing results to the actual artifact counts from fully excavated middens. They found that a representative rim sherd sample from even large middens could not be gained without excavating 40–45% of the whole. For middens smaller than 100–150 m^2, sampling of any fraction does not produce a consistently acceptable standard error. As Bellhouse & Finlayson note, further studies along these lines are crucial to developing effective mitigation methods where complete salvage of sites is not possible.

In the Draper project adjacent lands were all surveyed. Using this full coverage survey, Warrick has reconstructed the 200-year sequence of population growth, village fission, and later nucleation that created the Draper site (177:239–43). Although the Draper project has already made many such contributions (42, 45, 62, 121, 173), the data from this site still have much to contribute to Iroquoian studies.

Other village sequences with nucleated sites similar to Draper's have since been discovered (9, 117, 176, 178). The Coulter site has a community plan very similar to Draper's, undergoing a number of expansions (26); but this process appears to have occurred later than at Draper (177). A model of gradual incorporation of other communities into a core village to produce Draper-type settlements has been developed by Ramsden (126). In it, a new population is incorporated slowly into the existing village. Newcomers live first in houses constructed just outside the village palisade. As they become integrated, the palisade is dismantled and rebuilt to enclose the newcomers' residences. The model conforms with archaeological data and has important implications for Iroquoian sociopolitical evolution.

Warrick (174) has presented a contextual model of Iroquoian village life and social organization. In this model, change does not result from single causes, such as warfare or economy, but rather results over the long term from such factors as climate, space conservation, village socioeconomics, government, and demography. Warrick has proposed that households were composed of corporate kin groups that did not compete with each other for wealth but rather formed economic and political coalitions. The strength of the coalitions is reflected in the arrangements of village structures. Village organization varied from houses placed haphazardly in early villages to clusters of parallel houses in later ones. In large villages, these corporate coalitions were apparently clan based, with clusters of longhouses forming clan barrios around central plazas. The model allows study of societal change over both time and space and has been successfully applied at the Fonger site. This is the most explicit societal model yet proposed to explain Iroquoian development.

Researchers have increasingly recognized the diversity within and between local areas. Many see contemporaneous communities within site clusters as a better unit of analysis than larger national constructs such as "Huron" or "Neutral" (93, 177). Basing regional studies of this kind on the Iroquoian patterns of swidden horticulture and village relocation allows a community's history to be traced from one site to another across the landscape. Bradley (12) has enlarged upon Tuck's earlier work on the Onondaga (166), and workers at the Rochester Museum continue to expand upon Wray & Schoff's (187) earlier work (188, 189). Pearce (117) provided a sequence from Glen Meyer through Neutral times for the London, Ontario area, and Warrick (177) traced a Pickering-to-Huron sequence in the Draper area. Snow (143) noted that tracking specific communities may not be possible in all Iroquoian areas. There may be too much "noise" in the data (e.g. village fission, nucleation, or long distance relocation) to allow single communities to be tracked with confidence in clusters where more than two communities were moving.

The movement of a community from one site to another is difficult to track and apparently difficult to explicate. Tuck, for example, has never satisfactorily described the ceramic micro-traditions he uses to differentiate between his sequences for two Onondaga communities. However, a tight case can be developed from diverse lines of evidence such as settlement location in relation to arable land (10, 65, 178, 184), consistent village removal distance (179), incremental change in artifact seriation (87, 94, 135, 136), and knowledge of demographic changes (177) to infer successor villages. Full-coverage survey is also needed to insure generation of reliable sequences. Such data are available for some parts of New York and southern Ontario. This kind of analysis may be more difficult to apply in the hilly uplands of New York. Furthermore, the amount of land covered in survey, sites discovered, sites tested, and the community patterns available are all greater in Ontario, allowing much more detailed interpretation than can be supported in New York.

Understanding the continuity of communities within site clusters has led to reevaluation of J. Wright's conquest hypothesis (190), designed to explain the early Ontario Iroquoian sequence. Wright concluded that Glen Meyer populations were conquered by Pickering ones around AD 1300, ending the first half of the Iroquoian sequence in southern Ontario. This hypothesis, generally accepted for many years despite its inconsistency with what is known of warfare in pre-state contexts, has now been abandoned by several younger scholars, who adduce against it the continuity in community relocations during the time of the proposed conquest (52, 117, 184). Alternative hypotheses will likely supplant the conquest scenario.

Settlement Patterns and Subsistence

Owing to accumulation of data and to an emphasis on paleoenvironmental reconstruction, the diversity of settlement patterns both temporally and spatially is now being recognized.

Early Ontario Iroquoian sites of specialized function include fishing stations identified by Fox (50) and Noble (110) for the Glen Meyer. Seasonal fishing camps are located on the north shore of Lake Erie and villages are on the sand plain to the north. A similar pattern exists in the Pickering area, with fishing camps on Lake Ontario and in the Trent waterway/Rice Lake area (115, 185).

Williamson (184) has demonstrated other special-purpose camps among the Glen Meyer Iroquoians. Small site locations within historically documented mast forests, extensive nut remains, and the unsuitability of oak forest soils for horticulture indicate the sites were used for gathering and harvesting of nuts and exploitation of the deer attracted to the mast. At the Little site, Williamson (184) found a deer surround and butchering area dating to this time. Excavations recovered 10,000 deer elements from the features of this site.

While there are horticultural villages present on the adjacent Caradoc sand plain, these appear to have housed complete communities only during winter months. At other times, families and groups traveled out to the special extractive camps leaving an unknown fraction of the population in the main village. Full reliance on villages as permanent habitation appears not to have occurred until the Middle Iroquoian period.

Special-purpose sites have been identified by several people for the Middle Ontario Iroquoian stage (33, 40, 50, 80, 138, 195). Inferred site function ranges from canoe camps to fishing stations; additional site functions remain to be identified through the analysis of subsistence remains (33:351). "Non-village" settlements for the later Huron and Neutral have also been identified; these include horticultural hamlets, fishing stations, and hunting camps (51, 62, 75, 93, 98, 109, 112, 118, 127, 183, 192).

By later times, specialized sites were used for horticultural purposes as well as exploitation of other resources. These take the form of small cabins or hamlets near fields that were used as warm weather farming shelters. Several single houses were found around the early Neutral Lawson site (116), and such dwellings are believed to have existed in other regions (127, 176). Larger habitations, classified as hamlets, were used for similar purposes in Ontario (33, 44, 62, 183). Isolated cabins and small hamlets also appear in the Mohawk sequence, but whether these are associated with all later Iroquoian peoples is still not known.

Settlement and Sociopolitical Organization

Niemczycki's (107) regional study of Seneca and Cayuga development included a modeled settlement/community round for the Owasco/Oak Hill periods. She found that large communities formed by AD 1200, but these were unstable and fissioned. For the next century or so, people continued to practice a mixed subsistence of gathering, hunting, and fishing; corn was grown as a diet supplement. No villages from this time have been found, and Niemczycki has suggested the population lived in small camps or band-size groups similar to those of the earliest Owasco pattern. Not until AD 1300–1350 did stable villages coalesce again along with major dependence upon corn horticulture.

Niemczycki saw the same pattern in Tuck's Onondaga data. While these resemble the Ontario data, notably in the broad base and diversity of subsistence strategy, the lack of villages is a major difference. This difference may be more apparent than real, as early Ontario Iroquoian villages were sometimes rebuilt two or three times. Total occupation of any location could last for 50 years (177). Too few community plans have been excavated from New York to determine whether the same pattern could exist among Owasco peoples. Ritchie's excavations, as noted above, were too small to reveal whether the Ontario pattern holds in New York. This is a major data gap to be filled in the future.

One of the most significant differences between the different Iroquoian clusters is that although they experienced the same sorts of changes in habitation type, size, and organization, these appear to occur at different times. For example, the establishment of stable 1-ha villages appears to have occurred up to 200 years earlier in Ontario than in New York. The Mohawk seem to be the last group to have attained this size. Similarly, the nucleation of communities into large settlements of 1500–2000 people began at different times in the two groups. A better understanding of the chronology of these changes will add greatly to our ability to model these processes and discuss the evolution of these Iroquoian societies.

The repetition of these patterns and others (e.g. trends in longhouse size) implies important (if still incompletely understood) social innovations. Earlier communities became unstable as populations exceeded 200, but some later communities were stable at levels approaching ten times that size. Thus internal segmentation and village councils must have been among the innovations (49, 64:129–134; 159:37). Clearly Iroquoia is an important laboratory for the study of the evolution of tribal societies.

ENVIRONMENTAL CONTEXT AND ECOLOGICAL APPROACHES

Variation within and between communities—over time and across space—has been addressed through the placement of sites and sequences in increasingly detailed environmental contexts. This has led to a greater understanding of specific ecological relationships and related issues such as village growth, nucleation and relocation. Environmental context has been approached through the analysis of subsistence data and through settlement patterns.

While reports from the 1940s through the early 1970s included information on environmental setting and exploited resources (129, 130, 166, 186), they generally did not include close examination of environmental context and human ecology. Those looking at issues such as the *in situ* hypothesis or population growth at that time only superficially considered environmental variables and horticultural subsistence (191). Beginning in the 1970s, the stronger emphasis on environment and ecology that moved through archaeology as a whole (cf 16, 24, 131, 154, 172) was likewise seen in Iroquoian archaeology. It has resulted in more detailed recovery and reporting of subsistence remains, the use of explicit and quantifiable techniques for the study of land and resource use patterning, and the incorporation of environment into systemic models of change.

The application of over-generalized models of Iroquoian adaptation and settlement patterns (cf 46) has prevented full utilization of environmental variables and ecological models in the region. This once tended to keep the focus of researchers away from intra-regional variability. At present, however, the study of variability constitutes a major research trend.

Subsistence Remains

In site reports, Tuck (166) and Ritchie & Funk (130) identified and quantified faunal and floral remains for New York Iroquois sites they investigated in the 1960s as part of their settlement pattern studies. Comparison of broad changes over time allowed them to draw some general conclusions about changes in Iroquois subsistence adaptation. Later studies that have included more rigorous recovery and analytical techniques for faunal and floral remains represent a significant advancement.

The study of the Crawford Lake area and associated Iroquoian sites (43:31) involved the sampling of pollen from lake sediments and flotation recovery of seed remains. Important results include evidence for changes in local forest succession in association with the presence of corn pollen. Stewart's (153) analysis of the faunal assemblage from the complete excavation of the Nodwell site in southern Ontario (193) also advanced the study of subsistence remains. This resulted in the identification of patterns of resource use and seasonal activity within the village (153). Prevec's identification of Neutral faunal remains has led to inter-site comparisons and interpretation of changes in resource use associated with the growing fur trade during European contact (122). Junker-Andersen's (71) detailed analysis of the faunal remains from the historic period Mohawk Jackson-Everson site allowed reconstruction of resource use and dietary patterns, including the identification of some of the earliest known examples (middle 1600s) of European domesticated species on a Mohawk site. In general, fewer detailed analyses of site assemblages have been conducted in New York than in Ontario owing to a less active field work program.

Site reports that reflect current standards regarding the recovery and analysis of subsistence remains include the multicomponent Owasco-Historic period Boland site report (55, 124, 134) and the Late Middleport period Wiacek site report (92). These reports help researchers to assess specific resource use patterns, thereby enhancing our ability to assess possible variability between sites and sequences based on local environmental context. For example, the faunal remains at Wiacek indicate a tendency towards aquatic resources and mammals from a mature forest environment (92:129–30).

Fecteau (40) has made a significant contribution to the understanding of the evolution of horticulture at a regional scale. Based on the synthesis and analysis of reported data from southern Ontario, one conclusion is that domesticates spread east and north from southwestern Ontario with significant variations in the timing of the individual spread of corn, beans, and other major cultigens. For example, although corn occurs on Princess Point complex sites by AD 600, evidence for beans, squash, and sunflower does not appear until the middle 11th century (40:167–171). Monckton's (105) study of historic Huron plant remains is a source of detailed information on Huron plant use and diet. Important results include the discovery of an unexpectedly high dependence on noncultivated plants.

Campbell & Campbell's (17) analysis of mammal remains from 27 Neutral Iroquoian sites has been used to test hypotheses about climatic cooling and its effect on Iroquoian subsistence during the Little Ice Age. The increase in representation of field-dwelling species in the assemblages, however, cannot conclusively support a specific interpretation. The amount of analyzed and reported data available for Neutral sites is impressive, but this is not the case for all areas in Iroquoia.

Environmental Context and Settlement Patterns

Some recent studies of Iroquoian settlement ecology have used environmental data to model critical problems such as length of site occupation, hierarchy in site size and function, population growth, village nucleation, and reasons for site relocations. These studies, while analytically isolating environmental variables, allow for the incorporation of environmental context and ecological relationships into larger research questions and broader multi-causal models.

Trigger (156) was one of the first to attempt to assess the role of factors such as subsistence, trade, and warfare in historic period Iroquoian settlement patterns. Based on his ethnohistorical and archaeological analyses, he attempted to determine whether agricultural intensification was the cause or an effect of the Iroquoian warfare complex. A feature of this very preliminary study of ecology and settlement patterns was the focus on variability among four Iroquoian groups (Five Nations, Neutral, St. Lawrence, and Huron). By contrast, current research is focused on the variability within these groups. Trigger admits to his very general treatment of environmental variables, noting that he did not plot sites in relation to physical, climatic, or soil features. Heidenreich's (64) detailed study of the geography of historic Huron settlement patterns represents one of the first systematic analyses of these variables in relation to a reconstructed settlement-subsistence system, although the study is still broad and generalizing in its sub-regional scale of analysis.

Several researchers have focused on the study of soil productivity in relation to settlement pattern change. Sykes (155) examined the soils associated with Late Ontario Iroquoian sites identified as representing post-AD 1400 Huron village movements. Catchment analysis was employed to quantify the potential length of site occupation for each of eleven village sites. The results indicated that soils are not the most limiting factor in settlement patterns and that other variables such as firewood depletion, refuse accumulation, chronic warfare, and game scarcity should be considered (155). Studies with similar results include those of Bond (9) and Vandrei (171). Starna et al (151) have emphasized the additional limiting variable of insect infestation of horticultural fields. Warrick & Molnar's (178) analysis of a local site sequence in southern Ontario shows that villages located themselves adjacent to areas of tree growth suitable for village construction and firewood procurement. This entailed location next to regenerating fields from previous catchments or natural secondary growth and cedar swamps. Consistency of site relocation distance is used for the inference that catchment size was consistent and was conditioned by factors such as tolerable walking distance to fields.

Researchers have taken a number of other environmentally based approaches to settlement pattern issues. Examples include the exploration of prevailing winter winds as a variable determining longhouse orientation (32, 111) and the study of climatic stress on subsistence as an important factor in responses such as relocation, migration, and changing village size/density (113, 196). Some (10, 92) have used patterns of ecological succession as inferred from historic records to attempt reconstruction of horticultural field systems.

Settlement Type Diversity

A result of putting sites more explicitly into environmental contexts has been the recognition of variability in site function within sequences. The generalized notion of Iroquoian village has been replaced by a spectrum of site types including hamlets and camps. Such sites would have been used for horticultural production, fishing, hunting, and other forms of resource extraction. For example, Williamson (184, 185) has discussed variability detected through microenvironmental analysis of sites from the Glen Meyer phase. Using soil productivity and associated forest species in site catchments he was able to differentiate villages from hamlets and to suggest associated subsistence strategies (184, 185). A number of other studies have shown variation in settlement type (see the previous section).

Recently, several studies have used geographic information systems (GIS) to expand the archaeologists' ability to analyze site location and mobility patterns in relation to environmental parameters (1, 60, 68, 197). For example, Hunt (68) created a GIS data base for the analysis of site locations, soils, and climatic parameters in western New York State. He concluded that village relocation constituted an adaptive strategy intended to optimize productivity of swidden horticulture in the face of a deteriorating climate.

Environmentally Based Models of Change

An attempt by Campbell & Campbell (17) to relate changes in the faunal assemblage to increased growing season hazards resulting from the Little Ice Age is a good example of the development of specific ecological models that can lead to more general models of Iroquoian culture change. Recently a number of researchers have suggested the relevance of such external pressures as climate change in modeling the development of Iroquoian societies (68, 113, 145, 162:125, 174:135, 177:113–115; 196).

Wykoff (196) has made a case for incorporating a model of Iroquoian culture change based on the effects of global climatic events in the 13th century. The effects of the Medieval Maximum of solar activity on climate is proposed to have led to a concentration of Iroquoian peoples on the environmentally favorable Allegheny Plateau. This suggests an important link to the intensification of horticulture and village life. The study provides some of the theoretical and ecological background necessary for more detailed archaeological testing of areas such as the Allegheny Plateau. Snow (145) has pursued this issue and incorporated climate change into a larger model of Iroquoian migrations. His "incursion hypothesis" addresses Iroquoian origins prior to the traditional tribal territories and should lead to the testing of specific hypotheses about archaeological discontinuities prior to the Owasco period and about the southern periphery of Iroquoia.

O'Shea's (113) work on the use of wild resources among horticulturalists provides a theoretical framework for understanding the effects of environmental variability. Using the Huron as an example, he discusses the importance of risk-buffering strategies as a means for coping with uncertainty or seasonal variability in horticultural productivity. O'Shea notes that variability for the Huron might have been brought on by occupation of an area considered marginal for consistent growing seasons. It also might be brought about by increased annual fluctuations in climate usually associated with climatic deterioration, as in the case made by Wykoff (196) for other areas within the region. In the Huron case outlined by O'Shea, a marginal environment led to the need for a risk-buffering strategy. Trade between Huron and Algonquin neighbors involving maize for meat and fish was the primary strategy involved. This analysis not only puts such interaction into an ecological theoretical perspective on culture change, but also emphasizes the need to put Iroquoians into a larger sphere of relations outside Iroquoia.

DEMOGRAPHIC PROBLEMS

Iroquoia is a region in which demographic issues can be approached through both archaeology and biological anthropology. In each case, favorable conditions exist here that generally do not characterize other regions. The significance of demographic variables has been highlighted in recent years by the controversy over hypothesized 16th century epidemics. Dobyns (29–31) has taken the extreme view that many lethal but unrecorded epidemics swept across North America in the 16th century, such that any census data from the end of that century or the beginning of the next already reflected reduced populations. This allowed him to reconstruct population levels for AD 1500 larger than any other scholarly estimates.

Ubelaker (168, 169) offers estimates near the opposite extreme for North America. His estimates assume that few serious undetected epidemics occurred in the 16th century and that the severe epidemics during and after the 17th century were delayed in most regions. The difference between Ubelaker's and Dobyns's estimates is nearly an order of magnitude. Milner (104) is in agreement with Ubelaker, but Ramenofsky (125) sides with Dobyns. Snow & Lanphear (146, 147) have argued that documentary evidence from Iroquoia supports conclusions closer to those of Ubelaker than to those of Dobyns. Snow's Mohawk work and Warrick's (177) work in Ontario support this position archaeologically.

Archaeological Approaches

Archaeological approaches to demography have usually fallen into three categories: estimates based on (a) environmental carrying capacities, (b) inventoried burial populations, and (c) habitation areas. Estimates based on carrying capacities tend to be unrealistically high because they do not account adequately for short-term fluctuations (54, 141). Asch (6) was more successful with the second kind of approach, but the necessary 100% sample of burial data is not available for most periods and most regions. The third approach works well in Iroquoia for reasons unique to this region.

Iroquoian village sites tend to be compact, single-component sites of short longevity. Occupations of two or three decades are usually not confused by either earlier or later occupations on the same locations. Further, they tend to have been located on or near prime agricultural land, such that the discovery rate has been high in New York, Quebec, and Ontario. Finally, the longhouse, although somewhat variable over time and space, was a standardized residential structure. Counts of inhabitants can often be derived from archaeological floor plans with an accuracy of ±5% (148, 149).

This latter property of Iroquois settlements has been used to derive village population sizes for archaeological sites. Naroll (106) proposed using aggregate house areas to derive population. Only a few Iroquoian sites have been excavated completely enough to allow this approach. However, the uniform, compact, and bounded nature of Iroquoian sites does allow derivation of population from total village area. Warrick (177) has approached the problem by counting hearths per hectare of village area and multiplying hearths times a standard number of individuals. Snow (142) has used plans from completely excavated villages in combination with documentary data on the numbers of people per hearth and/or longhouse compartment to derive square meters of village area per person. The results of these two approaches are remarkably consistent. Iroquoian villages tended to provide about 20 m^2 per person except in cases of the very compact and often defensively sited villages of the 16th and earliest 17th centuries. In these cases the area per person dropped to as low as 12 m^2.

LeBlanc (91) and Wiessner (182) argued that the population-calculation technique described above is unreliable when applied broadly. However, within Iroquoia we appear to have the means in hand to derive populations that are valid for at least one small region for a few centuries. Warrick's results have led him to conclude that Ontario Iroquoian populations grew dramatically during the 14th and 15th centuries. They leveled off, at least in Huronia, in the 16th century, perhaps as a result of the rise of density-dependent diseases such as tuberculosis. Snow's results have led him to conclude that the Mohawk population grew rapidly in the century leading up to 1634, when the first serious exogenous smallpox epidemic struck. The growth was so rapid that it must have involved both endogenous growth and immigration. The latter factor helps to account for the disappearance of Iroquoian settlements from Jefferson County, New York, and Bradford County, Pennsylvania in the same era, but it also points out the problems involved in paleodemography. Any analysis must be set in regional context and take account of migration.

Throughout Iroquoia, sociopolitical innovations appear to have allowed local populations to rise to new critical sizes approaching 2000 in the 15th and 16th centuries. The larger populations may have been stabilized in part by density-dependent diseases such as tuberculosis. Regional limits to growth were imposed by deer and wapiti, which were critical resources because hides were needed for clothing (150).

Biological Approaches

Large ossuaries have been found in the northwestern part of Iroquoia. Susan Pfeiffer (120) has derived details of population structure from ossuaries, and has established the importance of tuberculosis as a Precolumbian disease in Iroquoian communities. Melbye (103) has followed Anderson (3) in deriving population structure from remains in the Fairty ossuary. Workers at the Rochester Museum have used burials from non-ossuary cemeteries in western New York to detect the incursion of Ontario Iroquoians (108) and to assess the movement of women between communities (133).

J. Wright & Anderson (194) attempted to assess the continuity or discontinuity between Middle Woodland populations and Late Woodland Iroquoian populations in southern Ontario. Unfortunately, their samples were too small, and appropriate statistical procedures had not yet been developed when they carried out their work. Archaeologists should use the current call for reburial in both the United States and Canada as an occasion to carry out this work promptly. Adequate skeletal populations and up-to-date statistical tests now exist that would allow us to determine whether known Iroquoian populations derived largely in situ from an earlier Point Peninsula population or largely intruded upon and displaced the earlier population.

The total number of Iroquoians around AD 1600 was probably about 95,000 (144). This estimate bears significantly on the current debate about the timing of the first arrival of Iroquoians in what are now New York and Ontario. Clermont (23) has argued that the growth rate of Iroquoians was too slow and the historic population too high for them to have grown to that size from a small founding population in a matter of six or seven centuries. The low natality of Iroquoian populations is well known (39). However, it was not so low as to preclude growth to over 95,000 from a founding population of only 500 in less then seven centuries (144). Thus so far none of the evidence from biological anthropology helps to force a choice between the in situ hypothesis and the hypothesis that Iroquoians arrived in the region after AD 900. Clearly, however, biological anthropology could be used to address this issue, which we hope will receive prompt attention.

Implications of Demography

Dincauze & Hasenstab (28) have examined the possibility that the intrusion of Iroquoians into the region was an indirect consequence of expansion at the core of Mississippian development around Cahokia. The hypothesis necessarily assumes that the intrusion occurred no earlier than the period AD 1150–1300, when Cahokia was at or nearing its peak. While the hypothesis is attractive as a derivative of core-periphery theory, most Iroquoian specialists are convinced that the Iroquoian lineage goes back to at least AD 900 in Ontario and New York.

Hasenstab has proposed a second alternative hypothesis, called the "predatory expansion hypothesis" (60:60–62). This hypothesis assumes no chain reaction from a Mississippian heartland, but instead rests on the simpler assumption that Iroquoians adapted so well to the region that they supplanted the previous occupants. Unfortunately, like the core-periphery one, this hypothesis is encumbered with the assumption that the expansion took place around AD 1400 owing to the climatic stresses of that time. But AD 900 was a time of climatic opportunity, not stress, an ecological setting that is more consistent with an adaptive expansion, and that is a more likely date for intrusion on archaeological grounds (60:170).

Argument from archaeological data led Snow to conclude that Iroquoians radiated into the region from central Pennsylvania around AD 900 (145). Their adaptive expansion was made possible by maize horticulture, compact matrilocal residence, and larger and more permanent villages than could be maintained by the people they displaced. This remains a testable alternative hypothesis to the in situ hypothesis, which has survived as a largely untested controlling model since its introduction by MacNeish (101) 40 years ago.

Early Iroquoian villages were smaller than later ones. Villages of no more than 200 inhabitants were typical (130, 177). Villages of the 16th century were much larger, accommodating up to 2000 inhabitants (42, 148, 177). The shift suggests that the threshold of political instability rose dramatically in a few centuries. Moreover, the villages that grew to hold as many as 2000 people were at the same time more compact than previous ones, and individual longhouses were much longer. Although some reports of very long longhouses may have resulted from the failure to detect the divisions between tandem longhouses during excavation, there is convincing evidence that at least some over 100 m long existed (166:79). The social and political implications of this profound demographic change are only beginning to be explored.

Many Iroquoianists judge that continued progress in demographic studies will depend upon careful reconstruction of village site sequences in all areas of Iroquoia. The sequences developed by Wray & Schoff (187), Tuck (166), Bradley (12), and Warrick & Molnar (178) are often cited as models that should be emulated elsewhere in the region. However, Niemczycki (107) has shown that even the relatively uncomplicated Seneca sequence may have been oversimplified and that the complex reality may be beyond our grasp. More complicated sequences like those presented by the Huron and Mohawk cases in the 16th and 17th centuries may well defy full resolution. Nevertheless, Pearce's (117) work shows that even when the details remain obscure, we can take a societal perspective with respect to large bodies of archaeological data that represent many communities interacting over time and space.

The view is widely held that we should exploit unique archaeological opportunities in Iroquoia in order better to understand early interaction between Iroquoian groups and later incorporation of interaction with Europeans into this system. The issue is important to our understanding both of the evolution of the League of the Iroquois and of 17th-century population decline. There are few regions where issues like these can be perceived with such clarity.

INTERACTION PATTERNS

The reconstruction of past interaction patterns and the examination of the role that trade and exchange, population movement, and social and political communication played in shaping Iroquoian cultural development are growing areas of interest in Iroquoian archaeology. The substantive contributions to the reconstruction of Iroquoian prehistory and culture process made over the last decade result directly from advances in method and theory, and from paradigmatic shifts in the discipline.

In the 1950s and 1960s interaction patterns did not receive much attention, as Iroquoian archaeologists embraced the in situ hypothesis (101) and internal explanations of Iroquoian cultural development (165). These trends in Iroquoian research were consistent with the general rejection of the causal role of external forces in favor of processual explanations that emphasized internal culture change.

In the 1970s a renewed interest in interaction patterns led a number of scholars to study the distribution of ceramic styles as indicators of information transfer and communication among native groups. Methodologically the roots of this work can be traced back to Deetz (27), Whallon (181), and Longacre (95), who used stylistic information to reconstruct descent systems and other aspects of internal social organization. Their techniques were later applied to the study of interaction patterns among regional populations.

In Iroquois archaeology, Engelbrecht's (35–38) may be the most notable among the many studies (14, 66, 102, 180) conducted using this approach. His analysis of the similarities among ceramic assemblages of tribal groupings in New York provided information on culture-historical trends and native interaction patterns, but it failed to detect evidence of the formation of the League of the Iroquois. While Engelbrecht's systematic analysis of a large data base, his emphasis on working with ceramic styles at the attribute level, and his reconstruction of protohistoric and early historic period interaction patterns are important contributions, the most lasting impression from such work is of the inherent limitations of the approach. Are the ephemeral characteristics of social and political interactions reflected in ceramic styles? Despite all the research conducted, the answer to this question remains inconclusive. Do exotic attributes and motifs represent trade and exchange of pottery, the transmission of ideas as a result of peaceful interaction, the adoption of captives as a result of warfare, or some other factor? Despite sophisticated data collection and analysis, comparisons of ceramic styles do not produce mutually exclusive and testable hypotheses. Perhaps the best testimony to the limitations of this line of study is the fact that we still do not know the significance of the large quantities of Huron and St. Lawrence Iroquoian pottery on many sites in southeast Ontario.

Advances in method and theory will help solve some of these problems. A middle range theory for ceramic analysis could contribute most to defining mutually exclusive material culture correlates for different categories of interaction. Much work was done in this field during the 1980s (4, 5, 128, 170), but little of it is directly applicable to Iroquoia, where pottery making does not appear to have been a craft specialization. Iroquoianists need to apply midrange studies of tribal interaction patterns themselves, in order to solve critical problems of Iroquoian archaeology. This is true not only for ceramic analyses, but for other approaches to the reconstruction and understanding of past interaction patterns as well. We hope to see substantive contributions in this area in the future.

In contrast, the 1980s did witness progress in the application of new techniques to the study of interaction, trade, and exchange. Contributions were made in the field of archaeometry, which holds the potential not only to resolve old issues regarding the meaning of exotic styles of ceramics on

Iroquoian sites, but also to address a host of new research questions about past interaction patterns, at one time largely beyond the grasp of archaeologists. Led by Trigger, a group of researchers in southeast Ontario were among the first to apply archaeometric techniques to the study of Iroquoian ceramics in an attempt to identify transported pottery, not by style, but by ceramic characterizations (163). They also explored the correlation between exotic styles and ceramic composition. This approach is significant because it allows archaeologists to reason about interaction and exchange using two independent lines of evidence.

This work served as a catalyst for further research (21, 25, 83–86, 164). While Trigger's initial effort helped to elucidate the patterns of interaction underlying stylistic distributions in southeast Ontario and the St. Lawrence Valley, more recent research has used archaeometric techniques to study interaction patterns with Algonkian groups on the periphery of Iroquoia (21, 25, 84, 164). Work on this neglected topic may yield insights into acculturation between groups of differing subsistence and sociopolitical organization. Finally, Kuhn (83) has employed trace element analysis to identify ceramic trade pipes in Iroquoian assemblages and trace changing interaction patterns between New York and southeast Ontario over time. The results of this work appear to suggest that the prehistoric period was characterized by a much higher degree of both local and long-distance interaction than has traditionally been assumed. The implications are significant because in this period Iroquoian communities were on the threshold of tribalization.

The application of archaeometric techniques to the study of past interaction patterns has not been limited to compositional analyses of ceramics. Much good work has been done using a variety of techniques to begin to characterize lithic sources as well. As a result of the work of Luedtke (96, 97), Lavin (90), Janusas (69), Kuhn & Lanford (88), Jarvis (70), and others (61, 114), archaeologists are beginning to establish a baseline for the characterization of a wide variety of lithic materials in the northeast. Important contributions to the study of the prehistoric procurement, transport, and exchange of lithics can be expected in the future, if only because lithic analyses have been so widely neglected in Iroquoian archaeology. As with ceramic characterization studies, there is much more to be done in this field.

Elemental analysis has also been applied to distinguish native copper from European varieties of copper and brass on those early protohistoric Iroquoian components so critical to our understanding of early European contacts and trade (11, 13, 48, 59). This should become standard procedure for archaeologists reporting on site assemblages with metal materials from that period. Such research is just one component of the ongoing interest in interaction and exchange patterns during the protohistoric period. Much of this work has focused on the occurrence, distribution, and meaning of shell (119), a trade material that can be identified without the need of rigorous elemental or compositional techniques.

Bradley (11–13) was among the first to focus attention on the southerly exchange network that brought marine shell, finished shell artifacts, and eventually European goods from the Atlantic coast, up the Susquehanna, and into all of Iroquoia. Although at times overstating the case (161), his work has clearly influenced the discipline, which had traditionally focused on the St. Lawrence corridor as the principal entry point for the nascent European trade. The results of field work carried out within the last decade have clearly dated the origins of the trade in marine shell back to the prehistoric period (12), as much as 50 years before European goods began passing through the same trade network. The results of this work have given Iroquoianists reason to pause and rethink their ideas regarding the sources, nature, and impact of the European trade on existing native interaction and exchange networks.

It is disappointing that the program of large-scale, systematic analysis of marine shell beads in Iroquoia begun by Lynn Ceci in the middle 1980s did not come to full fruition, owing to her untimely death. Her contributions to the field were significant (18–20), and her presence is missed. Ceci and her peers in shell bead research moved the focus of Iroquoian studies away from Iroquoian-European trade and toward intra-Iroquoian interaction patterns during the period of early European influences. This subtle reorientation has revitalized protohistoric and historic period Iroquoian research and opened new avenues of study that have yet to be fully explored.

European glass beads also have much to contribute to the study of trade networks. A standard typology for trade beads was developed by Kidd & Kidd (82), which has promoted much comparative work. Researchers such as Fitzgerald, I. Kenyon, and T. Kenyon have worked through the last decade to correlate the changes in bead assemblages with the establishment of European trading networks among the Iroquoians (47, 76, 77, 79). These observations have in turn prompted reappraisal of the cultural processes that have been dated using bead seriation (78, 132). Much more remains to be done in this vein.

Discussion of recent contributions to the field of trade and exchange during the period of early European contacts would not be complete without recognizing the work of Hamell (56–58), whose efforts over the past ten years have also had an important impact on the interpretation of early Iroquoian-European trade. Applying the approach of comparative ethnology, Hamell has successfully argued for the primacy of an emically based understanding of the symbolic role that early trade goods played in Iroquoian ideology and native belief systems. While the postprocessual movement in the discipline provided an atmosphere ripe for new semiotic interpretations of the archaeological record, Hamell's work avoided much of the excess that characterized structuralist archaeology in the 1980s. His work has had a strong and positive influence on the discipline, as evidenced by the incorporation of his theories into recent syntheses of Iroquoian culture process on the protohistoric horizon (12, 160). Whether or not entrenched cultural-materialist interpretations of other aspects of Iroquoian culture process will be reexamined as a result of these trends remains to be seen.

Despite many important contributions to the study of interaction patterns in Iroquoian archaeology, much remains to be done. A greater application of archaeometric techniques is needed in the Northeast, which still lags behind other regions. Iroquoianists need to adopt mid-range approaches to modeling past interaction patterns and their material correlates, rather than depending too heavily on the ethnohistoric literature. Continued progress in these areas could broaden our interpretation and understanding of Iroquoian prehistory, particularly regarding past interaction patterns.

Certain general theoretical changes over the past decade have been positive. Cultural materialist explanations of Iroquoian-European trade during the earliest periods of culture contact have largely been abandoned, yet the implications of semiotic theory for other aspects of prehistoric interaction systems, as well as for Iroquoian culture process in general, remain to be fully explored.

CONCLUSIONS

In part we have written this review to provide scholars working in Iroquoia with an assessment of the current state of our collective efforts, but we have also been motivated to inform other archaeologists about the potential of the region for addressing problems of general interest. Demography, exchange, settlement systems, subsistence, political development, European contact, adaptation, and related topics are all approachable in Iroquoian archaeology, and researchers in this international region are among the most active anywhere.

ACKNOWLEDGMENTS

In preparing this article we solicited wisdom from 80 colleagues, senior and junior. Thirty-four responded in detail, giving us valuable ideas and perspectives. They are Alan Beauregard, James Bradley, Hetty Jo Brumbach, Norman Clermont, Dena Dincauze, William Engelbrecht, William Fenton, Stuart Fiedel, William Fox, Robert Funk, Alexander von Gernet, John Hammer, Robert Hasenstab, Charles Hayes, Eleazer Hunt, Susan Jamieson, Mima Kapches, Rob MacDonald, Richard MacNeish, Ellis McDowell-Loudan, James Pendergast, Susan Prezzano, Peter Ramsden, Lorraine Saunders, Martha Sempowski, Michael Spence, William Starna, David Stothers, Lynne Sullivan, Peter Timmins, Bruce Trigger, Ron Williamson, James Wright, and William Wykoff. They have our thanks, our regrets that so much could not be included in a brief paper, and our absolution from error.

Literature Cited

1. Allen, K. M. S. 1990. Modelling early historic trade in the eastern Great Lakes Region using geographical information systems. See Ref. 2, pp. 319–29

2. Allen, K. M. S., Green, S. W., Zubrow, E. B. W., eds. 1990. *Interpreting Space: GIS and Archaeology*. London: Taylor & Francis

3. Anderson, J. E. 1963. The people of Fairty. *Natl. Mus. Can. Bull.* 193:28–129
4. Arnold, D. E. 1981. A model for the identification of non-local ceramic distribution: a view from the present. See Ref. 67, pp. 31–44
5. Arnold, D. E. 1985. *Ceramic Theory and Cultural Process.* Cambridge: Cambridge Univ. Press
6. Asch, D. 1976. *The Middle Woodland Population of the Lower Illinois Valley.* Northwest. Archaeol. Prog. Sci. Pap. 1
7. Bakker, P. 1990. A Basque etymology for the word "Iroquois." *Man in the NE* 40:89–93
8. Bellhouse, D. R., Finlayson, W. D. 1979. An empirical study of probability sampling designs. *Can. J. Archaeol.* 3:105–23
9. Bond, S. C. 1985. The relationship between soils and settlement patterns. In *The Mohawk Valley Project: 1982 Field Season Report*, ed. D. R. Snow, pp. 17–40. Albany: SUNY, Inst. NE Anthropol.
10. Bowman, I. 1979. The Draper site: Historical accounts of vegetation in Pickering and Markham townships with special reference to the significance of a large, even-aged stand adjacent to the site. See Ref. 62, pp. 47–58
11. Bradley, J. W. 1979. *The Onondaga Iroquois: 1500–1655, A study of acculturative change and its consequences.* PhD thesis, Syracuse Univ. Ann Arbor: Univ. Microfilms
12. Bradley, J. W. 1987. *Evolution of the Onondaga Iroquois: Accommodating Change 1500–1655.* Syracuse: Syracuse Univ. Press
13. Bradley, J. W. 1987. Native exchange and European trade: Cross-cultural dynamics in the sixteenth century. *Man in the NE* 33:31–46
14. Brumbach, H. J. 1975. "Iroquoian" ceramics in "Algonkian" territory. *Man in the NE* 10:17–28
15. Bursey, J. A. 1989. Further comments on the postmould clusters = sweat lodges dialogue. *Archaeol. Notes* 89(4):20–28
16. Butzer, K. W. 1971. *Environment and Archaeology.* Chicago: Aldine. 2nd ed.
17. Campbell, C., Campbell, I. D. 1989. The little ice age and Neutral faunal assemblages. *Ont. Archaeol.* 49:13–33
18. Ceci, L. 1977. *The effect of European contact and trade on the settlement pattern of Indians of Coastal New York, 1524–1665: The archaeological and documentary evidence.* PhD thesis. City Univ. New York
19. Ceci, L. 1982. The value of wampum among the New York Iroquois. *J. Anthropol. Res.* 38:97–107
20. Ceci, L. 1985. *Shell bead evidence from archaeological sites in the Seneca Region of New York State.* Presented at Annu. Conf. Iroquois Res., Rensselaerville, NY
21. Chapdelaine, C., Kennedy, G. G. 1990. The origin of the Iroquoian rim sherd from Red Bay. *Man in the NE* 40:41–43
22. Clarke, D. L. 1977. Spatial information in archaeology. In *Spatial Archaeology*, ed. D. L. Clarke, pp. 1–32. New York: Academic
23. Clermont, N. 1990. Why did the Saint Lawrence Iroquoians become horticulturalists? *Man in the NE* 40:75–79
24. Coe, M. D., Flannery, K. V. 1964. Microenvironments and Mesoamerican prehistory. *Science* 143:650–54
25. Crepeau, R. R., Kennedy, G. G. 1990. Neutron activation analysis of St. Lawrence Iroquoian pottery. *Man in the NE* 40:65–74
26. Damkjar, E. R. 1990. *The Coulter Site and Late Iroquoian Coalescence in the Upper Trent Valley.* Occas. Pap. NE Archaeol. 2. Dundas, Ont: Copetown Press
27. Deetz, J. 1965. *The Dynamics of Stylistic Change in Arikara Ceramics.* Urbana: Univ. Ill. Ser. Anthropol. 4
28. Dincauze, D. F., Hasenstab, R. J. 1989. Explaining the Iroquois: Tribalization on a prehistoric periphery. In *Centre and Periphery: Comparative Studies in Archaeology,* ed. T. C. Champion, pp. 67–87. London: Unwin Hyman
29. Dobyns, H. F. 1966. Estimating aboriginal American population: an appraisal of techniques with a new hemispheric estimate. *Curr. Anthropol.* 7:395–416
30. Dobyns, H. F. 1983. *Their Number Become Thinned: Native American Population Dynamics in Eastern North America.* Knoxville: Univ. Tenn. Press
31. Dobyns, H. F. 1989. More methodological perspectives on historical demography. *Ethnohistory* 36:285–99
32. Dodd, C. F. 1984. Ontario Iroquois tradition longhouses. *Archaeol. Survey Can. Mercury Ser.* 124:181–437
33. Dodd, C. F., Poulton, D., Lennox, P. A., Smith, D. G., Warrick, G. 1990. The Middle Ontario Iroquoian stage. See Ref. 34, pp. 321–60
34. Ellis, C. J., Ferris, N., eds. 1990. *The Archaeology of Southern Ontario to A.D. 1650.* Occas. Publ. London Chapter, Ont. Archaeol. Soc. 5
35. Engelbrecht, W. 1971. *A stylistic analysis of New York Iroquois pottery.* PhD thesis. Univ. Mich., Ann Arbor. Univ. Miocrofilms
36. Engelbrecht, W. 1972. The reflection of patterned behavior in Iroquois pottery decoration. *Penn. Archaeol.* 42:1–15
37. Engelbrecht, W. 1974. The Iroquois: patterning at the tribal level. *World Archaeol.* 6:52–65
38. Engelbrecht, W. 1979. Ceramic patterning between New York Iroquois sites. In *Spatial Organization of Culture,* ed. I. Hodder, pp. 141–52. London: Duckworth
39. Engelbrecht, W. 1987. Factors maintaining low population density among the prehistoric New York Iroquois. *Am. Antiq.* 52:13–27
40. Fecteau, R. D. 1985. *The introduction and*

diffusion of cultivated plants in southern Ontario. Master's thesis. York Univ., Ontario

41. Fenton, W. N. 1978. Northern Iroquoian culture patterns. See Ref. 158, pp. 296–321

42. Finlayson, W. 1985. *The 1975 and 1978 Rescue Excavations at the Draper Site: Introduction and Settlement Patterns. Archaeol. Survey Can. Mercury Ser.* 130

43. Finlayson, W. D., Byrne, R. 1975. Investigations of Iroquoian settlement patterns at Crawford Lake, Ontario—A preliminary report. *Ont. Archaeol.* 25:31–36

44. Finlayson, W. D., Pearce, R. J. 1989. Iroquoian communities in southern Ontario. In *Households and Communities,* ed. S. MacEacheran, D. Archer, R. Gavin, pp. 301–6. Alberta: Univ. Calgary Archaeol. Assoc.

45. Finalyson, W. D., Pihl, R. H. 1980. Some implications for the attribute analysis of rim sherds from the Draper site, Pickering Ontario. In *Proceedings of the 1979 Iroquois Pottery Conference,* ed. C. F. Hayes, pp. 113–31. Rochester Mus. Sci. Cent. Res. Rec. 13

46. Fitting, J. E. 1972. The Huron as ecotype: the limits of maximization on a western Great Lakes society. *Anthropologica* 14:3–18

47. Fitzgerald, W. R. 1983. Further comments on the Neutral glass bead sequence. *Archaeol. Notes* 83(1):31–46

48. Fitzgerald, W. R., Ramsden, P. G. 1988. Copper based metal testing as an aid to understanding early European-Amerindian interaction: scratching the surface. *Can. J. Archaeol.* 12:153–62

49. Forge, A. 1972. Normative factors in the settlement size of neolithic cultivators. In *Man, Settlement, and Urbanism,* ed. P. J. Ucko, R. Tringham, G. W. Dimbledy, pp. 363–76. London: Duckworth

50. Fox, W. A. 1976. The central north shore. In *The Late Prehistory of the Lake Erie Drainage Basin,* ed. D. Brose, pp. 162–92. Cleveland: The Cleveland Mus. Nat. Hist.

51. Fox, W. A. 1986. The culture history of Long Point: an interim report. In *Studies in Southwestern Ontario Archaeology,* ed. W. A. Fox, pp. 18–24. Occas. Publ. London Chapter, Ont. Archaeol. Soc. 1

52. Fox, W. A. 1990. The Middle Woodland to Late Woodland transition. See Ref. 34, pp. 171–88

53. Grassmann, T. 1952. The Mohawk-Caughnawaga excavation. *Penn. Archaeol.* 22:33–36

54. Grayson, D. K. 1974. The Riverhaven No. 2 vertebrate fauna: comments on methods in faunal analysis and on aspects of the subsistence potential of prehistoric New York. *Man in the NE* 8:23–39

55. Gremillion, K. J. 1990. Plant remains: 1984 season. See Ref. 124, pp. 135–41

56. Hamell, G. 1983. Trading in metaphors: the magic of beads. See Ref. 63, pp. 5–28

57. Hamell, G. 1984. Metaphor, myth and contemporary Iroquois history. *The Iroquoian: Bull. Lewis Henry Morgan Chapter NY State Archaeol. Assoc.* 9:24–31

58. Hamell, G. 1987. Mythical realities and European contact in the Northeast during the sixteenth and seventeenth centuries. *Man in the NE* 33:63–87

59. Hancock, R., Pavlish, L., Farquar, R., Salloum, R., Fox, W., et al. 1991. Distinguishing European trade copper and north eastern North American native copper. *Archaeometry* 33:69–86

60. Hasenstab, R. J. 1990. *Agriculture, warfare and tribalization in the Iroquois homeland of New York: A G.I.S. analysis of Late Woodland Settlement.* PhD thesis. Univ. Mass., Amherst

61. Hatch, J., Miller, P. 1985. Procurement, tool production, sourcing research at the Vera Cruz jasper quarry in Pennsylvania. *J. Field Archaeol.* 12:219–30

62. Hayden, B. 1979. *Settlement Patterns of the Draper and White Sites: 1973 Excavations.* Dept. Archaeol. Simon Fraser Univ. Publ. 6

63. Hayes, C. F. III, ed. 1983. In *Proceedings of the 1982 Glass Trade Bead Conference.* Rochester Mus. Sci. Cent., Res. Rec. 16

64. Heidenreich, C. E. 1971. *Huronia: A History and Geography of the Huron Indians 1600–1650.* Toronto: McClelland & Stewart

65. Horne, M. 1987. A preliminary examination of site selection criteria for Middleport-Neutral sites in the Waterloo region. *Kewa* 87(2):4–24

66. Horvath, S. 1979. A computerized study of Princess Point complex ceramics: Some implications of late prehistoric social organization in Ontario. In *The Princess Point Complex, Archaeol. Survey Can. Mercury Ser. 58,* pp. 310–17

67. Howard, H., Morris, E. L., eds. 1981. *Production and Distribution: A Ceramic Viewpoint.* BAR Int. Ser. 120. Oxford: BAR

68. Hunt, E. D. 1990. *A consideration of environmental, physiographic, and horticultural systems as they impact Late Woodland Settlement patterns in Western New York State: A geographic information system (GIS) analysis of site location.* PhD thesis. SUNY at Buffalo

69. Janusas, S. E. 1984. A petrological analysis of Kettle Point chert and its spatial distribution in regional prehistory. *Archaeol. Surv. Can. Mercury Ser.* 128

70. Jarvis, H. W. 1990. Instrumental neutron activation analysis on Onondaga Chert in the Niagara frontier. *Ont. Archaeol.* 51:3–15

71. Junker-Andersen, C. 1986. Faunal remains from the Jackson-Everson (NYSM 1213) site. See Ref. 89, pp. 93–160

72. Kapches, M. C. 1980. Wall trenches on

Iroquoian sites. *Archaeol. East. NA* 8:98–105
73. Kapches, M. C. 1984. Cabins on Ontario Iroquois sites. *NA Archaeol.* 5:63–71
74. Kapches, M. C. 1990. The spatial dynamics of Ontario Iroquoian longhouses. *Am. Antiq.* 55:46–67
75. Kenyon, I. 1972. The Neutral Sequence in the Hamilton Area. Presented at Annu. Meet. Can. Archaeol. Assoc., 5th, St. John's, Newfoundland
76. Kenyon, I. 1984. Sagard's "Rassade Rouge" of 1624. *Kewa* 84(4):2–14
77. Kenyon, I., Fitzgerald, W. R. 1986. Dutch glass beads in the Northeast: an Ontario perspective. *Man in the NE* 32:1–34
78. Kenyon, I., Fox, W. A. 1982. The Grimsby cemetery—a second look. *Kewa* 82(9):3–16
79. Kenyon, I., Kenyon, T. 1983. Commments on seventeenth century glass trade beads from Ontario. See Ref. 63, pp. 59–74
80. Kenyon, W. A. 1959. *The Inverhuron Site.* R. Ont. Mus. Art Archaeol. Div. Occas. Pap. 1
81. Kenyon, W. A. 1968. *The Miller Site.* R. Ont. Mus. Occas. Pap. 14
82. Kidd, K. E., Kidd, M. A. 1970. A classification system for glass beads for the use of field archaeologists. *Can. Hist. Sites Occas. Pap. Archaeol. Hist.* 1:45–89
83. Kuhn, R. D. 1985. *Trade and exchange among the Mohawk-Iroquois: a trace element analysis of ceramic smoking pipes.* PhD thesis. SUNY Albany
84. Kuhn, R. D. 1986. Interaction patterns in eastern New York: a trace element analysis of Iroquoian and Algonkian ceramics. *Bull. J. Archaeol. NY State* 92:9–21
85. Kuhn, R. D. 1986. Indications of interaction and acculturation through ceramic analysis. See Ref. 89, pp. 75–92
86. Kuhn, R. D. 1989. The trace element analysis of Hudson valley clays and ceramics. *Bull. J. Archaeol. NY State* 99:25–30
87. Kuhn, R. D., Bamann, S. E. 1987. Preliminary report on the attribute analysis of Mohawk ceramics. *Bull. J. Archaeol. NY State* 94:40–46
88. Kuhn, R. D., Lanford, W. A. 1987. Sourcing Hudson valley cherts from trace element analysis. *Man in the NE* 34:57–69
89. Kuhn, R. D., Snow, D. R., eds. 1986. *The Mohawk Valley Project: 1983 Jackson-Everson Excavations.* Albany: SUNY Inst. NE Anthropol.
90. Lavin, L. 1983. *Patterns of chert acquisition among Woodland groups with the Delaware Watershed: A lithological approach.* PhD thesis. New York Univ.
91. LeBlanc, S. 1971. An addition to Naroll's suggested floor area and settlement population relationship. *Am. Antiq.* 36:210
92. Lennox, P. A., Dodd, C. F., Murphy, C. R. 1986. *The Wiacek Site: A Late Middleport Component in Simcoe County, Ontario.* London, Ont: Ont. Minist. Transp.

Commun., Environ. Unit, Plan. Design Sect.
93. Lennox, P. A., Fitzgerald, W. R. 1990. The culture history and archaeology of the Neutral Iroquois. See Ref. 34, pp. 405–56
94. Lennox, P. A., Kenyon, I. 1984. Was that Middleport Necked or Pound Oblique? A study in Iroquoian ceramic typology. *Ont. Archaeol.* 42:13–26
95. Longacre, W. A. 1970. *Archaeology as Anthropology: A Case Study.* Tucson: Anthropol. Pap. Univ. Ariz. No. 17
96. Luedtke, B. E. 1978. Chert sources and trace element analysis. *Am. Antiq.* 43(3):413–43
97. Luedtke, B. E. 1979. The identification of sources of chert artifacts. *Am. Antiq.* 44(4):744–57
98. MacDonald, J. 1986. *The Varden Site: A Multi-Component Fishing Station on Long Point, Lake Erie.* Report. Toronto: Ont. Minist. Cult. Commun.
99. MacDonald, R. 1987. Notes on longhouse storage units. *Archaeol. Notes* 87(3):5–11
100. MacDonald, R. 1988. Ontario Iroquoian sweat lodges. *Ont. Archaeol.* 48:17–26
101. MacNeish, R. S. 1952. *Iroquois Pottery Types: A Technique for the Study of Iroquois Prehistory.* Natl. Mus. Can. Bull. 124
102. McPherron, A. 1970. On the sociology of ceramics: pottery style clustering, marital residence, and cultural adaptations of an Algonkian-Iroquoian border. In *Iroquois Culture, History and Prehistory, Proc. 1965 Conf. Iroquois Research,* ed. E. Tooker, pp. 101–7. Albany: SUNY Press
103. Melbye, J. 1981. *The Fairty ossuary revisited: Fertility and mortality among Iroquoian People of the 14th Century.* Presented at Annu. Meet. Can. Assoc. Phys. Anthropol.
104. Milner, G. R. 1980. Epidemic disease in the postcontact Southeast: a reappraisal. *Mid-Continental J. Archaeol.* 5:39–56
105. Monckton, S. 1990. *Huron paleoethnobotany.* PhD thesis. Univ. Toronto
106. Naroll, R. 1962. Floor area and settlement population. *Am. Antiq.* 27:587–89
107. Niemczycki, M. A. P. 1984. *The Origin and Development of the Seneca and Cayuga Tribes of New York State.* Rochester Mus. Sci. Cent. Res. Rec. 17
108. Niemczycki, M. A. P. 1988. Seneca tribalization: an adaptive strategy. *Man in the NE* 36:77–87
109. Noble, W. C. 1972. *Neutral settlement patterns.* Presented at Annu. Meet. Can. Archaeol. Assoc., 5th, St. John's, Newfoundland
110. Noble, W. C. 1975. Corn and the development of village life in southern Ontario. *Ont. Archaeol.* 25:37–46
111. Norcliffe, G. B., Heidenreich, C. E. 1974. The preferred orientation of Iroquoian longhouses in Ontario. *Ont. Archaeol.* 23:3–30

458   BAMANN ET AL

112. O'Brien, R. M. 1976. *An Archaeological Survey of Methodist Point Park Preserve.* Ont. Minist. Cult. Recreat. Hist. Plan. Res. Branch Res. Pap. 9
113. O'Shea, J. 1989. The role of wild resources in small-scale agricultural systems: tales from the lakes and plains. In *Bad Year Economics,* ed. P. Halstead, J. O'Shea, pp. 57–67. Cambridge: Cambridge Univ. Press
114. Pavlish, L. A., Hancock, R. G. V., Julig, P., D'Andrea, A. C. 1987. Systematic stratified INAA of two chert outcrops in southern Ontario. In *Annual Report of the Slowpoke Reactor Facility, July 1986 to June 1987.* Toronto: Univ. Toronto
115. Pearce, R. J. 1978. Archaeological investigations of the Pickering phase in the Rice Lake area. *Ont. Archaeol.* 29:17–24
116. Pearce, R. J. 1983. *The Windermere, Ronto and Smallman Sites: Salvage Excavations of Prehistoric Iroquoian Hamlets.* Mus. Indian Archaeol. Res. Rep. 13
117. Pearce, R. J. 1984. *Mapping middleport: a case study in societal archaeology.* PhD thesis. McGill Univ.
118. Pendergast, J. F. 1974. The Sugarbush site: a possible Iroquoian maple sugar camp. *Ont. Archaeol.* 23:31–61
119. Pendergast, J. F. 1989. The significance of some marine shell excavated on Iroquoian sites in Ontario. In *Proc. 1986 Shell Bead Conf.,* ed. C. F. Hayes III, 20:97–112. Rochester Mus. Sci. Cent. Res. Rec.
120. Pfeiffer, S. 1980. Spatial distribution of human skeletal material within an Iroquoian ossuary. *Can. J. Archaeol.* 4:169–72
121. Poulton, D. 1985. *An Analysis of the Draper Site Chipped Lithic Artifacts.* Mus. Indian Archaeol. Res. Rep. 15
122. Prevec, R., Noble, W. 1983. Historic Neutral Iroquois faunal utilization. *Ont. Archaeol.* 39:41–56
123. Prezzano, S. C. 1988. Spatial analysis of post moulds at the Sackett site, Ontario County, New York. *Man in the NE* 35:27–45
124. Prezzano, S. C., Steponaitis, V. P., eds. 1990. *Excavations at the Boland Site, 1984–1987: A Preliminary Report.* Res. Lab. Anthropol. Univ. NC, Chapel Hill Res. Rep. 9
125. Ramenofsky, A. F. 1987. *Vectors of Death: The Archaeology of European Contact.* Albuquerque: Univ. New Mexico
126. Ramsden, P. G. 1988. Palisade extension, village expansion and immigration in Iroquoian sites in the upper Trent valley. *Can. J. Archaeol.* 12:177–83
127. Ramsden, P. G. 1990. The Hurons: archaeology and culture history. See Ref. 34, pp. 361–84
128. Rice, P. M. 1981. Evolution of specialized pottery production: a trial model. *Curr. Anthropol.* 22:219–40
129. Ritchie, W. A. 1952. *The Chance Horizon: An Early Stage of Mohawk Iroquois Culture Development.* NY State Mus. Circ. 29
130. Ritchie, W. A., Funk, R. E. 1973. *Aboriginal Settlement Patterns in the Northeast.* Albany: NY State Mus. Sci. Serv. Mem. 20.
131. Sanders, W. T., Parsons, J. R., Santley, R. S. 1979. *The Basin of Mexico: Ecological Processes in the Evolution of a Civilization.* New York: Academic. 2 Vols.
132. Saunders, L. P., Sempowski, M. L. 1991. The Seneca site sequence and chronology: the baby or the bathwater? *Bull. J. Archaeol. NY State* 102:13–26
133. Sempowski, M. L., Saunders, L. P., Cervone, G. C. 1988. The Adams and Culbertson sites: a hypothesis for village formation. *Man in the NE* 35:95–108
134. Scarry, C. M. 1990. Plant remains: 1985–1987 seasons. See Ref. 124, pp. 143–59
135. Smith, D. G. 1983. *An Analytical Approach to the Seriation of Iroquoian Pottery.* Mus. Indian Archaeol. Res. Rep. 12
136. Smith, D. G. 1987. *Archaeological systematics and the analysis of Iroquoian ceramics: a case study from the Crawford Lake Area, Ontario.* PhD thesis. McGill Univ.
137. Smith, D. G. 1990. Iroquoian societies in southern Ontario: introduction and historic overview. See Ref. 34, pp. 279–90
138. Smith, S. 1979. *The Methodist Point Site.* Ont. Minist. Cult. Recreat. Hist. Plan. Res. Branch Res. Rep. 11
139. Snow, D. R. 1980. *The Archaeology of New England.* New York: Academic
140. Snow, D. R., ed. 1981. *Foundations of Northeast Archaeology.* New York: Academic
141. Snow, D. R. 1981. Approaches to cultural adaptation in the Northeast. See Ref. 140, pp. 97–138
142. Snow, D. R. 1986. *Historic Mohawk Settlement Patterns.* Presented at Annu. Meet. Can. Archaeol. Assoc., 19th, Toronto
143. Snow, D. R. 1991. Mohawk. *Bull. J. Archaeol. NY State* 102:34–39
144. Snow, D. R. 1992. Northern Iroquoian population growth and its implications for their origins. *Rech. Amérindiennes Québec.* In press
145. Snow, D. R. 1992. Paleoecology and the prehistoric incursion of northern Iroquoians into the lower Great Lakes region. In *Great Lakes Archaeology and Paleoecology: Exploring Interdisciplinary Initiatives for the Nineties,* ed. B. Warner, R. MacDonald. Waterloo: Q. Sci. Inst., Univ. Waterloo. In press.
146. Snow, D. R., Lanphear, K. M. 1988. European contact and Indian depopulation in the Northeast: the timing of the first epidemics. *Ethnohistory* 35:15–33
147. Snow, D. R., Lanphear, K. M. 1989. "More methodological perspectives": a rejoinder to Dobyns. *Ethnohistory* 36:299–304
148. Snow, D. R., Starna, W. A. 1989. Sixteenth century depopulation: a view from the Mohawk valley. *Am. Anthropol.* 91:142–49

149. Starna, W. A. 1980. Mohawk Iroquois populations: a revision. *Ethnohistory* 27:371–82

150. Starna, W. A., Relethford, J. H. 1985. Deer densities and population dynamics: a cautionary note. *Am. Antiq.* 50:825–32

151. Starna, W. A., Hammel, G. R., Butts, W. L. 1984. Northern Iroquoian horticulture and insect infestation: a cause for village removal. *Ethnohistory* 23:371–82

152. Steckley, J. L. 1989. Huron sweat lodges: the linguistic evidence. *Archaeol. Notes* 89(1):7–8, 14

153. Stewart, F. L. 1974. Faunal remains from the Nodwell Site (BcHi-3) and from four other sites in Bruce County, Ontario. *Archaeol. Surv. Canada, Mercury Ser.* 16

154. Struever, S. 1968. Flotation techniques for the recovery of small archaeological remains. *Am. Antiq.* 33:353–62

155. Sykes, C. M. 1980. Swidden horticulture and Iroquoian settlement. *Archaeol. East. NA* 8:45–52

156. Trigger, B. G. 1963. Settlement as an aspect of Iroquoian adaptation at the time of European contact. *Am. Anthropol.* 65:86–101

157. Trigger, B. G. 1968. The determinants of settlement patterns. In *Settlement Archaeology*, ed. K. C. Chang, pp. 53–78. Palo Alto: National

158. Trigger, B. G., ed. 1978. *Northeast: Handbook NA Indians*, Vol. 15. Washington: Smithsonian Inst.

159. Trigger, B. G. 1981. Prehistoric social and political organization: an Iroquoian case study. See Ref. 140, pp. 1–50

160. Trigger, B. G. 1985. *Natives and Newcomers: Canada's "Heroic Age" Reconsidered.* Montreal: McGill-Queen's Press

161. Trigger, B. G. 1987. *Introduction to Papers on the Beginnings of the Fur Trade.* Symp. 5th NA Fur Trade Conf. Montreal: Lake St. Louis Hist. Soc.

162. Trigger, B. G. 1990. Maintaining economic equality in opposition to complexity: an Iroquoian case study. In *The Evolution of Political Systems,* ed. S. Upham, pp. 119–45. Cambridge: Cambridge Univ. Press

163. Trigger, B. G., Yaffe, L., Diksic, M., Galinier, J.-L., Marshall, H., et al 1980. Trace element analysis of Iroquoian pottery. *Can. J. Archaeol.* 4:119–46

164. Trigger, B. G., Yaffe, L., Dautet, D., Marshall, H., Pearce, R. 1984. Parker Festooned pottery a the Lawson site: trace element analysis. *Ont. Archaeol.* 42:3–11

165. Tuck, J. A. 1968. *Iroquois cultural development in Central New York.* PhD thesis. Syracuse Univ.

166. Tuck, J. A. 1971. *Onondaga Iroquois Prehistory: A Study in Settlement Archaeology.* Syracuse: Syracuse Univ. Press

167. Tuck, J. A. 1978. Northern Iroquoian prehistory. See Ref. 158, pp. 322–33

168. Ubelaker, D. H. 1976. Prehistoric new world population size: Historical review

and current appraisal of North American estimates. *Am. J. Phys. Anthropol.* 45:661–65

169. Ubelaker, D. H. 1988. North American Indian population size, A.D. 1500 to 1985. *Am. J. Phys. Anthropol.* 77:289–94

170. Van der Leeuw, S. E. 1981. Ceramic exchange and manufacture: A "flow structure" approach. See Ref. 67, pp. 361–86

171. Vandrei, C. E. 1987. Observations on Seneca settlement in the early historic period. *Bull. J. Archaeol. NY State* 95:8–17

172. Vita-Finzi, C., Higgs, E. S. 1970. Prehistoric ecology in the Mount Carmel area of Palestine: site catchment analysis. *Proc. Prehist. Soc.* 36:1–37

173. Von Gernet, A. 1985. *Analysis of Intrasite Artifact Spatial Distributions: The Draper Site Smoking Pipes.* Mus. Indian Archaeol. Res. Rep. 16

174. Warrick, G. A. 1984. Reconstructing Ontario Iroquoian village organization. *Archaeol. Surv. Can. Mercury Ser.* 124:1–80

175. Warrick, G. A. 1988. Estimating Ontario Iroquoian village duration. *Man in the NE* 36:21–60

176. Warrick, G. A. 1988. *The Iroquoian Occupation of Southern Simcoe County: Results of the Southern Simcoe County Archaeological Project. Rep.* Toronto: Ont. Minist. Cult. Commun.

177. Warrick, G. A. 1990. *A Population history of the Huron-Petun, AD 900–1650.* PhD thesis. McGill Univ.

178. Warrick, G. A., Molnar, J. S. 1986. An Iroquoian site sequence from Innisfil township, Simcoe County. *Archaeol. Notes* 86(3):21–34

179. Warrick, G. A., Molnar, J. S., Fecteau, R. D. 1991. Iroquoian village ecology. *The Birdstone* 5:1–19

180. Weber, C. J. 1971. Types and attributes in Iroquois pipes. *Man in the NE* 2:51–65

181. Whallon, R. 1968. Investigations of late prehistoric social organization in New York State. In *New Perspectives in Archaeology,* ed. S. R. Binford, L. R. Binford, pp. 223–44. Chicago: Aldine

182. Wiessner, P. 1974. A functional estimator of population from floor area. *Am. Antiq.* 39(2):343–50

183. Williamson, R. F. 1983. The Robin Hood site: a study in functional variability in late Iroquoian settlement. *Monogr. Ont. Archaeol.* 1

184. Williamson, R. F. 1985. *Glen Meyer: people in transition.* PhD thesis. McGill Univ.

185. Williamson, R. F. 1990. The early Iroquoian period of southern Ontario. See Ref. 34, pp. 291–320

186. Wintemberg, W. J. 1936. *The Roebuck Prehistoric Village Site, Greenville County, Ontario.* Natl. Mus. Can. Bull. 83

187. Wray, C. F., Schoff, H. 1953. A preliminary report on the Seneca sequence in western New York, 1550–1687. *Penn. Archaeol.* 23:53–63

188. Wray, C. F., Sempowski, M. L., Saunders, L. P., Cervone, G. C. 1987. *The Adams and Culbertson Sites.* Rochester Mus. Sci. Cent. Res. Rec. 19

189. Wray, C. F., Sempowski, M. L., Saunders, L. P. 1991. *Tram and Cameron: Two Early Contact Era Seneca Sites.* Rochester Mus. Sci. Cent. Res. Rec. 21

190. Wright, J. V. 1966. *The Ontario Iroquois Tradition.* Natl. Mus. Can. Bull. 210

191. Wright, J. V. 1972. *Ontario Prehistory: An 11,000 Year Outline.* Ottawa: Natl. Mus. Can.

192. Wright, J. V. 1972. The Dougall site. *Ont. Archaeol.* 17:3–23

193. Wright, J. V. 1974. The Nodwell site. *Ar-chaeol. Surv. Can. Mercury Ser.* 22

194. Wright, J. V., Anderson, J. E. 1969. *The Bennett Site.* Natl. Mus. Can. Bull. 229

195. Wright, M. J. 1986. The Uren Site AfHd-3: an analysis and reappraisal of the Uren substage type site. *Monogr. Ont. Archaeol.* 2

196. Wykoff, M. W. 1988. *Iroquoian prehistory and climate change: notes for empirical studies of the Eastern Woodlands.* PhD thesis. Cornell Univ.

197. Zubrow, E. B. W. 1990. Modelling and prediction with geographic information systems: a demographic example from prehistoric and historic New York. See Ref. 2, pp. 307–18

Annu. Rev. Anthropol. 1992. 21:461-90

THINK PRACTICALLY AND LOOK LOCALLY: Language and Gender as Community-Based Practice

Penelope Eckert

Institute for Research on Learning, Palo Alto CA 94304

Sally McConnell-Ginet

Department of Modern Languages and Linguistics, Cornell University, Ithaca NY 14853-4701

KEYWORDS: sociolinguistic variation, interactional style, meaning and sexual politics

INTRODUCTION

How do gender and language interact? For the past 20 years or so, linguists, anthropologists, psychologists, sociologists, and feminist thinkers have explored many aspects of this question. There are now dozens of books and hundreds of course offerings on gender and language (14, 20, 41, 60, 67, 92, 98, 99), specialized articles are found in many journals and collections (15, 21, 59, 78, 87, 90, 109, 110, 115), and review articles continue to appear (8, 32, 47, 74, 76, 89). Topics treated include sexist, heterosexist, and racist language; interruptions; graffiti and street remarks; names and forms of address; politeness; tag questions; directives; motherese; children's talk during play; schoolroom discourse; bilingualism and language contact; metaphors; shifts in word meanings; the language of science, religion, and war; silence and volubility; intonation; emotional expressiveness; religious and political rhetoric; sociolinguistic variation; and language change. This list is far from comprehensive but its scatter suggests an absence of theoretical coherence in language and gender studies.

Partial integration of the range of linguistic phenomena that seem sensitive to gender is sometimes attempted by trying to explain them all in terms of a

461

0084-6570/92/1015-0461$02.00

general feature of gender identities or relations. The most influential frameworks in which this has been attempted can be thought of as emphasizing either gender difference or (men's) dominance. Thorne & Henley (108) highlighted these two modes of explanation in their early anthology, *Language and Sex: Difference and Dominance,* although they were ahead of their time in proposing that difference and dominance would probably both enter into explaining gender-language interactions.

We have organized much of our discussion around difference on the one hand (especially as a component of gender identities) and power on the other (especially male dominance as a component of gender relations). However, we have tried to shift attention away from an opposition of the two and toward the processes through which each feeds the other to produce the concrete complexities of language as used by real people engaged in social practice. In our second section, we discuss the separation between the sexes (allegedly producing distinctive female and male communicative cultures); there we also critically discuss sex as a determinant of social address and the resulting orientation toward linguistic variation and change. In our third section, we look at accounts of male power in language and the subordination of women at personal and at institutional levels; we briefly consider other kinds of hierarchical relations, such as those across class and racial boundaries; and we examine larger issues about language and power. But in both the second and third sections we note some of the ways that gender difference helps create hierarchical and other kinds of gender relations; and we indicate how those power relations in turn help construct "women", "men", and their language. Not only are difference and dominance both involved in gender, but they are also jointly constructed and prove ultimately inseparable. These constructions are different at different times and places, and the constructors are people, not faceless abstractions like "society." It is the mutual engagement of human agents in a wide range of activities that creates, sustains, challenges, and sometimes changes society and its institutions, including gender and language.

We aim here to encourage a view of the interaction of gender and language that roots each in the everyday social practices of particular local communities and sees them as jointly constructed in those practices. Thus we use our critical reviews of others' research primarily to hang flesh on the bones of a community-based practice orientation, within which we propose to think about language, about gender, and about their interaction as living social practices in local communities. To think practically and look locally is to abandon several assumptions common in gender and language studies: that gender can be isolated from other aspects of social identity and relations, that gender has the same meaning across communities, and that the linguistic manifestations of that meaning are also the same across communities.

To think practically about gender is to focus on the historical processes of constructing gender categories and power relations: "Gender" becomes a dynamic verb. We speak of practices (and traits and activities and values) as "gendered" where they enter in some important way into "gendering" people and their relations. That is, gendered practices construct members of a community "as" women or "as" men (or members of other gender categories), and this construction crucially also involves constructing relations between and within each sex. Looking locally, we see that the same community practices that help constitute a particular person as a woman may, for example, also help constitute her as "African-American" and "middle-class" and "a mother" and "a sister" and "a neighbor" and so on. We often speak of "women" and of "men" (or sometimes of "female" and "male"), referring to those so constituted in their own communities. But in talking globally, we do not want to suggest that gendered identities and relations have any common core "fixed" by their (initial classificatory) link to reproductive biology. Dichotomous sex-based categories often (not always!) provide an easily applicable way to sort an entire community into two non-overlapping groups. But the content of those categories (including the social relations within and between the groups) is constantly being constituted and in various ways transformed as the members of that community engage with one another in various practices. There is no guarantee that "women" (or "men") in a particular community will in fact constitute themselves as a coherent social group with distinctive common interests. Even practices closely tied to reproductive biology (e.g. those revolving around menstruation and the "disease" of PMS) are connected in complex ways to other social practices (e.g. class-related employment possibilities; see 71), thus making it problematic to speak of "women's" position or interest without reference to other factors.

It used to be fashionable to draw a sharp distinction between sex (biology and what it supposedly "determines"—i.e. femaleness or maleness) and gender (cultural beliefs and norms linked to sex, often more specifically a normative conception of individual attributes associated with sex—i.e. femininity or masculinity). Practice-theoretic approaches to gender make it clear, however, that this dichotomy cannot be maintained (e.g. 22). What looks like laudable terminological clarity in the service of workable analytical distinctions turns out to mask intellectual confusion. Bodies and biological processes are inextricably part of cultural histories, affected by human inventions ranging from the purely symbolic to the technological. It isn't that cultures simply "interpret" or assign "significance" as a cultural overlay to basically biological distinctions connected to sex; rather, social practices constitute in historically specific and changing ways not only gender (and sexual) relations but also such basic gender (and sexual) categories as "woman" and "man" and related categories such as "girl" or "lesbian" or "transsexual" or "lady" or "bitch." "Female" and "male" label distinctions in potential sexual reproductive roles: All cultures known to us sort people at birth into two groups on the basis of anatomical distinctions potentially relevant to those roles. Crucially, however, what is made of those categories and how they link to other sex-related categories and relations emerges only in the historical play of social practices, including their link to such phenomena as medical and technological changes in reproductive possibilities. "Defining" these various terms is not preliminary to but an ongoing component of developing a scholarly practice centered on questions of gender.

Language enters into the social practices that gender people and their activities and ideas in many different ways, developing and using category labels like "woman" and "man" being only a small part of the story. To understand precisely how language interacts with gender (and with other symbolic and social phenomena) requires that we look locally, closely observing linguistic and gender practices in the context of a particular community's social practices. Gumperz (42) defines a speech community as a group of speakers who share rules and norms for the use of a language. This definition suggests the importance of practice in delineating sociolinguistically significant groupings, but it does not directly address social relations and differentiation among members of a single community (though implicitly treating differentiation as revealing "sub-" communities). Nor does it make fully explicit the role of practice in mediating the relation between language and society.

To explore in detail how social practice and individual "place" in the community interconnect, sociolinguists need a conception of a community that articulates place with practice. We therefore adopt Lave & Wenger's notion of the "community of practice" (69, 116). A community of practice is an aggregate of people who come together around mutual engagement in an endeavor. Ways of doing things, ways of talking, beliefs, values, power relations—in short, practices—emerge in the course of this mutual endeavor. As a social construct, a community of practice is different from the traditional community, primarily because it is defined simultaneously by its membership and by the practice in which that membership engages. (This does not mean that communities of practice are necessarily egalitarian or consensual—simply that their membership and practices grow out of mutual engagement.) In addition, relations between and among communities of practice, and relations between communities of practice and institutions, are important: Individuals typically negotiate multiple memberships (in families, on teams, in workplaces, etc), many of them important for understanding the gender-language interaction. A focus on language and gender as practice within communities of practice can, we think, provide a deeper understanding of how gender and language may interact and how those interactions may matter.

DIFFERENCE: GENDER IDENTITIES

In thinking about gender, many start by looking at sex differences. We discuss two strands of sociolinguistic research that have emphasized differences among speakers. One strand starts with a view of gender differences as arising in female and male subcultures, each of which is characterized by gendered values and modes of interaction. These studies focus on an array of discourse phenomena as implementations of those values and interactional modes, analyzing cross-sex communicative problems as stemming from gender/cultural differences in norms of appropriate discourse. Language is of interest simply as part of communicative interaction: The larger inquiry is sociocultural, and so language is considered together with such nonverbal phenomena as gaze direction and posture.

The other strand comprises more extensive research from a wider range of research projects. It offers, however, no fully articulated conception of gender and focuses on linguistic phenomena at a structural level: Sex is seen as one of several attributes determining social address or "place" in a community (theoretically on a par with class, race, age) and also determining a distinctive relation to linguistic variation (e.g. pronunciation patterns or orientation toward standard grammar). Gender is of interest just because sex seems in many instances to correlate significantly with linguistic variation, often interacting with class and other components of social address: The starting point is linguistic variation within a population and its relation to social address and to structural linguistic change.

Sex as the Basis of Separate (but Equal) Subcultures

As we shall see in the section on power, below, many have argued that differences in women's and men's relations to language—both in systemic matters, such as how vowels are pronounced, and in the dynamics of conversational interaction—are produced by, and themselves help reproduce, male power. At least some analysts, however, have thought of individual cross-sex interactions as plagued by misunderstandings that cannot be explained adequately in terms of the man's control or the woman's submission. According to these researchers, such misunderstandings seem rather to reflect prevalent gender differences in preferred communicative styles and interactional strategies.

Gumperz and colleagues (43) have explained certain problematic interactions and social tension in encounters between members of different social groups as arising from unrecognized differences in the communication patterns those social groups favor. Originally applied to different ethnic, national, and regional groups, this model was extended to tensions between women and men by Maltz & Borker (70), who proposed that norms of friendly peer conversation are learned mainly in single-sex preadolescent peer groups, and that these norms are radically different for females and males, yet essentially the same within each sex across many different local communities. Adult women and men, then, may unwittingly bring different norms to their interactions, each assuming that the other is flouting established norms rather than adhering to a different but equally valid set: She assumes he means what she would mean by making (or not making) a particular conversational move, whereas his intended import is different; and he likewise misjudges her contributions to their exchange. The intended analogue is the young American woman responding with indignation to the British hotel clerk's "shall I knock you up in the morning," hearing a sexual proposition where wake-up service is being offered. Although this model does not account for why boys and girls develop different cultures along the same lines in distinct local communities, it implies that gender practices in the wider society (e.g. the United States) are the key.

Tannen (105) elaborates the Maltz-Borker picture, expanding considerably on the cultural models of male and female conversational practice. Although the general two-culture model does not in itself dictate a particular "essentialist" conception of how female interactional norms might differ from male, the model has in fact been coupled with a currently popular view of "women's" and "men's" ways of thinking and behaving (5, 35). The claim is that women emphasize connection with others, avoiding overt confrontations and direct disagreement, seeking empathy and understanding rather than guidance from their conversational partners, offering intimacy, suggesting or asking rather than directing or telling, preferring the tête-à-tête to talk in larger groups; boys continue boyish patterns of self-assertion into manhood, competing with one another to establish their individual claims to hierarchical status, proferring instruction rather than tea or sympathy, displaying their own ideas and claims for others to confirm but also engaging with relish in defending them against expected attacks of the sort they themselves frequently launch, seeking large audiences and avoiding showing themselves as vulnerable. Neither male nor female is culpable for misunderstandings and disappointments in cross-sex interaction, since each is simply continuing in the track established in the innocence of childhood. Where much work on language and gender ignores male behavior by treating it as a neutral norm from which women deviate, this work has the great merit of trying to account for men's behavior as well as women's. It also has the merit of recognizing that women are not defined simply in terms of their relation to men and that women may actively espouse values and pursue goals not set for them by men. The stereotypes are familiar, but they paint a much more positive view of the "female" subculture and sometimes a less flattering view of the "male" than may have been traditional.

What has seemed to many the most interesting consequence of the dual-culture model—namely, that cross-sex communicative problems derive from inadequate knowledge of interactional norms in the "other" culture—seems to suppose that people ignore all but the interactional possibilities predominant in their own gender-specific subcultures and make no real interactional choices, simply acting as passive sponges who soak up gendered identities. We do not deny that sex separation in childhood may result in gendering some adult interests, strategies, and social values, that such gender differentiation may go unnoticed, or that ignorance of it may cause misunderstandings. But the emphasis on separation and resulting ignorance misses people's active engagement in the reproduction of or resistance to gender arrangements in their communities. For example, indirect requests are a familiar interactional resource in many communities of practice. Every English speaker knows that an interrogative such as "do you think you can finish this by tomorrow?" can function as a polite request or a sugar-coated command, as well as a genuine information-seeking question. The misinterpretation of requests-masquerading-as-questions is likewise available to all speakers as a strategy of resistance: The child's "Not really, mom" in response to her "Would you like to set the table?" tries to read mom's directive literally, thus forcing her to display openly her actual coercive authority. When a man reads a woman's "no" as "yes" he actively exploits his "understanding" of the female style as different from his own—as being indirect rather than straightforward. His reading is possible not because his subculture taught *him* to encourage and welcome sexual advances by feigning their rejection; rather, he tells himself that such coyness is part of "femininity," a mode of being he views as significantly different from his own. The dual-culture approach posits the speakers' mistaken belief in shared norms and symbols. Gender relations in many actual communities of practice familiar to us, however, are often founded on (possibly mistaken) presuppositions not of sameness but of difference ("woman—the eternal mystery"). By taking separation as given, theorists ignore the place of this separation in the practice of the wider community. In fact, both real differences and the belief in differences serve as interactional resources in the reproduction of gender arrangements, of oppression, and of more positive liaisons.

The commonest criticism of the dual-culture model is that it ignores power (41, 48, 97). Where interpretations are disputed, whose cultural norms prevail? Dominance relations between cultures have indeed received little attention in Gumperz-style analyses of communicative conflict. But the dual-culture theory can certainly accommodate power asymmetries. The theory might well predict that those in the subordinated culture would be more likely to "understand" the interactive dialect of their oppressors than vice versa, on the direct analogy to the position of those who speak stigmatized vernaculars or minority languages (Black English Vernacular or Spanish in New York City, for example). But the appeal of the theory is that it minimizes blame for cross-cultural tensions for both the dominating and the dominated group: There is no more agency (and hence no more responsibility) in becoming an interrupter rather than a "good listener" than there is in becoming a speaker of Quechua rather than English. To deny agency and assume interactional difficulties arise simply from insufficient knowledge of differences is to preclude the possibility that people sometimes use differences (and beliefs about differences) strategically in constructing their social relations. In other words, dual-culture theory cannot recognize, let alone explain, strategic appeals to (real or perceived) differences. Yet strategic appeals to difference in constructing gender relations are apparent from even casual observation of social practice: Careful examination of unsatisfactory social relations in cases where cultural separation is more pervasive (e.g. different racial groups) may well also show uses of difference (or beliefs about it) in constructing dominance and other relations. The dual-culture theorists are right in insisting on the importance of interactional devices in gender relations, but their "no-fault" analysis makes it virtually impossible to see how gender differences in interactional strategies are constructed and how interactional strategies (more precisely, strategists) construct gender relations from a repertoire of similarities and differences and ideas about them.

Sex as Social Address

Sociolinguists working in the quantitative paradigm pioneered by Labov have found significant correlations within geographic communities between linguistic variables and speakers' demographic characteristics—socioeconomic class, race, age, and sex (65, 114). The most striking findings concern phonological variation. Variationists have garnered empirical data that describe the spread of patterned sound shifts through and between communities. Regular, systematic sound change appears to enter communities through the speech of the locally oriented working- and lower-middle-class population, and then to move upwards through the socioeconomic hierarchy. People tend to develop and regulate their linguistic repertoire through contact with language used by those they speak with regularly. Thus the partial separation between classes, racial groups, and generations—the relatively infrequent contact across these social boundaries—seems to affect linguistic change much as physical and political divisions do. Social addresses, however, are not all equal. In a sense, variationists consider gender precisely because sex differences in variation emerge even in communities where the sexes are not systematically separated the way socioeconomic or racial groups are. Some such differences may result from different kinds of contact outside the home community—contacts that might significantly affect exposure to standard dialects or to vernacular varieties not heard at home (9, 62). Because most gender differences in variation cannot be explained in this way, however, sociolinguists have reasoned thus about gender identity: If it isn't separation that differentiates the sexes in their linguistic behavior then it must be some aspect of the distinctive content of their gendered personalities or social positions. Differences in the use of linguistic variables, then, reflect sex-based differences in social practice.

Variation studies have used correlations to determine the role of linguistic variables in social practice. Sociolinguistic variables are seen as passive "markers" of the speaker's place in the social grid (particularly in the socioeconomic hierarchy). Correlation of a linguistic variable (or a certain frequency of its use) with a demographic category gives a rudimentary social meaning to that variable within the community: The variable "means" membership in the demographic group correlated with its use. Speakers are seen as making strategic use of sociolinguistic markers in order to affirm membership in their own social group, or to claim membership in other groups to which they aspire. According to this idea working-class speakers use local vernacular variables to claim the local goods and services due authentically local people (64); the hypercorrect patterns in the formal speech of the lower middle class assert membership in the middle class (66). Variables that women use more than men throughout different strata of a community signal female identity in that community (49), and men who rarely use those variables thereby signal their male identity (45, 62). In all these cases, identity, interpreted in terms of place in the social grid, is seen as given, and manipulation of the linguistic repertoire is seen as making claims about these given identities.

Analysts have, however, recognized linguistic variation as doing more than just marking group membership. The fact that the middle class is more resistant to phonological change than the working class has been attributed to the nature of class-based participation in the marketplace (93), and class differences in variation have been attributed to class-based differences in social network structure (80). A variety of patterns of variation have been associated with social network and local orientation (63, 66, 106). Nichols (83) found linguistic behavior among women differentiated by whether or not they had access to the marketplace (in the sense of opportunities for paid work); the different forms of women's and men's participation in the marketplace accounted for language differences across gender boundaries (teaching school requires greater adherence to standard language norms than construction work, for example). Milroy (80) has found complex relations between linguistic differences among women and market-related differences in their social network structure (whether, for example, coworkers are also neighbors or kin).

Although explanations of language variation are becoming more sophisticated as ethnographic studies provide more richly textured data and analyses, the relations between variation and social practice, and between variation and gender, require further elucidation. Finding practice-based explanations of sex correlations will require a significant leap beyond the correlational and class-based modes of explanation used so far. Explanations that do recognize the contributions of practice to variation have typically tried to infer psychological dynamics from correlations rather than from observations of gender dynamics in the communities from which the correlations have been extracted. Speakers who use language patterns that mark (i.e. that are statistically associated with) the social stratum above their own are characterized as upwardly mobile, prestige oriented, and/or insecure. Such correlational interpretation of linguistic variables involves a certain circularity. For example, a number of studies find that women make greater use than men of historically conservative variants. These variants have been interpreted as prestige markers, and women's greater use of them has been said to reflect status consciousness or prestige orientation. But no independent evidence is offered that the patterns in question have (only) the social meaning analysts have assigned on a correlational basis. How they figure in the social practice of the women and men using them has not been examined in detail. When other correlations have emerged in which women have made greater use of historically innovative variants than men, these innovative variants have also been interpreted as prestige markers, maintaining the characterization of women as prestige oriented (62, 113). What is at issue is not whether women in a particular community are or are not upwardly mobile or status conscious. Our methodological point is rather that the social meanings of linguistic variables cannot be ascertained merely on the basis of the social address of those who use them most frequently. Nor are linguistic variables unambiguous (13, 16). A variable acquires multiple meanings through the uses made of it in communities of practice. In this respect it is like other informationally rich symbols (cf the discussion of indirect requests above, p. 467, and of tag questions and rising intonations on declaratives below, p. 478).

A Community-Based-Practice View of Difference

What many of the studies cited above have found are *tendencies* toward gender-differentiated practice that have implications for language. It is important to remember that statements like "women emphasize connection in their talk whereas men seek status" are statistical generalizations. We must take care not to infer from such unmodified claims about "women" and "men" that individuals who don't fit the generalization are deviants from some "normative" gender model. This is especially true when women and men are characterized as "different" from one another on a particular dimension. If gender resides in difference, what explains the tremendous variability we see in actual behavior *within* sex categories? Is this variability statistical noise in a basically dichotomous gender system? Or are differences among men and among women also important aspects of gender? Tomboys and goody-goodies, homemakers and career women, body builders and fashion models, secretaries and executives, basketball coaches and French teachers, professors and students, mothers and daughters—these are all categories of girls and women whose mutual differences are part of their construction of themselves and each other as gendered beings. When femaleness and maleness are differentiated in terms of such attributes as power, ambition, physical coordination, rebelliousness, caring, or docility, the role of these attributes in creating and texturing important differences among very female identities and very male identities tends to become invisible. Analysts all too often slide from statistical generalizations to quasi-definitional or prototypical characterizations of "women" and of "men," thus inaccurately homogenizing both categories and marginalizing those who do not match the prototypes.

The point here is not that statistical generalizations about the females and the males in a particular community are automatically suspect. But to stop with such generalizations or to see finding such "differences" as the major goal of investigations of gender and language is problematic. Correlations simply indicate areas where further investigation might shed light on the linguistic and other practices that enter into gender dynamics in a community. An emphasis on difference as constitutive of gender draws attention away from a more serious investigation of the relations among language, gender, and other components of social identity. Gender can be thought of as a sex-based way of experiencing other social attributes such as class, ethnicity, or age (and also less obviously social qualities like ambition, athleticism, musicality, and the like). To examine gender independently as if it were just "added on" to such other aspects of identity is to miss its significance and force. Certainly to interpret broad sex patterns in language use without considering other aspects of social identity and relations is to paint with one eye closed. Speakers are not assembled out of independent modules: part European American, part female, part middle-aged, part feminist, part intellectual.

Abstracting gender from other aspects of social identity also leads to premature generalization even about "normative" conceptions of femaleness and maleness. While neither of the two strands of research discussed above is theoretically committed to a "universalizing" conception of women or of men, research in both has tended to take gender identity as given, at least in broad strokes at a global level. Although many of the most audible voices in both the dual-culture and the social-address traditions have indicated clearly that the particular content of gender identities is variable cross-culturally, they have nonetheless spoken of "women" and of "men" in ways that underplay not only cross-cultural differences but also the variability within each gender class for a given culture, much of which is highly structured socially. The strong temptation (one we have sometimes succumbed to ourselves) is to apply theoretical accounts of gender difference globally to women and men.

The portrayal of women as self-effacing, indirect, and particularly concerned with connection derives from research on the American white middle class. Drawing on contrasts with Samoa, Ochs (85) suggests that this "mainstream" American stereotype of women's speech owes much to child-centered mothering practices. Tannen's research on interactions between ethnicity and preference for directness (102) casts doubt on a simple relation between gender and indirection, and African American women have also protested unwarranted assumptions that directness contradicts universal norms of womanhood (81). One might still maintain that most women are less direct than most men in each of these local communities, but research in Madagascar showing most women as direct and most men as indirect (56) contradicts even this weak version of the generalization. Lakoff (68) proposes that women's linguistic patterns, whatever they may be, will be seen as somehow improper; but this is a generalization about evaluation, not linguistic behavior. Once we raise the question of just who might "see" women's language as deficient, a question that Lakoff ignores by using agentless passives and faceless abstractions like "the culture," it becomes apparent that in few communities will evaluations of women's (or of men's) speech be completely uniform. Not only may people recognize diversity among women and among men in their ways of speaking; one person may celebrate the very same gendered stereotype another depre-

cates. There may be statistically significant correlations between sex and preferred interactional styles and norms that hold across different communities of
practice, related to one another via their orientation to common structures and
institutions (e.g. to a national state, mass media, educational systems). Some
correlations may even hold globally (though only a wide range of detailed
local studies could establish these). But such observations would not demonstrate that gender can be isolated from other dimensions of social life, as
having some "essence" to be abstracted from the varied sociohistorical circumstances in which people become "women" and "men."

Rather than try to abstract gender from social practice, we need to focus on
gender in its full complexity: how gender is constructed in social practice, and
how this construction intertwines with that of other components of identity and
difference, and of language. This requires studying how people negotiate
meanings in and among the specific communities of practice to which they
belong.

What, then, is the relation between gender differences and communities of
practice? People's access and exposure to, need for, and interest in different
communities of practice are related to such things as their class, age, and
ethnicity, as well as to their sex. Working-class people are more likely than
middle-class people to be members of unions, bowling teams, and close-knit
neighborhoods. Upper-middle-class people are more likely than working-class
people to be members of tennis clubs, orchestras, and professional organizations. Men are more likely than women to be members of football teams,
armies, and boards of directors. Women are more likely to be members of
secretarial pools, aerobics classes, and consciousness raising groups. These
aspects of membership combine in complex ways. For example, associated
with differences in age, class, and ethnicity are differences in the extent to
which the sexes belong to different communities of practice. And different
people—for a variety of reasons—will articulate their multiple memberships
differently. A female executive living in a male-dominated household will
have difficulty articulating her membership in her domestic and professional
communities of practice; a male executive "head of household" will likely
have no such trouble. A lesbian lawyer "closeted" within the legal community
may also belong to a "women's" community whose membership defines itself
in opposition to the larger heterosexual world. The woman who scrubs toilets
in the households of these two women may be a respected lay leader in her
local church, facing still another set of tensions in negotiating multiple memberships. Gender is also reproduced in differential forms of participation in
particular communities of practice. Women tend to be subordinate to men in
the workplace; women in the military do not engage in combat; and in the
academy, most theoretical disciplines are overwhelmingly male, with women
concentrated in descriptive and applied work that "supports" theorizing.
Women and men may also participate differently in single-sex communities of
practice. For example, if all-women's groups do in fact tend to be more

egalitarian than all-men's groups, as some current literature claims, then women's and men's forms of participation in such groups will differ. Relations within same-sex groups will, of course, be related in turn to the place of such groups in the larger society. Only recently, for example, have women's sports begun to receive significant recognition, and men's sports continue to involve far greater visibility, power, and authority. This articulation with power outside the team in turn translates into different possibilities for relations within. Further, the relations among communities of practice when they come together in overarching communities of practice also reproduce gender arrangements. For example, the relation between male varsity sports teams and cheerleading squads illustrates a more general pattern of men's organizations and women's auxiliaries. Umbrella communities of this kind do not offer all members the same status. When several families get together for a meal and the women team up to do the serving and cleaning up while the men watch football, gender differentiation (including differentiation in language use) is being reproduced within the family on an institutional level.

The individual's development of gender identity within a community of practice [e.g. the Philadelphia neighborhood of working class African American families Goodwin (38, 39, 40) describes] is inseparable from the continual construction of gender within that community of practice, and from the ongoing construction of class, race, and local identities. Nor can it be isolated from that same individual's participation and construction of gender identity in other communities of practice (e.g. her "scholastic-track" class in an integrated school outside the neighborhood). Speakers develop linguistic patterns as they act in their various communities. Sociolinguists have tended to see this process as one of acquisition of something relatively "fixed." Like social identity, the symbolic value of a linguistic form is taken as given, and the speaker simply learns it and uses it either mechanically or strategically. But in practice, social meaning, social identity, community membership, and the symbolic value of linguistic form are constantly and mutually constructed. (Indeed the variationists' circular construction of the social meaning of variables can be seen as part of this process.) And the relation between gender and language resides in the modes of participation available to various individuals within various communities of practice as a direct or indirect function of gender. These modes of participation determine not only the development of particular strategies of performance and interpretation, but more generally access to meaning and to meaning-making rights.

People use the attribution of difference to construct social hierarchies. In hierarchies, dominant community members attribute deviance only to subordinates; their own distinctive properties they consider unremarkable—the norm. Even if subordinate members are not seen explicitly as deficient, they are disadvantaged by this process of nonreciprocal difference attribution because social practices and institutions favor the interests of "normal" participants (6). Many of the studies reviewed here offer evidence elucidating the power dynamics of gender differences in language use. Not all of the authors cited note this aspect of the phenomena they discuss, but recasting their work within such a framework gives us a rich picture of the dynamics of linguistic power.

POWER: GENDER RELATIONS

Power is not all that connects gender identities to gender relations (consider, for example, intimacy and desire). Differences between and within gender groups can support collaborative efforts in community endeavors, dividing labor and drawing on multiple talents (72), and can function in structuring desire (and not only heterosexual desire; see 61). But interest in power has been the engine driving most research on language and gender, motivated partly by the desire to understand male dominance and partly by the desire to dismantle it (sometimes along with other social inequalities).

Janus-like, power in language wears two faces. First, it is situated in and fed by individual agency; situated power resides primarily in face-to-face interactions but also in other concrete activities like reading or going to the movies. Second, it is historically constituted and responsive to the community's coordinated endeavors; social historical power resides in the relation of situated interaction to other situations, social activities, and institutionalized social and linguistic practices. This duality of power in language derives directly from the duality of social practice: Individual agents plan and interpret situated actions and activities, but their planning and interpretation rely on a social history of negotiating coordinated interpretations and normative expectations (and in turn feed into that history). And the duality of social practice is directly linked to the duality of meaning. What speakers "mean" in their situated utterances and how their interlocutors interpret them is the situated face of meaning; its historical community face involves the linguistic system(s) with conventionalized meanings and usage norms to which utterance meanings are oriented. The real power of language, its social and intellectual value, is found in the interplay between these two aspects of meaning and in the room for development afforded by the adaptability of conventions (e.g. indirection, irony, metaphor, pervasive vagueness, and ambiguity).

The overwhelming tendency in language and gender research has been to emphasize either speakers and their social relations (e.g. women's disadvantages in conversation) or the meanings and norms encoded in the linguistic systems and practices historically available to them (such sexist patterns as conflating generic human with masculine in forms like "he" or "man"). But linguistic forms have no power except as given in people's mouths and ears (or via other media); talk about meaning that leaves out the people who mean is at best limited. We begin by looking at power in situated interactions, then expand the discussion to include more explicit considerations of the community's attempted coordination of symbolic practices (and control of their potential power). We emphasize the existence of alternatives to androcentric world views and practices, moving finally to consideration of power and gender dynamics and change in communities of practice.

Interactional Reproduction of Gender and Male Power

Lakoff blazed new ground some 20 years ago by hypothesizing that gender difference in the use of English among mainstream white middle-class Americans helped maintain male dominance (67). She followed a long tradition in characterizing "women's language" as different from the standard set by men in being polite, tentative, indirect, imprecise, noncommital, deferential, closer to norms of grammatical "correctness" and less colloquial, emotionally expressive but euphemistic, and so on. However, she departed radically from the misogynistic tradition that gave rise to such stereotypes by arguing that this sort of speech was forced on girls and women as the price of social approval for being appropriately "feminine." At the same time, she saw women's language as keeping them from becoming effective communicators in positions where they might act as independent and nonsubordinate agents. Although challenges have been mounted to many of Lakoff's proposed formal characterizations of "women's language" and to the functions (and hence "meanings") she assigns to those forms, her ideas have been important in suggesting that genderized language use might figure in reproducing men's advantage over women at both personal and institutional levels.

Lakoff's early work prompted analysts to consider how language might connect to men's dominance in the professions and public life. She argued that norms of conversational interaction operative in mainstream American middle-class communities put a woman speaker in a double bind. Behavior that satisfies what is expected of her as a woman disqualifies her in the marketplace: To speak "as a woman" is to speak "as an underling"; and authoritative speech is, according to Lakoff, incompatible with cultural norms of femininity. Lakoff also proposed that linguistic conventions put women at an expressive disadvantage by encoding an androcentric (more specifically a misogynistic) perspective on women themselves. Lakoff not only noted explicitly insulting terms for referring to and addressing women, but also used linguistic techniques to highlight the problematic assumptions that underlie the widespread use of such apparently innocent words as "lady" and "girl."

Impressed by the suggestion that institutionalized male power might be instantiated in everyday linguistic exchanges, investigators began in the mid-1970s to look at such exchanges as potential arenas of sexual politics. A variety of approaches were taken to investigating institutionalized male power in interactions. One was to test gender stereotypes—particularly to assess the empirical evidence on the portrayals of gendered speech in the scholarly literature on language and gender (23, 25). Another kind of study granted (provisionally) the accuracy of stereotypical characterizations of the form of gendered speech but then reanalyzed the functions of those forms, seeing "women's" interactional moves in cross-sex contexts as resisting or coping with the dominance embodied in "men's" moves and as sometimes having other functions as well (29, 73). These studies, too, sought to efface the misogynist underpinnings of many prevalent beliefs about gender differences in language. A different but related strategy has been to examine interaction in single-sex groups, often in order to explore the possible dimensions of gender-specific verbal cultures [55; a study by Goodwin (38) has been widely cited as evidence for separate cultures but is not understood as such by its author]. The emphasis of all these efforts has been on women's language, since an important motivation of the work was to attack casual (and often demeaning) female stereotypes. Of course, these scholars also wanted to compensate for the fact that much sociolinguistic investigation had ignored women's language use.

One stereotype to come under empirical scrutiny early was that of the talkative woman. Swacker (100) showed that, given the task of describing a picture, the college men in her study talked far longer than the women and tended also to make more positive (if incorrect) statements; women were more tentative in the face of insufficient information. These intriguing results raise questions about how the men and women interpreted their obligations and rights in the context of the task. There are clearly situations in which men are expected and licensed to talk more, and others in which women are; and men and women have differential rights and obligations to talk about particular topics. There is not likely to be a simple relation between amount of talk and gender, or for that matter between amount of talk and power. There are enormous cultural differences in the relationship between power/authority and verbosity (1, 8, 95).

Swacker's speakers were performing solo, doing what was asked of them without threat of competition or benefit of cooperation. Conversational interactions offer other complications, interruptions being one important focus for exploring gender and power in language use. Early studies found that men interrupt more than women (in same-sex and in cross-sex interactions) and that women get interrupted more than men (36, 117, 118, 120); similar patterns of dominant interrupters seemed to emerge in asymmetries of parent-child and doctor-patient interaction. Recent reviews of research on sex differences in amount of speech and on interruptions and overlapping speech show, however, that matters are considerably more complicated (53, 54, 101, 104) than such observations might suggest. First of all, identification of interruptions that usurp others' speaking rights creates serious analytical problems; overlaps and speaker changes interpreted as disruptive interruptions are formally no different from those that function as supportive devices in conversation. Furthermore, conversational turn-taking norms and behavior are not the same in all regional or ethnic groups or situations, and investigation in a variety of settings does not give a clear picture of connections between gender and interruptions even for middle-class whites. Edelsky (28) and Coates (19) found women in certain informal situations regularly overlapping their speech, and

LANGUAGE AND GENDER AS PRACTICE 477

Kalčik's study of women's rap groups (55) notes continual collaboration in topic development as supported by overlaps and mutual sentence completion.

In addition, control is not always a matter of monopolizing "air-time" or of other forms of overt bullying. Control can be exercised through refusing to talk (29, 51, 58) or through making someone else talk (17). An individual's conversational contribution is evaluted in retrospect, and inasmuch as silence can signal the inappropriateness or unsatisfactoriness of the preceding turn, it can be a powerful tool for devaluing contributions. In the same way, an individual may continue to provide talk in order to fill in the threatening silence offered by the interlocutor. Such talk may then be evaluated—by both parties—as idle chatter. The potential for devaluation of women's contributions (by both men and women) under these circumstances is tremendous. This interactional construction of the worth of what is said, of the weightiness of different speakers' words for ongoing community-wide purposes, contributes to the development and maintenance of a community history. Such a history tends to reproduce androcentric values in its ongoing conventions and norms—in familiar messages and in the unexamined assumptions that hide in the historically constituted backgrounds against which discourses unfold within the community. A contributor not accorded attention and respect will find her capacity reduced for full participation in the social elaboration of thought, meaning, and community values. The cycle may be vicious in even subtler ways. Strategies undertaken in recognition of situational disadvantage often additionally convey recognition (and at least apparent acceptance) of subordination. Faced with less than energetic participation from the interlocutor, for example, a person may well employ compensatory linguistic strategies to establish the right to talk. Fishman's (29) study of several graduate student couples showed women having considerable difficulty introducing topics and starting conversations with their male partners. They fell back on such strategies as the opening questions that children use to get the floor—"Do you know what?" Announcing perceived lack of entitlement in this way ultimately confirms both partners in their views of the locus of control. As O'Barr & Atkins (84) noted, powerless strategies reproduce powerlessness, signaling the lack of authority (and presumptive value in the community) of their users.

Pointing to the fact that devaluation and limited authority tend to reproduce themselves must not be seen as "blaming the victim" for interactional failures but as showing how dominance can be exercised in the absence of overt coercion. The cycle for a woman may start with social devaluation of her speech, and that devaluation may handicap her capacity for effective speech even where interlocutors might be disposed to treat her as a valued colleague in common enterprises. (Such dispositions are hardly commonplace.) Women and men may utter the same linguistic form but not be able to accomplish the same things by doing so because both men and women presume the lesser value of women's contributions to community endeavors. The power lies not in the forms themselves but in the complex web that connects those forms to those who utter and interpret them and their kinds of membership in the community of practice in which the utterance occurs. Two linguistic forms have been highlighted as evidence of women's interactive insecurity—tag questions ("We should leave, shouldn't we?") and rising "question" intonation in declarative sentences ("My name is Lee?"). It was early recognized that the tag form could carry an intonation that seemed more nearly coercive than insecure or deferential; early quantitative studies of tag questions (23, 25) did not directly examine whether the forms they counted encoded tentativeness and insecurity, however, but concentrated on whether or not they characterized women's speech "in general," finding different sex correlations in quite different situations. However, it has been pointed out (17) that, even keeping intonation constant, tag questions can be heard in exactly the same conversational setting as either deferential or threatening, depending on relations among the participants and the activities in which they are engaged. Similar comments have been made about interpretation of rising intonations in contexts of assertion. Guy et al (45) provide quantitative evidence that Australian women use more rising intonations than men do overall, and suggest that this is a result of women's tentativeness. In an ethnographic study, McLemore (79) showed that rising intonation could be a powerful strategy within a Texas sorority; one speaker reported, however, that she would never use such an intonation in a male-dominated situation, because there it would sound "weak." Even within the sorority, the power of the rise correlated with its user's social position (pledges, for example, sounded "weak" when using repeated rises). This leads us to the more general observation that speech strategies are evaluated in the context of the identities of the participants and their status in specific interactions. The same language may be interpreted differently, for example, depending on whether it is used by a man or a woman. As Lakoff has pointed out, a woman using the same powerful language strategies as a man might well be evaluated as more aggressive than the man. Conversely, language strategies that are heard as powerful when used by a man (e.g. slow, measured delivery) may well not be heard as such when employed by a woman.

Alternative and Changing Norms and Conventions

It can be discouraging to survey the ways women's linguistic "differences" from men can disadvantage women as agents reshaping the linguistic norms of their communities. However, we have many indications that this situation can be challenged successfully. Male "control" in situated interactions and in the course of shaping evolving community norms is at best partial and certainly not monolithic. Both women and men have complex arrays of "interests" to further through their actions and have ambivalent connections to community endeavors.

Some of the studies cited above emphasize women's agency, their active participation in interactions. In addition, a number of researchers (re)examining women's participation in linguistic practices find this active agency important not just for the individual agents but for developing socially viable countercurrents and giving alternative meanings to linguistic strategies and forms. Although some "coping" practices ultimately help maintain existing inequities (simply making them more "bearable" for the oppressed), other countercurrents have more potential for transforming communities.

Politeness, for example, is often associated with women's language use. Researchers have tended to see politeness as either passive enforced deference (e.g. 67) or willful "prissy" avoidance of real social engagement (for an early critique of this view see 2). As noted above in the discussion of variation and adherence to "standard language" norms, women's alleged "correctness" can also be viewed as evidence that they are repressed prigs (the "schoolmarm" image) or timid and unimaginative shrinking violets. Alternative functional characterizations may be somewhat more positive, linking women's politeness and correctness to their nurturing roles and to the educative and "civilizing" functions they often serve.

Quite different interpretations have seen these same "women's" linguistic features arising as (partial) strategic solutions to the problems posed for women by their social oppression. Trudgill (113) proposed that women's relative phonological conservatism in Norwich England reflects a symbolic compensation for a lack of access to the marketplace. Eckert (26, 27) has expanded on this view, arguing that women are constrained in a variety of ways to accumulate symbolic capital more generally. Deuchar (24) has argued, furthermore, that where women's language is more standard than men's it may serve to defend them against accusations of stupidity or ignorance, thus increasing the likelihood that they will be recognized as agents capable not only of communicating but also of creating meanings, as not only consumers but also producers of symbols. Speculations like these gain support from observations of such "women's language" features as politeness and "correctness" in the context of community practice.

Community-based studies show clearly, for example, that politeness is not simply a matter of arbitrary conventional norms constraining individuals ("Ask Kim nicely!") but of intricate and connected strategies to foster social connections and potential alliances and to subvert institutionalized status advantages (see 12 for a general account). Brown (11) examines language use in a Mayan community where in-marrying women are structurally subordinated in many ways, including being subjected to physical violence from husbands and mothers-in-law. Although they do defer to men, they accord respect to other women and foster positive affiliative ties both with other women and with men. In general, they fine-tune their politeness strategies to enhance their individual positions, even using the forms of respect ironically as weapons in such rare (and socially problematic) activities as direct confrontation in the courtroom (10). Lack of other resources having forced these women to develop such nuanced linguistic skills, they actively use them to lessen their social disadvantage and increase their social power (albeit only in limited ways).

A number of community studies detail other concrete ways women refuse to accept passively certain problematic features of their participation in community practices, often reevaluating those practices from alternative perspectives. Radway (92), for example, found that a number of women who were avid readers of "bodice-ripping" romances exercised considerable selectivity in their reading and were not, as some critics argued, simply feeding a perverse masochism produced by a misogynistic culture. They actively sought visions of capable women and (at least eventually) admiring and respecting men; they saw their own reading activities as having educational value and as asserting their own self-worth and entitlement to pleasure. They recognized, however, that others did not share their assessment. Furthermore, as Radway points out, reading romances may have prevented their issuing more fundamental challenges to the unsatisfactory state of gender relations in their communities of practice, including in their marriages.

Studies that emphasize access as a determining factor in the "acquisition" of language varieties have an underlying functionalist flavor. Specific language varieties are associated with specific situations; speakers are then cast both as passive users of whatever language varieties they happen to come into contact with and as passive participants in whatever situations they happen to find themselves in. But language choice can be an important strategy for gaining control over one's exposure to people, situations, and opportunities. Gal's study (33) of language shift in a Hungarian-speaking agricultural community in Austria shows young women emerging as leaders in social change and language shift as part of a move to gain greater control over their own lives—and young men holding back in order to maintain control over theirs. In this male-dominated peasant community, women see their interests as conflicting with those of local men. By rejecting Hungarian for German, they reject the roles and identity of a peasant wife in a male-dominated agricultural community, in favor of greater access to jobs and marriage partners in the emerging local industrial economy. Their local male peers' retention of Hungarian, on the other hand, is consonant with the greater attractiveness for men of the traditional agricultural life.

Harding's (46) description of women's verbal behavior in a Spanish village might seem to support either Tannen's generalized claim that women seek connection or less flattering views of women as "gossips." But Harding's rich ethnographic observations show that this behavior plays a different role in overall practice. Though formal authority and political power in the village are vested in men, the men depend on their wives for information (obtained through talk with other women); this information is offered to husbands in forms designed to influence their evaluation of affairs and their subsequent decisions. Thus the women gain considerable influence over many important matters in the community, though that influence is exercised only with the cooperation of men and only within the general parameters of existing practices and relations.

Misogyny in evaluating women's speech (e.g. trivializing it as "gossip") has certainly been prevalent, and sexist patterns of language use are now well documented. Baron (3) provides a useful historical perspective, and Frank & Treichler (31) offer a superb summary of the field accompanied by excellent annotated bibliographies. Much of this work has focused on American English [and on heterosexual white middle-class speakers thereof; but see (47, 119)]; but the project of documenting male dominance in speech evaluation, and that of documenting misogyny and heterosexism in widespread usage patterns and rhetorical practices, have recently become international (50, 52, 86, 112). Scholars have also begun to study linguistic androcentrism in such enterprises as science and philosophy (30, 82).

Women do not always accept views excluding them from active participation in shaping the community's endeavors and practices. Visible and effective resistance has characterized the (mainly white and middle-class) feminist movement, ranging from new publications like *Ms.*, to consciousness-raising groups, to assertiveness training, to nonsexist language guidelines (see 31; for Canada's bilingual situation, see 57). Just as striking though less visible in the mainstream are the many refusals to accept wholeheartedly women's relegation to inferior status. Martin's (71) compelling ethnographic study of ways of talking about women's reproductive experiences shows that although authoritative (mainly male) voices in the community (e.g. the medical establishment) do sometimes enforce views of women as under these authorities' control ("managing childbirth"), women can see themselves as active agents. Class privilege may make resistance to predominant views of gender less likely. For example, middle-class women tend to accept the medical model of menstruation, childbirth, and menopause far more readily than do working-class women. Why? Perhaps because the middle-class women far more often depend directly for their personal and economic well-being on men much like those in the medical establishment: Doctors' wives or daughters or sisters have a general interest in doctors' continued authority, and some middle-class women (indeed increasingly many these days) aspire to be accepted as members of that medical establishment themselves.

Some feminists have spoken of men's "control" of language: Men set norms that limit and devalue "women's language" and they appropriate meaning-making for themselves. Male-controlled meaning leads not only to what is called sexist language but also to exclusion of women's contributions from the wide range of cultural values and from what counts as knowledge. Language has been described as "man made" (99) and, more recently, as shaped in and serving the interests of a "patriarchal universe of discourse" (87). The claim is that men (sometimes "modified": e.g. elite white heterosexual men) derogate women and their language and impose on women definitions of reality that serve men's interests at the expense of women's, suppressing or at least ignoring women's meanings. There are subtle as well as simplistic versions of the view that men have shaped language as an instrument for their own sexual, social, political, and intellectual ends. Even the subtlest versions fail to show how norms and conventions might confer or sustain privilege without overt coercion or conscious direction. Nor have their proponents investigated the complex ways linguistic power relates to gendered individuals, including resistant practices like those mentioned above.

Ultimately the view that males have made language an instrument of their own purposes also misses the real potency of language by assuming its meanings float in the ether, unattached to social and linguistic practices. McConnell-Ginet (75, 77) explains semantic change as possible precisely because linguistic forms do not come permanently glued to meanings but are endowed with meanings in the course of social practice. The history of linguistic and social practice constrains but does not determine what a speaker can mean. Male domination in conversation, then—be it subtle or overt—can impose male-oriented meanings on linguistic forms and reinforce them; but meanings are never uniform, nor can they be completely controlled. There is always room for resistance, challenge, and alternatives. Male-centered perspectives can seem to infect "the language" itself, but protection afforded them by existing linguistic conventions of meaning is never complete: Such conventions (and thus "the language") must be continuously sustained in ongoing interactions. Thus we cannot separate so-called "semantic" issues from the kinds of interactive dynamics we have discussed above; on the contrary, it is through these dynamics (including the ways individual interactions connect to wider community practices and institutions) that "the language" and conventions for using it are constituted.

The fact that in most societies familiar to us there are more stereotypes of female language than of male indicates the pervasiveness of the view that women and their relation to language are deviant or "other." Ironically, however, the cumulative effect of a new research focus on women has been to perpetuate this view of men as "normal" and women as needing to be studied. For example, many still refer to the study of language and gender as the study of "women's language." Just as racial privilege maintains the illusion that racial difference resides in people of color, and as heterosexual privilege sustains the illusion that differences in sexuality reside in lesbians and gay males, male privilege sustains the myth that male talk and male meaning-making are not gendered. Such privilege affects the interpretation of speech differences; it also affects how people use language to represent and direct their own and others' thought and action. "Women's words" have too often been interpreted by analysts from male-centered perspectives that ignore multiple possibilities of meaning: To mount any real challenge to women's linguistic disadvantage, we must shift scholarly attention to "men's words" and to language more generally. Black & Coward suggest (7) that men's linguistic advantage over women, in our own and other Western cultures, may derive primarily from the fact that in many communities of practice there exist familiar ways of talking and thinking—roughly what they and other theorists call "discourses"—that constitute men as ungendered autonomous beings and women as gendered and dependent on men. Such discourses involve more than use of such so-called masculine generic forms as "he" or "man," extending to a more general presumption that maleness is a norm while femaleness is a special condition—a presumption that supports a wide range of linguistic and other social practices. One need not believe the presumption to fall into its trap. Even someone attacking the privilege of "white, male heterosexuals" can slip and imply that "most Americans" are in that category, and feminists can eloquently defend the rights of "women and other (!) minorities." The "majority" here is quite clearly not a literal one, yet we have almost certainly ourselves lapsed into such profoundly problematic misstatements (though not, we hope, in this review).

Community Practices and Linguistic Power

As we have seen, sexual asymmetries in culturally sanctioned power can be both deeper and more subtly connected to language than is suggested by accounts of enforced female deference or male tyranny in local speech activities. Language is a key symbolic and communicative resource, central to developing the ways of thinking and doing that give communities of practice their character. As the preceding sections show, dominance relations among individuals or groups cannot be assessed simply by surveying who says what to whom. Relations of equality or dominance are partly produced in and through what is said (and through histories of similar utterances and their interpretations), as are the speaker and the auditor. The utterance "How about some more coffee, hon?" must be understood in light of two quite different practices when spoken, on the one hand, by a wife holding her empty cup up to her husband and, on the other, by a young male airline passenger to the middle-aged woman pushing the refreshment cart. A marriage creates a persistent community of practice typically involving a rich array of couple-specific practices. The airplane is a very short-lived community involving limited and routine practices common to many similar communities. In both cases power relations derive in part from such conversational exchanges and their place in community practice.

Dominance is sustained by privileging in community practice a particular perspective on language, obscuring its status as one among many perspectives, and naturalizing it as neutral or "unmarked." The privileged can assume their own positions to be norms toward which everyone else orients; they can judge other positions while supposing their own to be invulnerable to less privileged assessment. This privileged relation to a symbolic system, which we shall call symbolic privilege, carries with it interpretive and evaluative authority that requires no explanation or justification.

Symbolic privilege is not, of course, absolute; it is a matter of degree. Nor is a person's rank in symbolic privilege fixed. A woman might have considerable symbolic privilege in her neighborhood but rank low in her office; she might exercise considerable authority in talk about nutrition but not in discussion of finance. Symbolic privilege in some communities of practice may extend far beyond local settings, perhaps through institutions and practices associated with them. Treichler (111) recounts the lovely story of a woman collecting citations for the *Oxford English Dictionary* who used in, and then collected from, her own published writings words and meanings she wanted "authorized" by dictionary inclusion. Symbolic privilege is seldom so obvious or so self-consciously wielded.

Symbolic resources do, of course, mediate access to material resources, but they are ultimately more difficult to monopolize and control. The function and meaning of linguistic forms must be created by situated use if language is to serve the changing needs of communities. A language that cannot grow or change is a defective social and cognitive instrument. Growth and change may threaten established linguistic privilege.

EPILOG

Despite the studies of language and gender discussed above we do not yet have a coherent view of the interaction of gender and language. Existing theories have tended to draw on popular conceptions of gender—e.g. as a set of sex-determined attributes of individuals (a kind of "femininity" or "masculinity," often associated with a particular division of social activities such as childcare or making war), or as a relation of oppression of females by males. As we have emphasized, gender cannot be understood simply as a matter of individual attributes: Femininity connects to masculinity, femininities and masculinities connect to one another, and all connect to other dimensions of social categorization. Nor is gender reducible to a relation between "women" and "men" as undifferentiated groups. Rather, gender is constructed in a complex array of social practices within communities, practices that in many cases connect to personal attributes and to power relations but that do so in varied, subtle, and changing ways.

Although a number of scholars have attempted to understand language as rooted in social practice, relatively little progress has been made in explaining how social practices relate to linguistic structures and systems. With only a few exceptions (e.g. 7, 32), linguists have ignored recent work in social theory that might eventually deepen our understanding of the social dimensions of cognition (and of the cognitive dimensions of social practice). Even less attention has been paid to the social (including the linguistic) construction of gender categories: The notions of "women" and "men" are typically taken for granted in sociolinguistics. Nor has much attention been given to the variety of ways gender relations and privilege are constructed. Dominance is often seen as either a matter of deference and/or coercion; other aspects of gender relations—e.g. sexual attraction—are typically ignored. Theoretical work in gender studies (e.g. 6, 22, 96, 107) is still not well known among theorists of society and culture (but see 37 as an interesting contribution), and sociolinguistic studies have only rarely taken advantage of recent developments in understanding gender (but see e.g. 39).

Sociolinguists working on questions of language and gender need to build bridges to other communities of scholarly practice whose endeavors focus more centrally on gender. Many linguists talk about gender only because sex has seemed to emerge as a significant variable in their study of phenomena like variation, intonation, or the use of indirection in discourse. They try to elucidate particular aspects of language use or linguistic structure; they seldom hold themselves accountable to gender theory, or even to linguistic theory beyond their own area of specialization. Others who talk about language do so from an interest not in language itself but in gender (not always an analytical or intellectual interest); such scholars may miss insights into the detailed workings of language that linguistics can provide. No community of intellectual practice yet centers on the interactions of gender and language. It is therefore impossible at this point to share approaches to the important questions or evaluations of interim answers.

Investigators have not neglected to look at others' observations before proposing accounts of gender and language interactions. Citations abound in support of claims that women's language reflects conservatism, prestige consciousness, upward mobility, insecurity, deference, nurturance, emotivity, connectedness, sensitivity to others, and solidarity; and that men's language reflects toughness, lack of affect, competitiveness, and independence. But the observations on which such claims are based have all been made at different times and in different circumstances with different populations. One seldom finds good evidence from social practice for the gender characterizations made (evidence of the kind provided by Brown for her claim (11) that the Mayan women in the Mexican village of Tenejapa are politer than their male peers), and it is rarer still to find evidence from social practice of the comparability of observations made in distinct local communities.

It seems clear that the content of gender categories and their connections to linguistic behavior can only be determined by ethnographic study. Such study will likely demonstrate that gender categories intertwine with other social classifications (e.g. class, age, race) within communities of practice; the categories' content and their connections with linguistic behavior will likely work differently in distinct communities of practice. But, as we have noted, there are also deeper difficulties than those posed by premature generalization across communities about gender-language correlations. First, such generalizations tend to forestall close examination of how features like vernacular use (variously interpreted as discussed above, pp. 469, 479) might enter into the social practices of the community. Which activities and situations promote use of the vernacular by those who "tend" to avoid it and for those who "tend" to favor it?

Second, to ask how "women" (or "men") behave "as a group" is to focus on gender conformity and ignore intragender differences (especially challenges to gender hegemony). Suppose in a particular community a given woman uses more (or a given man less) vernacular than other female and male community members, respectively. Are there patterns of exception to community-wide generalizations that can be explained by a deeper understanding of the community's social practices? Can looking at these patterned exceptions yield insight into mechanisms of social and linguistic change?

Third, focus on gender content diverts attention from what may ultimately prove the far more interesting question: How does social practice "use" gender differences (seen as central to gender "content") in constructing gender relations and other social relations (and vice versa). What role does language play in this reciprocal construction of gender difference and gender relations? The diversity of gender differences and relations across and within communities should help us better understand the possible parameters of interaction between language and gender (and, more generally, among language, thought, and society).

Every informed and detailed study of a single language contributes to our understanding of linguistic universals, and every informed and detailed study of a social group contributes to our understanding of social and cultural universals. Both linguists (e.g. 18) and anthropologists (e.g. 34) have argued, however, that such universals are more formal than substantive. Linguists and anthropologists generally agree that comparative studies are essential to getting a grip on the ranges of human language, thought, and social life. We have nothing so grandiose in mind as a detailed theory of the general principles and parameters of gender and language interactions. We certainly are not recommending linguistic theory as a model for thinking about those interactions. What we do want to stress, however, is the great variability both in the factors that constitute gender—the character of gender differences and beliefs about them—and in relations between genders. The latter include not only sex-linked power asymmetries but also other aspects of social ties and social relations [including connections to other social hierarchies and to what Connell (22) dubs the "cathexis" complex of desire, liking, and aversion]. We still have little idea of what general principles may be at play in the joint construction of gender differences and gender relations.

Significant further advances in the study of language and gender must involve unprecedented integration. Such integration can come only through the intensive collaboration of people working in a variety of fields and a variety of communities. Language and gender studies, in fact, require an interdisciplinary community of scholarly practice. Isolated individuals who try to straddle two fields can often offer insights, but progress depends on getting people from a variety of fields to collaborate closely in building a common and broad-based understanding. Collaboration is needed among people in different fields and among people doing similar work in more than one community. A collaborative effort among ethnographers in many different communities might arrive at a view of gender dynamics across communities rich enough to begin to permit generalizations about the relation to language of those dynamics. These would not simply be studies of women or of men. These studies would explore how "women" and "men" are constructed as social categories. They would also explore how these constructions link to relations among those constructed as "women" and among those constructed as "men" (including those constructed as atypical or deviant members of their categories) as well as to relations between those assigned to different categories. These studies would be studies not of language in isolation from other social practices but of the linguistic dimensions of social practice [and, more generally, the complex social and cognitive character of so-called "(socio)linguistic competence"]. By approaching both gender and language as constructed in communities of practice, we may be able to strengthen claims about the social and cognitive importance of their interaction. We may likewise succeed in enriching our view of social conflict and change, thus deepening our understanding of the profoundly historical character of gender, of language, and of their connections.

ACKNOWLEDGMENTS

The authors thank the many colleagues from whom we have learned about language, gender, and their interaction, including especially the participants in our 1991 Linguistic Society of America Summer Institute course. We also owe a lot to the others who have worked on these topics, including many scholars whose work we have not happened to cite. Special thanks to Carl Ginet and Sandra Bem for helpful comments and encouragement at critical stages; to Nancy Henley, Cheris Kramarae, and Barrie Thorne for suggested references; to Etienne Wenger for a useful evening of talk about communities of practice; to the computer folks who tried to make our e-mail connections work; and to Karen Powell for assembling the bibliography. Each of us thanks the other for intellectual and other kinds of companionship, and we agree to share authorial responsibility completely. Our names appear in alphabetical order.

Literature Cited

1. Albert, E. M. 1972. Culture patterning of speech behavior in Burundi. See Ref. 44, pp. 72–105
2. Angle, J., Hesse, S. 1976. *Hoity-Toity Talk and Women*. Work. Pap. 131. Cent. Res. Soc. Organ., Univ. Mich.
3. Baron, D. 1986. *Grammar and Gender*. New Haven: Yale Univ. Press
4. Bauman, R., Sherzer, J., eds. 1974. *Explorations in the Ethnography of Speaking*. Cambridge: Cambridge Univ. Press
5. Belenky, M. F., Goldberg, N. R., Tarule, J.M. 1986. *Women's Ways of Knowing*. New York: Basic Books
6. Bem, S. L. 1993. *The Lenses of Gender: Transforming the Debate on Sexual In-*

equality. New Haven: Yale Univ. Press. In press

7. Black, M., Coward, R. 1990. Linguistic, social and sexual relations. See Ref. 15, pp. 111–33

8. Borker, R., Maltz, D. 1989. Anthropological perspectives on gender and language. In *Gender and Anthropology: Critical Reviews for Research in Teaching,* ed. S. Morgen, pp. 411–37. Washington, DC: Am. Anthropol. Assoc.

9. Bortoni-Ricardo, S. M. 1985. *The Urbanization of Rural Dialect Speakers.* Cambridge: Cambridge Univ. Press

10. Brown, P. 1990. Gender, politeness, and confrontation in Tenejapa. *Discourse Process.* 13:123–41

11. Brown, P. 1980. How and why are women more polite: Some evidence from a Mayan community. See Ref. 78, pp. 111–36

12. Brown, P., Levinson, S. 1987. *Politeness: Some Universals in Language Use.* Cambridge: Cambridge Univ. Press

13. Brown, P., Levinson, S. 1979. Social structure, groups and interaction. In *Social Markers in Speech,* ed. K. R. Scherer, H. Giles, pp. 291–342. Cambridge: Cambridge Univ. Press

14. Cameron, D. 1985. *Feminism and Linguistic Theory.* London: Macmillan

15. Cameron, D. 1990. *The Feminist Critique of Language: A Reader.* London/New York: Routledge

16. Cameron, D., Coates, J. 1988. Some problems in the sociolinguistic explanation of sex differences. See Ref. 21, pp. 13–26

17. Cameron, D., McAlinden, F., O'Leary, K. 1988. Lakoff in context: The social and linguistic function of tag questions. See Ref. 21, pp. 74–93

18. Chomsky, N. 1986. *Knowledge of Language: Its Nature, Origin and Use.* New York: Praeger

19. Coates, J. 1988. Gossip revisited: Language in all-female groups. See Ref. 21, pp. 94–122

20. Coates, J. 1986. *Women, Men and Language.* London: Longman

21. Coates, J., Cameron, D., eds. 1988. *Women in Their Speech Communities: New Perspectives on Language and Sex.* London / New York: Longman

22. Connell, R. W. 1987. *Gender and Power.* Stanford, CA: Stanford Univ. Press

23. Crosby, F., Nyquist, L. 1977. The female register: An empirical study of Lakoff's hypothesis. *Lang. Soc.* 6:313–22

24. Deuchar, M. 1988. A pragmatic account of women's use of standard speech. See Ref. 21, pp. 27–32

25. Dubois, B. L., Crouch, I. 1975. The question of tag questions in women's speech: They don't really use more of them, do they? *Lang. Soc.* 4:289–94

26. Eckert, P. 1990. Cooperative competition in adolescent girl talk. *Discourse Process.* 13:92–122

27. Eckert, P. 1990. The whole woman: Sex and gender differences in variation. *Lang. Variation Change* 1:245–67

28. Edelsky, C. 1981. Who's got the floor? *Lang. Soc.* 10:383–421

29. Fishman, P. M. 1983. Interaction: The work women do. See Ref. 109, pp. 89–102

30. Fox Keller, E. 1987. The gender/science system: Or is sex to gender as nature is to science? *Hypatia* 2

31. Frank, F. W., Treichler, P. A. 1989. *Language, Gender, and Professional Writing: Theoretical Approaches and Guidelines for Nonsexist Usage.* New York: Modern Language Assoc.

32. Gal, S. 1991. Between speech and silence: The problematics of resesarch on language and gender. In *Gender at the Crossroads of Knowledge: Feminist Anthropology in the Postmodern Era,* ed. M. DiLeonardo, pp. 175–203. Berkeley: Univ. Calif. Press

33. Gal, S. 1978. Peasant men can't get wives: Language change and sex roles in a bilingual community. *Lang. Soc.* 7:1–16

34. Geertz, C. 1973. *The Interpretation of Cultures.* New York: Basic Books

35. Gilligan, C. 1982. *In a Different Voice.* Cambridge: Harvard Univ. Press

36. Gleason, J. B., Greif, E. B. 1983. Men's speech to young children. See Ref. 109, pp. 140–50

37. Goffman, E. 1977. The arrangement between the sexes. *Theory Soc.* 4.301–32

38. Goodwin, M. H. 1980. Directive-response speech sequences in girls' and boys' task activities. See Ref. 78, pp. 157–73

39. Goodwin, M. H. 1991. *He-Said-She-Said.* Bloomington: Indiana Univ. Press

40. Goodwin, M. H. 1990. Tactical uses of stories: Participation frameworks within girls' and boys' disputes. *Discourse Process.* 13:33–72

41. Graddol, D., Swann, J. 1989. *Gender Voices.* Oxford: Basil Blackwell

42. Gumperz, J. J. 1972. Introduction. See Ref. 44, pp. 1–25

43. Gumperz, J. J., ed. 1982. *Language and Social Identity.* Cambridge: Cambridge Univ. Press

44. Gumperz, J. J., Hymes, D., eds. 1972. *Directions in Sociolinguistics.* New York: Holt, Rinehart & Winston

45. Guy, G., Horvath, B., Vonwiller, J., Daisley, E., Rogers, I. 1986. An intonational change in progress in Australian English. *Lang. Soc.* 15:23–52

46. Harding, S. 1975. Women and words in a Spanish village. In *Toward an Anthropology of Women,* ed. R. R. Reiter, pp. 283–308. New York: Monthly Review Press

47. Henley, N. M. 1992. Ethnicity and gender issues in language. In *Handbook of Cultural Diversity in Feminist Psychology,* ed. H. Landrine. Washington DC: Am. Technol. Assoc. In press

48. Henley, N., Kramarae, C. 1991. Gender, power, and miscommunication. In *Problem*

Talk and Problem Contexts, ed. N. Coupland, H. Giles, J. Wiemann, pp. 18–43. Newbury Park, CA: Sage

49. Hindle, D. 1979. The social and situational conditioning of phonetic variation. Dissertation. Univ. Penn.

50. Hiraga, M. K. 1991. Metaphors Japanese women live by. Work. Pap. Lang., Gender, Sexism 1:38–57

51. Houston, M., Kramarae, C. 1991. Speaking from silence: Methods of silencing and resistance. Discourse Soc. 2:387–99

52. Ide, S., McGloin, N. H., eds. 1990. Aspects of Japanese Women's Language. Tokyo: Kurosio

53. James, D., Clarke, S. 1992. Women, men and interruptions: A critical review. See Ref. 103. In press

54. James, D., Drakich, J. 1992. Understanding gender differences in amount of talk: A critical review of research. See Ref. 103. In press

55. Kalčik, S. 1975. "… like Ann's gynecologist or the time I was almost raped": Personal narratives in women's rap groups." J. Am. Folklore 88:3–11

56. Keenan, E. 1974. Norm-makers, norm-breakers: Uses of speech by men and women in a Malagasy community. See Ref. 4, pp. 125–43

57. King, R. 1991. Talking Gender: A Guide to Nonsexist Communication. Toronto: Copp Clark Pitman/Longman

58. Komarovsky, M. 1962. Blue-Collar Marriage. New Haven/London: Yale Univ. Press

59. Kramarae, C. 1988. Technology and Women's Voices: Keeping in Touch. New York/London: Routledge & Kegan Paul

60. Kramarae, C. 1981. Women and Men Speaking: Frameworks for Analysis. Rowley, MA: Newbury House

61. Krieger, S. 1983. The Mirror Dance: Identity in a Women's Community. Philadelphia: Temple Univ. Press

62. Labov, W. 1991. The intersection of sex and social class in the course of linguistic change. Lang. Variation Change 2:205–51

63. Labov, W. 1972. The linguistic consequences of being a lame. In Language in the Inner City, ed. W. Labov, pp. 255–92. Philadelphia: Univ. Penn. Press

64. Labov, W. 1980. The social origins of sound change. In Locating Language in Time and Space, ed. W. Labov, pp. 251–65. New York: Academic

65. Labov, W. 1966. The Social Stratification of English in New York City. Washington, DC: Cent. Appl. Linguist.

66. Labov, W. 1972. Sociolinguistic Patterns. Philadelphia: Univ. Penn. Press

67. Lakoff, R. 1975. Language and Woman's Place. New York: Harper & Row

68. Lakoff, R. T. 1990. Talking Power: The Politics of Language in Our Lives. New York: Basic Books

69. Lave, J., Wenger, E. 1991. Situated Learning: Legitimate Peripheral Participation. Cambridge: Cambridge Univ. Press

70. Maltz, D. N., Borker, R. A. 1982. A cultural approach to male-female miscommunication. See Ref. 43, pp. 196–216

71. Martin, E. 1987. The Woman in the Body: A Cultural Analysis of Reproduction. Boston: Beacon Press

72. McConnell-Ginet, S. 1980. Difference and language: A linguist's perspective. In The Future of Difference, ed. H. Eisenstein, pp. 157–66. Boston: G. K. Hall

73. McConnell-Ginet, S. 1983. Intonation in a man's world. See Ref. 109, pp. 69–88

74. McConnell-Ginet, S. 1988. Language and gender. In Linguistics: The Cambridge Survey, ed. F. J. Newmeyer, pp. 75–99. Cambridge: Cambridge Univ. Press

75. McConnell-Ginet, S. 1984. The origins of sexist language in discourse. In Discourses in Reading and Linguistics, ed. S. J. White, V. Teller, pp. 123–35. Ann. NY Acad. Sci.

76. McConnell-Ginet, S. 1983. Review article. Language 59:373–91

77. McConnell-Ginet, S. 1989. The sexual (re)production of meaning: A discourse based theory. See Ref. 31, pp. 35–50

78. McConnell-Ginet, S., Borker, R. A., Furman, N., eds. 1980. Women and Language in Literature and Society. New York: Praeger

79. McLemore, C. 1992. The interpretation of L*H in English. In Linguistic Forum 32, ed. C. McLemore. Austin: Univ. Texas Dep. Linguist. Cent. Cogn. Sci. In press

80. Milroy, L. 1980. Language and Social Networks. Oxford: Blackwell

81. Morgan, M. 1992. Indirectness and Interpretation in African American Women's Discourse. Pragmatics. In press

82. Moulton, J. 1983. The adversary paradigm in philosophy. In Discovering Reality, ed. S. Harding, M. B. Hintikka. Boston/Dordrecht: Reidel

83. Nichols, P. C. 1983. Linguistic options and choices for black women in the rural south. See Ref. 109, pp. 54–68

84. O'Barr, W. M., Atkins, B. K. 1980. "Women's language" or "powerless language"? See Ref. 78, pp. 93–110

85. Ochs, E. 1991. Indexing gender. In Rethinking Context, ed. A. Duranti, C. Goodwin. Cambridge: Cambridge Univ. Press

86. Pauwels, A., ed. 1987. Women and Language in Australian and New Zealand Society. Mosman, NSW: Aust. Professional Publ.

87. Penelope, J. 1990. Speaking Freely: Unlearning the Lies of the Fathers' Tongues. New York: Pergamon

88. Penfield, J. 1987. Women and Language in Transition. Albany, NY: SUNY Press

89. Philips, S. U. 1980. Sex differences and language. Annu. Rev. Anthropol. 9:523–44

90. Philips, S. U., Steele, S., Tanz, C., eds. 1987. Language, Gender, and Sex in Com-

parative Perspective. Cambridge: Cambridge Univ. Press
91. Poynton, C. 1989. *Language and Gender.* Oxford: Oxford Univ. Press
92. Radway, J. A. 1984. *Reading the Romance: Women, Patriarchy, and Popular Literature.* Chapel Hill, NC: Univ. NC Press
93. Sankoff, D., Laberge, S. 1978. The linguistic market and the statistical explanation of variability. In *Linguistic Variation: Models and Methods,* ed. D. Sankoff, pp. 239–50. New York: Academic
94. Sattel, J. 1983. Men, inexpressiveness and power. See Ref. 109, pp. 119–24
95. Scollon, R., Scollon, S. B. K. 1980. *Athabaskan-English Interethnic Communication.* Fairbanks: Cent. Cross-cultural Stud., Univ. Alaska
96. Segal, L. 1990. *Slow Motion: Changing Masculinities, Changing Men.* New Brunswick, NJ: Rutgers Univ. Press
97. Singh, R., Lele, J. K. 1990. Language, power and cross-sex communication in Hindi and Indian English revisited. *Lang. Soc.* 19:541–46
98. Smith, P. M. 1985. *Language, the Sexes and Society.* Oxford: Blackwell
99. Spender, D. 1980. *Man Made Language.* London: Routledge & Kegan Paul
100. Swacker, M. 1975. The sex of speaker as a sociolinguistic variable. See Ref. 108, pp. 76–83
101. Swann, J. 1988. Talk control: An illustration from the classroom of problems in analysing male dominance of conversation. See Ref. 21, pp. 123–40
102. Tannen, D. 1982. Ethnic style in male-female communication. See Ref. 43, pp. 217–31
103. Tannen, D., ed. 1992. *Gender and Conversational Interaction.* Oxford: Oxford Univ. Press
104. Tannen, D. 1989. Interpreting interruption in conversation. *Pap. 25th Annu. Meet. Chicago Linguist. Soc., Part 2: Parasession on Language and Context.* Chicago: Univ. Chicago Press
105. Tannen, D. 1990. *You Just Don't Understand: Women and Men in Conversation.* New York: Morrow
106. Thomas, B. 1988. Differences of sex and sects: linguistic variation and social networks in a Welsh mining village. See Ref. 21, pp. 51–60
107. Thorne, B. 1990. Children and gender: Constructions of difference. In *Theoretical Perspectives on Sexual Difference,* ed. D. Rhode, pp. 100–12. New Haven: Yale Univ. Press
108. Thorne, B., Henley, N., eds. 1975. *Language and Sex: Difference and Dominance.* Rowley, MA: Newbury House
109. Thorne, B., Kramarae, C., Henley, N., eds. 1983. *Language, Gender and Society.* Rowley, MA: Newbury House
110. Todd, A. D., Fisher, S. 1988. *Gender and Discourse: The Power of Talk.* Norwood, NJ: Ablex
111. Treichler, P. A. 1989. From discourse to dictionary: How sexist meanings are authorized. See Ref. 31, pp. 51–79
112. Trömmel-Plötz, S. 1982. *Frauensprache - Sprache der Vernderung.* Frankfurt-am-Main: Fischer
113. Trudgill, P. 1972. Sex, covert prestige and linguistic change in the urban British English of Norwich. *Lang. Soc.* 1:179–95
114. Trudgill, P. 1974. *The Social Differentiation of English in Norwich.* Cambridge: Cambridge Univ. Press
115. Vetterling-Braggin, M., ed. 1981. *Sexist Language: A Modern Philosophical Analysis.* Totowa, NJ: Littlefield, Adams & Co.
116. Wenger, E. 1993. *Communities of Practice.* New York: Cambridge Univ. Press. In press
117. West, C., Zimmerman, D. H. 1983. Small insults: A study of interruptions in cross-sex conversations between unacquainted persons. See Ref. 109, pp. 102–17
118. West, C., Zimmerman, D. H. 1977. Women's place in everyday talk: Reflections on parent-child interaction. *Soc. Probl.* 24:521–29
119. Wolfe, S. J. 1988. The rhetoric of heterosexism. In *Gender and Discourse: The Power of Talk,* ed. A. D. Todd, S. Fisher, pp. 199–244. Norwood, NJ: Ablex
120. Zimmerman, D., West, C. 1975. Sex roles, interruptions and silences in conversation. See Ref. 108, pp. 105–29

Annu. Rev. Anthropol. 1992. 21:491–516

SOCIAL ANTHROPOLOGY OF TECHNOLOGY

Bryan Pfaffenberger

Division of Humanities, School of Engineering and Applied Science, University of Virginia, Charlottesville, Virginia 22901

KEYWORDS: activity systems, technological change, sociotechnical systems, ritual, artifacts

At the onset of the 20th century, anthropologists such as Balfour, Marett, and Haddon could readily identify three spheres of strength in anthropological research: material culture, social organization, and physical anthropology (49). The study of technology and material culture, however, was about to be jettisoned, and with stunning finality. By 1914, Wissler (103:447) complained that the study of these subjects "has been quite out of fashion." Researchers were giving their attention to "language, art, ceremonies, and social organization" in place of the former almost obsessive concentration on the minute description of techniques and artifacts, and on the tendency to study artifacts without regard for their social and cultural context. As I aim to show in this chapter, the anthropological study of technology and material culture is poised, finally, for a comeback, if in a different guise. Its findings may significantly alter the way anthropologists analyze everyday life, cultural reproduction, and human evolution.

If this all-but-forgotten field is to play such a role, it must overcome nearly a century of peripheral status. In anthropology's quest for professionalism, material-culture studies came to stand for all that was academically embarrassing: extreme and conjectural forms of diffusionist and evolutionist explanation, armchair anthropology, "field work" undertaken by amateurs on collecting holidays, and the simplistic interpretation of artifacts shorn of their social and cultural context. Malinowski, for instance, condemned the "purely technological enthusiasms" of material culture ethnologists and adopted an "intransigent position" that the study of "technology alone" is "scientifically sterile" (69:460). The study of technology and material culture, a topic that

491

0084-6570/92/1015-0491$02.00

was (and is still) perceived as "dry, even intellectually arid and boring" (92, 5), was relegated to museums, where—out of contact with developments in social anthropology and deprived of ethnographic experience—museum scholars lacked the resources to advance the field. For their part, cultural anthropologists argued that studying techniques and artifacts could only deflect anthropologists from their proper role—that is, from studying culture. Kroeber & Kluckhohn, for example, dismissed the term *material culture* out of hand, arguing that "what is culture is the *idea* behind the artifact" (55:65). "Accordingly," Kroeber argued, "we may forget about this distinction between material and nonmaterial culture, except as a literal difference, that is sometimes of practical convenience to observe" (54:296). For anthropology, jettisoning material culture studies was a necessary step in establishing the scientific basis, the intellectual appeal, and the distinctive subject matter of the discipline.

Periodic attempts have been made to revive the seriously ill patient (e.g. 21, 34, 49, 59, 65, 66, 85, and 88), with their pace quickening in the 1980s (43, 44, 62, 63, 72, 73, 84, 92, 96). Yet, arguably, no real resuscitation has taken place, owing largely to the continued insouciance with which Anglo-American anthropologists regard the study of material culture and technology. In a recent restatement of the Kroeber & Kluckhohn view, Bouquet (13:352) condemns the "recent bids to reinstate the 'materiality' of material culture," as if such bids stemmed from some Philistine conspiracy, against which she prefers recognition of the "hegemony of linguistic approaches to the object world." Noting that the excesses of early material-culture scholars were rightly pilloried, Sillitoe laments that the "mud seems to have stuck more to artifacts and their study ... than to the [evolutionists'] wild-guess theories," which have themselves enjoyed a modest comeback (92, p. 6). As it stands, a topic with which anthropology was once closely identified—the cross-cultural study of technology and material culture—has been largely taken up by scholars working in other fields, such as the history of technology and the interdisciplinary field known as science and technology studies (STS), or by anthropologists with marginal appointments in museums or in the general studies divisions of engineering and technical colleges.

Despite the peripheral status of the anthropology of technology and material culture, compelling questions remain: What is technology? Is technology a human universal? What is the relationship between technological development and cultural evolution? Are there common themes in the appropriation of artifacts that bridge capitalist and precapitalist societies? How do people employ artifacts to accomplish social purposes in the course of everyday life? What kind of cultural meaning is embodied in technological artifacts? How does culture influence technological innovation—and how does technological innovation influence culture?

These questions are far from trivial—and, arguably, only anthropology can answer them. No other discipline offers sufficient comparative depth or appropriate methodologies. The challenge still remains, as Malinowski himself put it, to understand the role of technology as "an indispensable means of approach to economic and sociological activities and to what might be called native science" (69:460). And the challenge is even greater now that scholars generally concede that language, tool use, and social behavior evolved in a process of complex mutual interaction and feedback. Summing up the consensus of a conference titled "Tools, Language, and Intelligence: Evolutionary Implications," Gibson concludes that "We need to know more about the ways in which speaking, tool-using, and sociality are interwoven into the texture of everyday life in contemporary human groups" (29:263).

In this chapter, I argue that social anthropology has already discovered a great deal about human technological activity—especially when anthropological findings are interpreted in the context of recent, stunning advances in the sociology of scientific knowledge (11), the history and sociology of technology, and the emergent field known as science and technology studies (STS). Collectively, these fields, without much anthropological involvement, have developed a concept, the *sociotechnical system* concept (48), that refuses to deny the *sociality* of human technological activity. Developed mainly in social and historical studies of industrial societies, the sociotechnical system concept, I seek to show, serves fruitfully to integrate anthropological findings about *pre*industrial societies into a coherent picture of the universals of human technology and material culture. The central objective of this review, then, is to convey the sociotechnical system concept to an anthropological audience, and to show how it resolves key controversies within anthropology. The results should prove of interest to anthropologists working in fields as diverse as cultural ecology, ritual, symbolic anthropology, ethnoarchaeology, archaeology, and human evolution studies.

One reason for the rapid advance of STS is its refusal to accept the myths of science and technology at face value. Mulkay (74), for example, shows that sociology's refusal to develop a sociological analysis of scientific knowledge stems from sociologists' uncritical acceptance of a mythic Standard View of science. I suggest that the achievement of a truly *social* anthropology of technology likewise requires extending anthropology's recent productive venture into reflexivity (18, 70)—specifically, by making the mythic Standard View of technology explicit, and resolutely questioning its implications. For this reason, this essay begins with the Standard View of technology, and although its purpose is to present the sociotechnical system concept and explore its implications for anthropology, it is organized as a series of attacks on the implications of the Standard View.

THE STANDARD VIEW OF TECHNOLOGY

Like the Standard View of science (74: 19-21), the Standard View of technology underlies much scholarly as well as popular thinking. A master narrative of modern culture, the Standard View of technology could be elicited, more or less intact, from any undergraduate class. Occasionally, it is made explicit in anthropological writings (e.g. 39). By suggesting that such a Standard View exists, I do not mean to imply that every scholar who has advanced some part of it necessarily endorses the rest. In what follows, I deliberately use the masculine pronoun to stand for humankind; to do otherwise would strip the Standard View of its gender ideology.

Necessity is the mother of invention. As Man has been faced with severe survival challenges, certain extraordinary individuals have seen, often in a brilliant flash of inspiration, how to address the challenge of Need by applying the forces, potentialities, and affordances of Nature to the fabrication of tools and material artifacts. The power of Nature is there, waiting to be harnessed, to the extent that the inventor can clear away the cobwebs of culture to see the world from a purely utilitarian standpoint. In this we see Man's thirst for Progress.

Form follows function. To be sure, Man decorates his tools and artifacts, but artifacts are adopted to the extent that their form shows a clear and rational relationship to the artifacts' intended function—that is, its ability to satisfy the need that was the raison d'être of the artifact's creation. Thus, a society's material culture becomes a physical record of its characteristic survival adaptation; material culture is the primary means by which society effects its reproduction. The meaning of human artifacts is a surface matter of style, of surface burnish or minor symbolization.

By viewing the material record of Man's technological achievements, one can directly perceive the challenges Man faced in the past, and how he met these challenges. This record shows a unilinear progression over time, because technology is cumulative. Each new level of penetration into Nature's secrets builds on the previous one, producing ever more powerful inventions. The digging stick had to precede the plough. Those inventions that significantly increase Man's reach bring about revolutionary changes in social organization and subsistence. Accordingly, the ages of Man can be expressed in terms of technological stages, such as the Stone Age, the Iron Age, the Bronze Age, and so on. Our age is the Information Age, brought on by the invention of the computer. Overall, the movement is from very simple tools to very complex machines. It was also a movement from primitive sensorimotor skills (techniques) to highly elaborate systems of objective, linguistically encoded knowledge about Nature and its potential (technology).

Now, we live in a material world. The result of the explosion of technological knowledge has been a massive expansion of Man's reach, but with lamentable and unavoidable social, environmental, and cultural consequences: We live in a fabricated environment, mediated by machines. Technology was more authentic when we used tools, because we could control them. Machines, in contrast, control us. Thus one can identify a Great Divide or Rupture when Man lost his authenticity as a cultural creature, his Faustian depth as a being living in a world of cultural meaning, and gave himself over to a world ruled by instrumentalism and superficiality. This Rupture was the Industrial Revolution, which launched the Age of the Machine. As the primacy of function over aesthetics rips through culture, we increasingly live in a homogenous world of functionally driven design coherence. Our culture has become an inauthentic one in which reified images of technology predominate. We can define ourselves only by purchasing plastic,

ersatz artifacts made far away. To retain some measure of authenticity the young
must be brought into direct contact with the great works of art and literature.

The Standard View of technology appears to be a pillar of Modernism, a cultural, literary, and artistic period noted for its extreme ambivalence toward technology. According to most scholars (e.g. 40), Modernism reached its apex between the two World Wars. In essence, Modernism represents a struggle to find a stable ground of being within the promise and peril of science and technological development. Like Siva in Hindu iconography, technology is seen through the Modernist lens as both creator and destroyer, an agent both of future promise and of culture's destruction. Echoed perfectly in the Standard View of technology, Modernism amounts to

> an extraordinary compound of the futurist and the nihilistic, the revolutionary and the conservative, the romantic and the classical. It was the celebration of a technological age and a condemnation of it; an excited acceptance of the belief that the old regimes of culture were over, and a deep despairing in the face of that fear (15:46).

Modernism is an almost unavoidable response, as Bradbury & McFarlane put it, to the "scenario of our chaos" (15:27). Accordingly, any attempt to grasp the role of human technological activity must begin by questioning the Standard View's assumptions, which could, if left unexamined, color anthropological thought.

"NECESSITY IS THE MOTHER OF INVENTION"

The Standard View puts forth a commonsense view of technology and material culture that accords perfectly with our everyday understanding. All around us are artifacts originally developed to fulfill a specific need—juicers, word processors, vacuum cleaners, and telephones; and apart from artifacts that are decorative or symbolic, the most useful artifacts—the ones that increase our fitness or efficiency in dealing with everyday life—are associated each with a specific Master Function, given by the physical or technological properties of the object itself. Extending this commonsense view one quickly arrives at a theory of technological evolution (parodied by 4:6): People need water, "so they dig wells, dam rivers and streams, and develop hydraulic technology. They need shelter and defense, so they build houses, forts, cities, and military machines ... . They need to move through the environment with ease, so they invent ships, chariots, charts, carriages, bicycles, automobiles, airplanes, and spacecraft."

The New Archaeology, which sought to put archaeology on a firm modernist footing, puts forward a view of technology and artifacts firmly in accord with the Standard View and its presumption of need-driven technological evolution. Culture, according to Binford (7), is an "extrasomatic means of adaptation"; thus technology and material culture form the primary means by which people establish their viability, given the constraints imposed upon them by their environment and the demands of social integration. It follows, as Binford argued in 1965 (8), that every artifact has two dimensions, the primary, referring to the instrumental dimension related to the artifact's function, and the secondary, related to the artifact's social meaning and symbolism. Echoing this view, Dunnell makes explicit the connection that is assumed between an artifact's function and group survival: The artifact's function is that which "directly enhances the Darwinian fitness of the populations in which they occur" (23:199). Style, in contrast, is something added on the surface, a burnish or decoration, that might play some useful role in symbolizing group solidarity but is decidedly secondary. In the Modernist view, there are universal human needs, and for each of these there is an ideal artifact. For the primitive technologist, discovering such an artifact is like discovering America: It was there before the explorers finally found it—and to the extent that anyone bothers to look, it will be found, and inevitably adopted (although it might be resisted for a time). The tale of Man's rise, then, is the story of increasing technological prowess, as digging sticks develop into ploughs, drums into telephones, carts into cars.

The Standard View of technology offers a seemingly "hard" or "tough-minded" view of artifacts and technological evolution, but there is ample evidence that its "hardness" dissolves when examined critically. What seems to us an incontrovertible need, for which there is an ideal artifact, may well be generated by our own culture's fixations. Basalla (4:7–11) demonstrates this point forcefully with respect to the wheel. First used for ceremonial purposes in the Near East, the wheel took on military applications before finally finding transport applications. In Mesoamerica, the wheel was never adopted for transport functions, given the constraints of terrain and the lack of draught animals. Even in the Near East, where the wheel was first invented, it was gradually given up in favor of camels. Basalla comments, "A bias for the wheel led Western scholars to underrate the utility of pack animals and overestimate the contribution made by wheeled vehicles in the years before the camel replaced the wheel" (4:11). Against all Modernist bias, Basalla's view echoes the findings of recent social anthropologists who have argued that it is impossible to identify a class of "authentic" artifacts that directly and rationally address "real" needs (2, 22:72; 87). Culture, not nature, defines necessity. One could reassert that a "hard" or "tough-minded" approach requires the recognition, after all, that people must eat, and so on, but it is abundantly evident that a huge variety of techniques and artifacts can be chosen to accomplish any given utilitarian objective (91).

The supposed functions of artifacts, then, do not provide a clear portrait of a human culture's needs (38), and what is more, one cannot unambiguously infer from them precisely which challenges a human population has faced. The natives of chilly Tierra del Fuego, after all, were content to do without clothing. Accordingly, some archaeologists and social anthropologists would break radically with the Standard View in asserting that material culture does not play a decisive role in shaping a human group's adaptation to its environment. Golson (32) notes that a basic stone toolkit survives intact through "revolutionary" changes in subsistence in both the classic Old World sites and in the New Guinea highlands. A survey of the New Guinea tools, Golson concludes, "revealed none that is indispensable to any form, from the simplest to the most complex, of Highlands agricultural practice, except the stone axe or adze and the digging stick which are not only common to all but also serviceable in other than agricultural contexts" (32:161). Summarizing the evidence from social anthropology, Sahlins (86:81) puts this point well: "For the greater part of human history, labor has been more significant than tools, the intelligent efforts of the producer more significant than his simple equipment." Sahlins' view is echoed by Lemonnier (62:151), who notes that the "search for correspondences between technical level and 'stage' of economic organization does not seem likely to lead to a theory of the relation between technical systems and society, other than one so over-simplified and general that it quickly loses all interest." Material culture alone provides only a shadowy picture of human adaptations.

If techniques and artifacts are not the linchpins of human adaptation, as is so often surmised, then radical redefinitions are in order. It is not mere technology, but technology in concert with the social coordination of labor, that constitutes a human population's adaptation to its environment. In most preindustrial societies, technology plays second fiddle to the human capacity to invent and deploy fabulously complex and variable social arrangements. How, then, should we define technology? Spier (93:2), for instance, defines technology as the means by which "man seeks to modify or control his natural environment." This definition is clearly unsatisfactory. It assumes, a priori, that Man's inherent aim is domination or control of nature; and, anyway, it is wrong, since (as has just been argued) techniques and artifacts are secondary to the social coordination of labor in shaping human adaptations. One could broaden the definition of technology to include the social dimension. But because the term "technology" so easily conjures up "merely technical" activity shorn of its social context (77), I believe it preferable to employ two definitions, the one more restricted, and the other more inclusive. *Technique* (following 62, 63) refers to the system of material resources, tools, operational sequences and skills, verbal and nonverbal knowledge, and *specific* modes of work coordination that come into play in the fabrication of material artifacts. *Sociotechnical system,* in contrast, refers to the distinctive technological activity that stems from the linkage of techniques and material culture to the social coordination of labor. The proper and indispensable subjects of a social anthropology of technology, therefore, include all three: techniques, sociotechnical systems, and material culture.

The sociotechnical system concept stems from the work of Thomas Hughes on the rise of modern electrical power systems (45, 46; for applications of the concept, see 68, 81). According to Hughes, those who seek to develop new technologies must concern themselves not only with techniques and artifacts; they must also engineer the social, economic, legal, scientific, and political context of the technology. A successful technological innovation occurs only when all the elements of the system, the social as well as the technological, have been modified so that they work together effectively. Hughes (45) shows how Edison sought to supply electric lighting at a price competitive with natural gas (economic), to obtain the support of key politicians (political), to cut down the cost of transmitting power (technical), and to find a bulb filament of sufficiently high resistance (scientific). In a successful sociotechnical system, such as the electric lighting industry founded by Edison, the "web is seamless": "the social is indissolubly linked with the technological and the economic" (60:112). In short, sociotechnical systems are heterogeneous constructs that stem from the successful modification of social and nonsocial actors so that they work together harmoniously—that is, so that they resist dissociation (60:166–17)—i.e. resist dissolving or failing in the face of the system's adversaries. One or more sociotechnical systems may be found in a given human society, each devoted to a productive goal.

Extending Hughes's concept, Law (60) and Latour (57) emphasize the difficulty of creating a system capable of resisting dissociation. A system builder is faced with natural and social adversaries, each of which must be controlled and modified if the system is to work. Some of them are more obdurate, and some of them more malleable, than others. In illustrating this point, Law shows that the sociotechnical system concept applies fruitfully to the study of preindustrial technology, in this case the rise of the Portuguese mixed-rigged vessels in the 14th and early 15th centuries. The real achievement, argues Law, was not merely the creation of the mixed-rigged vessel, with its increased cargo capacity and storm stability. Equally important was the magnetic compass, which allowed a consistent heading in the absence of clear skies; the simplification of the astrolabe, such that even semieducated mariners could determine their latitude; exploration that was specifically intended to produce tables of data, against which position could be judged; and an understanding of Atlantic trade winds, which allowed ships to go forth in one season and come back in another. To achieve the necessary integration of all these factors, the system builders had to get mariners, ship builders, kings, merchants, winds, sails, wood, instruments, and measurements to work together harmoniously. The system they created resisted dissociation; they were able to sail out beyond the Pillars of Hercules, down the coast of Africa, and soon around the globe.

Although it is no easy trick to construct a system resistant to dissociation, sociotechnical systems are not inevitable responses to immutable constraints; they do not provide the only way to get the job done. People unfamiliar with technology usually gravely understate the degrees of latitude and choice open to innovators as they seek to solve technical problems (48). More commonly, one sees a range of options, each with its tradeoffs, and it is far from obvious which, if any, is superior. In virtually every technical area, there is substantial latitude for choice. For instance, Lemonnier (62) points to the apparently arbitrary variation of techniques as one moves across the New Guinea highlands; such variation is to be found, Lemonnier notes, even among those "functional" (as opposed to "stylistic") aspects of a tool that are directly implicated in its action upon material (62:160). It would be wrong to attribute a system's "success" (i.e. in resisting dissociation) to the choice of the "correct" technique or social-coordination method.

By analogy to the sociology of scientific knowledge (11), this point can be formulated as a *principle of symmetry*. In the sociology of scientific knowledge, this principle countered an older sociology of science that explained the success of a theory by its conformity to the Truth, while ascribing the failure of another theory to social factors (bias, influence, "interests," etc). The principle of symmetry calls for precisely the same kind of social explanation to be used in accounting for the success as well as the failure of a theory—or, by extension, of a sociotechnical system. Accordingly, it would violate the principle of symmetry to argue that one system succeeds because its builders chose the "right" techniques, the ones that really "work." Of apparently successful systems, we can say only that the system builders have apparently succeeded in bringing to life one out of a range of possible systems that could achieve its goal (e.g. trapping wild pigs, growing rice, or sailing down the coast of Africa). Such a system could be viewed as an adaptation, in line with cultural ecology, but only by abandoning the *post hoc, ergo propter hoc* fallacy of functionalism. That a sociotechnical system develops does not imply that it is the logical system, or the only possible system, that could have developed under the circumstances; social choice, tactics, alternative techniques, and the social redefinition of needs and aspirations all play a role in the rise of sociotechnical systems.

An additional example, south Indian temple irrigation, should help to clarify the sociotechnical system concept and its implications. A marked characteristic of agriculture in medieval south India was the royal donation of wastelands to communities of Brahmans, who in turn were encouraged to organize and supervise agricultural production. They did so by investing the lands in newly constructed temples, which provided a locus of managerial control for the construction, maintenance, and management of complex irrigation systems (42, 67) that successfully resisted drought and led to a majestic efflorescence of south Indian Hindu culture. The heterogeneous quality of such a system is immediately evident. The system linked into a cohesive, successful system actors such as kings, canal-digging techniques, dams, flowing water, modes of coordinating labor for rice production, agricultural rituals, deities, notions of social rank and authority, conceptions of merit flowing from donations, conceptions of caste relations and occupations, conceptions of socially differentiated space, religious notions of the salutary effect of temples on the fertility of the earth, economic relations (land entitlements), trade, temple architecture, and knowledge of astrological and astronomic cycles (used to coordinate agricultural activities). A human sociotechnical system links a fabulous diversity of social and nonsocial actors into a seamless web (47).

Any sociotechnical system shows the imprint of the context from which it arose, since system builders must draw on existing social and cultural resources. But it is important to stress that every sociotechnical system is in principle a de novo construct; to make the system work, system builders draw from existing resources but modify them to make them function within the system. In this sense, sociotechnical-system building is almost inevitably *sociogenic* (56): Society is the result of sociotechnical-system building. The distinctive social formation of medieval south India, for instance, is in almost every instance attributable to the achievement of the sociotechnical system of temple irrigation. The system of temple irrigation draws on old ideas of gods, kings, water, dams, castes, gifts, and all the rest, but it transforms every one of these ideas in important ways. In this sense, the sociotechnical system concept is in accord with the structuration theory of Giddens (30): People construct their social world using the social resources and structures at hand, but their activities modify the structures even as they are reproduced.

A sociotechnical system, then, is one of the chief means by which humans produce their social world. Yet sociotechnical systems are all but invisible through the lenses provided by Western economic, political, and social theory, as Lansing (56) discovered in his study of Balinese irrigation. From the standpoint of Western theory, irrigation is organized either by the despotic state, as Wittfogel argued, or by autonomous village communities, as anthropologists argued in reply. Invisible within this discourse, Lansing found, was the Balinese water temple, a key component in a *regional* sociotechnical system devoted to the coordination of irrigation. Lansing discovered that the rites in these Balinese water temples define the rights and responsibilities of subsidiary shrines (and with them, the *subaks,* or local rice-growing collectivities, that line the watershed) through offerings and libations of holy water. By symbolically embedding each local group's quest for water within the supra-local compass of temple ritual, water temples encourage the cooperation necessary to ensure not only the equitable distribution of water but also the regulated flow of inundation and fallowing that proves vital for pest control and fertility. Tellingly, the solidarity that is created is not political; the king has obvious interests in promoting this kind of solidarity but does not actively intervene within it. And neither is this solidarity purely economic; it crosscuts other arenas of economic integration. A sociotechnical system engenders a distinctive form of social solidarity that is neither economic nor political (47); that is why it took so long for these systems to be "discovered" by anthropologists indoctrinated with classical social theory.

Sociotechnical systems have remained equally invisible through the lens provided by the Standard View of technology, which refuses to deal with the ritual dimension of technical activity. According to the Standard View, and to virtually every anthropological definition of technology, a technique is an *effective* act (62:154, citing 71), as opposed to magic or religion. Spier makes this commonsense assumption explicit in excluding from "technology" any "magico-religious means" by which people seek to control nature (93:2). Such a view forestalls any consideration of the crucial role that ritual institutions play in the coordination of labor and the network's legitimation (24, 35, 83, 95,), a point that should already be apparent from the south Indian and Balinese examples already discussed. Among the Montagnards of highland Vietnam (19), agriculture is no mere matter of material culture and manual labor. On the contrary, ritual is a key component of agricultural work; the rites call forth social groups to engage in specific activities, and they provide a metacommentary on the entire productive process. Sociotechnical systems may very well include ritual components with explicit productive goals that we find "false," such as enhancing the fertility of the earth; but to ignore them is to miss the crucial role they play in the coordination of labor. I would therefore argue that the social anthropology of technology, against all common sense, should adopt a principle of absolute impartiality with respect to whether a given activity "works" (i.e. is "technical") or "doesn't work" (i.e. is "magico-religious"); only if we adopt such impartiality do the social dimensions of sociotechnical activity come to the fore (80).

The labor-coordination role of ritual is surprisingly widespread, and for good reason: Ritual works surpassingly well to coordinate labor under conditions of statelessness or local autonomy. Among the Piaroa of lowland south America, for example, shamanic rituals employ scarce mystical knowledge to transfer mystical powers of fertility and increase to people who feel themselves in need of such powers; Granero views such rituals as an *"essential part of the productive practices of Piaroa society"* (35:665, Granero's emphasis). Given their access to what Granero tellingly calls the "mystical means of reproduction," shamans legitimately claim the right to solicit and coordinate agricultural labor, as well as organize trade (1986). Under stateless or locally autonomous conditions, rituals provide the ideal medium for the coordination of labor in that they virtually rule out dissent (9): "you cannot argue with a song." In Sri Lanka, 19th-century civil servants meticulously recorded the rites of the threshing floor, which required economically significant transactions to be conducted with a superstitious scrupulousness of detail, and a special, virtually incomprehensible language. This ritual language required participants to adopt an "odd shibboleth," as one observer termed it, for these vital economic transactions; the limited vocabulary sharply constrained what could be said (79). Thus another key feature of sociotechnical systems is their *silence,* the relatively insignificant role played by human language as against nonverbal communication in ritual (28) as a coordinator of technical activities.

Here we see yet another reason for the invisibility of such systems within the compass of Western social theory, which excessively privileges language over nonverbal cognition and behavior (10).

A successful sociotechnical system achieves a stable integration of social and nonsocial actors, but it is no static thing: Keeping the network functioning requires constant vigilance, and it may also require additional technical or social modification. Every sociotechnical system must cope with what Hughes calls *reverse salients,* areas of obduracy or resistance that prevent the system from expanding or threaten it with dissociation. On reaching the Indies, the Portuguese found that Muslims had monopolized the trade with Hindu princes; the Portuguese response was to work a good deal to make the cannon lighter and more powerful (60:127–28). Sociotechnical systems also betray a characteristic life cycle (46) as they grow from invention, small-scale innovation, growth and development, and a climax of maximum elaboration and scope, followed by senescence and decay, until the system disappears or is replaced by a competing system. Such life cycles may be visible in the myriad cycles of innovation, growth, efflorescence, and decay that characterize the archaeological record.

The sociotechnical system concept, in sum, suggests that mere necessity is by no means the mother of invention, just as production alone is by no means the sole rationale for the astonishing linkages that occur in sociotechnical systems (cf 5). To be sure, sociotechnical-system builders react to perceived needs, as their culture defines them. But we see in their activities the essentially creative spirit that underlies sociogenesis, which is surely among the supreme modes of human cultural expression. Basalla (4:14) puts this point well: A human technology is a "material manifestation of the various ways men and women throughout time have chosen to define and pursue existence. Seen in this light, the history of technology is part of the much broader history of human aspirations, and the plethora of made things are a product of human minds replete with fantasies, longings, wants, and desires." Basalla's point suggests that no account of technology can be complete that does not consider fully the *meaning* of sociotechnical activities, and in particular, the nonproductive roles of technical activities in the ongoing, pragmatic constitution of human polities and subjective selves. Sociotechnical systems can be understood, as I argue in the next section, only by acknowledging that they produce power and meaning as well as goods.

"THE MEANING OF AN ARTIFACT IS A SURFACE MATTER OF STYLE"

The commonsense Modernism of the Standard View desocializes human technological activity, as has just been argued, by reducing the creativity of sociotechnical-system building to the doctrine of Necessity. In precisely the same way, the Standard View desocializes the meaning of technological artifacts by reducing this meaning to the artifact's alleged function, with a residual and secondary role left for the relatively superficial matter (it is claimed) of style. To recapture the sociality of human artifacts, it is necessary to turn this distinction upside down. I begin, therefore, by arguing that the supposedly "hard" part of the artifact, its function, is in reality the "softest," the one that is most subject to cultural definition.

Archaeologists commonly distinguish function and style, as has already been noted. But as Shanks & Tilley argue,

> It is impossible to separate out style and the function [for instance] in either vessel shape or projectile point morphology. There is no way in which we can meaningfully measure and determine what proportion of a vessel's shape performs some utilitarian end, the remainder being assigned to the domain of style. To take a chair—what proportion of this is functional as opposed to stylistic? No answer can be given; the style inheres in the function and vice versa. Furthermore, ascribing any specific or strictly delimited function to an object is in many, if not all cases, an extremely dubious exercise. A chair may be to sit on, it nominally fulfills this function, but chairs can also be used for standing on, or for knocking people over the head with, as pendulums, rulers, or almost anything else. This is not to deny the banal point that objects have uses and may normally be used in just one way, but it is to suggest that such a position represents, at best, a starting point rather than an end point for archaeological analysis (91:92).

The views of Shanks & Tilley are echoed by Norman (75:9), who calls attention to an artifact's *affordances*. An affordance is a perceived property of an artifact that suggests how it should be used. Affordances are inherently multiple: Differing perceptions lead to different uses. You can drink water from a cup to quench thirst, but you can also use a cup to show you are well bred, to emphasize your taste in choosing decor, or to hold model airplane parts. But is not such a point just so much strained, special pleading? Everyone knows that chairs are *primarily* for sitting in; despite "minor" variations associated with specific historical styles and tastes, isn't the chair's function the pre-eminent matter? Such a distinction between function and style is common sense only to the extent that we ignore a key component of technology, ritual. In the preceding section I stressed ritual's prominent role in coordinating labor in sociotechnical systems. Here, I emphasize the equally prominent role of ritual in defining the function of material culture.

To illustrate this point with a convenient and simple example, I draw on the work of K. L. Ames on Victorian hallway furnishings (1). Ames notes that the hallway was the only space in the Victorian house likely to be used by both masters and servants. Masters and visitors of the masters' class would pass through the hall, while servants and tradesmen would be asked to sit there and wait. Ames calls attention to the contradictory character of these artifacts: They had to be visually appealing to the master class as they passed through the hall; but if they included seats, they had to be austere, without upholstery, and uncomfortable, befitting the lower social status of the messenger boys, book agents, census personnel, and soap-sellers who were made to wait there. Plain and uncomfortable, the bench echoed the design of servants' furnishings, which resembled (in the words of a servant quoted by Ames) the furnishings of a penal colony. With such constant reminders of their status, the servants would have no occasion to compare their status favorably with that of their master and mistress. Peers and people of higher status, Ames notes, were shown past the bench and directly into the house. In short, the Victorian hallway is a special space devoted to the enactment of entry rituals.

As the Victorian hallway bench suggests, style and function cannot be distinguished as easily as the Standard View would claim. What appears in a naive analysis to be the superficial matter of "style" (the bench's austerity) turns out, thanks to Ames' deeper contextual reading of hallway artifacts, to be the very "function" of the artifact (to remind servants of their status)! Note that here the function of the artifact (to be attractive to masters and remind servants of their station) can be known only by comprehending the perceived social role that the artifact is designed to fulfill; this perceived social role, in turn, can be known only from a contextual analysis that fully explores the dimensions of Victorian class sensibilities. I do not mean that the flatness and discomfort of the Victorian hallway bench were intended merely to "reflect" Victorian class sensibilities. When employed in a ritual context, the bench was obviously intended to *construct* Victorian statuses in ways not obvious outside the ritual context. With this analysis in view, one can argue that the dimension of an artifact identified by archaeologists, historians, and collectors as "style" once formed part of a now lost ritual system, and for that reason now stands out oddly and mysteriously against the artifact's supposed "function." In short, the distinction between "function" and "style" is a product of the *decontextualization and dehistoricization of artifacts* (see 43:107–20 for an excellent illustration of this point).

Daniel Miller's work among south Indian potters (72) demonstrates that artifacts play key roles in *framing* ritual activities—that is, in providing cues that establish the cultural significance of the events taking place. In a little-understood process that is unconscious and nonverbal, frames—though inconspicuous—play an important social role, establishing the context within which social action takes on meaning. For Miller artifacts are on the one hand extremely visible and omnipresent; yet on the other hand, they operate silently and invisibly (73:109). As many anthropologists have discovered, people find it difficult and pointless to talk about the meaning of artifacts: When pressed, informants resort to their last-ditch tactic, "Our ancestors did it this way" (62:165). Once again we meet a familiar theme: the silence of human technological activity and its invisibility within the compass of theories that assign excessive privilege to speech and writing.

Miller's work among south Indian potters shows the cross-cultural relevance of my point about Victorian hallway artifacts—namely, that the "style" of an artifact, when restored fully to its cultural context, turns out to be its "function." But what is even more important, Miller's work suggests that this "function" of artifacts may inspire artifact diversity, a key feature of human technology. When many versions of an artifact are available, they can play many roles in social life. Miller concludes: "Technology could be analyzed as the *systematic exploitation of the range of methods used in order to produce patterned variation* (72:201, my emphasis). Pushing this point further, one can argue that a major rationale for the creation of sociotechnical systems, beyond mere Necessity, is the elaboration of the material symbols that are indispensable for the conduct of everyday life. And one can identify here another form of linkage, as yet unexplored: the linkage between the rituals that coordinate labor and the rituals that frame human social behavior by employing material artifacts as cues. It seems likely that such linkages amount to a formidable apparatus of domination, even under conditions of statelessness, thus belying the mythos of egalitarianism in stateless societies.

If no form of domination goes unresisted, then one would expect artifacts to be employed in redressive rituals that are specifically designed to mute or counter the invidious status implications of the dominant ritual system. I therefore see the social use of artifacts, paraphrasing Richard Brown (12:129), as a process of nonverbal communication. In this process, each new act of ritual framing is a statement in an ongoing dialogue of ritual statements and counterstatements. In the counterstatements, people whose status is adversely affected by rituals try to obtain or modify valued artifacts, in an attempt to blunt or subvert the dominant rituals' implications. These statements, and their subsequent *counterstatements,* help to constitute social relations as a *polity.* I therefore call attention to *redressive* technological activities, which are interpretive responses to technological domination, to highlight the political dimension of technology. I call this polity-building process a *technological drama.*

A technological drama (78, 82) is a discourse of technological "statements" and "counterstatements" in which there are three recognizable processes: *technological regularization, technological adjustment,* and *technological reconstitution.* A technological drama begins with technological regularization. In this process, a design constituency creates, appropriates, or modifies a technological production process, artifact, user activity, or system in such a way that some of its technical features embody a political aim—that is, an intention to alter the allocation of power, prestige, or wealth (57). Because a sociotechnical system is so closely embedded in ritual and mythic narrative, the technological processes or objects that embody these aims can easily be cloaked in myths of unusual power. Ford's assembly line, for example, was cloaked in the myth that it was the most efficient method of assembling automobiles—a myth indeed, since Norwegian and Swedish experiments have shown that team assembly and worker empowerment are just as efficient. The myth masked a political aim: Ford saw the rigid and repetitive work roles as a way of domesticating and controlling the potentially chaotic and disruptive workforce of Southern and Eastern European immigrants (94:153). The stratifying role of the Victorian hallway bench, to cite another example, was cloaked in a myth of hygiene, which ascribed its plainness to its function in seating those who had recently sojourned in the filthy streets (1, 27).

Like texts, the technological processes and artifacts generated by technological regularization are subject to multiple interpretations, in which the dominating discourse may be challenged tacitly or openly. I call such challenges *technological adjustment* or *technological reconstitution*. In technological adjustment, impact constituencies—the people who lose when a new production process or artifact is introduced—engage in strategies to compensate the loss of self-esteem, social prestige, and social power caused by the technology. In this process they make use of contradictions, ambiguities, and inconsistencies within the hegemonic frame of meaning as they try to validate their actions. They try to control and alter the discourse that affects them so invidiously, and they try to alter the discursively regulated social contexts that regularization creates. Police whose movements are tracked by surveillance systems, for example, become adept at finding bridges and hills that break the surveillance system's tracking signal. They can then grab a burger or chat with another cop without having their location logged. Adjustment strategies include appropriation, in which the impact constituency tries to gain access to a process or artifact from which it has been excluded (e.g. 17). Before the personal computer, computer enthusiasts and hobbyists learned how to hack their way into mainframe systems—as did the youthful Bill Gates (now the CEO of Microsoft Corporation), who was reputed to have hacked his way into systems widely thought to be impregnable. In technological reconstitution, impact constituencies try to reverse the implications of a technology through a symbolic inversion process I call *antisignification*. Reconstitution can lead to the fabrication of counterartifacts (e.g. 51), such as the personal computer or "appropriate technology," which embody features believed to negate or reverse the political implications of the dominant system.

Following Victor Turner (97:91–94, 98:32), I choose the metaphor of "drama" to describe these processes. A technological drama's statements and counterstatements draw upon a culture's root paradigms, its axioms about social life; in consequence, technological activities bring entrenched moral imperatives into prominence. To create the personal computer, for example, was not only to create new production processes and artifacts, but also to bring computational power to the People, to deal the Establishment a blow by appropriating its military-derived tools, and to restore the political autonomy of the household vis-à-vis the Corporation. Here we see the dimension of desire that Basalla (4) emphasizes: To construct a sociotechnical system is not merely to engage in some creative or productive activity. It is to bring to life a deeply desired vision of social life, often with a degree of fervor that can only be termed millenarian.

In any explanation of the motivations underlying sociotechnical-system building and artifact appropriation the role of such activities in the subjective processes of self-definition deserves emphasis (22). In the grip of what Miller calls the mass culture critique, we tend to treat contemporary acts of artifact appropriation in capitalist society "as so tainted, superficial, and trite that they could not possibly be worth investigating." Materialistc people, in addition, are seen as "superficial and deluded, and are unable to comprehend their position" (73:166). Yet, as Miller stresses (73:86–108) there are good grounds for arguing that artifacts play a key role cross-culturally in the formation of the self: Artifact manipulation and play, for example, provide the conceptual groundwork for the later acquisition of language (100). We learn early, argues Miller (73:215), that artifacts play key roles in a "process of social self-creation" in which artifacts are "directly constitutive of our understanding of ourselves and others." In this sense contemporary societies, despite the rise of the Consumer Culture, possess much in common with preindustrial societies (2, c.f. 14:228–9): Artifacts are multiplied, elaborated, appropriated, and employed in framing activities as a form of self-knowledge and self-definition, a contention supported by the dizzying and unfathomable array of spectacular artifacts now collecting dust in ethnological museums. Miller's point leads directly to a consideration of a third contention of the Standard View, the doctrine that technological evolution has proceeded from simple to complex, and has deprived modern Man of his authenticity.

"A UNILINEAR PROGRESSION … FROM SIMPLE TOOLS TO COMPLEX MACHINES"

It would be idiotic to deny that contemporary humans know a great deal more about technology than did our predecessors. History shows cumulative trends in virtually every field of technological endeavor. But the sociotechnical system concept leads to the equally inescapable conclusion that an enormous amount of human knowledge about building sociotechnical systems has been utterly and irretrievably lost. I argue here that the extent of this loss can be appreciated only by understanding the heterogeneous nature of sociotechnical systems and by radically questioning the Standard View's assumption that the evolution of technology may be described as the shift from Tool to Machine. Such an analysis will raise equally radical questions about the Standard View's notion of Rupture.

   In a preindustrial society, people do not often talk about the technical knowledge they possess. In studying weavers in Ghana, for instance, Goody was surprised by the insignificant role of questioning and answering in the teaching of apprentices (33). Although highly elaborate systems of ethnobotanical classification may play key roles in subsistence systems, an enormous amount of technological knowledge is learned, stored, and transmitted by experiential learning, visual/spatial thinking, and analogical reasoning. Bloch

(10:187) describes the nonlinguistic learning that takes place, a form of learning very incompletely understood in the cognitive sciences:...

> Imagine a Malagasy shifting cultivator with a fairly clear, yet supple mental model, perhaps we could say a script, stored in long-term memory, of what a 'good swidden' is like; and that this model is partly visual, partly analytical (though not necessarily in a sentential logical way), partly welded to a series of procedures about what you should do to make and maintain a swidden. This Malagasy is going through the forest with a friend who says to him, 'Look over there at that bit of forest, that would make a good swidden.' What happens then is that, after a rapid conceptualization of the bit of forest, the model of 'the good swidden' is mentally matched with the conceptualized area of forest, and then a new but related model, 'this particular place as a potential swidden,' is established and stored in long-term memory.

Bloch argues that the linguistically derived theory of human cognition is insufficient because it cannot account for the speed with which we perform daily tasks such as identifying a 'good swidden.' It cannot account, as Miller notes (73:102), for our ability to absorb almost instantly the social implications of a furnished interior "consisting of a combination which is not only almost certainly in some degree unique, but some of whose basic elements may also be new to us." As we use technology for practical and social purposes, then, we draw on a nonverbal form of human cognition whose capabilities clearly form an enormous, but heretofore little recognized, component of our species' everyday intelligence. The portion of technical knowledge that people can verbalize represents only the tip of the iceberg.

The notion that technology is applied science—that it represents the practical use of logically-formulated, linguistically-encoded knowledge—is very misleading. A sociotechnical system is much better described as an *activity system,* a domain of purposive, goal-oriented action in which knowledge and behavior are reciprocally constituted by social, individual, and material phenomena (64, 102). As Janet and Charles Keller have emphasized, and as Bloch's example so tellingly illustrates, an activity system constantly fluxes between being and becoming: "Action has an emergent quality which results from the continual feedback from external events to internal representations and from the internal representations back to enactment" (52:2). Crucial to this process is an equally flexible cycling among alternative cognitive modes, including visual/spatial thinking and linguistic/classificatory thinking (53). Visual/spatial thinking is widespread in all technological activity systems, including today's high technology. (25, 26, 101, 99). But visual/spatial thinking is silent. Competent producers and users rarely mention it. This kind of knowledge is lost, sometimes irretrievably, in the wake of technological "progress." Recreation of a system that has been lost is virtually impossible. We have no idea how some preindustrial artifacts were made, let alone how highly effective activity systems were so successfully coordinated under preindustrial conditions.

When one views a sociotechnical system as a complex heterogeneous linkage of knowledge, ritual, artifacts, techniques, and activity, it is apparent that much more than visual/spatial knowledge about manufacture can be lost when a system dissociates. A human sociotechnical system involves the coordination of a massively complex network; in the case of Portuguese naval expansion this network consisted of such entities as kings and queens, ships, crews, winds, cannons, maps, sails, astrolabes, Muslims, and gold. Viewed as an activity system, a sociotechnical system must include all the conceptual, visual, experiential, tactile, and intuitive knowledge necessary to modify these diverse elements so that they work together harmoniously. Even in the most "primitive" sociotechnical systems, such as those of contemporary hunters and gatherers living in marginal environments (e.g. 61), the scope of knowledge integration involved is phenomenal. The complexity of any human sociotechnical system is belied by the simplicity of its tools (32).

All human sociotechnical systems, whether "primitive" or "preindustrial," are enormously complex and inherently heterogeneous. Through recognition of this fact one can begin a critique of the notion of Rupture that figures so prominently in the Standard View. According to the Standard view, tool use is *authentic* and fosters *autonomy;* one owns and controls one's own tools and isn't dependent on or exploited by others. When we use machines, in contrast, we must work at rhythms not of our own making, and we become ensnared in the supralocal relations necessary for their production, distribution, and maintenance. To the extent that we become dependent on machines we do not own, the stage is set for exploitation. We become divorced from nature, and our conceptions of the world become pathological, through a process called *reification* (a malady frequently asserted to occur only in industrial societies). According to the doctrine of Rupture, reification occurs because we employ objects as a means of knowing ourselves. When these objects are no longer our own authentic products, as is the case with industrially produced artifacts, our attention is deflected from critical self-awareness to the incompletely understood Other who generates the artifact (73:44).

The concept of sociotechnical systems enables us to see to what degree the doctrine of Rupture overstates the consequences of the transition from Tool to Machine. Although one would be foolish to deny the significant consequences of the machine's rise, preindustrial sociotechnical systems were themselves complex and exploitive—frequently more so than the Standard View acknowledges. A preindustrial sociotechnical system unifies material, ritual, and social resources in a comprehensive strategy for societal reproduction. In the course of participation in such a system, many if not most individuals find themselves playing dependent and exploited roles. By no means is reification restricted to industrial technology. As Lansing notes for Bali,

> Water temples establish connections between productive groups and the components of the natural landscape that they seek to control. The natural world surrounding each village is not a wilderness but an engineered landscape of rice

terraces, gardens, and aqueducts created by the coordinated labor of generations. Anthropomorphic deities evoke this residual human presence in an engineered landscape ... . Each wier is the origin of an irrigation system, which has both physical and social components. The concept of the deity of the wier evokes the collective social presence at the weir, where free-flowing river water becomes controlled irrigation water (56:128).

It would appear, then, that preindustrial sociotechnical systems have much in common with today's machine-based technological systems: Both rely extensively on nonverbal cognition, both show enormous complexity and elaboration, and both seem to generate reified notions rather than "authentic" self-awareness. Moreover, the conditions of freedom in preindustrial societies are falsely represented by focusing on the allegedly nonconstraining nature of tool (as opposed to machine) use. Any sociotechnical system, ancient or modern, primitive or industrialized, stems from the efforts of system builders who attempt to create a network capable of resisting dissociation. As previously argued, the use of ritual to coordinate productive activity in preindustrial sociotechnical systems amounts to a form of domination and control, even under stateless conditions. One can suggest, in fact, that both modern devices and preindustrial systems of ritual coordination are machines, as Latour (57:129) defines the term: "A machine, as the name implies, is first of all a machination, a stratagem, a kind of cunning, where borrowed forces keep one another in check so that none can fly apart from the group." Latour refers here to the role that machines play in uniting the constituent elements of modern sociotechnical systems: Machines tie the assembled forces to one another in a sustainable network (see 57:103–44 for telling discussions of the diesel engine, the Kodak camera, and the telephone). To argue thus is not to deny that the rise of the machine has brought about important, if as yet incompletely understood, alterations in human sociotechnical activity. It is to stress that the Standard View, with its division of human history into the Age of the Tool and the Age of the Machine, substantially overstates the political and subjective implications of the rise of machines (50:174).

What can the sociotechnical systems concept tell us about another kind of rupture, the kind produced when a modern industrial technology or artifact is adopted by a "traditional" society? A variant of the Standard View, perfectly expressed in the film "The Gods Must Be Crazy," alleges that the world-wide distribution of industrial artifacts will inevitably tear out the foundations of "authentic" traditional cultures and draw all the peoples in the world within the grip of consumer ideology. Implicit in this view is a strong version of technological determinism, the doctrine that because there is only one way to make or use a material artifact, every culture that adopts it will be forced to develop the same social and labor relations. Because social information is so crudely encoded in artifacts, however, it is extremely unlikely that a transferred artifact will succeed in bringing with it the ideological structure that produced it. For example, Hebdige (41) shows how motor scooters were deliberately developed in Italy to signify the feminine as opposed to the masculine motorbike: The motor was covered and quiet, the curves were soft and the shapes rounded, and so on. In Britain in the 1960s, however, the motor scooter was adopted by Mods, male and female, for whom it signified a European ("soft") image, as against the Rockers, who appropriated the motorcycle to signify an American ("hard") image.

Thus the "recipient" (appropriating) culture can reinterpret the transferred artifact as it sees fit. No less should be expected of people in so-called "traditional societies." According to the sociotechnical systems model, no such thing as a "traditional society" exists. Every human society is a world in the process of becoming, in which people are engaged in the active technological elaboration, appropriation, and modification of artifacts as the means of coming to know themselves and of coordinating labor to sustain their lives. New resources are unlikely to be ignored if they can be woven into an existing or new activity system. An artifact's determinative implications for labor in one context may be nullified if it is adopted to fulfill an essentially expressive function, as is the case for many "showpiece" industrial installations in Third World countries.

In a recent important essay, Schaniel (89) has stressed that the adoption of artifacts does not necessarily imply the adoption of the system of logic that produced the technology. Schaniel illustrates this point by discussing the history of Maori appropriation of iron artifacts. In the first phase, the Maori ignored the artifacts, seeing little or no value in them. After some experimentation, the Maori found that hoes and spades could be worked into their indigenous system of agriculture. European observers were shocked to find that the Maori bound their hoes to short handles and used this implement from the squatting position. The favorite implement for levering up the ground remained the digging stick. The Maori later modified the digging stick by affixing to it a short piece of straight iron (89:496). Schaniel concludes that "the process of adopting and adapting introduced technology ... does not imply that introduced technology does not lead to change, but the change is not pre-ordained by the technology adapted ... . The process of technological adaptation is one where the introduced technology is adopted to the social processes of the adopting society, and not vice-versa" (89:496–98).

That said, the appropriation of modern technology, whether for productive or symbolic purposes, may bring with it what Pelto calls "de-localization," the irreversible growth of dependence on nonlocal sources of energy (76:166–68). As Pelto's study of the snowmobile in Lapland suggests, de-localization may expand the geographical scope within which people actively appropriate artifacts, with extensive implications for social and cultural change. It would be wrong, however, to try to predict the trajectory of such change from a technical analysis of the transferred technology, as the extensive literature on the social impact of the Green Revolution attests. According to some studies (36, 37), the Green Revolution invariably leads to "techno-economic differentiation" and the growth of a pauper class because rich farmers disproportionately benefit from the extra-local resources (high-yielding varieties, pesticides, herbicides, and fertilizers). Other studies report that Green Revolution technology does not necessarily produce socioeconomic differentiation, so long as countervailing customs assure the equitable use of agricultural inputs (3, 20, 31). In assessing the social and cultural impact of de-localization, however, it is important to bear in mind that assuming technological determinism is much easier than conducting a fully contextual study in which people are shown to be the active appropriators, rather than the passive victims, of transferred technology (79).

Sharp's famous analysis of steel axes among "stone-age" Australians illustrates the peril of reading too much technological determinism into a single case. Sharp showed how missionaries, by providing stone axes to women and young men, whose status had previously been defined by having to ask tribal elders for these artifacts, brought down a precariously legitimated stratification system. However, any status differentiation system that depends on sumptuary regulations, rules that deny certain artifacts to those deemed low in status, is vulnerable to furious adjustment strategies if such artifacts suddenly become widely available; culture contact and technology transfer are by no means required to set such processes in motion. The process Sharp described is not constitutive of technology transfer per se; a clear analogue is the erosion of the medieval aristocracy's status as peasants freed themselves from sumptuary regulations and acquired high-status artifacts (73:135–36).

Where technological change has apparently disrupted so-called "traditional societies," the villain is much more likely to be colonialism than technology. Colonialism disrupts indigenous political, legal, and ritual systems, and in so doing, may seriously degrade the capacity of local system-builders to function effectively within indigenous activity systems. In colonial Sri Lanka, the liberal British government was obsessed with the eradication of multiple claims to land, which were perceived to discourage investment and social progress. The legal eradication of such claims destroyed the ability of native headmen to adjust holdings to changing water supply levels and undermined the traditional basis by which labor was coordinated for the repair of dams and irrigation canals. Village tanks and canals fell into disrepair as impecunious villagers allowed their lands to be taken over by village boutique owners and moneylenders (79). This example suggests that it is not transferred technology, but rather the imposition of an alien and hegemonic legal and political ideology—arguably, technicism, but not technology—that effects disastrous social change in colonized countries.

It is when sociotechnical systems come into direct competition, as is the case in advanced technological diffusion, that spectacular disintegrations of indigenous systems can occur. The sudden deployment of a competing system may outstrip the capacity of indigenous system participants to conceptualize their circumstances and make the necessary adjustments; their mode of deploying resources, material and human, no longer works. Latour (58:32) comments:

> The huge iron and steel plants of Lorraine are rusting away, no matter how many elements they tied together, because the world [their builders] were supposing to hold has changed. They are much like these beautiful words Scrabble players love to compose but which they do not know how to place on the board because the shape of the board has been modified by other players.

CONCLUSIONS

Against the Standard View's exaggerated picture of technological evolution from simple tools to complex machines, the sociotechnical system concept puts forward a universal conception of human technological activity, in which complex social structures, nonverbal activity systems, advanced linguistic communication, the ritual coordination of labor, advanced artifact manufacture, the linkage of phenomenally diverse social and nonsocial actors, and the social use of diverse artifacts are all recognized as parts of a single complex that is simultaneously adaptive and expressive.

The sociotechnical systems of the Machine Age do differ from their preindustrial predecessors, but the Standard View grossly exaggerates these differences. For example, most modern definitions of technology assert that, unlike their preindustrial predecessors, modern technological systems are systems for the application of science, drawing their productive power from objective, linguistically encoded knowledge (e.g. 16). But on closer examination we see here the influence of Standard View mythology. Historians of technology tell us that virtually none of the technologies that structure our current social landscape were produced by the application of science; on the contrary, science and organized objective knowledge are more commonly the *result* of technology. The principles of thermodynamics, for example, were discovered as scientists sought to determine how devices actually worked and what their operating parameters were (26). The notion that modern technology is efffective because it is founded in objective, "true" knowledge violates the principle of symmetry advanced earlier in this essay, even as it denigrates the achievements of preindustrial sociotechnical systems. As Lansing notes (56), Balinese water temples were more effective managers of irrigation than the all-but-disastrous Green Revolution techniques have been.

By jettisoning material-culture studies in the early 20th century, anthropology lost one means of developing a holistic, multi-disciplinary approach to culture. By reinstating the social anthropology of technology and material culture, we lay the foundation once again for fruitful communication among social anthropologists, ethnoarchaeologists, archaeologists, and students of human evolution. Besides challenging certain myths about technology that social anthropologists often take for granted, I hope this essay helps to raise the level of such interdisciplinary discourse. For example, efforts are now underway to comprehend human evolution in terms of the complex interplay among "tools, language, and intelligence" (29). From the perspective of this essay, such an effort is misconceived: It overprivileges tools and language, and disguises the truly significant phenomena—namely, sociotechnical systems and nonverbal cognition. To grasp the evolutionary significance of human technological activity, I suggest that anthropologists lay aside the myths of the Standard View ("necessity is the mother of invention," "the meaning of an artifact is a surface matter of style," and "the history of technology is a unilinear progression from tools to machines"), and view human technological activity using the concept of the sociotechnical system. Once we do so, we can begin to construct hypotheses about the *universals* of human technology—universals that highlight what is distinctly *human* about activities as diverse as making stone tools and launching space vehicles.

Literature Cited

1. Ames, K. 1978. Meaning in artefacts: hall furnishings in Victorian America. *J. Interdis. Hist.* 9:19–46
2. Appadurai, A. 1986. Introduction: commodites and the politics of value. In *The Social Life of Things: Commodities in Cultural Perspective,* ed. A. Appadurai, pp. 3–61. Cambridge: Cambridge Univ. Press
3. Attwood, D. 1979. Why some of the poor get richer: economic change and mobility in rural Western India. *Curr. Anthropol.* 20:495–514
4. Basalla, G. 1988. *The Evolution of Technology.* Cambridge: Cambridge Univ. Press
5. Baudrillard, J. 1975. *The Mirror of Production,* transl. M. Poster. St. Louis: Telos Press
6. Bijker, W., Hughes, T., Pinch, T., eds. 1987. *The Social Construction of Technological Systems: New Directions in the Sociology and History of Technology.* Cambridge: MIT Press
7. Binford, L. 1962. Archaeology as anthropology. *Am. Antiq.* 28:217–25
8. Binford, L. 1965. Archaeological systematics and the study of culture process. *Am. Antiq.* 31:203–10
9. Bloch, M. 1974. Symbol, song, dance, and the features of articulation. *Eur. J. Sociol.* 15:55–81.
10. Bloch, M. 1991. Language, anthropology, and cognitive science. *Man* 26:183–98
11. Bloor, D. 1991. *Knowledge and Social Imagery.* Chicago: Univ. Chicago Press. 2nd. ed.
12. Brown, R. 1987. *Society as Text: Essays on Rhetoric, Reason, and Reality.* Chicago: Univ. Chicago Press
13. Bouquet, M. 1991. Images of artefacts. *Crit. Anthropol.* 11:333–56
14. Bourdieu, P. 1984. *Distinction: A social Critique of the Judgement of Taste.* London: Routledge and Kegan Paul.
15. Bradbury, M., McFarlane, J. 1976. The name and nature of modernism. In *Modernism,* ed. M. Bradbury, J. McFarlane, pp. 19–55. Harmondsworth: Penguin
16. Bruzina, R. 1982. Art and architecture, ancient and modern. *Res. Philos. Technol.* 5:163–87
17. Burke, P. 1978. *Popular Culture in Early Modern Europe.* London: Temple Smith
18. Clifford, J., Marcus, G., eds. 1986. *Writing Culture: The Poetics and Politics of Ethnography.* Berkeley: Univ. Calif. Press.
19. Condominas, G. 1986. Ritual technology in swidden agriculture. In *Rice Societies: Asian Problems and Prospects,* ed. I. Norlund, S. Cederroth, I. Gerden. pp. 29–37. Riverdale: Curzon Press
20. Coward, E. 1979. Principles of social organization in an indigenous irrigation system. *Hum. Organ.* 38:35–43
21. Digard, J.-P. 1979. La technologie en anthropologie: fin de parcours ou nouveau souffle? *L'Homme* 19:105–40
22. Douglas, M., Isherwood, B. 1979. *The World of Goods.* New York: Basic Books
23. Dunnell, R. 1978. Style and function: a fundamental dichotomy. *Am. Antiq.* 43:192–202
24. Flannery, K. V., Marcus, J. 1976. Formative Oaxaca and the Zapotec cosmos. *Am. Sci.* 64:374–83
25. Ferguson, E. S. 1977. The mind's eye: nonverbal thought in technology. *Science* 197:827–36
26. Fores, M. 1982. Technological change and the "technology" myth. *Scand. Econ. Hist. Rev.* 30:167–88
27. Forty, A. 1986. *Objects of Desire.* New York: Pantheon
28. Gell, A. 1975. *Metamorphosis of the Cassowaries.* London: Athlone Press

29. Gibson, K. 1991. Tools, language, and intelligence: evolutionary implications. *Man* 26:255–64
30. Giddens, A. 1979. *Central Problems in Social Theory*. London: MacMillan
31. Goldman, H., Squire, L. 1982. Technical change, labor use, and income distribution in the Muda irrigation project. *Econ. Dev. Cult. Change* 30:753–76
32. Golson, J. 1977. Simple tools and complex technology. In *Stone Tools as Cultural Markers: Change, Evolution, and Complexity*, ed. R. Wright, pp. 154–161. Canberra: Australian Inst. Aborig. Stud.
33. Goody, E. 1978. Toward a theory of questions. In *Questions and Politeness: Strategies in Social Interaction*, ed. E. Goody. Cambridge: Cambridge Univ. Press
34. Gould, R. 1968. Living archaeology: the Ngatatjara of Western Australia. *Southwest. J. Anthropol.* 24:101–22
35. Granero, F. 1986. Power, ideology, and the ritual of production in lowland south America. *Man* 21:657–79
36. Griffin, K. 1974. *The Political Economy of Agrarian Change: An Essay on the Green Revolution*. Cambridge: Harvard Univ. Press
37. Grotsch, K. 1972. Technical change and the destruction of income in rural areas. *Am. J. Agric. Econ.* 54:326–41
38. Hally, D. 1985. The identification of vessel function: a case study from northwest Georgia. *Am. Antiq.* 51:267–95
39. Harris, M. 1968. *The Rise of Anthropological Theory*. New York: Crowell
40. Harvey, D. 1989. *The Condition of Postmodernity: An Enquiry into the Origins of Cultural Change*. Oxford: Blackwell
41. Hebdige, D. 1981. Object as image: the Italian scooter cycle. *Block* 4:39–56
42. Heitzman, E. 1987. Temple urbanism in medieval south India. *J. Asian Stud.* 46:791–826
43. Hodder, I. 1985. *Reading the Past: Current Approaches to Interpretation in Archaeology*. Cambridge: Cambridge Univ. Press
44. Hodder, I., ed. 1989. *The Meaning of Things: Material Culture and Symbolic Expression*. London: Unwin Hyman
45. Hughes, T. 1983. *Networks of Power: Electrification in Western Society, 1880–1930*. Baltimore: Johns Hopkins Univ. Press
46. Hughes, T. 1987. The evolution of large technological systems. See Ref. 6, pp. 51–82
47. Hughes, T. 1989. *American Genesis: A Century of Innovation and Technological Enthusiasm, 1870–1970*. New York: Penguin
48. Hughes, T. 1990. From deterministic dynamos to seamless-web systems. In *Engineering as a Social Enterprise*, ed. H. Sladovich, pp. 7–25. Washington: Natl. Acad. Press
49. Hutton, J. H. 1944. The place of material culture in the study of anthropology. *J. Roy. Anthropol. Inst.* 74:1–6
50. Ingold, T. 1988. Tools, minds, and machines: an excursion into the philosophy of technology. *Techniques et Cultures* 12:151–76
51. James, S. 1979. Confections, concoctions, and conceptions. *J. Anthropol. Soc. Oxford* 10:83–95
52. Keller, C., Keller, J. 1991a. *Thinking and Acting with Iron*. Urbana: Beckman Inst.
53. Keller, C., Keller, J. 1991b. Imaging in iron or thought is not inner speech. Presented at Wenner-Gren Found. Anthropol. Res. Symp. No. 112, Rethinking Linguistic Relativity
54. Kroeber, A. L. 1948. *Anthropology*. New York: Harcourt & Brace
55. Kroeber, A., Kluckhohn, C. 1952. *Culture: A Critical Review of Concepts and Definitions*. Cambridge: Harvard Univ. Press
56. Lansing, S. 1991. *Priests and Programmers: Technologies of Power in the Engineered Lanscape of Bali*. Princeton: Princeton Univ. Press
57. Latour, B. 1987. *Science in Action: How to Follow Scientists and Engineers Through Society*. Cambridge: Harvard Univ. Press
58. Latour, B. 1986. The Prince for machines as well as for machinations. Paper read at the Seminar on Technology and Social Change, Univ. of Edinburgh (June 12–13, 1986)
59. Lauer, P., ed. 1974. *Readings in Material Culture*. Brisbane: Queensland Univ. Anthropol. Mus.
60. Law, J. 1987. Technology and heterogeneous engineering: the case of Portuguese expansion. See Ref. 6, pp. 111–34
61. Lee, R. 1979. *The !Kung San: Men, Women, and Work in a Foraging Society*. Cambridge: Cambridge Univ. Press
62. Lemonnier, P. 1986. The study of material culture today: toward an anthropology of technical systems. *J. Anthropol. Archaeol.* 5:147–86
63. Lemonnier, P. 1989. Bark capes, arrowheads, and Concorde: on social representations of technology. See Ref. 44, pp. 156–71
64. Leont'ev, A. 1981. The problem of activity in psychology. See Ref. 102, pp. 37–71
65. Leroi-Gourhan, A. 1943. *Evolution et techniques. L'homme et la matière*. Paris: Albin Michel
66. Leroi-Gourhan, A. 1945. *Evolution et techniques. Milieu et techniques*. Paris: Albin Michel
67. Ludden, D. 1985. *Peasant Society in South India*. Princeton: Princeton Univ. Press
68. MacKenzie, D. 1987. Missile accuracy: a case study in the social processes of technological change. See Ref 6, pp. 195–222
69. Malinowski, B. 1935. *Coral Gardens and Their Magic*. London: Routledge
70. Marcus, G., Fischer, M. 1986. *Anthropol-*

ogy as Cultural Critique: An Experimental Moment in the Human Sciences. Chicago: Univ. Chicago Press.

71. Mauss, M. 1983. *Sociologie et anthropologie.* Paris: Presses Universitaires de France

72. Miller, D., ed. 1983. Things ain't what they used to be." *Roy. Anthropol. Inst. News* 59:5–16

73. Miller, D. 1987. *Material Culture and Mass Consumption.* London: Basil Blackwell

74. Mulkay, M. 1978. *Science and the Sociology of Knowledge.* London: George Allen and Unwin

75. Norman, D. 1988. *The Psychology of Everyday Things.* New York: Basic Books

76. Pelto, P. 1973. *The Snowmobile Revolution: Technology and Social Change in the Arctic.* Menlo Park, CA: Benjamin Cummings

77. Pfaffenberger, B. 1988. Festishized objects and humanized nature: toward an anthropology of technology. *Man* 23:236–52

78. Pfaffenberger, B. 1988. The social meaning of the personal computer, or, why the personal computer revolution was no revolution. *Anthropol. Q.* 61:39–47

79. Pfaffenberger, B. 1990. The harsh facts of hydraulics: technology and society in Sri Lanka's colonization schemes. *Technol. Cult.* 31:361–97

80. Pfaffenberger, B. 1990. The Hindu temple as a machine, or the Western machine as a temple. *Techniques et Cultures* (16):183–202

81. Pfaffenberger, B. 1990. *Democratizing Information: Online Databases and the Rise of End-User Searching.* Boston: G. K. Hall

82. Pfaffenberger, B. 1992. Technological dramas. *Sci., Technol., Human Values* 17. In press

83. Rappaport, R. A. 1971. Ritual, sanctity, and cybernetics. *Am. Anthropol.* 73:59–76

84. Reynolds, B. 1983. The relevance of material culture to anthropology. *J. Anthropol. Soc. Oxford* 14:209–17

85. Richardson, M., ed. 1974. *The Human Mirror: Material and Spatial Images of Man.* Baton Rouge: Louisiana State Univ. Press

86. Sahlins, M. 1972. *Stone Age Economics.* Chicago: Aldine

87. Sahlins, M. 1976. *Culture and Practical Reason.* Chicago: Univ. Chicago Press

88. Sayce, R. 1933. *Primitive Arts and Crafts: An Introduction to the Study of Material Culture.* Cambridge: Cambridge Univ. Press

89. Schaniel, W. 1988. New technology and cultural change in traditional societies. *J. Econ. Issues* 22:493–98

90. Scheffler, I. 1967. *Science and Subjectivity.* New York: Knopf

91. Shanks, M., Tilley, C. 1987. *Social Theory and Archaeology.* Albuquerque: Univ. New Mexico Press

92. Sillitoe, P. 1988. *Made in Niugini: Technology in the Highlands of Papua New Guinea.* London: Brit. Mus.

93. Spier, R. 1970. *From the Hand of Man: Primitive and Preindustrial Technologies.* Boston: Houghton-Mifflin

94. Staudenmaier, J. 1989. The politics of successful technologies. In *In Context: History and the History of Technology,* ed. H. Cutliffe, R. Post, pp. 150–71. Bethlehem: Lehigh Univ. Press

95. Tennekoon, S. 1988. Rituals of development: the accelerated Mahaweli development program of Sri Lanka. *Am. Ethnol.* 15:294–310

96. Tilley, C. 1990. *Reading Material Culture.* Oxford: Blackwell

97. Turner, V. 1957. *Schism and Continuity in an African Society: A Study of Ndembu Village Life.* Manchester: Manchester Univ. Press

98. Turner, V. 1974. *Dramas, Fields, and Metaphors: Symbolic Action in Human Society.* Ithaca: Cornell Univ. Press

99. Vicente, W. 1984. Technological knowledge without science: the innovation of flush riveting in American airplanes, ca. 1930–1950. *Technol. Cult.* 25:540–76

100. Vygotsky, L. 1978. *Mind in Society.* Cambridge: Harvard Univ. Press

101. Wallace, A. 1978. *Rockdale: The Growth of an American Village in the Early Industrial Revolution.* New York: Alfred A. Knopf

102. Wertsch, J., ed. 1981. *The Concept of Activity in Soviet Psychology.* Armonk, NY: M. E. Sharpe

103. Wissler, C. 1914. Material cultures of the North American Indians. *Am. Anthropol.* 16:447–505

Annu. Rev. Anthropol. 1992. 21:517–36

ARCHAEOLOGICAL RESEARCH ON STYLE

Michelle Hegmon

Department of Sociology and Anthropology, New Mexico State University, Las Cruces, New Mexico 88003

KEYWORDS: material culture, information, artifact analysis

A consideration of material culture style has been a part of archaeology almost from the beginning. However, only in the past few decades have many archaeologists begun to question and discuss explicitly what style is and how it can be used [summaries of these trends can be found in a recent review in this series (99) and elsewhere (16, 36a)]. Recent examinations of style by archaeologists (17:1) and by an art historian (117:253) both cite Gadamer's (36:466) statement that "the notion of style is one of the undiscussed self-evident concepts upon which our historical consciousness is based." These researchers then go on to argue that archaeologists no longer share a united approach to style. Various kinds of style have been defined (e.g. 135, 112–114), and it sometimes appears that archaeologists have as many approaches to style as we have works on the topic.

In reviewing the literature, however, I found that despite different labels, archaeologists generally agree on what is meant by style and are able to launch profitable discussions of stylistic variation (e.g. 99) or of particular styles (e.g. 42) without lengthy preamble. Archaeologists have a common ground for considering style, though it is manifested in various definitions. At the core of the definitions used by a number of archaeologists with very different theoretical perspectives are two basic tenets. First, *style is a way of doing something*

517

0084-6570/92/1015-0517$02.00

(e.g. 66, 112, 139), and second, *style involves a choice* among various alternatives (20:365; 47:591; 112).

If archaeologists can agree on so basic an issue, then why the debate? Why another review of style and archaeology fewer than ten years after the last (99)? Why so many recent books on style and related topics (12, 17, 65, 122)? The source of the debate becomes apparent, of course, when the various definitions are examined in more detail. According to Sackett, style (in traditional archaeological approaches) involves choice between functionally equivalent alternatives, and a style is "a highly specific and characteristic manner of doing something, which, by its very nature is peculiar to a specific time and place" (112:63; 113–115). Wiessner argues that "style is a form of non-verbal communication through doing something in a certain way that communicates information about relative identity" (139:107). Finally, Hodder states that "style is 'a way of doing,' where 'doing' includes the activities of thinking, feeling, being" (66:45). Thus for Sackett, style bears particularly on time-space systematics, for Wiessner it has a communicative function, and for Hodder it relates to cognitive processes.

Thus, despite this general agreement that style is a way of doing, debate arises about specifics: What, if anything, does style do? How does style relate to social and cultural processes? How is it best analyzed and studied archaeologically? Here I focus primarily on these questions, on style in artifacts (rather than architecture, mortuary practices, etc), and on work done in the past 15 years.

STYLE AND FORMAL VARIATION: HISTORICAL PERSPECTIVES AND ANALYTICAL RIGOR

In past decades—including the early years of the New Archaeology—many archaeologists defined style as a component of material culture, that is, as formal variation not determined by technological constraints (4:25; 110:321). Style was studied primarily as a diagnostic code for us to interpret (120:287; see also 16:9); and the distribution of styles or "stylistic variability" (4:203) was analyzed to define space-time systematics and gain information about prehistoric social groups. While this approach can be criticized for treating style as a passive phenomenon (119:89; 140), it is also worthy of praise, especially in terms of the analytical process. When style is defined as a component of material culture, a close analytical link is maintained between the object of study (i.e. patterns of formal variation) and the subject (i.e. style).

More recently, archaeologists have attempted to understand style from a more active perspective. The various definitions of style presented above, along with other perspectives on style and material culture articulated recently (e.g. 61, 89, 118, 119, 140), consider style to be a component of human activity. While this perspective is obviously attractive in view of current anthropological interests, it is somewhat problematic analytically because it separates the subject (style as a component of human activity) from the object of study (material culture variation). While archaeologists are often skilled at developing effective bridging arguments that relate subject and object (e.g. 96), it is all too easy in stylistic research to ignore rather than recognize and bridge the subject-object gap. As Conkey (16:10–11) notes, material culture variation is sometimes treated *as if* it were human activity or stylistic communication.

As the active perspective on style has become more widely accepted in recent years, archaeologists have made considerable progress in bridging the gap between understanding style as a component of human activity, on the one hand, and analysis of material culture variation, on the other. Researchers (e.g. Conkey, cited above) have explicitly recognized the potential problem. Ten years ago Sackett wrote that style "is conceived as one kind of meaning that can be read into form, and not necessarily a property of form as such. Thus, while I may often refer figuratively in what follows to 'stylistic variation' among objects, this literally should be taken to mean formal variation that we happen to regard as being stylistically significant" (112:64). More recently Sackett (115:32) has directed his attention to understanding "where, in formal variability, does style reside?"

As archaeologists explore various dimensions of style both as a component of human activity and as material culture variation, the relationship between the two is becoming better understood. A number of researchers define certain kinds of style or components of style very tightly, and then consider specific patterns of material variation that can be closely linked to those aspects of style (e.g. 30, 32, 84, 101). Others focus on understanding causes of material variation, including production, exchange, and technological function, and consider style as a component of that variation (e.g. 43, 98). Finally, a number of archaeologists and ethnologists are adopting material culture as social production as their research subject (e.g. 2, 61, 65, 89, 118, 119, 125).

Here I trace the analytical process that links material culture variation, style, and human activity. In the section that follows, I explore the development of an active interpretation of style. Next I consider definitions of various kinds of style. I then consider work focused on the sources of material variation, including socio-cultural correlates and technology.

STYLE AS INFORMATION AND COMMUNICATION

In 1977, Martin Wobst proposed what has come to be known as the information-exchange theory of style. He argued that style *functions* in cultural systems as an avenue of communication, and he defined style as "that part of the formal variability in material culture that can be related to the participation of artifacts in processes of information exchange" (140:321). Although the general idea of style as communication was not previously unknown (e.g. 4:20–30; 15:85; 120:304), stylistic communication was rarely discussed explicitly in archaeology. Rather, style was often treated as a passive phenomenon, with a minimal role in cultural systems. In some cases style was specifically contrasted to function (e.g. 29, 111:370). However, since 1977, treatment of style has changed profoundly (at least in Anglo-American archaeology), and discussion of information and/or communication has become almost de rigueur in research on style, whether Wobst is cited or not.

Emphasis on information and communication is a positive development. It assures that style will no longer be relegated automatically to a passive or residual role. However, information is so broad a concept that it can become almost meaningless. The information contained in style can be interpreted as anything from prehistoric symbolism to a chronological indicator (see 17:3; 107:244–45). As Hantman (44:37) notes, the information-exchange model "can easily become a post-hoc explanation for any and all prehistoric stylistic patterns."

Recent research has made significant progress towards refining both Wobst's (140) formulation and the broad concept of stylistic information by making explicit various factors relating to style, information, and material culture variation.[1] First, some of Wobst's specific predictions have been challenged and refined. In his presentation of the information exchange theory, Wobst, working within a functionalist and systems-theory paradigm, argued that because style is a relatively expensive form of communication, stylistic information exchange will only be used in certain contexts so as to maximize efficiency. While this argument makes sense theoretically, in many empirical cases human material practices seem less than efficient; and inefficiency or excess can convey important information, particularly information about power or status [e.g. Hawaiian feather cloaks (30) or Kuba brocaded textiles (127:222; see discussion in 69)].

In general, researchers agree that the use of style is more complex than would be expected if efficiency were the only consideration. Specifically, at least two of Wobst's arguments have been disputed. First, although he suggested that "only simple invariate and recurrent messages will normally be transmitted stylistically" (140:323), in many cases style conveys fairly complex and/or ambiguous information—as, for example, in Shipibo-Conibo Quenea designs (23, 37). Wiessner (137:162; 139:111) argues that ambiguity of stylistic information, rather than being inefficient, may be an important strategy in social relations. Second, Wobst (140) suggested that because stylistic messages are most useful in communicating with persons who do not know the sender well, stylistic information will be found primarily in visible contexts. While these predictions hold in some cases, a number of studies dispute the importance of visibility and argue that subtle variation may convey important information in close social relations (e.g. 20:378; 27, 59:55; see also 99:130–

---

[1]
  Unfortunately Wobst has not elaborated on his original statement, nor has he discussed in print others' use of his ideas.

32). In a cross-cultural comparison, Jones and I (69) found that the importance of visibility and social distance varies with the kind of information transmitted stylistically. Material visible only in private is more likely to convey messages about ritual or belief systems, whereas highly visible material often indicates group or ethnic boundaries.

Dietler & Herbich (27) devote considerable effort to criticizing the information-exchange approach. They argue that their data on Luo (western Kenya) pottery decoration contradicts the expectations developed by Wobst (140) because the decoration requires little effort and is rarely associated with highly visible beer pots. They also state that the decoration conveys little information (27:158). It therefore appears that Luo pottery decoration does not fit the information-exchange theory's definition of style and cannot be used to refute the theory. Rather, the association among low visibility, little effort, and little information content in Luo pottery tends to *support* the general expectations of the information-exchange theory (see further discussion in 69). An important point brought out by this debate is that, according to the information-exchange theory, *not all* material variation is style; rather, style is that part of variation that conveys information (140:321).

The recognition that information exchange does not explain all aspects of style or material culture variation is a second major advance in the application of the information-exchange theory. During the initial heyday of information exchange, many researchers—including myself (51)— embraced information exchange and rejected other perspectives. Now many researchers recognize that information exchange emphasizes only one component of style—that is, the *use* of style-bearing objects—while it gives little consideration to the production and perpetuation of style. As a result, perspectives that emphasize learning and tradition [what have been dubbed the "learning-interaction" and "normative" theories (4, 98)] are no longer rejected out of hand [see the discussion by Conkey (16:6)].

Kintigh (70) and Hill (56) explicitly apply both the learning-interaction and information-exchange theories. Kintigh (70) suggests that subtle aspects of design on Cibola ceramics are more likely to be a product of learning, while more visually distinct attributes are more likely to have been used in information exchange (70:372; see also 128). Hill proposes an evolutionary framework that combines the two theories in a different way. He argues that a pool of stylistic variation exists and is maintained primarily through processes of learning and interaction. Cultural selection then perpetuates those aspects of style that are useful, for information exchange or other reasons.

Very recently, a number of archaeologists, working from widely divergent theoretical perspectives, have continued to explore various aspects of style. Braun (10) takes an evolutionary approach similar to Hill's, though Braun focuses on understanding why certain stylistic practices persist transgenerationally. At the opposite end of the theoretical spectrum, Hodder (60) reconsiders what might be called a normative view of material culture and emphasizes interpretations within an historical context (see also 63). Other researchers have recently focused on how style is learned and how material culture is produced (e.g. 23, 27). Although many of these researchers do not explicitly draw on the information-exchange theory, and some (e.g. 60) explicitly eschew the functionalism of information exchange, all employ an active view of style and consider its cultural role and/or function.

Finally, the information-exchange theory, as first proposed, considered style to be active, in the sense that it functions in a cultural system; however, the theory gave little consideration to the active role of the people who create and use the style (C. Sinopoli, personal communication). Recent work, however, has explicitly considered the active use of style in individuals' social strategies (e.g. 135–138) and as social production that is created and manipulated by social actors (119:98). Thus the active perspective on style originally developed as part of Wobst's (140) information-exchange theory has been broadened to include active human agents.

While the information-exchange theory and the active view of style it exemplifies provide archaeologists with significant analytical potential, they also tempt the scholar into confounding style as subject and material variation as object. Fortunately, as more researchers accept a view of style and information exchange as active processes, they reassess Wobst's predictions, consider where information exchange does and does not apply, and broaden the perspective to include human actors. Scholars are also currently devoting more attention to what kinds of information are conveyed stylistically and in what kinds of situations.

KINDS OF STYLE

Researchers have recognized that no single theory can explain all aspects of style or all facets of material culture variation, and they have likewise recognized that style is not a unidimensional phenomenon. In the past few years a number of archaeologists have identified various kinds of style, which may co-occur on the same object and be interpreted in different situations. Fruitful approaches have been developed by Sackett (112–115; cf 5) and Wiessner (135–139) and have been advanced by others (e.g. 84, 101, 101a). Sackett argues that style resides in the choices made by artisans, particularly choices that result in the same functional end. He calls the results of such choices *isochrestic variation*—variants that are "equivalent in use" (112:72–73). He suggests that such choices are learned or socially transmitted, and variation may therefore reflect both social interaction and historical context. Sackett (113–115) contrasts his isochrestic approach to what he calls the *iconological* approach (used by Wiessner and others), which, he says, holds that style, by definition, has as its "primary function the symbolic expression of social information" (112:82).

Wiessner (135) proposes a multi-faceted view of style (see also 136–138). Drawing on Wobst (140) and a number of social theorists, she argues that style transmits information about personal and social identity that is used in the "fundamental human cognitive process of identification via comparison" (138:58). Wiessner (135) describes two kinds of style that convey different kinds of information, though both may be conveyed by the same objects. *Emblemic* style has a distinct referent and often carries information about groups and boundaries. *Assertive* style has no distinct referent but carries information about vaguer (or less easily verbalized) notions often relating to individual identity and expression.

In a series of exchanges and later statements, Sackett (113–115) and Wiessner (137, 139) argue that several different kinds of stylistic communication and/or variation can coexist and be subjected to separate analysis. Although he emphasizes isochrestic variation, which bears only a tenuous relationship to active social processes, Sackett does not reject the iconological approach. Instead, he (113:158) considers the possibility that although isochrestic variation is not necessarily imbued with social information, it may, under certain circumstances, take on iconographic cultural meanings—e.g. when an "unconscious" tradition becomes ethnically significant in times of ethnic conflict. Wiessner (137, 139) emphasizes the universal aspects of style used in social comparison (i.e. iconographic style); but she also recognizes that some components of material culture are best explained as isochrestic variation.

Others have expanded these perspectives and developed archaeological applications. Macdonald (84) relates Wiessner's two kinds of style directly to social behaviors he calls panache and protocol. Protocol, a "set of social processes ... aimed at the promotion of group identity" (84:53), results in emblemic style, while panache—social processes that emphasize the individual—results in assertive style. Macdonald goes on to develop archaeological implications for these kinds of styles in mortuary analyses, and applies the concepts of protocol and panache to data from the American Plains.

In an elegant application, Plog (101) argues that different patterns of ceramic design variation manifested by different traditional ceramic types in the American Southwest are evidence of different kinds of styles. Strongly covarying designs on an early decorated type are interpreted as isochrestic variation, whereas increasingly variable designs on later types are more likely symbolic—that is, assertive or emblemic style. One later type tends to be associated with the Chaco regional system and/or with ceremonial structures; and this type has strongly covarying designs. Plog (101) argues that these invariant designs may involve iconographic style, indicative of special status.

Franklin (32, 33) also considers emblemic style in contrast to what she calls stochastic style. She does not define stochastic style explicitly but notes that it "relates to the individual's perception of the world from a culturally-shaped perspective" and varies independently of ethnographic boundaries (32:122). She argues that because Australian rock art does not vary in ways that would be expected if it were emblemic style (i.e. stylistic differences do not coincide with tribal or ethnic differences), it is best explained as exemplifying stochastic style.

The delineation of multiple kinds of style represents an advance in the development of an active concept of style. This perspective makes clear that style can have many roles, including—in the case of isochrestic variation—relatively inactive ones. Unfortunately, researchers who have applied this multi-dimensional concept have assumed or defined slightly different kinds of style. Wiessner (135) distinguishes assertive and emblemic styles; Sackett (113–115) uses isochrestic variation and iconological style; Plog (101) uses isochrestic variation, symbolic style, and iconographic style; Franklin (32) uses emblemic and stochastic style. While a proliferation of new definitions and concepts is an important aspect of the development of a new perspective, future work will probably be most productive if it builds on the concepts already defined (e.g. 84). Research that develops archaeological applications, including means of identifying different kinds of style (e.g. 101), would be particularly valuable.

THE SOCIO-CULTURAL SIGNIFICANCE OF STYLE AND MATERIAL CULTURE

The relationship among material culture, style, and socio-cultural processes is central to much research on style, whether the goal is to understand social production in a given context (118, 119) or to make inferences about prehistoric social organization (55, 80).

Much anthropological research has been done on this relationship. Ethnologists have explored the symbolic significance of design iconography (e.g. 37, 92), ethnoarchaeologists have attempted to discern the material correlates of social groups (e.g. 43), and social theorists have investigated the role of material culture in social strategies (e.g. 2, 89, 118, 119). Here I consider these issues in relation to style in four interrelated subsections covering (a) symbolic meanings, (b) learning and interaction, (c) social distinctions, and (d) power relations.

Structure and Symbolic Meaning

Anthropologists—as well as art historians and other researchers—have long noted and investigated the structural and symbolic meanings of art and material culture style (6, 38:94–120; 79:245–73). Consideration of these meanings takes many forms. Many authors draw parallels between the organization of designs, on the one hand, and social and/or environmental organization on the other (e.g. 1, 3, 88). Arnold (3:71) suggests that designs on pottery in Quinua, Peru "are organized by the same structural principles that organize the environmental and social space in the community." Others consider the specific symbolic/iconographic content of designs (e.g. 37, 92,). Shanks & Tilley

(119:98–99) suggest that material culture can be regarded as a structured sign system.

In recent years, a number of researchers have related the symbolic content of material culture to the operation of society (e.g. 8, 20, 59, 66, 86, 126, 134). Hodder (59:58–86; 67) considers how calabash containers and their decorations—which are made and used by women—represent symbolic and structural contrasts between milk and blood, or women and young men. He links these contrasts to the structure of social relations, particularly to dominance by older men, and suggests that calabash and spear styles may function as a sort of silent discourse by means of which women and young men maintain solidarity and possibly disrupt the dominance of older men. David et al (20) interpret Mafa and Bulahay pottery decoration in terms of the symbolic parallels between pots and people. In their elegant essay, "Why pots are decorated," they assert in explanation that pots are like people. Pottery helps to reinforce social values: "Designs on pottery, far from being 'mere decoration,' art for art's sake, or messages consciously emblemic of ethnicity, are low-technology channels through which society implants its values in the individual—every day at mealtimes" (20:379). Braithwaite (8) argues that decoration on pottery is a form of symbolic and ritual discourse used primarily in stressful interactions between men and women.

Although our ability to identify specific meanings in the archaeological record is limited, archaeologists have made considerable headway in the interpretation of meaning in style and material culture. Some postprocessual archaeologists argue that style and other aspects of material culture should be interpreted only within their specific cultural and historical context because style is the result of "specific historical practices ... in given conditions" (118:148–49). Furthermore, "artifacts and social acts draw their meaning from the roles they play, their use, and in the daily patterns of existence" (61:4). These researchers' insistence on this level of specificity sometimes limits their interpretations to ethnographic, ethnohistorical, or historical contexts, including a study of beer cans (118). However, several studies working with well-researched cases have been able to interpret the meaning of style and material culture in the prehistoric archaeological record (see 39 and 58 for examples within the post-processual paradigm, or 49 for a more general application).

Other archaeologists have sought to interpret stylistic meanings at a more general level. Although we cannot generally determine what every detail of material culture means, it is often possible to understand the general range of meanings conveyed by a class of artifacts (30:74; 73, 104:359–60). This approach involves considering the dimensions of stylistic variation (e.g. diversity, redundancy, structural regularity) in relation to other evidence. For example, I have interpreted a high degree of ceramic design diversity associated with relatively strong architectural boundedness as a stylistic expression of small-scale social differentiation, although I was not able to ascertain the specific kinds of boundaries that may have been expressed stylistically (52, 53;

see 9, 25 for related interpretations of diversity; also 78). A number of other researchers have also presented interpretations that emphasize such dimensions of stylistic variation. Crown (19) argues that standardized representational designs on Salado polychrome pottery are some form of ritual symbolism. Pollock (104) interprets increases in design redundancy on Susiana ceramics—which are associated with increases in settlement complexity—as representative of increases in vertical stratification. Finally, Braun (11) suggests that increases in the amount of decoration and decorative diversity on prehistoric Woodland pottery result from an increase in the expression of social identities and social differences.

Learning and Interaction

The burgeoning archaeological interest in style in the last several decades was inspired, at least in part, by the ceramic sociology studies of the 1960s (e.g. 55, 80). A basic premise of these studies was that material similarity is directly related to social interaction and shared learning contexts. Although many of the methods and specific results of these studies have been criticized (e.g. 97, 124), the studies inspired profitable research into sources of material culture variation. One topic that has received considerable attention [including work by one of the original "ceramic sociologists" and his students (41, 43, 81)] is the effect of learning and production on material culture variation.

Results of various studies suggest that the association between style and learning or production context is variable and context dependent. In analyses of Kalinga pottery Graves (41, 43) found only weak association between work groups and design similarity. Similarly, Hardin (34) found that Tarascan pottery design styles in most cases did not parallel work groups. Among the Shipibo-Conibo, DeBoer (23:103) found that "learning may lead to similarity or difference depending on the context." That is, a woman generally learns from her mother and adopts some aspects of her mother's style, though she may also develop a different style either because of differences in talent or because of a deliberate attempt to distance self from mother. At the pueblo of Zuni, where pottery-making is taught in a fairly formal setting (associated with the high school), different styles of design are strongly associated with different teachers (48:55). Finally, Luo potting communities have distinctive decorative "microstyles" (27).

The relationship between style or stylistic variation and the organization of production has also been a focus of research, particularly for scholars of complex societies (e.g. 18, 31, 108, 123, 133a). There appears to be a general relationship between style and production at some levels (e.g. between the scale of production and standardization). However, many aspects of style and material culture are affected by various cultural factors (such as prestige systems) and therefore bear little direct relationship to the organization of production (133a). The location of production does not necessarily coincide with stylistic similarities and differences. While different materials are often made in different places, in a number of cases stylistically similar materials were found to have been produced at different locations (e.g. 19, 45, 141).

Although the association of learning/production context and stylistic similarity is far from absolute, some important insights can be gained by comparing these data. Longacre (82:8) suggests that the link between learning and material similarity is strong in cases where instruction is more formal (as at Zuni). The link between learning context and material similarity also appears to be stronger in cases (including Zuni and Shipibo-Conibo) where designs have more explicit symbolic content. In addition, the learning/production context may be expressed at one level of stylistic variation but not another. Several producer-groups (including the Luo and Zuni) have distinctive "micro-styles," though they conform to a broader stylistic (possibly ethnic) tradition [a possibility considered by Kintigh (70)]. Finally, in a number of cases (including the Luo, Tarascans, and Kalinga), stylistic distinctions may be understood only by the producers or a limited subset of society (27, 34, 83).

Social Distinctions

Archaeologists have a long, and sometimes notorious, history of correlating styles of material culture and social groups, such as the European Neolithic Beaker Folk and the Hohokam Red-on-Buff Culture. At the same time, we have also recognized that material culture is not necessarily isormorphic to living cultures (13:41). No longer is the association between material culture and living cultures taken for granted. Instead, the archaeological interpretation of cultural identity is an active topic of research (122). Although the relationship is complex, there is a fairly strong association between material culture and social units at many levels, from the individual to the ethnic group.

Wiessner (135–139) and others (23, 84) have discussed the use of style for individual expression, including artistic expression. At a slightly broader, though still intra-societal level, numerous ethnographic studies document the association of certain styles with various intra-societal groups, including Kalinga age cohorts (41, 43), Masai age grades (72), Hopi political factions (142), and Maori sub-tribes (86). Stylistic distinctions at the level of the individual or intra-societal group are potentially problematical archaeologically because they are unlikely to create spatially distinct patterns in the archaeological record. However, stylistic distinctions should result in a greater degree of stylistic diversity; thus analyses of diversity or stylistic variability may reveal the existence of intra-societal boundaries or distinctions (10, 52, 53; see also 138).

In many cases material culture differences are associated with ethnic differences (e.g. 23, 83, 122, 135, 140). Kalinga vessel shape or profile seems "to be actively employed as a marker of important social boundaries ... at the regional level" (83:105). In the Baringo District (Western Africa) some forms of material culture (including dress and to some extent pots and stools) clearly distinguish ethnic and tribal groups, though other forms cross-cut ethnic boundaries (59). Ethnic groups (including the Shipibo-Conibo) in the Ucayali Basin (Peru), have distinct styles that "almost certainly constitute a form of iconologic signaling in which adjacent and competing riverine groups distinguish themselves in a stylistically indelible manner (i.e. through tattooing and head-flattening)" (23:86). Washburn (132; see also 129, 130), argues that certain aspects of material culture—what she calls basic-level features such as design symmetry—are most likely to display ethnic identity, and she documents these kinds of ethnic distinctions in a number of cases, including those of Lao and Bakuba weavers. An important component of many studies that associate material culture and ethnicity is the understanding that the association is not automatic, a result of some kind of mental template; rather, style—a way of making or decorating material culture—is an active component of group definition. In several cases material culture differences are associated with competition and tend to increase as social tensions increase (23, 57, 59, 83, 94, 140).

While this association between material culture differences and ethnic differences encourages archaeological application, it clearly cannot be taken for granted. At least one volume (122), as well as other recent research (e.g. 7, 73, 86), has been devoted to elucidating the material expression of cultural differences. The process is complex. Cultural identity and ethnicity are not clear-cut concepts; they are often difficult to define even with ethnographic data. A number of authors illustrate cases in which perceived cultural differences have no material component (26), or in which certain material distinctions parallel ethnic distinctions while others cross-cut them (59). In other cases, ethnic distinctions, while present, are considered passive epiphenomena of other kinds of expression (73).

Despite the potential pitfalls, archaeologists have identified what appear to be spatially distinct social units in the archaeological record (e.g. 44, 57, 98, 116, 141). Although an absence of archaeologically observable stylistic boundaries is difficult to interpret, the presence of such boundaries can be interpreted, with some confidence, as an indication of social distinctions. The development of stylistic boundaries or changes in their distribution can be interpreted in terms of changes in the social units.

Power and Social Inequality

The control of material goods and manipulation of ideology are often central to the definition of rank and the exercise of power in complex societies. The style of the material culture may be an important component of these power manipulation strategies. Elites often have exclusive access to certain kinds of goods, and elite status is frequently reinforced in iconography (e.g. 30, 54). Recently, researchers have studied how elites acquire and manipulate status symbols and how the meanings of those symbols may change (30, 85, 91, 105, 121). Because much of this work considers material culture in general rather than style per se, I do not review it in detail here; but at least one point that runs through this work is directly relevant to this discussion: Analyses of style with respect to power relations must consider how people who are trying to gain or maintain power manipulate material culture. Such considerations promote an active view of style and the people who make it and thus have important implications for the development of an active view of style at a broader level.

STYLE AND TECHNOLOGY

Recent research has both increased the precision of our understanding of style and broadened our conception of what style is. No longer opposed to function, style is seen as *having* a function. Similarly, style is no longer conceived as separate from technology and production. Rather, a technology (that is, a way of doing something) can have style. Although research linking style and technology has been fairly infrequent, some important advances have been made.

First, archaeologists often struggle with the problem of how to identify style, particularly in nondecorative components of material. Painted decorations on a pot are good candidates for stylistic analysis, but what about the rim profile and temper? Sackett's (112) concept of isochrestic variation—variation that results from a choice between technologically equivalent alternatives—takes steps towards resolving this problem. Isochrestic variation can include components of material culture that are intrinsic to an object's technological function or to the technology involved in that object's production. For example, isochrestic variation in lithic technology can encompass choice of raw materials, reduction technique, or tool shape (112:105). Sackett (112–115) focuses primarily on style or isochrestic variation in artifacts, but others have linked style and technology at a broader level.

In 1977 (the year the information-exchange theory was published), a volume edited by Lechtman & Merrill (75) advanced the concept of technological styles. The contributors considered not only artifacts but also "the activities which produce the artifacts" to be stylistic (75:5). Unfortunately, many authors in the volume used what would today be considered a fairly passive definition of style,[2] and the concept of technological styles has not been widely applied (but see 14 for a recent work on technological styles). More research in this direction would probably be fruitful. Lemonnier (76, 77) also uses the general concept of technological style, though he uses different terminology and does not site Lechtman & Merrill's work. Lemonnier focuses on "technological systems," which include everything from garden preparation to the kinds of plants used in men's and women's capes. He argues that these "technological systems" (which are ways of doing something and therefore could be called

---

2

For example, Lechtmen considers style to be "the manifest expression, on the behavioral level, of cultural patterning that is usually neither cognitively known nor even knowable by members of a cultural community" (75:4).

styles of technology) are "signifying systems" (76:174) used in ethnic and gender relations.

Interest in the relationship between style and technology has important implications. As Sackett's (112–115) work demonstrates, understanding that style can include technological choices helps us determine what components of artifacts should be included in stylistic analyses and increases the kinds of information that can be gained from the study of production systems. Production is no longer merely a factor that needs to be controlled-for before stylistic analysis can be done, nor must production be considered only in economic terms. Instead, production can be a subject of interest for archaeologists concerned with issues related to style.

ANALYTICAL APPROACHES

As archaeologists became increasingly interested in style in the 1960s and 1970s, they developed an array of methods with which to analyze styles of material culture. One of the most significant advances of earlier research was the development of systematic and replicable systems of classification and quantification as a basis for stylistic analysis. Researchers developed methods of analysis (directed primarily at decoration) that eventually included a hierarchy of attributes—ranging from the shapes of individual forms to the overall design configuration [e.g. 98, 106; see review in Plog (99:128–33)]. Recent research includes extensive application and occasional refinement of these methods (e.g. 19, 53, 102). Washburn (e.g. 129, 130, 132) has continued to pursue symmetry analysis and has published a comprehensive guide to the technique (133).

For the most part, however, recent advances emphasize not new techniques of classification and analysis but new applications of developed techniques.[3] Archaeologists have increasingly combined and extended analytical techniques, to great benefit. These combinations fall into two general categories. First, researchers often draw from more than one analytical system and consider different components of material. For example, in research on ceramic designs from the Southwest (52, 53), I considered both the appearance of design elements (triangles, lines, etc) on the ceramic assemblage as a whole (sherds and whole vessels) and the layout and symmetry of designs on only whole vessels or large portions of vessels. For similar approaches, see combined work by Lathrap and Washburn (74, 131), and by Braun (11). Researchers have also combined analyses of specific attributes and typological

---

[3] One exception is work by Jernigan (68), who developed a new method of analysis based on design schema. However, Jernigan's work has been criticized (28, 101a) because the schemata—which are emic units of design—are vaguely defined, and the analysis is not replicable.

analyses in order to interpret the kind of information or kind of style conveyed by each type (53, 101).

Second, rather than concentrating solely on one class of material culture, a number of archaeologists and ethnoarchaeologists have broadened their approaches to consider style in multiple media. For example, Hays (50) considers designs on various Basketmaker III (7th century AD) media (including ceramics, rock art, and textiles) from the American Southwest. She interprets the role of the designs (e.g. in relation to gender and as a possible indicator of ethnic differences) based on their occurrence on different material and in different contexts. DeBoer (24) considers different ways in which design styles are applied to different media in Andean South America. The Shipibo-Conibo use complex and symbolically significant Quenea designs on many different media (pottery, textiles, clothing, etc), while the Cache apply different designs to different media. DeBoer (24) contrasts the *pervasive* design system of the Shipibo-Conibo with the *partitive* system of the Cache. He relates these differences both to the stability of designs over time and to the level of meaning attached to the designs; he finds that the Shipibo-Conibo pervasive designs are both more stable and more meaningful (see also the discussion in 69; see 39, 59, 64, 126 for other examples of cross-media analyses of style).

CONCLUSIONS

In this review I have treated the study of style in archaeology, considering primarily style in portable artifacts. Other current issues and applications of stylistic analysis should be acknowledged. These include the evolution of style (7, 87:314; 109), the use of stylistic analysis in chronological studies (19, 71, 102, 103), art historical/classical perspectives on style (22, 117), stylistic diffusion (21, 71), and studies of architecture or burial practices (e.g. 35, 90, 95).

As research on style has proliferated, so has the variety of research perspectives. Fortunately, in a very encouraging development, researchers are increasingly replacing debates about which theory of style or kind of analysis is correct with the conclusion that many perspectives may be applicable, depending on the problem at hand. This multi-level/multi-dimensional approach is apparent in consideration of issues ranging from the definition of various kinds of style to analyses that combine classification of separate design elements with studies of design symmetry. The broad perspective gained by such an approach helps to foster, if not a sense of unity, at least a level of tolerance that often draws together disparate viewpoints.

The general perspective on style taken by many researchers also fosters a degree of unity in archaeological approaches to style. Most research on style at least considers the active role of style, whether or not such an active perspective is central to the research. Work such as Wiessner's (135–139)—which focuses on style as a means of defining the self or group—considers the role of style and stylistic information in social relationships. Shanks & Tilley (118, 119) also emphasize the role of style, although they see style (or art) as "social production" and a form of ideology. Finally, researchers who focus on understanding sources of material culture variation—and who do not take an active view of style—often still consider whether or not the material culture conveys information and in what contexts (e.g. 27). Thus the role of style can be a unifying concept for these disparate perspectives.

We are still far from an integrated theory of style, and some have suggested that such a theory is neither possible nor necessary (17:2–3). We also lack integration on a more modest level. Although we understand many aspects of style and have extensive data on material culture variation, we have not yet put all the pieces together. Archaeology lacks a synthetic perspective that integrates the many sources of empirical data with conceptual approaches to style. The information is available, however, so the time for such integration may be near.

ACKNOWLEDGMENTS

I am grateful to James Allison, Robert Bolin, Stephen Plog, and Carla Sinopoli for their comments and advice on this paper.

Literature Cited

1. Adams, M. J. 1973. Structural aspects of a village art. *Am. Anthropol.* 75:265–79
2. Appadurai, A., ed. 1986. *The Social Life of Things: Commodities in Cultural Perspectives.* Cambridge: Cambridge Univ. Press. 329 pp.
3. Arnold, D. E. 1983. Design structure and community organization in Quinua, Peru. See Ref 129, pp. 56–73
4. Binford, L. R. 1972. *An Archaeological Perspective.* London: Seminar Press
5. Binford, L. R. 1989. Styles of style. *J. Anthropol. Archaeol.* 8:51–67
6. Boas, F. 1955. *Primitive Art.* Reprint. Dover Publ., New York. Orig. publ. 1927, Oslo: H. Aschehoug and Co.
7. Boyd, R., Richerson, P. J. 1987 The evolution of ethnic markers. *Cult. Anthropol.* 2:65–79
8. Braithwaite, M. 1982. Decoration as ritual symbol: a theoretical proposal and ethnographic study in southern Sudan. See Ref. 58a, pp. 80–88
9. Braun, D. P. 1985. Ceramic decorative diversity and Illinois Woodland regional integration. See Ref. 93, pp. 128–53
10. Braun, D. P. 1990. Style and selection. See Ref. 12
11. Braun, D. P. 1991. Why decorate a pot? Midwestern household pottery, 200 B. C.–A. D. 600. *J. Anthropol. Archaeol.* 10:360–97

12. Carr, C., Neitzel, J., eds. 1990. *Style, Society, and Person.* Cambridge: Cambridge Univ. Press. In press
13. Childe, V. G. 1951. *Social Evolution.* London: Watts and Company
14. Childs, S. T. 1991. Style, technology, and iron smelting furnaces in Bantu-speaking Africa. *J. Anthropol. Archaeol.* 10:332–59
15. Clarke, D. 1968. *Analytical Archaeology.* London: Methuen
16. Conkey, M. 1990. Experimenting with style in archaeology: some historical and theoretical issues. See Ref. 17, pp. 5–17
17. Conkey, M., Hastorf, C., eds. 1990. *Uses of Style in Archaeology.* Cambridge: Cambridge Univ. Press. 124 pp.
18. Costin, C. L. 1991. Craft specialization: issues in defining, documenting, and explaining the organization of production. In *Archaeol. Method Theory* 3:1–56
19. Crown, P. L. 1990. Converging traditions: Salado Polychrome ceramics in Southwestern prehistory. Presented at Annu. Meet. Soc. Am. Archaeol., 55th, Las Vegas
20. David, N., Sterner, J., Gavua, K. 1988. Why pots are decorated. *Curr. Anthropol.* 29:365–89
21. Davis, D. D. 1983. Investigating the diffusion of stylistic innovations. *Adv. Archaeol. Method Theory* 6:53–89
22. Davis, W. 1990. Style and history in art history. See Ref. 17, pp. 18–31

23. DeBoer, W. R. 1990. Interaction, imitation, and communication as expressed in style: the Ucayali experience. See Ref. 17, pp. 82–104
24. DeBoer, W. R. 1991. The decorative burden: design, medium and change. See Ref. 81, pp. 144–61
25. DeBoer, W. R., Moore, J. A. 1982. The measurement and meaning of stylistic diversity. Ñawpa Pacha 20:147–62
26. DeCorse, C. R. 1989. Material aspects of Limba, Yalunka and Kuranko ethnicity: archaeological research in northeastern Sierra Leone. See Ref. 122, pp. 125–40
27. Dietler, M., Herbich, I. 1989. Tich Matek: the technology of Luo pottery production and the definition of ceramic style. World Archaeol. 21:148–64
28. Douglass, A. A., Lindauer, O. 1988. Hierarchical and nonhierarchical approaches to ceramic design analysis: a response to Jernigan. Am. Antiq. 53:620–26
29. Dunnell, R. C. 1978. Style and function: a fundamental dichotomy. Am. Antiq. 43:192–202
30. Earle, T. K. 1990. Style and iconography as legitimation in complex chiefdoms. See Ref. 17, pp. 73–81
31. Feinman, G. M. 1985. Changes in the organization of ceramic production in prehispanic Oaxaca, Mexico. See Ref. 93, pp. 194–223
32. Franklin, N. R. 1986. Stochastic vs emblemic: an archaeologically useful method for the analysis of style in Australian rock art. Rock Art Res. 3:121–24
33. Franklin, N. R. 1989. Research with style: a case study from Australian rock art. See Ref. 122, pp. 278–90
34. Friedrich, M. H. 1970. Design structure and social interaction: archaeological implications of an ethnographic analysis. Am. Antiq. 35:332–43
35. Fritz, J. M. 1987. Chaco Canyon and Vijayanagara: proposing spatial meaning in two societies. In Mirror and Metaphor: Material and Social Constructions of Reality, ed. D. W. Ingersoll, Jr., G. Bronitsky, pp. 313–49. Landham, MA: University Press of America
36. Gadamer, H. G. 1965. Wahrheit und Methode. Tübingen: Mohr. 2nd ed.
36a. Gebauer, A. B. 1987. Stylistic analysis: A critical review of concepts, models, and applications. J. Danish Archaeol. 6:223–23
37. Gebhart-Sayer, A. 1985. The geometric designs of the Shipibo-Conibo in ritual context. J. Latin Am. Lore 11(2):143–75
38. Geertz, C. 1983. Local Knowledge: Further Essays in Interpretive Anthropology. New York: Basic
39. Gibbs, L. 1987. Identifying gender representation in the archaeological record: a contextual study. See Ref. 62, pp. 79–89
40. Deleted in proof
41. Graves, M. W. 1981. Ethnoarchaeology of Kalinga ceramic design. PhD thesis. Univ. Ariz., Tucson. 360 pp.
42. Graves, M. W. 1982. Breaking down ceramic variation: testing models of White Mountain Redware design style development. J. Anthropol. Archaeol 1:305-54
43. Graves, M. W. 1985. Ceramic design variation within a Kalinga village: temporal and spatial processes. See Ref. 93, pp. 5–34
44. Hantman, J. L. 1983. Social networks and stylistic distributions in the prehistoric plateau southwest. PhD thesis. Ariz. State Univ., Tempe
45. Hantman, J. L, Plog, S. 1982. The relationship of stylistic similarity to patterns of material exchange. In Contexts of Prehistoric Exchange, ed. T. K. Earle, J. E. Ericson, pp. 237–63. New York: Academic
46. Deleted in proof
47. Hardin, M. A. 1984. Models of decoration. In The Many Dimensions of Pottery: Ceramics in Archaeology and Anthropology, ed. A. C. Pritchard and S. E. van der Leeuw, pp. 575–607. Amsterdam: Univ. Amsterdam
48. Hardin, M. A. 1991. Sources of ceramic variability at Zuni Pueblo. See Ref. 81, pp. 40–70
49. Hays, K. A. 1989. Katsina depictions on Homol'ovi ceramics: toward a fourteenth century pueblo iconography. Kiva 54:297–311
50. Hays, K. A. 1991. Social contexts of style and information in a seventh century Basketmaker community. Presented at Annu. Meet. Soc. Am. Archaeol., 56th, New Orleans
51. Hegmon, M. 1986. Information exchange and integration on Black Mesa, Arizona, A. D. 931–1150. See Ref. 100, pp. 256–81
52. Hegmon, M. 1992. Boundary-making strategies in early pueblo societies: style and architecture in the Kayenta and Mesa Verde regions. In The Ancient Southwestern Community: Models and Methods for the Study of Prehistoric Social Organization, ed. W. H. Wills, R. D. Leonard. Albuquerque: Univ. New Mexico Press. In press
53. Hegmon, M. 1992. The Social Dynamics of Pottery Style in the Early Puebloan Southwest. Cortez, CO: Crow Canyon Archaeol. Cent. In press
54. Helms, M. W. 1987. Art styles as interaction spheres in Central America and the Caribbean: polished black wood in the Greater Antilles. In Chiefdoms in the Americas, ed. R. D. Drennan, C. A. Uribe, pp. 67–84. Lanham, MD: University Press of America
55. Hill, J. N. 1970. Broken K Pueblo: prehistoric social organization in the American Southwest. Anthropol. Pap. Univ. Ariz. No. 18
56. Hill, J. N. 1985. Style: a conceptual evolutionary framework. See Ref. 93, pp. 362–85
57. Hodder, I. 1979. Economic and social stress and material culture patterning. Am. Antiq. 44:446–54

58. Hodder, I. 1982. Sequences of structural change in the Dutch Neolithic. See Ref. 58a, pp. 162–77
58a. Hodder, I., ed. 1982. *Symbolic and Structural Archaeology.* Cambridge: Cambridge Univ. Press. 188 pp.
59. Hodder, I. 1982. *Symbols in Action.* Cambridge: Cambridge Univ. Press
60. Hodder, I. 1982. Theoretical archaeology: a reactionary view. See Ref. 58a, pp. 1–16
61. Hodder, I. 1985. Postprocessual archaeology. *Adv. Archaeol. Method Theory* 8:1–26
62. Hodder, I., ed. 1987. *The Archaeology of Contextual Meanings.* Cambridge: Cambridge Univ. Press
63. Hodder, I. 1987. The contextual analysis of symbolic meanings. See Ref. 62, pp. 1–10
64. Hodder, I. 1987. Contextual archaeology: an interpretation of Catal Hüyük and a discussion of the origins of agriculture. *Inst. Archaeol. Bull.* 24:43–56
65. Hodder, I., ed. 1989. *The Meaning of Things.* London: Unwin Hyman
66. Hodder, I., 1990. Style as historical quality. See Ref. 17, pp. 44–51
67. Hodder, I. 1991. The decoration of containers: an ethnographic and historical study. See Ref. 81, pp. 71–94
68. Jernigan, E. W. 1986. A non-hierarchical approach to ceramic decoration analysis: a Southwestern example. *Am. Antiq.* 51:3–20
69. Jones, K., Hegmon, M. 1991. The medium and the message: a survey of information conveyed by material culture in middle range societies. Presented at Annu. Meet. Soc. Am. Archaeol., 56th, New Orleans
70. Kintigh, K. 1985. Social structure, the structure of style, and stylistic patterns in Cibola pottery. See Ref. 93, pp. 35–74
71. Kojo, Y. 1991. *Rethinking methods and paradigms of ceramic chronology.* PhD thesis, Univ. Ariz., Tucson
72. Larick, R. 1985. Spears, style, and time among Maa-speaking pastoralists. *J. Anthropol. Archaeol.* 4:201–15
73. Larick, R. 1991. Warriors and blacksmiths: mediating ethnicity in East African spears. *J. Anthropol. Archaeol.* 10:299–331
74. Lathrap, D. W. 1983. Recent Shipibo-Conibo ceramics and their implications for archaeological interpretation. See Ref. 129, pp. 25–39
75. Lechtman, H., Merrill, R. S., eds. 1977. *Material Culture, Styles, Organization, and Dynamics of Technology.* 1975 Proc. Am. Ethnol. Soc. St. Paul, Minnesota: West
76. Lemonnier, P. 1986. The study of material culture today: toward an anthropology of technical systems. *J. Anthropol. Archaeol.* 5:147–86
77. Lemonnier, P. 1989. Bark capes, arrowheads and the Concorde: on social representations of technology. See Ref. 67, pp. 156–71
78. Leonard, R. D., Jones, G. T., eds. 1989. *Quantifying Diversity in Archaeology.* Cambridge: Cambridge Univ. Press

79. Lévi-Strauss, C. 1963. *Structural Anthropology.* New York: Basic
80. Longacre, W. A. 1970. Archaeology as anthropology: a case study. Anthropol. Pap. Univ. Ariz. No. 17
81. Longacre, W. A., ed. 1991. *Ceramic Ethnoarchaeology.* Tucson: Univ. Arizona Press
82. Longacre, W. A. 1991. Ceramic ethnoarchaeology: an introduction. See Ref. 81, pp. 1–10
83. Longacre, W. A. 1991. Sources of ceramic variability among the Kalinga of northern Luzon. See Ref. 81, pp. 95–111
84. Macdonald, W. K. 1990. Investigating style: an exploratory analysis of some Plains burials. See Ref. 17, pp. 52–60
85. McGuire, R., Paynter, R., eds. 1991. *The Archaeology of Inequality.* London: Basil Blackwell
86. Mead, H. M. 1990. Tribal art as symbols of identity. In *Art and Identity in Oceania,* ed. A. Hanson, L. Hanson, pp. 269–81. Honolulu: Univ. Hawaii Press
87. Meltzer, D. J. 1981. A study of style and function in a class of tools. *J. Field Archaeol.* 8: 313–26
88. Merrill, E. B. 1987. Art styles as reflections of sociopolitical complexity. *Ethnology* 26:221–30
89. Miller, D. 1982. *Artefacts as Categories.* Cambridge: Cambridge Univ. Press
90. Miller, D. 1985. Ideology and the Harappan civilization. *J. Anthropol. Archaeol.* 4:34–71
91. Miller, D., Tilley, C. 1984. *Ideology, Power and Prehistory.* Cambridge: Cambridge Univ. Press
92. Munn, N. D. 1986. *Walbiri Iconography: Graphic Representation and Cultural Symbolism in a Central Australian Society.* Chicago: Univ. Chicago Press. 2nd ed.
93. Nelson, B. A., ed. 1985. *Decoding Prehistoric Ceramics.* Carbondale: Southern Illinois Univ. Press
94. Osborn, A. 1989. Multiculturalism in the eastern Andes. See Ref. 122, pp. 141–56
95. Parker Pearson, M. 1982. Mortuary practices, society and ideology: an ethnoarchaeological study. See Ref. 58a, pp. 99–114
96. Peebles, C., Kus, S. 1977. Some archaeological correlates of ranked societies. *Am. Antiq.* 42:421–28
97. Plog, S. 1978. Social interaction and stylistic similarity: a reanalysis. *Adv. Archaeol. Method Theory,* 1:143–82
98. Plog, S. 1980. *Stylistic Variation in Prehistoric Ceramics.* Cambridge: Cambridge Univ. Press
99. Plog, S. 1983. Analysis of style in artifacts. *Annu. Rev. Anthropol.* 12:125–42
100. Plog, S., ed. 1986. *Spatial Organization and Exchange: Archaeological Survey on Northern Black Mesa.* Carbondale: Southern Illinois Univ. Press. 377 pp.
101. Plog, S. 1990. Sociopolitical implications

of stylistic variation in the American Southwest. See Ref. 17, pp. 61–72

101a. Plog, S. 1992. Approaches to the study of style: complements and contrasts. See Ref. 12

102. Plog, S., Hantman, J. L. 1986. Multiple regression analysis as a dating method in the American Southwest. See Ref 100:87–114

103. Plog, S., Hantman, J. L. 1990. Chronology construction and the study of prehistoric culture change. *J. Field Archaeol.* 17:439–56

104. Pollock, S. M. 1983. Style and information: an analysis of Susiana ceramics. *J. Anthropol. Archaeol.* 2:354–90

105. Pollock, S. M. 1983. *The symbolism of prestige.* PhD thesis. Univ. Mich., Ann Arbor

106. Redman, C. L. 1978. Multivariate artifact analysis: a basis for multidimensional interpretations. In *Social Archaeology: Beyond Subsistence and Dating,* ed. C. L. Redman et al, pp. 159–92. New York: Academic

107. Rice, P. M. 1987. *Pottery Analysis: A Sourcebook.* Chicago: Univ. Chicago Press

108. Rice, P. M. 1989. Ceramic diversity, production, and use. See Ref. 78, pp. 109–17

109. Rindos, D. 1989. Undirected variation and the Darwinian explanation of culture change. *Adv. Archaeol. Method Theory* 1:1–45

110. Sackett, J. R. 1973. Style, function and artifact variability in palaeolithic assemblages. In *The Explanation of Culture Change,* ed. C. Renfrew, pp. 317–25. London: Duckworth

111. Sackett, J. R. 1977. The meaning of style: a general model. *Am. Antiq.* 42:369-80

112. Sackett, J. R. 1982. Approaches to style in lithic archaeology. *J. Anthropol. Archaeol.* 1:59–112

113. Sackett, J. R. 1985. Style and ethnicity in the Kalahari: a reply to Wiessner. *Am. Antiq.* 50:154–59

114. Sackett, J. R. 1986. Isochrestism and style: a clarification. *J. Anthropol. Archaeol.* 5:266–77

115. Sackett, J. R. 1990. Style and ethnicity in archaeology: the case for isochrestism. See Ref. 17, pp. 32–43

116. Sampson, C. G. 1988. *Stylistic Boundaries among Mobile Hunter-Foragers.* Washington, DC: Smithsonian Inst. Press

117. Sauerländer, W. 1983. From stilus to style: reflections on the fate of a notion. *Art Hist.* 6:253–70

118. Shanks, M., Tilley, C. 1987. *Reconstructing Archaeology: Theory and Practice.* Cambridge: Cambridge Univ. Press.

119. Shanks, M., Tilley, C. 1987. *Social Theory and Archaeology.* Albuquerque: Univ. New Mexico Press

120. Shapiro, M. 1953. Style. In *Anthropology Today,* ed. A. L. Kroeber, pp. 287–312. Chicago: Aldine

121. Shennan, S. J. 1986. Interaction and change in third millennium B. C. western and central Europe. In *Peer Polity Interaction,* ed. C. Renfrew, S. Shennan, pp. 137–48. Cambridge: Cambridge Univ. Press

122. Shennan, S. J., ed. 1989. *Archaeological Approaches to Cultural Identity.* London: Unwin Hyman. 317 pp.

123. Sinopoli, C. M. 1988. The organization of craft production at Vijayanagara, South India. *Am. Anthropol.* 90:580–97

124. Stanislawski, M. B. 1973. Review of "Archaeology as anthropology: a case study." *Am. Antiq.* 38:117–21

125. Thomas, N. 1991. *Entangled Objects.* Cambridge: Cambridge Univ. Press

126. Tilley, C. 1984. Ideology and the legitimation of power in the Middle Neolithic of Southern Sweden. See Ref. 91, pp. 111–46

127. Vansina, J. 1978. *The Children of Woot: A History of the Kuba Peoples.* Madison: Univ. Wisconsin Press

128. Voss, J. A. 1980. *Tribal emergence during the neolithic of northwestern Europe.* PhD thesis. Univ. Mich., Ann Arbor. 371 pp.

129. Washburn, D. K., ed. 1983. *Structure and Cognition in Art.* Cambridge: Cambridge Univ. Press

130. Washburn, D. K. 1983. Symmetry analysis of ceramic design: two tests of the method on Neolithic material from Greece and the Aegean. See Ref. 129, pp. 138–64

131. Washburn, D. K. 1983. Toward a theory of structural style in art. See Ref. 129, pp. 1–7

132. Washburn, D. K. 1989. The property of symmetry and the concept of ethnic style. See Ref. 122, pp. 157–73

133. Washburn, D. K., Crowe, D. 1987. *Symmetries of Culture: Theory and Practice of Plane Pattern Analysis.* Seattle: Univ. Washington Press

133a. Wattenmaker, P. A. 1990. *The social context of specialized production: reorganization of household craft and food economies in an early Near Eastern State.* PhD thesis. Univ. Mich., Ann Arbor

134. Welbourn, A. 1984. Endo ceramics and power strategies. See Ref. 91, pp. 17–24

135. Wiessner, P. 1983. Style and social information in Kalahari San projectile points. *Am. Antiq.* 49:253–76

136. Wiessner, P. 1984. Reconsidering the behavioral basis for style: a case study among the Kalahari San. *J. Anthropol. Archaeol.* 3:190–234

137. Wiessner, P. 1985. Style or isochrestic variation? A reply to Sackett. *Am. Antiq.* 50:160–66

138. Wiessner, P. 1989. Style and changing relations between the individual and society. See Ref. 65, pp. 56–63

139. Wiessner, P. 1990. Is there a unity to style? See Ref. 17, pp. 105–12

140. Wobst, H. M. 1977. Stylistic behavior and information exchange. In *For the Director: Research Essays in Honor of James B. Griffin,* ed. C. E. Cleland, pp. 317–42. Ann

Arbor: Mus. Anthropol. Anthropol. Pap. 61, Mus. Michigan

141. Wright, R. 1986. The boundaries of technology and stylistic change. In *Ceramics and Civilization,* ed. W. D. Kingery, 2. Columbus, OH: Am. Ceramic Soc.

142. Wyckoff, L. L. 1985. *Designs and Factions: Politics, Religion, and Ceramics on the Hopi Third Mesa.* Albuquerque: Univ. New Mexico Press

Annu. Rev. Anthropol. 1992. 21:537–64

BEYOND ART: Toward an Understanding of the Origins of Material Representation in Europe

KEYWORDS: Paleolithic art, body ornamentation, prehistoric Europe, Aurignacian, Upper Paleolithic technology

Randall White

Department of Anthropology, New York University, New York, NY 10003

> *Through the coloring of metaphor, the nonverbal perception of existing structures, and the symbolic imagination, humans have the unique capacity to create new things (52:38).*

INTRODUCTION

In the pages that follow, I seek not to provide a comprehensive review of explanations for the "origins of art," but to accomplish three complementary tasks:

First, I attempt to reorient, in a direction more satisfying to anthropology, research that seeks to understand or explain that phenomenon generally recognized as the first "art." I propose a framework that focuses on material forms of representation and that seeks to understand them as metaphorically based, socially meaningful constructs.

Second, I provide a broad, critical evaluation of the current record pertaining to the earliest material representations, echoing and elaborating upon Chase & Dibble's (23) skepticism about alleged symbolic objects dating to before the Middle/Upper Paleolithic transition.

Third, I present an overview of Aurignacian material representation, the operational chain that produced it, and the patterning inherent in it.

I conclude by reaffirming my previously stated view (123) that the invention of material forms of representation went hand in hand with a major social transformation across the Middle/Upper Paleolithic transition in Europe. In

0084-6570/92/1015-0537$2.00

addition, I attempt to understand the advantages and cultural evolutionary consequences of metaphorically based material representations. This concern with metaphor and its relationship to "the origins of art" stems directly from Knecht's (52, 53) probing and fresh analysis of the foundations of innovation in early Upper Paleolithic organic projectile technology. I have taken many of her insights, notably her emphasis on the role of nonverbal thought in techno- logical innovation, and aimed them at the question of "art" in the Aurignacian.

BACKGROUND TO THE PROBLEM

Since the discovery in the mid-19th century of engraved bone and antler objects, and somewhat later of painted and engraved images on cave walls, there have been frequent attempts to explain the origins of "Paleolithic art" (19, 25, 34, 39, 42, 49, 72, 74, 102). In almost all cases, including the most recent examples, these attempts have been made by art historians, developmental psychologists, nonanthropologically trained archaeologists, or devoted ama- teurs. Few anthropologically satisfying models for art origins have been devel- oped.

Partly as a result of being the work of nonarchaeologists, many treatises on the origins of "art" have mistakenly focused on cave art (especially cave painting, and especially Lascaux and Altamira). In reality, three-dimensional animal and human sculptures, engraved and painted blocks, and simple "non- figurative" motifs appeared at least 15,000 years before the first cave was painted. In other words, studies that purport to deal with the origins of "art" have often ignored the first half of art history. As Delluc & Delluc (35) have pointed out, the period from the first visual representations at about 35,000 years ago until the painting of Lascaux is as great as the period from Lascaux to Picasso!

A more serious problem, as Conkey (29, 30) has frequently noted, is the reliance on the concept of "art" as if it were a universal category of human existence. This fetishization of a recently derived historical category is particu- larly serious in art history (18:1), which, "never having really broken with the tradition of the *amateur*, gives free rein to celebratory contemplation and finds in the sacred character of its object every pretext for a hagiographic hermeneu- tics superbly indifferent to the question of the social conditions in which works are produced and circulate."

Two modern anthropological themes have been entirely missing from the literature on the origins of art: a broader concern with *material culture* (2, 31, 120), and a sophisticated formulation of the notion of the *social construction of meaning* (10, 56, 113) and the related issue of representation. As a result, "origins of art" articles usually end up speculating about the process by which "art" (almost always conceived as graphic depiction) was "discovered," rather than illuminating the broader social, technological, and ideational contexts and processes that made complex representational systems possible, desirable, and useful.

With roots in art history and/or psychology, origins models are almost always derived from developmental psychology with overwhelming confidence in the notion that Piagetian ontogeny recapitulates phylogeny (34, 72, 73, 74). Thus, the development of "art" in human history is presumed to be mirrored in the process by which modern children learn to depict (34, 73). Remarkably, the desirability and utility of "art" are treated as self-evident. In other words, once it was discovered that lines and objects could stand for things, "art" spread rapidly because its value (usually phrased as giving pleasure to its creators) was self-evident. This view is similar to the old notion that plant and animal domestication were so self-evidently useful that we need not explore why they came about, only how.

I find this view unfruitful, and I wish to recontextualize the question by shifting the focus from "art" to the material construction and representation of meaning, and by applying this broader conception to what we know of the material record for such representation. I argue here that the value of material representation was not self-evident at the outset and that like all inventions, material representation was contingent upon, coherent with, and dialectically related to the contemporaneous neurological, social, technological, and ideational context.

Another flaw in models of the origins of "art" is equally serious: They restrict themselves to graphic depiction. Despite dozens of demonstrations in modern social anthropology that personal adornment is one of the most powerful and pervasive forms in which humans construct and represent beliefs, values, and social identity, the thousands of body ornaments known from the beginning of the Upper Paleolithic have been ignored in the fetishization of "art" as depiction (34) and the trivialization of bodily adornment as "decorative art" or "trinkets" (3). Such an attitude toward body ornaments is totally unfounded and prevents a more thoroughgoing understanding of prehistoric societies. Personal ornaments, perhaps more than any other aspect of the archaeological record, are a point of access for archaeologists into the social world of the past.

The neglect of personal ornaments is surprising on two counts: They are a commonly encountered part of the archaeological record, and ethnographers currently see body ornamentation as a significant source of insight into social and cosmological aspects of human cultures. The view of personal adornment taken here is coherent with that of T. Turner (113:112) who argues that "The surface of the body, as the common frontier of society, the social self, and the psycho-biological individual, becomes the symbolic stage upon which the drama of socialisation is enacted, and bodily adornment in all its culturally multifarious forms, from body-painting to clothing and from feather headdresses to cosmetics, becomes the language through which it is expressed." According to Andrew Strathern (103:15), "What people wear, and what they do to and with their bodies in general, forms an important part of the flow of information—establishing, modifying, and commenting on major social categories, such as age, sex and status, which are also defined in speech and in actions. Whatever the precise origins of clothing, then, they can be sought only within the general context of the development of social communication and of society itself."

The argument presented here—that preserved representations, the images that they comprise, and the material qualities inherent in them are value-laden symbolic representations/constructions—raises a fundamental question: How is it that particular images, objects, materials, colors, forms, and textures come to have—indeed, first came to have—value and to carry meaning within a given social and symbolic context? Beidelman (9) has eloquently argued that much of the answer to this question lies squarely within the domain of social psychology and psycho-linguistics. Nevertheless, archaeology's ability to answer this question hinges in part on whether there are cross-cultural generalities in the rendering valuable of particular kinds of objects and images for purposes of social display. Indeed, choice of rare and exotic materials; labor-, skill-, and knowledge-intensive production; and metaphorical reference to valued or sacred subjects are virtually universal in their effectiveness in constructing meaning and communicating social identity in the ethnographic present. I argue below that these also characterize even the very first personal ornaments in the archaeological record.

REPRESENTATION AND MATERIALITY

The argument here is not that material forms of representation signal the origins of representation per se. In my view, linguistic representation was prerequisite to other forms of representation. As Quine (98:3) noted long ago, "Conceptualization on any considerable scale is inseparable from language." As I will show below, the conceptual complexity evident in the earliest known corpus of material representation is considerable. Rather, I argue that tangible, visible, material representations have a value, immediacy, authority, and duration quite different from those of linguistic representations. I am in firm disagreement with Davidson & Noble (33), who view depiction as prerequisite to language.

For me, the great innovation was in the *material rendering* or *objectivation* (10) of concepts, forms, emotions, social relations, etc—a process that Hallowell (48) referred to as "extrinsic symbolization." Representational objects thus become part of what Berger & Luckmann (10) call "the reality of everyday life," and for them (p. 35) "The reality of everyday life is not only filled with objectivations; it is only possible because of them. I am constantly surrounded by objects that 'proclaim' the subjective intentions of my fellow men ... ." Such is the power and evolutionary significance of *material* representations, and to repeat, it is quite probably *material forms* of representation that we are monitoring in the archaeological record, not representation itself or the emergence of the capacity for it.

But materiality implies cultural production involving, minimally: (*a*) selection and procurement of raw materials, (*b*) transformation of these into conventional forms via a set of techniques and relations of production, and (*c*) the exchange/display/use of the finished objects. Each of these operational stages is of course played out in a particular social and cultural, not to mention, physical environment. Such an operational chain in the construction of representational objects leaves significant traces in the archaeological record (30, 60, 61, 63, 64, 66, 99, 127) and raises for archaeologists the distinct possibility of studying, literally, the construction of meaning and its socio-spatial distribution. Thus, we can respond directly to the important sociological question of how "subjective meanings become objective facticities" (10:18).

To some considerable degree all objects, and not merely those that we artificially privilege as "art" objects, are cultural representations (57, 58, 133). As Knecht (52, 53) has shown so forcefully, Aurignacian split-based point technology exhibits a set of underlying technological principles that represent a choice from among several other possibilities. Thus it is easy to imagine split-based antler points acting to reflect or represent a particular cultural or regional identity in the way imagined by Sackett (100) for hammers and screwdrivers. More for lack of space than lack of interest, however, I restrict my discussion here to objects presumed to be largely representational in intent.

Apart from the fact that representational objects come to form part of our cultural environment, what is it about material forms of representation that makes them so useful or desirable? Weiner (117, 118) argues that because objects endure beyond a single human life they can play a critical role in social reproduction and continuity. Moreover, objects have histories (see also 24 for an East African example) that link them to ancestors, a fact that imbues them with political authority that words and actions lack. Finally, Weiner proposes that objects are remote from the wearer/giver and can, therefore, carry messages too dangerous or controversial for words (see also 10:30–34). On a more obvious level, they are highly visible and interpretable given a shared system of meaning (15, 16, 134) and have the effect of communicating not only intra-group distinctions but regional affiliations and group membership as well (27).

The complex process of constructing social and political identities with material objects is well illustrated by Weiner's (119) description of shell and seed ornaments being bestowed upon a child by its father in an attempt to enhance its "social beauty." According to Weiner (119:61), "Once a child wears shell decorations, it has entered, if only minimally, into the world of politics."

METAPHOR AND MATERIALITY

The concept of representation has widely varied usages in anthropology and semiotics, ranging from the literal (e.g. *This drawing represents a horse*) to the metaphorical and metonymical (e.g. *This drawing, by virtue of being a horse, represents intelligence*). Two of the most recent articles on the origins of "art"

(34, 49) exemplify the former usage. Indeed, Halverson (49) suggests that Paleolithic cave paintings may have represented nothing more than the esthetic pleasure derived from depiction (i.e. they were devoid of representational value or meaning). As we shall see, however, even the oldest known Upper Paleolithic depictions were highly skewed with respect to subject matter, style, technique, and spatial distribution, indicating a complex conceptual and organizational underpinning that is probably based on metaphor.

Lakoff & Johnson (56:5) consider that "the essence of metaphor is understanding and experiencing one kind of thing in terms of another." Moreover, they note (p. 3) that "metaphor is pervasive in everyday life, not just in language but in thought and action. Our ordinary conceptual system, in terms of which we both think and act, is fundamentally metaphorical in nature."

Nisbet (87:4) observes that "Metaphor is, at its simplest, a way of proceeding from the known to the unknown. It is a way of cognition in which the identifying qualities of one thing are transferred in an instantaneous, almost unconscious flash of insight to some other thing that is, by remoteness or complexity, unknown to us." And further, on the same page, "Metaphor is our means of effecting instantaneous fusion of two separated realms of experience into one illuminating, iconic, encapsulating image."

While metaphor has traditionally been viewed as a poetic device, Lakoff & Johnson, like V. Turner (114), construct a powerful argument that metaphor is at the very heart of perception, conception, and, most important for our purposes here, representation. Turner (p. 25) goes so far as to suggest the likelihood that "scientists and artists both think primordially in such images; metaphor may be the form of what M. Polanyi calls 'tacit knowledge.'"

Two sub-classes of metaphor are important to recognize: *metonymy:* using one entity to refer to another that is related to it (56:36)—e.g. *The Times hasn't arrived at the press conference yet*; and *synecdoche:* a special case of metonymy where the part stands for the whole (p. 36)—e.g. *We need some new blood in the organization.*

If metaphor pervades not only language, but thought and action as well, there ought to be such things as material metaphors, and they ought to be observable today and detectable in the archaeological record. Moreover, the absence of metaphorical thought in our hominid ancestors would have had severe consequences for their ability to deal with intangibles like time and death, which modern humans understand and organize metaphorically.

Indeed, we know from the ethnographic record (and from any evocative piece of modern "art") that material metaphors exist. In the domain of personal adornment, Strathern & Strathern (104:176) observe, parts of animals or plants are used to associate the wearer with the qualities of the whole organism. "If we turn to self-decoration itself, there also we find a lack of representational art. The process of decoration in Hagen is not representational but metonymical; that is, when Hageners wish to associate themselves with magically powerful things, such as birds, they do not construct masks, carvings, or paintings of these. Instead they actually take parts of the birds, their feathers, and attach these to themselves as decorations." Precisely the same sort of metonymical system has been documented by Kuper (55) for the Swazi, who maintain a rich ceremonial body decoration composed of animal parts. Among the Swazi two of the cosmologically and socially most important species, the elephant and the lion, are the subject of a rich folklore that places great value upon certain of their fundamental social behaviors. In body decoration, they are represented metonymically by ivory and lion-skin, respectively. According to Kuper (55:621), "The lion and the elephant appear together in Swazi cosmology as the most powerful and dominant in both the untamed world of nature, and the world of men."

Ethnographically the range of animal and plant species chosen for the decorative value of their parts is usually quite constant within the same tribe and among closely related tribes. This homogeneity is probably due to the fact that their value as ornaments derives from a deeply imbedded and widely shared cosmological structure with respect to particular species—usually those of peripheral dietary significance. In other words, animals of great cosmological value or power are often used in the construction and communication of social identities. Therefore, while body decoration and graphic representation are intensely social phenomena, part of their power and legitimacy in constructing social identity and meaning is drawn from the fact that they implicate a deeply held and widely shared cosmology.

It has long been observed that animals and their biological and social characteristics have served as metaphors for human social distinctions. As Lévi-Strauss observed (70:13), "The animal world and that of plant life are not utilized merely because they are there, but because they suggest a mode of thought. The connection between the *relation of man to nature* and the *characterization of social groups,* which Boas thought to be contingent and arbitrary, only seems so because the real link between the two orders is indirect, passing through the mind." I return to the important subject of metaphor when I examine Aurignacian representational objects, arguing that the invention of material representations, particularly metaphorical ones, was critical to virtually every aspect of the explosive transformation in European culture that we have come to know as the Middle/Upper Paleolithic transition.

MATERIAL REPRESENTATION AND THE MIDDLE/UPPER PALEOLITHIC TRANSITION

Two contradictory views have emerged concerning the nature of the Middle/Upper Paleolithic transition in Europe. Some authors (23, 83, 84), including myself (123, 124, 129), have persistently viewed the transition as abrupt and revolutionary in all of its various aspects (art, body ornamentation, bone/antler technology, etc). Pigeot (95) has recently argued that even stone tool technology reveals fundamental cognitive differences between the late

Mousterian and the early Upper Paleolithic. This work is most compatible with a "replacement" model for the emergence of anatomically modern humans in Europe (106, 107).

Others, working from the same published record, argue that the "real" transition occurred not at the Middle/Upper Paleolithic boundary but 15,000 years later, at the late Glacial maximum (71, 105). It will be clear below that the latter position, which in my opinion is founded on an "in situ evolution" view of the emergence of biologically modern humans in Europe, contradicts the archaeological record of the European Early Upper Paleolithic. It glosses over thousands of body ornaments (127–129) and bone/antler implements (52, 69), not to mention hundreds of engraved/incised objects, many of them three-dimensional representations (45, 47, 126, 127).

I have recently argued (127) that what is revolutionary about the Early Upper Paleolithic in comparison to the Mousterian is the existence of a metonymical quality to objects transformed into that which we recognize as "art" and personal adornment. In other words, particular forms, designs, and qualities were of interest to Mousterians but were never dissociated from their natural context. For example, a Mousterian biface from a Périgord surface site has a band of golden color running through it, which has been retained along one edge of the tool, apparently at the expense of bilateral symmetry. This tool very much resembles Mousterian flint tools from England and France that retain naturally embedded fossils (88, 89). Mousterians occasionally collected the fossils they encountered, such as the fossil shark's tooth from Darra-I-Kur in Afghanistan (38), the Nummulite fossil from Tata (115) in Hungary, and the fossil shells and blocks of pyrite from the Grotte de l'Hyène at Arcy-sur-Cure (41). Peculiar forms and qualities were collected and examined but apparently never transferred to new contexts—a transfer that is the basis of metaphorical thought.

"Symbolic" qualities have been claimed for certain objects of pre-Upper Paleolithic age, but upon closer examination such claims are highly doubtful. Because a critical discussion of the full range of alleged pre-Upper Paleolithic representational forms is excluded by space limitations, I direct the reader to Leonardi's (65) thorough and skeptical inventory of most of these objects and to Chase & Dibble's (23) less comprehensive but excellent critical review. I wish to note, however, that I am doubtful about Leonardi's view (65:99) that an incised bone from Pêch de l'Azé, a piece engraved with angular marks from L'Ermitage and some incisions on stone from the Abri Tagliante indicate a figurative intent, *"si vague soit-elle."* Like an Acheulean example from Polignac in France (26), none of these exhibit the continuity through time or formal redundancy that would argue in favor of their being purposeful, not to mention representational. Moreover, there is nothing to suggest that a single zig-zag incision from the Mousterian of Bacho Kiro (77), while perhaps purposeful (carnivore gnawing remains to be fully excluded), is necessarily representational.

Mania & Mania (75) have published recently a series of marked bones from the German Acheulean site of Bilzingsleben, claiming that the markings were purposeful and probably symbolic in intent. I doubt this interpretation and find no greater patterning in these marks than on the wooden cutting board in my kitchen.

Otte (92, 93) has recovered from the Mousterian-age layers at Sclayn in Belgium a series of bear teeth with grooves at the enamel-root junction, which he suggests may be Mousterian pendants. However, they are purely paleontological specimens, unassociated with archaeological material. Moreover, Gautier (40) has convincingly shown the presence of identically thinned bear teeth in modern populations of bears, apparently the result of oral digestive processes (116), often involving dietary grit. I found these teeth entirely unlike any purposely manufactured pendants that I have seen, in that no tool traces are present.

Two "pendants" from La Quina (80) have been proposed by Marshack (78, 79) to be Mousterian in age. The first is a fox canine, the root of which is alleged to have the initial traces of the manufacture of a hole by gouging. While Combier (26) questions its artificial nature, my objections concern the very complicated stratigraphy of this site (80, 81), excavated in 1905, long before credible stratigraphic controls were employed in Paleolithic archaeology. Because it has been recognized for many years that the stratigraphy of La Quina (*amont*), from which the tooth comes, is subject to major revision, there are serious doubts about the piece's Mousterian provenience. Moreover, even Martin recognized that final Mousterian and basal Aurignacian levels were in contact at La Quina (81:18).

The second object from La Quina is a reindeer phalange that has "perhaps" been pierced by human action. However, after initially suggesting that this piece was a pendant, the excavator, Martin, rejected this possibility and argued instead for carnivore perforation. I have seen numerous similar examples from Aurignacian levels, none of which, in my opinion, can be attributed to human activity. Chase & Dibble (23) share this view for pierced phalanges recovered by Bordes from the Mousterian levels at Combe-Grenal. Indeed, Chase (22) has documented one modern example that he found in a coyote coprolite and that was apparently produced by gnawing or by gastric erosion.

In Central Europe, the German site of Bocksteinschmiede has yielded two possible gouged pendants (121) associated with a Micoquian (dated elsewhere to as late as 45,000 BP (1) or late Mousterian industry. Although, in my opinion both objects are probably natural (carnivore perforation?), the vestigial metapodial is somewhat similar to pierced moose metapodials from the Aurignacian at the Moravian site of Mladec (90). To this point, none of the other "terminal Mousterian" sites from Central Europe has yielded personal ornaments.

Possible decorative objects have been reported from pre-Upper Paleolithic time outside of Europe: A single pierced shell was recovered from Border

Cave (8) in South Africa and "a few Mediterranean *Glycymeris* sp. shells were collected in the lower Mousterian layers" of Qafzeh in Israel (7). Not having personally examined these objects or photos of them, I can make no assessment.

In sum, most of the supposed personal ornaments and purposeful markings attributed to the European Acheulean and Mousterian are dubious on either stratigraphic or taphonomic grounds. Even if we were to accept all of the even remotely credible specimens, it is clear that, unlike the case in the Upper Paleolithic that follows, there is no continuity or redundancy in form. Over the course of hundreds of thousands of years there are no two objects that are alike and there is certainly no gradual evolutionary trajectory.

It may be the case, as Leroi-Gourhan (quoted in 26:72) argued, that "Derrière les orbites proéminentes des Paléanthropiens, quelque chose se passait déja qui allait prendre beaucoup d'importance par la suite." However, accepting even one or two of the supposed personal ornaments at face value renders the relative explosion of beads and pendants (and graphic imagery) at the beginning of the Upper Paleolithic all the more interesting! If Neandertals were mentally capable of representation, why did material representation not become fixed as an enduring part of their adaptation when it has such obvious selective advantage? I have suggested elsewhere (122, 127, 128) that the answer lies in the emergence of new kinds of social systems that rendered both possible and useful the sharing and reproduction through time of complex ideas, conventional representational forms, and hence complex systems of meaning and social action.

AURIGNACIAN MATERIAL REPRESENTATION IN EUROPE

The earliest fully credible material representations in Europe are the pierced animal teeth (Figure 1) recovered by Kozlowski (54) from Bacho Kiro Cave in Bulgaria, from an Aurignacian level dated to >43,000 by the traditional radiocarbon method. Recent thermoluminescence (TL) dates from El Castillo in Spain have now pushed back the basal Aurignacian, with bone/antler implements, to the vicinity of 40,000 BP (11, 20, 21). From a similar Aurignacian assemblage at nearby El Pendo (43) were recovered pierced animal teeth and a steatite facsimile of a vestigial deer canine, in an Aurignacian level underlying two Castelperronian levels. At Mladec in Czechoslovakia a group of pierced moose telemetacarpals and numerous pierced animal teeth were found in what is accepted as a very early Aurignacian assemblage (perhaps 40,000 BP) associated with early modern human skeletal material (90). It remains to be seen whether similar assemblages in France and Italy (13, 14), almost all of which contain at least some personal ornaments, will be found to be equally early once the traditional limits imposed by radiocarbon dating have been overcome by TL applications.

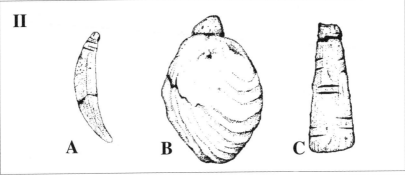

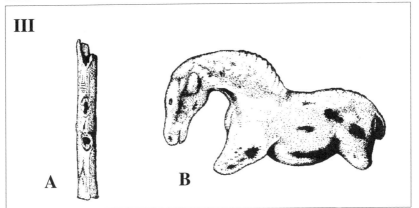

Figure 1   Various representational objects from the early Upper Paleolithic.

I: Examples of pierced teeth from Aurignacian and Castelperronian contexts (roughly actual size). A: Castelperronian from Arcy-sur-Cure; B: Aurignacian I from Brassempouy; C: Aurignacian I from La Quina; D and E: Early Aurignacian from Bacho Kiro.

II: Examples of objects grooved for suspension (roughly actual size). A,B: Castelperronian from Arcy-sur-Cure; C: Aurignacian I from Abri Blanchard.

III: Evidence of complex representation from Aurignacian I contexts. A: Broken bird-bone flute from Isturitz (roughly half actual size; after 94); B: Sculpted ivory horse from the Aurignacian I of Vogelherd (somewhat larger than actual size)

Marshack (79) attempts to bolster the presumption that symbolic behavior characterized Neandertals and evolved *gradually* into its prominent role in the Upper Paleolithic (presumably as part of the process that saw Neandertals evolve gradually into anatomically modern humans!). In doing so, he gives the mistaken impression that the personal ornaments from Castelperronian levels at Arcy-sur-Cure pre-date Aurignacian materials in Western Europe. Remarkably, this argument ignores the fact that in Western Europe the Castelperronian developed several thousand years after the first appearance of the Aurignacian (85), and overlies Aurignacian levels at El Pendo (11), Roc de Combe (17, 59), and Le Piage (59). Indeed, the famous but poorly published Castelperronian body ornaments, bone/antler implements, and decorated objects from the Grotte de Renne at Arcy-sur-Cure (67, 68, 86, 110, 111, 131) are radiocarbon dated to no older than 33,000 BP. In other words, Aurignacian personal ornaments had been well established for as long as 10,000 years by the time there is evidence that the Castelperronians (apparently Neandertals) began producing them.

Interesting questions arise at Arcy, one of only two Castelperronian sites (50) to have yielded personal ornaments. It has recently been observed (131) that the personal ornaments (Figure 1) and incised objects from the Castelperronian at Arcy are typically "Aurignacian" in technology, raw material, and form. Either Castelperronians were working on an Aurignacian model, they were scavenging objects from contemporaneous Aurignacian sites, or the Arcy objects are the product of stratigraphic mixture with the overlying Aurignacian levels.

In sum, personal ornaments first appear in Europe in Aurignacian levels dated to around 40,000 BP. There is no indisputable evidence for such objects in Mousterian/Castelperronian contexts that pre-date or are contemporaneous with the initial Aurignacian presence in Europe.

In the past two decades, social anthropologists have tended to view social identity as being constructed and communicated through the medium of bodily adornment. At the same time, new interest has arisen in what Appadurai (2) has called "the social life of things." Unfortunately, the very social anthropologists who espouse a concern with the material construction of social identity and meaning seldom address the material means by which natural substances are transformed into objects that act as social signifiers. Thus, we frequently lack an integration of technology and social dynamics through which we might gain access to the culturally embedded technological production sequences from which socially meaningful decorative styles emerge. In the remainder of this chapter, I take this notion of the construction of social identity and meaning literally by examining the materials, technologies, and subject-matters of Aurignacian material representation in Europe.

I include in my discussion representations of all sorts, but only those that can be considered among the first such objects created by humans. Therefore, I discuss only artifacts attributed to the Aurignacian archaeological culture of Europe, which dates to the period from about 40,000 until about 28,000 years ago, and which left a rich archaeological record of images and personal ornaments.

Over the past five years I have studied approximately 5,000 pierced objects and associated production debris from Western, Central, and East European Aurignacian sites dating from ~40,000–28,000 BP. These objects, to the extent that they have even been recognized previously, have been conventionally assigned to the category of body ornaments. Roughly one third of these objects are pierced teeth and shells, while the remainder are carefully formed ivory and soft stone beads. In this same period, I have examined virtually all of the known Aurignacian "art" objects, some of which are also pierced for suspension.

My presentation here follows my research design, which is to (re)construct operational chains for each class of material representation. For each class of object I speak to the following topics: raw material choice and acquisition; techniques of production and labor investment; use and use-context; and subject-matters, motifs, and metaphors. Since these are topics not addressed through the archaeological record until recently, the existing data base is not always adequate to a full discussion. Therefore, what follows is to some degree a patchwork quilt that perhaps raises more questions than it resolves. However, I hope it begins to move us beyond the sterility of the question of the "origins of art."

Raw Material Choice and Acquisition

There is considerable overlap among different classes of Aurignacian material representation in the raw materials employed. The full range preserved in the record (Table 1) includes various mineral and animal substances, including limestone, schist, talc-schist, steatite, mammalian teeth, bone, antler and ivory, fossil and contemporary species of marine and freshwater shells, fossil coral, fossil belemnite, jet, lignite, hematite, and pyrite. However, this relatively extensive list should not be taken to suggest a kind of random use of materials encountered in the environment. A number of pronounced choices were made, which I discuss below.

Personal ornaments are frequently manufactured of materials exotic to the regions in which they are found. This is especially true of shells (109, 112) and rare minerals, but may also be true of ivory, at least in the southwest French Aurignacian, although this remains to be firmly demonstrated. In general, there appears to be a source-distance gradient, with rare minerals falling off with distance North from the Pyrenees, and Atlantic and Mediterranean shell species becoming more attenuated as one proceeds into the French interior. Figurative and quasi-figurative objects show a distinct difference from personal ornaments in that their supports are, nearly without exception, of local materials (ivory and limestone in southern Germany; limestone in southwest France; and steatite in Austria).

Techniques of Production and Labor Investment

The operational chain for Aurignacian ivory and stone beads varies both intra- and inter-regionally. In France, beads of the commonest form (Figure 2), represented by more than 1000 specimens, have been called basket-shaped. Found in large quantities early in this century at Abri Blanchard, Abri Casta- net, Abri de la Souquette, Isturitz, and Saint Jean de Verges, these have now been radiocarbon dated by Delporte at Brassempouy to between 33,000 and 32,000 years ago. They were created from pencil-like rods of ivory or steatite that were then circumincised and snapped into cylindrical blanks from one to two centimeters long. These were then bilaterally thinned at one end to form a sort of stem. A perforation was then created at the junction of the stem and the unaltered end. This was usually done by gouging from each side, rather than by rotational drilling. These rough-outs were then ground and polished into their final basket shape using hematite as an abrasive.

Ivory beads in south German Aurignacian sites (46), also radiocarbon dated to between 33,000 and 32,000 years ago, are substantially different, although the basic principle of reducing an ivory baton was the same (Figure 3). In the case of Geissenklosterle, for example, a baton elliptical in section was cir- cumincised and snapped into a series of blanks. The individual blanks were then thinned and perforated by gouging. In this case, however, two holes

Table 1 Raw materials used in Aurignacian representational objects

Limestone	occasional objects of suspension
	support material for several dozen figurative and quasi-figurative engravings and patterned arrangements of incisions and punctuations
	one case of a cervid tooth facsimile
Ivory	hundreds of objects of suspension
	about two dozen 3-D and bas-relief sculptures including animals, humans, and therianthropes, and facsimiles of teeth and shells
Hematite/Manganese	occasional objects of suspension
	occasional painted lines on limestone supports
	one case of a painted animal image on a limestone support
Schist	numerous objects of suspension
Talc-Schist, Pyrite and Steatite	numerous objects of suspension
	occasional cervid tooth facsimiles
	one case of a 3-D anthropomorphic sculpture
Mammalian Teeth	hundreds of objects of suspension, with special selection of fox canines, cervid vestigial canines, wolf/hyena carnassials and bovid incisors
	occasional examples of horse incisors and human molars
	one case of a phallus sculpted from the base of a bovid incisor
Bone	occasional objects of suspension
	frequent support material for patterned arrangements of incisions and punctuations
Antler and Horn	occasional objects of suspension
	one case of a bovid horn-core sculpted into a "phallus"
Fossil and Contemporary Shells, Including Coral and Belemnite	hundreds of objects of suspension with fewer than a dozen species making up more than 90% of the several hundred known specimens
Jet and Lignite	occasional objects of suspension

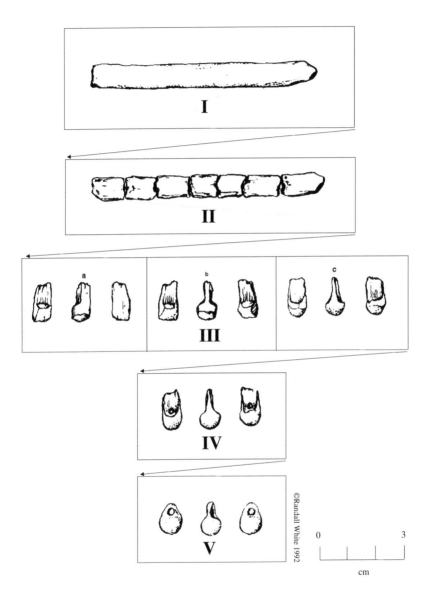

Figure 2 The production sequence for ivory and steatite basket-shaped beads from French Aurignacian I contexts

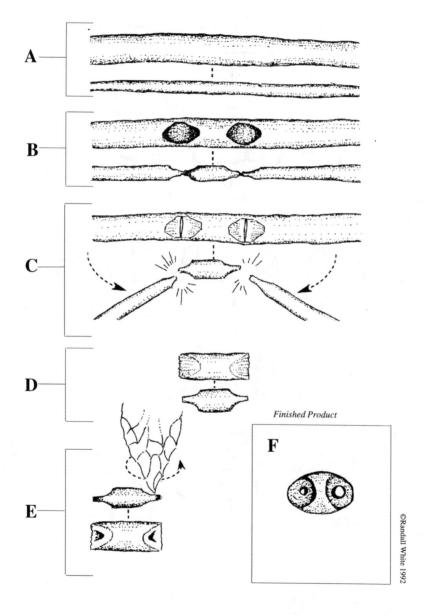

Figure 3   The production sequence for manufacturing two-holed beads from German Aurignacian I contexts (after 46)

separated by a bulge were dug into the blank. This type of bead is as unknown in France as the basket-shaped form is in Germany.

At least two variations of this basic reduction principle were known in the Belgian Aurignacian (62, 91), although there are serious uncertainties about cultural attribution of many of the Belgian specimens (36, 37). At Spy, ivory rods more or less flat in section were roughed out and perforated before they were detached from the larger mass. A variation on this approach existed at Goyet, where the baton was semicylindrical in section. These were segmented, perforated, and then detached from the larger mass prior to grinding and polishing.

I have studied in detail the Aurignacian-age ornament assemblage from the lower level at the site of Kostenki 17 in the Don Valley of Russia, excavated by Boriskovsky, by Rogachev, and most recently by Praslov. Charcoal associated with this assemblage, which Praslov and Rogachev have labelled the Spitsinskaya culture, has been dated to 32,700(+2000, -1600) BP and 36,400(+1700, -1400) BP (51, 97).

None of the ornaments at Kostenki 17 was manufactured of ivory; instead all were created from a variety of rare but apparently local raw materials. There are eight soft stone pendants from Kostenki 17, three of schist, three of limestone (one of which may be zoomorphic), and two of talc. In most cases, the holes were well executed, having been drilled from each side. The three schist pendants are all roughly the same size and totally natural in form. They are quite asymmetrical in outline.

Perhaps the most original component of the ornamental assemblage from Kostenki 17 is a group of perforated marine fossils that fall into two categories of raw material: fossil coral, and fossil belemnites. The three fossil coral polyps were perforated from one side only, and the holes are very delicate. There are four belemnite fossil beads, for which no production debris was found. Spectacularly beautiful in color and translucence, these might easily be mistaken for amber. Their form results from an operational chain that begins with the natural cylindrical form of the belemnites. These were split down the center, and each half, which was then semi-cylindrical in section, was subdivided into segments. It is noteworthy that this splitting-and-segmenting approach is precisely the technique that Knecht (52) has observed for the reduction of antlers into spear-points in contemporaneous sites in Central and Western Europe.

Three of these segments were then perforated near one end by means of fine, biconical rotational drilling. The fourth was conically drilled from the outside in. The distal and proximal ends were smoothed by polishing, as were the lateral margins. Two different taxa of belemnites are represented by two examples each. The primary difference between them is the presence on one form of fine transverse ripples, which have a remarkable visual and tactile effect.

In general then, ivory and steatite beads were produced by a set of regionally specific, highly standardized techniques. The end-products themselves are highly standardized in both size and form (129). Formation of such beads is labor intensive, especially when executed in ivory. Experiments conducted with elephant ivory at New York University (NYU), using faithful replicas of Aurignacian tool-forms, suggest an average time per basket-shaped bead of well in excess of one hour.

Mammalian teeth and marine shells show considerable variation in perforation techniques (108, 109, 112). Only on rare occasions, however, were they perforated by rotational drilling. Usually, preliminary gouging, thinning, or pecking was followed by pressure piercing. Much less time is involved here than for production of formed beads, since teeth already come in a more-or-less finished package except for the perforation.

Figurative and quasi-figurative images share many of the techniques employed in the production of personal ornaments. In the case of ivory and steatite three-dimensional sculptures, a larger mass was reduced by gouging, grinding, and polishing, the final stages probably being accomplished through the use of fine metallic abrasives (hematite powder). An experimental reconstruction of the famous Vogelherd horse (Figure 1) took Hahn (45) 35–40 hours to accomplish.

Engraved limestone slabs show a different, but no less complicated and labor-intensive set of techniques (35). Large, local limestone slabs frequently had their surfaces prepared by abrasion. Then, the representations themselves were applied in a remarkable diversity of line-types reflecting processes of engraving, pecking, chiseling, gouging, etc (35) that Delluc & Delluc have reconstructed experimentally.

Painted images are rare in the Aurignacian and are almost always composed of simple lines that do not seem to constitute figurative images (35, 44, 46). The sole exception is a remarkable bichrome painting of a bovid from Abri Blanchard (35), which falls outside of the range of anything else known from the Aurignacian. I have recently suggested (130) the possibility that this image is actually Gravettian in age.

Use and Use-Context: Sewing or Stringing?

Unfortunately, there are no Aurignacian burials prior to those of Cro-Magnon at around 30,000–28,000 BP. Therefore, lacking direct association between Aurignacian beads and human skeletons, we are obliged to design research strategies to demonstrate, first, that these were indeed objects of suspension and, second, precisely how they were suspended. At NYU we are at the outset of a combined scanning-electron-microscopy/experimental-replication program that has already yielded to McLean (82) clues about the attachment of Aurignacian basket-shaped beads. Her preliminary results suggest that these were sewn on, as inferred from examples of possible scoring of the necks of beads, perhaps to hold the thread in place.

Inter-Regional Context

Conkey (29, 30, 32) has justly advised against sweeping approaches to the origins and evolution of "art" that are not temporally and geographically situated. Here I examine only the first known material representation in Europe, which seems to appear everywhere on that continent within a relatively short time. However, there are quantitative and qualitative differences in Aurignacian representational objects that go beyond the different bead production sequences mentioned above. For example, except for a couple of questionable cases in southwest France (130, 131), three-dimensional animal sculptures in ivory are limited to central Europe. Engraved limestone blocks are limited to a small area of southwest France and exhibit subject matters entirely different from those of the German sculptures. Ivory beads and pierced teeth and shells are present but relatively rare in central Europe, while they are super-abundant in France and well represented in Eastern Europe.

These regional differences in Aurignacian-age representational inventories probably indicate that the Aurignacian culture as it has been constructed based upon stone-tool and antler weapon inventories is probably a complex mosaic of regional cultures with significantly different systems of meaning and representation.

Intra-Regional Context

Within these regions, which remain poorly defined, there are significant quantitative and qualitative differences among penecontemporaneous Aurignacian sites. For example, most limestone engravings and personal ornaments in the Périgord come from a half dozen (Abri Blanchard, Abri Castanet, Abri de la Souquette, Abri du Laussel, Grand Abri de la Ferrassie, Abri Cellier) of the more than 60 Aurignacian sites excavated to date (125). Indeed, three of these sites are situated within 100 m of each other and probably represent different areas of the same Aurignacian occupation (129). Most other Aurignacian sites have yielded only small numbers of personal ornaments and decorated objects. The same pattern can be discerned in the German Aurignacian with respect to ivory sculptures (44); three sites have yielded virtually all known examples.

It is tempting to raise the possibility that, as Conkey (28, 32), Bahn (4, 5), and I (123, 124) have proposed for "portable art"–rich sites in the French and Spanish Magdalenian, these Aurignacian sites represent seasonal aggregation sites characterized by intense levels of social, ceremonial, and exchange activities. However, seasonal estimates (96) and settlement/subsistence reconstructions such as those for other Upper Paleolithic periods remain unavailable for the French and German Aurignacian.

Intra-Site Context

It has been inadequately recognized that there are major differences between German and French Aurignacian sites yielding material representations when viewed from the perspective of the size and spatial location of figurative objects. Hahn (45) shows distribution maps of the sculpted ivory figures from Vogelherd, Geissenklosterle, and Hohlenstein-Stadel, all of these sites being shallow caves. In all cases the sculptures are tucked away in the back (Hohlenstein) or along one wall (Geissenklosterle, Vogelherd). In the latter two sites, which have yielded several figures, these are clustered in a tiny area of the archaeological "surface," as if purposely cached or buried. In contrast, engraved blocks in the French Aurignacian are found exclusively in rock shelters and are arranged primarily along the lip of the talus, or along the back wall, giving the effect of delimiting the "living area" (35). They would have been visible to the occupants continuously.

With respect to personal ornaments, the low frequencies in the German sites do not allow any statements about spatial clustering. In the major French sites, all excavated before 1935, horizontal provenience information for most personal ornaments is simply not available.

Subject-Matters, Motifs, and Metaphors

In a remarkably thorough and empirically grounded treatise on the sculpted ivory figures in the German Aurignacian, Hahn (45) makes the following observations:

1. All sculptures show patterned markings that do not seem to represent the texture or color of the animals coats. Rather the different types of marking are patterned by species, and thus probably should be interpreted as information supplementary to the animal image itself. Generally, the rib-cage and abdomen are outlined by notches or crosses, and the major axes of the body (the back, the legs) are outlined by notches. Such markings may have provided schematic information on anatomy. More difficult to explain are instances where the entire body is covered with signs, notably punctuations.
2. The sculptures vary greatly in size and apparent function. The smallest examples were pendants. Medium-sized and large versions show no obvious function.
3. The animal species represented were available in the local environment, but there is no quantitative similarity between the fauna hunted and that represented. A high percentage of carnivores seems to exclude hunting magic as an explanation.
4. Except for a single horse, only the largest and strongest species (mammoth, rhinoceros, bison, lion, and bear) were represented, and then only adults. Where sex is determinable, only males are indicated.
5. Some of the animals are shown in a "neutral" posture, but four pieces (the horse, two lions, and the bear) are in offensive, perhaps even attacking or menacing, postures.
6. Three of the figures are anthropomorphic, one very schematic, and the other two actually therianthropic. These therianthropes, especially the human/felid statuette from Hohlenstein Stadel, show a conceptual assimilation of humans and animals.

7. Spatially, mammoths are segregated from other herbivores as well as carnivores and anthropomorphs, the latter showing similar distributions.
8. Power and strength are the dominant themes (metaphors in the terms developed earlier) represented; female imagery is absent.
9. On the whole, the complex patterning observed implies an underlying
   magico-religious system.

The nature of representation itself is very different in the southwest French
Aurignacian, although there are certain areas of overlap. First, most figurative
representation is in two dimensions, and few of these images are of animals.
Those animals that do exist are barely intelligible. I attribute this to the significant conceptual differences between two- and three-dimensional representation. Reducing a large horse to a three-dimensional scale model is a task very
different from that of reducing the same horse to a two-dimensional surface
that gives the illusion of three-dimensionality. Two-dimensional figurative
representation involves many visual tricks, and it may well be that Aurignacian
people had not mastered them. For this reason, Aurignacian material representations may have been among the first to have existed. Rather than looking for
prototypes, we might well imagine that they are the prototypes for later developments in representational techniques.

There is a serious problem of subject recognition in analyzing the several
dozen French Aurignacian engraved blocks. A complex array of punctuations,
cup-marks, incisions, and notches (see 35 for a comprehensive inventory)
appear, few of which form coherent natural images. The dominant form of
engraved sign has traditionally and uncritically been identified as the human
vulva (6). Several dozen of these have been identified, but it is not at all clear
that they represent a single coherent image class. These and other arrangements of cup-like marks may represent animal hoof-prints—a tantalizing possibility, since the the association of an animal and its hoof-print might
constitute a kind of natural symbol: In the absence of two-dimensional conventions for credible depiction, the removal of a hoof-print from its original
context by mimicking it on stone seems to make sense as one of the earliest
forms of symbolic representation—a textbook case of metonymy.

I do not claim to be able to identify Aurignacian signs as hoofs or vulvae. If
they were so intended, then they are simple and elegant metonyms, as are the
hundreds of pierced animal teeth in the French Aurignacian, and perhaps
especially the several facsimiles of animal teeth, and shells in steatite, ivory
and limestone. These teeth and facsimiles, like the German animal figurines,
bear no quantitative resemblance to midden-bone inventories from the sites in
which they were found. For participants in the societies concerned, they were
presumably evocative of valued qualities ascribed to the animals represented.

Several ivory facsimiles of marine shells from the French Aurignacian have
been reported, six from the site of La Souquette alone (127:Figure 21.6).
Equally interesting is the close similarity between, on the one hand, patterned
arrangements of tiny punctuations on bone, antler, and ivory objects, some of

which have been interpreted as calendric or notational (76), and, on the other hand, natural punctuated designs found on shells from the same archaeological levels (123). While some examples are more convincing than others, the transfer of such natural patterns to new contexts is one more indication that the fundamentals of metaphor were being played out in material form.

A final example (Figure 4) is a unique and ambiguous object from La Souquette (127:99) which seems to link metaphorically two quite different objects. The object in question began as a standard Aurignacian split-based point manufactured of reindeer antler. At some stage in its history it was transformed into what appears to be a marine mammal, perhaps a seal, by the narrowing of the point and the creation of a hole where one would expect such an animal's eye. The split base, which remained unaltered, seems to represent the animal's flippers. This object is rendered all the more remarkable by the fact that a seal mandible (the only example known from an Aurignacian level) was found in the more-or-less contiguous Aurignacian site of Abri Castanet, some 250 km from the late Pleistocene Atlantic shore.

Perhaps the most unexpected representational object that has survived from the Aurignacian is a multi-holed wind instrument, frequently described as a flute (Figure 1), from the early Aurignacian at the site of Isturitz in southwestern France (94). This flute, manufactured of bird bone (another metaphorical relationship?), indicates that music was part of the earliest representational environment that Aurignacian people had created.

As in the case of the German figurines, there are hundreds of limestone, bone, antler, and ivory objects in the French Aurignacian that bear simple but patterned arrangements of incisions and notches. It is uncertain whether any of these can be accounted for by the metaphorical model suggested here, and the motivation for them remains obscure (but see 101). However, we should be cautious about assuming a priori, with Boas (15), that no relationship between the form of such objects and their meaning was intended.

BACK TO "WHY?"

In concluding, let me emphasize some directions for thinking about why material forms of representation exploded onto the scene between 40,000 and 30,000 years ago in Europe.

It is my view that two- and three-dimensional representation was an invention and like all inventions had to be coherent in and useful to its cultural context in order to be adopted. I presume that, on several occasions prior to the Upper Paleolithic, the ability to use lines and materials to represent natural objects was recognized and perhaps even accomplished in isolated instances.

I presume that Neandertals recognized the evident association between different animal tracks and the species they could expect to find if they followed them. We should consider the possibility, however, that metaphor was not part of their neurological and behavioral repertoire. As Lakoff & Johnson (56:239) have noted for modern humans "It is as though the ability to compre-

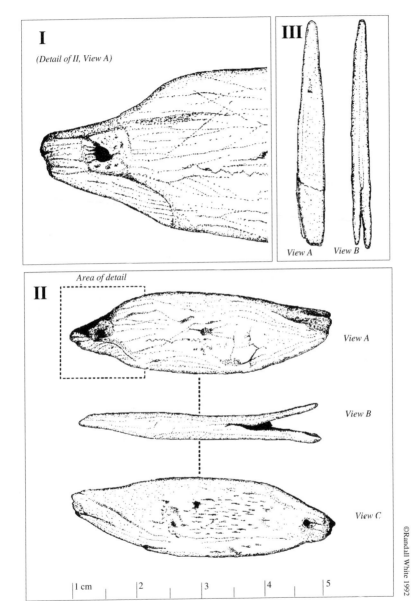

Figure 4 The transformed split-based antler point from Abri de lat Souquette

I: Detail of perforated and altered area

II: Three views of "seal"

III: Example of typical unaltered form of Aurignacian I split-based point

hend experience through metaphor were a sense, like seeing or touching or hearing, with metaphors providing the only ways to perceive and experience much of the world. Metaphor is as much a part of our functioning as our sense of touch, and as precious." The absence of this sense in Neandertals could certainly be imagined to produce what Binford (12) has described as a lack of planning depth. Modern cultures have pervasive metaphors by which time is understood and organized. Our own metaphors include "time is a moving object" and "time is a commodity" (56: Ch. 9). Although we know that metaphoric capacity is neurologically based, the study of endocasts seems incapable of resolving this question.

However, presuming Neandertals and contemporaneous *Homo sapiens sapiens* outside of Europe to have had the neurological capacity for metaphor, we must admit that what was missing prior to the Upper Paleolithic was a social context in which the invention of material forms of representation would be perceived as advantageous. We have seen in the ethnographic record that material forms of representation are frequently about political authority and social distinctions. Personal ornaments, constructed of the rare, the sacred, the exotic, or the labor/skill-intensive, are universally employed, indeed essential, to distinguish people and peoples from each other.

Conventionally executed and valued figurative imagery operates in much the same fashion, especially when it is concentrated in special locations within regions, and when its subject matter is fundamentally different between regions, as we have seen for the European Aurignacian. As Weiner has noted, objects are powerful social and political devices that transcend generations and have histories of their own. The Vogelherd ivory statuettes, found in precisely the same part of the cave, but in two successive and distinct occupational levels, imply this kind of transcendence.

The objectivation of metaphorically grounded representation also has powerful implications for technological innovation (52, 53). Nonverbal thought (i.e. thinking in images) appears essential to any significant degree of invention and innovation, and the ability to externalize, communicate, and share such images may have had powerful implications for the demographic expansion of Upper Paleolithic human populations.

It is likely that in this complex amalgam of technological innovation, increasingly strained human/land relationships, and the emergence of an internally and externally differentiated sociopolitical world is to be found the reason that material representation came to be valued by people of the Aurignacian and all of their descendants in the Upper Paleolithic and beyond.

ACKNOWLEDGMENTS

Discussions with several students and colleagues over the past few years have had an impact on my thinking on the subject of material representation. They include Margaret Conkey, Kathleen Ehrhardt, Anne Hendrickson, Heidi Knecht, Joann McLean, Fred Myers, Magen O'Farrell, Anne Pike-Tay, Bambi Schieffelin, and Annette Weiner. Of course, I accept full responsibility for deficiencies in the present work. The research was supported by grants from the National Science Foundation, the Wenner-Gren Foundation and the J. S. Guggenheim Foundation.

Literature Cited

1. Allsworth-Jones, P. 1987. *The Szeletian.* Oxford: Oxford Univ. Press
2. Appadurai, A. 1986. *The Social Life of Things.* Cambridge: Cambridge Univ. Press
3. Bahn, P. 1977. Seasonal migration in Southwest France during the late Glacial period. *J. Archaeol. Sci.* 4(3):245–57
4. Bahn, P. 1982. Inter-site and inter-regional links during the Upper Palaeolithic: the Pyrenean evidence. *Oxford J. Archaeol.* 1(3):247–68
5. Bahn, P. 1984. *Pyrenean Prehistory: A Palaeoeconomic Survey of the French Sites.* Warminster: Aris and Phillips
6. Bahn, P. 1986. No sex, please, we're Aurignacians. *Rock Art Res.* 3:99–120
7. Bar-Yosef, O. 1989. Upper Pleistocene cultural stratigraphy in southwest Asia. In *The Emergence of Modern Humans: Biocultural Adaptations in the Later Pleistocene,* ed. E. Trinkaus, pp. 154–80. Cambridge: Cambridge Univ. Press
8. Beaumont, P., de Villiers, H., Vogel, J. 1978. Modern man in sub-Saharan Africa prior to 49,000 B. P.: a review and evaluation with particular reference to Border Cave. *S. African J. Sci.* 74:409–19
9. Beidelman, T. 1968. Some Nuer notions of nakedness, nudity, and sexuality. *Africa* 38(2):1–131
10. Berger, P. Luckmann, T. 1966. *The Social Construction of Reality.* Garden City: Doubleday
11. Bernaldo de Quiros, F., Cabrera Valdès, V. 1992. Early Upper Paleolithic industries of Cantabrian Spain. In *Before Lascaux: The Complex Record of the Early Upper Paleolithic,* ed. H. Knecht, A. Pike-Tay, R. White. Boca Raton: CRC Press. In press
12. Binford, L. 1984. *Faunal Remains from Klasies River Mouth.* New York: Academic
13. Blanc, A. 1953. Nuovo giacimento paleolitico ai Balzi Rossi di Grimaldi. *Paleontog. Ital.* 50(3)
14. Blanc, A., Segre, A. 1953. *Excursion au Mont Circé: le Volcan latial, le Mont Circé.* Roma-Pisa: IVth Int. Cong. INQUA
15. Boas, F. 1955. *Primitive Art.* New York: Dover
16. Bogatyrev, P. 1971 [1937]. *The Function of Folk Costume in Moravian Slovakia.* The Hague: Mouton
17. Bordes, F., Labrot, J. 1967. La stratigraphie du gisement du Roc de Combe (Lot) et ses implications. *Bull. Soc. Préhist. Française* 64:29–34
18. Bourdieu, P. 1977. *Outline of a Theory of Practice.* Cambridge: Cambridge Univ. Press
19. Breuil, H. 1925. Les origines de l'art. *J. Psychol. Norm. Pathol.* 22:290–96
20. Cabrera Valdès, V. 1984. El *Yacimiento de la Cueva de* Castillo (Puente Viesgo, Santander). Madrid: Cons. Super. Invest. Cien. Inst. Españ. Prehist.
21. Cabrera Valdès, V., Bischoff, J. 1989. Accelerator C14 dates for early Upper Paleolithic (basal Aurignacian) at El Castillo cave (Spain). *J. Archaeol. Sci.* 16:577–84
22. Chase, P. 1990. Sifflets du Paléolithique moyen (?). Les implications d'un coprolithe de coyote actuel. *Bull. Soc. Préhist. Française* 87(6):165–67
23. Chase, P., Dibble, H. 1987. Middle Paleolithic symbolism: a review of current evidence and interpretations. *J. Anthropol. Archaeol.* 6(3):263–96
24. Cole, H. 1979. Living art among the Samburu. In *The Fabrics of Culture,* ed. J. M. Cordwell, R. A. Schwarz, pp. 88–102. The Hague: Mouton
25. Collins, D., Onians, J. 1978. The origins of art. *Art Hist.* 1(1):1–25
26. Combier. J. 1988. Témoins moustériens d'activités non utilitaires. In *De Néandertal à Cro-Magnon,* ed. C. Farizy, pp. 69–72. Nemours: Musée de Préhistoire d'Isle de France
27. Conkey, M. 1978. Style and information in cultural evolution: towards a predictive model for the Paleolithic. In *Social Archeology: Beyond Subsistence and Dating,* ed. C. Redman et al, pp. 61–85. New York: Academic
28. Conkey, M. 1980. The identification of prehistoric hunter-gatherer aggregation sites: the case of Altamira. *Curr. Anthropol.* 21:609–30
29. Conkey, M. 1983. On the origins of Paleolithic art: a review and some critical thoughts. In *The Mousterian Legacy: Human Biocultural Change in the Upper Pleistocene,* ed. E. Trinkaus, pp. 201–27. Oxford: Brit. Archaeol. Rep. 164
30. Conkey, M. 1987. New approaches in the search for meaning? A review of research in 'Paleolithic Art.' *J. Field Archaeol.* 14(4):413–30
31. Conkey, M. 1989. The place of material culture in contemporary anthropology. In *Perspectives on Anthropological Collections from the American Southwest: Proceedings of a Symposium,* ed. A. Hedlund, pp. 13–32. Tempe: Arizona State Univ. Res. Pap. 40
32. Conkey, M. 1990. L'art mobilier et l'établissement de géographies sociales. In

L'Art des Objets au Paléolithique 2, ed. J. Clottes, pp. 163–72. Paris: Ministère de la Culture

33. Davidson, I., Noble, W. 1989. The archaeology of perception: traces of depiction and language. *Curr. Anthropol.* 30(2):125–55
34. Davis, W. 1986. The origins of image-making. *Curr. Anthropol.* 27:193–215
35. Delluc, B., Delluc, G. 1978. Les manifestations graphiques aurignaciennes sur support rocheux des environs des Eyzies (Dordogne). *Gallia Préhist.* 21:213–48
36. Dewez, M. 1969. *Révision des successions chronologiques observées à la grotte de Spy (Belgique).* Stuttgart: Int. Kongress Speleol.
37. Dewez, M. 1981. Spy: cent ans de fouilles et de découvertes. *Bull. ASBL Ardenne Gaume* 13:25–42
38. Dupree, L. 1972. Prehistoric research in Afghanistan (1959–1966). *Trans. Am. Philos. Soc.* 62:14–32
39. Eaton, R. 1978. The evolution of trophy hunting. *Carnivore* 1(1):110–21
40. Gautier, A. 1986. Une histoire de dents: les soi-disant incisives travaillées du Paléolithique moyen de Sclayn. *Helinium* 26:171–81
41. Girard, C. 1978. *Les Industries Moustériennes de la Grotte de l'Hyène à Arcy-sur-Cure (Yonne). XIe Supplement à Gallia Préhistoire.* Paris: CNRS
42. Gombrich, E. 1960. *Art and Illusion.* London: Phaidon
43. Gonzalez-Echégaray, J. 1980. El yacimiento de la Cueva de "el Pendo" (excavaciones 1953–57). *Biblio. Praehist. Hispana* 17:1–270
44. Hahn, J. 1972. Aurignacian signs, pendants and art objects in Central and Eastern Europe. *World Archaeol.* 3:252–56
45. Hahn, J. 1986. *Kraft und Aggression: Die Botschaft der Eiszeitkunst im Aurignacien Suddeutschlands?* Tubingen: Archaeol. Venatoria
46. Hahn, J. 1988. *Das Geissenklösterle I.* Stuttgart: Konrad Theiss Verlag
47. Hahn, J. 1990. Fonction et signification des statuettes du Paléolithique supérieur européen. In *L'Art des Objets au Paléolithique 2*, ed. J. Clottes, pp. 173–84. Paris: Ministère de la Culture
48. Hallowell, A. I. 1960. Self, society and culture in, phylogenetic perspective. In *The Evolution of Man: Mind, Culture and Society,* ed. S. Tax, pp. 309–71. Chicago: Univ. Chicago Press
49. Halverson, J. 1987. Art for art's sake in the Paleolithic. *Curr. Anthropol.* 28(1):63–89
50. Harrold, F. 1988. The Chatelperronian and the early Aurignacian in France. In *The Early Upper Paleolithic: Evidence from Europe and the Near East,* ed. J. Hoffecker C. Wolf, pp. 157–92. Oxford: Brit. Archaeol. Rep. 437

51. Hoffecker, J. 1988. Early Upper Paleolithic sites of the European USSR. See Ref 50, pp. 237–72
52. Knecht, H. 1991. *Technological innovation and design during the Early Upper Paleolithic: a study of organic projectile technologies.* PhD thesis, New York Univ.
53. Knecht, H. 1992. The role of innovation in changing early Upper Paleolithic organic projectile technologies. *Techniques et Culture* 17. In press
54. Kozlowski, J., ed. 1982. *Excavation in the Bacho Kiro Cave, Bulgaria: Final Report.* Warsaw: Polish Sci. Publ.
55. Kuper, H. 1973. Costume and cosmology: the animal symbolism of the Ncwala. *Man* 8(4):613–30
56. Lakoff, G., Johnson, M. 1980. *Metaphors We Live By.* Chicago: Univ. Chicago Press
57. Larick, R. 1985. Spears, style and time among Maa-speaking pastoralists. *J. Anthropol. Archaeol.* 4(1):206–20
58. Larick, R. 1991. Warriors and blacksmiths: mediating ethnicity in East African spears. *J. Anthropol. Archaeol.* 10(4):299–331
59. Laville, H., Rigaud, J.-Ph., Sackett, J. 1980. *Rock Shelters of the Périgord.* New York: Academic
60. Lechtman, H. 1977. Style in technology: some early thoughts. In *Material Culture: Styles, Organization and Dynamics of Technology,* ed. H. Lechtman, R. Merril, pp. 3–20. St. Paul, MN: Am. Ethnol. Soc.
61. Lechtman, H. 1984. Andean value systems and the development of prehistoric metallurgy. *Tech. Cult.* 25(1):1–36
62. Lejeune, M. 1987. *L'Art Mobilier Paléolithique et Mésolithique en Belgique.* Treignes: Éditions du Centre d'Etudes et de Documentation Archéologiques
63. Lemonnier, P. 1983. L'étude des systèmes techniques, une urgence en technologie culturelle. *Techniques et Culture* 1:11–34
64. Lemonnier, P. 1986. The study of material culture today. *J. Anthropol. Archaeol.* 5:147–86
65. Leonardi, P. 1976. Les incisions préleptolithiques du Riparo Tagliante (Vérone) et de Terra Amata (Nice) en relation au problème de la naissance de l'art. *Att. Acad. Naz. Lincei,* pp. 35–104
66. Leroi-Gourhan, A. 1945. *Evolution et Techniques. Vol. 2: Milieu et Techniques.* Paris: Editions Albin Michel
67. Leroi-Gourhan, A. 1961. Les fouilles d'Arcy-sur-Cure (Yonne). *Gallia Préhistoire* 4:3–16
68. Leroyer, C., Leroi-Gourhan, Arl. 1983. Problème de chronologie: le Castelperronien et l'Aurignacien. *Bull. Soc. Préhist. Française* 80(2):41–44
69. Leroy-Prost, C. 1975. L'industrie osseuse aurignacienne: Essai regional de classification: Poitou, Charentes, Périgord. *Gallia Préhist.* 18:65–156

70. Lévi-Strauss, C. 1963. *Totemism*. Boston: Beacon Press
71. Lindly, J., Clark, G. 1990. Symbolism and modern human origins. *Curr. Anthropol.* 31(3):233–61
72. Luquet, G.-H. 1926. Les origines de l'art figuré. *Ipek* 2:1–28
73. Luquet, G.-H. 1930. *L'Art Primitif*. Paris: Gaston Doin
74. Luquet, G.-H. 1930. *The Art and Religion of Fossil Man*. New Haven: Yale Univ. Press
75. Mania, D., Mania, U. 1985. Deliberate engravings on bone artefacts of Homo erectus. *Rock Art Res.* 5:91–107
76. Marshack, A. 1972. *The Roots of Civilization*. London: Weidenfeld and Nicolson
77. Marshack, A. 1982. Non-utilitarian fragment of bone from the Middle Palaeolithic layer. In *Excavation in the Bacho Kiro Cave, Bulgaria: Final Report*, ed. J. Kozlowski, p. 117. Warsaw: Polish Scientific Publishers
78. Marshack, A. 1990. Early hominid symbol and evolution of the human capacity. In *The Emergence of Modern Humans: An Archaeological Perspective*, ed. P. Mellars, pp. 457–98. Edinburgh: Edinburgh Univ. Press
79. Marshack, A. 1991. Response to Davidson. *Rock Art Res.* 8:47–58
80. Martin, H. 1909. *Recherches sur l'évolution du Moustérien dans le gisement de la Quina (Charente)*. Paris: Schleicher
81. Martin, H. 1931. *La Station Aurignacienne de la Quina*. Angouleme: Extrait du Bulletin de la Société Archéologique et Historique de la Charente
82. McLean, J. 1991. *A study of the fabrication and use of Aurignacian I beads from Abri Blanchard*. Masters thesis, New York Univ.
83. Mellars, P. 1973. The character of the Middle-Upper Palaeolithic transition in southwest France. In *The Explanation of Culture Change, ed.* C. Renfrew, pp. 255–76. London: Duckworth
84. Mellars, P. 1989. Major issues in the emergence of modern humans. *Curr. Anthropol.* 30(3):349–85
85. Mercier, N., Valladas, H., Joron, J.-L., Reyss, J.-L., Lévêque, F., Vandermeersch, B. 1991. Thermoluminescence dating of the late Neanderthal remains from Saint-Césaire. *Nature* 351:737–39
86. Movius, H. 1969. The Chatelperronian in French archaeology: the evidence of Arcy-sur-Cure. *Antiquity* 43:111–23
87. Nisbet, R. 1969. *Social Change and History: Aspects of the Western Theory of Development*. London: Oxford Univ. Press
88. Oakley, K. 1971. Fossils collected by the earlier palaeolithic men. *Mélanges de Préhistoire, d'Archéocivilisation et d'Ethnologie Offerts à André Varagnac*, pp. 581–84. Paris

89. Oakley, K. 1973. Fossil shell observed by Acheulian man. *Antiquity* 47:59–60
90. Oliva, M. 1987. *Aurignacien na Morave*. Kromeriz: Studie muzea Kromerizska
91. Otte, M. 1974. Observations sur le débitage et le façonnage de l'ivoire dans l'Aurignacien en Belgique. In *Prémier Colloque International sur l'Industrie de l'Os dans la Préhistoire*, ed. H. Camps-Fabrer, pp. 93–96. Paris: CNRS
92. Otte, M., Léotard, J.-M., Schneider, A.-M., Gautier, A. 1983. Fouilles au grottes de Sclayn (Namur). *Helinium* 23:112–38
93. Otte, M., Cordy, J.-M., Magnon, D. 1985. Dents incisées du Paléolithique moyen. *Cah. Préhist. Liègoise* 1:80–84
94. Passemard, E. 1944. La caverne d'Isturitz en Pays Basque. *Préhistoire* 9:1–84
95. Pigeot, N. 1991. Reflexions sur l'histoire technique de l'homme: De l'evolution cognitive à l'evolution culturelle. *Paléo* 3:167–200
96. Pike-Tay, A. 1991. *Red Deer Hunting in the Upper Paleolithic of South-West France: A Study in Seasonality*. Oxford: Brit. Archaeol. Rep. 569
97. Praslov, N., Rogachev, A. 1982. *Palaeolithic of the Kostenki-Borschevo Area on the River Don: Results of Field Excavations (in Russian)*. Leningrad: Nauka
98. Quine, W. 1960. *Word and Object*. Cambridge: MIT Press
99. Renfrew, C. 1986. Varna and the emergence of wealth in prehistoric Europe. In *The Social Life of Things*, ed. A. Appadurai, pp. 141–68. Cambridge: Cambridge Univ. Press
100. Sackett, J. 1973. Style, function and artifact variability in Paleolithic assemblages. In *The Explanation of Culture Change, ed.* C. Renfrew, pp. 317–25. London: Duckworth
101. Sauvet, G. 1990. Les signes dans l'art mobilier. In *L'Art des Objets au Paléolithique 2*, ed. J. Clottes, pp. 83–100. Paris: Ministère de la Culture
102. Stoliar, A. 1985. *Proisxozdenie Izobrazitel'nogo Iskusstva (The Origin of Figurative Art)*. Moscow: Iskusstva
103. Strathern, And. 1981. Introduction. *Man as Art*, ed. M. Kirk, pp. 15–36. New York: Viking
104. Strathern, And., Strathern, M. 1971. *Body Decoration in Mount Hagen*. Toronto: Univ. Toronto Press
105. Straus, L., Heller, C. 1988. Explorations of the twilight zone: the early Upper Paleolithic of Vasco-Cantabrian Spain and Gascony. See Ref. 50, pp. 97–133
106. Stringer, C. 1989. Documenting the origin of modern humans. See Ref. 7, pp. 67–96
107. Stringer, C. 1989. The origin of early modern humans: a comparison of the European and non-European evidence. See Ref. 78, pp. 232–44

108. Taborin, Y. 1977. Quelques objets de parure. Etude technologique: les percements des incisives de bovinés et des canines de renard. In Méthodologie Appliquée à l'Industrie de l'Os Préhistorique, ed. H. Camps-Fabrer, pp. 303–10. Paris: CNRS

109. Taborin, Y. 1987. Les Coquillages dans la Parure Paléolithique en France. Paris: Thèse de Doctorat d'Etat, Université de Paris I

110. Taborin, Y. 1988. Les prémices de l'expression symbolique. In De Néandertal à Cro-Magnon, ed. C. Farizy, pp. 73–75. Nemours: Musée de Préhistoire d'Isle de France

111. Taborin, Y. 1990. Les prémices de la parure. In Paléolithique Moyen Récent et Paléolithique Supérieur Ancien en Europe, ed. C. Farizy, pp. 335–44. Nemours: Mem. Mus. Préhist. l'Isle de France, 3

112. Taborin, Y. 1992. Shells of the French Aurignacian and Périgordian. See Ref. 11, In press

113. Turner, T. 1980. The social skin. In Not Work Alone, ed. J. Cherfas, R. Lewin, pp. 112–245. Beverley Hills: Sage

114. Turner, V. 1974. Dramas, Fields and Metaphors: Symbolic Action in Human Society. Ithaca: Cornell Univ. Press

115. Vertès, L. 1964. Tata: Eine Mittelpaläolithische Travertin-Siedlung in Ungarn. Budapest: Akadémiai Kiadoac

116. Wallace, J. 1979. Approximal grooving of teeth. Am. J. Phys. Anthropol. 40:385–90

117. Weiner, A. 1980. Reproduction: a replacement for reciprocity. Am. Ethnol. 7(1):71–85

118. Weiner, A. 1985. Inalienable wealth. Am. Ethnol. 12(2):210–27

119. Weiner, A. 1987. The Trobriand Islanders of Papua, New Guinea. New York: Holt, Rinehart and Winston

120. Weiner, A., Schneider, J., eds. 1989. Cloth and Human Experience. Washington: Smithsonian Inst. Press

121. Wetzel, R., Bosinski, G. 1969. Die Bocksteinschmiede im Lonetal (Markung Rammingen, Kreis Ulm). Stuttgart: Veröffentlichungen des Staatlichen Amtes für Denkmalpflege Stuttgart, Reihe A

122. White, R. 1982. Rethinking the Middle/Upper Paleolithic transition. Curr. Anthropol. 23(2):169–92

123. White, R. 1982. The manipulation and use of burins in incision and notation. Can. J. Anthropol. 2(2):129–35

124. White, R. 1983. Changing land use patterns across the Middle/Upper Paleolithic transition: the complex case of the Périgord. See Ref. 29, pp. 113–21

125. White, R. 1985. Upper Paleolithic Land-Use in the Périgord: A Topographic Approach to Subsistence and Settlement. Oxford: Brit. Archaeol. Rep. 253

126. White, R. 1986. Dark Caves, Bright Visions: Life in Ice Age Europe. New York: Am. Mus. Nat. Hist.

127. White, R. 1989. Visual thinking in the ice age. Sci. Am. 260(7):92–99

128. White, R. 1989. Toward a contextual understanding of the earliest body ornaments. See Ref. 7, pp. 211–31

129. White, R. 1989. Production complexity and standardization in early Aurignacian bead and pendant manufacture: evolutionary implications. See Ref. 78, pp. 366–90

130. White, R. 1992. Bone, antler and ivory objects from abri Blanchard, commune de Sergeac (Dordogne), at the Logan Museum of Anthropology, Beloit College. In French Paleolithic Collections in the Logan Museum of Anthropology, ed. R. White, L. Breitborde, pp. 97–119. Beloit, WI: Logan Mus. Bull. 1(2)

131. White, R. 1992. A social and technological view of Aurignacian and Castelperronian personal ornaments in France. In El Origen del Hombre Moderno en el Suroeste de Europa, ed. V. Cabrera Valdès. Madrid: Ministerio de Educacion y Ciencia. In press

132. White, R., Knecht, H. 1992. The abri Cellier (or la Ruth [sic]), commune de Tursac (Dordogne): results of the 1927 Beloit College excavations. In French Paleolithic Collections in the Logan Museum of Anthropology, ed. R. White, L. Breitborde, pp. 39–96. Beloit, WI: Logan Mus. Bull. 1(2)

123. Wiessner, P. 1984. Reconsidering the behavioral basis of style. J. Anthropol. Archaeol. 3:190–234

134. Wobst, M. 1977. Stylistic behavior and information exchange. In For the Director: Essays in Honor of James B. Griffin, ed. C. Cleland, pp. 317–42. Ann Arbor: Anthropol. Pap. Univ. Michigan 61

AUTHOR INDEX

Lewis-Williams, J. D., 311
Lewontin, R., 384
Lex, B., 309
Leyshon, W. C., 155
Lhote, H., 130
Li, T. K., 149, 150
Li, V. H., 367
Lieber, M., 27
Lieberman, S. S., 13, 420, 421
Lienhardt, G., 115
Linares, O. F., 337
Lincoln, B., 340
Lindauer, O., 530
Linde, C., 215
Lindly, J., 544
Linton, R., 339
Little, B. B., 158, 159
Little, L. R., 159
Little, M. A., 146
Littleton, C. S., 340
Litvin, J., 178, 187, 191, 193
Liu, A. Y.-C., 409
Livingstone, F. B., 334, 336
Livingstone, M. B. E., 157
Lloyd, G., 95
Loadholt, C. B., 155
Locke, R. G., 312
Lofgren, O., 208, 214
Lofgren, R. P., 146
Lokesh, B., 146
Lombardi, C., 176, 184
Longacre, W. A., 451, 524, 526
Lonnerdal, B., 183, 187, 189, 196
Loomis, W. F., 148
Lopez, T., 182
Lopez de Romana, G., 182
Lopreato, J., 333
Lorona, L. V., 25
Lothrop, J. C., 55
Louillot, G., 36
Lourandos, H., 54
Lovejoy, C. O., 407, 413, 422, 428
Lowell, A. E., 146
Lowenthal, D., 113
Lowenthal, I. P., 26
Lowes, S., 33
Lowy, M., 359, 363
Lozanoff, S., 287, 289
Lucas, A., 197
Luckham, R., 363, 365, 366, 371
Luckmann, T., 93, 538, 540, 541
Lucy, J. A., 383, 390–94
Ludden, D., 499
Luedtke, B. E., 452
Luft, F. C., 154
Luhrmann, T. M., 211, 218
Lukacs, G., 104
Luker, K., 207, 209
Lukes, S., 96, 346, 383
Lumley, B., 263

Lumsden, C. J., 332
Luquet, G.-H., 538, 539
Lutes, V., 182
Lynch, D. O., 371
Lynch, K., 114
Lynch, M., 210, 212
Lynch, R., 318
Lyon, W. S., 323
Lyons, J., 103, 387
Lytle, C. M., 363

M

Ma, K., 262
Macaulay, S., 358
MacCurdy, G. G., 69
MacDonald, J., 441
MacDonald, R., 438
Macdonald, W. K., 519, 522, 527
MacGregor, G. A., 154
MacKenzie, D., 497
MacLarnon, A. M., 144
MacLaury, R. E., 392, 393
MacLean, C. J., 155
MacLean, W. C. Jr., 182, 187, 189, 190
MacLeod, J., 207, 208, 210, 216
Macnamara, J., 387
Macnamara, J. T., 387
MacNeish, R. S., 449, 450
Maddock, K., 369
Madhavapeddi, R., 157
Madow, W. G., 300
Madsen, D. B., 47, 52
Madsen, R., 208, 209, 212, 214, 215
Magid, A. A., 126
Magne, M. P. R., 55
Magnon, D., 545
Mahalanobis, P. C., 10
Mahieu, W. de, 102, 115
Mahmoud, D. A., 187
Makiesky-Barrow, S., 26, 27
Maksud, M. G., 160
Maley, J., 125
Malina, R. M., 158, 159
Malinowski, B., 96, 102, 103, 491, 493
Mallory, J. P., 336, 337, 340
Maloiy, G. M. O., 416
Malotki, E., 98, 390
Maltz, D., 102, 461, 476
Maltz, D. N., 215, 465
Manelis Klein, H. E., 382
Manganaro, M., 212
Manguin, E., 125
Mania, D., 545
Mania, U., 545
Mann, B., 205
Mann, G. V., 146
Manners, R., 33, 34
MANNHEIM, B., 381–406; 397, 398
Manning, F. E., 27

Manning, P., 210, 212
Mansbach, I., 184
Manson, P. M., 289, 295
Mansour, M., 192–96
Manwell, C., 128
Marchand, J. W., 381
Marchini, J. S., 155, 156
Marcus, G., 209, 211, 493
Marcus, J., 337, 346, 501
Marcus, L., 284
Margen, S., 159
Maril, R. L., 207, 210
Markman, E. M., 387
Marks, A. E., 126
Marles, A., 32
Marsh, J. L., 289, 295
Marshack, A., 544, 545, 548, 558
Marshall, F., 133, 137
Marshall, H., 452
Marshall, L., 178, 193
Marshall, M., 339
Marshall, W. K., 22, 32
Martin, E., 206, 216, 463, 481
Martin, H., 545
Martin, J. R., 382
Martin, R. B., 409
Martin, R. D., 144, 413
Martin, W. E., 205
Martines, J., 176, 184
Martinez, C., 160, 195, 196
Martinez-Alier, V., 27
Martorell, R., 159, 160, 176, 182, 183, 187, 195, 197
Martyna, W., 388
Masayesva-Jeanne, L., 390
Massey, L. K., 146
Mata, L. J., 184
Mather, L., 360, 362
Mathiot, M., 388, 392
Matsuda, M. J., 363, 370
Mauss, M., 43, 94, 95, 97, 108, 501
Mawson, A., 132
Maxwell, R., 93
May, P. A., 151
Mayer, A., 363
Maynard, D. W., 362
Mayr, E., 11, 384
Mazess, R. B., 143, 161
McAlinden, F., 477, 478
McCabe, T., 264
McCarron, D. A., 154
McClellan, C., 48
MCCONNELL-GINET, S., 461–90; 388, 461, 474, 476, 482
McCracken, R. D., 147, 148
McCron, R., 265
McDaniel, C. K., 381, 392
McDaniel, D. O., 68, 83
McDaniel, E. G., 146
McDonald, M., 179
McDonogh, G., 109

SUBJECT INDEX

structures of knowledge among
consciousness and, 311–12

E

East Africa
early pastoralism in, 132–34
East Asia
shamanic authority in, 317–18
Ecological succession
Iroquoian settlement patterns and, 445
Ecstasy, 310
Efficiency
stylistic information exchange and, 520
Egalitarianism
American, 215
Elites
style and, 528–29
Embedded mobility, 57
Emblemic style, 523–24
Enculturation
mobility and, 59
Endorphins
shamanism and, 311
Engineering beam
primate limb bone diaphyses and, 408
English class subcultures, 265–71
English language
gendered pronouns of, 387–90
Environmental change
beneficial traits made harmful by, 151–55
Environmentalism
neo-shamanism and, 322
Environmental variability
Iroquoian society and, 446
Epidemics
Iroquoian communities and, 447
Erysipelothrix
rheumatoid arthritis and, 84
Eskimo
arthritis in, 70, 71–72, 75–76, 78, 81, 83
diet of
heart disease and, 146
Estimators
in morphometrics, 285–86
Ethanol
metabolism of
population variations in, 149–51
Ethnic identity
design symmetry and, 528
Ethnicity
politics and, 28
preference for directness and, 471
Ethnocentrism
literature on infant feeding and, 172
Ethnographic experimentation
fictionalization in, 213
Ethnography
Caribbean
boundaries of observation and analysis
and, 33–35
comparative, 20
Euclidean distance matrix analysis
in morphometrics, 293–95
Europe
marriage rules in

historical change in, 347–48
material representation in
Aurignacian, 546–58
Paleolithic, 543–46
Evolutionary culture theory, 331–50
cultural selection in, 344–50
descent in, 333–40
family-tree hypothesis in, 333–34
modification in, 341–50
natural selection in, 343–44
propositions of, 331
transmission forces in, 341–43
Evolutionary time
morphology in, 296
Exogamy, 348–49
Expert systems
working-class resistance to, 216
Extrinsic symbolization, 540

F

Factor analysis
in quantitative archaeology, 247
Family
in American culture, 218–20
post-modern, 219
Family-tree hypothesis
in evolutionary culture theory, 333–34
Fats
in breast milk, 183
Fatty acids
in breast milk, 183
Fava beans
antimalarial action of, 145
consumption of
beneficial effects of, 145
Fecundity
mobility and, 59
Female identity
linguistic variables signaling, 469
Female infanticide
growth rate among travelers and, 46
Feminism
cultural analysis and, 264
subculture theory and, 270
Femoral diaphyseal circumference
as body size indicator, 426–27
Fictionalization
in ethnographic experimentation, 213
Finite-element scaling analysis
change in form calculated by, 288
in morphometrics, 286–90
Fishers
arthritis among, 71–72
Fish oils
ischemic heart disease and, 146
Food
bacterial contamination of
early infant feeding and, 194
Food processing
advantages of, 146–47
Food production
ceramic tradition and, 127
Foods
advantages of, 145–46
Food storage

in quantitative archaeology, 242
Locational clustering
  in quantitative archaeology, 242, 248–49
Locomotor behavior
  primate
    compact bone microstructure and, 428
Logistical mobility, 44
Log-linear model
  in quantitative archaeology, 242
Long bone
  diaphyseal cross-sectional geometry in, 412–21
  structural organization of, 409
Lorisines
  long-bone diaphyseal structure in, 414
  long-bone structural properties of, 415–16
Loris tardigradus
  long-bone structural properties of, 415–16
Lowland savanna pastoral neolithic, 132

M

Macaca fascicularis
  femur of
    barrel morphology of, 414
Macaques
  humerus/femur rigidity ratio in, 414
Maize
  alkali processing of, 146–47
Malaria
  diet and, 145–46
Male/female work patterns
  mobility and, 44
Male identity
  linguistic variables signaling, 469
Male power
  interactional reproduction of gender and, 475–78
Malnutrition
  body size and, 157–61
  prolonged breastfeeding and, 174
Manioc
  consumption of
    malaria and, 145–46
Mannheim, B., 381–400
Manual labor
  as essence of masculinity, 274
Maranao
  disputing among
    role of law in, 361
Marie-Strümpell disease, 68
Marine invertebrates
  egg size and life history variables in
    Procrustes analysis and, 292
Maroon
  gender roles among, 26
Marriage
  conflict-management processes and, 360
  middle-class, dual-career
    gender equality in, 219
  working-class
    gender segregation in, 219
Marriage rules
  Western European
    historical change in, 347–48
Masculinity

manual labor as essence of, 274
Material culture
  analytical approaches to, 530–31
  function of
    ritual and, 503
  social anthropology of, 491–514
  style in, 524–29
  structural/symbolic meanings of, 524–26
  variation in
    learning and, 526–27
Materiality, 540–41
Material objectivation, 540
Material representation
  Aurignacian in Europe, 546–58
  materiality and, 540–41
  metaphor and, 541–43
  origins of, 537–60
  Paleolithic transition and, 543–46
Maternal nutrition/health
  breastfeeding and, 181–83
Mathematical reasoning
  in archaeology, 233–34, 241
Matrifocality, 26
Maya genetic unit
  radiation of, 340
Meaning
  social construction of, 538
Media culture, 222
Melanesian initiation rites
  transmission of knowledge and, 343
Menstruation
  hormonal suppression of
    breastfeeding and, 183
Mental illness
  shamanic behavior and, 309
Meratus
  shamanism among, 319
Metaphor
  cognitive schemas and, 393
  material representation and, 541–43
  Neandertals and, 560
Metonymy
  in material representation, 542–43
Mexican-Americans
  diabetes mellitus among, 151–52
Mexico
  village and national courts in
    relationship of, 359
Middle class
  phonological change among, 469
Migration
  permanent
    population growth and, 45
Milk letdown reflex, 180
Millenarianism
  futurity in, 115–16
Misogyny
  in language usage patterns, 481
Mobility, 43–60
  demography and, 58–59
  effects of, 57–59
  embedded, 57
  enculturation and, 59
  fecundity and, 59
  foraging and, 45, 46–48
  housing and, 56–57

CUMULATIVE INDEXES

CONTRIBUTING AUTHORS, VOLUMES 14–21

602 INDEXES

CHAPTER TITLES, VOLUMES 14–21

ANNUAL REVIEWS INC.

a nonprofit scientific publisher
4139 El Camino Way
P. O. Box 10139
Palo Alto, CA 94303-0897 • USA

Annual Reviews Inc. publications may be ordered directly from our office; through booksellers and subscription agents, worldwide; and through participating professional societies.
Prices are subject to change without notice.   ARI Federal I.D. #94-1156476

- **Individuals:** Prepayment required on new accounts by check or money order (in U.S. dollars, check drawn on U.S. bank) or charge to MasterCard, VISA, or American Express.
- **Institutional Buyers:** Please include purchase order.
- **Students: $10.00 discount** from retail price, per volume. Prepayment required. Proof of student status must be provided. (Photocopy of Student I.D. is acceptable.) Student must be a degree candidate at an accredited institution. Order direct from Annual Reviews. Orders received through bookstores and institutions requesting student rates will be returned.
- **Professional Society Members:** Societies who have a contractual arrangement with Annual Reviews offer our books at reduced rates to members. Contact your society for information.
- **California orders** must add applicable sales tax.
- **CANADIAN ORDERS:** We must now collect 7% General Sales Tax on orders shipped to Canada. Canadian orders will not be accepted unless this tax has been added. Tax Registration # R 121 449-029. **Note:** Effective 1-1-92 Canadian prices increase from USA level to "other countries" level. See below.
- **Telephone orders,** paid by credit card, welcomed. Call Toll Free **1-800-523-8635** (except in California). California customers use 1-415-493-4400 (not toll free). M-F, 8:00 am - 4:00 pm, Pacific Time. Students ordering by telephone must supply (by FAX or mail) proof of student status if proof from current academic year is not on file at Annual Reviews. Purchase orders from universities require written confirmation before shipment.
- **FAX: 415-855-9815   Telex: 910-290-0275**
- **Postage paid by Annual Reviews** (4th class bookrate). UPS domestic ground service (except to AK and HI) available at $2.00 extra per book. UPS air service or Airmail also available at cost. UPS requires street address. P.O. Box, APO, FPO, not acceptable.
- **Regular Orders:** Please list below the volumes you wish to order by volume number.
- **Standing Orders:** New volume in the series will be sent to you automatically each year upon publication. Cancellation may be made at any time. Please indicate volume number to begin standing order.
- **Prepublication Orders:** Volumes not yet published will be shipped in month and year indicated.
- **We do not ship on approval.**

ANNUAL REVIEWS SERIES *Volumes not listed are no longer in print*	Prices, postpaid, per volume		Regular Order Please send Volume(s):	Standing Order Begin with Volume:
	Until 12-31-91 USA & Canada / elsewhere	After 1-1-92 USA / other countries (incl. Canada)		
Annual Review of ANTHROPOLOGY				
Vols. 1-16 (1972-1987)	$33.00/$38.00 ⎫			
Vols. 17-18 (1988-1989)	$37.00/$42.00 ⎬ $41.00/$46.00			
Vols. 19-20 (1990-1991)	$41.00/$46.00 ⎭			
Vol. 21 (avail. Oct. 1992)	$44.00/$49.00	$44.00/$49.00	Vol(s)._____	Vol._____
Annual Review of ASTRONOMY AND ASTROPHYSICS				
Vols. 1, 5-14, (1963, 1967-1976)				
16-20 (1978-1982)	$33.00/$38.00 ⎫			
Vols. 21-27 (1983-1989)	$49.00/$54.00 ⎬ $53.00/$58.00			
Vols. 28-29 (1990-1991)	$53.00/$58.00 ⎭			
Vol. 30 (avail. Sept. 1992)	$57.00/$62.00	$57.00/$62.00	Vol(s)._____	Vol._____
Annual Review of BIOCHEMISTRY				
Vols. 30-34, 36-56 (1961-1965, 1967-1987)	$35.00/$40.00 ⎫			
Vols. 57-58 (1988-1989)	$37.00/$42.00 ⎬ $41.00/$47.00			
Vols. 59-60 (1990-1991)	$41.00/$47.00 ⎭			
Vol. 61 (avail. July 1992)	$46.00/$52.00	$46.00/$52.00	Vol(s)._____	Vol._____

ANNUAL REVIEWS SERIES *Volumes not listed are no longer in print*	Prices, postpaid, per volume		Regular Order Please send Volume(s):	Standing Order Begin with Volume:
	Until 12-31-91 USA & Canada / elsewhere	After 1-1-92 USA / other countries (incl. Canada)		

Annual Review of BIOPHYSICS AND BIOMOLECULAR STRUCTURE

Vols. 1-11	(1972-1982)	$33.00/$38.00		
Vols. 12-18	(1983-1989)	$51.00/$56.00 } $55.00/$60.00		
Vols. 19-20	(1990-1991)	$55.00/$60.00		
Vol. 21	(avail. June 1992)	$59.00/$64.00 $59.00/$64.00	Vol(s)._____	Vol.____

Annual Review of CELL BIOLOGY

Vols. 1-3	(1985-1987)	$33.00/$38.00		
Vols. 4-5	(1988-1989)	$37.00/$42.00 } $41.00/$46.00		
Vols. 6-7	(1990-1991)	$41.00/$46.00		
Vol. 8	(avail. Nov. 1992)	$46.00/$51.00 $46.00/$51.00	Vol(s)._____	Vol.____

Annual Review of COMPUTER SCIENCE

Vols. 1-2	(1986-1987)	$41.00/$46.00 $41.00/$46.00		
Vols. 3-4	(1988, 1989-1990)	$47.00/$52.00 $47.00/$52.00	Vol(s)._____	Vol.____

Series suspended until further notice. Volumes 1-4 are still available at the special promotional price of $100.00 USA /$115.00 other countries, when all 4 volumes are purchased at one time. Orders at the special price must be prepaid.

Annual Review of EARTH AND PLANETARY SCIENCES

Vols. 1-10	(1973-1982)	$33.00/$38.00		
Vols. 11-17	(1983-1989)	$51.00/$56.00 } $55.00/$60.00		
Vols. 18-19	(1990-1991)	$55.00/$60.00		
Vol. 20	(avail. May 1992)	$59.00/$64.00 $59.00/$64.00	Vol(s)._____	Vol.____

Annual Review of ECOLOGY AND SYSTEMATICS

Vols. 2-18	(1971-1987)	$33.00/$38.00		
Vols. 19-20	(1988-1989)	$36.00/$41.00 } $40.00/$45.00		
Vols. 21-22	(1990-1991)	$40.00/$45.00		
Vol. 23	(avail. Nov. 1992)	$44.00/$49.00 $44.00/$49.00	Vol(s)._____	Vol.____

Annual Review of ENERGY AND THE ENVIRONMENT

Vols. 1-7	(1976-1982)	$33.00/$38.00		
Vols. 8-14	(1983-1989)	$60.00/$65.00 } $64.00/$69.00		
Vols. 15-16	(1990-1991)	$64.00/$69.00		
Vol. 17	(avail. Oct. 1992)	$68.00/$73.00 $68.00/$73.00	Vol(s)._____	Vol.____

Annual Review of ENTOMOLOGY

Vols. 10-16, 18	(1965-1971, 1973)			
20-32	(1975-1987)	$33.00/$38.00		
Vols. 33-34	(1988-1989)	$36.00/$41.00 } $40.00/$45.00		
Vols. 35-36	(1990-1991)	$40.00/$45.00		
Vol. 37	(avail. Jan. 1992)	$44.00/$49.00 $44.00/$49.00	Vol(s)._____	Vol.____

Annual Review of FLUID MECHANICS

Vols. 2-4, 7	(1970-1972, 1975)			
9-19	(1977-1987)	$34.00/$39.00		
Vols. 20-21	(1988-1989)	$36.00/$41.00 } $40.00/$45.00		
Vols. 22-23	(1990-1991)	$40.00/$45.00		
Vol. 24	(avail. Jan. 1992)	$44.00/$49.00 $44.00/$49.00	Vol(s)._____	Vol.____

Annual Review of GENETICS

Vols. 1-12, 14-21	(1967-1978, 1980-1987)	$33.00/$38.00		
Vols. 22-23	(1988-1989)	$36.00/$41.00 } $40.00/$45.00		
Vols. 24-25	(1990-1991)	$40.00/$45.00		
Vol. 26	(avail. Dec. 1992)	$44.00/$49.00 $44.00/$49.00	Vol(s)._____	Vol.____

Annual Review of IMMUNOLOGY

Vols. 1-5	(1983-1987)	$33.00/$38.00		
Vols. 6-7	(1988-1989)	$36.00/$41.00 } $41.00/$46.00		
Vol. 8	(1990)	$40.00/$45.00		
Vol. 9	(1991)	$41.00/$46.00 $41.00/$46.00		
Vol. 10	(avail. April 1992)	$45.00/$50.00 $45.00/$50.00	Vol(s)._____	Vol.____